Second Edition

Lesson Planner

World Link

Developing English Fluency

Susan Stempleski
Nancy Douglas
James R. Morgan

2

HEINLE
CENGAGE Learning™

Australia • Brazil • Japan • Korea • Mexico • Singapore • Spain • United Kingdom • United States

HEINLE
CENGAGE Learning™

World Link Lesson Planner 2: Developing English Fluency
2nd Edition

Susan Stempleski
Nancy Douglas
James R. Morgan

Publisher: Sherrise Roehr
Senior Development Editor: Katherine Carroll
Senior Development Editor: Jennifer Meldrum
Development Editor: Michael Poor
Director of Global Marketing: Ian Martin
Senior Product Marketing Manager: Katie Kelley
Assistant Marketing Manager: Anders Bylund
Content Project Manager: John Sarantakis
Senior Print Buyer: Mary Beth Hennebury
Composition: PreMediaGlobal
Cover/Text Design: Page2 LLC
Cover Image: iStockphoto

ISBN-13: 978-1-111-06189-0
ISBN-10: 1-111-06189-0

Heinle
20 Channel Center Street
Boston, MA 02210
USA

Cengage learning is a leading provider of customized learning solutions with office locations around the globe, including Singapore, the United Kingdom, Australia, Mexico, Brazil, and Japan. Locate our local office at **international.cengage.com/region**

Cengage Learning products are represented in Canada by Nelson Education, Ltd.

Visit Heinle online at **elt.heinle.com**
Visit our corporate website at **cengage.com**

Printed in the United States of America
2 3 4 5 6 7 8 9 10 - 14 13 12 11

Contents

World Link Program Walk Through	Tiv
Professional Development Pages by Dr. Andy Curtis	T10
Resource Integration Guide	T21

Lesson Plans and Student Book pages with Answer Keys are found on facing pages (2a and 2)

Unit 1	2a, 2
Unit 2	12a, 12
Unit 3	22a, 22
Review Units 1-3	32a, 32
Unit 4	36a, 36
Unit 5	46a, 46
Unit 6	56a, 56
Review Units 4-6	66a, 66
Unit 7	70a, 70
Unit 8	80a, 80
Unit 9	90a, 90
Review Units 7-9	100a, 100
Unit 10	104a, 104
Unit 11	114a, 114
Unit 12	124a, 124
Review Units 10-12	134a, 134
Language Summaries	138
Grammar Notes	144
Index	T155
World Link 2 Audio Scripts	T156
World Link 2 Workbook Answer Key	T171
Video Quick Start Guide	T178
Video Worksheets	T186
Video Scripts	T222
Video Worksheet Answer Key	T240

Lesson Planner Features

This *World Link, Second Edition* Lesson Planner is designed to make your preparation as simple as possible, allowing you to maximize actual classroom teaching time.

What's new?

- Resource Integration Guide
- Teacher's Resources CD-ROM
- Interleaved Lesson Planner pages
- Point-of-use:
    - Teaching Tips
    - Language Tips
    - Grammar Tips
    - Culture Tips
- Writing Prompts
- Teaching Options
- Extra! Expansion activities
- Large Class Options

Culture Tips give insight into different world cultures.

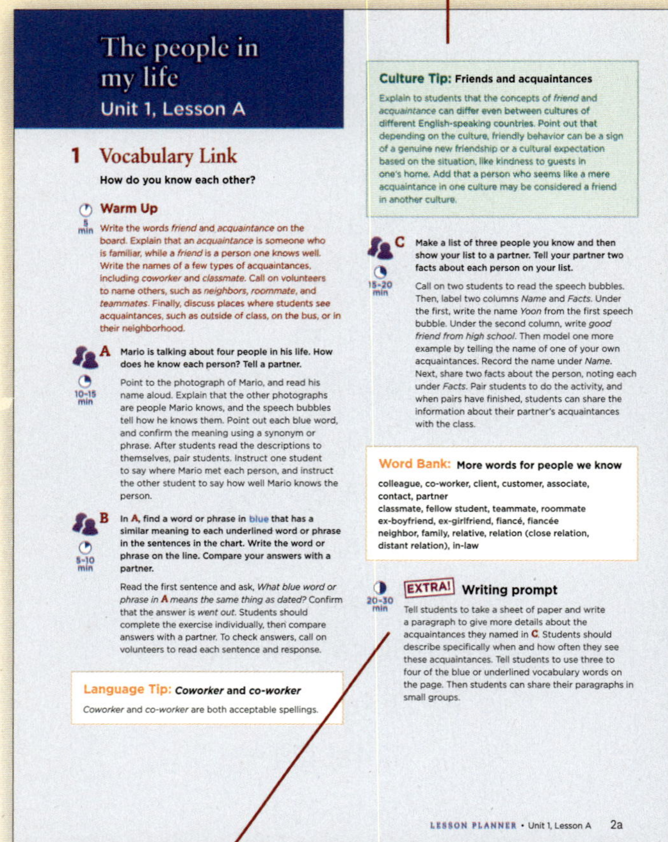
The people in my life
Unit 1, Lesson A

1 Vocabulary Link
How do you know each other?

Warm Up (5 min)
Write the words *friend* and *acquaintance* on the board. Explain that an *acquaintance* is someone who is familiar, while a *friend* is a person one knows well. Write the names of a few types of acquaintances, including *coworker* and *classmate*. Call on volunteers to name others, such as *neighbors*, *roommate*, and *teammates*. Finally, discuss places where students see acquaintances, such as outside of class, on the bus, or in their neighborhood.

A Mario is talking about four people in his life. How does he know each person? Tell a partner. (10-15 min)
Point to the photograph of Mario, and read his name aloud. Explain that the other photographs are people Mario knows, and the speech bubbles tell how he knows them. Point out each blue word, and confirm the meaning using a synonym or phrase. After students read the descriptions to themselves, pair students. Instruct one student to say where Mario met each person, and instruct the other student to say how well Mario knows the person.

B In A, find a word or phrase in blue that has a similar meaning to each underlined word or phrase in the sentences in the chart. Write the word or phrase on the line. Compare your answers with a partner. (5-10 min)
Read the first sentence and ask, *What blue word or phrase in A means the same thing as dated?* Confirm that the answer is *went out*. Students should complete the exercise individually, then compare answers with a partner. To check answers, call on volunteers to read each sentence and response.

Language Tip: *Coworker* and *co-worker*
Coworker and *co-worker* are both acceptable spellings.

Culture Tip: Friends and acquaintances
Explain to students that the concepts of *friend* and *acquaintance* can differ even between cultures of different English-speaking countries. Point out that depending on the culture, friendly behavior can be a sign of a genuine new friendship or a cultural expectation based on the situation, like kindness to guests in one's home. Add that a person who seems like a mere acquaintance in one culture may be considered a friend in another culture.

C Make a list of three people you know and then show your list to a partner. Tell your partner two facts about each person on your list. (15-20 min)
Call on two students to read the speech bubbles. Then, label two columns *Name* and *Facts*. Under the first, write the name *Yoon* from the first speech bubble. Under the second column, write *good friend from high school*. Then model one more example by telling the name of one of your own acquaintances. Record the name under *Name*. Next, share two facts about the person, noting each under *Facts*. Pair students to do the activity, and when pairs have finished, students can share the information about their partner's acquaintances with the class.

Word Bank: More words for people we know
colleague, co-worker, client, customer, associate, contact, partner
classmate, fellow student, teammate, roommate
ex-boyfriend, ex-girlfriend, fiancé, fiancée
neighbor, family, relative, relation (close relation, distant relation), in-law

EXTRA! Writing prompt (20-30 min)
Tell students to take a sheet of paper and write a paragraph to give more details about the acquaintances they named in C. Students should describe specifically when and how often they see these acquaintances. Tell students to use three to four of the blue or underlined vocabulary words on the page. Then students can share their paragraphs in small groups.

LESSON PLANNER • Unit 1, Lesson A 2a

7 Communication
Veronica's Restaurant

Warm Up (10-15 min)
Call on a few students to name their favorite restaurant. Follow up with questions on the food served there, plus details about the setting, like whether it is crowded, expensive, small, large, fancy, or casual. Write adjectives students use in their responses on the board. Then, divide the class into small groups. Appoint one student in each group to label a sheet of paper with two columns, *Popular Restaurants* and *Unpopular Restaurants*, and record the groups' responses. Tell groups they have 3 minutes to brainstorm as many adjectives as possible about both popular and unpopular restaurants. After time is up, review and discuss the responses. Were groups' responses similar or different? Did any adjectives appear in both columns?

A Look at the pictures of Veronica's Restaurant. Talk about the changes you see. Use the adjectives in the box to help you. (10-15 min)
Read the list of adjectives in the box, and ask volunteers to explain them in synonyms, brief definitions, or examples. Then, explain that students will use them to compare the pictures. Read the example comparison in the speech bubble while students look carefully at the pictures. Tell students to work in pairs, taking turns making comparisons between the old and new restaurants, and then ask each pair to share one comparison with the class.

EXTRA! Write a review (15-20 min)
After students complete the exercise, ask them to write a short review of the new Veronica's. Tell them to write at least two comparisons that describe the changes she made to her restaurant. Ask students to read the review aloud to a partner.

B With a partner, make a fifteen-second radio advertisement for the new Veronica's using your ideas from A. Write your ideas below. Then practice the announcement aloud. (15-20 min)
Talk about TV and radio advertisements for restaurants, naming details that interest audiences, such as a new menu or dishes, friendly service, or prices. Read the example sentences in the speech bubble. Explain that a successful ad should be attention-grabbing, descriptive of a restaurant's best features and enticing. Then assign students to small groups to work on their ads.

B Teaching Option Writing
Students can write a print or television advertisement instead of a radio ad.

C Present your radio advertisement to the class. Whose was the best? Why? (10-15 min)
Call on one pair at a time to present their ad. Then ask students what they remember from the ads they heard. Ask them, *Is the ad they remember most clearly the best one? Why?* or *Why not?*

Teaching Tip: Evaluating a presentation
Explain that students' presentations will be evaluated by these criteria: *interesting*, *loud enough*, and *clear*. Make an evaluation form with four columns, listing each of the criteria and a final column labeled *Notes*. You may ask the other students to copy the columns along the top of their own sheets of paper, and to write the names of presenters along the left margin. After each presentation, ask the class to mark the first three columns with a check mark if the presentation was interesting, loud enough, and clear, and to write any extra notes in the last column. Having students take notes on other presenters keeps them listening actively.

Teaching Tip: Model presentations
Before students speak in front of the class, provide guidance on public speaking. Tell students to speak clearly and look in the direction of their listeners. Help them understand the importance of these tips by modeling an ideal presentation, as well as showing what a presentation looks and sounds like when the presenter does not speak clearly and looks away from viewers.

Large Class Option
Pairs can present in small groups rather than in front of the whole class. When each pair in the group is finished, you can regroup students to see additional presentations. Each student can still record the information in a brief evaluation. After that, instruct students to write one detail they liked about each presentation, as well as one way to improve it. Collect the notes and scan over them. Select the ones that seem most helpful, and read them anonymously to the class.

EXTRA! Practice phrases (10-15 min)
Practice using phrases *a little* and *much* with comparisons. Give examples of a comparison, such as *Apples are better than oranges*. Explain how phrases change it: *Apples are a little better than oranges. Apples are much better than oranges.* Have students work with a new partner to revise their radio ads using the phrases *a little* and *much*. Share a few with the class.

LESSON PLANNER • Unit 2, Lesson A 16a

Extra! expansion activities offer additional reading practice and additional communication activities.

Teaching Options provide alternative activities that could be done instead of or in addition to the book activity.

Large Class Options offer suggestions on how to do the activity in a class of 50 or more students.

Point-of-use Teaching Tips, Language Tips, and Grammar Tips give teachers important information and strategies for teaching with *World Link*.

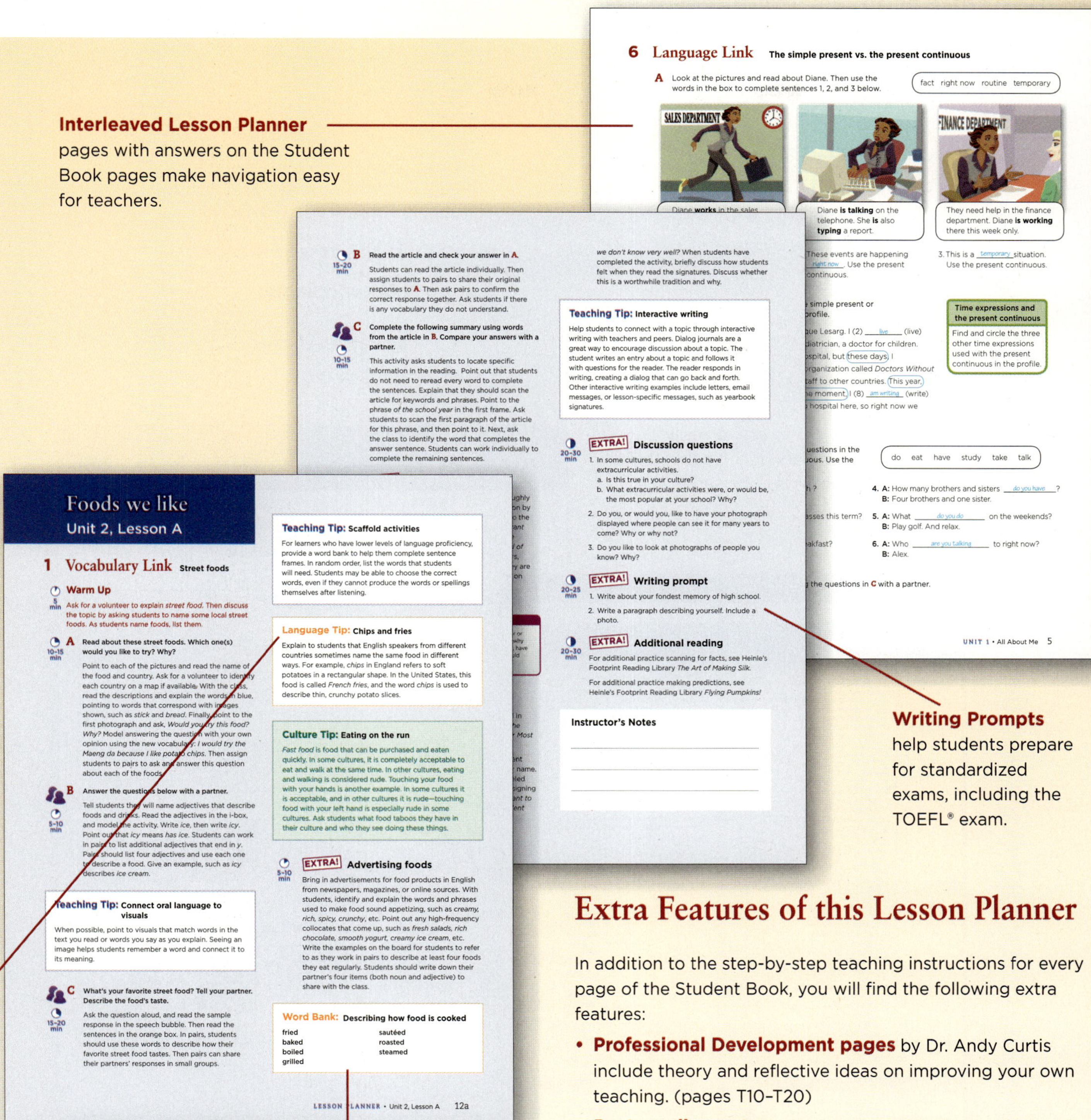

Interleaved Lesson Planner pages with answers on the Student Book pages make navigation easy for teachers.

Writing Prompts help students prepare for standardized exams, including the TOEFL® exam.

Word Banks provide additional related vocabulary.

Extra Features of this Lesson Planner

In addition to the step-by-step teaching instructions for every page of the Student Book, you will find the following extra features:

- **Professional Development pages** by Dr. Andy Curtis include theory and reflective ideas on improving your own teaching. (pages T10–T20)
- **Post-reading notes** contain suggestions for a number of follow-up activities, giving opportunities for your students to work with the readings in a variety of ways.
- **Discussion questions** encourage students to communicate with each other using the unit theme and language.
- **Additional reading suggestions** including Heinle's Footprint Reading Library and Foundations Reading Library.

Additional Resources included in the World Link Lesson Planner

- Video resources including:
  - Video Quick Start Guide
  - Video Scripts
  - Video Worksheets (three worksheets per unit)
- Workbook Answer Keys
- Audio Scripts

Resource Integration Guide

This time-saving tool allows you to easily coordinate the wide variety of components and support offered in the *World Link* series.

Teacher's Resources CD-ROM included in the Lesson Planner features photocopiable:

- Communicative activities
- Graphic organizers

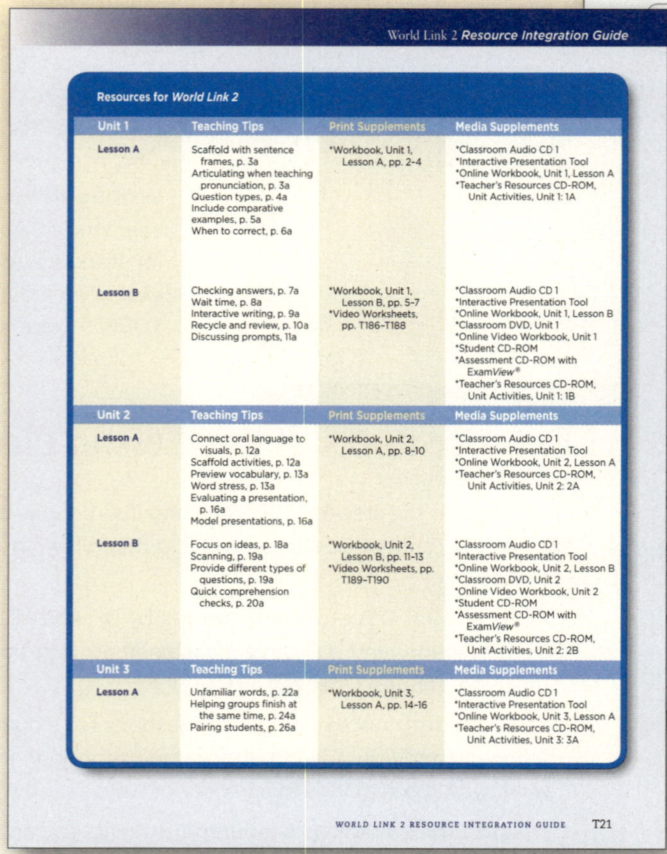
World Link 2 *Resource Integration Guide*

Resources for *World Link 2*

Unit 1	Teaching Tips	Print Supplements	Media Supplements
Lesson A	Scaffold with sentence frames, p. 3a Articulating when teaching pronunciation, p. 3a Question types, p. 4a Include comparative examples, p. 5a When to correct, p. 6a	*Workbook, Unit 1, Lesson A, pp. 2-4	*Classroom Audio CD 1 *Interactive Presentation Tool *Online Workbook, Unit 1, Lesson A *Teacher's Resources CD-ROM, Unit Activities, Unit 1: 1A
Lesson B	Checking answers, p. 7a Wait time, p. 8a Interactive writing, p. 9a Recycle and review, p. 10a Discussing prompts, 11a	*Workbook, Unit 1, Lesson B, pp. 5-7 *Video Worksheets, pp. T186-T188	*Classroom Audio CD 1 *Interactive Presentation Tool *Online Workbook, Unit 1, Lesson B *Classroom DVD, Unit 1 *Online Video Workbook, Unit 1 *Student CD-ROM *Assessment CD-ROM with Exam*View*® *Teacher's Resources CD-ROM, Unit Activities, Unit 1: 1B
Unit 2	**Teaching Tips**	**Print Supplements**	**Media Supplements**
Lesson A	Connect oral language to visuals, p. 12a Scaffold activities, p. 12a Preview vocabulary, p. 13a Word stress, p. 13a Evaluating a presentation, p. 16a Model presentations, p. 16a	*Workbook, Unit 2, Lesson A, pp. 8-10	*Classroom Audio CD 1 *Interactive Presentation Tool *Online Workbook, Unit 2, Lesson A *Teacher's Resources CD-ROM, Unit Activities, Unit 2: 2A
Lesson B	Focus on ideas, p. 18a Scanning, p. 19a Provide different types of questions, p. 19a Quick comprehension checks, p. 20a	*Workbook, Unit 2, Lesson B, pp. 11-13 *Video Worksheets, pp. T189-T190	*Classroom Audio CD 1 *Interactive Presentation Tool *Online Workbook, Unit 2, Lesson B *Classroom DVD, Unit 2 *Online Video Workbook, Unit 2 *Student CD-ROM *Assessment CD-ROM with Exam*View*® *Teacher's Resources CD-ROM, Unit Activities, Unit 2: 2B
Unit 3	**Teaching Tips**	**Print Supplements**	**Media Supplements**
Lesson A	Unfamiliar words, p. 22a Helping groups finish at the same time, p. 24a Pairing students, p. 26a	*Workbook, Unit 3, Lesson A, pp. 14-16	*Classroom Audio CD 1 *Interactive Presentation Tool *Online Workbook, Unit 3, Lesson A *Teacher's Resources CD-ROM, Unit Activities, Unit 3: 3A

WORLD LINK 2 RESOURCE INTEGRATION GUIDE T21

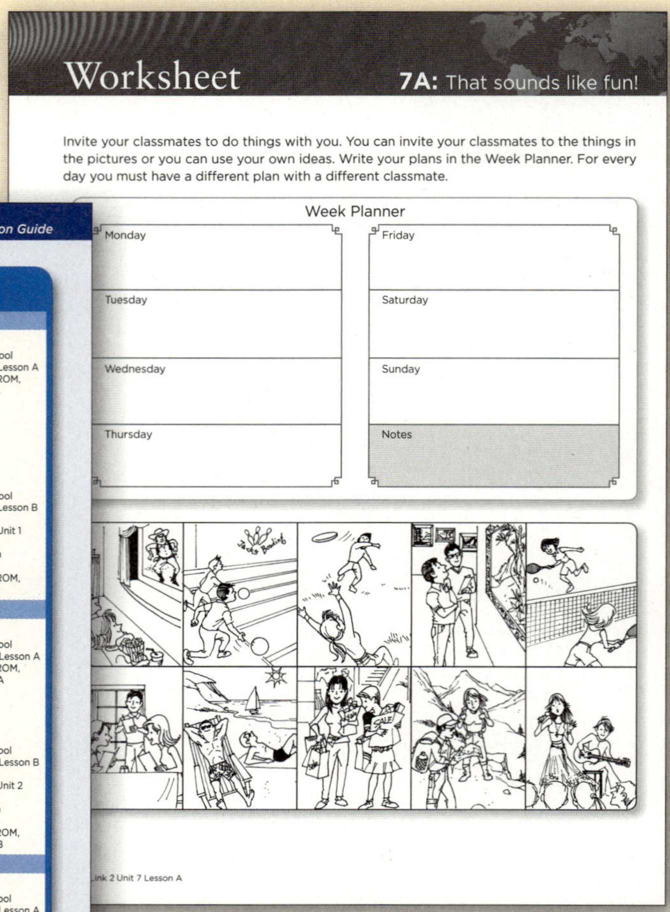
Worksheet **7A:** That sounds like fun!

Invite your classmates to do things with you. You can invite your classmates to the things in the pictures or you can use your own ideas. Write your plans in the Week Planner. For every day you must have a different plan with a different classmate.

Week Planner

Monday	Friday
Tuesday	Saturday
Wednesday	Sunday
Thursday	Notes

…nk 2 Unit 7 Lesson A

More Teacher Resources

The *World Link* series offers additional Teacher Resources including:

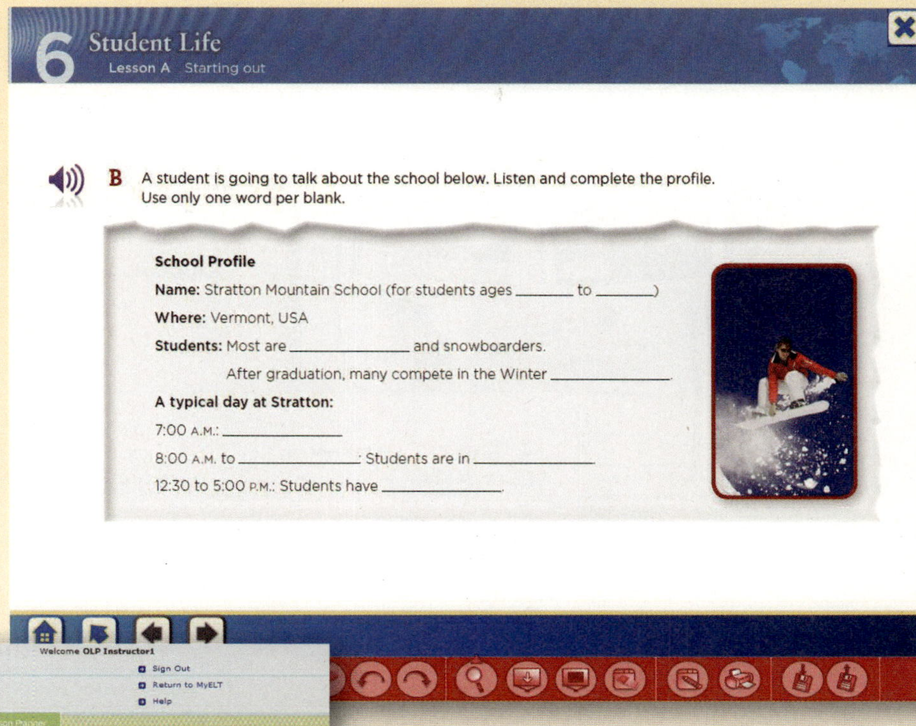

Interactive Presentation Tool

Delivered on a CD-ROM, the Interactive Presentation Tool combines Student Book, Workbook, video, audio, and other resources for use in the classroom with an interactive whiteboard or data projector with computer.

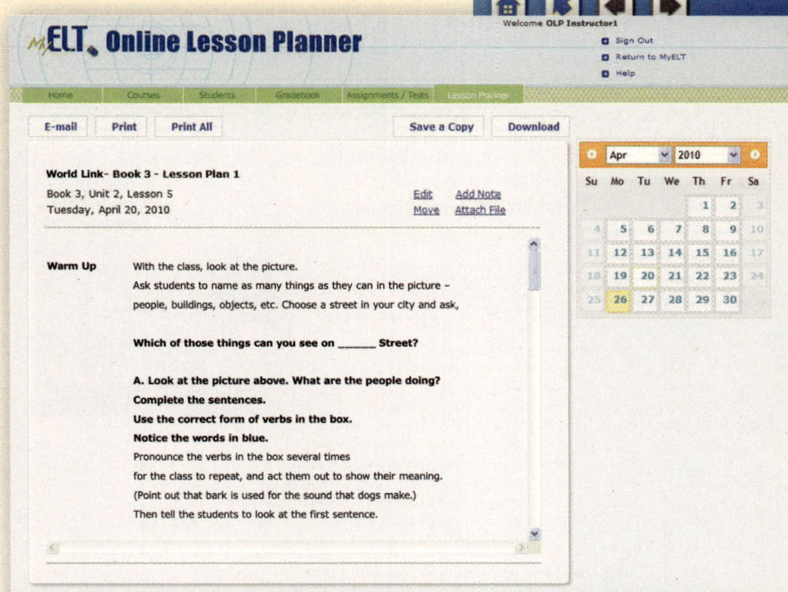

Online Lesson Planner

Perfect for the busy teacher, the Online Lesson Planner is a web-based tool that allows *World Link* users to create and customize lesson plans for their classes. Then save and share them in a range of formats.

ExamView® Assessment Suite

Assessment CD-ROM with Exam*View*®

Includes Placement Test!

The Assessment CD-ROM with Exam*View*® is a test-generating software with a data-bank of ready-made questions designed to allow teachers to carry out assessment quickly and conveniently.

Student Book Features

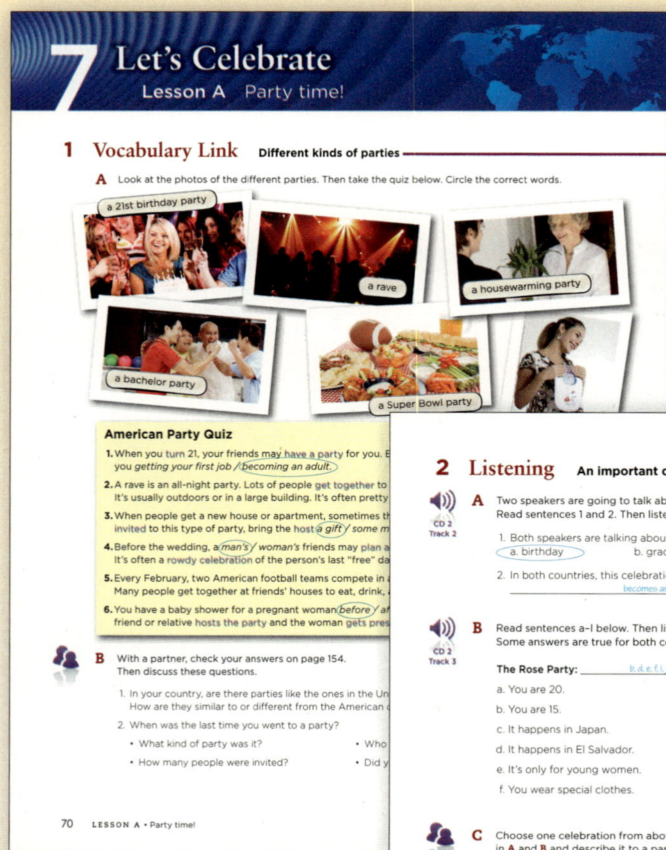

Vocabulary Link dynamically introduces the vocabulary through the use of word families and useful expressions.

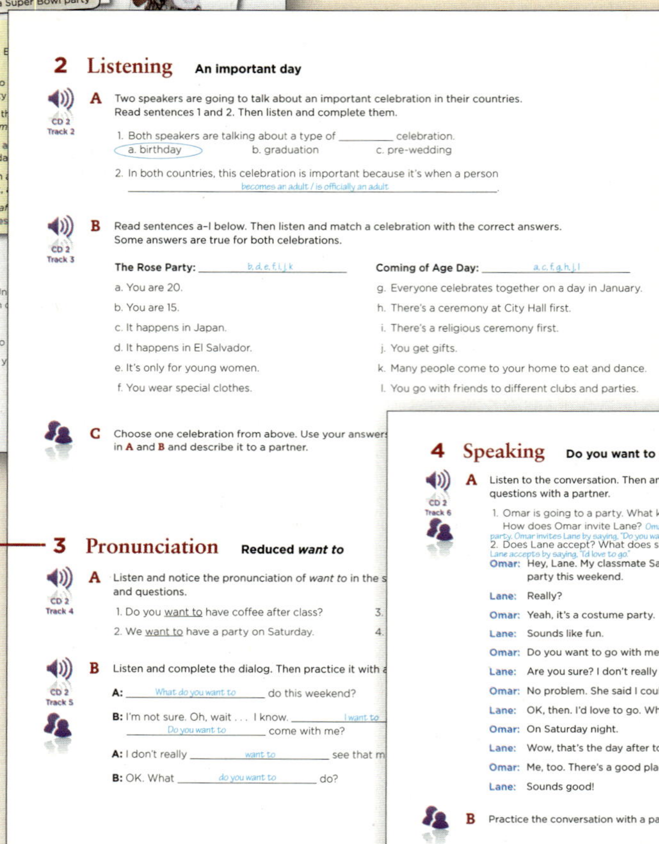

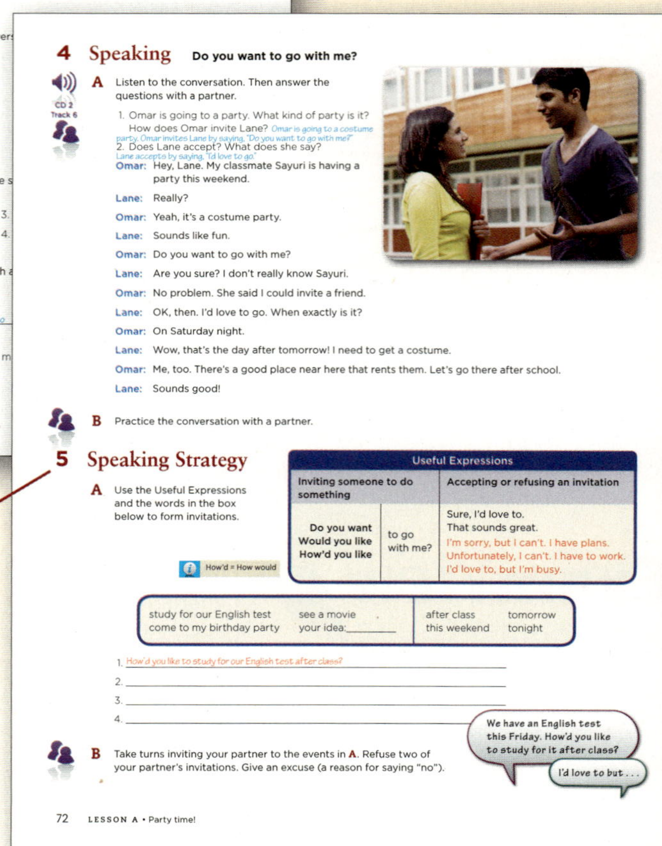

Pronunciation exercises give students item-specific practice with reductions, stress, rhythm, intonation, and troublesome minimal pairs.

Speaking and Speaking Strategy sections give students guided support while leading them to produce the language fluently.

Listening sections use listening tasks to focus students' attention, and are accompanied by open-ended Ask & Answer discussion and critical thinking opportunities.

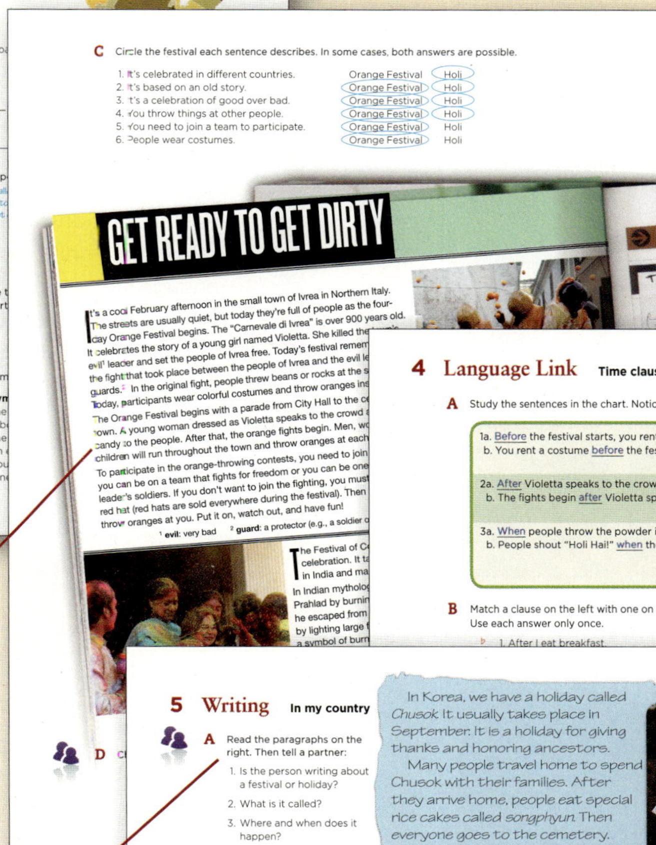

Language Link introduces the essential grammar either inductively or deductively with the purpose of assuring accuracy and appropriateness of language.

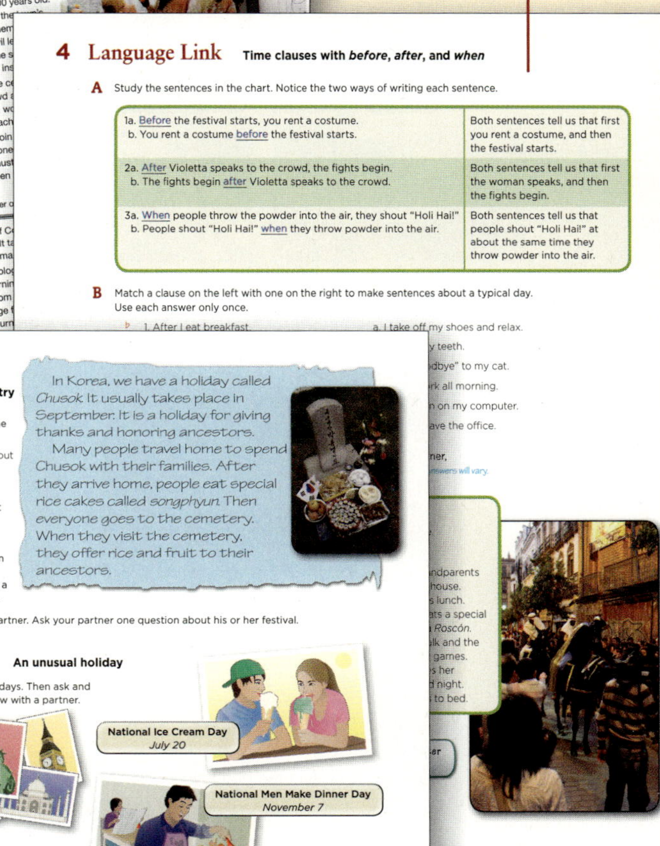

Readings feature high interest topics in a variety of styles.

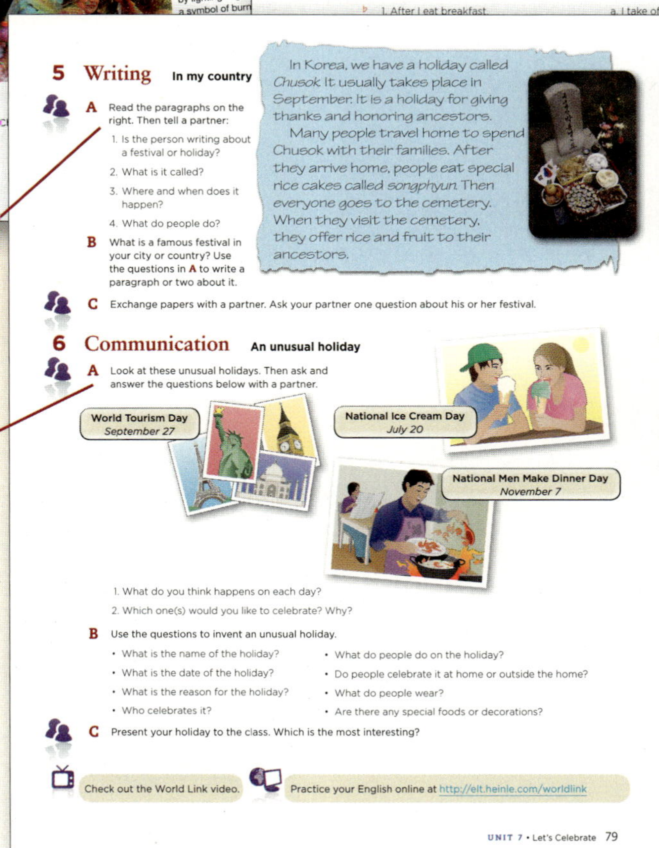

Writing sections reinforce the structures, vocabulary, and expressions learned.

Communication sections include fun tasks and engaging activities to provide learners with opportunities for realistic, meaningful communication using target language.

Student Book Features (continued)

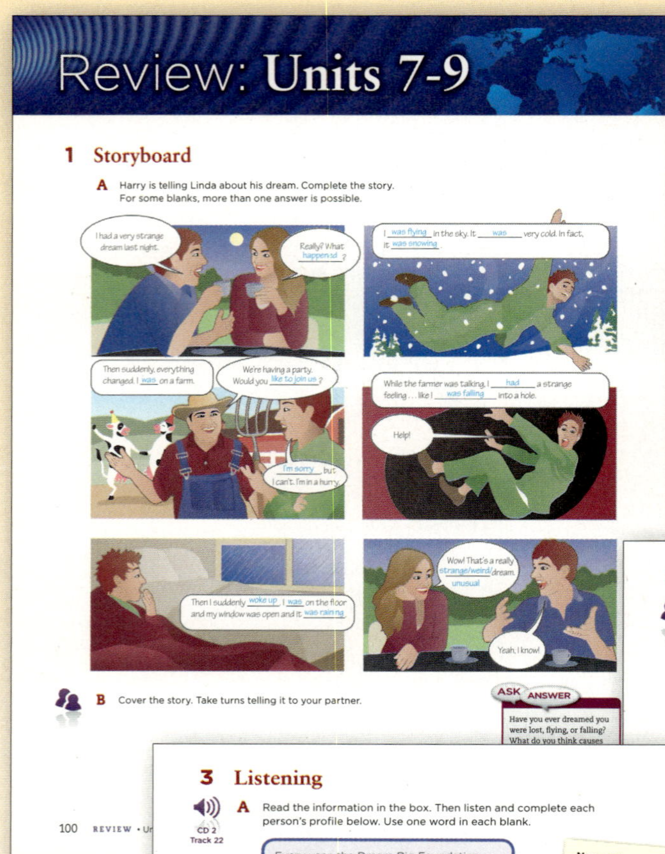

Review: Units 7-9

1 Storyboard

A Harry is telling Linda about his dream. Complete the story. For some blanks, more than one answer is possible.

B Cover the story. Take turns telling it to your partner.

ASK ANSWER
Have you ever dreamed you were lost, flying, or falling? What do you think causes

Review sections appear every three units and actively engage students in utilizing the language learned with the intention of mastering fluency.

2 See It and Say It

A Yesterday there was a movie premiere at the Galaxy Theater. Look at the picture. What were the people doing when the movie star arrived? Tell your partner.

...you know. Write the name of the movie on the sign in the picture.
...r to the premiere. Your partner should ask one or two questions.

...you like to see the new ...movie with me?
Sure. When?
After class.
I'd love to, but . . .

...s to see the movie.
...nd accepting or refusing invitations.

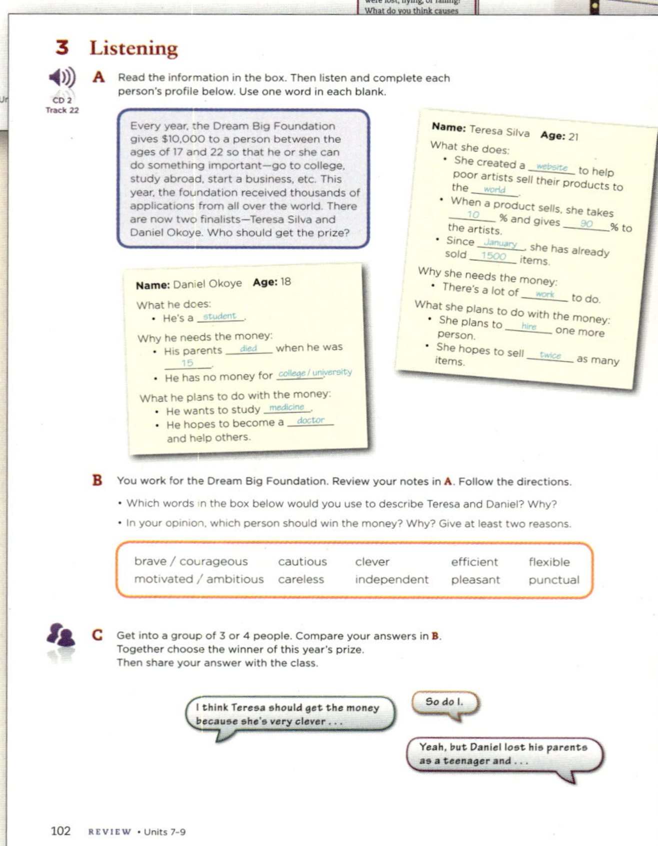

3 Listening

A Read the information in the box. Then listen and complete each person's profile below. Use one word in each blank.

CD 2 Track 22

Every year, the Dream Big Foundation gives $10,000 to a person between the ages of 17 and 22 so that he or she can do something important—go to college, study abroad, start a business, etc. This year, the foundation received thousands of applications from all over the world. There are now two finalists—Teresa Silva and Daniel Okoye. Who should get the prize?

Name: Daniel Okoye **Age:** 18
What he does:
- He's a student.

Why he needs the money:
- His parents died when he was 15.
- He has no money for college / university.

What he plans to do with the money:
- He wants to study medicine.
- He hopes to become a doctor and help others.

Name: Teresa Silva **Age:** 21
What she does:
- She created a website to help poor artists sell their products to the world.
- When a product sells, she takes 10 % and gives 90 % to the artists.
- Since January, she has already sold 1500 items.

Why she needs the money:
- There's a lot of work to do.

What she plans to do with the money:
- She plans to hire one more person.
- She hopes to sell twice as many items.

B You work for the Dream Big Foundation. Review your notes in **A**. Follow the directions.
- Which words in the box below would you use to describe Teresa and Daniel? Why?
- In your opinion, which person should win the money? Why? Give at least two reasons.

brave / courageous	cautious	clever	efficient	flexible
motivated / ambitious	careless	independent	pleasant	punctual

C Get into a group of 3 or 4 people. Compare your answers in **B**. Together choose the winner of this year's prize. Then share your answer with the class.

I think Teresa should get the money because she's very clever . . .
So do I.
Yeah, but Daniel lost his parents as a teenager and . . .

World Link Workbook and Online Workbook

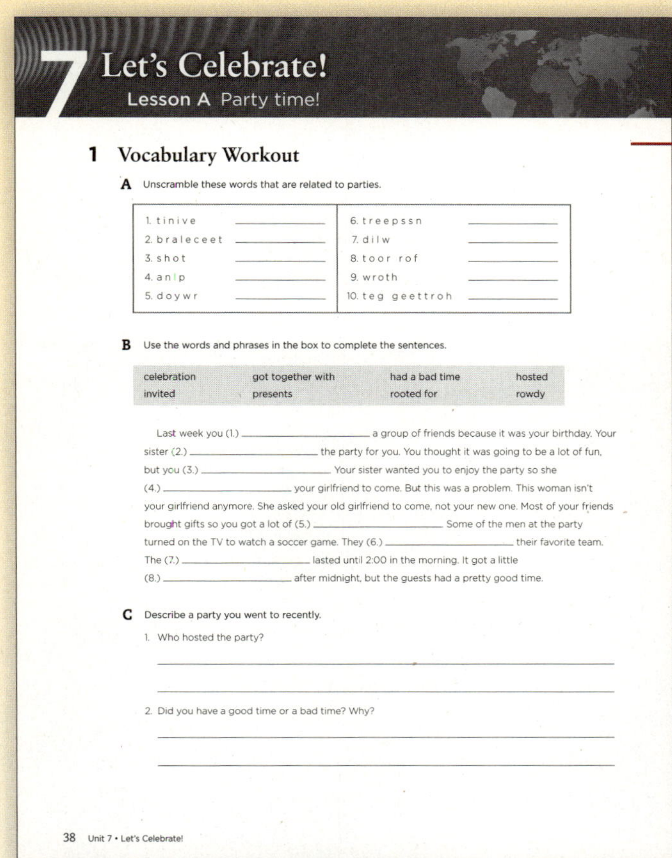

7 Let's Celebrate!

Lesson A Party time!

1 Vocabulary Workout

A Unscramble these words that are related to parties.

1. tinive	________	6. treepssn	________
2. braleceet	________	7. dilw	________
3. shot	________	8. toor rof	________
4. anip	________	9. wroth	________
5. doywr	________	10. teg geettroh	________

B Use the words and phrases in the box to complete the sentences.

celebration	got together with	had a bad time	hosted
invited	presents	rooted for	rowdy

Last week you (1.) ________ a group of friends because it was your birthday. Your sister (2.) ________ the party for you. You thought it was going to be a lot of fun, but you (3.) ________. Your sister wanted you to enjoy the party so she (4.) ________ your girlfriend to come. But this was a problem. This woman isn't your girlfriend anymore. She asked your old girlfriend to come, not your new one. Most of your friends brought gifts so you got a lot of (5.) ________. Some of the men at the party turned on the TV to watch a soccer game. They (6.) ________ their favorite team. The (7.) ________ lasted until 2:00 in the morning. It got a little (8.) ________ after midnight, but the guests had a pretty good time.

C Describe a party you went to recently.

1. Who hosted the party?

____

2. Did you have a good time or a bad time? Why?

____

38 Unit 7 • Let's Celebrate!

Workbook options reinforce vocabulary, skills, and structures taught in the core materials.

Online Workbook is a web-based resource that gives learners personalized access to a range of automatically graded exercises.

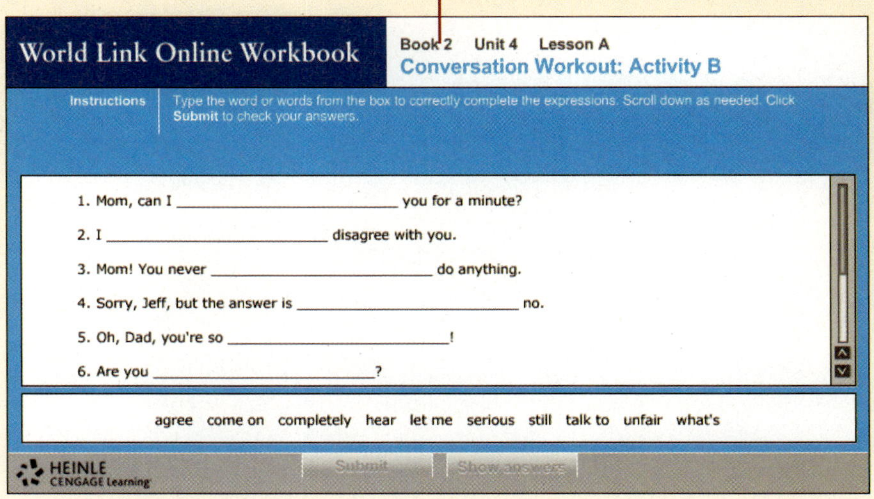

World Link Online Workbook

Book 2 Unit 4 Lesson A

Conversation Workout: Activity B

Instructions Type the word or words from the box to correctly complete the expressions. Scroll down as needed. Click **Submit** to check your answers.

1. Mom, can I ________ you for a minute?
2. I ________ disagree with you.
3. Mom! You never ________ do anything.
4. Sorry, Jeff, but the answer is ________ no.
5. Oh, Dad, you're so ________!
6. Are you ________?

agree come on completely hear let me serious still talk to unfair what's

HEINLE CENGAGE Learning

Submit Show answers

World Link Video Program

Created specifically for English Language Learners

- 4-level Video Program, from false beginner to high intermediate
- Three clips per unit: a TV talk show ("Good Morning World"), an engaging sitcom ("City Living"), and real life interviews. ("Global Viewpoints")
- Available on DVD, Student CD-ROM, through the Online Video Workbook, and on the Interactive Presentation Tool
- Resources for teachers (in Lesson Planner) include
    - Photocopiable Video Worksheets and Videoscripts
    - Quick Start Video Scripts Guide

Can be used as a stand-alone program for the lab, in the classroom, or for self-study.

NEW! Video segment – "Good Morning World" – for each unit

"Good Morning World" features interviews, discussions, and performances in the style of TV talk shows. The hosts, Jay and Kim, welcome different guests and discuss various topics related to the unit themes and recycle the language used in World Link.

The sitcom style of "City Living" expands on the language practiced in the lesson, providing an opportunity to see it used in natural settings and situations.

"Global Viewpoints" features interviews with students and professional people from around the world, sharing their opinions on issues related to the topic of each unit.

Online Video Workbooks feature activities that correspond with the video units including a variety of task-based activities.

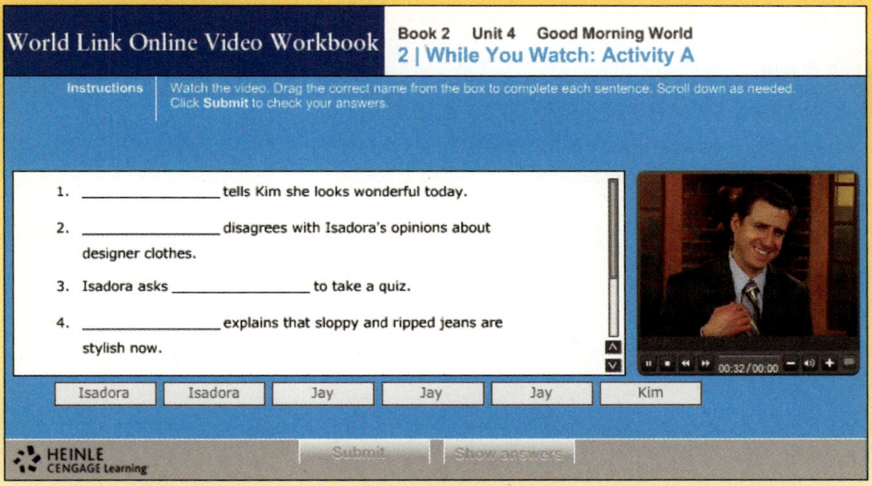

Website

The *World Link* website provides resources for both teachers and students which help link students' learning to the outside world.

Part One: Engaging in Professional Development

This section of the *World Link Lesson Planner* is designed to help you make your *World Link* textbook part of your professional development. Although English language teachers often do not think of their textbooks as part of their professional development, we believe that the *World Link* textbooks can and should be part of it, and in this section, we show you how.

The exercises in this section were designed so you can complete all of them individually, but if you can find a colleague to do them together with you, you will both learn more.

In the first part of this section, Engaging in Professional Development, we will look at the following questions:

What kind of an English language teacher are you?
What does "professional development" mean to you?

A Describing Yourself

At the beginning of a course, we often ask our students to describe themselves, but how often do we describe ourselves?

Task 1

Write an *X* on each of the lines below, nearest to the end that best describes the kind of English language teacher you are.

new teacher ________________ experienced teacher

focused on structure ________________ focused on meaning

teacher-centered ________________ student-centered

aim for accuracy ________________ aim for fluency

teach for examination purposes ________________ teach for communicative purposes

Task 2

Circle a number for each statement that follows, to show how you feel about each statement.

1 = Strongly Disagree 2 = Disagree	3 = Agree 4 = Strongly Agree

A good English language teacher knows all the grammar rules of English.

1 2 3 4

A good English language teacher is aware of his or her students' feelings about English language and culture.

1 2 3 4

A good English language teacher is aware of his or her own feelings about English language and culture.

1 2 3 4

A good English language teacher gives clear and concise feedback.

1 2 3 4

A good English language teacher loves English.

1 2 3 4

There are many more qualities and characteristics of a good English language teacher, but the important point is to know what we mean when we think or talk about being "a good English language teacher."

Task 3

Complete the statement below in 50 words or fewer, and share your completed statement with another teacher who has completed the same exercise.

In my particular teaching and learning context, the ideal English language teacher is someone who . . .

____

____

____

____

B Starting Your Own Autobiography

Many English language teachers ask their students to write about themselves, and most English language teachers ask their students to do fill-in-the-blank activities. But how often do we write descriptions of ourselves and fill in the blanks?

Task 4

Fill in the blanks in the short passage below.

I first became interested in being an English language teacher in ____________________ (time/place). My first position as an English language teacher was in ______________ (place). I felt _______________ (feelings) before my first lesson. The students were _______________ (adjective) and I felt _______________ (feelings) when that first lesson was over! I now feel ______________ (feeling) when a lesson is over.

I enjoy being an English language teacher because _______________ (reason). One of the main challenges I face as an English language teacher is _______________ (challenge). If I had the chance, I would make the following changes to my life and work as an English language teacher: ____.

This exercise is called Starting Your Own Autobiography because it is just a beginning. You could continue, and write about your first day, first week, or first semester as an English language teacher. Writing about our own early experiences as a teacher is one way to reflect on those times and to think about how we've changed since then—and what has remained unchanged.

So far, you have completed four short, simple tasks to help you think about the kind of English language teacher you are. It's important to know who we are and what we do before we try to develop professionally, because all professional development is based on personal development.

Try the next two tasks to help you describe who you are and what you do as an English language teacher.

Task 5

Imagine you meet someone at a party who's never heard of teaching English as a second or foreign language. They ask you what you do, and you tell them, "I'm an English language teacher." They reply, *"An English language teacher? What's an English language teacher? What do English language teachers do? What do you do?"*

How would you reply?

____

____

____

As English language teachers, we work mostly with words. But English language teachers (and students) are also often very visual, and many of us use a lot of pictures, drawings, photographs, and other images in our classrooms.

Task 6

In the box below draw a small, simple picture that shows what you do and how you feel about being an English language teacher. Using a spider map (See the Teacher's Resources CD-ROM for an example), write one key word or phrase in the center of the box, then draw lines coming out from that center, with a word or phrase at the end of each line that describes what you do and how you feel about being an English language teacher.

As we explained at the start of this section, you can complete exercises alone, but if you can find one or more teachers to do them with, you will all learn more. The Task 6 activity is a good example. To learn the most about yourself from this activity, you and another teacher should each draw your spider map on large, blank sheets of paper, then show them to each other and talk about what each picture represents.

C What Is Professional Development?

There is a strong link between personal and professional development. So, it will help you to write your own personal definition of professional development here:

Task 7

For me, "professional development" means . . .

____

____

____

____

It is important to stress that "professional development" does not only mean going to conferences, reading books, or writing papers. Although these are very helpful professional development activities, they are just three possible ways from a large number and a wide variety of different ways, which we will learn more about in this section of the book.

Task 8

Check (✓) the professional development activities that you have tried. If you have tried the activity, what did you learn? If you have not tried this activity before, why not?

☐ Keeping a teaching journal/diary

Tried and learned ________________________________

____

Not tried because ________________________________

____

☐ Watching yourself teaching on video

Tried and learned ________________________________

____

Not tried because ________________________________

____

☐ Watching another teacher teaching

Tried and learned ________________________________

____

Not tried because ________________________________

____

☐ Having another teacher watch you teaching

Tried and learned ________________________________

____

Not tried because ________________________________

____

☐ Teaching together with another teacher

Tried and learned ________________________________

____

Not tried because ________________________________

____

☐ Creating a teaching portfolio

Tried and learned ________________________________

____

Not tried because ________________________________

____

☐ Writing a "teaching philosophy" (a statement of your pedagogic beliefs)

Tried and learned ________________________________

____

Not tried because ________________________________

____

The first few tasks in this section helped you to think about who you are and what you do. Then, we asked you to think about what you understand by the term professional development, what developmental activities you've engaged in, and what you have learned from those activities.

Let's now return to the question we asked at the very beginning: What is professional development?

Professional development is anything you choose to do because you want to be better at what you do. Choice and trust are two essential features of professional development. You can be required to have another teacher in your classroom, observing you. But if you didn't choose to have that person there, and if you don't trust the person, there will be little or no development.

Professional development is also about change. But it's not always about changing what you do. It can be about changing the way you think about what you do. In this section, you have completed various tasks. If you carried out these activities carefully and thoughtfully, then you were engaged in professional development. If you learned anything about your professional self from doing these activities, then you were engaged in professional development.

Drawing Relationships: Bringing together the different parts of our work

As we mentioned earlier, English language teachers (and learners) are often very visual. So, another way of thinking about professional development is to use simple shapes to show complex relationships. Here's an example, based on three key aspects of professional development we've discussed:

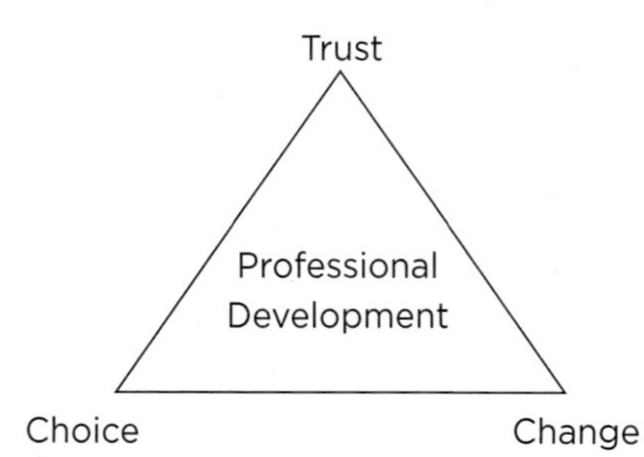

One interpretation of this diagram might be: Trusting yourself and others, engaging in professional development because you choose to do so, and willingness to change are all necessary for professional development to take place.

Another example:

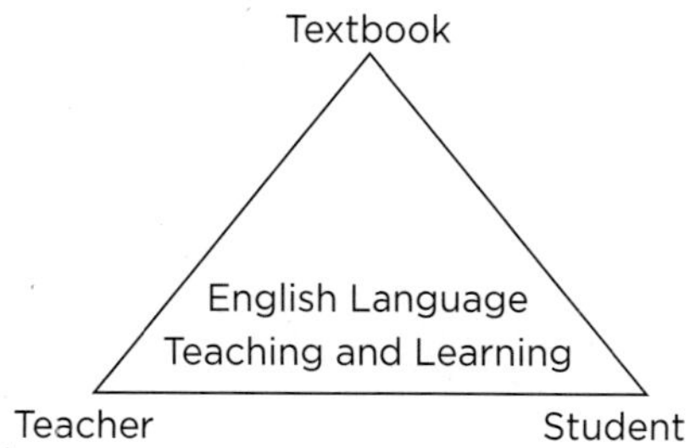

An interpretation of the diagram above might be: English language teachers and students work together, using English language textbooks, to teach and learn the language.

Task 9

Try to put into your own words what this next diagram shows:

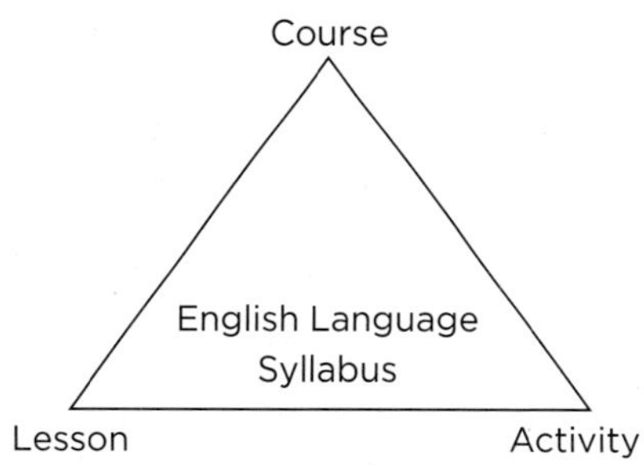

In professional development, teachers often talk about *reflective practice*. This means thinking about what we do so we can understand more, and then make changes so we can do what we do better.

Task 10

Think of three aspects of what you do as an English language teacher, and label the three corners of the triangle below. In the middle of the triangle, write what it is that connects the three corners, then write a brief description of how the three are connected.

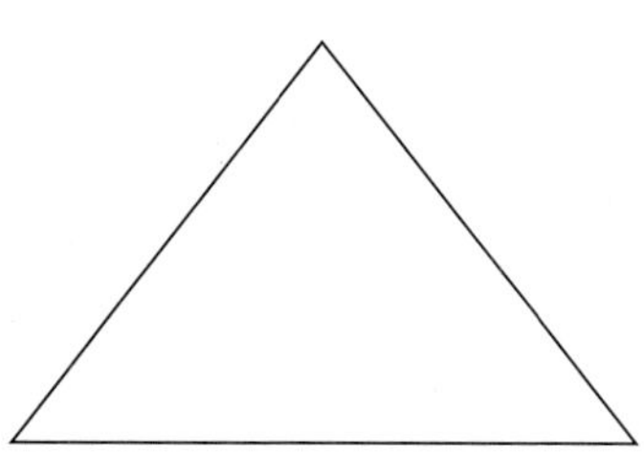

Making Connections: Picturing Professional Development

English language teachers also often make use of analogies in their teaching, so that simple language can be used to express complex thoughts.

Analogies are powerful ways of helping us understand what we think and mean and say. For example, we could say, "Being an English language teacher is like being the captain of a ship, because we are all working together on a voyage of discovery."

Task 11

Complete the same sentence, but with your own analogy:

In my teaching and learning context, being an English language teacher is like ______________________________

____

because ______________________________

____

An activity like this can be part of your professional development because, even though it seems short and simple, it may require a lot of thought to create a good analogy and then describe it in clear and concise language.

Change and Professional Development

As we said earlier, development is all about change—changing what we do, how we do it, and how we think about what we do. Before we can engage in professional development, we should take some time to look at our feelings about change.

Task 12

Circle a number for each statement below to show how you feel about the statement.

1 = Strongly Disagree
2 = Disagree
3 = Agree
4 = Strongly Agree

Change is difficult.

1 2 3 4

Change takes a long time.

1 2 3 4

Change takes a lot of energy.

1 2 3 4

Change is complex.

1 2 3 4

Change is painful.

1 2 3 4

Change is usually negative.

1 2 3 4

Once you have read all the statements on page T13 and circled a number for each one, add up your total score. If you have a total score of more than 20, you have probably had a lot of experience of dealing with challenging change. If you have a total of between 12 and 15, the changes you have experienced may have been largely positive, and with a score of 10 or less, you may have experienced relatively little change or few changes, so far.

Most of us tend to naturally resist change, as we are often "creatures of habit"—we like things to stay the same. But change is one of the only things we can be sure of in modern life. It is sometimes even said that "change is the only constant"!

Task 13

Think of an important change in your life—either personal or professional. Was it difficult and complicated? Did it take a lot of time and energy? Are things better now, because of the change?

Make a few brief notes about this change. How would you describe it to a friend? Once you have made a few notes, use these to describe your change to a friend or colleague, and ask them to do the same with you:

____

____

____

____

____

Change may be difficult, and it may even be painful, but the one thing worse than changing is *not* changing. As teachers, we are preparing our students for a constantly changing world. If we are to help them, we must be willing and able to change, grow, and develop. It is even possible that change is at the heart of all teaching and learning.

Here are some ways to make change less difficult:

1. Break it down into small steps.
2. Set yourself realistic, achievable goals at each step.
3. Expect resistance and identify where there will be areas of resistance.
4. Think of ways to overcome this resistance; for example, think of the benefits of the change.
5. Allow enough time for each step to be completed.
6. Reward yourself as you achieve each goal and complete each step.

D The Language of Professional Development

Like all professions, teaching has it own language which teachers can use to talk about teaching. Within this language of the profession there are a number of words and phrases that are commonly used when talking about professional development.

As a language teacher you know that when learning a language, it is not necessary to remember all the meanings of all the words, but it is important to be familiar with them. This task has, then, been created to help you become more familiar with some commonly used terms related to teacher professional development.

As English language teachers, we often ask our students to complete "matching" activities, linking a word with its meaning. So, let's do one of those activities here.

Task 14

Match some simple definitions with some of the words and phrases most commonly used to describe different approaches to professional development for language teachers. (Check your answers on page T20.)

Word or Phrase

1. Case studies
2. Action research
3. Teaching portfolio
4. Mentoring
5. Development
6. Reflective practice
7. Teaching journal
8. Shock language
9. Peer observation
10. Team teaching
11. Training
12. Coaching
13. Awareness
14. Attitude

a. Structured, systematic ways of thinking about what we do and who we are

b. A diary of significant events and moments in our teaching day

c. Short stories based on real teaching and learning events with different endings

d. Sudden and complete immersion in a new and unfamiliar language

e. Being conscious of your psychological state and of your external environment

f. A set of skills acquired for the completion of particular tasks

g. Two (or more) teachers observing each other's teaching and giving feedback

h. A collection of documents and texts that illustrate different aspects of our work

i. Two (or more) teachers planning, preparing, and teaching together

j. A senior teacher helps a junior teacher to develop his or her knowledge and skills

k. A structured, step-by-step investigation of some aspect of our teaching, our students, etc.

l. Two teachers at the same level help each other to develop in a number of different and agreed upon areas.

m. Becoming better at what you do through growth and change

n. Ways of understanding and responding to ourselves, others, and events

E Painless Professional Development: *Is It Really Possible?*

There are many reasons why many English language teachers do not engage in as much professional development as they might like to do. As we discussed earlier, development requires change, and change can be difficult. Two other common problems are a lack of time and a lack of money. What are some of the obstacles to professional development that you face in your teaching and learning context?

Although there may be challenges to overcome, there are many reasons why we should engage in professional development.

Task 15

Circle a number for each of the statements that follow to show whether each reason for engaging in professional development is important for you or not.

1 = Not Important
2 = Important
3 = Very Important

To keep up to date with new developments in ELT

1 2 3

To maintain an interest in and enthusiasm for teaching

1 2 3

To keep our teaching creative and enjoyable

1 2 3

To meet and exchange ideas with other teachers

1 2 3

To develop new skills needed for new technology

1 2 3

To avoid "teacher burnout"

1 2 3

To increase and improve job security

1 2 3

To be promoted to a more senior position

1 2 3

To improve salary and status

1 2 3

To learn about new approaches to English language teaching and learning

1 2 3

There are many other reasons for engaging in professional development. Can you identify some of them?

In the same way that change does not have to be painful, professional development does not necessarily need a lot of additional time and money. It is possible to engage in professional development by doing what we are already doing, but doing it with more awareness and more reflection than we usually do.

F Making Your Textbook Part of Your Professional Development

To review some of the main points we have discussed so far:

Professional development is anything you choose to do because you want to be better at what you do.

Professional development does not only mean going to conferences, reading books, or writing papers. There are many different ways to grow professionally.

We also touched upon various types of professional development activities, e.g.,

Teaching journal	Team teaching
Case studies	Mentoring
Action research	Coaching
Teaching portfolio	Peer observation

But one method that few English language teachers think of is using their English language textbook as part of their professional development.

In these pages, you have so far completed 15 different tasks. If you completed each of these tasks carefully and thoughtfully, you were actively engaged in professional development.

But what about the textbook itself? How can an English language textbook be part of an English language teacher's professional development?

Most English language teachers do not think of their textbooks as tools for professional development. Some of the reasons are:

1. Textbooks are used to teach students, so they are not thought of as ways for teachers to learn about teaching.
2. Textbooks are part of our regular, routine, everyday classroom work.
3. Professional development is still often thought of as doing something different, something "extra," or going somewhere else, away from where we are now.

But here are some reasons why you should think of your textbooks as a part of your professional development.

1. Careful and thoughtful use of any kind of teaching material can be part of a teacher's professional development process.
2. Deciding which textbook to use is in itself a professional decision, drawing on your knowledge, skills, and experience.
3. The way in which a textbook is used—which units are used, which are not, what supplementary material you provide, etc.—also requires a lot of knowledge, skills, and experience.

Part Two: Pursuing Professional Development Using Your Textbook

At the end of Part One, we said:

Careful and thoughtful use of any kind of teaching material can be part of a teacher's professional development process.

Also in Part One, we defined *reflective practice* as a set of structured and systematic ways of thinking about what we do as English language teachers, including the ways in which we use materials.

Reflective practice is an important component of professional development, and can be thought of as a kind of "stepping back." As we do this, we create the necessary distance to see ourselves, and what we do, more clearly.

If you take time to reflect on the ways in which you use your English language textbook, you can make this part of your professional development. Part Two: Pursuing Professional Development Using Your Textbook has been created and designed to help you do this.

At the end of Part One, we also said:

Deciding which textbook to use is in itself a professional decision, drawing on your knowledge, skills, and experience.

It is true that not all English language teachers are allowed to choose the textbooks they believe would work best for them and for their students. Many teachers are simply given books selected by someone else, or textbooks assigned according to standardized, national exams. But even if we do not choose the textbook we work with, there are ways, even in this situation, to create opportunities for professional development. In Part Two we will explore some of these opportunities.

If you do decide or help to decide which English language textbooks you and your students use, then you are making important decisions because the textbooks we choose and use can directly affect the quality and quantity of English language teaching and learning in our classrooms.

A What Is Teaching?

Task 16

In the space below, write your own personal definition of teaching.

Teaching is . . .

____

____

____

There are as many different meanings of teaching as there are teachers, because teaching—like learning—is a personal experience. As it is a unique experience, it is never exactly the same for any two teachers or for any two students. Compare your definition with the description below of how teaching and learning happens.

Teaching and learning are the result of a series of choices and decisions made by the teacher and by the students. Sometimes, the choices and decisions are made together, between students and teachers, and sometimes they are made independently. Teaching—like learning—is about making choices and making decisions.

In a single English language lesson, the teacher—and the students—may make hundreds of moment-to-moment choices and decisions.

B Making Choices and Decisions about Textbooks as Part of Our Professional Development

Although choices and decisions are similar, they are not exactly the same. For example, in an English language class, a teacher may choose between one student and another, both of whom have raised their hands to answer a question. But decisions in classrooms are often a little more complicated, for example, deciding whether or not to continue with a particular activity, as your decision here will affect the timing for the rest of the lesson.

In the English language classroom, there are so many decisions being made that teachers are unaware of many—or even most—of them. But away from the classroom, we can reflect on our decisions so we can understand better why we decided to follow one course of action rather than another.

So, if we think carefully about why we decide to use one textbook over another, we are engaged in a professional development process.

If we think and talk with other teachers about the strengths and weaknesses of one textbook compared to another, we are engaged in professional development.

If we read a short article about how to evaluate textbooks, so that our decisions are informed not only by our knowledge, skills, and experiences, but also by a systematic way of assessing textbooks, then we are also engaged in professional development.

Thinking about the decisions we make when we select an English language textbook can become part of our professional development. But once the decision about which textbook to use has been made, there are many other decisions that need to be made as well.

C Sharing and Charting Your Professional Development

These activities are designed so that they can be carried out by one person, but as teaching and learning are interactive events, you will learn more from these activities if you work on them with another teacher, or with a group of teachers, that you know and trust.

Sharing is an important part of your professional development. Even if you are all using different English language textbooks, you can still learn a lot from each other by exchanging ideas and experiences, as the challenges you face and the decisions you make are often similar.

We have left spaces for you to write your responses to the different tasks and activities in this section for two reasons.

First, your notes will help you share your thoughts with other teachers. But your notes may also form an important part of documenting your professional development, even if you work by yourself.

Development, growth, and change—like teaching and learning—are often invisible, so it is important to keep a record of your development, for yourself and for others.

D Comparing Textbooks

Task 17

If you decided to use this *World Link* textbook, on what did you base that decision?

I decided to use this *World Link* textbook because . . .

____

____

____

____

____

If the decision to use this textbook was made by someone else, talk with them about that decision.

Task 18

Think of some other English language textbooks you have used recently. How is this *World Link* textbook similar to those other textbooks, and in what ways is it different from those textbooks?

Similarities

1. ____________________

2. ____________________

3. ____________________

Differences

1. ____________________

2. ____________________

3. ____________________

A good English language textbook should help the teacher and the students learn more, and learn more effectively and more enjoyably. Your textbook should add to your lesson, not detract from it.

Task 19

How could this *World Link* textbook help develop your English teaching?

____

____

____

____

E Getting to Know Your *World Link* Textbook

When we make decisions, we generally base those decisions on our knowledge, skills, and experiences.

If we are to make the most of our textbooks and use them as part of our professional development, we must have a thorough knowledge of the textbook.

How well do you know your *World Link* textbook?

Task 20

Complete this short quiz and see how much you know!

Q1. How many units are there in your *World Link* textbook?

____

Q2. True or False? The first part of each unit is called Lesson A, and is made up of seven main parts. __________

Q3. Can you name all the parts of Lesson A in the right order?

1. ____________________
2. ____________________
3. ____________________
4. ____________________
5. ____________________
6. ____________________
7. ____________________

Q4. True or False? The second part of each unit is called Lesson B, and is made up of six main parts. __________

Q5. Can you name all the parts of Lesson B in the right order?

1. ____________________
2. ____________________
3. ____________________
4. ____________________
5. ____________________
6. ____________________

Q6. Can you give the unit number and title of two of the units in your *World Link* textbook?

Unit number: ____________________

Unit title: ____________________

Unit number: ____________________

Unit title: ____________________

Q7a. How many Review Units are there in this textbook?

____

Q7b. How many units are reviewed in each Review Unit?

____

Q8. Who are the writers of this textbook?

____

____

Q9. Where, when, and by whom was this textbook published?

____

F Exploring Our Decisions by Asking Questions

The key to making your textbooks part of your professional development is to keep asking questions that explore the decisions you make as you use the textbook.

Before you use a textbook, it is important to consider it in its entirety, then make decisions about individual units, and finally make decisions about the different parts within each unit.

Task 21

Here are some examples of questions you should consider before starting to use your *World Link* textbook.

Q1. Do you plan to use all 12 of the units in the textbook? If so, why? If not, which units will you not use, and why?

____

____

Q2. Do you intend to use the units in the order in which they are presented? If yes, why?

____

____

____

Q3. If you plan to change the order of the units and present them in a different sequence, why, and which sequence do you plan to use?

Reason(s) for changing the sequence:

____

____

____

Alternative sequence:

____

____

____

G Adopting and Adapting Your English Language Textbook

The questions in Task 21 are related to adapting your *World Link* textbook to your local teaching and learning context, as every student and every teacher is unique, as we discussed earlier, and every teaching and learning context is unique. Because of this uniqueness, once a textbook has been chosen, or adopted, it may also then need to be "localized," or adapted.

Task 22

What are some aspects of your English language teaching and learning environment that make it different from others?

____

____

Task 23

Describe the students with whom you expect you will be using this book.

Q1. First language: ______________________________

Q2. Age range: ______________________________

Q3. Number of years they have studied English:

____

Q4. English language ability levels:

____

Q5. Reasons for learning English:

____

Q6. What makes these students different from other students?

____

____

____

____

Q7. You are unique, too! What makes you different from other English language teachers you work with?

____

____

____

____

In Part One, we talked about the importance of change in professional development.

Task 24

Are there any changes you plan to make to your *World Link* textbook to adapt it to your English language teaching and learning environment?

If so, what kinds of changes will you make?

____

____

____

Task 25

Are there any changes you will make to your *World Link* textbook to adapt it to your English language students?

If so, what kinds of changes will you make?

____

____

____

Task 26

Are there any changes you will make to your *World Link* textbook to adapt it to your teaching style(s)? If so, what kinds of changes will you make?

____

____

____

There are other questions you could ask yourself as well, including: What local objects and artifacts can I—and my students—bring in to supplement and localize the material in the textbook? These "pedagogical artifacts" are sometimes called "realia."

H Before, During, and After

Another way of using our textbooks as part of your professional development is to make it a focus of your pre-lesson, during-lesson, and post-lesson reflection.

We have already looked at many examples of some of the questions you might ask before and during the lesson, related to your textbook. But there are many questions you should ask afterwards. These include:

- Did that unit or lesson work the way I thought it would? If not, how was it different? It is important to remember here that a lesson may go better than you thought it would, so "different" can be "different but better" as well as "different and worse" than you thought it would be!
- If I had to re-teach the same lesson, using the same unit, what would I do the same, what would I do differently, and why?
- Were the materials at the right level for my students? If so, how do I know? If not, what changes can I make so that the material matches the students' levels more closely?
- Did students appear to understand all of the instructions for all of the exercises?

I Conclusion

We hope we have helped you to start thinking of your *World Link* textbook as part of your professional development. By using your textbook carefully, thoughtfully, and reflectively, your textbook can help you learn as well as help you teach. Good luck! Enjoy!

Answers to Task 14

1. c, 2. k, 3. h, 4. j, 5. m, 6. a, 7. b, 8. d, 9. g, 10. i, 11. f, 12. l, 13. e, 14. n

Resources for *World Link 2*

Unit 1	Teaching Tips	Print Supplements	Media Supplements
Lesson A	Scaffold with sentence frames, p. 3a Articulating when teaching pronunciation, p. 3a Question types, p. 4a Include comparative examples, p. 5a When to correct, p. 6a	*Workbook, Unit 1, Lesson A, pp. 2–4	*Classroom Audio CD 1 *Interactive Presentation Tool *Online Workbook, Unit 1, Lesson A *Teacher's Resources CD-ROM, Unit Activities, Unit 1: 1A
Lesson B	Checking answers, p. 7a Wait time, p. 8a Interactive writing, p. 9a Recycle and review, p. 10a Discussing prompts, p. 11a	*Workbook, Unit 1, Lesson B, pp. 5–7 *Video Worksheets, pp. T186–T188	*Classroom Audio CD 1 *Interactive Presentation Tool *Online Workbook, Unit 1, Lesson B *Classroom DVD, Unit 1 *Online Video Workbook, Unit 1 *Student CD-ROM *Assessment CD-ROM with Exam*View*® *Teacher's Resources CD-ROM, Unit Activities, Unit 1: 1B
Unit 2	**Teaching Tips**	**Print Supplements**	**Media Supplements**
Lesson A	Connect oral language to visuals, p. 12a Scaffold activities, p. 12a Preview vocabulary, p. 13a Word stress, p. 13a Evaluating a presentation, p. 16a Model presentations, p. 16a	*Workbook, Unit 2, Lesson A, pp. 8–10	*Classroom Audio CD 1 *Interactive Presentation Tool *Online Workbook, Unit 2, Lesson A *Teacher's Resources CD-ROM, Unit Activities, Unit 2: 2A
Lesson B	Focus on ideas, p. 18a Scanning, p. 19a Provide different types of questions, p. 19a Quick comprehension checks, p. 20a	*Workbook, Unit 2, Lesson B, pp. 11–13 *Video Worksheets, pp. T189–T190	*Classroom Audio CD 1 *Interactive Presentation Tool *Online Workbook, Unit 2, Lesson B *Classroom DVD, Unit 2 *Online Video Workbook, Unit 2 *Student CD-ROM *Assessment CD-ROM with Exam*View*® *Teacher's Resources CD-ROM, Unit Activities, Unit 2: 2B
Unit 3	**Teaching Tips**	**Print Supplements**	**Media Supplements**
Lesson A	Unfamiliar words, p. 22a Helping groups finish at the same time, p. 24a Pairing students, p. 26a	*Workbook, Unit 3, Lesson A, pp. 14–16	*Classroom Audio CD 1 *Interactive Presentation Tool *Online Workbook, Unit 3, Lesson A *Teacher's Resources CD-ROM, Unit Activities, Unit 3: 3A

Resources for *World Link 2*

Lesson B	Using parts of speech, p. 27a Understanding a chart, p. 28a	*Workbook, Unit 3, Lesson B, pp. 17–19 *Video Worksheets, pp. T192–T194	*Classroom Audio CD 1 *Interactive Presentation Tool *Online Workbook, Unit 3, Lesson B *Classroom DVD, Unit 3 *Online Video Workbook, Unit 3 *Student CD-ROM *Assessment CD-ROM with Exam*View*® *Teacher's Resources CD-ROM, Unit Activities, Unit 3: 3B
Review Unit 1–3			
	Repetition, p. 32a Conversation practice, p. 32a Order of details, p. 33a Choices, p. 34a Ask and reinforce, p. 35a Small group work, p. 35a		*Classroom Audio CD 1 *Interactive Presentation Tool
Unit 4	**Teaching Tips**	**Print Supplements**	**Media Supplements**
Lesson A	Assigning partners, p. 36a Read, look up, and speak, p. 38a Performing in class, p. 38a Group work, p. 40a	*Workbook, Unit 4, Lesson A, pp. 20–22	*Classroom Audio CD 1 *Interactive Presentation Tool *Online Workbook, Unit 4, Lesson A *Teacher's Resources CD-ROM, Unit Activities, Unit 4: 4A
Lesson B	Explaining vocabulary, p. 41a Vocabulary notebooks, p. 41a Vocabulary notebook follow-up, p. 41a Maintaining the energy, p. 44a	*Workbook, Unit 4, Lesson B, pp. 23–25 *Video Worksheets, pp. T195–T197	*Classroom Audio CD 1 *Interactive Presentation Tool *Online Workbook, Unit 4, Lesson B *Classroom DVD, Unit 4 * Online Video Workbook, Unit 4 *Student CD-ROM *Assessment CD-ROM with Exam*View*® *Teacher's Resources CD-ROM, Unit Activities, Unit 4: 4B
Unit 5	**Teaching Tips**	**Print Supplements**	**Media Supplements**
Lesson A	Completing a conversation, p. 47a Explaining vocabulary, p. 50a	*Workbook, Unit 5, Lesson A, pp. 26–28	*Classroom Audio CD 1 *Interactive Presentation Tool *Online Workbook, Unit 5, Lesson A *Teacher's Resources CD-ROM, Unit Activities, Unit 5: 5A

Resources for *World Link 2*

Lesson B	Dictation, p. 51a Prediction, p. 52a Peer feedback, p. 54a	*Workbook, Unit 5, Lesson B, pp. 29–31 *Video Worksheets, pp. T198–T200	*Classroom Audio CD 1 *Interactive Presentation Tool *Online Workbook, Unit 5, Lesson B *Classroom DVD, Unit 5 *Online Video Workbook, Unit 5 *Student CD-ROM *Assessment CD-ROM with Exam*View*® *Teacher's Resources CD-ROM, Unit Activities, Unit 5: 5B
Unit 6	**Teaching Tips**	**Print Supplements**	**Media Supplements**
Lesson A	Monolingual dictionaries, p. 56a Inductive learning, p. 59a	*Workbook, Unit 6, Lesson A, pp. 32–34	*Classroom Audio CD 1 *Interactive Presentation Tool *Online Workbook, Unit 6, Lesson A *Teacher's Resources CD-ROM, Unit Activities, Unit 6: 6A
Lesson B	Errors in communication, p. 65a	*Workbook, Unit 6, Lesson B, pp. 35–37 *Video Worksheets, pp. T201–T203	*Classroom Audio CD 1 *Interactive Presentation Tool *Online Workbook, Unit 6, Lesson B *Classroom DVD, Unit 6 *Online Video Workbook, Unit 6 *Student CD-ROM *Assessment CD-ROM with Exam*View*® *Teacher's Resources CD-ROM, Unit Activities, Unit 6: 6B
Review Unit 4–6			
	Choral repetition, p. 66a		*Classroom Audio CD 1 *Interactive Presentation Tool
Unit 7	**Teaching Tips**	**Print Supplements**	**Media Supplements**
Lesson A	Stand and deliver, p. 72a Vocabulary one-on-one, p. 73a	*Workbook, Unit 7, Lesson A, pp. 38–40	*Classroom Audio CD 2 *Interactive Presentation Tool *Online Workbook, Unit 7, Lesson A *Teacher's Resources CD-ROM, Unit Activities, Unit 7: 7A
Lesson B	Performance targets for speakers in class, p. 77a Guessing before reading (or listening), p. 77a	*Workbook, Unit 7, Lesson B, pp. 41–43 *Video Worksheets, pp. T204–206	*Classroom Audio CD 2 *Interactive Presentation Tool *Online Workbook, Unit 7, Lesson B *Classroom DVD, Unit 7 *Online Video Workbook, Unit 7 *Student CD-ROM *Assessment CD-ROM with Exam*View*® *Teacher's Resources CD-ROM, Unit Activities, Unit 7: 7B

Resources for *World Link 2*

Unit 8	Teaching Tips	Print Supplements	Media Supplements
Lesson A	Repetition by backward build-up, p. 82a Photographs, p. 82a	*Workbook, Unit 8, Lesson A, pp. 44–46	*Classroom Audio CD 2 *Interactive Presentation Tool *Online Workbook, Unit 8, Lesson A *Teacher's Resources CD-ROM, Unit Activities, Unit 8: 8A
Lesson B	Unfamiliar vocabulary in reading texts, p. 87a Accommodating late finishers, p. 87a	*Workbook, Unit 8, Lesson B, pp. 47–49 *Video Worksheets, pp. T207–T209	*Classroom Audio CD 2 *Interactive Presentation Tool *Online Workbook, Unit 8, Lesson B *Classroom DVD, Unit 8 *Online Video Workbook, Unit 8 *Student CD-ROM *Assessment CD-ROM with Exam*View*® *Teacher's Resources CD-ROM, Unit Activities, Unit 8: 8B

Unit 9	Teaching Tips	Print Supplements	Media Supplements
Lesson A	Review, p. 91a Reading speed, p. 92a Partner work, p. 92a Learner's dictionary, p. 93a	*Workbook, Unit 9, Lesson A, pp. 50–52	*Classroom Audio CD 2 *Interactive Presentation Tool *Online Workbook, Unit 9, Lesson A *Teacher's Resources CD-ROM, Unit Activities, Unit 9: 9A
Lesson B	Standardized tests, p. 96a Competitive games, p. 99a	*Workbook, Unit 9, Lesson B, pp. 53–55 *Video Worksheets, pp. T210–T212	*Classroom Audio CD 2 *Interactive Presentation Tool *Online Workbook, Unit 9, Lesson B *Classroom DVD, Unit 9 *Online Video Workbook, Unit 9 *Student CD-ROM *Assessment CD-ROM with Exam*View*® *Teacher's Resources CD-ROM, Unit Activities, Unit 9: 9B
Review Unit 7–9			
	Correcting grammar in speaking activities, p. 100a Class controlled dictation, p. 102a Competition in the classroom, p. 103a		*Classroom Audio CD 2 *Interactive Presentation Tool

Resources for *World Link 2*

Unit 10	Teaching Tips	Print Supplements	Media Supplements
Lesson A	Listening, p. 105a Students who were absent for A, p. 108a	*Workbook, Unit 10, Lesson A, pp. 56–58	*Classroom Audio CD 2 *Interactive Presentation Tool *Online Workbook, Unit 10, Lesson A *Teacher's Resources CD-ROM, Unit Activities, Unit 10: 10A
Lesson B	Using a dictionary while reading, p. 109a Referents in readings, p. 111a	*Workbook, Unit 10, Lesson B, pp. 59–61 *Video Worksheets, pp. T213–T215	*Classroom Audio CD 2 *Interactive Presentation Tool *Online Workbook, Unit 10, Lesson B *Classroom DVD, Unit 10 *Online Video Workbook, Unit 10 *Student CD-ROM *Assessment CD-ROM with Exam*View*® *Teacher's Resources CD-ROM, Unit Activities, Unit 10: 10B
Unit 11	**Teaching Tips**	**Print Supplements**	**Media Supplements**
Lesson A	Teaching inductively, p. 117a Setting up groups, p. 118a	*Workbook, Unit 11, Lesson A, pp. 62–64	*Classroom Audio CD 2 *Interactive Presentation Tool *Online Workbook, Unit 11, Lesson A *Teacher's Resources CD-ROM, Unit Activities, Unit 11: 11A
Lesson B	Paraphrasing instructions, p. 121a Extensive reading, p. 121a	*Workbook, Unit 11, Lesson B, pp. 65–67 *Video Worksheets, pp. T216–T218	*Classroom Audio CD 2 *Interactive Presentation Tool *Online Workbook, Unit 11, Lesson B *Classroom DVD, Unit 11 *Online Video Workbook, Unit 11 *Student CD-ROM *Assessment CD-ROM with Exam*View*® *Teacher's Resources CD-ROM, Unit Activities, Unit 11: 11B
Unit 12	**Teaching Tips**	**Print Supplements**	**Media Supplements**
Lesson A	Role plays, p. 126a Inductive vs. deductive learning, p. 127a	*Workbook, Unit 12, Lesson A, pp. 68–70	*Classroom Audio CD 2 *Interactive Presentation Tool *Online Workbook, Unit 12, Lesson A *Teacher's Resources CD-ROM, Unit Activities, Unit 12: 12A

Resources for *World Link 2*

Lesson B	Authentic reading material, p. 131a	*Workbook, Unit 12, Lesson B, pp. 71-73 *Video Worksheets, pp. T219-T221	*Classroom Audio CD 2 *Interactive Presentation Tool *Online Workbook, Unit 12, Lesson B *Classroom DVD, Unit 12 *Online Video Workbook, Unit 12 *Student CD-ROM *Assessment CD-ROM with Exam*View*® *Teacher's Resources CD-ROM, Unit Activities, Unit 12: 12B
Review Unit 10–12			
	"Assistant Teachers" for in-class correction, p. 136a Alphabet/spelling review, p. 137a		*Classroom Audio CD 2 *Interactive Presentation Tool

Second Edition

World Link

Developing English Fluency

Susan Stempleski
Nancy Douglas
James R. Morgan

2

HEINLE
CENGAGE Learning™

Australia • Brazil • Japan • Korea • Mexico • Singapore • Spain • United Kingdom • United States

HEINLE
CENGAGE Learning™

World Link 2: Developing English Fluency
2nd Edition

Susan Stempleski
Nancy Douglas
James R. Morgan

Publisher: Sherrise Roehr
Senior Development Editor:
Jennifer Meldrum
Senior Development Editor:
Katherine Carroll
Director of Global Marketing:
Ian Martin
Senior Product Marketing Manager:
Katie Kelley
Assistant Marketing Manager:
Anders Bylund
Content Project Manager:
John Sarantakis
Senior Print Buyer:
Mary Beth Hennebury
Composition: Bill Smith Group
Cover/Text Design: Page2 LLC
Cover Image: iStockphoto

Library of Congress Control Number: 2009939402
Student Book:
ISBN-13: 978-1-4240-5502-9
ISBN-10: 1-4240-5502-4
Student Book with Student CD-ROM:
ISBN-13: 978-1-4240-6819-7
ISBN-10: 1-4240-6819-3

Heinle
20 Channel Center Street
Boston, MA 02210
USA

Cengage learning is a leading provider of customized learning solutions with office locations around the globe, including Singapore, the United Kingdom, Australia, Mexico, Brazil, and Japan. Locate our local office at:
international.cengage.com/region

Cengage Learning products are represented in Canada by Nelson Education, Ltd.

Visit Heinle online at **elt.heinle.com**
Visit our corporate website at **cengage.com**

Photo Credits: 2: center image copyright CURAphotography 2008/ Used under license from Shutterstock.com, top right bobbieo/iStockphoto.com, center right Photos.com , center left Creatas Images/Jupiterimages **3:** top left The Photo Works / Alamy, top left iofoto/istockphoto.com, top right Trista Weibell/iStockphoto.com, top right Oleg Prikhodko/iStockphoto.com **7:** center image copyright Adam Tinney 2009 / Used under license from Shutterstock.com, center left Laurence Gough/iStockphoto.com, center right Thinkstock/Jupiter Images **8:** top image copyright qingqing 2009/Used under license from Shutterstock.com, center pippa west/iStockphoto.com, bottom image copyright Felix Mizioznikov 2009 / Used under license from Shutterstock.com **9:** copyright 2005 PhotoDisc Inc., **10:** top right image copyright Francesco Ridolfi 2009 / Used under license from Shutterstock.com, center left Michael McDonnell/Hulton Archive/Getty Images, bottom left UPI Photo/Obama Press Office / Landov **12:** top left sébastien Baussais / Alamy, top center Kate Tero/danleap/iStockphoto.com, center right Niamh Baldock / Alamy, top right image copyright Faraways 2009/Used under license from Shutterstock.Com **13:** all images copyright 2005 PhotoDisc Inc. **14:** top right image copyright Gina Smith 2009 / Used under license from Shutterstock.com **17:** center right image copyright Tomo Jesenicnik 2009 / Used under license from Shutterstock.com **19:** Reuters/CORBIS **20:** top left image copyright Elena Elisseeva 2009 / Used under license from Shutterstock.com, top center Directphoto.org / Alamy, top right SGM/Stock Connection/Aurora Photos, bottom left Chang W. Lee /The New York Times **21:** Fausto Albuquerque / Alamy **22:** center right Courtesy of SWNS, bottom right Ever /iStockphoto.com **23:** © Iofoto | Dreamstime.com **24:** belknap/iStockphoto.com **27:** top left image copyright Yuri Arcurs 2009 / Used under license from Shutterstock.com, center right Todd Arena/iStockphoto.com, center left Larry Williams/Blend Images/Jupiter Images, top right Joe Sohm/Visions of America LLC / Alamy **28:** Markus Divis/ Mac99/iStockphoto.com **29:** top right Jarno Gonzalez Zarraonandia/iStockphoto.com, bottom left image copyright Jarno Gonzalez Zarraonandia 2009 / Used under license from Shutterstock.com **30:** Jacom Stephens/iStockphoto.com **31:** center left AP Photo/Eric Gay, center JTB Photo/Japan Travel Bureau/PhotoLibrary, center right Ed Darack/Science Faction/Encyclopedia/Corbis **33:** top left image copyright Pamela Corey 2009/Used under license from Shutterstock.Com, top left image copyright Apollofoto/used under license from www.shutterstock.com, top right Ana Abejon/iStockphoto.com, top right image copyright Lev Olkha/used under license from www.shutterstock.com **34:** top left MR.SURAKIT HARNTONGKUL/iStockphoto.com, top Dale Berman/iStockphoto.com, top image copyright Denis Pepin 2009/Used under license from Shutterstock.Com, top right image copyright Josh Resnick 2009/Used under license from Shutterstock.com **35:** center left www.iStockphoto.com, center Andrzej Gibasiewicz/iStockphoto.com, center right Jonathan Larsen/iStockphoto.com, center right Jeremy Voisey/iStockphoto.com **37:** Gary Woodard | Dreamstime.com **38:** Jupiterimages/Pixland/Jupiter Images **41:** top left Maria Taglienti-Molinari/Hulton Archive/Getty Images, top right Pat Thielen / Alamy, center left Peter Beavis /Stone/Getty Images, center right image copyright AYAKOVLEVdotCOM 2009 / Used under license from Shutterstock.com, bottom left © Markfgd | Dreamstime.com, bottom right Scott Griessel/iStockphoto.com **42:** top left image copyright CREATISTA 2009 / Used under license from Shutterstock.com, top center Sorsillo | Dreamstime.com, top center Konstantynl Dreamstime.com, top right image copyright andesign101 2009 / Used under license from Shutterstock.com **44:** image copyright Carlos E. Santa Maria 2009 / Used under license from Shutterstock.com **46:** top right Getty Images/Photos.com/Jupiterimages, center right Catherine Yeulet/iStockphoto.com **48:** top right SZE FEI WONG/iStockphoto.com, center right Ice | Dreamstime.com **49:** image copyright Monkey Business Images 2009 / Used under license from Shutterstock.com **51:** center left image copyright Rui Vale de Sousa 2009 / Used under license from Shutterstock.com, center © Aladin66 | Dreamstime.com, center right hfng/iStockphoto.com **53:** top right Digital Vision/Getty Images/RF, bottom right Alistair Laming / Alamy, **55:** Michael Klinec / Alamy **57:** Ben Blankenburg/iStockphoto.com **58:** © Tissiana | Dreamstime.com **59:** all images

Printed in the United States of America
1 2 3 4 5 6 7 8 9 10 - 14 13 12 11 10

Acknowledgments

Thank you to the educators who provided invaluable feedback throughout the development of the second edition of the *World Link* series: Rocio Abarca, Instituto Tecnológico de Costa Rica / FUNDATEC; Anthony Acevedo, ICPNA (Instituto Cultural Peruano Norteamericano); David Aduviri, CBA (Centro Boliviano Americano) - La Paz; Ramon Aguilar, Universidad Tecnológica de Hermosillo; Miguel Arrazola, CBA (Centro Boliviano Americano) - Santa Cruz; Cecilia Avila, Universidad de Xalapa; Isabel Baracat, CCI (Centro de Comunicação Inglesa); Andrea Brotto, CEICOM (Centro de Idiomas para Comunidades); George Bozanich, Soongsil University; Emma Campo, Universidad Central; Martha Carrasco, Universidad Autonoma de Sinaloa; Herbert Chavel, Korea Advanced Institute of Science and Technology; Denise de Bartolomeo, AMICANA (Asociación Mendocina de Intercambio Cultural Argentino Norteamericano); Rodrigo de Campos Rezende, SEVEN Idiomas; John Dennis, Hokuriku University; Kirvin Andrew Dyer, Yan Ping High School; Daniela Frillochi, ARICANA (Asociación Rosarina de Intercambio Cultural Argentino Norteamericano); Jose Gonzales, ICPNA (Instituto Cultural Peruano Norteamericano); Marina Gonzalez, Instituto Universitario de Lenguas Modernas; Robert Gordon, Korea Advanced Institute of Science and Technology; Gu Yingruo, Research Institute of Xiangzhou District, ZhuHai; Yo-Tien Ho, Takming University; Roxana Jimenez, Instituto Tecnológico de Costa Rica / FUNDATEC; Sirina Kainongsuang, Perfect Publishing Company Limited; Karen Ko, ChinYi University; Ching-Hua Lin, National Taiwan University of Science and Technology; Simon Liu, ChinYi University; Maria Helena Luna, Tronwell; Ady Marrero, Alianza Cultural Uruguay Estados Unidos; Nancy Mcaleer, ELC Universidad Interamericana de Panama; Michael McCallister, Feng Chia University Language Center; José Antonio Mendes Lopes, ICBEU (Instituto Cultural Brasil Estados Unidos); Leonardo Mercado, ICPNA (Instituto Cultural Peruano Norteamericano); Tania Molina, Instituto Tecnológico de Costa Rica / FUNDATEC; Iliana Mora, Instituto Tecnológico de Costa Rica / FUNDATEC; Fernando Morales, Universidad Tecnológica de Hermosillo; Vivian Morghen, ICANA (Instituto Cultural Argentino Norteamericano); Niu Yuchun, New Oriental School Beijing; Elizabeth Ortiz, COPEI (Copol English Institute); Virginia Ortiz, Universidad Autonoma de Tamaulipas; Peter Reilly, Universidad Bonaterra; Ren Huijun, New Oriental School Hangzhou; Andreina Romero, URBE (Universidad Rafael Belloso Chacín); Adelina Ruiz, Instituto Tecnologico de Estudios Superiores de Occidente; Eleonora Salas, IICANA (Instituto de Intercambio Cultural Argentino Norteamericano); Mary Sarawit, Naresuan University International College; Jenay Seymour, Hong-ik University; Huang Shuang, Shanghai International Studies University; Sávio Siqueira, ACBEU (Asociação Cultural Brasil Estados Unidos) / UFBA (Universidade Federal da Bahia); Beatriz Solina, ARICANA (Asociación Rosarina de Intercambio Cultural Argentino Norteamericano); Tran Nguyen Hoai Chi, Vietnam USA Society English Training Service Center; Maria Inés Valsecchi, Universidad Nacional de Río Cuarto; Patricia Veciño, ICANA (Instituto Cultural Argentino Norteamericano); Punchalee Wasanasomsithi, Chulalongkorn University; Tomoe Watanabe, Hiroshima City University; Tomohiro Yanagi, Chubu University; Jia Yuan, Global IELTS School.

(Photo credit continued from copyright page) copyright 2005 PhotoDisc Inc **61:** center left copyright 2005 PhotoDisc Inc., center right Typhoonski | Dreamstime.com **62:** top left image copyright Cristian M 2010 / Used under license from Shutterstock.com, top right Barsik | Dreamstime.com, bottom left copyright 2005 PhotoDisc Inc., bottom center copyright 2005 PhotoDisc Inc. **63:** top image copyright Paul Banton/used under license from www.shutterstock.com, center right image copyright Yuri Arcurs 2010/used under license from www.shutterstock.com **65:** JEFF J MITCHELL/Reuters/Corbis **70:** top left image copyright Dmitriy Shironosov 2009 / Used under license from Shutterstock.com, tcenter 1 design/iStockphoto.com, top right Edward Bock/iStockphoto.com, center left Asia Images Group/Getty images, center image copyright Lisa F. Young 2009 / Used under license from Shutterstock.com, center right image copyright Jim Cox 2009 / Used under license from Shutterstock.com **72:** Monkeybusi | Dreamstime.com **74:** bottom left nathewise/Dreamstime.com, bottom center Lauri Patterson/iStockphoto.com, bottom right Jack Puccio/iStockphoto.com, center left Mfelixphoto/Dreamstime LLC, center image copyright Anatema 2009/ Used under license from Shutterstock.com, center right Loretta Hostettler/iStockphoto.com, top left Hans F. Meier/iStockphoto.com, top center image copyright Maria Yfanti 2009/ Used under license from Shutterstock.com, top right image copyright RoJo Images 2009/ Used under license from Shutterstock.com **75:** center left Damian Palus/iStockphoto.com, center right Image copyright Stavchansky Yakov 2009/Used under license from Shutterstock.com, center right JIMIN LAI/AFP/Getty Images **76:** center right image copyright liotru 2009 / Used under license from Shutterstock.com, top right Goncaloferreira| Dreamstime.com **77:** center right Vicki Couchman/Axiom /PhotoLibrary, bottom left Martinlouis | Dreamstime.com **78:** Valeria73 | Dreamstime.com 79: Michel Setboun/Corbis **80:** left © Linqong | Dreamstime.com, right Everett Collection **82:** image copyright James Steidl/ 2009/ Used under license from Shutterstock.com **84:** left David Calicchio/Dreamstime, right image copyright dundanim 2009 / Used under license from Shutterstock.com **85:** left Lifetime TV / Courtesy: Everett Collection, right FILM 4/CELADOR FILMS/PATHE INTERNATIONAL / THE KOBAL COLLECTION/Picture Desk **86:** James Arrington/iStockphoto.com **87:** top center Astroid / Dreamstime.com, top right Christie Gardner/iStockphoto.com **88:** GERARD JULIEN/AFP/Getty Images **90:** Copyright © Yoav Levy / Phototake -- All rights reserved. **94:** center right iStockphoto.com, center right © Golden Pixels LLC / Alamy, bottom left Gene Chutka/iStockphoto.com, bottom right Steven Braun / iStockphoto.com **95:** left Alaska Stock Images / Alaska Stock / PhotoLibrary, right © Pzaxe | Dreamstime.com **96:** bottom left Afby71 / Dreamstime.com, bottom center Nancy Wegard/Liaison/Getty Images Entertainment /Getty Images, bottom center image copyright haider 2010 / Used under license from Shutterstock.com, bottom right image copyright Flashon Studio 2010/Used under license from shutterstock.com **99:** center left © Doug Berry/iStockphoto.com, center © Visions of America LLC / Alamy, center right image copyright Lisa F. Young 2010 / Used under license from Shutterstock.com, bottom left image copyright MARKABOND 2010 / Used under license from Shutterstock.com, bottom center © Marvin Dembinsky Photo Associates / Alamy, bottom right Image copyright CandyBoxPhoto 2010/Used under license from Shutterstock.com, top left Vladimir Godnik/Getty Images, top center Gene Chutka/iStockphoto.com, top right Ben Blankenburg/iStockphoto.com **103:** image copyright Sergej Razvodovskij 2010 / Used under license from Shutterstock.com **104:** Cammerayda... | Dreamstime.com **106:** Luis Sandoval Mandujano/erlucho/iStockphoto.com **111:** top right Rcphoto | Dreamstime.com, center right Jinxy Productions/Blend Images/Jupiter Images **113:** center left Leslie Banks/iStockphoto.com, bottom center digitalskillet/iStockphoto.com, bottom center image copyright Andrew Lever 2009/Used under license from Shutterstock.com, bottom right Steve Cole/iStockphoto.com **114:** top right image copyright Solid Web Designs LTD 2008/ Used under license from Shutterstock.com, center right Djmodena/Dreamstime LLC, left image copyright Alex Melnick 2010/ Used under license from Shutterstock.Com **115:** top left Image copyright jossnat 2009/Used under license from Shutterstock.com, top right mbbirdy/iStockphoto.com **116:** UPPA/Photoshot **118:** top left marco betti / Alamy, center left copyright 2005 PhotoDisc Inc., center copyright 2005 PhotoDisc Inc. **119:** top right Stéphane Bidouze/ iStockphoto.com, center right San Jose Mercury News 2009/Newscom **120:** top right gchutka/iStockphoto .com, center right Inga Ivanova/iStockphoto.com **121:** top right © Riekefoto | Dreamstime.com, bottom right Brendan McDermid/Reuters/CORBIS **122:** left Krzysztof Chrystowski/iStockphoto.com, center Scott Olson/ Getty Images, right image copyright Baloncici 2010/Used under license from Shutterstock.com **123:** ROBYN BECK/AFP/Getty Images **127:** bottom left Image copyright Losevsky Pavel 2010/Used under license from Shutterstock.com, bottom right Josh Hodge/iStockphoto.com **128:** - Backpack image copyright chungking 2010 / Used under license from Shutterstock.com, Bottled Water image copyright R. Gino Santa Maria 2009/ Used under license from Shutterstock.com, Canned Food doram/iStockphoto.com, Chewing Gum Jesus Jauregui/iStockphoto.com, Cooking Pot image copyright vnlit 2010 / Used under license from Shutterstock.com, First Aid Kit DNY59/iStockphcto.com, Flashlight Sergey Plakhotin / iStockphoto.com, Lighter Eldad Carin/iStockphoto.com, Money image copyright Bob Cheung 2009 / Used under license from Shutterstock.com, Plastic Plates and Cups Nancy Tripp/iStockphoto.com, Sleeping Bag image copyright ericlefrancais 2010 / Used under license from Shutterstock.com, Swiss Army Knife rphotos/iStockphoto.com, Tent image copyright Yuriy Kulyk 2010 / Used under license from Shutterstock.com, Thermos image copyright Karel Slavík 2010 / Used under license from Shutterstock.com, Cell Phone image copyright jocicalek 2008/Used under license from Shutterstock.com, **131:** l copyright 2005 PhotoDisc Inc., center right image copyright thumb 2010/ Used under license from Shutterstock.com **132:** Alex Segre / Alamy **133:** image copyright Jason Maehl 2010 / Used under license from Shutterstock.com **136:** image copyright Phase4Photography 2008/Used under license from Shutterstock.com

Scope & Sequence

Unit/Lesson	Vocabulary Link	Listening	Language Link
Unit 1: All About Me			
Lesson A The people in my life p. 2 **Lesson B School days** p. 7	* **How do you know each other?** p. 2 *acquaintances, work together* * **I'm taking a class.** p. 7 *take a class, pass a test, get a good grade*	* **How do you know Michael?** p. 3 Make and check predictions Draw conclusions * **GBL Learning Center** p. 8 Listen for gist and details	* **The simple present vs. the present continuous** p. 5 * **Review of the simple past** p. 10
Unit 2: Let's Eat!			
Lesson A Foods we like p. 12 **Lesson B Eating well** p. 17	* **Street foods** p. 12 *fried, sweet, salty* * **What's their secret?** p. 17 *cut back, eat out, protect*	* **Foods of the southern United States** p. 13 Make and check predictions Listen for facts * **The Slow Food Movement** p. 18 Make and check predictions Infer information	* **The comparative form of adjectives** p. 15 * **The superlative form of adjectives** p. 20
Unit 3: Unsolved Mysteries			
Lesson A What a coincidence! p. 22 **Lesson B Mysteries of the world** p. 27	* **What are the chances?** p. 22 *luckily, unfortunately, take a chance* * **An unsolved mystery** p. 27 *mysterious, theory, prove*	* **Lucky you!** p. 23 Listen for gist Categorize information * **Full moon fever** p. 28 Use visuals to aid in listening Understand cause and effect	* **Stative verbs** p. 25 * **Modals of present possibility** p. 30
Review Units 1–3 p. 32			
Unit 4: Today's Trends			
Lesson A Family trends p. 36 **Lesson B Fashion trends** p. 41	* **Family trends** p. 36 *average, percent, twice as high* * **Fashion trends** p. 41 *conservative, sporty, casual*	* **Still at home** p. 37 Listen for main idea and details Determine a speaker's attitude * **You've got the look.** p. 42 Listen for gist and details Make and check predictions	* **Quantity expressions** p. 39 * **Giving advice with *could, should, ought to,* and *had better*** p. 44
Unit 5: Out and About			
Lesson A Running errands p. 46 **Lesson B This is my neighborhood.** p. 51	* **Handy Helpers** p. 46 *take a break, make an appointment, pick up/drop off* * **How's your commute?** p. 51 *running late, take a bus, stuck in traffic*	* **I'm calling because . . .** p. 47 Choose an appropriate response * **Commuters around the globe** p. 52 Listen for main idea and details Infer information	* **Polite requests with modal verbs and *mind*** p. 49 * **Intensifiers: *really, very, pretty*** p. 54
Unit 6: Student Life			
Lesson A Starting out p. 56 **Lesson B After graduation** p. 61 **Review Units 4–6** p. 66	* **Applying to college** p. 56 *apply (to/for), competition, recommendation, get accepted* * **One of these days . . .** p. 61 *the day after tomorrow, in the near future*	* **Not your typical school** p. 57 Make and check predictions Draw conclusions * **Career Day** p. 62 Infer information Listen to sequence events	* **Plans and decisions with *be going to* and *will*** p. 59 * **Predictions with *be going to* and *will*** p. 64
Review Units 10–12 p. 134			

Pronunciation	Speaking & Speaking Strategy	Reading	Writing	Communication
Reduction of present continuous *-ing* ending p. 3	**I'd like you to meet . . .** p. 4 Introducing a person Responding to introductions	**A book of memories** p. 8 Skim for the main idea Summarize a text	**The first day of class** p. 11 Write about a time you attended a class for the first time	* **Is it you?** p. 6 Guessing classmates' identities based on their habits * **Class awards** p. 11 Selecting classmates to receive different awards
Sentence stress and rhythm p. 13	**How about Thai food?** p. 14 Making and responding to suggestions	**The healthiest people in the world** p. 18 Use the title and photo to make predictions Scan to find information and complete a chart	**Restaurant review** p. 21 Write a review of a restaurant you know	* **Veronica's Restaurant** p. 16 Creating a radio advertisement for an improved restaurant * **Comparing foods** p. 21 Creating a menu for a new restaurant
Past tense vowel shifts p. 23	**I bet she's good at math.** p. 24 Talking about possibility	**Mysterious artwork** p. 28 Use photos to make predictions Identify main ideas in paragraphs	**A strange event** p. 30 Write your own ending to a story	* **Strange but true stories** p. 26 Retelling a story and discussing possibilities * **What's your theory?** p. 31 Discussing theories of unsolved world mysteries
Unstressed *of* in rapid speech p. 37	**I know what you're saying, but . . .** p. 38 Disagreeing	**Trendspotting** p.42 Make predictions Understand text organization Draw conclusions	**What's your advice?** p. 45 Write a letter requesting advice	* **What should they do?** p. 40 Giving an opinion about what a person should do * **Do you need a makeover?** p. 45 Using a survey to determine your partner's trendiness
Reduced forms of *could you* and *would you* p. 47	**I'd like to make an appointment.** p. 48 Making appointments	**Surprising neighborhoods** p. 52 Use photos to make predictions Categorize information	**Come to my neighborhood** p. 54 Write about your neighborhood	* **My *benriya* service** p. 50 Creating an errand/chore service * **Improving your community** p. 55 Proposing a plan to make your community a better place
Reduced pronunciation of *going to* p. 57	**Look on the bright side.** p. 58 Offering another point of view	**An opportunity of a lifetime** p. 62 Make and check predictions Guess the meaning of words from context	**My life now and in the future** p. 65 Write predictions about your future	* **Find someone who . . .** p. 60 Talking to people about their plans for the future * **Predicting the future** p. 65 Using a profile to make predictions about someone's future

Scope & Sequence

Unit/Lesson	Vocabulary Link	Listening	Language Link
Unit 7: Let's Celebrate			
Lesson A **Party time!** p. 70 Lesson B **Festivals and holidays** p. 75	* **Different kinds of parties** p. 70 *get together, have a good time, throw a party* * **International festivals** p. 75 *take place, first prize, perform*	* **An important day** p. 71 Listen for main idea Categorize information * **The Race of Hope** p. 76 Listen for main idea and key details Draw conclusions	* **Similarity and agreement with *so, too, either, neither*** p. 73 * **Time clauses with *before, after,* and *when*** p. 78
Unit 8: Storytelling			
Lesson A **What's the story?** p. 80 Lesson B **Happily ever after** p. 85	* **I love that show!** p. 80 *the same old story, a happy ending, predictable* * **Modern fairy tales** p. 85 *struggle, survive, incredible*	* **One sentence at a time** p. 81 Listen for details Listen to sequence events * **The moral of the story is . . .** p. 86 Identify key details in a story Draw conclusions	* **Past continuous vs. simple past** p. 83 * **Adverbs of manner** p. 88
Unit 9: The World of Work			
Lesson A **Work history** p. 90 Lesson B **Dream jobs** p. 95	* **Job qualities** p. 90 *knowledgeable, punctual, pleasant* * **Not your typical job** p. 95 *demanding, hazardous, rewarding*	* **It's hard work.** p. 91 Infer information Make and check predictions Determine a speaker's attitude * **It's worth it.** p. 96 Listen for the gist and details Infer information	* **The present perfect; *for* and *since*** p. 93 * **Verb + infinitive** p. 98
Review Units 7–9 p. 100			
Unit 10: Telecommunications			
Lesson A **Telephoning** p. 104 Lesson B **Cell-phone society** p. 109	* **Give me a call.** p. 104 *on the phone, hang up, wrong number* * **How polite are you?** p. 109 *rude, raise your voice, banned*	* **On the phone** p. 105 Choose an appropriate response * **Do you mind?** p. 110 Listen for gist Draw conclusions	* **Permission with *may, can, could, would / do you mind if . . .*** p. 107 * **Verb + gerund vs. verb + infinitive** p. 112
Unit 11: Technology Today			
Lesson A **Then and now** p. 114 Lesson B **Making life better** p. 119	* **They make life easier.** p. 114 *portable, durable, convenient* * **Too much plastic** p. 119 *reduce, prevent, restore*	* **Predicting the future** p. 115 Answer factual detail questions * **Now you see it.** p. 120 Listen for main ideas and details Listen to sequence events	* ***Used to*** p. 117 * ***As . . . as*** p. 122
Unit 12: Let's Go Somewhere!			
Lesson A **Before you go** p. 124 Lesson B **Adventures in traveling** p. 129	* **Tasks before a trip** p. 124 *empty the trash, exchange money, water the plants* * **Airline travel** p. 129 *boarding pass, carry-on, check in*	* **While we're away, could you . . . ?** p. 125 Listen for details Identify speakers * **A long weekend** p. 130 Listen for facts	* **Modal verbs of necessity** p. 127 * **The present perfect for indefinite time** p. 132
Review Units 10–12 p. 134			

Pronunciation	Speaking & Speaking Strategy	Reading	Writing	Communication
Reduced *want to* p. 71	**Do you want to go with me?** p. 72 Inviting someone to do something Accepting or refusing an invitation	**Get ready to get dirty** p. 76 Categorize information Guess the meaning of words from context	**In my country** p. 79 Write a description of a festival	* **Party planning** p. 74 Planning parties and deciding which one to attend * **An unusual holiday** p. 79 Inventing a new and unusual holiday
Was* vs. *wasn't*; *were* vs. *weren't p. 81	**So then what happened?** p. 82 Telling a story	**The Cinderella story** p. 86 Identify main ideas in paragraphs Scan for details	**A fairy-tale diary** p. 89 Tell a story from another person's point of view	* **Who's telling the truth?** p. 84 Listening to two stories and determining who is telling the truth * **Guess who I am** p. 89 Acting in English and seeing if others can guess who you are
Reduced *for* in time expressions p. 91	**Tell me a little about yourself.** p. 92 Interviewing for a job	**I love my job.** p. 96 Skim for the gist Summarize a text	**Writing about jobs** p. 98 Write about a job or a job interview	* **I really want this job!** p. 94 Role playing a real job interview * **Guess my job!** p. 99 Playing a guessing game to discover classmates' jobs
Repeating to clarify information p. 105	**May I speak to Lisa, please?** p. 106 Using the telephone	**Phone free in the car?** p. 110 Understand main ideas and supporting details Understand referents	**Opinions about cell phones** p. 112 Write your opinion about cell phones	* **Good news!** p. 108 Role playing a telephone call that brings good news * **How young is too young?** p. 113 Role playing a discussion about children and cell phones
Pronunciation of *s* in *used to* and *use / used* p. 115	**The fact is . . .** p. 116 Stating facts	**Rescue robots** p. 120 Understand a sequence of events Guess the meaning of words from context	**Comparing two products** p. 122 Write about two brands of the same item	* **Things have changed.** p. 118 Talking about how your life has changed in the last five years * **Design your own robot.** p. 123 Presenting your ideas for a new robot
Reduced *have to* and *has to* p. 125	**I can't remember where it is.** p. 126 Saying you've forgotten something	**Traveling alone** p. 130 Make predictions from titles and photos Find examples to support answers	**Travel experiences** p. 132 Write about a place you've visited	* **What should we take?** p. 128 Deciding what items to take on a camping trip * **Find someone who has . . .** p. 133 Surveying the class about their travel experiences

Language Summaries p. 138 **Grammar Notes** p. 144

1 All About Me

Lesson A The people in my life

1 Vocabulary Link How do you know each other?

A Mario is talking about four people in his life. How does he know each person? Tell a partner.

Cintra and I **went out** in the past, but she's not my girlfriend anymore. We're **just friends** now.

I met Tomas and Silvia in college. We **attended** the same school. They both live in different cities now, but we're still **close friends**.

Adrian and I **work together**. He's a nice guy, but to be honest, he's just an **acquaintance**. I don't know him very well.

Cintra was Mario's girlfriend. Now they are just friends. Adrian and Mario are coworkers. Tomas and Silvia are Mario's close friends. They went to the same college.

B In **A**, find a word or phrase in blue that has a similar meaning to each underlined word or phrase in the sentences in the chart. Write the word or phrase on the line. Compare your answers with a partner.

Words used to talk about ...		
friends	**workmates**	**classmates**
1. Cintra and I dated in the past. *went out* 2. He's someone I know, but not very well. *acquaintance* 3. We're not dating now. *just friends* 4. We're still good friends. *close friends*	5. We're coworkers. *work together*	6. We went to the same school. *attended*

C Make a list of three people you know and then show your list to a partner. Tell your partner two facts about each person on your list.

So, who is Yoon?

He's a good friend. We went to high school together.

The people in my life

Unit 1, Lesson A

1 Vocabulary Link

How do you know each other?

Warm Up

5 min

Write the words *friend* and *acquaintance* on the board. Explain that an *acquaintance* is someone who is familiar, while a *friend* is a person one knows well. Write the names of a few types of acquaintances, including *coworker* and *classmate*. Call on volunteers to name others, such as *neighbors*, *roommates*, and *teammates*. Finally, discuss places where students see acquaintances, such as outside of class, on the bus, or in their neighborhood.

A **Mario is talking about four people in his life. How does he know each person? Tell a partner.**

10–15 min

Point to the photograph of Mario, and read his name aloud. Explain that the other photographs are people Mario knows, and the speech bubbles tell how he knows them. Point out each blue word, and confirm the meaning using a synonym or phrase. After students read the descriptions to themselves, pair students. Instruct one student to say where Mario met each person, and instruct the other student to say how well Mario knows the person.

B **In A, find a word or phrase in blue that has a similar meaning to each underlined word or phrase in the sentences in the chart. Write the word or phrase on the line. Compare your answers with a partner.**

5–10 min

Read the first sentence and ask, *What blue word or phrase in **A** means the same thing as dated?* Confirm that the answer is *went out*. Students should complete the exercise individually, then compare answers with a partner. To check answers, call on volunteers to read each sentence and response.

Language Tip: *Coworker* and *co-worker*

Coworker and *co-worker* are both acceptable spellings.

Culture Tip: Friends and acquaintances

Explain to students that the concepts of *friend* and *acquaintance* can differ even between cultures of different English-speaking countries. Point out that depending on the culture, friendly behavior can be a sign of a genuine new friendship or a cultural expectation based on the situation, like kindness to guests in one's home. Add that a person who seems like a mere acquaintance in one culture may be considered a friend in another culture.

C **Make a list of three people you know and then show your list to a partner. Tell your partner two facts about each person on your list.**

15–20 min

Call on two students to read the speech bubbles. Then, label two columns *Name* and *Facts*. Under the first, write the name *Yoon* from the first speech bubble. Under the second column, write *good friend from high school*. Then model one more example by telling the name of one of your own acquaintances. Record the name under *Name*. Next, share two facts about the person, noting each under *Facts*. Pair students to do the activity, and when pairs have finished, students can share the information about their partner's acquaintances with the class.

Word Bank: More words for people we know

colleague, co-worker, client, customer, associate, contact, partner
classmate, fellow student, teammate, roommate
ex-boyfriend, ex-girlfriend, fiancé, fiancée
neighbor, family, relative, relation (close relation, distant relation), in-law

EXTRA! Writing prompt

20–30 min

Tell students to take a sheet of paper and write a paragraph to give more details about the acquaintances they named in **C**. Students should describe specifically when and how often they see these acquaintances. Tell students to use three to four of the blue or underlined vocabulary words on the page. Then students can share their paragraphs in small groups.

2 Listening How do you know Michael?

Skills: Listen for gist; Listen for details; Make and check predictions; Draw conclusions

Warm Up

5 min

List key words discussed in prior activities that define relationships, such as *family*, *neighbor*, *classmate*, and *coworker*. Call on volunteers to describe a person they know who falls under each category.

> **Teaching Tip: Scaffold with sentence frames**
>
> Prior to class discussions, post a few sentence frames that students can use to begin their responses. Frames should begin the statement, and allow students to finish it. Read the frames aloud, and model a response to get the discussion started.

A **Look at the pictures below. How do you think the people in each picture know each other? Tell a partner.**

5-10 min

Assign students to pairs. List two to three details that pairs should try to guess about each photograph, such as how the people met each other and how close they are. After partners are finished, call on students to share their responses with the class.

B **Listen to the conversations and number the pictures in A in the order (1, 2, 3) you hear them. One picture is extra.**

CD 1 Track 2 · 10-15 min

Play the first conversation, and pause. Tell students to write number 1 in the photo of people who are talking in the recording. Then continue the audio. Check answers with the class. Ask students which words helped them find the correct answers.

C **Look at your answers (1, 2, 3) in B and listen again. Which sentence is true about the people in each photo? Circle the correct answer.**

CD 1 Track 2 · 10 min

Tell students to look at the photograph they labeled number 1. Then read aloud 1a, 1b, and 1c. Ask students to choose which statement is true about photo number 1. Then repeat the process for photos 2 and 3. Play the audio again and check the correct answers.

D **Look again at the pictures in A. Who are the people? How do they know each other? Tell a partner.**

10 min

Students can work with the same partner they worked with in activity **A** to describe how the people in each photograph know each other.

Point out details that students should include, such as where and when they met, and how they know each other now.

EXTRA! Writing prompt

10 min

Tell students to write a few sentences about one person they know whom a person in the photographs makes them think of. For example, the baby boy in the photo could remind a student of their baby brother or nephew. Students should describe how they know this person, along with ways he or she is similar to the person in the photograph.

3 Pronunciation

Reduction of present continuous *-ing* ending

A **Listen to the conversations. Notice how the underlined verbs are pronounced. Then practice with a partner.**

CD 1 Track 3 · 10-15 min

Read the dialogs, carefully pronouncing the verbs ending in *-ing*. Then read it quickly with the reduced form. Ask students what the difference is. Repeat the reduced form and the class repeats after you. Assign students to pairs. As partners practice together, listen closely to their pronunciation of *-ing* at the end of verbs, and correct pronunciation when necessary.

B **Practice reading the sentences below with a partner. Use the reduced pronunciation of *-ing*.**

10 min

In the same pairs, students should read each sentence aloud to their partner. Tell partners to listen for the reduced *-in'* sound.

C **Now listen and check your pronunciation.**

CD 1 Track 4 · 10 min

Now, play the audio of the same sentences the students just practiced. Call on students to say whether their initial pronunciation was correct or incorrect.

> **Teaching Tip: Articulating when teaching pronunciation**
>
> Sometimes when teachers are teaching pronunciation, they slow down and pronounce words slowly and articulately. This does not help students understand faster speakers. For example, in class, teachers might pronounce *-ing* very clearly, but in everyday speech speakers usually say *-in'*. Try not to overemphasize pronunciation in class, as this will hinder students' comprehension later.

2 Listening **How do you know Michael?**

A Look at the pictures below. How do you think the people in each picture know each other? Tell a partner.

B Listen to the conversations and number the pictures in **A** in the order (1, 2, 3) you hear them. One picture is extra.

CD 1 Track 2

C Look at your answers (1, 2, 3) in **B** and listen again. Which sentence is true about the people in each photo? Circle the correct answer.

CD 1 Track 2

1. a. They're dating. b. They're acquaintances. c. They're just friends.
2. a. They went to the same school. b. They're just friends. c. They're coworkers.
3. a. They're in the same class. b. They're acquaintances. c. They're close friends.

D Look again at the pictures in **A**. Who are the people? How do they know each other? Tell a partner.

3 Pronunciation **Reduction of present continuous *-ing* ending**

A Listen to the conversations. Notice how the underlined verbs are pronounced. Then practice with a partner.

CD 1 Track 3

1. **Clara:** Now I remember you. How are you doing?
   Rakesh: Fine. How about you?

2. **Lisa:** Hey, Josh. Are you busy?
   Josh: Yeah. I'm writing a paper for my English class.
   Lisa: OK. Talk to you later.

B Practice reading the sentences below with a partner. Use the reduced pronunciation of *-ing.*

1. I'm trying to finish my homework.
2. I'm fixing my car.
3. She's working in her garden.
4. We're going to the movies.

C Now listen and check your pronunciation.

CD 1 Track 4

4 Speaking **I'd like you to meet . . .**

CD 1 Track 5

A Listen to the conversations. Who is meeting for the first time?

Conversation 1

Maria: Hi, Junko.

Junko: Hi, Maria. It's good to see you again! How are you?

Maria: Fine. How about you?

Junko: Pretty good.

Maria: Oh, and this is my friend Ricardo. We both go to City University.

Junko: Hey, Ricardo. Nice to meet you.

Ricardo: Yeah, you too.

Conversation 1: Junko and Ricardo are meeting for the first time.

Conversation 2

Mr. Otani: Morning, Miriam.

Miriam: Good morning, Mr. Otani. . . . Oh, Mr. Otani, I'd like you to meet Andres Garcia. He started working here yesterday. Andres, Mr. Otani is our V.P. of Sales.

Mr. Otani: Nice to meet you, Andres.

Andres: It's very nice to meet you, too, Mr. Otani.

Conversation 2: Andres and Mr. Otani are meeting for the first time.

ASK ANSWER

What does Maria say to introduce Ricardo?
What does Miriam say to introduce Andres?

Conversation 1: Maria says, "This is my friend Ricardo."
Conversation 2: Miriam says, "Mr. Otani, I'd like you to meet Andres Garcia."

B Practice both conversations with two partners.

5 Speaking Strategy

A Work in groups of three: Student A, Student B, and Student C.

1. Student A: Choose a famous person to be. Write down your identity on a piece of paper and give it to Student B.
2. Student B: Read the identity of Student A. Then introduce Student A to Student C formally.
3. Change roles and follow steps 1 and 2 again.

Useful Expressions

	Introducing a person to someone else	Responding to introductions
formal ↑	Mr. Otani, **I'd like to introduce you to** Andres.	It's (very) nice to meet you. (It's) nice / good to meet you, too.
	Mr. Otani, **I'd like you to meet** Andres.	
↓	Junko, **this is** Ricardo. Junko, **meet** Ricardo.	Nice / Good to meet you. You, too.
informal	Junko, Ricardo.	

B Now introduce the "famous friends" you met in **A** to your other classmates. Use a formal or informal style.

Ana, I'd like you to meet ________. (name)

It's nice to meet you, ________. (name)

It's nice to meet you too, Ana.

4 Speaking I'd like you to meet...

Warm Up

5 min

Ask, *In what situations or places do we need to introduce one friend to another? Do you enjoy introducing people? Why or why not?* Then ask students what they want to know about a person when they first meet him or her for the first time. Discuss responses.

Teaching Tip: Question types

Generally, try to ask open-ended and short-answer questions rather than yes/no questions when possible to maximize students' opportunities to practice language by putting thoughts into English words.

CD 1 Track 5

10 min

A Listen to the conversations. Who is meeting for the first time?

Tell students that they will read and hear a conversation among three people, and they need to figure out which two people are meeting for the first time. Play the audio. Call on students to answer the questions *Who is meeting for the first time?* Then ask students which words and phrases helped them find the answer.

Culture Tip: Terms of respect

Explain that in English-speaking cultures, terms of respect include titles for people with certain jobs (such as Dr. Lopez or Judge Li) or those who are older than others in the group (Mr. Hansen or Mrs. Fernandez). Commonly used titles are *Mr., Mrs., Ms., Miss, and Dr.* Remind students that we use these titles with last names, not first names. *Mrs. Teresa Valero* and *Mrs. Valero* are correct; *Mrs. Teresa* is incorrect.

5 min

B Practice both conversations with two partners.

Put students in groups of three to role play each conversation. Remind students to try to sound like they are speaking rather than reading. When pairs have finished, they can switch roles and read the conversations again.

ASK ANSWER

Read aloud the two questions and call on volunteers. Ask them to point to parts of text that support their answers.

5 Speaking Strategy

10–15 min

A Work in groups of three: Student A, Student B, and Student C.

Introduce the Useful Expressions, and say them for the class to repeat. Discuss situations that require formal style, like class or workplace discussions. Ask students to name some informal situations. Next, brainstorm some names of famous people that students know, such as politicians, celebrities, and athletes. Put students into groups of three, and assign the roles of A, B, and C. As students complete steps 1–3, walk around listening for the introductions and help groups stay on task. Each group should rotate roles so everyone plays each role.

5 min

B Now introduce the "famous friends" you met in A to your other classmates. Use a formal or informal style.

Explain that students will introduce their "famous friends" to classmates. Ask for volunteers to read aloud the dialog using the speech bubbles, inserting the names of famous people they reviewed in the prior activity. Finally, ask groups to turn to neighbors and use the dialog to introduce their "famous friends." Groups can rotate a few times to practice the introductions.

Culture Tip: Body language

In some cultures there is specific body language that accompanies introductions. With the class, talk about the titles, phrases, and body language used in local introductions. How do introductions differ between very young people and those who are much older? What is considered polite or rude? Ask students to share things they have heard about other cultures.

10 min

EXTRA! Correct the introduction

This activity helps students to practice using phrases for introductions. Divide the class into two teams. Write a sentence used in introductions, and include an error. For example, write, *Mr. Otani, I would like to introduce to Andres*. Call on a student from Team A. Ask the student to find and correct the error (missing *you* after introduce). If he or she gets the answer correct, Team A gets a point. If not, Team B gets a turn. Present 10 or more introduction sentences with errors. After all sentences have been corrected, the team with the most points wins.

6 Language Link

The simple present vs. the present continuous

Warm Up

5 min

On the board label two columns: *Every Day* and *Right Now*. Ask students to share a few activities or tasks they do every day. Model one response, such as *Every morning I drive to work*. Record this and other responses under *Every Day*. Next, ask students to name activities they are doing right now. Give an example, such as *I am talking*. Record this and other responses under *Right Now*.

A 5–10 min

Look at the pictures and read about Diane. Then use the words in the box to complete sentences 1, 2, and 3 below.

Review the present and present continuous. Point to the columns from the Warm Up activity, and explain that the verbs under *Every Day* are present, and those under *Right Now* are present continuous. Ask, *Which form uses -ing?* The present continuous uses *-ing*. Then, tell students to look at the pictures while you read the text. Point out the box on the upper right with the words *fact, right now, routine, temporary*, explaining vocabulary as needed. Tell students that they will use these words to complete the activity. Check answers with the class.

Teaching Tip: Include comparative examples

When students learn a new verb tense, list the tense in a column alongside other tenses, including simple present. This allows students to see how the current tense compares to those they already know. In addition, present sentence pairs that show the new tense and old tense in examples side by side. This helps students understand the meaning of the new tense.

Grammar Tip: The present continuous

The main use of the present continuous is to talk about events in progress at the time of speaking (the use taught in this unit). It is also used to talk about repeated temporary events *(I usually work in the afternoon, but this month I'm working nights.)* and processes of change *(The national economy is getting better.)*. The present continuous can also be used to talk about future time, with events that are planned: *I'm leaving on vacation tomorrow*. Along with the other continuous tenses, the present continuous is not used with verbs of thinking and sensing: *It smells good*, not *It's smelling good*.

B 5–10 min

Veronique Lesarg is a doctor. Use the simple present or present continuous to complete her profile.

Read the information in the box about time expressions. Point back to the expression *right now*, and explain that similar phrases include *this minute* or *at the moment*. Explain that actions happening now can apply to those lasting a day (*today*), a week (*this week*), or longer. Ask for volunteers to name examples, and list or supplement correct responses, such as *this year*, *this month*, and other phrases. Check responses as a class, and be sure to ask students the reason why each tense was chosen.

Grammar Tip: Verbs that are not used in present continuous

Some verbs should generally not be used in present continuous forms. These verbs involve emotions and senses. Examples include *see*, *hear*, *agree*, *believe*, *like*, and *love*. These verbs can express temporary thoughts or feelings, but unlike other temporary actions, these verbs are expressed in present tense.

C 10–15 min

Complete these sentences to make questions in the simple present or the present continuous. Use the verbs in the box.

Introduce using present and continuous present in questions. Write this pair of questions using present tense and continuous tense: *A) Why do you study at this school? B) Why are you studying for the test right now?* Underline the phrases *do you study* and *are you studying*. Ask a volunteer which question is present continuous. Students can complete the questions individually, and then check the answers as a class.

D 5–10 min

Now take turns asking and answering the questions in C with a partner.

Assign students to pairs. First, one student should ask each question, while his or her partner answers. Then, partners should change roles. Review responses with the class by calling on students and asking one of the questions.

6 Language Link **The simple present vs. the present continuous**

A Look at the pictures and read about Diane. Then use the words in the box to complete sentences 1, 2, and 3 below.

fact	right now	routine	temporary

Diane **works** in the sales department. She always **arrives** at work at 8:00 a.m.

Diane **is talking** on the telephone. She **is** also **typing** a report.

They need help in the finance department. Diane **is working** there this week only.

1. Sentence 1 states a general __fact__. Sentence 2 talks about a habit or __routine__. Use the simple present.
2. These events are happening __right now__. Use the present continuous.
3. This is a __temporary__ situation. Use the present continuous.

B Veronique Lesarg is a doctor. Use the simple present or present continuous to complete her profile.

My name (1) ___is___ (be) Veronique Lesarg. I (2) ___live___ (live) in Montreal. I (3) ___am___ (be) a pediatrician, a doctor for children. I usually (4) ___work___ (work) in a hospital, but (these days), I (5) ___am volunteering___ (volunteer) for an organization called *Doctors Without Borders*. They (6) ___send___ (send) staff to other countries. (This year,) I (7) ___am working___ (work) in Africa. (At the moment,) I (8) ___am writing___ (write) to you from a small village. There's no hospital here, so right now we (9) ___are building___ (build) one.

Time expressions and the present continuous

Find and circle the three other time expressions used with the present continuous in the profile.

C Complete these sentences to make questions in the simple present or the present continuous. Use the verbs in the box.

do	eat	have	study	take	talk

1. **A:** Why ___are you studying___ English ?
   B: I need it for my work.
2. **A:** ___Are you taking___ any other classes this term?
   B: Yes, I am—two business classes.
3. **A:** When ___do you eat___ breakfast?
   B: About 7:00, usually.
4. **A:** How many brothers and sisters ___do you have___?
   B: Four brothers and one sister.
5. **A:** What ___do you do___ on the weekends?
   B: Play golf. And relax.
6. **A:** Who ___are you talking___ to right now?
   B: Alex.

D Now take turns asking and answering the questions in **C** with a partner.

7 Communication **Is it you?**

A Take a sheet of paper and cut it into five strips.
On strips 1-3, write the following:

1. a routine you never change
2. an unusual habit
3. a general fact about yourself

Continue your list.
On strips 4 and 5, write the following:

4. an activity you are doing these days
5. why you are studying English

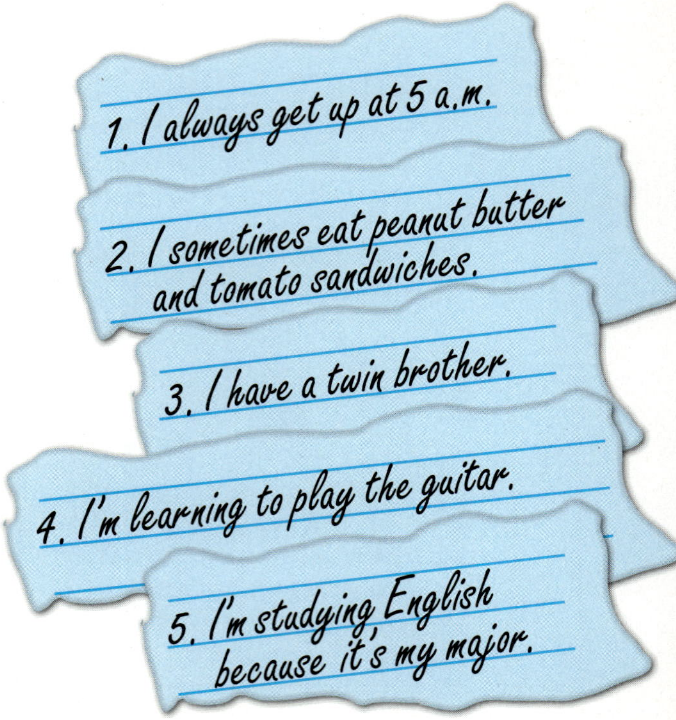

B Give your papers to the teacher. Your teacher will mix up the papers and give you five new sentences.

C Talk to your classmates.
Ask questions to find out who wrote each sentence.

D Tell the class an interesting fact you learned about one of your classmates.

7 Communication Is it you?

Warm Up

5-10 min

Write the words *routine* and *habit*. Explain that a *routine* is something a person does each day at a certain time, like getting up and eating breakfast. Point out that a habit is an action or a behavior pattern. Habits can be good or bad. Ask students for examples of good and bad habits (such as reviewing materials every day after class and smoking). In small groups, students can list examples of several routines and habits.

A 10-15 min

Take a sheet of paper and cut it into five strips. On strips 1–3, write the following:

(See Student Book page 6 for complete instructions.)

Read the instructions and the sample answers aloud. Tell students to complete the first item individually. Then ask them to share their responses aloud. As they write answers to the remaining items, you can walk around the room to spot check student's work for accuracy. Provide corrective feedback when an answer indicates a student has misunderstood a word or question.

EXTRA! Writing prompt

15-20 min

Ask students to choose one of their responses and write a journal entry about it. Explain that they should explain the information and how it affects their feelings, life, or health. Responses can be one or more paragraphs.

B 5 min

Give your papers to the teacher. Your teacher will mix up the papers and give you five new sentences.

Next, collect the sentence strips, mix them up, and redistribute them. Explain that students will form questions from the sentences to find their classmates who wrote them.

C 15-20 min

Talk to your classmates. Ask questions to find out who wrote each sentence.

Together, practice phrasing questions using the sample answers: *Do you always get up at 5 a.m.? Do you sometimes eat peanut butter and tomato sandwiches?* Ask students to stand up and circle the room, asking questions to locate the students whose responses they received.

Teaching Tip: When to correct

Avoid correcting every mistake students make. In writing samples, find one or two repeated errors or common errors to correct and explain. With each writing assignment, focus on a different point so that eventually many of them will be covered. In speaking, only correct student errors that interfere with the listeners' comprehension of words or ideas.

D 15-20 min

Tell the class an interesting fact you learned about one of your classmates.

Call out the name of a student and ask students who spoke with this classmate to share an interesting fact about him or her. Try to call out each student's name so that classmates learn at least two or three facts about every student.

Instructor's Notes

School days
Unit 1, Lesson B

1 Vocabulary Link I'm taking a class.

Warm Up

5 min

Ask students to name some activities they enjoy doing and list responses, which may include sporting activities, clubs, and music or academic lessons outside of regular classes. Next, read through the list, and ask the class how each activity is useful for students. Explain that activities and extra studies are sometimes necessary for college or job preparation.

Culture Tip: Extracurricular activities

Colleges in English-speaking countries often expect students to prove active participation in extracurricular activities. *Extracurricular activities* are those that are done in addition to regular school work and after school hours. These activities show that students have skills above studying. For example, some schools have a school newspaper. Students who participate write articles, take photographs, conduct interviews, and complete other tasks that journalists do. Other extracurricular activities include sports, language clubs, playing an instrument, volunteer work, or holding a part-time job.

A **Read the statements and match each person with his or her picture below. Then tell a partner: What is each person doing? Why?**

15 min

With the class, discuss each photograph. Ask volunteers to describe what the people in the pictures are doing. Then read sentences 1–3. Explain the vocabulary in blue, along with brief definitions or synonyms. Then pair up students to reread the sentences and identify the student each describes.

B **Complete the sentences with the correct form of the blue word(s) in A.**

15–20 min

Point to the list of the vocabulary words in blue that the class reviewed in a prior activity. Ask brief questions to reinforce students' comprehension and memory of each word. For example, ask, *What is another way to say 'I need to go to practice soccer'*? After reviewing the words, students can complete the activity. Check the answers together as a class. Give students a chance to ask questions.

Teaching Tip: Checking answers

There are many ways to check answers to activities in the student book and workbook, all with advantages and disadvantages.

- Teacher reads the answers aloud, students check their work—the fastest way, but allows the least student involvement.
- Teacher calls on students to give their answers—also fast, but may make students feel anxious.
- Students check their answers from an answer key when they are finished—allows students to work at their own pace, but requires preparation.
- Students correct each other's work—gives students more responsibility, but they may not correct all mistakes.
- Volunteers each write the answer to one question on the board—gives the class an opportunity to work with common errors, but uses a lot of class time.
- Teacher corrects outside of class—an opportunity for detailed feedback, but requires a lot of work from the teacher.

ASK ANSWER

Read the questions aloud. Students can discuss the answers with a partner and write a one- or two-sentence response. Collect responses and read them anonymously to the class.

Instructor's Notes

All About Me

Lesson B School days

1 Vocabulary Link **I'm taking a class.**

A Read the statements and match each person with his or her picture below. Then ask a partner: What is each person doing? Why?

1. "My parents think playing sports is important. So, after school, I have soccer practice every day. I also take tennis lessons for an hour on the weekend."
2. "I'm taking a class to prepare for the university entrance exam. The class meets for three hours a day. It's a lot of work, but I need help to pass the test."
3. "Two months ago, I was failing math—getting D's and F's. Now a tutor comes to my house and helps me with my homework, and I'm finally getting a good grade in the class!"

B Complete the sentences with the correct form of the blue word(s) in **A**.

1. I can't go to the movies with you. I ___have___ baseball ___practice___ this afternoon.
2. Tyler never studies, so now he is ___getting___ a bad ___grade___ in all his classes.
3. Maiko studied really hard and she ___passed___ the test!
4. This term, I'm ___taking___ two business classes at City University.
5. Our English class ___meets___ on Tuesdays and Thursdays.
6. To ___prepare___ for tomorrow's class, please read pages 20 to 45.
7. My piano ___lesson___ is only for 30 minutes. After that, we can go to the store.
8. Liam ___is failing OR failed___ his biology class, so he has to retake it next term.
9. Nico is a ___tutor___ . He helps children with their homework.

ASK ANSWER

1. How are you doing in school? Do you get good grades?
2. Are you taking any special classes or lessons now (or did you in the past)? If yes, why? How often do (*or* did) the classes meet?

2 Listening GBL Learning Center

A Look at the places listed below. Why do people go to these places? What do they learn? Discuss your ideas with a partner.

a language institute | a sports camp | a test preparation center

B You are going to hear a radio ad. Listen. Which place in **A** is the ad talking about? What does the place help people do? *a test preparation center. It helps people prepare for exams.*

CD 1 Track 6

C Listen to the rest of the radio ad. Match each person to his or her job and his or her results. Some answers are extra. One answer is used two times.

CD 1 Track 7

1. 

2. 

3. 

a. doctor
b. engineer
c. soccer player
d. student

e. score went up 50 points
f. score went up 15 points
g. passed the first time
h. failed and then passed

The first woman is probably studying in the U.S. now because she got a better score on the TOEFL. The man probably moved up in his job and now makes more money. The second woman is probably in medical school.

ASK ANSWER
Think about the three people in the listening and their results. What do you think they are doing now?

3 Reading A book of memories

A Skim the reading on page 9. Look quickly at the title, photo, and the first and last sentence in each paragraph. Then complete the sentence below.

A yearbook is _____ for a certain school year.

a. a list of the most popular students
b. a book used to prepare for exams
(c.) a collection of student photos and activities
d. a record of students' grades

2 Listening GBL Learning Center

Skills: Listen for gist; Listen for details; Draw conclusions

Warm Up

5–10 min

Ask, *What tests do people need to take for a job or to get into college?* Students might list national exams, school essays, or international English exams, such as IELTS or TOEFL. Ask students if they plan to take one of these tests or if they took one already. How do people study for these exams?

A 5–10 min **Look at the places listed below. Why do people go to these places? What do they learn? Discuss your ideas with a partner.**

Read each term, with students repeating after you. Explain each term, emphasizing that these are all places people go for intensive study or practice. Tell students that words like *center* and *institute* often are used in names of places for learning or training, as well as the words *academy, clinic, college,* and *school*. Explain that *camp* is usually used for sports, though *computer camps* do exist. Then pair up students to discuss the questions. Call on pairs to share their answers.

Teaching Tip: Wait time

When you call on students to respond, give them several seconds to produce an answer. Sometimes students need a few moments to process and then say their response in English.

B CD 1 Track 6, 5–10 min **You are going to hear a radio ad. Listen. Which place in A is the ad talking about? What does the place help people do?**

Read the questions with the class. Then play the audio. Replay if necessary. Call on a student to give the answer. Ask which words and phrases helped him or her find the answer.

C CD 1 Track 7, 10–15 min **Listen to the rest of the radio ad. Match each person to his or her job and his or her results. Some answers are extra. One answer is used two times.**

Tell students that each person in the photos holds one or more of the jobs listed. Read the list of jobs aloud. Then read e. through h. Explain that each statement describes one or more of the people shown. Finally, play the audio. Check answers as a class.

ASK ANSWER

Students can work in small groups to discuss the question and then report their ideas to the class.

3 Reading A book of memories

Skills: Skim for the main idea; Make and check predictions; Summarize a text

Warm Up

5 min

Ask students what objects or situations remind them of friends and teachers from prior school years. Ask whether students save objects like notes, pictures, programs from plays, or letters from friends. Then, explain that a *yearbook* is a book that shows photographs of people and events over a school year. Point out the photo on page 9.

Language Tip: Compound words

Explain that a *compound word* is one word made up of two or more words put together. Write the example *yearbook*. Circle *year*, and underline *book*. Repeat that a yearbook is a book that represents a year in school. Point out that compound words can often be figured out by examining the meanings of the words that have been combined.

A 5–10 min **Skim the reading on page 9. Look quickly at the title, photo, and the first and last sentence in each paragraph. Then complete the sentence below.**

Review tips on skimming. For example, suggest that students form questions to answer as they skim, and that they look for keywords to spot important sections of text. When they find answers and important sections, remind students to slow down and read for information, and then speed up again until they locate the next section of text that needs careful attention.

B 15-20 min **Read the article and check your answer in A.**

Students can read the article individually. Then assign students to pairs to share their original responses to **A**. Then ask pairs to confirm the correct response together. Ask students if there is any vocabulary they do not understand.

C 10-15 min **Complete the following summary using words from the article in B. Compare your answers with a partner.**

This activity asks students to locate specific information in the reading. Point out that students do not need to reread every word to complete the sentences. Explain that they should scan the article for keywords and phrases. Point to the phrase *of the school year* in the first frame. Ask students to scan the first paragraph of the article for this phrase, and then point to it. Next, ask the class to identify the word that completes the answer sentence. Students can work individually to complete the remaining sentences.

5-10 min

EXTRA! Rephrase sentences

Now that students have read the article thoroughly and completed activity **C**, check comprehension by asking them to rephrase the sentences in **C**. Do the first example. Write, *A yearbook shows important events from the school year*. Point out that the meaning is the same as *A yearbook is a record of the school year*. Allow students to work in pairs, and assign each pair two sentences. When they are finished, check responses as a class by calling on volunteers.

ASK ANSWER

Ask students to tell the class about their own school and whether or not students received yearbooks. Ask students to name reasons why students may or may not wish to have a yearbook record. Finally, have students work in small groups to list three sections that they would include in a yearbook and why.

20-30 min

EXTRA! Post-reading

1. Tell students to think about details included in yearbooks. For example, ask, *Why include the photograph and name of the Class Clown or Most Likely to Succeed?*
2. Assign students to small groups. Each student should label a sheet of paper with his or her name. Tell students to write a message on the labeled sheet of each group member as if they are signing his or her yearbook. Ask, *What would we want to tell close friends? What might we tell a student we don't know very well?* When students have completed the activity, briefly discuss how students felt when they read the signatures. Discuss whether this is a worthwhile tradition and why.

Teaching Tip: Interactive writing

Help students to connect with a topic through interactive writing with teachers and peers. Dialog journals are a great way to encourage discussion about a topic. The student writes an entry about a topic and follows it with questions for the reader. The reader responds in writing, creating a dialog that can go back and forth. Other interactive writing examples include letters, email messages, or lesson-specific messages, such as yearbook signatures.

20-30 min

EXTRA! Discussion questions

1. In some cultures, schools do not have extracurricular activities.
   a. Is this true in your culture?
   b. What extracurricular activities were, or would be, the most popular at your school? Why?
2. Do you, or would you, like to have your photograph displayed where people can see it for many years to come? Why or why not?
3. Do you like to look at photographs of people you know? Why?

20-25 min

EXTRA! Writing prompt

1. Write about your fondest memory of high school.
2. Write a paragraph describing yourself. Include a photo.

20-30 min

EXTRA! Additional reading

For additional practice scanning for facts, see Heinle's Footprint Reading Library *The Art of Making Silk.*

For additional practice making predictions, see Heinle's Footprint Reading Library *Flying Pumpkins!*

Instructor's Notes

B Read the article and check your answer in **A**.

Yearbooks in the United States

Most high schools in the United States publish a yearbook once a year, usually in the spring. It is a record of the school year—a "book of memories" for the students.

Inside a yearbook is each student's photo. The seniors are graduating soon, and their photos appear first. Next are the juniors. They are one year behind the seniors. Then come the sophomores, or second-year students. The last photos are the first-year students, the freshmen. The yearbook is not only about students. The teachers have photos, too.

The yearbook also has photos and descriptions of sports teams, academic subjects, and extracurricular activities. These are activities students do after school, such as the chess club and Spanish club. There is even a yearbook club. Students in this club write, design, and take photos all year for the yearbook. At the end of the year, the book is printed.

In the yearbook, some students receive special titles. The seniors vote and choose the "class clown" (a funny student), the "most likely to succeed" (a student who got the best grades), and the "best dressed" (a student with a good fashion sense). There are also other awards and categories.

Students usually sign each other's yearbooks. This is especially important for the seniors because they are graduating. Students write notes to each other, such as, "We had a lot of fun," or "I'll never forget you." They also write about all the fun and funny experiences they shared in school together.

C Complete the following summary using words from the article in **B**. Compare your answers with a partner.

A yearbook is a (1) ___record___ of the school year. You will find each student's (2) ___photo___ in a yearbook. Photos of the (3) ___seniors___ come first. The yearbook features (4) ___sports___ teams, academic subjects, and extracurricular activities. There are many clubs: the (5) ___yearbook___ club makes the yearbook. Seniors vote and give some students (6) ___titles___ such as "class clown." Students (7) ___sign___ their classmates' yearbooks. The yearbook is truly a book of (8) ___memories___ .

ASK ANSWER

Did/Does your high school have a yearbook? If yes, what is it like?
If no, would you like to have one? What would you put in your school yearbook?

4 Language Link **Review of the simple past**

A Read about Diego's high school experiences. Underline the regular simple past verbs. Circle the irregular ones. Then tell a partner: what happened to Diego?

> In high school, I studied a lot and got good grades. But the first time I took the university entrance exam, I failed. That was hard. To prepare for the next exam, I went to a test prep center. Two good things happened there: I met my girlfriend in the class. And the next time, I passed the entrance exam!

B Look at the high school photos of these two famous people. Complete each profile with the correct past tense verbs from the box. Then fill in their names.

act	become	die	go	take	write

Her mother (1) ___died___ when she was six years old. In high school, she (2) ___took___ drama and dance classes. She (3) ___went___ to New York in 1977, and later she (4) ___became___ a very famous singer. She also (5) ___wrote___ books for children and (6) ___acted___ in movies.

Her name is (7) ___Madonna___ Louise Ciccone.

be	divorce	enter	move	run	win

He (1) ___was___ born in Hawaii to an American mother and a Kenyan father. His parents (2) ___divorced___ and later he (3) ___moved___ with his family to Indonesia and then again to the U.S. In 1988, he (4) ___entered___ Harvard Law School and in 2008, he (5) ___ran___ for President of the United States. He (6) ___won___ .

His name is (7) ___Barack___ ___Obama___ .

C Choose a person in **B** and write 3 or 4 questions about him or her. Then ask your partner the questions.

> In high school, what classes did she take?

Answers will vary.

____

____

____

4 Language Link

Review of the simple past

Warm Up

5 min

Briefly review past tense verbs by discussing activities that students enjoyed in prior school years. Model a few examples of activities you enjoyed in complete sentences. Write statements, such as, *I played sports. I read books. I studied a lot. I had three close friends.* Underline the verbs, and identify each as regular or irregular. Next, go around the room, so each student can share one activity they enjoyed in past tense.

Teaching Tip: Recycle and review

Vary the ways you recycle and review what students have learned. During warm ups, move quickly and do activities, such as labeling parts of speech, choosing or creating the correct verb form, fill in the blank, true or false, and others like this. Each of these question types can be used to quiz students on grammar points or vocabulary.

Grammar Tip: Simple past

The simple past is used for facts, routines, and actions completed in the past.

A Read about Diego's high school experiences. Underline the regular simple past verbs. Circle the irregular ones. Then tell a partner: what happened to Diego?

15-20 min

Read the paragraph aloud. Guide students through the first sentence. Then students can continue working individually. To check answers, copy the paragraph on the board, and ask volunteers to mark the correct responses.

B Look at the high school photos of these two famous people. Complete each profile with the correct past tense verbs from the box. Then fill in their names.

10 min

Tell students to work individually to fill in the blanks. If they have difficulty with the irregular forms, allow them to use the Grammar Notes on page 145 of their books. When all students are ready, check answers with the class. Then assign students to pairs to practice the sentences orally.

EXTRA! Verb chart

10-15 min

Ask students to fill out a verb chart to keep handy. Label two columns: *Simple Present* and *Simple Past*. List about 15 common verbs under *Simple Present*, and direct students to fill in the forms under *Simple Past*. Check them together. Recommend that students keep the list handy. When they need to use either form in the future, refer them to the chart to either find the verb in question, or record new verbs that are not already listed.

EXTRA! Writing prompt

15 min

Students can write a brief profile (like the ones in **B**) about themselves, someone they know, or a famous person. They should include interesting facts and details and write in the past tense.

C Choose a person in B and write 3 or 4 questions about him or her. Then ask your partner the questions.

10-15 min

Read the example question in the callout. Together, brainstorm topics that might be of interest, such as subjects studied, friends, hobbies or extracurricular activities, former jobs, and talents of the individuals described in the paragraph. Tell students that they may use these topics as they write questions.

Instructor's Notes

5 Writing The first day of class

Warm Up

5 min

Ask students to recall their first day of English class and call on volunteers to share what they remember. Then read the description of a student's first day. Ask, *How was your first day similar to this student's? How was it different?*

A **Think about your first day in English class. On a separate piece of paper, explain what happened on that day.**

10 min

Tell students to prepare by listing details about people, discussions, or other aspects of the first day of English class. The list can be notes, not complete sentences. Students should review their list and decide which details to include in their writing. Remind students to write about how each detail affected their feelings about class.

B **Exchange papers with a partner. Tell the class about your partner's memories.**

10–15 min

Students should read their partner's papers and ask questions. Go around the room calling on each student to share a few details about his or her partner's first day in class.

B Teaching Option **Support/challenge**

To challenge stronger students, ask them to write a one-page essay. To make the activity easier for students who need support, ask them to write a paragraph. If necessary, remind students about the parts of an essay or a paragraph.

B Teaching Option **Speaking**

Emphasize speaking in this activity by having students interview each other about their first day of English class using details in their partner's paper as a basis for questions. Ask students to form five questions to ask their partners, write the questions, and then ask them. Students should record their partner's response by each question. Then call on each pair to share a few responses with the class.

6 Communication Class awards

Warm Up

5 min

Ask volunteers to describe people who are either friendly or funny, or who demonstrate great fashion sense, art skills, or singing abilities. Then, remind students that yearbooks single out students whose peers think they best display these qualities.

Check out the World Link Video. Practice your English online at http://elt.heinle.com/worldlink

A **Work with a partner. Look at the awards below. Invent one more award for number 6.**

10 min

Give pairs time to review the awards and brainstorm one more. Tell them to think of traits that make a person stand out, such as being helpful or dependable. Go around the room, and ask each pair to name the trait they listed.

Teaching Tip: Discussing prompts

Discuss writing prompts before students begin writing. Class discussions help students to prepare their thoughts, as well as supply concepts and vocabulary they may need for the writing assignment.

B **Who would be the best person in your class to receive each award in A? Write the names under the awards.**

10–15 min

Students can work with the same partner as in activity **A**. They should discuss students from class who might receive each award, and then choose one name to write in the blank.

C **Tell the class your choices in A. Explain your reasons.**

10 min

Starting with the first award, call on several pairs to tell which classmate they named and why. Then continue to the next award. For the last award, call on as many pairs as time allows to share which award they listed.

Large Class Option

For large classes, pairs can write the names of classmates who should receive each award, along with the reasons. Ask pairs to record their names at the top and pass their papers to the front of the classroom. For each award, read a few responses.

Next, play *Guess Who?* Use information from the responses to describe a person in the class or a person described during activity A. For example, *Some people feel this person should receive the Class Artist award. She always does artistic projects that are creative and colorful.* Call on volunteers to name the student.

World Link Video and World Link Website

Remind students of the value of further practice outside the classroom. Ask students who have watched the video or done online practice to share their experiences.

5 Writing The first day of class

A Think about your first day in English class. On a separate piece of paper, explain what happened on that day.

B Exchange papers with a partner. Tell the class about your partner's memories.

I remember our first English class. I didn't know anyone. I sat next to Anika. She was really nice. When the class started, the teacher asked me a question but I got nervous and couldn't answer. Later, we played a game and I talked a lot.

6 Communication Class awards

A Work with a partner. Look at the awards below. Invent one more award for number 6.

1. Name: ____________________

2. Name: ____________________

3. Name: ____________________

4. Name: ____________________

5. Name: ____________________

6. Name: ____________________

B Who would be the best person in your class to receive each award in **A**? Write the names under the awards.

C Tell the class your choices in **A**. Explain your reasons.

> We chose Carlos as the "friendliest." On the first day of class, he said "hello" to everyone. He also helped . . .

Check out the World Link video.

Practice your English online at http://elt.heinle.com/worldlink

2 Let's Eat!

Lesson A Foods we like

1 Vocabulary Link Street foods

A Read about these street foods. Which one(s) would you like to try? Why?

Street Foods
from around the World

Are you hungry and looking for a fast, inexpensive, and tasty snack? Here are three traditional street foods from around the world.

***Paletas* (Mexico)**

What it is: A popsicle, usually made with juice or water and pieces of fresh fruit. Sometimes, red chili pepper is also added to a paleta. It's the perfect mix of sweet and spicy flavors!

***Doner kebap* (Turkey)**

What it is: Pieces of juicy meat (usually lamb or chicken) served on a thin piece of bread with different sauces. It's delicious!

***Maeng da* (Thailand)**

What it is: Water beetles (a kind of insect) are fried in oil and then salt is added. The result: a salty snack that tastes like potato chips!

Food • 27

> ***-y*** = "full of something": salty, spicy, oily, healthy, tasty, juicy

B Answer the questions below with a partner.

1. Read the note above. Then find two other adjectives in **A** that end in *-y*.
2. Choose four words from the note. Think of a matching food for each one.

C What's your favorite street food? Tell your partner. Describe the food's taste.

> Near my house, you can buy churros on the street. They're fried pieces of dough with sugar added. They're sweet and delicious!

Describing how something tastes

This soup **is** tasty/delicious/terrible/sweet/salty/spicy.

This tea **tastes** good/delicious/terrible/sweet/salty/spicy.

This meat **tastes like** chicken.

Foods we like

Unit 2, Lesson A

1 Vocabulary Link Street foods

Warm Up

5 min

Ask for a volunteer to explain *street food*. Then discuss the topic by asking students to name some local street foods. As students name foods, list them.

A 10–15 min

Read about these street foods. Which one(s) would you like to try? Why?

Point to each of the pictures and read the name of the food and country. Ask for a volunteer to identify each country on a map if available. With the class, read the descriptions and explain the words in blue, pointing to words that correspond with images shown, such as *stick* and *bread*. Finally, point to the first photograph and ask, *Would you try this food? Why?* Model answering the question with your own opinion using the new vocabulary: *I would try the Maeng da because I like potato chips*. Then assign students to pairs to ask and answer this question about each of the foods.

B 5–10 min

Answer the questions below with a partner.

Tell students they will name adjectives that describe foods and drinks. Read the adjectives in the i-box, and model the activity. Write *ice*, then write *icy*. Point out that *icy* means *has ice*. Students can work in pairs to list additional adjectives that end in *-y*. Pairs should list four adjectives and use each one to describe a food. Give an example, such as *icy* describes *ice cream*.

Teaching Tip: Connect oral language to visuals

When possible, point to visuals that match words in the text you read or words you say as you explain. Seeing an image helps students remember a word and connect it to its meaning.

C 15–20 min

What's your favorite street food? Tell your partner. Describe the food's taste.

Ask the question aloud, and read the sample response in the speech bubble. Then read the sentences in the orange box. In pairs, students should use these words to describe how their favorite street food tastes. Then pairs can share their partners' responses in small groups.

Teaching Tip: Scaffold activities

For learners who have lower levels of language proficiency, provide a word bank to help them complete sentence frames. In random order, list the words that students will need. Students may be able to choose the correct words, even if they cannot produce the words or spellings themselves after listening.

Language Tip: Chips and fries

Explain to students that English speakers from different countries sometimes name the same food in different ways. For example, *chips* in England refers to soft potatoes in a rectangular shape. In the United States, this food is called *French fries*, and the word *chips* is used to describe thin, crunchy potato slices.

Culture Tip: Eating on the run

Fast food is food that can be purchased and eaten quickly. In some cultures, it is completely acceptable to eat and walk at the same time. In other cultures, eating and walking is considered rude. Touching your food with your hands is another example. In some cultures it is acceptable, and in other cultures it is rude—touching food with your left hand is especially rude in some cultures. Ask students what food taboos they have in their culture and who they see doing these things.

5–10 min

EXTRA! Advertising foods

Bring in advertisements for food products in English from newspapers, magazines, or online sources. With students, identify and explain the words and phrases used to make food sound appetizing, such as *creamy, rich, spicy, crunchy*, etc. Point out any high-frequency collocates that come up, such as *fresh salads, rich chocolate, smooth yogurt, creamy ice cream*, etc. Write the examples on the board for students to refer to as they work in pairs to describe at least four foods they eat regularly. Students should write down their partner's four items (both noun and adjective) to share with the class.

Word Bank: Describing how food is cooked

fried	sautéed
baked	roasted
boiled	steamed
grilled	

2 Listening

Foods of the southern United States

Skills: Make and check predictions; Listen for facts (including negative factual information)

Warm Up

5 min

Review the adjectives used to describe food. List five or six foods that students know, and call on students to describe the taste. Write the adjectives students say.

Teaching Tip: Preview vocabulary

Before listening to or reading new material, preview keywords, words that cannot be figured out by context, or words that are highlighted. This helps students understand the message by giving them information to build on.

A Look at the four photos below. What do you think each food tastes like? Tell your partner.

5-10 min

Tell students they will need to use background knowledge about foods they know to guess what the foods pictured taste like. Ask if any students have had these foods before. With a partner, students should name familiar foods that might taste similar to the foods pictured in the photos.

B Listen to Bill and Marta's conversation. Complete the information about the food.

CD 1 Track 8
10-15 min

Tell students they will hear a conversation between two people, one of whom has tried the foods in the photographs. Tell students to listen carefully for the foods Marta names to fill in the blanks. Play the audio one or more times, and then check answers with the class.

C Listen to the rest of the conversation. Write the words used to describe the foods. Then circle the food Marta *didn't* like. Why didn't she like it?

CD 1 Track 9
10 min

Tell students that now they will hear the whole conversation, and that they should listen closely to how Marta describes the foods. Point out the butter on the grits and ask, *How can we describe a food that tastes like butter? Buttery.* Play the audio at least twice, allowing time in between for students to mark their answers.

ASK ANSWER

Students can discuss these questions in small groups. Then follow up with a whole-class discussion. Ask questions that will prompt students to use the vocabulary to describe their regional foods.

EXTRA! Ask classmates a question

10-15 min

Tell students to circle the room asking classmates the name of a food they would like to try. Students can record both the classmates' names and their responses. Next, lead a class discussion about the responses. Ask questions like, *What food does Logan want to try? Which classmates want to try a new fruit? How many classmates want to try a vegetable?* Discuss responses aloud.

3 Pronunciation

Sentence stress and rhythm

A Listen and repeat the sentences. Note where the stress falls.

CD 1 Track 10
10-15 min

Review the idea of stress—important words or parts of words that sound "louder" or "stronger" in a sentence. Tell students to listen for the stress in the two sentences. Play the audio several times. Say the sentences for the class to repeat in chorus, then in rows, and individually. Then assign students to a partner and tell them to take turns reading the sentences several times. Walk around listening for correct stress. Remind students that speaking with correct sentence stress and rhythm will help make their English sound more natural.

Teaching Tip: Word stress

Unlike many other languages, English does not have one set pattern for which syllables receive stress in a word. Students need to learn the correct stress for each new vocabulary item they acquire.

B Circle the stressed syllables in these sentences. Then listen and check your answers. Practice saying the sentences with a partner.

CD 1 Track 11
10 min

Ask students which types of words were stressed in the sentences in **A**. *Nouns and adjectives.* Tell students to pay close attention to these words as they do this activity.

2 Listening Foods of the southern United States

A Look at the four photos below. What do you think each food tastes like? Tell your partner.

CD 1 Track 8

B Listen to Bill and Marta's conversation. Complete the information about the food.

CD 1 Track 9

C Listen to the rest of the conversation. Write the words used to describe the foods. Then circle the food Marta *didn't* like. Why didn't she like it? Marta didn't like the Mississippi mud pie because it was too sweet.

1. The chicken was delicious.
2. The grits tasted like oatmeal with a strong buttery flavor.
3. The tomatoes were oily, but they went well with the chicken and grits.
4. The dessert was a thick, chocolate pie. It was too sweet.

ASK ANSWER

Do these four foods sound good to you? Why or why not?
Is your hometown (or region) famous for a special food? Describe it.

3 Pronunciation Sentence stress and rhythm

CD 1 Track 10

A Listen and repeat the sentences. Note where the stress falls.

ORanges are SWEETer than GRAPEfruit.   PoTAto chips are SALtier than CRACKers.

CD 1 Track 11

B Circle the stressed syllables in these sentences. Then listen and check your answers. Practice saying the sentences with a partner.

1. Math is harder than English.
2. Apples are juicier than carrots.
3. The curry is spicier than the chili.
4. January is colder than February.

4 Speaking **How about Thai food?**

CD 1 Track 12

A Listen to the conversation. Then answer the questions.

1. What are Jose and Jill going to eat for dinner? Thai food
2. How do Jose and Jill make suggestions? Underline the words.

Jose: So, Jill, where do you want to go to dinner tonight?

Jill: I don't know. Why don't we go to the pizza place on the corner?

Jose: Pizza again? I don't really feel like it.

Jill: OK, how about Thai food instead?

Jose: Fine with me. Where do you want to go?

Jill: Well, Thai House is near here. And there's another place — The Thai Cafe — but it's downtown.

Jose: Thai House is closer. Let's go there.

Jill: Sounds good!

B Practice the conversation with a partner.

5 Speaking Strategy

Useful Expressions

<table>
<tr><th colspan="3">Making suggestions</th><th>Responding to suggestions</th></tr>
<tr><td colspan="3">Statements</td><td rowspan="5">Great idea!
(That) sounds good (to me).
Fine with me.
I don't really want to.
I don't really feel like it.</td></tr>
<tr><td>Let's</td><td>have</td><td>Thai food for dinner.</td></tr>
<tr><td colspan="3">Questions</td></tr>
<tr><td>Why don't we</td><td>have</td><td rowspan="2">Thai food for dinner?</td></tr>
<tr><td>How / What about</td><td>having</td></tr>
</table>

A Study the Useful Expressions. Then complete the dialogs below with a partner. Sometimes more than one answer is possible.

1. **A:** Let's stop at that cafe for coffee.
   B: Sounds good!
2. **A:** What time do you want to meet in the morning?
   B: Why don't we meet at 7:00?
   A: That's a little early. How/What about meeting at 8:00 instead?
   B: Fine with me. See you then.
3. **A:** What do you want to do today?
   B: How/What about going to the beach?
   A: I don't feel like it. Let's see a movie instead.
   B: OK, sounds good.

B Get into a group of three and do the following.

1. On your own: think of two restaurants that are good for a meal.
2. Suggest one of the restaurants to your partners. They can accept or refuse. If a person refuses, he or she should say why and suggest another restaurant.
3. Change roles and repeat steps 1 and 2.

4 Speaking How about Thai food?

Warm Up

5 min

Ask students to talk about their favorite restaurant. Ask them why it is their favorite place to eat out. Students can describe the food, the service, or the décor.

CD 1 Track 12

10 min

A Listen to the conversation. Then answer the questions.

Tell students they will hear a conversation between two friends who are making plans to go to a restaurant. Play the audio one or more times while students read along. Students should complete the questions independently. Check the answers as a class. Explain that *Let's* is more direct and informal, while *Why don't we...?* And *How about...?* are slightly more formal.

5 min

B Practice the conversation with a partner.

Assign pairs to practice the dialog. Then students should switch roles. Finally, they should change partners and practice the dialog with their new partner.

B Teaching Option

Instead of role playing the dialog as written, each pair of students can choose three suggestions in the dialog and rewrite them to form new suggestions. Then partners share their dialogs with another pair.

5 Speaking Strategy

10–15 min

A Study the Useful Expressions. Then complete the dialogs below with a partner. Sometimes more than one answer is possible.

Introduce the expressions in the box, saying them for the class to repeat. Point out that each sentence under *Making suggestions* is a way of suggesting a plan or idea, and each sentence under *Responding to suggestions* is a polite way of saying yes or no. Put students in pairs to complete the dialogs using the Useful Expressions. Check answers as a class, and ask for alternative answers in sentences where more than one is possible.

Culture Tip: Rejecting suggestions

When rejecting a suggestion, native speakers of English usually give an explanation—even if it's not completely honest. Omitting an excuse can sound too blunt or rude.

In some Asian cultures (like China and Japan), it is rude to reject a suggestion directly. An invitee may not commit to the suggestion while never saying *no* directly. Do not push for another answer. It is considered rude to make someone commit when they are trying to be polite to you by not saying no.

15 min

B Get into a group of three and do the following.

(See Student Book page 14 for complete instructions.)

Tell students to think of their three favorite restaurants and why they like them. Call on three volunteers to read the speech bubbles. Then, put students into groups and explain that the group will choose which one of the favorite restaurants to go to. Require that each group member make a suggestion or express an alternative choice. After groups practice and change roles and repeat, they can share their restaurant choice with the class.

Word Bank: More places to eat

café, coffee shop, tea room, coffee house, bakery
diner, deli *or* delicatessen
trattoria, bistro, tapas bar
steakhouse, barbeque restaurant
snack bar, food court, concession stand, cafeteria
raw bar, oyster bar, sushi bar
pub, bar and grill, tavern, inn

Instructor's Notes

6 Language Link

The comparative form of adjectives

Warm Up

5 min

Ask students to recall adjectives they have learned in this lesson. List the adjectives, and add *delicious*. Name a food, such as chicken, and give an example description: *chicken is delicious*. Repeat by naming several foods that students can describe for the class using adjectives.

A Read the advertisement. Underline all the adjectives. Then tell a partner: How are the underlined adjectives similar? How are they different?

10-15 min

With the class, read the advertisement. Give students time to complete the underlining task. Then pair students to compare answers. Walk around and look at students' work. Call on pairs to read the first two adjectives, and write these on the board. Repeat twice with the remaining adjectives. Ask students to tell you the difference between the pairs of adjectives on the board. Point out that three of them end in *-er*. Confirm that *-er* at the end of the words means *more than*. Together, work out the rules for the comparative form of adjectives. Use and show students the explanations and examples in the Grammar Notes on page 145.

B Complete the chart with the missing words. Then check your answers with a partner.

10-15 min

Explain that the underlined words in **A** are *comparatives*: adjectives that compare things or show how they are different. Write the word pair *big* and *bigger*. Demonstrate their meanings with nearby objects, such as books. Hold up a book, and say, *This is big.* Hold up the larger book and say, *This is bigger*. Remind students that the *-er* at the end means *more.* Explain that some comparisons are formed by adding the word *more* before the adjective instead of *-er* at the end. Write the example word pair *delicious* and *more delicious*. After students fill in the chart, check answers together.

EXTRA! Name the comparison

15-20 min

Help students practice forming comparisons. List several adjectives from completed activities, such as *spicy*, *delicious*, *sweet*, *salty*, *oily*, *large*, *good*, and others. Ask volunteers to name the comparative form that means *more than*. List each comparative by the corresponding adjective. Tell students to copy the list onto a sheet of paper. Then put students in pairs to quiz one another by having one student name the adjective and the other name the comparative. Finally, when pairs have reviewed each adjective, instruct them to quiz each other on the spellings of comparatives.

C Complete the sentences with the comparative form of the adjective in parentheses.

10-15 min

Read the example. Point out the word *than.* Explain that *than* is often used in sentences that compare two things. Then read the i-box and the example sentence again. Students should complete the sentences individually. Check answers with the class.

C Teaching Option Support/challenge

Students can work in pairs to practice saying sentences using comparatives. They should listen for their partner's answer and see if they have written the same one. For stronger students, pairs should talk about real foods they have eaten. Do the first example: *Indian food is spicier than Japanese food.*

Language Tip: *good, better, best*

Explain that while comparatives require either *more* before a word or *-er* after a word, it is incorrect to use the two together. Write an incorrect example: *Rice is more healthier than bread*. Correct the example with input from students.

D Think of foods to compare using the adjectives in the box. Then say sentences comparing the foods with a partner.

10-15 min

Ask a volunteer to read the adjectives. Individually, students should review the list and write down two foods that each describes. Then assign students to pairs to practice saying sentences about the foods their partners wrote down.

World Link

Ask students to name popular desserts in different countries or local desserts they like. Then read the question and confirm the answer.

Instructor's Notes

6 Language Link **The comparative form of adjectives**

A Read the advertisement. Underline all the adjectives.Then tell a partner: How are the underlined adjectives similar? How are they different?

The pairs of adjectives all describe the restaurant and its food. Both large and larger, for example, describe the size of the portions. Spicy and spicier both describe how the chicken tastes.

*How the adjectives are different: Larger, spicier, more spacious, and better all show that now the food has more of that particular characteristic or quality. (The portions were **large**. Now they are **larger**.)*

B Complete the chart with the missing words. Then check your answers with a partner.

The comparative form of adjectives					
One syllable		Two syllables		Three or more syllables	
sweet	sweeter	simple	*simpler*	*refreshing*	more refreshing
large	*larger*	*spicy*	spicier	delicious	*more delicious*
big	bigger	*crowded*	more crowded	interesting	*more interesting*

Notice! The comparative form of *good* is *better*.

C Complete the sentences with the comparative form of the adjective in parentheses.

1. The red curry is ___*spicier*___ than the green curry. (spicy)
2. Cherry candy is ___*sweeter*___ than real cherries. (sweet)
3. Wow! This apple pie is ___*more delicious*___ than my Mom's! (delicious)
4. Our English teacher is ___*more popular*___ than our math teacher. (popular)
5. You're a ___*better*___ cook than I am. (good)
6. She is really embarrassed. Her face is ___*redder*___ than an apple! (red)

The comparative is often followed by *than* when comparing two things.

D Think of foods to compare using the adjectives in the box. Then say sentences comparing the foods with a partner.

good healthy refreshing salty sweet

Apples are healthier than potato chips.

WORLD LINK

Hot bananas served with a spicy chocolate sauce is a popular dessert in…
a. Morocco
b. Guatemala
c. India

7 Communication Veronica's Restaurant

A Look at the pictures of Veronica's Restaurant. Talk about the changes you see. Use the adjectives in the box to help you.

clean	new	happy
bright	big	cheerful
messy	old	dirty
good	bad	nice
beautiful		

The old Veronica's

The new Veronica's

The old Veronica's was dirty.
The new Veronica's is cleaner.

B With a partner, make a fifteen-second radio advertisement for the new Veronica's using your ideas from **A**. Write your ideas below. Then practice saying the announcement aloud.

____

____

____

____

C Present your radio advertisement to the class.
Whose was the best? Why?

Come and see the new Veronica's!
It's bigger and better than ever!

7 Communication

Veronica's Restaurant

10-15 min

Warm Up

Call on a few students to name their favorite restaurant. Follow up with questions on the food served there, plus details about the setting, like whether it is crowded, expensive, small, large, fancy, or casual. Write adjectives students use in their responses on the board. Then, divide the class into small groups. Appoint one student in each group to label a sheet of paper with two columns, *Popular Restaurants* and *Unpopular Restaurants,* and record the groups' responses. Tell groups they have 3 minutes to brainstorm as many adjectives as possible about both popular and unpopular restaurants. After time is up, review and discuss the responses. Were groups' responses similar or different? Did any adjectives appear in both columns?

A 10-15 min **Look at the pictures of Veronica's Restaurant. Talk about the changes you see. Use the adjectives in the box to help you.**

Read the list of adjectives in the box, and ask volunteers to explain them in synonyms, brief definitions, or examples. Then, explain that students will use them to compare the pictures. Read the example comparison in the speech bubble while students look carefully at the pictures. Tell students to work in pairs, taking turns making comparisons between the old and new restaurants, and then ask each pair to share one comparison with the class.

15-20 min

EXTRA! Write a review

After students complete the exercise, ask them to write a short review of the new Veronica's. Tell them to write at least two comparisons that describe the changes she made to her restaurant. Ask students to read the review aloud to a partner.

B 15-20 min **With a partner, make a fifteen-second radio advertisement for the new Veronica's using your ideas from A. Write your ideas below. Then practice the announcement aloud.**

Talk about TV and radio advertisements for restaurants, naming details that interest audiences, such as a new menu or dishes, friendly service, or prices. Read the example sentences in the speech bubble. Explain that a successful ad should be attention-grabbing, descriptive of a restaurant's best features, and enticing. Then assign students to small groups to work on their ads.

B Teaching Option Writing

Students can write a print or television advertisement instead of a radio ad.

C 10-15 min **Present your radio advertisement to the class. Whose was the best? Why?**

Call on one pair at a time to present their ad. Then ask students what they remember from the ads they heard. Ask them, *Is the ad they remember most clearly the best one? Why?* or *Why not?*

Teaching Tip: Evaluating a presentation

Explain that students' presentations will be evaluated by these criteria: *interesting*, *loud enough*, and *clear*. Make an evaluation form with four columns, listing each of the criteria and a final column labeled *Notes*. You may ask the other students to copy the columns along the top of their own sheets of paper, and to write the names of presenters along the left margin. After each presentation, ask the class to mark the first three columns with a check mark if the presentation was interesting, loud enough, and clear, and to write any extra notes in the last column. Having students take notes on other presenters keeps them listening actively.

Teaching Tip: Model presentations

Before students speak in front of the class, provide guidance on public speaking. Tell students to speak clearly and look in the direction of their listeners. Help them understand the importance of these tips by modeling an ideal presentation, as well as showing what a presentation looks and sounds like when the presenter does not speak clearly and looks away from viewers.

Large Class Option

Pairs can present in small groups rather than in front of the whole class. When each pair in the group is finished, you can regroup students to see additional presentations. Each student can still record the information in a brief evaluation. After that, instruct students to write one detail they liked about each presentation, as well as one way to improve it. Collect the notes and scan over them. Select the ones that seem most helpful, and read them anonymously to the class.

10-15 min

EXTRA! Practice phrases

Practice using phrases *a little* and *much* with comparisons. Give examples of a comparison, such as *Apples are better than oranges*. Explain how phrases change it: *Apples are a little better than oranges. Apples are much better than oranges.* Have students work with a new partner to revise their radio ads using the phrases *a little* and *much*. Share a few with the class.

Eating well
Unit 2, Lesson B

1 Vocabulary Link

What's their secret?

5 min

Warm Up

Ask students to think about their diet and lifestyle. Ask, *Do you eat healthy foods? What foods?* Then ask, *Besides eating right, what habits are healthy?* Suggest exercising, not smoking, and relaxing if students do not.

Language Tip: Effect

You may need to explain *effect* as it is used in the title of the article. As a noun, an effect is an inevitable result of something. For example, the *ripple effect* describes an effect that spreads to other things, based on the way ripples travel across calm water when something breaks the surface. Other commonly used examples include *greenhouse effect, placebo effect,* and *domino effect*.

15–20 min

A Read the article below. Then answer the questions with a partner.

Read the article with the class, and allow students time to think about it. Then point out the words in blue. Write them on the board and ask volunteers to explain or give synonyms for these words. If students are hesitant to offer suggestions, remind them to use the context and think about what words or phrases could be substituted for the words in blue. Then pair students to answer the questions. When pairs have finished, discuss with the class Dr. Miller's list of healthy habits, and ask students to name specific examples of green vegetables, types of fish, foods that contain red meats, different unhealthy habits, and various ways of exercising from walking to playing sports.

A Teaching Option Support/challenge

To make this activity easier, reword the questions into true and false statements. For example, reword the first question into this statement: *True or False: The countries are similar because people there eat fish.* After pairs answer the questions, provide the answers for them to self-check. To make the activity more challenging, after students talk to their partner, have them use the information to write comparisons about healthy and unhealthy habits. For example, *Eating fresh foods is healthier than eating processed foods*. Ask them to share their responses aloud.

15–20 min

B Which statements would Dr. Miller agree with? Explain your answers to a partner.

Read the statements aloud to the class. After each one, ask, *Would Dr. Miller agree?* Instruct students to answer in writing. After students have answered all of the questions, assign them to pairs. Each student should explain his or her responses to a partner. Review the correct answers, and call on volunteers to give the reasons. If necessary, ask guiding questions. For example, for the first item, ask, *What type of meat is hamburger? Does Dr. Miller feel that is a healthy meat?*

5–10 min

C Discuss the questions with a partner.

Read the questions aloud. Answer one yourself as a model. Then ask students to think about their own habits and answer the questions with a partner. Tell them to form comparative statements about which partner's habits are healthier and why.

10–15 min

EXTRA! Discussion

Review the foods and habits that produce the Jungle Effect, and ask students whether the local culture reflects these habits. Ask students to explain the similarities and differences, using comparative adjectives whenever possible.

Instructor's Notes

Lesson B Eating well

1 Vocabulary Link What's their secret?

A Read the article below. Then answer the questions with a partner.

1. How are the five countries in the article similar?
2. Why are these people's traditional diets special?

1. These countries all have some of the healthiest people in the world.
2. Their traditional diets are special because the things they eat and drink increase their energy, help them think better, and protect against dangerous diseases like cancer and heart failure.

yourhealth*.com

Your Health

Mexico, Japan, Cameroon, Iceland, and Greece. What do these five countries have in common? In her book, *The Jungle Effect*, Dr. Daphne Miller says these places have some of the healthiest people in the world.

What's their secret? Dr. Miller says these people's traditional diets have important health benefits. The things they eat and drink increase their energy, help them think better, and protect against dangerous diseases like cancer.

Dr. Miller says a healthy diet and lifestyle are important. She says we should…

- eat more green vegetables, fish, yogurt, corn, beans, and spices.
- cut back on red meat and processed* foods.
- eat out in restaurants less.
- eliminate unhealthy habits, like smoking.
- get plenty of exercise.

*_**processed**_: instant (pre-made)

B Which statements would Dr. Miller agree with? Explain your answers to a partner.

1. People should eat more hamburgers.
   1. Dr. Miller would not agree with this statement.
2. Don't smoke.
   2. Dr. Miller would agree with this statement.
3. Don't eat instant noodles too often.
   3. Dr. Miller would agree with this statement.
4. Cook at home more.
   4. Dr. Miller would agree with this statement.
5. Going to the gym once a month is enough.
   5. Dr. Miller would not agree with this statement.
6. Salmon, spinach, and black beans make up a healthy meal.
   6. Dr. Miller would agree with this statement.

C Discuss the questions with a partner.

Do you have a healthy diet and lifestyle? Why or why not?

How often do you eat or drink the things listed in the article?

Word Partnership *diet*
balanced/healthy/unhealthy/strict/traditional **diet**

2 Listening **The Slow Food Movement**

A Discuss the questions with a partner.

1. We often hear about "fast food" and "instant food." What is it?
2. How often do you eat it?

CD 1
Track 13

B You are going to hear two people talking about the Slow Food Movement.

1. Which statements below do you think its members believe?
2. Listen and circle the correct answer(s).

> A **movement** is a group of people who have the same beliefs or ideas.
>
> A **member** is a part of the group.

People should ______________.

a. serve food slowly
b. eat no fast or instant foods
c. learn to prepare their own meals
d. grow food slowly and carefully

C Read the six statements below. Then listen again. For each sentence, choose *T* (true), *F* (false), or *NS* (not said). Explain your answer choices to a partner.

CD 1
Track 13

Mr. Moretti thinks . . .

1. most Slow Food members are Italian.	T	F	NS
2. eating a slow food diet is difficult for busy people.	T	F	NS
3. a slow food diet has many health benefits.	T	F	NS
4. a slow food diet is good for the environment.	T	F	NS
5. you should learn your grandparents' recipes.	T	F	NS
6. more stores are selling slow food items these days.	T	F	NS

ASK ANSWER

Would you join the Slow Food Movement? Why or why not?

3 Reading **The healthiest people in the world**

A Look quickly at the title, picture, and reading on page 19. Then try to guess the answers to 1 and 2 below. Explain your ideas to a partner.

1. The reading is mainly about ______________.

   a. people from around the world
   b. healthcare for older people
   c. a group of people from Japan
   d. older people in the United States

2. What is unusual about these people?

   a. Most of them are women.
   b. A large number live to age 100 or older.
   c. They have the spiciest food in the world.
   d. There are only 100 of them in the world.

B Now read the article and check your answers to 1 and 2 in **A**.

2 Listening The Slow Food Movement

Skills: Make and check predictions; Listen for gist; Listen for details; Infer information

5–10 min

Warm Up

Ask students what kinds of foods they prepare at home. List responses. Ask students how long it takes to prepare these foods. Then, discuss reasons why people might eat food that is quick to get, even if it is less healthy.

5–10 min

A Discuss the questions with a partner.

After students work in pairs, review *fast food* and *instant food*. Ask volunteers to define *fast food* and *instant food*. Confirm that fast foods can be purchased quickly in a restaurant, and give examples like hamburgers, pizza, and fried chicken. Confirm that instant foods, such as macaroni and cheese, frozen dinners, and canned foods, are prepared quickly at home, often by boiling or microwaving. Ask a few students what types of fast foods and instant foods they eat and how often.

Culture Tip: Drive-through

Explain that the fast-food trend first became popular in the United States and then spread to other English-speaking countries, as the global pace of life became quicker. If necessary, confirm that a *drive-through restaurant* is one where customers can order, pay for, and take out food without leaving their car. Point out that this makes fast-food ordering even faster. Ask students how fast food and drive-through style eating is viewed in their culture.

CD 1 Track 13
5–10 min

B You are going to hear two people talking about the Slow Food Movement.

Ask students to guess what *slow food* means. Confirm that it means fresh foods that are cooked naturally. Read the box defining *movement* and *member*. Then play the audio.

Teaching Tip: Focus on ideas

Explain to students that they can understand the main idea of a conversation even before they are able to understand every single word. Instruct them to try not to get "stuck" on one or two words they do not know, but rather to listen for and focus on details they can understand.

CD 1 Track 13
10–15 min

C Read the six statements below. Then listen again. For each sentence, choose *T* (true), *F* (false), or *NS* (not said). Explain your answer choices to a partner.

Read the sentences with the class. Tell students to listen for keywords to help them hear the answers. Then play the audio.

ASK ANSWER

After students complete the sentence and talk to their partners, you can follow up by calling on each student to tell whether he or she would join the Slow Food Movement, and ask why or why not. Write reasons on the board.

3 Reading

The healthiest people in the world

Skills: Use the title and photo to make and check predictions; Scan for specific information to complete a chart; Read for details

5 min

Warm Up

Tell students to keep their books closed, and ask students, *Who are the healthiest people in the world? Where are some places that people live a very healthy life? How does this compare with your own country?*

5–10 min

A Look quickly at the title, picture, and reading on page 19. Then try to guess the answers to 1 and 2 below. Explain your ideas to a partner.

Tell students that they will use the title and picture to make predictions about the reading. They should make guesses about the answers to the questions before talking with a partner. After pairs have finished, call out each letter after questions 1 and 2, and ask for a show of hands for students who chose that answer. Call on a few volunteers to explain why they chose that answer. Ask students what predictions they were able to make from the title and picture.

15 min

B Now read the article and check your answers to 1 and 2 in A.

Tell students that they will now look back through the article and read it more slowly and carefully. Tell them to circle any vocabulary they don't understand. Before checking answers, explain words they have questions about. Check with a show of hands how many students correctly predicted the answers.

C 10–15 min **Scan the article and complete the chart below. You have two minutes.**

Tell students that they should not reread the article word-for-word, but should scan the text for the answers to the questions. Suggest that they look for keywords in the questions to help them spot the information in the text. Ask which keywords students will scan for in the text to complete the exercise. Give an example if needed. *Will you look for the word* lifestyle? (No.) *Will you look for the word* eat? (Yes.) As you confirm the answer, point to the word *eat* in the phrase *What they eat*.

Teaching Tip: Scanning

Scanning is a challenging skill that students need to practice. Give them helpful tips, such as looking at the beginning of a page or paragraph to find important ideas. Remind students to look for keywords as they scan to help them locate information. Point out that scanning has a different purpose from reading. Explain that the goal of reading is understanding most or all of the ideas in the text, whereas the aim of scanning is finding specific information.

ASK ANSWER

Ask students to explain to a partner why Okinawans live so long. Then, instruct partners to discuss the lifestyles in their country. Students should share their partners' responses with the class.

Culture Tip: Okinawa

Okinawa is a group of islands in Japan, about 70 miles (112 km) long and 7 miles (11 km) wide. Before becoming part of Japan in the 19th century, Okinawa was an independent kingdom. The islands have a subtropical climate with beautiful natural scenery, and are very popular with tourists. Fishing, cattle raising, and sugar refining are important in the economy. Farmers grow rice, soybeans, and pineapples there, and factory workers produce textiles, sake (rice wine), and lacquerware.

EXTRA! Post-reading

10–20 min

1. With the class, talk about reasons why people want to learn about centenarians. Ask, *Why do we study their lifestyles? Why do a high number of centenarians in one place show that the people have healthy lifestyles?*

2. Students can do further research on centenarians on the Internet or using print resources like encyclopedias and share what they learn with the class. What regions besides Okinawa have large numbers of centenarians?

EXTRA! Discussion questions

20–30 min

1. In some countries, people tend to dislike and avoid fast food.
   a. Is this true in your culture? Do you know anyone who loves fast food?
   b. Do you enjoy eating fast food or fresh food more? Why?

2. Would you like to live to be a centenarian? Why or why not?

EXTRA! Writing prompt

15–20 min

1. Tell students to write a few sentences about their lifestyle. What healthy habits do you have? Which habits are unhealthy? Which habits do you want to change?

2. Ask students to answer this question: What can the world learn from centenarians?

Teaching Tip: Provide different types of questions

During class discussions, keep all students engaged by using different types of questions geared toward students with varying proficiencies. Ask advanced speakers open-ended questions, or questions that are answered with an explanation, such as, *Why do centenarians live so long?* If students have difficulty answering an open-ended question, rephrase the question to include embedded answer choices: *Do centenarians live 100 or 10 years?* If beginners have difficulty with those types of questions, try questions that can be answered with a word or phrase or multiple choice questions, such as *How many years do centenarians live?*

EXTRA! Additional reading

20–30 min

For additional practice making predictions, see Heinle's Footprint Reading Library *Butler School*.

For additional practice reading for details, see Heinle's Footprint Reading Library *Capoeira: The Fighting Dance*.

Instructor's Notes

The Healthiest Lifestyle in the World?

In many countries around the world, people are living longer than before. People have healthier lifestyles, and healthcare is better, too.

Okinawa is an island off the coast of Japan. The people on Okinawa, the Okinawans, may have the longest lives and healthiest lifestyles in the world.

Researchers did a study. They started by looking at city and town birth records from 1879. They didn't expect to find many centenarians (hundred-year-olds) in the records, so they were very surprised to find so many old and healthy people living in Okinawa. The United States, for example, has 10 centenarians per 100,000 people. In Okinawa there are 34 centenarians per 100,000 people!

What is the Okinawans' secret? First, they eat a healthy diet that includes fresh fruits and vegetables. They also eat fish often and drink plenty of water and green tea. But researchers think that the Okinawans have other healthy habits as well. They don't do hard exercise such as weightlifting or jogging. Instead, they prefer relaxing activities like gardening and walking. Researchers say that older Okinawans also have a good attitude[1] about aging. They sit quietly and relax their minds with deep breathing exercises. They also enjoy massage.

[1] **attitude:** the way you think or feel about something

C Scan the article and complete the chart below. You have two minutes.

Okinawan Centenarians

What they eat	What they drink
fresh fruit and vegetables	a lot of water
fish	green tea
How they exercise	**How they relax**
gardening	deep breathing exercises
walking	massage

ASK ANSWER

Why do Okinawans live so long? Give some reasons.
Do people in your country have healthy lifestyles? Give examples.

4 Language Link **The superlative form of adjectives**

A Read the information about the restaurants. Then complete the sentences below with the correct form of each adjective.

A
opened: 1942
dinner menu: 40 euros

B
opened: 1925
dinner menu: 60 euros

C
opened: 1886
dinner menu: 80 euros

Restaurant A is *old*.

Restaurant B is *older* than Restaurant A.

Restaurant C is **the oldest** restaurant.

Restaurant A is *expensive*.

Restaurant B is *more expensive* than Restaurant A.

Restaurant C is *the* most *expensive* restaurant.

B Complete the chart with the missing words. Then check your answers with a partner.

The superlative form of adjectives					
One syllable		Two syllables		Three or more syllables	
sweet	the sweetest	simple	*the simplest*	*expensive*	the most expensive
large	*the largest*	*spicy*	the spiciest	delicious	*the most delicious*
big	the biggest	*crowded*	the most crowded	interesting	*the most interesting*

Notice! The superlative form of *good* is *the best.*

C Complete the restaurant profile with the superlative form of the adjectives in parentheses. Then answer these questions:

1. Why is this restaurant unusual? Why do people like it?
2. Does it sound interesting to you? Why or why not?

The restaurant is unusual because people eat their meals in a completely dark room. People like it because it's unusual, the food is good, and it's a good place to go on a first date.

Are you looking for an interesting place to have a meal? One of (1) *the most unusual* (unusual) places in the world is Beijing's Dark Restaurant—where you eat in a completely dark room! Dark Restaurant is one of (2) *the trendiest* (trendy) spots* in China. For many, it is also (3) *the most popular* (popular) place to go on a first date. "It's (4) *the best* (good) way to get to know someone," says Zhi-ying Chen, a visitor to the restaurant. "In the dark, you can relax and talk." Chen adds, "I also had one of (5) *the most delicious* (delicious) meals of my life." His girlfriend agrees. "It was (6) *the weirdest* (weird) but (7) *the most interesting* (interesting) eating experience I ever had!"

**spot = place*

D Work with a partner. Use these adjectives to talk about restaurants you know.

noisy	trendy	cheap
boring	romantic	bad

Bob's Bistro is the noisiest restaurant I know.

4 Language Link

The superlative form of adjectives

Warm Up

5 min

Briefly review comparative forms from Lesson A by pointing to or sketching pairs of objects and asking students to use a comparative adjective to describe them. For example, hold up a pencil, and say *small*. Hold up a paperclip, and call on a student. The student says the comparative form *smaller*.

15–20 min

A Read the information about the restaurants. Then complete the sentences below with the correct form of each adjective.

After students read, review the information about the restaurants with questions such as, *Which restaurant opened in 1925?* If necessary, explain that the *euro* is a unit of money similar to the dollar, yen, and peso. Write the adjectives *nice, nicer, nicest*. Explain that *nicer* is a comparison between two, and *nicest* compares three or more. Then, write the adjectives *old* and *expensive*. Explain that students will use three forms of *old* in the first set of frames and forms of *expensive* in the second set. If necessary, do the first frame together. Students can complete the others individually. Check the answers.

Teaching Tip: Quick comprehension checks

During lessons, do quick comprehension checks by asking questions about vocabulary words, topics, and details. Call on students who do not volunteer, as well as those who do. Provide explanations when necessary. Rather than repeating information the same way it was said before, say it using simpler words or examples that are likely to be familiar to students.

10 min

B Complete the chart with the missing words. Then check your answers with a partner.

Tell students to work individually to fill in the spaces. Remind them that some comparisons use *-er* and *-est*, but others use *more* and *most*. When all students are ready, assign students to pairs check answers. Call on individuals to read responses aloud. Write the answers on the board.

Grammar Tip: *good, better, best*

Explain to students that some comparative forms do not look similar to the adjective. Give examples like *good, better, best*, along with *bad, worse, worst*. Practice using these words in sentences with frames, such as *Broccoli is _____, and carrots are _____. Celery is the ______!*

20–30 min

EXTRA! Comparative game

Divide the class into two sides. Call on one student from Side A. Ask a question about the restaurants using a comparative or superlative. The student should answer by identifying the correct restaurant. If the answer is correct, Side A gets a point. If the answer is incorrect, call on the first student from Side B to try. If the student answers correctly, Side B gets a point and another turn. Repeat the process several times. If you run out of questions about the three restaurants shown, to extend the activity, use objects around the room or pictures of Veronica's Restaurant from Lesson A. When you have asked 20 questions, the side with the most points wins.

10–15 min

C Complete the restaurant profile with the superlative form of the adjectives in parentheses. Then answer these questions:

(See student book page 20 for complete instructions.)

Do the first example as a class, calling on a volunteer to supply the answer. Point out that this superlative, *most unusual*, did not require a stem change. Instead, *most* was placed in front of the adjective. Check answers together as a class. Tell students to read the article. As a class, discuss what the people in the article like about Dark Restaurant and the students' responses to questions 1 and 2.

10 min

D Work with a partner. Use these adjectives to talk about restaurants you know.

Point to the adjectives and ask, *What familiar restaurants can you describe using these words?* Read the example, then ask volunteers to provide responses. Finally, ask students to work with a partner to talk about restaurants they know.

5 Writing **Restaurant review**

Warm Up

5 min Discuss online reviews. Ask students whether they read reviews of restaurants before trying a new place and why or why not.

A 10 min **You are a restaurant reviewer for a popular website. Choose a restaurant you know and make some notes. Then write a review.**

Read the review. Students should work in pairs to identify three topics in the review. Confirm that the topics are food, staff, prices, and popularity of the restaurant. Ask, *What does the first sentence tell readers?* Point out that it clearly tells the writer's opinion about the restaurant. Point out the superlative adjective *best*. Tell students they will write a review about a restaurant they know. First, instruct them to prepare brief notes about their opinion of the restaurant and its food, staff, and prices, and other topics they feel are important. Remind students that the first sentence of the review should sum up their overall opinion. Students should use their notes to complete the review.

B 10-15 min **Read your partner's review. Do you want to try the restaurant? Why?**

Direct students to exchange restaurant reviews with a partner. Ask partners to read the reviews silently. Then, give pairs time to ask questions about any information in the review. Next, call on students to tell the class the name of the restaurant their partner reviewed and whether they want to eat there and why or why not.

B **Teaching Option** Speaking

After reading students' reviews, pair them up to give interviews with a partner. Each student should ask questions about the restaurant that his or her partner reviewed, while the partner answers the questions. The questions should include information from the student's review, but questions can also address other topics. Tell students to make their best guess for questions they don't know the answers to. After they practice, ask pairs to perform their interviews for the class.

6 Communication **Comparing foods**

Warm Up

5 min With the class, list dishes that students like that are spicy, sweet, expensive, and traditional. If necessary, explain that *expensive* means costs a lot of money, and *traditional* foods are those that have been eaten in a place for a long time. List a few examples of each.

A 10-15 min **Complete this chart with foods you know.**

As students complete the chart, walk around helping them with spelling and answer any questions they may have about the activity. Spot check answers and provide suggestions if needed.

B 10-15 min **Compare your list with a partner's. Tell your partner which food you think is...**

Assign students into pairs, and ask partners to exchange lists. Give students a few minutes to review his or her partner's list and ask any questions about it. Then, ask that one student answer the questions using foods from his or her partner's list. Point to and read the example aloud. The pairs switch roles and repeat.

C 15-20 min **With your partner, create a menu for a new restaurant using many of the foods your group's members have written. Divide the menu into sections (appetizers, entrées, drinks, desserts). Include prices.**

Tell students they will create a menu with a partner. With the class, review the main sections of a menu and talk about typical menu layouts. Then instruct pairs to brainstorm the names of foods that belong to each section and write their lists of foods in the appropriate sections.

D 5-10 min **Post your menus for the class to see. Who has the best menu? Why?**

Students may tape their menus to the wall so that everyone can see them. Give students the chance to ask questions of the pairs or small groups about their menus.

World Link Video and World Link Website

Remind students of the value of further practice outside the classroom. Ask students who have watched the video or done online practice to share their experiences.

Check out the World Link Video. Practice your English online at http://elt.heinle.com/worldlink

5 Writing **Restaurant review**

A You are a restaurant reviewer for a popular website. Choose a restaurant you know and make some notes. Then write a review.

Amazon Sun [★★★★★]

Amazon Sun is the best Brazilian restaurant in town. The food is delicious, the staff is friendly, and the prices are moderate. One of the tastiest dishes on the menu is the feijoada completa — a traditional dish of meat, beans, and Brazilian spices. It's excellent!

Amazon Sun is also one of the trendiest places to go these days, so be sure to make a reservation. Enjoy!

Restaurant: Amazon Sun
Food: Brazilian
Prices: Moderate
Location: Downtown
Service: Friendly

B Read your partner's review. Do you want to try the restaurant? Why?

6 Communication **Comparing foods**

A Complete this chart with foods you know.

Spicy foods	Sweet foods	Expensive foods	Traditional foods

B Compare your list with a partner's.
Tell your partner which food you think is . . .

I think tiramisu is the most delicious food on the list.

the most delicious	the most expensive	the hardest to prepare at home
the cheapest to buy	the healthiest	the worst for you

C With your partner, create a menu for a new restaurant using many of the foods your group's members have written. Divide the menu into sections (appetizers, entrées, drinks, desserts). Include prices.

D Post your menus for the class to see. Who has the best menu? Why?

Check out the World Link video.

Practice your English online at http://elt.heinle.com/worldlink

3 Unsolved Mysteries

Lesson A What a coincidence!

1 Vocabulary Link What are the chances?

A Look at the pictures and the title of the article below. What do you think it's about? Tell your partner.

B Now read the article. Then put the events of the story in order from 1–8.

- __7__ Carmen read the letter.
- __3__ The couple parted.
- __1__ Carmen went to England.
- __8__ Steve and Carmen got together again.
- __2__ Carmen met Steve. They fell in love.
- __6__ Years later, workmen found the letter.
- __5__ Carmen's mother got the letter but then she lost it.
- __4__ Steve wrote a letter to Carmen.

Letter reunites* lovers

In the mid 1990s, Carmen Ruiz Perez and Steve Smith met and fell in love. Carmen, from Spain, was studying in Steve's hometown of Devon, England. They dated for a year, but then Carmen got a job in Paris and the couple had to separate.

After Carmen left, Steve realized he still loved her. Did she love him? He took a chance and wrote a letter to Carmen's address in Paris. Unfortunately, she no longer lived there. Luckily, Steve had Carmen's home address in Spain. He sent a letter to her mother's house. Her mother got the letter, but it fell behind a piece of furniture in her house and was lost. Steve never heard from Carmen.

Several years later, workmen were fixing her mother's house and they found the letter by accident**. What good luck! Carmen read the note and contacted Steve. The couple met and soon married. Steve says he's lucky to have Carmen. "I missed my chance with her the first time. But in the end, everything worked out for the best."

* reunite: to bring two or more things together again

** by accident: by chance, without planning

C Find a word or phrase in blue in the article that has the opposite meaning of each word or phrase in the chart. Compare answers with a partner.

word or phrase	opposite
reunite	separate
unfortunately	luckily
on purpose	by accident
bad luck	good luck
unlucky	lucky
didn't try something difficult or risky	took a chance
ended badly	worked out
had an opportunity to do something	missed a chance

ASK ANSWER

Retell Steve and Carmen's story in your own words. Why was this couple lucky?

What a coincidence!

Unit 3, Lesson A

1 Vocabulary Link

What are the chances?

Warm Up

5 min

Ask students if they have ever sent an important message that the person didn't get. Ask one or two students to share what the message said and what happened as a result. If students are unable to think of examples, share a story of your own.

A **Look at the pictures and the title of the article below. What do you think it's about? Tell your partner.**

5–10 min

Tell students to look at the envelope and the photograph. Explain that looking at a title and photos before they read something can help them better understand the information in a reading. Assign students to pairs to talk about their predictions. Then call on two or three pairs to make their predictions.

B **Now read the article. Then put the events of the story in order from 1–8.**

10–15 min

Write these words on the board: *parted, got together, by accident*. Call on a volunteer to read each of the eight sentences. Tell the students to think about what these words might mean as they read about Carmen and Steve. To check answers, call on students to dictate the sentences to you in the correct order and write them on the board. Finally, ask students about the three words you wrote on the board before they read. What do they think the words mean? How did they figure them out?

> **Teaching Tip: Unfamiliar words**
>
> Putting possibly unfamiliar words on the board lets students know that it's OK if they don't know them. Students are then more likely to try to guess the meanings from context and continue reading.

C **Find a word or phrase in blue in the article that has the opposite meaning of each word or phrase in the chart. Compare answers with a partner.**

15–20 min

First, review the title of the article with the group. Did Carmen and Steve think they would get back together? What were the chances that they would? Were the chances good or bad? Point out that in the chart, on the right, *take a chance* means to try something difficult or risky—something that might not succeed. The opposite, on the left, is to *not* try. Tell students to work independently to find words in the article that mean the opposite of the words on the left. Students can check answers with a partner.

EXTRA! Dictation

20 min

Dictate the first paragraph of the article "Letter Reunites." Review the words *comma* and *period* by writing the punctuation symbols on the board and asking what these are called. Read the paragraph aloud at normal speed while students read it silently. Then with books closed, read the paragraph again at normal speed. Read it a third time in small chunks, reading each chunk *twice*. Say "comma," or "period," as needed. Finally, read it once more at normal speed. Before you begin, put these words on the board for the students to refer to if needed: mid 1990s, Ruiz Perez, Devon.

In the mid 1990s, / Carmen Ruiz Perez / and Steve Smith / met and fell in love. / Carmen, from Spain, / was studying in Steve's hometown / of Devon, England. / They dated for a year, / but then / Carmen got a job in Paris / and the couple had to separate.

Instructor's Notes

2 Listening Lucky you!

Skills: Identify the main idea; Listen for gist; Categorize information

Warm Up

5 min

Write *Good luck!* on the board. Ask students when they might say *Good luck!* to someone. Before an exam? Before dinner? Before watching television? Before a job interview? When they say *Good luck!* to someone, what do they mean?

A Discuss the questions with a partner.

5-10 min

Read the questions aloud or call on a student to read them. If you think students may need some help thinking of what to say, briefly answer each question yourself. Assign students to pairs to talk about their answers. Follow up the second question with the group. Ask students what things their partners do for good luck. Write a quick, informal list on the board.

B You are going to hear a man give a talk. Listen and choose the best title for it.

CD 1 Track 14, 10-15 min

Read the possible titles aloud or choose a student to read them. Play the audio. Then replay it, pausing after the sentence, "So the question is: why are some people lucky but others aren't?" Write that sentence on the board, then ask which title is the best. Ask why b. is the answer. See if a student can tell you that it states the main idea of the talk.

C Listen. Circle the correct answer.

CD 1 Track 15, 15-20 min

Read the six incomplete sentences. Explain the phrases *listen to their feelings* (in 3) and *focus on the facts* (in 4). Play the rest of the talk from where you paused it in **B**. Don't let students complete the sentences yet, but just listen. Play the talk again while students complete the sentences. Check answers by writing them on the board.

ASK ANSWER

Remind students that in **A**, they said that they were lucky or unlucky. According to the talk in **C**, were they right or wrong? Students can discuss these questions in pairs, or you can lead a discussion with the whole class.

World Link

With the class, talk about other lucky things they know of around the world. A four-leafed clover is considered lucky in the U.S. (most clovers have three leaves). The color red and the number 8 are lucky in China. Tell students that lucky things are called "good luck charms."

EXTRA! Good luck charms

20-30 min

Ask students if they carry or have any good luck charms. If students have them with them, encourage them to show the class. In small groups or as a class, students can answer these questions about good luck charms: *1. Do you believe that things can bring you luck? 2. Do you have a good luck charm? 3. What other things do people do for luck?*

3 Pronunciation Past tense vowel shifts

A Complete the sentences below with the past tense form of each verb.

10-15 min

If students are already somewhat familiar with irregular past tense forms and their pronunciation, they can complete the task individually. Walk around as they work to spot-check their answers.

B With a partner, say both the present and past tense forms of each verb in A. What do you notice about the vowels in these verbs?

5-10 min

Write two or three regular verbs on the board in the present and past tenses. Remind students that only their endings change in speaking and writing. Contrast this with the irregular verbs in the exercise. Assign students to pairs and ask them to think about the changes they see and hear between the present and past tense forms.

C Listen to the sentences in A. How was your pronunciation of the verbs?

CD 1 Track 16, 10 min

Play the audio pausing after each sentence so that students can repeat them.

D Practice saying the sentences with a partner.

5-10 min

Students can begin by saying alternate sentences. Then each student can try to tell the whole story without looking at the book. Their partner can say the verb of each sentence to prompt him or her.

Instructor's Notes

2 Listening **Lucky you!**

A Discuss the questions with a partner.

1. Do you think you're a lucky person? Why or why not?
2. Do you ever do things for good luck? For example, do you wear a certain color or say special words?

CD 1 Track 14

B You are going to hear a man give a talk. Listen and choose the best title for it.

a. Good Things Happen . . . by Accident!
b. Why Are Some People Luckier Than Others?
c. Better Luck Next Time!
d. Beliefs About Luck Around the World

CD 1 Track 15

C Listen. Circle the correct answer.

1. Lucky / Unlucky people are very careful.
2. Lucky / Unlucky people take chances.
3. Lucky / Unlucky people listen to their feelings.
4. Lucky / Unlucky people focus on the facts.
5. Lucky / Unlucky people expect bad things to happen.
6. Lucky / Unlucky people expect good things to happen.

ASK ANSWER

Are you more of a lucky or an unlucky person?

WORLD LINK

The Maneki Neko (or the "Lucky Cat") is often seen in homes, businesses, and restaurants around the world. It was first used in ____________.
a. China
b. India
c. Japan

3 Pronunciation **Past tense vowel shifts**

A Complete the sentences below with the past tense form of each verb.

1. I heard (hear) an interesting story on the radio last night.
2. Steve and Carmen met (meet) in England.
3. Later, she took (take) a job in Paris and they separated.
4. Steve knew (know) he still loved Carmen so he wrote (write) a letter to her.
5. Carmen's mother got (get) the letter, but then she lost (lose) it.
6. Later, workmen found (find) the letter and Carmen read (read) it. What luck!
7. I thought (think) this was a good story.

B With a partner, say both the present and past tense of each verb in **A**. What do you notice about the vowels in these verbs?

CD 1 Track 16

C Listen to the sentences in **A**. How was your pronunciation of the verbs?

D Practice saying the sentences with a partner.

4 Speaking I bet she's good at math.

CD 1 Track 17

A Nico and Sandra are talking about a news article. Listen and answer the questions.

1. What did a woman in New York City do? *1. She guessed the correct number of candies in a jar and won $25,000.*
2. How did she do it? *2. Maybe she guessed or maybe she's good at math.*
3. What is she going to do now? *3. Maybe the woman is going to go on vacation or use the money for school.*

Sandra: Anything interesting in today's news?

Nico: Yeah, I'm reading about a woman in New York City. She just won $25,000.

Sandra: That's a lot of money. Did she win the lottery?

Nico: No, she guessed the correct number of candies in a jar.

Sandra: Really? How many were there?

Nico: 7,954.

Sandra: Wow. That was a lucky guess!

Nico: Oh, I doubt she guessed. I bet she's good at math. The article says she won a similar contest in the past.

Sandra: So, what's she going to do with the money?

Nico: I don't know. She'll probably go on vacation or use it for school.

B Practice the conversation with a partner.

5 Speaking Strategy

A On the lines below, write two things about yourself that are true. Write one thing that is a lie.

Example answers:
I have a dog.
I play drums in a band.
My uncle lives in Germany.

Useful Expressions: Talking about possibility	
Saying something is likely	
I bet (that)	Marco plays drums in a band.
Marco **probably**	plays drums in a band.
Maybe / Perhaps	Marco plays drums in a band.
To disagree that it is likely	
I doubt (that)	Marco plays drums in a band.

B Get into a group of 3-4 people and do the following:

1. One person tells the group his or her sentences.
2. The others . . .
   - ask the speaker questions to find out which sentence is a lie.
   - use the Useful Expressions to discuss their ideas.
   - guess which sentence is a lie. If you guess correctly, you get a point.
3. Change roles and repeat steps 1 and 2.

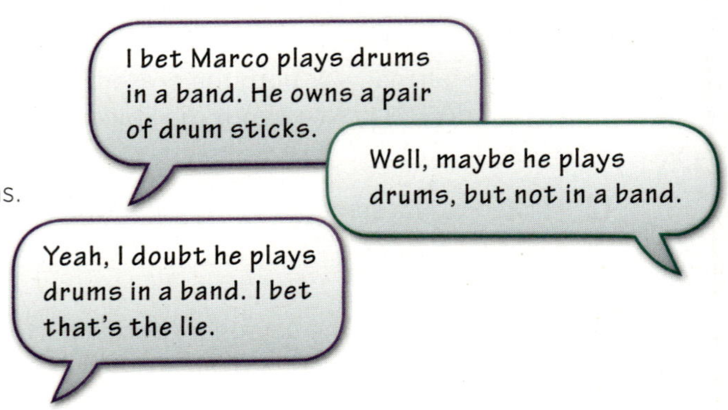

4 Speaking **I bet she's good at math.**

Warm Up

5 min

Ask students if they have ever tried to guess, for example, how many things are in a bowl or how much something weighs. Why were they guessing? To win something, or just for fun? Did they guess the right answer?

A CD 1 Track 17 10 min

Nico and Sandra are talking about a news article. Listen and answer the questions.

Tell the students to read the conversation as they listen to it. Play the audio once or twice and tell students to listen for Nico's and Sandra's answers to the questions. Discuss the students' answers and play the audio again to check them. Then read the conversation line by line so that the students can repeat it.

B 5 min

Practice the conversation with a partner.

Students can switch roles or partners for more practice.

5 Speaking Strategy

A 5 min

On the lines below, write two things about yourself that are true. Write one thing that is a lie.

Introduce the Useful Expressions and say them for the class to repeat. Point out that three of the expressions use *that*, but it can also be omitted. Tell students they are going to play a game to practice using these expressions.

To bring students' attention back to the activity, read the directions. Tell students that they do not have to write anything serious or important for the true and untrue statements. Give some simple examples to help them get started, such as, *I have two sisters. I was born in Sydney. I don't like tomatoes.* As students write, walk around the room helping with ideas as needed.

Note: The word *lie* might be a bit strong for your students. Remind them that this is only a game and it need not be a serious lie. If students still feel uncomfortable, suggest that they perhaps say something that is true about someone else and see if others can guess if it is also true about them.

B 5 min

Get into a group of 3–4 people and do the following:

(See student book page 24 for complete instructions.)

Put students into groups, and tell them to keep track of their points. As groups work, walk around listening for the Useful Expressions.

Culture Tip: Disagreeing politely

In English, if you disagree with someone and say nothing more, it can sound impolite or unfriendly. It may end the conversation. When you disagree, go on to say why, or suggest a different idea of your own. Then the conversation can continue in a friendly way.

Teaching Tip: Helping groups finish at the same time

A common situation in group work is that one group completes the task long before the others—or long after.

Here are some approaches you can take with a group that finishes too quickly:

- Check to be sure they have understood the task and completed all parts correctly.
- Give them additional questions.
- Have the group prepare a written report of their ideas, answers, etc.

With a group that finishes too slowly:

- Tell them to omit parts of the task.
- Take over briefly as discussion leader to help them move along.
- Set a time limit. Tell them, *I'll ask for your answers in 5 minutes.*

6 Language Link Stative verbs

Warm Up

5 min

With the class, talk about the five traditional senses: sight or vision, hearing, taste, smell, and touch. The senses are nouns; what verbs go with each one?

A 5-10 min

Look at the chart of stative verbs below. Then add the verbs in the box to the chart.

Introduce the first four categories of stative verbs. Explain that *Other verbs* lists common and useful stative verbs which do not fall into any one category. Read each verb in the chart and ask for a volunteer to explain or give a synonym for each one. Do the same for the verbs in the box. Students can complete the chart individually. Check answers as a class.

B 5-10 min

These sentences use stative verbs. The sentences in Column A are correct. The ones in Column B are incorrect. What can you say about stative verbs? Tell a partner.

Pair students to study the correct and incorrect use of stative verbs. Tell students to look carefully at the differences between the sentences. Then call on three or four pairs to tell the class what they can say about stative verbs, based on the chart. Repeat their correct ideas and write them on the board.

Word Bank: Stative verbs

Thinking verbs	Having verbs	Feeling verbs	Sensing verbs
agree	keep	adore	feel
disagree	owe	dislike	touch
doubt	possess	(not) mind	
imagine		prefer	
realize		value	
recognize		want	
remember			
suppose			

Language Tip: Stative verbs

Activity **B** shows that it's incorrect to use the progressive with stative verbs. However, some stative verbs do have non-stative meanings, for example, "Are you having a good time?" In addition, even with the same meaning, it's sometimes fine to say, for example, "It's late. I'm thinking we should take a taxi," or "This is so cool! I'm loving it!" The action is taking place very much in the present moment, and the progressive expresses this well. The simple present is also correct, of course.

C 10-15 min

Read the paragraph below. If an underlined verb is used incorrectly, circle it and correct it. Then take turns reading the paragraphs aloud with a partner.

Before students begin, give them a few minutes to read the paragraph. Ask them questions to bring out the main points of the story so that they understand it while they're working with the verbs. Check answers as a class. Then pair up students to practice reading aloud.

Culture Tip: Lotteries

Lotteries are common in many countries and on the Internet. People buy a ticket to have a chance at winning large cash prizes. Most lotteries are licensed or run by governments, for which they are a source of revenue. In the United States, there is no national lottery, but most states have one, and 40 to 50 percent of adults play regularly.

Instructor's Notes

6 Language Link **Stative verbs**

A Look at the chart of stative verbs below. Then add the verbs in the box to the chart.

hate	hear	like	own	smell	understand

Stative Verbs				
Thinking verbs	**Having verbs**	**Feeling verbs**	**Sensing verbs**	**Other verbs**
believe	belong	appreciate	hear	seem
know	have	hate	see	look
think	own	like	smell	mean
understand		love	taste	cost
				need

B These sentences use stative verbs. The sentences in Column A are correct. The ones in Column B are incorrect. What can you say about stative verbs? Tell a partner.

Column A (correct)	Column B (incorrect)
I own more than 100 books.	~~I am owning more than 100 books.~~
We know many words in English.	~~We are knowing many words in English.~~
He seems like a nice person.	~~He is seeming like a nice person.~~

C Read the paragraphs below. If an underlined verb is used incorrectly, circle it and correct it. Then take turns reading the paragraphs aloud with a partner.

Winning the lottery—to most people, it seems like great luck. Unfortunately, for the winners, it's often the opposite. Ian Walters, for example, won a million pounds in a lottery in the UK five years ago. "When you win the lottery, suddenly you are having (have) a lot of money," he explains. "You are thinking (think) it will last forever, and you spend it quickly." And then one day, the money is gone. "Two years ago, I had a big house," Ian says. "These days, I'm living with my sister and I'm working in a small cafe. Luckily, I still am owning (own) my car." So, what's Ian's advice? "In the past, I believed money could buy happiness," he says. "Now I am knowing (know) this isn't true."

7 Communication **Strange but true stories**

A Work with a partner. Choose one story—Story A or Story B—below. Cover the other story up—do not read it. Read the story you chose. Think about answers to these questions as you read:

1. Who is the story about?
2. What happened?

Story A

David Brown and Michelle Kitson met in an unusual way. One night, David went out with his friends. The next morning, he woke up, thinking of a phone number. He didn't know whose it was, so he texted the person. "Did I meet you last night?" he asked in his message. In another town, Michelle got David's text. She didn't know him. She answered, "No. Who are you and where are you from?" David answered and the two continued texting. Finally, David took a chance and asked to meet Michelle. She agreed and now they are dating. David still can't believe his good luck. Why did he dream about Michelle's phone number? He still can't explain it.

Story B

On the morning of February 19, Corina Sanchez said goodbye to her husband and 17-year-old son and went to work. "It was a typical day," Corina remembers. "But then at lunchtime, I started to feel strange—really nervous—but I didn't know why. Two hours later, I got a phone call from my son—he was in a car accident!" Luckily, Corina's son wasn't hurt, but how did she know something was wrong? She still can't explain it.

B Work again with your partner and do the following:

Student A: In your own words, tell your story to your partner.
Student B: Listen to your partner's story. Take notes to answer the questions. Then switch roles.

1. Who is the story about? ______________________
2. What happened? ______________________
____

C Can you explain what happened to David and Corina? Discuss your ideas with your partner. Then compare your ideas with another pair. Which explanation is the best?

How did David know Michelle's phone number?

Well, I bet he ...

7 Communication

Strange but true stories

Warm Up

5 min

With books closed, tell students they're going to read two stories about things that happened that people could not explain. Ask if something like that has ever happened to them. Was it a good thing or a bad thing?

A 15–20 min

Work with a partner. Choose one story – Story A or Story B – below. Cover the other story up – do not read it. Read the story you chose. Think about answers to these questions as you read:

(See student book page 26 for complete instructions.)

Preview the questions with the class. Tell students they will be telling their story to a partner without looking at the book, so they need to be clear about what happened. Emphasize that it's important to not read the other story. If they do, their partner will have no reason to tell them the story, and they will not get the practice they need. One partner should choose Story A and the other Story B.

Teaching Tip: Pairing students

Because of the pair work in **B**, you may want to make sure that the same number of students reads each story. If you assign the stories, the faster readers could read the longer story. In a large class, this also minimizes the confusion when it's time to form pairs. If you have an odd number of students, you can work with one student.

B 25–30 min

Work again with your partner and do the following:

(See student book page 26 for complete instructions.)

Tell students that this is a conversation, not just one person talking and one person writing. As students talk, walk around and ask the storytellers a few questions. Check the note takers' work to make sure they are getting the main ideas in the right order. To follow up, ask one storyteller and one note taker (who writes on the board) to go to the front of the class for the same conversation. The other students listen and watch. If the students listening think something is not clear (in the story or the notes), they should comment or ask a question.

C 10–15 min

Can you explain what happened to David and Corina? Discuss your ideas with your partner. Then compare your ideas with another pair. Which explanation is the best?

Point out the example in the speech bubbles for starting the discussion. Then review the Useful Expressions on page 24. Students should use their notes from **B** to talk about the story they didn't read. Remind students that if they disagree with someone's idea, they need to say why they think it's wrong or give an idea of their own.

C Teaching Option **Telling a story collectively**

Instead of working in pairs, brainstorm story ideas with the whole class. Give one or two ideas yourself to start things off. Then have students continue the story. Each student can add a sentence or various students can chime in with ideas. Encourage all students to participate.

EXTRA! Writing prompt

20–30 min

Write one of the stories you heard—your own or someone else's. Explain why you think things happened. If you don't know why, give one or two possible reasons, and say why you don't agree.

Instructor's Notes

Mysteries of the world

Unit 3, Lesson B

1 Vocabulary Link

An unsolved mystery

Warm Up

5 min

With books closed, remind students that in the stories on page 26, the strange event happened to just one person (David and Corina). The experience described on this page has happened to many people around the world. Ask if anyone knows what *hum* means. If possible, have a student explain it and demonstrate a hum for a few seconds. Tell students they are going to read about a hum that only some people all over the world can hear.

A Read the information below. What is "The Hum"? Who hears it? What causes it?

10–15 min

Before reading, tell students to look at the photos and scan the speech bubbles to find out where the people are from. As students read, walk around to help with vocabulary. Students can answer the questions with a partner. Check answers as a class.

EXTRA! Make inferences

5–10 min

Ask students, *Which sentences mean "I don't understand The Hum?"*, and *Which sentence means "I hate The Hum?"* Give them these possible answers:

a. It's driving me crazy!
b. I don't know what to think.
c. It just doesn't make sense.

B Match words 1–8 to their definitions (a–f). Some definitions match more than one word.

15–20 min

Do the first one as a class. Model reading the answer, *Mysterious means strange or unusual.* Tell students to complete 2–8 on their own. Allow them to refer to the speech bubbles so those who need it can get more practice getting the meaning from context. While students work, walk around reminding students to look back at the words in context. When all students have finished, call on a volunteer to read each of the answers, following the model above. Ask a few students how they were able to figure out the meanings. Did looking at the words in context help?

Language Tip: *Explanation*

In this context the correct answer for *explanation* is *a. guess or idea* because these are possible explanations. In other contexts and the more standard definition of *explanation* is *a reason*.

Teaching Tip: Using parts of speech

Show students that they can use parts of speech to help match the words and definitions. For example, in activity **B**, four definitions (a–f) are verbs, one is a noun, and one is an adjective. Ask students to identify the parts of speech. The same is true of the words (1–8). Point out that students can now match parts of speech to find the correct answers.

C Write the noun or verb form of these words. Then compare your answers with your partner.

10–15 min

Pair up students and tell them to focus on spelling when comparing answers. Review spelling as you check answers. Students can spell out the words as you write them on the board. Write exactly what they say. If they say the wrong letter, other students will correct it.

EXTRA! Talking about possibility

10–15 min

Students can use the Useful Expressions in Lesson A to talk about words and definitions in **B**. Review the expressions on page 24. Then tell students to use them when discussing the words in pairs. Write the following parts of sentences on the board to help students form sentences with the expressions. *I bet mysterious means . . . Maybe explanation means . . . I doubt that prove means . . . . Perhaps it means . . . .* While students practice speaking, walk around listening for correct use of the expressions.

ASK ANSWER

As a class, review the theories in **A** (all expressed by Jacqui Moore). Then students can ask and answer in pairs, or in groups, to share more ideas.

Unsolved Mysteries

Lesson B Mysteries of the world

1 Vocabulary Link An unsolved mystery

A Read the information below. What is "The Hum"? Who hears it? What causes it? See answer at bottom of the page.

"I hear a low humming sound all the time. It sounds like a car engine. It's very **mysterious**. I hope someone **solves** this **mystery** soon because it's driving me crazy!" —*Alan Black, England*

"No one can **figure out** the source of the humming sound. We have a lot of **theories**, but no answers yet."—*Dr. Harini Gupta, scientist, India*

"I first heard 'The Hum' in the 1970s. Only some people can hear it. There are lots of possible **explanations**: electrical wires, traffic noise, cell phone towers ... I don't know what to think." —*Jaqui Moore, Australia*

"We're **investigating** 'The Hum'. I can't even **prove** it exists because I can't hear a thing. But many people say that they hear it. It just doesn't **make sense**." —*Brian Lam, police officer, U.S.*

B Match words 1–8 to their definitions (a–f). Some definitions match more than one word.

a. a guess or idea
b. to show that something is definitely true
c. to find an answer to a question or problem
d. to study something closely to find the truth
e. to be logical or understandable
f. strange or unusual

___f___ 1. mysterious
___c___ 2. figure out
___e___ 3. make sense
___a___ 4. explanation
___d___ 5. investigate
___a___ 6. theory
___b___ 7. prove
___c___ 8. solve

C Write the noun or verb form of these words. Then compare your answers with your partner.

Noun	Verb
explanation	explain
investigation	investigate
solution	solve
proof	prove

ASK ANSWER

Look again at the theories in **A**. Can you think of other explanations for "The Hum"?
In your opinion, which explanation makes the most sense?

"The Hum" is a low humming sound that sounds like a car engine. Only some people can hear "The Hum," and these people hear the sound all the time. No one knows exactly what causes "The Hum." Some theories suggest it is caused by electrical wires, traffic, or maybe cell phone towers.

2 Listening **Full moon fever**

A Look at the chart. What do you think it's showing us? Tell a partner.

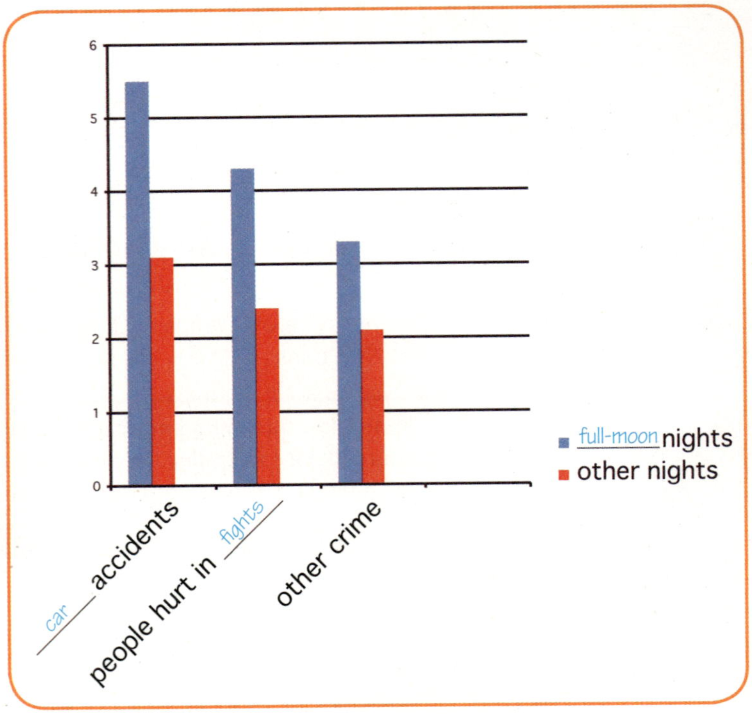

B You are going to hear a news report. Do the following:

CD 1 Track 18

1. Listen and complete the chart in **A**.
2. What are officials planning to do? Write your idea and then tell a partner.
   London officials are planning to put more police on the street on full moon nights.

C Look at your answer to question 2 in **B**. Why are officials planning to do this? Listen to the rest of the report. Complete the sentences below.

CD 1 Track 19

1. The city needs more ___police___.
2. ___Full moon___ nights are ___brighter___ than other nights.
3. More people ___go out___.

ASK ANSWER

What are London officials planning to do? Why? Use your answers in **B** and **C** to explain.

What are some beliefs about the moon in your country?

3 Reading **Mysterious artwork**

A Look at the title and photos on page 29 and answer the questions below. Then read the interview once to check your answers.

1. What do you think the things in the photos are?
2. Who do you think made them?

B Read the passage again. Then write the questions below in the correct places in the interview. Two questions are extra.

- What was the purpose of the lines?
- How do the local people feel about the lines?
- What exactly are the Nazca Lines?
- Who created these unusual ground drawings?
- How did they do it—especially without modern technology?
- Can anyone visit the Nazca Lines?

2 Listening Full moon fever

Skills: Predict the topic and organize information; Use visuals to aid in listening; Understand cause and effect

Warm Up

5 min

Ask students if they have heard stories about people acting differently when the moon is full. What have they heard? Have they experienced or witnessed anything themselves?

A **Look at the chart. What do you think it's showing us? Tell a partner.**

5–10 min

With the class, talk about the words at the bottom of the chart. Are they generally good things or bad things? What do the blue and red bars show?

B **You are going to hear a news report. Do the following:**

CD 1 Track 18

5–10 min

(See student book page 28 for complete instructions.)

Read question 1 to the students. Point out the three places where they must complete the chart. Read question 2 and explain *officials* if necessary. Then play the audio. Give students time to talk with a partner and compare their charts and their answers to the question.

> **Teaching Tip: Understanding a chart**
>
> Reading charts is a part of reading. Use the chart on page 28 to help students enhance their reading skills.
>
> Discuss the chart fully with the whole class. Say that the numbers at the left mean 100, 200, and so on. Ask these questions, and tell students to answer with *about*.
>
> 1. How many car accidents are there on full moon nights? (About 550.)
> 2. How many car accidents are there on other nights? (About 300.)
> 3. How many people are hurt in fights on full moon nights? (About 425.)
> 4. How many are hurt in fights on other nights? (About 230.)
> 5. How many other crimes are there on full moon nights? (About 320.)
> 6. How many other crimes are there on other nights? (About 200.)

C **Look at your answer to question 2 in B. Why are officials planning to do this? Listen to the rest of the report. Complete the sentences below.**

CD 1 Track 19

15–20 min

Read the three incomplete sentences. Tell students that the completed sentences explain why officials are planning to put more police on the street. Play the audio once while students listen. The second time they hear the audio they should complete the sentences.

> **ASK ANSWER**
>
> Walk around listening to responses while students are asking and answering the questions in pairs. Remind them to close their books when answering and to use their own words.

3 Reading Mysterious artwork

Skills: Use photos to make predictions; Identify main ideas in paragraphs; Read closely for details

Warm Up

5 min

Talk about artwork from the past that is too big to be in a museum. Write a list on the board (you could start the list with the Statue of Liberty). Where is this artwork? Ask who has seen any of it.

A **Look at the title and photos on page 29 and answer the questions below. Then read the interview once to check your answers.**

15–20 min

With books closed, write the two questions on the board. Tell students there are two photos to look at and read the questions. Give students just 20–30 seconds with their books open to look at the photos. Then they should close their books again before talking with their partner. When pairs have finished talking, call on three or four for their answers. List these answers on the board. Then tell students to read the interview on their own. After students have finished reading, call on volunteers to answer the questions. Review the predictions on the board. Were any correct? If so, ask the student who predicted correctly how they did it.

B **Read the passage again. Then write the questions below in the correct places in the interview. Two questions are extra.**

15–20 min

Read the six questions. Write these terms on the board: *local people, Nazca Lines,* and *ground drawings*. Ask about the meanings when students finish reading. Check answers as a class. Ask students, *Which was the easiest question to place? Which was the most difficult? Why?*

10-15 min

C The statements below are wrong. Change them so that they are correct. Underline the sentence(s) in the interview that helped you make your changes.

Choose one or two students to do this exercise at the board while the others work in their seats. Correct the sentences on the board with the whole class.

10-15 min

D Look back at the four questions in the interview. Take turns asking and answering these with a partner. When you answer a question, use your own words. Try not to look back at the reading.

Tell students that when they are trying to recall parts of the interview to answer the questions, they should concentrate on remembering keywords and facts, not a whole sentence. They should then explain the fact or idea in their own words.

Culture Tip: 200 B.C. and 7th century A.D.

The interview dates the Nazca people "in the area from 200 B.C. to the 7th century A.D." 200 B.C. was the first year of the 2nd century B.C. (200–101). The 7th century A.D. was 601–700.

15-20 min

EXTRA! Post-reading

What are some places that you would like to visit? What do you like about them? Would you like to visit the Nazca lines? Why or why not?

15-20 min

EXTRA! Discussion questions

1. The Nazca Lines are in danger from tourism. There is no way to protect them. Is it important to keep tourists away from the lines? Or should everyone be able to see them?
2. It is possible that the Nazca Lines were made just to be beautiful? Do you think this is likely?
3. Some people believed that the Nazca Lines were made by visitors from another planet. For a minute, imagine such visitors today. Do you think they would be a good thing for Earth or not?

15-20 min

EXTRA! Writing prompt

Ask students to write five to six sentences about whether people living today should care about the Nazca Lines and/or other old wonders. Students should express their opinions and provide reasons that support those opinions. Some other questions students may want to consider: *Why is there curiosity about the Nazca Lines? Can people today learn anything from the Nazca Lines or other ancient artworks? Is it important to protect such sites?*

20-30 min

EXTRA! Additional reading

For more practice making predictions, see Heinle's Footprint Reading Library *Blue Cows?*

For more practice reading at this level, see Heinle's Page Turners Reading Library *Danny Dark.*

Instructor's Notes

MYSTERIOUS ARTWORK

Interviewer: The Nazca Desert in Peru is home to one of the most unusual sites in the world. In this issue, we talk with Dr. Gabriel Reyes about the Nazca Lines and why they are one of history's greatest mysteries.

So, Dr. Reyes, tell us: What exactly are the Nazca Lines?

Dr. Reyes: On the ground for almost 60 kilometers (37 miles) in the Peruvian desert are hundreds of line drawings of different animals, humans, insects, and other symbols. These drawings, known as the Nazca Lines, are very large. Some are over 200 meters (600 feet) long and can only be seen correctly from the sky.

Interviewer: Who created these unusual ground drawings?

Dr. Reyes: For years, people had different theories. Some thought visitors from another planet drew them—maybe because the lines are best seen from a plane. Today, though, scientists believe the Nazca people created the images. They lived in the area from 200 B.C. to the 7th century A.D. and probably made the drawings over 1,500 years ago.

Interviewer: 1,500 years ago? How did they do it—especially without modern technology?

Dr. Reyes: Most likely they used simple tools. A team probably planned what they wanted a certain image to look like. Then they worked together and made the drawings in the desert ground. They didn't need planes or other modern equipment.

Interviewer: What was the purpose of the lines?

Dr. Reyes: Good question. We still can't figure out why the Nazca people drew these large pictures on the ground - images you can really only see from the sky. Many scientists think the images might be religious symbols. Others believe the lines may be a large map; perhaps the Nazca people used the lines to find water in the desert. Still others think the lines were a special type of calendar. As I say, scientists are still investigating.

C The statements below are wrong. Change them so they are correct. Underline the sentence(s) in the interview that helped you make your changes.

1. North Americans probably created the lines in the year 1500 A. D.
   1. The Nazca people of South America (Peru) probably created the lines 1,500 years ago.
2. The lines are small and must be looked at closely on the ground.
   2. The lines are very large and are best seen from the sky (in a plane).
3. It was probably difficult for people to make the lines without modern tools.
   3. It wasn't difficult for people to make the lines without modern tools.
4. Scientists now know what the Nazca Lines were used for—a calendar.
   4. Scientists still can't figure out what the Nazca Lines were used for—maybe they were religious symbols, a large map, or a calendar.

D Look back at the four questions in the interview. Take turns asking and answering these with a partner. When you answer a question, use your own words. Try not to look back at the reading.

4 Language Link Modals of present possibility

A Look at the picture and read the question and the answers in the chart. Then complete sentences 1 and 2 below with the correct modals.

1. Use ___may, might, or could___ to say something is possible.
2. Use ___can't or couldn't___ to say something is not possible.

Who's that man with Marta?			
Subject	Modal	Main Verb	
He	**may** **might** **could**	be	her dad. They look alike.
	can't **couldn't**	be	her brother. He's much older than Marta.

B Read the note about short answers. Then complete the dialogs below. Practice them with a partner.

1. A: Is Luis from Brazil?
   B: He ___may/might/could be___. He visits Sao Paulo all the time.
2. A: How old is Alice?
   B: I don't know. She ___may/might/could be___ 30 or 35.
   C: She ___can't/couldn't be___. She graduated from college in 1980.
3. A: Do you think "The Hum" is real?
   B: It ___may/might/could be___. A lot of people hear it.
4. A: Where's Jane?
   B: I'm not sure. She ___may/might/could be___ with Myra. They always hang out together.
   A: She ___can't/couldn't be___. Myra is on vacation.
5. A: Are Yuko's parents in Japan now?
   B: They ___can't/couldn't be___ there. I just saw them yesterday.

Short answers (with *be*)

Is that Marta's brother?
It **might/could** be.
It **can't/couldn't** be.

C Read each situation. Think of two possible explanations for each one.

1. Your friend isn't answering her cell phone.
2. You received a mysterious package in the mail.
3. The teacher isn't here today.
4. A new student in our class is quiet.

1. The batteries may/might/could be dead. OR She may/might/could be at school and she left her phone at home.
2. It may/might/could be from a relative. OR It may/might/could be some books. OR It can't/couldn't be a birthday present—it's not my birthday!
3. She may/might/could be busy. OR She may/might/could be sick.
4. He may/might/could be shy. OR He may/might/could be nervous.

5 Writing A strange event

A Read the paragraph on the right. Then write one or two more paragraphs to finish the story.

Danny woke up. "What was that noise?" he wondered. It was dark and Danny couldn't see. He turned on the light and looked at the clock. It was 2:00 a.m. Bang! There was the noise again. "What could it be?" Danny thought nervously. His parents weren't at home and his sister was at a friend's house. Danny opened his bedroom door and walked out to investigate. . . .

B Exchange your story with a partner. As you read your partner's story, answer the questions. Then tell your partner your answers.

1. What was the sound Danny heard?
2. What is a good title for your partner's story?

4 Language Link

Modals of present possibility

Warm Up

5 min

Ask factual questions about people you and the students know. Ask, for example, how old they are or where they live. Then ask, *Are you sure?* The students answer *yes* or *no*.

15-20 min

A Look at the picture and read the question and the answers in the chart. Then complete sentences 1 and 2 below with the correct modals.

To begin, ask questions about Marta and the man in the photo: *How old is Marta? How old is the man? Is she his sister? His daughter?* Students should answer *Possibly* or *I don't know*. Then read and explain the chart. Students can complete the sentences, and then check answers as a class.

10 min

B Read the note about short answers. Then complete the dialogs below. Practice them with a partner.

Remind students of the questions they answered in **A**. Now they can use modals in their answers. Tell students to complete the dialogs with *may be, might be, could be, can't be,* or *couldn't be.* Write the five phrases with modals on the board. Model the dialogs alone or with a student. Have students repeat before practicing in pairs.

Language Tip: Modals of present possibility

Modals express a speaker's attitude or opinion about a situation. Because two speakers may feel differently about the same situation, it is difficult to learn the precise meanings of modals by listening to native speakers. Although they often use *may, might,* and *could* slightly differently, this is not necessary for efficient communication.

15-20 min

C Read each situation. Think of two possible explanations for each one.

Read the situations with the class. Then pair students. Walk around as the students discuss the situations. Help with vocabulary and ideas if necessary. To follow up, ask the students to share their explanations, and list them on the board.

C Teaching Option Dialogs

Students can do the exercise as dialogs using the situation in **C** and their own explanations. For example:

1. A: Yuko isn't answering her cell phone.
   B: It might be turned off.
   A: Or the battery could be dead.

5 Writing A strange event

Warm Up

5 min

Ask who has seen the 1990 comedy movie "Home Alone." What happened in the movie? (A young boy is left at home by mistake when his family goes away for Christmas. He defends his house against two comical burglars.)

10-15 min

A Read the paragraph on the right. Then write one or two more paragraphs to finish the story.

Read the paragraph aloud while students read it silently. Students work alone to finish the story in two more paragraphs. Walk around helping students with questions and ideas as needed.

A Teaching Option Process Writing (1)

Pre-writing has already been done for the students in the form of the first paragraph about Danny. The next steps are writing the rough draft and rereading to correct and improve it. As students write, walk around and remind them to write steadily, with little revising and correcting at this stage. When they finish, tell them to reread their work and improve it without rewriting it.

30-35 min

B Exchange your story with a partner. As you read your partner's story, answer the questions. Then tell your partner your answers.

Walk around as students are reading and talking about their stories. Remind them to answer the two questions about their partner's story. Ask the two questions of several students.

B Teaching Option Process Writing (2)

The next step is getting feedback from another student. The papers will be too messy for the partner to read. Tell students to read their paper aloud while the partner follows along. This should be a conversation about the story. Both students can interrupt with questions, suggestions, and comments. When they have discussed both stories, they separate again and rewrite their stories, revising them as needed. At this point, students have practiced about half of the writing process.

6 Communication What's your theory?

Warm Up

5–10 min

On the board, write *Sasquatch* and *Bigfoot.* These are two names for the same thing. Ask what students know about this mysterious creature. If they have no information, here is some you can share.

People report:

- A large animal like a man or an ape
- 7–8 feet tall
- Covered with hair like an ape or a bear
- Smells bad
- Very large footprints
- Stands up straight, walks on two feet
- Reported all over North America

Talk about mysterious creatures like Sasquatch. Ask, *Do you believe they exist? Do you want them to exist?*

A 5–10 min

Look at the photos and read the notes about these unsolved mysteries. Then answer the question below about each.

Talk about the photos with the class. Have the students heard of any of these mysteries before? What have they heard? Ask a volunteer to explain the word *creature.* Where has the student seen or heard that word before? Ask another volunteer to describe the pyramids in Egypt. Finally, ask a third student to show with his or her hands the size of a basketball. Then, students can read the descriptions and answer the questions on their own. While the students are working, walk around to help with vocabulary, and ask a few questions about the readings.

B 10–15 min

Work in a group of 3 or 4 people. Discuss your answers to the question in A. Which is the most likely explanation?

Review modals of present possibility on page 30. Write these phrases on the board: *It might be . . . , It may be . . . , They could be . . . , They can't be . . . , It couldn't be . . . .* Tell students that they must give an opinion and a reason. *(They might be lights from a car. Maybe the sky reflects them.* or *They can't be car lights. They're too big.)* Put students in groups to discus the answers and decide on likely explanations.

C 10 min

Can you think of other unsolved mysteries like the ones in A? What do you think they are? Tell your group about them.

Walk around to hear some of the conversations and ask a few questions. If some of the groups have interesting information, ask them to tell the class.

C Teaching Option **Internet search**

There is a lot of information about unsolved mysteries on the web. Tell students to do a search using the keywords *mysterious creatures.* Ask them to choose one creature, take notes, and report back to the class.

Large Class Option

In a large class, it isn't practical for every student to report information to the whole group. Instead, have them report to smaller groups. Each group chooses the most interesting information and that student reports to the class. Alternatively, students can write the information they found and hand it in.

World Link Video and World Link Website

Remind students of the value of further practice outside the classroom. Ask students who have watched the video or done online practice to share their experiences.

Instructor's Notes

Check out the World Link Video. Practice your English online at http://elt.heinle.com/worldlink

6 Communication **What's your theory?**

A Look at the photos and read the notes about these unsolved mysteries. Then answer the question below about each.

The Chupacabra

The Yonaguni Monument

The Marfa Lights

What: It's a creature about 1.2 meters (4 feet) tall with red eyes and big teeth. It can jump high. It kills animals and drinks their blood. It's seen only at night.

Where: All over North and South America and parts of Russia

When: Was first seen in 1995

What: It's a large underwater rock formation—about 25 meters (82 feet) high. It looks like pyramids seen in Egypt and the Americas.

Where: In the Pacific Ocean, near Japan

When: Was discovered in 1986

What: They're lights that appear suddenly in the night sky. Often, there are two or three of them. They are about the size of a basketball. Sometimes they fly close to people's houses.

Where: In the desert near the town of Marfa, Texas (U.S.)

When: Were first seen in 1883

What do you think each thing is?

a. a large dog or other animal
b. a man in a costume
c. a terrible monster
d. your idea: ___________

a. an underwater city
b. an old Japanese pyramid
c. nothing, just some rocks
d. your idea: ___________

a. lights from a car or plane
b. some kind of strange weather
c. space aliens
d. your idea: ___________

B Work in a group of 3 or 4 people. Discuss your answers to the question in **A**. Which is the most likely explanation?

The Marfa Lights might be lights from a car or plane...

No, they can't be because...

C Can you think of other unsolved mysteries like the ones in **A**? What do you think they are? Tell your group about them.

Check out the World Link video.

Practice your English online at http://elt.heinle.com/worldlink

Review: Units 1-3

1 Storyboard

A Susan, Maya, and Bruno work together. Look at the pictures and complete the conversations. For some blanks, more than one answer is possible.

B Practice the conversation with two people. Then change roles and practice again.

C Introduce a friend to another friend. Invite both friends out to dinner.

Review: Units 1–3

1 Storyboard

Warm Up

5–10 min

List and read aloud these words and phrases: *1) introductions 2) acquaintances 3) street foods 4) extracurricular activities 5) luck 6) investigations*. Call on volunteers to explain one of these terms and to give an example that they learned about in class or from personal experiences. Explain that in the review unit, students will review what they have learned and have a chance to ask any remaining questions.

5–10 min

A Susan, Maya, and Bruno work together. Look at the pictures and complete the conversations. For some blanks, more than one answer is possible.

Discuss the people and events shown in the pictures. Ask students to predict who is meeting for the first time. Point to picture 5, and ask what word is shown in the callout. *Seafood.* Ask students to guess what is being said. Stronger classes can complete the conversation independently. For weaker classes, pair students to work together. Check answers, affirming alternative responses when appropriate.

> **Teaching Tip: Repetition**
>
> Incorporate frequent repetition of vocabulary words and grammatical structures to help students remember them. Repetition can be done verbally, in writing, pair practice, or through games. Daily vocabulary practice can be done as a routine at the beginning of class, between activities, or as a class wrap up. List words that were recently reviewed, along with a few from classes prior, and call on students to explain using definitions and examples.

10–15 min

B Practice the conversation with two people. Then change roles and practice again.

Pair students to practice the conversation. Ask them to imagine that they are speaking in real life, rather than reading, and to use expressive voices. Model reading the lines in the first picture with expression. After groups complete the conversation once, students should change roles and say the lines again. This time, tell speakers to use alternative responses for items that were listed during the class discussion. Walk around as students practice, and provide suggestions on expression or varying responses.

10–15 min

C Introduce a friend to another friend. Invite both friends out to dinner.

Give students a chance to practice introductions and inviting friends to dinner. Assign students to new groups of three. Ask them to apply what they have learned to create a conversation. Call on a few groups to perform their introductions and invitations for the whole class.

> **Teaching Tip: Conversation practice**
>
> In activities where students are reading a conversation rather than creating their own, students should pay special attention to pronunciation. Practice reading the words naturally, paying attention to the individual sounds, stresses, and intonations.

> **Culture Tip: Buying lunch**
>
> In English-speaking countries, students and coworkers often share lunch together in restaurants because lunch tends to cost less than dinner. In these cultures, males and females eat together. In addition, each person usually pays for his or her own meal. This popular tradition is called *going Dutch*. It is unusual, even strange, for one person to offer to pay for everyone.

Instructor's Notes

2 See It and Say It

Warm Up

5-10 min

Ask students if they have ever met again someone they knew a long time ago. *Where did they meet? What did they talk about? What questions did they ask one another?*

A 5-10 min

Below is a page from Anna Lopez's high school yearbook. She graduated in 1998. Read what her classmates wrote in her yearbook. How did Anna know each person? Discuss your ideas with a partner.

Remind students of the school tradition of signing yearbooks. Ask who might sign a student's yearbook. If needed, suggest responses, such as a best friend, classmate, boyfriend, girlfriend, or teammate. Then, explain that each person wrote a note in Anna Lopez's yearbook, and point to her photograph. Next, read each note aloud. Assign students to pairs, and ask them to describe the relationship between Anna and each person shown. Check answers as a class by calling on volunteers. Follow up by asking how students got the answer.

B 10-15 min

Look at the people in A as they are today.

Point to the pictures, and read aloud the names of the people shown. Explain that each pair knows each other now, and they knew each other in the past. Tell students that some event led these people to meet again. Ask each student to work individually to answer each of the three questions. Read the questions aloud, and explain any word or phrase that students do not understand. After each student writes a response, assign students to pairs to share their stories.

Word Bank: Meeting people

coincidence
by chance
unexpected
realize
recognize

20-30 min

EXTRA! Writing prompt

Ask students to write a story about a person they either knew before and met again or with whom they shared an unexpected connection. Tell them to include information on how they met the person and why their meeting was unexpected or special.

Teaching Tip: Order of details

Explain that it is important to write details in the correct order so that readers clearly understand the message. Point out that in stories, events are placed in the order of time. To demonstrate, write a three-sentence story in order, and then out of order. Remind students that reading their own writing aloud can help them identify details that are out of order or that require other changes to make sense.

Instructor's Notes

2 See It and Say It

Anna and Bobby were probably acquaintances. They didn't know each other very well.
Anna and Rachel were good friends. Anna probably went out with Michael.

A Below is a page from Anna Lopez's high school yearbook. She graduated in 1998. Read what her classmates wrote in her yearbook. How did Anna know each person? Discuss your ideas with a partner.

Sorry I didn't get to know you better, Anna. Good luck in college! Bobby

Hey, Anna! Best friends 4-ever! Rachel

Michael Evans

We're graduating, but you'll always be my girl, Anna. ~Michael

Bobby Leong

Anna Lopez

Rachel Williams

B Look at the people in **A** as they are today.

1. Bobby and Anna work together. Maybe Bobby works for Anna. Rachel is dating Michael, or they could be married.

1. What are their relationships now?
2. Choose one of the pictures below. Make up a story about it. Answer these questions:
   - What happened to the people in your picture after high school?
   - How did they meet again?
3. Tell your partner the story of your picture.

Bobby and Anna

Rachel and Michael

3 Listening

A Look at the photos below. What words would you use to describe these things? Tell your partner.

B Four people are going to talk about their eating habits. Listen. Which food does each person like or eat a lot? Match a speaker (1, 2, 3, or 4) with the correct photo(s).

CD 1
Track 20

C Read sentences 1–3 below. Then listen. Choose the correct answer for each sentence.

CD 1
Track 21

1. If you *get in shape*, you . . .
   a. gain weight.
   (b.) do things to be healthier.
   c. don't do much exercise.

2. If food tastes *bland*, it has . . .
   a. a strong taste.
   b. a lot of spices in it.
   (c.) no flavor.

3. If you *have a sweet tooth*, you . . .
   (a.) like sugary foods.
   b. can't eat sweets.
   c. are a good cook.

D Work with a partner and do the following:

1. Write three more food or drink items in the chart below.

food or drink item	Speaker 1	Speaker 2	Speaker 3	Speaker 4
1. pizza				
2. a glass of milk				
3. ____________				
4. ____________				
5. ____________				

CD 1
Track 20

2. Listen again. Which speaker (1, 2, 3, or 4) probably eats the items on your list often? Check (✓) the correct person.
3. Discuss your answers with a partner. Talk about the possibilities.

ASK ANSWER

Which person (1, 2, 3, or 4) are you most like?

I doubt that Speaker 1 eats pizza because...

3 Listening

Warm Up

5 min

Label two columns: *Food* and *Adjective*. Ask students to name their favorite foods, and list responses under the *Food* column. Then, point to a food listed, and call on a student to give one word that describes its taste or texture. If students need help recalling adjectives, suggest those reviewed in prior lessons, such as *sweet*, *salty*, *delicious*, *bitter*, *crunchy*, *oily*, *spicy*, or *soft*.

A Look at the photos below. What words would you use to describe these things? Tell your partner.

10–15 min

Assign students to pairs, and explain that they will write a list of words to describe the foods shown. Point to the list of adjectives the class just generated, and tell students they may use words from this list or other adjectives they know. Check answers orally by pointing to the photographs one at a time and calling on a few pairs to share adjectives they listed to describe the foods shown.

B Four people are going to talk about their eating habits. Listen. Which food does each person like or eat a lot? Match a speaker (1, 2, 3, or 4) with the correct photo(s).

CD 1 Track 20

5 min

Tell students they will hear a conversation between four speakers, and then number the boxes to show which speaker likes that food. Play the audio all the way through the first time to familiarize students with the voices of the speakers. Play the audio again so students can complete the activity. Finally, review the correct answers, and play back the parts of the recording that revealed the food each speaker likes.

C Read sentences 1–3 below. Then listen. Choose the correct answer for each sentence.

CD 1 Track 21

10–15 min

Remind students to listen for keywords to help them identify the question being addressed. Play the audio twice. When students have answered the questions, ask volunteers to share their responses and tell what part of the recording helped them identify the correct answer. To check understanding of the words and phrases in blue, ask a few volunteers to use those words in new sentences. Write those sentences on the board.

Teaching Tip: Choices

Try to provide choices that give students a chance to speak, write, or read about topics most interesting to them. In writing activities, for example, offer two or three prompts, and allow each student to choose the one most interesting to him or her, if appropriate for the goal of the activity. When sharing information with a partner, when possible, give students a choice of which question(s) to answer or expand on. Occasionally, allow students to choose points to evaluate or analyze as they work.

D Work with a partner and do the following:

10–15 min

(See student book page 34 for complete instructions.)

After students list foods, explain that they will check the boxes to show which speaker might eat each food. Tell students that the audio will be played two times. Then assign students to pairs to discuss and compare their answers. Read the speech bubble about Speaker 1, and explain that students may use similar phrases as they express their ideas.

ASK ANSWER

Read the question aloud. Then model a response based on your own food preferences. Ask students to share their response to the question with their partner.

EXTRA! True or false game

15–20 min

Write 10 statements taken from the recording. Make five of the statements very similar to the original, except change one detail that makes the statement false. Explain to students that they will play a game. Divide the room into two teams. Call on the first team member from Side A. Read statement 1, and ask, *Is this true or false?* If the player is correct, the team gets a point. If not, Team B gets a turn. If the statement is false, the responding team member gets a chance to correct the statement for 3 points. If he or she misses again, the next player from the other side gets a chance. Continue until all statements have been reviewed. The team with the most points wins.

4 Wonders of the World

Use the adjectives in the box to ask and answer questions about these monuments with a partner.

5–10 min

Explain that the "Wonders of the World" are places, both natural and man-made, on Earth that are special or amazing. Point to each, and read the name aloud. If available, show on a map the country where each site is located. Next, read the adjectives aloud. Call on volunteers to give a synonym or brief definition of each. Read the question and answer in the speech bubble to model the activity. Assign students to pairs to ask and answer questions. Call on a few pairs to share one or two of their questions and answers.

Teaching Tip: Ask and reinforce

During class discussions, take responses from volunteers, and call on students who tend to stay quiet to be sure they understand the discussion. For example, do quick comprehension checks to ensure that students understand the vocabulary to use in activities by asking, *What does this word mean?* If the student cannot provide a definition, give the response in a short phrase or synonym that might be familiar. Use the word in a quick example or sketch that demonstrates the meaning. Do not speak directly to one student, but to the whole class as you explain.

5 I'm Reading an Interesting Book.

5–10 min

A Choose three words from the box. Write three sentences about yourself in your notebook. Use the simple present or the present continuous.

Write a pair of sentences using simple present and present continuous, such as *I read* and *I am reading*. Ask, *Which sentence shows present continuous? How are these sentences different?* Confirm that the sentence in the present continuous shows what you are doing at this moment, whereas the other shows an activity you generally do. Review the differences further if students have difficulty understanding. Next, tell students to write sentences about themselves using either tense, as long as the idea is expressed correctly. Collect responses and read several anonymously, providing corrections when needed.

Teaching Tip: Small group work

Increase each student's speaking time by using small groups of about three students. Structure group activities in a way that requires every student to speak. One way to do this is to ask a leader to record responses, and to require that each student provides one response during the group discussion. When possible, group students for the most effective communication, such as placing talkative students together, rather than two talkative students with one quiet student.

10–15 min

B Work in small groups. Read one of your sentences. Each person in your group asks a question about your sentence.

Divide the class into groups of three. Call on three volunteers to read the sample responses, so that one student reads each item by the letter A, another reads B, and the third reads C. Then ask each group to choose the student who will read his or her sentence first, and proceed as other members ask questions. Continue the activity until all group members have read their statements.

Instructor's Notes

4 Wonders of the World

Use the adjectives in the box to ask and answer questions about these monuments with a partner.

beautiful	interesting	popular	strange
impressive	old	remote	tall

Which monument is the oldest?

Well, the statues on Easter Island look old, but I bet the Roman Colosseum is older.

5 I'm Reading an Interesting Book.

A Choose three words from the box. Write three sentences about yourself in your notebook. Use the simple present or the present continuous.

eat	know	like	study
read	own	work	

B Work in small groups. Read one of your sentences. Each person in your group asks a question about your sentence.

I always eat cereal for breakfast.

What kind of cereal do you eat?

Wheat flakes.

Why do you always eat cereal?

I don't have time in the morning. It's quick and easy.

4 Today's Trends

Lesson A Family trends

1 Vocabulary Link Family trends

thousands of women = many thousands
a thousand women = exactly 1,000

trend = a change or development toward something different

A Complete the sentences below with a word or phrase from the box. Compare your answers with a partner.

half	percent	thousands

American Family Trends

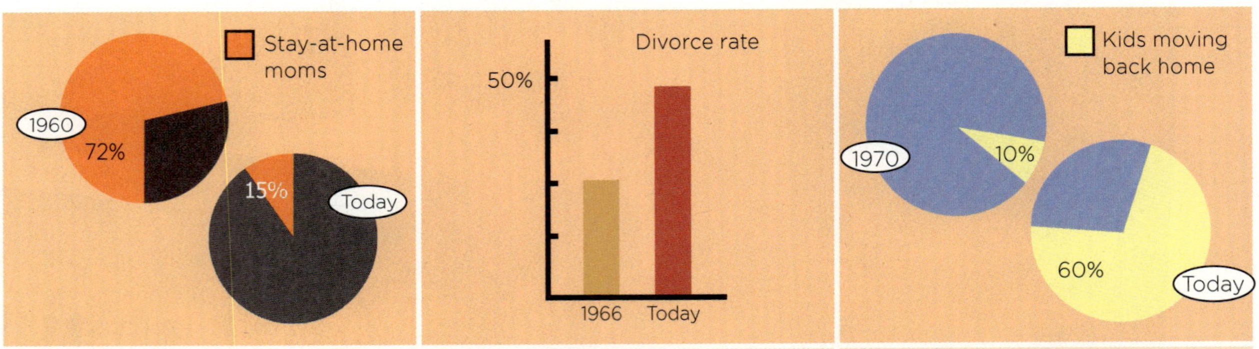

In 1960, over 70 percent of homes had a working father and stay-at-home mother. Today, this number has dropped to 15 percent because ___thousands___ of women now have jobs outside the home.

The number of divorces today is almost twice as high as in 1966. In the 1960s, a quarter (25%) of all marriages ended in divorce. Today, nearly ___half___ (50%) of all marriages end in divorce.

The average American leaves home between the ages of 18 and 20. In 1970, 10% of these people moved back with their parents after leaving home. Today, that number has risen to sixty ___percent___.

B Find a blue word or phrase in **A** that has a similar meaning to each word or phrase below.

1. almost ___nearly___
2. more than ___over___
3. two times as high as ___twice as high as___
4. usual, typical ___average___
5. fifty percent ___half___
6. increased ___risen___
7. decreased ___dropped___
8. twenty-five percent, one-fourth ___a quarter___

C Complete the sentences with a blue word in **A**. Which words are used to talk about an exact number or amount? Which talk about an approximate (not exact) amount?

1. Mary's birthday is next month. She's ___almost OR nearly___ 12 years old.
2. ___Half___ of 40 is 20.
3. There were ___thousands___ of people at the concert—maybe 20,000 or more.
4. Bob is ___over___ 30. Maybe he's 34 or 35.
5. Class A has 15 people and B has 30. Class B is ___twice___ as big as Class A.

ASK ANSWER

In your opinion, which trends in **A** are positive? Which are negative? Why?

Are these trends similar or different in your country? Explain.

Family Trends

Unit 4, Lesson A

1 Vocabulary Link Family trends

Warm Up

5 min

Ask students what they know (or can guess) about families in their country 50 years ago. Do they think most mothers worked outside the home 50 years ago? What about now? Do they think there were more divorces 50 years ago or now? Fifty years ago, did many adult children move back with their parents after they left home? What about now?

Read the info box aloud. Write on the board: *20,000* and *1,000*. Ask students to say *thousands of* and *a thousand* with these plural nouns: families, children, parents, marriages, divorces. Randomly point to the numbers on the board to cue each phrase (*thousands of parents, thousands of marriages, a thousand children*, etc.).

A Complete the sentences below with a word or phrase from the box. Compare your answers with a partner.

10–15 min

Before pair work, tell students to look at the three pairs of graphs about American families. Discuss them with the class. What are the dates in each pair of graphs? What three aspects of family life are changing?

Read the definition in the box. Then ask students *What is the trend in stay-at-home mothers in American families? Up or down? What is the trend in divorces? Up or down? What is the trend in adult children returning to live at home?*

B Find a blue word or phrase in **A** that has a similar meaning to each word or phrase below.

5–10 min

While students are working, walk around the room checking their work. If there are mistakes, tell the students how many are wrong (not what is wrong). Tell them to find the mistakes and correct them.

C Complete the sentences with a blue word in **A**. Which words are used to talk about an exact number or amount? Which talk about an approximate (not exact) amount?

5–15 min

After checking students' answers, write *Exact amount* and *Approximate amount* on the board. Ask students to tell you where to write each blue word, under *Exact amount* or *Approximate amount*. If your students know enough vocabulary, ask them to suggest other words for each list. Add them to the lists on the board.

Word Bank: Adjectives for numbers and statistics

exactly, precisely
approximately, about, around, roughly
over, more than
nearly, almost, close to, practically
under, less than, fewer than

ASK ANSWER

If your students are not yet ready to discuss the trends, form pairs or groups comprising stronger and weaker students to describe or summarize them briefly. When they understand the trends, open up the discussion to their opinions.

Teaching Tip: Assigning partners

Even if the seating arrangement in your classroom is fixed, it's good to have students work with a variety of partners during pair work. They can work with students of different ability levels, and also get to know their classmates better, building a feeling of community. Without changing seats, students can work with the person on either side, or turn around to face the person behind. Consider changing partners for every activity, or for every class period.

Culture Tip: Non-traditional families

A "traditional" family in most English-speaking countries means a father and mother and their children. However, there are many kinds of families. Which are typical in your students' country(ies)?

- Single-parent families—a mother or father alone raising children
- Blended or step-families—two divorced people marry, bringing with them children from their previous families
- Adoptive families—parents raising children they have adopted
- Grandparents raising their grandchildren when the parents are unable to care for them
- Multiple wives married to one man
- Cousins being raised together as siblings

2 Listening Still at home

Skills: Identify the main idea; Listen for details; Determine a speaker's attitude

Warm Up

5 min

Ask the students at approximately what age people in their country usually get married. If they are from the same country, do they agree on the age or disagree? At what age do they think most people *want* to get married?

A You will hear three people talking. Listen and answer the question.

CD 1 Track 22 · 10–15 min

Tell students that the three speakers are from different countries. Read the three trends aloud before playing the audio.

B Look at your answer in A and read the questions below. Then listen again and answer the questions.

CD 1 Track 22 · 10–20 min

Point to the answers and the countries. Tell students that there is more than one answer for each country.

C Listen again and connect the information in the three columns.

CD 1 Track 22 · 10–20 min

Copy the three columns on the board. Point to each column and name it (countries, people's ages, actions). Show students that they connect countries to ages and also events to ages. Look at the example together.

C Teaching Option Support/challenge

Copy the exercise on the board three times. To challenge stronger students, ask three volunteers to work at the board while the others work in their seats. This supports students who are less confident by letting them see what the more confident students are doing at the board. They may copy the answers, but they are also likely to understand them better in the end. Correct the work on the board with the whole class.

D Tell a partner about the trends in Italy, Japan, and the UK. Use your answers in B and C to help you.

5–10 min

Students should say at least two sentences about each country, taking turns so that each one speaks about each country. Follow up by asking several students to say their sentences for the class.

3 Pronunciation

Unstressed *of* in rapid speech

A Listen. Notice the pronunciation of the word *of*.

CD 1 Track 23 · 10–15 min

Write these phrases on the board: *most of my, a lot of people, part of becoming*. Tell students to notice *of* as they listen. After playing the recording, pronounce the phrases on the board as in the recording: *mosta my, a lotta people, parta becoming*. Point out that *of* is followed by a consonant (*m, p,* and *b*). Refer students to the rule in the information box. Play the audio again so that students can verify what they heard.

Language Tip: Pronunciation of *of* in isolation

When we slow down, the pronunciation of *of* is different. Point out that the last sound is /v/, not /f/. Read aloud slowly, pronunciation of *of* is /əv/.

B Listen and complete the sentences. Then practice saying them aloud.

CD 1 Track 24 · 10–15 min

Read the incomplete sentences aloud. Play the audio, and ask a volunteer to write the answers on the board. Read each completed sentence with students repeating. Tell students to turn to a partner to practice saying the sentences.

Language Tip: Right or wrong?

Students may have opinions about this kind of rapid-speech pronunciation. Some may enjoy sounding more like native speakers of American English, while others may consider it sloppy or uneducated. (In fact, many linguists do not usually think of pronunciation as correct or incorrect. They are interested in how people really talk, and they understand that languages change constantly.) In rapid speech, pronouncing *of* as /əv/ before a consonant sounds too careful and formal to most native speakers of American English. In slower speech (like that of most learners), it is more appropriate.

2 Listening Still at home

CD 1 Track 22

A You will hear three people talking. Listen and answer the question.

What trend are the people talking about?

a. people getting married later
(b.) children living with their parents longer
c. people having fewer children

CD 1 Track 22

B Look at your answer in **A** and read the questions below. Then listen again and answer the questions.

1. In each place, what is causing this trend? Match the places with the reasons from the box.

Italy ___a, c___
Japan ___a, d___
the UK ___a, b___

a. Housing costs are high.	c. Getting a job is difficult.
b. Education is expensive.	d. People are waiting to get married.

2. Which person does NOT think the trend is good?

a. Alessandro   b. Aya   (c.) Evan

CD 1 Track 22

C Listen again and connect the information in the three columns.

Italy	18–24	people get married
Japan	30	people leave home
the UK	28–29	
	36	

D Tell a partner about the trends in Italy, Japan, and the UK. Use your answers in **B** and **C** to help you.

In Italy, the average age that people leave home is 36. People wait to move out because ...

3 Pronunciation Unstressed *of* in rapid speech

CD 1 Track 23

A Listen. Notice the pronunciation of the word *of*.

1. Most of my friends still live with their parents.
2. A lot of people are getting married later.
3. Leaving your parents' house is part of becoming an adult.

Note: In rapid speech, the final *f* sound in *of* is usually dropped before a consonant sound.

CD 1 Track 24

B Listen and complete the sentences. Then practice saying them aloud.

1. ___None of___ the kids in my family still live at home.
2. ___A couple of___ my friends are studying in New York City.
3. ___Thousands of___ people get divorced every year.
4. ___Most of___ them have children.

4 Speaking **I know what you're saying, but . . .**

CD 1 Track 25

A Listen to the conversation. Then answer the questions with a partner.

1. Carla and her dad are fighting about something. What?
   Carla wants to go to a concert, but her father says "no."
2. Who do you agree with—Carla or her dad?

Carla: Dad, can I talk to you for a minute?

Dad: Sure, what's up?

Carla: Well, my friend Marta is going to see a concert tomorrow night and she invited me to go.

Dad: Tomorrow night? But tomorrow's Tuesday. Sorry, Carla, but no.

Carla: Dad! You *never* let me do anything.

Dad: That's not true, Carla. You do lots of things. But the concert ends late and you have school on Wednesday.

Carla: I know what you're saying, Dad, but it's just one night. And all of my friends are going.

Dad: Sorry, Carla, but the answer is still "no."

Carla: Oh, Dad, you're so unfair!

B Practice the conversation with a partner.

5 Speaking Strategy

Useful Expressions: Disagreeing

Politely	Strongly
I know what you're saying, but . . .	That's not true.
Sorry, but I disagree. / I don't agree.	I totally / completely disagree.
I hear you, but . . . [very informal]	Oh, come on! / Are you serious? [very informal]

A Work with a partner. One person is the parent. The other person is the son or daughter.

1. Choose a situation from the box. Think of reasons for and against it.
2. Create a new conversation similar to the one above. In your dialog, use at least two Useful Expressions.

B Get together with another pair.

- **Pair 1:** Perform your dialog for another pair.
- **Pair 2:** Listen. Who do you agree with—the parent or child? Why?

C Switch roles and do **B** again.

Parents: Your son or daughter wants to . . .

- go on a date
- visit another country by himself or herself
- get a part-time job
- your own idea: ______________

4 Speaking

I know what you're saying, but . . .

Warm Up

5 min

Ask students, *In your country (or your family), do parents and children sometimes disagree? What do they disagree about? Do they argue? Who usually wins?*

Culture Tip: Family arguments

In many countries children, even adult children, do not argue with their parents. It is considered disrespectful or even shameful. While in other countries children often argue with their parents and may even express anger. This is not usually considered good behavior, but it is tolerated.

CD 1 Track 25

10–15 min

A Listen to the conversation. Then answer the questions with a partner.

With the comprehension questions on the board and books closed, play the audio once. Students can check their answers with the person sitting next to them, or you can check the answers with the class. Play the audio again while students follow in their books. Then answer any questions students have about vocabulary or the situation of the speakers. Play the audio a third time, line-by-line, so that students can repeat it. When repetition of a line is ragged, model it yourself so they can try again.

10 min

B Practice the conversation with a partner.

Put students in pairs to practice the conversation. Remind them to look at their partner when they speak, and to say as much as they can before looking down to refresh their memories. Emphasize that it is just as important for the partner to look at the speaker. There should be eye contact whenever someone is speaking.

Teaching Tip: Read, look up, and speak

Practice of a written conversation feels more natural if students maintain eye contact when speaking to each other. Students should read a line or two, then look up at their partner and say the lines, or as much of them as possible. When they get stuck, they can look down and read, but look up again before speaking. The partner also should maintain eye contact with the speaker (not look at the book to see what he or she has to say next). The conversation will not flow like spontaneous speech, but it will feel more like it, and students will understand what they're saying.

5 Speaking Strategy

15–20 min

A Work with a partner. One person is the parent. The other person is the son or daughter.

Introduce the Useful Expressions. Tell students to look at the conversation in **A** again. Ask *who says I know what you're saying, but...* (Carla). Ask *who says sorry* and *how many times* (Dad, two times). Read the other Useful Expressions. Ask who might say each one, Carla or her dad, and where in the conversation they might say it. Read the lines aloud with the new expressions.

Discuss the situations in the box. Would students expect most parents to say yes or no in these situations? Does it make a difference if the child is a boy or a girl? Age 15 or 18? What would their own parents say (or what would they say to their children)?

Read aloud the guidelines for the pair work task. If students are not the right age to be the child in the conversation, tell them to decide how old the child is.

20–30 min

B Get together with another pair.

Each pair should perform their conversation at least twice, or until the other pair understands it well. The pairs can ask questions between performances. Then all four students should discuss the situation and the interaction. Each student should give his or her opinion about whom they agree with.

Teaching Tip: Performing in class

If possible, pairs should stand while they perform, and don't let them read their parts. If they forget the exact words, they should express the same idea as well as they can. Their partner will have to adjust to the new words, so he or she has to be listening carefully.

Follow up by asking for a show of hands: In any pairs, did the parent finally say yes? Have those pairs say what the situation was and why the parent finally agreed.

5–10 min

C Switch roles and do B again.

Students can switch roles with their own partner in the same conversation, or they can find a new partner and improvise a new conversation while they act it out.

6 Language Link **Quantity expressions**

Warm Up

5–10 min

Tell students to think of a family that they know (not their own, in case they might not want to share personal information). Ask for a show of hands for each of these questions. *Do they live in a big city? Do they live in a house or an apartment? Do they have a car? Does the wife work outside the home? Are there children in the family?* On the board, write the number of hands on each question over the number of students in the class (for example, *Big city:* $\frac{2}{25}$). Leave the information on the board. Comment on the information using the quantity expressions in the information box.

A 15–20 min

Read the information about six families from around the world. Then write *all, most, a lot, some, a couple,* or *none* in the blanks below.

Introduce the expressions in the information box. Use them to comment on the information on the board. (*Only a couple of the families live in big cities. Some of them live in apartments, but most of them live in houses . . . .*) With books open, ask students to identify the six flags. Read the information in the chart aloud, pointing to each column. Tell students that the six families are not necessarily typical of their countries (a typical American family includes children, although some don't; a typical Indian family does not speak English at home, although some do).

Students can complete the sentences and check answers on the board.

Culture Tip: Own or rent a home

One family pattern that varies around the world is owning or renting one's home. According to a study at the University of California at Los Angeles, 78% of people in Hungary own their homes, compared with 66% in the United States, 53% in the U.K., and only 35% in Sweden.

B 10–15 min

Complete the sentences below with the correct word(s).

Read the sentences aloud. Point out that the choice is between *most* and *most of, some* and *some of*, etc. Explain the information in the i-box—examples of when and when not to use *of* with these expressions. General groups do not need *of.* Examples are *most mothers, some teachers, all people.* Specific or limited groups need *of.* Groups are specific if they begin with *the*, or if they're expressed with a possessive or pronoun. Examples are *all of the people I know, some of my friends,* and *most of us.* Do the exercise on the board with the whole class.

C 15–20 min

Tell your partner about the families you know using *all (of), most (of), a lot (of), some (of), a couple (of),* or *none (of)*. Use the list below.

Pair up students and ask them to talk about some of the families they know. They can talk about the mothers, the fathers, the children, etc. Since these are specific groups (only people they know), most of their sentences should use *of.* Check some of their answers with the whole class. Then tell them to talk about people in general (mothers, fathers, children, etc.). None of these sentences should use *of.*

Finally, divide the class into groups of four or five. Ask each group to make a list of six statements, three about specific groups of people (*the people in this town, our friends,* etc.) and three about people or groups of people in general (*grandparents, boys, students,* etc.). Each group should choose the best sentence and write it on the board. Correct and discuss the sentences with the whole class.

Instructor's Notes

6 Language Link **Quantity expressions**

100%	all (of)
↑	most (of)
	a lot (of)
	some (of)
↓	a couple (of)
0%	none (of)

A Read the information about six families from around the world. Then write *all, most, a lot, some, a couple,* or *none* in the blanks below.

a couple = two

	the SHAW family	the IKEDA family	the OLIVEIRA family	the CHOI family	the DEMIR family	the KUMAR family
hometown	Chicago	Tokyo	Sao Paulo	Seoul	Istanbul	New Delhi
language	English	Japanese	Portuguese	Korean	Turkish	English
housing	house	apartment	apartment	apartment	apartment	apartment
transportation	car	subway	bus	car	car	bus
wife works	restaurant	office	hotel	office	office	office
children	no	yes	yes	yes	yes	yes

1. ___All___ of the families live in big cities.
2. ___A couple___ of the families speak English.
3. ___None___ of them speak French.
4. ___Most___ of the families live in apartments.
5. ___Some___ of them own cars.
6. ___All___ of the families have a working wife.
7. ___A lot___ of the wives work in an office.
8. ___Most___ of the families have children.

B Complete the sentences below with the correct word(s).

1. Most / Most of people want to be happy.
2. Most / Most of my friends speak English, but none / none of them speak it at home.
3. Some / Some of students live with their families because it's cheaper.
4. Most / Most of our neighbors have children; a couple / a couple of them have pets, too.
5. All / All of parents want their children to do well in school.
6. Some / Some of the teachers at my school are really strict.

Using *of*

(students everywhere) **Most students** work hard.

(specific students) **Most of the students** <u>in my class</u> work hard.

Not: ~~Most of students in my class work hard.~~

C Tell your partner about the families you know using *all (of), most (of), a lot (of), some (of), a couple (of),* or *none (of).* Use the list below.

have children	speak English
have a stay-at-home wife	own more than one car

WORLD LINK

By 2015, it's estimated that over ____ of the world's population will live in cities.
a. 30%
b. 50%
c. 70%

7 Communication What should they do?

A Read each situation below. For each one, choose the answer you agree with or write your own idea.

Luis has an older brother and sister. They both go to City University and Luis's father wants him to go there, too. Luis doesn't want to, but if he doesn't go to City, his father will not pay for his school. What should Luis do?

1. Go to City University like his father wants.
2. Start at City University and then later transfer (change) to another school.
3. Get a job, save his money, and pay for his own education.
4. Your idea: ______________________

Yukiko's sixteen-year-old brother is hanging out with some bad people. He isn't going to class and he is fighting at school. Yukiko is worried about her brother. What should she do?

1. Wait a little longer. Maybe things will change.
2. Talk to her brother. Tell him her feelings.
3. Tell her parents about her brother.
4. Your idea: ______________________

Josh is dating a girl named Holly. Josh loves Holly, but Josh's parents don't like her. This weekend is Josh's birthday. His parents are having a big party and they have invited all of his friends—except Holly. What should Josh do?

1. Talk to his parents and tell them to invite Holly.
2. Just bring Holly to the party.
3. Skip the party and spend the day with Holly.
4. Your idea: ______________________

B Get into a group of four or five people. Talk about your opinions in **A** with your group. Explain the reasons for your choice.

I think Luis should go to City University.

Yeah, I agree . . .

Sorry, but I totally disagree with both of you. I think . . .

C Look back at each situation in **A**. How many people in your group agreed with answers 1, 2, or 3? How many came up with their own answers? Compare your results with another group.

Most of the people in our group think Luis should go to City University.

Only one person in our group thinks Luis should go to City University. Most of us think . . .

7 Communication

What should they do?

Warm Up

5 min

Ask students, *When you have a problem, do you ask anyone for advice? Who do you ask? Do you usually feel better after you talk to them? Do you take their advice?*

A Read each situation below. For each one, choose the answer you agree with or write your own idea.

15–20 min

Read each situation and answers 1–3 aloud, or call on students to read them. Answer any questions about vocabulary, but try to get students to guess the meanings first. After reading each situation, tell students to close their books. Ask questions to help them understand and remember the details. (For example, *Are Luis's brother and sister older or younger? Are they in college? Where do they go to school? Is Luis in college yet? Does he want to go to college? What is the problem between Luis and his father?*)

After reviewing the situations, tell students to decide which answer they agree with. They should think about why they chose that answer and why they disagree with the others. They will need to explain this in **B**. To prepare for **B**, students can work alone or with a partner.

B Get into a group of four or five people. Talk about your opinions in A with your group. Explain the reasons for your choice.

10–15 min

Write the Useful Expressions from page 38 on the board. Quickly review the expressions to refresh students' memory of them. Ask three students to demonstrate the conversation. They should read the speech bubbles and complete them with their own reasons for agreeing or disagreeing.

Assign groups. If students were partners in **A**, they should be in different groups in **B**. While they're talking, go from group to group to listen, help with vocabulary, and participate.

C Look back at each situation in A. How many people in your group agreed with answers 1, 2, or 3? How many came up with their own answers? Compare your results with another group.

10–20 min

When the two groups get together, students can discuss their ideas again in the larger group. They might also try to come up with a new option for one of the situations.

Teaching Tip: Group work

Group work can be more useful for students if specific responsibilities are assigned. As students become accustomed to taking on these different responsibilities, group work becomes more efficient, more communicative, and more motivating. Doubling roles as suggested here takes pressure off individuals and encourages spontaneous communication about their tasks and the topic. These roles and responsibilities are suggested:

- Leaders: one or two students who ask questions and make sure that all group members participate in the discussion. If there are two, they can consult with each other and take turns.
- Secretaries: one or two students who take notes on the ideas expressed and conclusions reached by the group. If there are two, they can compare notes and be sure nothing is missed. If they both miss something, they should call a time out and check with the group members.
- Reporters: one or two students who present the group's results to the whole class. They should consult with the secretaries to be sure they cover the important points.

Reporters should participate actively in the discussion. Leaders and secretaries can also participate, although they need to concentrate on their assigned responsibilities. Secretaries can also serve as reporters, or one secretary and one leader can report. With frequent group work, all students will have repeated opportunities to experience each role.

Large Class Option

Assigning and doubling responsibilities as described above means there can be more students in each group. With two leaders, two secretaries, and two reporters, there might be as many as eight or even 10 students per group. This reduces the number of groups in the class, makes it possible for you to spend time with each group, and generally keeps things moving.

Instructor's Notes

Fashion trends
Unit 4, Lesson B

1 Vocabulary Link Fashion trends

Warm Up

5 min

With books closed, ask students, What is a piece of clothing that you used to really like to wear, but now is out of style? Why did you used to like it? What's wrong with it now?

A Read about some of these decades' popular fashions. Then, with a partner, use the words in blue to describe each photo on the time line.

15–20 min

Introduce the words in the information box. Then hold up the book and point to the photographs. Ask students if they would wear any of these styles today (or wore them in the past). Write the blue words for "The 80s" on the board and read the text aloud. Ask students which description has no photo. (The preppy look—if possible, bring in a photo.) Let students add any other words they don't understand to the list for "The 80s." Then explain the listed words. Do the same for "The 90s" and "The 00s" (say *oh-ohs*).

Pair students and tell them to describe the photos using as many of the listed words as possible and other vocabulary they know. Students should make original sentences, not just read the text. Model the exercise for them. (*His suit is conservative. Her dress has big shoulders.*)

Teaching Tip: Explaining vocabulary

Students should explain any words they can to each other. They can point to pictures, describe the words, give native-language equivalents, or give words with the opposite meaning. Students with bilingual dictionaries can look words up for the class. Finally, explain any remaining words yourself.

Teaching Tip: Vocabulary notebooks

Require students to keep a list of new words in a special pocket notebook, a separate section of their class notebook, or on their handheld device. They should list high-interest words or words that they think are especially useful. Every student's list will be unique. Periodically, ask a student to share some of the words in his or her vocabulary notebook with the class, or several students can share in small groups.

B Discuss the questions with a partner.

10 min

To prepare for pair work, discuss current styles with the class. Students may be able to name styles in the native language, but not in English. Make a list of English terms on the board for them to refer to. Read the adjectives in the box. Most are in the text in **A**, but *fun, stylish,* and *unique* are new. Walk around while students are talking to help with vocabulary.

EXTRA! Fashion trends

15–20 min

Ask students to bring in old photos of themselves. They can describe their hair and clothing and the trends at the time when the photo was taken. If students don't have photos, you can bring in photos of different fashion trends that you find online for students to describe.

Teaching Tip: Vocabulary notebook follow-up

If students have vocabulary notebooks, ask several students what words from this lesson they will be adding to their notebooks. Ask why they chose those words—are they especially interesting, or useful, or both? Write their choices on the board.

Instructor's Notes

Lesson B Fashion trends

1 Vocabulary Link Fashion trends

A Read about some of these decades' popular fashions. Then, with a partner, use the words in blue to describe each photo on the time line.

> **in** = popular, fashionable
> **a look** = a style

What was in?

The 80s

- Conservative business suits with big shoulders for both men and women
- Casual but sporty clothes known as the "preppy" look
- Bright colors and big jewelry
- Dramatic makeup and hairstyles and the color black—especially with punks and goths

The 90s

- Grunge: a casual—almost sloppy—look of ripped jeans and old shirts
- Hip-hop fashion: baseball caps, oversized shirts, and baggy pants

The 00s

- skinny (fitted) jeans
- Pointy shoes and boots for both men and women
- Body piercings
- Retro 80s fashion (dramatic hairstyles, bright colors)

B Discuss the questions with a partner.

1. What styles are "in" today? Describe each look.
2. Which words describe your look? What clothes do you usually wear?

Describing your look

casual / comfortable, colorful, conservative, dramatic, fun, retro, sloppy, sporty, stylish, unique

2 Listening **You've got the look.**

A With a partner, describe the people's clothes in the photos below.

B Listen to a makeover TV show. Number the people (1, 2, or 3) that the speakers talk about. One picture is extra.

CD 1 Track 26

If you **get a makeover**, you do things to make yourself more attractive.

C Look at your answers (1, 2, and 3) in **B**. Then do the following:

CD 1 Track 27

1. What style problem does each person have? Can you guess what the solutions are?
2. Listen to the rest of the show and complete the chart below. Use only one word per blank.

ASK ANSWER
Do you agree with the hosts' suggestions? Why or why not?

Style Problem	Style solution
Brad's look is too conservative / sloppy.	He could wear a nice new shirt.
Tamara's clothes are too baggy / sporty.	She should wear something more fitted, like a pair of skinny jeans and a fun top.
Mimi's look is too casual / mismatched.	She should choose a single style and one or two colors that match.

3 Reading **Trendspotting**

A Read the job advertisement. What do you think a *trendspotter* does? Who would hire a trendspotter?

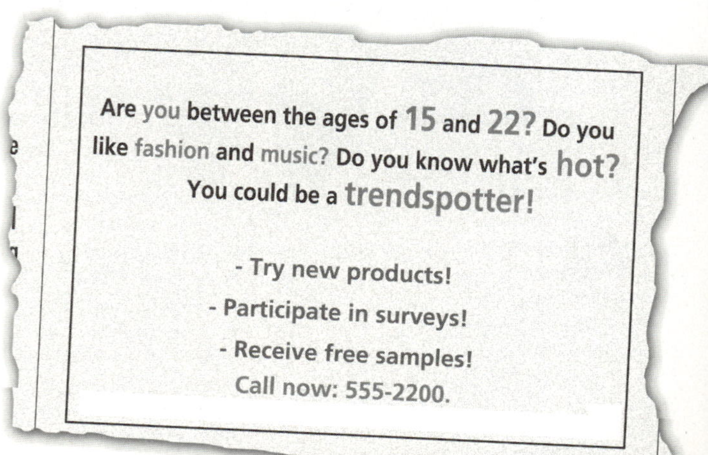

2 Listening You've got the look.

Skills: Listen for gist; Listen for details; Make and check predictions; Take notes

Warm Up

5 min

With books closed, tell students that some TV reality shows are called "makeover" shows. They show an ordinary person's clothing or home being changed and made fashionable by style experts. Ask what makeover shows are currently on TV. How many of the students watch them? Why do they like them (or not like them)?

A **With a partner, describe the people's clothes in the photos below.**

5 min

With the class, brainstorm words that may be needed to describe the photos (but don't designate them for a specific photo). Write the words on the board for reference before beginning pair work.

B **Listen to a makeover TV show. Number the people (1, 2, or 3) that the speakers talk about. One picture is extra.**

CD 1 Track 26

10–15 min

Tell students they will hear the recording only once to answer the questions. After checking answers, play it again to confirm the answers. For the second listening, hold up your book and point to the photographs as each feature is mentioned in the recording.

C **Look at your answers (1, 2, and 3) in B. Then do the following:**

CD 1 Track 27

20–25 min

(See student book page 42 for complete instructions.)

Read the two questions. Put students in pairs to answer the questions. They should use the names *Brad* (1), *Tamara* (2), and *Mimi* (3), and answer in complete sentences. Call on students to give their answers. Write some of their sentences on the board; repeat the others to acknowledge them.

Read the chart. Don't explain vocabulary in advance; students will be able to figure out many words as they listen to the recording. They will hear the opinions of Lisa and Marco from the TV show in order to fill in the chart. Tell them they will hear the recording three times. The first time they should just listen. The second and third times they can complete the chart. Ask three volunteers to write the chart on the board, one for each person (Brad, Tamara, Mimi). Review the answers on the board and have the class correct any mistakes. Then play the audio again. Point to each answer on the board as it is heard in the recording.

ASK ANSWER

Write this question on the board and ask for a show of hands, yes or no: *Do you agree that the three people needed to change their looks?* Put students in groups of four or five. Read the two questions in the box and tell students to discuss them in addition to the question on the board. One or two students should report the opinions expressed in the group.

3 Reading Trendspotting

Skills: Make and check predictions; Infer information; Read for details; Understand text organization; Draw conclusions

Warm Up

5–10 min

With books closed, ask students, *What are some products that are especially popular with teenagers? How do you think companies know what teenagers will buy?*

A **Read the job advertisement. What do you think a *trendspotter* does? Who would hire a trendspotter?**

10–15 min

Tell students that this is an advertisement for a job. Read the two questions and write them on the board. Do not pre-teach vocabulary; students should know most words or be able to guess them as they read. Pair students to read the advertisement and figure out vocabulary. They can also ask other students about vocabulary (in English). If they can't guess *trendspotter* from the context, break up the word for them. They know *trend*. They know *-er* means *a person who does something*. Tell them that *spot* means *see*, *notice*, or *identify*. So, a *trendspotter* is *a person who identifies trends*. Call on several students to give their answers to the two questions.

Language Tip: Advertisement

Some native speakers of American English say *ad ver TIZE ment;* others say *ad VER tis ment*. Both are correct. The short form is *ad,* pronounced like *add*.

Instructor's Notes

B 20–25 min

Brooke is 18 years old. She works as a trendspotter. What does she do? Read her blog postings and check your answers in A.

On the board, write the three trendspotter activities from the ad in **A** (*Try new products!*, etc.). Tell students to read Brooke's blog and list the things she does. Are they the same or similar to the things in the ad? Or are they different? After reading, pair students to discuss their answers. There may be different opinions about what is "similar" and what is "different."

Follow up with some of the interesting expressions in Brooke's blog posts. Write these sentences on the board and tell students to find sentences with the same meaning in the blog posts.

- Now I'm going to tell you something surprising. (*Guess what!*)
- I'm sorry we didn't see them. (*Too bad we missed them.*)
- Things we don't have to pay for (*free stuff*).
- Definitely! (*All the way!*)
- I don't like it very much. (*It's OK.*)
- Absolutely not! (*No way!*)

C 15–20 min

Check (✓) the sentence(s) Brooke would say about being a trendspotter. Compare your answers with a partner.

Give students time to answer the questions. Tell them to underline the place where they found each answer. Assign pairs to compare answers. They should also compare the information they underlined for each answer.

D 10–15 min

Below are extra sentences from the reading. Add each one to the correct place in the reading. One sentence is extra.

Write the sentences on the board with these words underlined. Tell students that when the sentences are in the right place, the underlined words will mean the same as something in the previous sentence.

- Yesterday, they were here in the studio. (the rock group called *Gifted*)
- I can't wait for our next meeting. (extra sentence does not go in the reading)
- Then she gave us a tour of the studio. (Mandy)
- There were about 10 of us. (we)

ASK ANSWER

Read the questions and put students in groups to discuss them. To follow up, ask if anyone thought that it is a bad idea for companies to use trendspotters, *and* who also said they would like to be a trendspotter. Is this a contradiction? Or is it understandable?

EXTRA! Post-reading

15–25 min

Tell students to look for something outside of class that they think is very trendy. Ask them to photograph it and bring the photo to class—one photo per student. They can print their photo or just bring their cell phone or camera. In groups of four to six, have them look at each other's photos and talk about the trends they illustrate.

EXTRA! Discussion questions

20–30 min

1. Are you interested in trends? Interested in some trends but not others? Are your friends interested (or not interested) in the same trends?
2. How do you think trends get started? Have you ever noticed a trend beginning? What was it?
3. Who are the trendiest people you know? Are they popular? Are they fun? Are they friends of yours? Are you one of them?

EXTRA! Writing prompt

15–20 min

1. Are you good at spotting trends? If so, why are you good at it? If not, why not?
2. "Teenagers worry too much about having the right 'stuff.' Things just aren't that important." Agree or disagree with this statement. Give reasons for your position. Mention a teenager you know.
3. Companies get useful information about products and advertising from young trendspotters. The trendspotters have fun and get free stuff. Is there anything wrong with this?

EXTRA! Additional reading

20–30 min

For more practice making predictions, see Heinle's Footprint Reading Library *Wind Power.*

For practice giving your opinion, see Heinle's Footprint Reading Library *Dangerous Dining.*

B Brooke is 18 years old. She works as a trendspotter. What does she do? Read her blog postings and check your answers in **A**.

Home | About | Archives | Mail | RSS

March 17

Part-time Job

0 Comments | Posted by Brooke

Today I started my new part-time job as a trendspotter. I was nervous and didn't know what to expect. Well, guess what! It was a lot of fun! I'm telling all my friends, "You should think about becoming a trendspotter, too!"

This morning, we had to report to a recording studio by 10 a.m. The "Trends Coordinator," Mandy, explained the schedule. Then she gave us a tour of the studio. That was really cool!

Next we sat around a big table in a room. There were about ten of us. Mandy gave each person three cards. One card said "Yes—All the way!" Another said, "It's OK." The third one said, "No way!" We listened to about 10 different songs. After each song, we had to hold up a card. They played some hip-hop, rock, heavy metal, and dance music. The heavy metal was "No way" for me!

March 24

Gifted

0 Comments | Posted by Brooke

Do you know the rock group called "Gifted"? They're really popular right now. Yesterday, they were here in the studio. Too bad we missed them. Anyway, they have a new CD coming out on Jtunz soon. We saw six different CD covers. (I guess they are trying to choose one.) This time, we didn't have any cards. Instead, we just talked about the covers we liked. Mandy asked us questions: "Which ones do you like?" "Why do you like them?" "Would you buy a CD with this cover?"

We finished at 12:30. We meet again next week at a boutique downtown. We will look at some new fashions. Each week we go to a different location. Oh, and we also received a music gift card for our work. This "job" doesn't pay, but we get free stuff!

That's all for now!

C Check (✓) the sentence(s) Brooke would say about being a trendspotter. Compare your answers with a partner.

____ It's kind of boring.

____ You can make good money.

✓ You get free things.

____ You work with famous people.

✓ People ask your opinion about lots of things.

✓ You work once a week at different places.

D Below are extra sentences from the reading.
Add each one to the correct place in the reading.
One sentence is extra.

Yesterday, they were here in the studio.

I can't wait for our next meeting! *extra sentence—not in the text*

Then she gave us a tour of the studio.

There were about ten of us.

ASK ANSWER

Why do you think companies use trendspotters? Do you think it's a good idea?

Would you like to be a trendspotter? Why or why not?

4 Language Link

Giving advice with *could, should, ought to,* and *had better*

A Read the question about cell phones and the three answers. Then complete the sentences with the modal verbs in blue.

Q: I want to buy a new cell phone. What should I do?

A1: You could ask your friends or a salesperson for their suggestions.

A2: You should read *Consumer Advice* magazine. They rate the different phones.

A3: You'd better be careful. Some of the best cell phones are really expensive.

you'd better = you had better

In A1, ___could___ is used to make a suggestion (about two or more things).

In A2, ___should___ is used to give advice. Ought to can also be used to give advice.

In A3, ___'d better (had better)___ is used to give stronger advice. It can sound like a warning.

B Complete the conversations with the expressions in the boxes. Use each expression only once.

Negative forms

You shouldn't wear a T-shirt to a job interview. It's too casual.

We'd better not drive to the concert. It'll be hard to park.

shouldn't | could | ought to

Betsy: I don't know what to wear to the party tonight.

Carla: You (1) ___could___ wear your new skinny jeans or black pants.

Betsy: It's a formal dress party.

Carla: Oh, then you (2) ___shouldn't___ wear jeans. They're too casual. You definitely (3) ___ought to___ wear the black pants.

had better | could | had better not

Fred: I still don't understand this grammar.

Doug: You (4) ___had better___ get some help or you will fail the test. It's on Thursday.

Fred: Maybe I (5) ___could___ take the test on Friday. That would give me extra time.

Doug: Well, you (6) ___had better not___ delay. There's not much time!

C You are going to an informal party. Your partner is going to a formal party. Look at the list and give advice to each other.

arrive a little late	wear casual clothes	bring a friend who wasn't invited
bring food for the party	wear a suit or a nice dress	bring flowers or champagne to the host

"You could wear a suit or nice dress."

"You shouldn't wear casual clothes."

4 Language Link

Giving advice with *could, should, ought to,* and *had better*

Warm Up

5 min

Ask, *Who has bought a cell phone recently?* (or MP3 player, video game, bicycle, car). *How did you decide what kind to buy? Did you ask anyone for advice? Who did you ask? Why?*

10–15 min

A Read the question about cell phones and the three answers. Then complete the sentences with the modal verbs in blue.

Read the (Q) question aloud. Ask, *What do I want to do?* (buy a cell phone) *And what do I want first?* (advice). Point to the words in blue in the three answers, pronounce them, and have students repeat. Tell students that the three modals have similar meanings, but they're not exactly the same. Students can do the exercise on their own, then check answers as a class.

15–20 min

B Complete the conversations with the expressions in the boxes. Use each expression only once.

Read the instructions and the negative forms in the box. Note that *ought to* has no negative form—use *shouldn't* instead. Tell students to complete the first conversation. To check answers, choose two students to read the dialog aloud. Write their answers on the board as they say them. Ask the class if the answers are correct, and change them if they're wrong. Model the conversation taking both parts yourself with students repeating. Students can practice it in pairs. Do the same with the second conversation.

20–25 min

C You are going to an informal party. Your partner is going to a formal party. Look at the list and give advice to each other.

Introduce the actions in the box, read the phrases aloud, and tell students to repeat. Some of the actions may be controversial. Even if your students are from the same country, there may be different opinions about some of the advice—is it appropriate for a casual party, appropriate for a formal party, or never appropriate? Students should discuss the actions in groups and clarify their opinions before practicing. Tell students that the phrases in the box are for giving advice. If your students need more support, put these first lines on the board to get them started:

I'm going to a party tonight and I want to wear my new jeans.

I'm going to a party tonight but my cousin is visiting me.

I'm going to a party tonight and I'd like to bring something.

I'm going to a party tonight and I don't know what to wear.

Culture Tip: Bringing a friend

When you are invited to someone's house, is it appropriate to bring a friend? Different cultures have very different opinions. In Mexico, for example, it is quite common to do this, even for a dinner party. In the United States, however, it is generally not done, especially for a formal party or dinner. It could be appropriate for a large, casual party, with younger people.

Culture Tip: Arriving at a party

If you are invited to a person's house for dinner at 7:00, what time do you arrive? In many South American countries it could be as late as 8:00, or even 9:00! In the U.K., you would arrive between 7:00 and 7:15. Don't arrive early because maybe the host won't be prepared.

Teaching Tip: Maintaining the energy

When you stop to practice the advice and discuss vocabulary, the activity may lose some of its energy. When possible, keep the momentum going by moving on without defining all words. Allow students to continue working if they have a general understanding.

Instructor's Notes

5 Writing What's your advice?

Warm Up

5 min

Write this saying on the board and discuss it with the class: *You never get a second chance to make a first impression.* Consider what contributes to a person's first impression. What are some situations where your first impression is very important?

A Read the post from Sad Sam in Seattle. What is his problem?

10 min

Read the post aloud or ask a student to read it. Ask students what kind of website this post might be on. (Possible answers: a newspaper's website, an information site like about.com.) Ask students to explain Sam's problem in their own words, without looking at the book. Tell them to look at the picture. Do they agree that Sam has a problem? Do they think they can help him?

B Now write a response to Sam. Give him some advice. Then share your writing with a partner.

25–30 min

Allow students to write their response at their own pace. As students finish, pair them to discuss their work. Each student should read his or her paper aloud while his or her partner reads along silently. Students should make sure they understand everything before commenting. The first comment should be something—anything—about the paper that the partner likes. After that, comments should focus on how to improve the paper. Is anything not clear? What would make it clearer? Would more details make it more interesting? What kind of details? Where? Put these guidelines on the board for reference while students are working. Finally, ask a few students to read their papers. Then their partners can tell the class what they said about the paper.

B Teaching Option **Process writing**

Extend the assignment to include more of the steps of process writing. Students have already generated ideas (in **A**) and written a first draft and gotten feedback (in **B**). You can go on to tell students to improve their work based on any good ideas they got from their partner, or ideas they had while reading and discussing it. When ready, you can have students edit (correct) their work and make a final draft.

6 Communication

Do you need a makeover?

Warm Up

5 min

Magazines and websites often have quizzes to tell you how intelligent you are, what kind of friend you are, etc. What other topics have students seen in quizzes? Do they think such quizzes are fun? Do they believe the results?

A Ask your partner the questions. Check (✓) your partner's answers.

10 min

One or more students can read the quiz items aloud. Answer any questions about vocabulary. In pairs, the students should ask and answer the quiz questions. The student answering the question should have his or her book closed. The student asking the question should look up at his or her partner when they speak, then look down again to check the box and get ready to ask the next question.

B Calculate your partner's score. Use the table.

5 min

Students write the total score for their partner. They do not tell their partner their score. There is no need to go over this exercise with the class.

C Read the appropriate advice to your partner. What does your partner think of the advice?

15–20 min

Read each paragraph aloud with students repeating. Answer any questions about vocabulary or general meaning. Pairs may read the advice to each other more than once, if needed. Then the same pairs should give each other their scores, and read the corresponding advice to their partners. Give students a few minutes to react to their scores. Then ask for a show of hands: *Who agreed with their score and the advice? Who disagreed? Is anyone going to take the advice? What are they going to do?*

World Link Video and World Link Website

Remind students of the value of further practice outside the classroom. Ask students who have watched the video or done online practice to share their experiences.

Check out the World Link Video. Practice your English online at http://elt.heinle.com/worldlink

5 Writing What's your advice?

Ask Susie Style

Home About Archives Mail RSS

Dear Susie Style,

I need your help! I can't get a job. Everywhere I go, I get the same answer: "No!" My friend says that my appearance is the problem. Here is a picture of me. What do you think? What should I do?

Sad Sam in Seattle

A Read the post from Sad Sam in Seattle. What is his problem?

B Now write a response to Sam. Give him some advice. Then share your writing with a partner.

6 Communication Do you need a makeover?

A Ask your partner the questions. Check (✓) your partner's answers.

How often do you . . .	often	sometimes	never
1. wear "the same old thing"?	☐	☐	☐
2. buy something because it's cheap?	☐	☐	☐
3. wear something comfortable but mismatched?	☐	☐	☐
4. wear something until it's completely worn out?	☐	☐	☐
5. leave the house without looking in the mirror?	☐	☐	☐
6. read fashion magazines about new trends?	☐	☐	☐
7. change your hairstyle?	☐	☐	☐
8. go to concerts and listen to new music?	☐	☐	☐

B Calculate your partner's score. Use the table.

	for questions 1–5	or questions 6–8
often	score 2 points	score 0 points
sometimes	score 1 point	score 1 point
never	score 0 points	score 2 points

C Read the appropriate advice to your partner. What does your partner think of the advice?

0-3 points: You know what's "in" and have a great sense of style. Keep up the great work!	**4-7 points:** You have a good sense of style, but you could change a few things or just try to do something new every week.	**8-12 points:** Your look definitely needs an update. You could change something about your clothing or hairstyle. You should also try to go out more and see what's happening.	**13–16 points:** You scored a lot of points. You'd better think about getting a complete makeover!

Check out the World Link video.

Practice your English online at http://elt.heinle.com/worldlink

5 Out and About

Lesson A Running errands

1 Vocabulary Link Handy Helpers

A Read the ad below and answer the questions with a partner.

1. What does Handy Helpers do?
   Handy Helpers does chores and runs errands for busy people.
2. Which items on the to-do list are errands?
   Which are chores? Write *E* for *errand* or *C* for *chore* next to each item.

an errand: a short trip you make to do or get something

a chore: work you do regularly at home

Handy Helpers

Are you a busy person? Do you have too much to do—even on the weekends? Would you like more time to relax? If you answered "yes" to any of these questions, it's time to contact Handy Helpers!

We'll do your chores or run your errands so you can take a break. To learn more about us and the services we offer, call or e-mail us today!

Click here to make a personal to-do list

My to-do list

- ❑ take the dog for a walk E
- ❑ go grocery shopping E
- ❑ do the dishes C
- ❑ sweep the floors and vacuum the rugs C
- ❑ pick up the dry cleaning E
- ❑ mail a package E
- ❑ do the laundry C
- ❑ take Marty to soccer practice E
- ❑ make dinner C

Other

- ❑ make an appointment to get a haircut
- ❑ make a dinner reservation at restaurant

B Complete the sentences below with the correct form of a word or phrase in blue from **A**.

1. All my clothes are dirty. I need to do the ___laundry___!
2. Kira's not home. She ___took___ her younger brothers ___to___ a movie.
3. My tooth hurts. I need to ___make an appointment___ to see the dentist.
4. The rug in the bedroom is dusty. Can you ___vacuum___ it?
5. Can you ___mail___ these letters at the post office?
6. I'd like to ___make a reservation___ for six people at 7:00 tonight. Is a table available?
7. Let's ___do___ the dinner dishes now.
8. Before you ___run___ any errands, you should ___make___ a list of the things you need to do.
9. Susan always ___picks up___ her children after they finish school.
10. I'm really tired. Let's ___take___ a ___break___. We can study again tomorrow.

C Which phrases in **A** use *do*, *make*, or *take*? Complete the chart below. Can you think of other phrases that start with these words? Add them.

do	the chores, ___the dishes___, ___the laundry___
make	dinner, an appointment, ___a reservation, a list___
take	(the dog for) a walk, someone to a place, ___a break___

ASK ANSWER

What chores or errands do you do?
When do you do them?

Running errands

Unit 5, Lesson A

1 Vocabulary Link Handy Helpers

Warm Up

5 min

With books closed, ask students, *What are some things you always have to do around the house? For example, cleaning? Do you enjoy doing any of them? Which ones do you really dislike?*

A Read the ad below and answer the questions with a partner.

10-15 min

Point to the i-box, and ask a student to read it aloud. Explain that errands are done outside the home and chores inside, or in the yard.

Tell students to look at the to-do list, and ask them which phrases they already understand. Write these phrases on the board, and confirm the meanings. Pronounce the other phrases in the list with students repeating. Answer questions about vocabulary. Spot-check their understanding by asking several students what some of the phrases mean.

Point to the two questions and read them aloud. Put students in pairs to read the ad and answer the questions. Check answers with the whole class, and answer any questions they have. Follow up by asking if they would like some help with their chores and errands. How much do they think Handy Helpers would charge?

Language Tip: Handy Helpers

Handy Helpers is a proper noun, and in English, it's singular. It takes singular verb forms: *Handy Helpers does chores and runs errands for busy people.* However, the pronoun is plural and verb forms agree: *They do chores and run errands for busy people.*

B Complete the sentences below with the correct form of a word or phrase in blue from A.

10-15 min

Read the instructions. Students can work alone or in pairs to complete the sentences. Check answers with the whole class. Write the numbers 1–10 on the board. Call on students to read a sentence aloud. Write their answers on the board as they speak. Other students should raise their hands and correct any they think are wrong. Confirm the answers when they are all correct on the board.

C Which phrases in A use *do, make,* or *take*? Complete the chart below. Can you think of other phrases that start with these words? Add them.

15-20 min

Read the instructions and show students they need to refer back to the ad in **A** to complete the chart. Students can work in pairs. When they have written all the *do, make, take* phrases from **A**, tell them to continue adding other phrases they know with verbs and nouns that go together.

For *make*, there is only one write-on line. Students will most likely pair *make* with *make a reservation* from the to-do list. But, note that *make a list* is also possible.

While students are working, write three lists on the board with the same information as the chart. When you check answers, continue the lists with the students' additional collocations, and add some of your own.

Word Bank: Phrases with *do, make, take*

do homework
do your best

make a (phone) call
make a snack
make breakfast, lunch, dinner, coffee, tea
make money
make friends

take a shower/bath
take a message
take a test, exam, quiz
take a class

ASK ANSWER

Read the questions aloud. Tell students that *when* means *what time of day* and also *how often*. If time and interest allow, you may want to include additional questions, for example:

What chores and errands do people actually enjoy?

Which ones do they dislike the most?

Does anyone in the group have no responsibilities at home?

Assign groups of four or five to discuss their answers. You can follow up with informal questions to some of the groups, or assign reporters in advance and have them report more formally to the whole class.

2 Listening I'm calling because ...

Skills: Listen for gist; Listen for details; Identify situations; Choose an appropriate response

Warm Up

5 min

With books closed, say, *Many people make phone calls for their jobs, and everyone makes personal phone calls.* Ask, *What personal calls do you make that are not to your family or friends? Do you call the doctor? The police?* Write their answers on the board in list form.

A CD 1 Track 28 5–10 min

You are going to hear four different phone calls. Read the sentences below. Then listen and circle the correct word(s) to complete each sentence.

Use the information box to explain *drop off* and contrast it with *pick up*. Read each sentence aloud twice—once with each answer. Students should repeat after you. Answer any questions about vocabulary or meaning.

With books closed, play the recording once. Then with books open, but without listening again, tell students to complete as many sentences as they can. Play the recording again one dialog at a time so that students can check their answers and complete the missing ones. Pause the recording after each dialog to discuss the answer with the class. If needed, play the dialog once more to confirm the answers.

B CD 1 Track 28 5–10 min

Read the statements below. Then listen to each phone call again. What would the person in each conversation say next? Choose the best answer.

With books closed, ask students what they remember of the four conversations in **A**. Who was called? (Examples: a restaurant, a dry cleaner). What did the caller want? (Examples: to change a reservation, to pick up his pants). Students need to choose the next thing that will be said in each dialog. Play the audio again. This time, pause between calls in order to give students a chance to read the possible answers and choose one. When you check the answers as a class, ask students to explain why the other answers would NOT work in these conversations.

ASK ANSWER

As a class, brainstorm a list of appointments on the board.

Ask the whole group the second question. Add these extra questions on the board. *Some popular restaurants don't take reservations. Would you wait in line to get in? How long would you wait? Or would you go somewhere else?* Students can discuss their answers in groups of three to five.

Teaching Tip: Completing a conversation

Asking students to complete a conversation requires students to 1) understand what is being said, 2) identify the situation, and 3) understand what makes the most sense as a reply. Being able to identify why a different answer would NOT work is equally as important as understanding why the correct answer does work. Ask students to justify their answer in order to show that they truly understand the language and are not just guessing.

EXTRA! Listening expansion

20–25 min

Have students continue the conversation until its logical conclusion. Then have students listen to the conversations again. This time they should complete the conversation until it ends naturally. This could be one more line or more.

3 Pronunciation

Reduced forms of *could you* and *would you*

A CD 1 Track 29 10–15 min

Listen to these sentences. Notice the reduced pronunciation of *could you* and *would you* in each sentence.

Explain the instructions. Write *could you* and *would you* on the board. Pronounce them unreduced and then reduced (*could you, couldja*). Explain that this is how American English speakers usually pronounce these phrases.

Play the recording once, then again, pausing after each sentence for students to repeat. Ask a few individuals to read a sentence. Correct their pronunciation if necessary. Then have the whole group repeat the sentences again, either reading the sentences yourself or playing the recording again.

B CD 1 Track 30 10–15 min

Listen to these sentences. Circle the words you hear.

Tell students to look at the sentences. Both phrases are correct; only the sound is different. Check answers, and play the recording again to confirm them.

C 10 min

With a partner, practice reading the sentences in B. Use reduced forms of *could you* and *would you*.

In pairs, students take turns saying the sentences. Walk around listening to their pronunciation and helping as needed. Continue the exercise until you have heard everyone.

2 Listening I'm calling because . . .

CD 1 Track 28

A You are going to hear four different phone calls. Read the sentences below. Then listen and circle the correct word(s) to complete each sentence.

1. The woman is calling to make / change a reservation.
2. The man wants to know when he can drop off / pick up his dry cleaning.
3. The man is calling to make / change an appointment.
4. The girl wants her friend to take her to school / the doctor's office.

drop off: to bring and leave something somewhere; opposite = *pick up*

CD 1 Track 28

B Read the statements below. Then listen to each phone call again. What would the person in each conversation say next? Choose the best answer.

1. a. Yes, eight o'clock is fine. We'll see you then.
   b. No, sorry; but she'll call you back tonight.
   c. Sure. How's 7:30?
2. a. Great. I'll be in this afternoon.
   b. OK, thanks. I'll bring them in today.
   c. No, sorry. That doesn't work for me.
3. a. Yes, there are ten.
   b. Because I need to see the dentist.
   c. I'm sorry, but do you have something later?
4. a. OK, I'll see you at school later.
   b. Sure. I'll pick you up in ten minutes.
   c. Yes, it is.

ASK ANSWER

For what things do you usually make an appointment?

When you go to a restaurant, do you usually make a reservation?

3 Pronunciation Reduced forms of *could you* and *would you*

CD 1 Track 29

A Listen to these sentences. Notice the reduced pronunciation of *could you* and *would you* in each sentence.

1. Could you open the window? It's hot in here.
2. Would you hold the door for me? Thanks.
3. Could you drop me off at school?
4. Would you help me lift this box?

CD 1 Track 30

B Listen to these sentences. Circle the words you hear.

1. That radio is really loud. Could you / Would you turn it down, please?
2. I think the computer is broken. Could you / Would you please look at it?
3. The phone's ringing. Could you / Would you answer it, please?
4. Let me see if he's in his office. Could you / Would you hold for a moment?

C With a partner, practice reading the sentences in **B**. Use reduced forms of *could you* and *would you.*

4 Speaking **I'd like to make an appointment.**

CD 1 Track 31

A Listen to the conversation. Then answer the questions with a partner.

1. Why is Minh calling ISS Language Center?
   He wants to make an appointment to see the student counselor.
2. When is he planning to go there?
   He's planning to go in tomorrow at 4:15.

Martina: Hello, ISS Language Center. This is Martina.

Minh: Yeah, hi. I'm in a TOEFL class that starts next week. I'd like to make an appointment to see the student counselor first.

Martina: Sure. I can help you with that. Let's see . . . can you come in tomorrow at 10:30?

Minh: No, that time isn't good for me. Do you have anything later in the day?

Martina: Let me check. . . . OK, how's 4:15?

Minh: That's perfect.

Martina: Great. Now, I just need to get your name.

Minh: It's Minh Nguyen.

Martina: Could you spell your last name for me, please?

Minh: Sure, it's N-G-U-Y-E-N.

B Practice the conversation with a partner.

5 Speaking Strategy

reschedule = to change to a different day or time

Useful Expressions: Making appointments	
Explaining why you're calling	
I'm calling to / **I'd like to**	make an appointment to see a counselor. make a dental / doctor's / hair appointment. reschedule my appointment / our meeting.
Scheduling the time	
Can you come in tomorrow **at** 2:00? **Can you make it** tomorrow **at** 2:00? **How's / What about** tomorrow **at** 4:00?	That's perfect. / That works great. No, that day / time isn't good for me.

A With a partner, read the situation below and create a new conversation similar to the one in Speaking. In your dialog, use at least two Useful Expressions.

Student A: You want to make an appointment to get a haircut on Thursday afternoon.

Student B: You're a hairstylist at a hair salon. The only appointment you have on Thursday is at 11:30 A.M. You have some afternoon appointments on the weekend.

B Switch roles. You and your classmate meet every Tuesday to practice English.

Student A: You need to reschedule your meeting for later in the week. Wednesday at 1:00 is best for you, but you can also meet on Friday.

Student B: You can only meet on Thursday or Friday after 1:00.

Hi, Alex. What's up?

I'm calling to . . .

4 Speaking

I'd like to make an appointment.

5 min

Warm Up

With books closed, ask, *Have you ever made an appointment with someone at this school? Did you make it over the phone or in person? What information did they ask you for?*

CD 1 Track 31

10–15 min

A Listen to the conversation. Then answer the questions with a partner.

Put the students in pairs and read the two comprehension questions. With books closed, play the audio while students read along. Give them a little time to discuss their answers. Play the audio again and check answers on the board. Answer any questions about vocabulary. Play the audio a third time, sentence by sentence, and have students repeat.

10 min

B Practice the conversation with a partner.

While students are practicing, walk around to comment, guide them, and answer questions. Speak with as many pairs as possible. They can look at the book while practicing, but remind them to always look at their partner when either of them is speaking.

B Teaching Option Support/challenge

If some pairs that work fast seem bored and ready to stop, tell them to close their books and say the conversation (approximately) from memory. Tell them if they get stuck, they can open their books and look at the conversation again for 30 seconds before closing it and continuing. If possible, check back to see how they are doing.

5 Speaking Strategy

30–45 min

A With a partner, read the situation below and create a new conversation similar to the one in Speaking. In your dialog, use at least two Useful Expressions.

Introduce the expressions for making appointments. Use the information box to explain *reschedule*. Model the *Explaining* sentences one by one with students repeating. Ask, *In the dialog, what does Martina say to this request?* Do the same with the *Scheduling* sentences. Ask, *In the dialog, what time does Martina suggest first? What does Minh say? What does he say the second time?*

Read the situation aloud. With books closed, ask two students to describe the situation in their own words. Correct any inaccuracies or let the other students comment.

In pairs, have students develop a conversation and practice it. They can write it down if they wish, but they may not look at the paper when performing.

Culture Tip: Appointments

In most English-speaking countries, arriving on time for an appointment is considered polite. For hair, doctor, or school appointments, you are expected to arrive a few minutes *before* your appointment so you are already settled with your coat hung up when the office is ready for you. Arriving on time is acceptable, but arriving late is considered rude. Some places will even cancel your appointment if you arrive later than 10 minutes after your appointed time.

In many Latin American countries, the time you should arrive depends on what type of appointment it is. It is usually considered fine if you arrive 15–30 minutes late for hair or doctor appointments, since it is expected that they are running behind, too. What are the rules for arriving at appointments in your students' culture(s)?

25–30 min

B Switch roles. You and your classmate meet every Tuesday to practice English.

This conversation is more realistic if B doesn't know when A is free, and vice versa, so do the activity with books closed. Bring in slips of paper with the situations for Student A and Student B. Tell students to repeat the opening lines of the conversation in the speech bubbles. Then they can look at their slips of paper and immediately begin to make up a conversation. When they have a good conversation and have practiced it, they can perform it for the whole group.

Large Class Option

Divide the class into groups of four or six. With books open, explain the instructions and the situations. The group collaborates in writing a conversation. Each student copies or learns it, and they practice it in pairs. Finally, one pair from each group performs for the whole class or for another group. (If there is an odd number of students, form one group of five and tell them to make a copy for you. When the group is ready to practice in pairs, join them and practice with the extra student.)

6 Language Link

Polite requests with modal verbs and *mind*

Warm Up

5 min

On the board, write this question (see page 47, Pronunciation): *Could you turn the radio down?* Under it write: *Turn the radio down,* and *Turn that radio down!* Read the three sentences with appropriate tone and emphasis (and reduction of *could you*). Discuss the three sentences with the class. Which sentence is more polite?

A 15–25 min **Study the chart. Then read the short dialogs below and complete the sentences.**

Point to the title (*Polite requests with modal verbs and mind*) and read it aloud. Ask students to name some modal verbs they know. Present the chart. Point out the titles of the two columns. Read the informal requests aloud one by one with students repeating. Remind students to reduce *could you* and *would you*. Point out that *can you* and *will you* are not reduced. Model the informal responses with students repeating.

Move on to *mind*. Tell students to say the request and the answers after you. Write the request on the board. Cross out *mind* and write *dislike*. Explain that *mind* means something like *dislike*. Write *Would you help me, please? Sure.* Tell students that the questions and the answers mean the same.

Discuss grammar. Ask, *What verb form is* help? (base form) *What verb form is* helping? (*-ing* form). Ask students to try to state the rule (*-ing* form after *mind*; base form after modal + *you*).

Read the two dialogs and the questions aloud and give students time to answer the questions. For more support, let them work in pairs. Check answers.

10–15 min

EXTRA! Additional practice

Tell students to work in pairs and write two more request dialogs, one with *Would you mind* and one with just *Would you*. Tell them to add this sentence to Speaker B's answer: *I'd be happy to.* Have two or more pairs work at the board and check their dialogs with the whole class. Tell students that both responses must mean *yes* because of the additional sentence. The dialog with *mind* must say *no* to mean *yes*.

Language Tip: Requests with *mind*

You may notice that native speakers sometimes answer a request with *Would you mind* by saying *Sure! I'll be happy to,* etc., to agree. They are answering the intent of the question, not its grammar.

B 10–15 min **Find the error(s) in each dialog and correct them. Then practice the dialogs with a partner.**

Some of the errors are with grammar and others with usage. As students work on their corrections, walk around the room checking their work. Point to dialogs that still have errors. Note who has correct dialogs and call on those pairs when checking answers.

When all corrections have been made, model the dialogs, have students repeat (with reductions where appropriate), and tell them to practice.

C 5–10 min **Write a request for each situation. Use the words in parentheses.**

Tell students to write two requests for each situation, one with *mind* and one without.

D 15–20 min **With a partner, take turns making and responding to the requests in C. Refuse (say "no" to) one request and give a reason why.**

Choose two students to model the example dialog. Tell students to use all six requests they wrote in **C** and answer three of them "no," with a reason.

Instructor's Notes

6 Language Link Polite requests with modal verbs and *mind*

A Study the chart. Then read the short dialogs below and complete the sentences.

Making Requests			Responding to Requests
informal	**Can / Will** you **Could / Would** you	help me, please?	OK. / Sure, no problem. / I'd be glad to. / Certainly. / Of course. Sorry, but . . .
formal	**Would you mind**	helping me, please?	No, not at all. / No, I'd be glad to. Sorry, but . . .

1. **A:** Would you mind taking the dog for a walk?
   B: No, not at all.

2. **A:** Could you open the window?
   B: Sorry, but I think it's locked.

Speaker A's request is more formal in dialog (1) / 2.

Speaker B says "No, I can't" to Speaker A in dialog 1 / (2).

B Find the error(s) in each dialog and correct them. Then practice the dialogs with a partner.

1. A: Can you spelling your last name for me, please?
   Can you spell your last name for me please?
   B: Of course. It's C-U-E-N-D-E.
2. A: The phone's ringing. Would you answer it, please?
   B: Yes, I would.
   Yes, no problem. OR Yes, I'd be glad to. OR Certainly. OR Of course.
3. A: I can't go to class today. Could you take notes for me?
   B: No, I'd be glad to.
   Sure, I'd be glad to.
4. A: Would you mind to do the dishes tonight? I'm tired.
   Would you mind doing the dishes tonight? I'm tired.
   B: No, not at all.

C Write a request for each situation. Use the words in parentheses.

1. Your roommate is going grocery shopping. (pick up / some milk)
   Can/Will/Could/Would you pick up some milk, please? Would you mind picking up some milk, please? (more formal)
2. You didn't understand something your teacher said. (repeat / again)
   Can/Will/Could/Would you repeat that again, please? Would you mind repeating that again, please? (more formal)
3. You and your friend are leaving a party. Your friend drove, but you didn't. You're really tired. (drive / home)
   Can/Will/Could/Would you drive me home, please? Would you mind driving me home, please? (more formal)

D With a partner, take turns making and responding to the requests in **C**. Refuse (say "no" to) one request and give a reason why.

Can you pick up some milk, please?

Sorry, but I'm not coming home first. I need to run errands. I'm afraid the milk will get warm.

7 Communication **My *benriya* service**

A Read the information below. Then tell a partner: What does a *benriya* do? Do you think it is a good service?

Need help or have a problem? Hire a *benriya*!

In Japan, a *benriya* is a person who fixes things, does household chores, and runs errands. *Benriyas* also do other annoying or difficult tasks for you. For example, they can . . .

- break up with your boyfriend or girlfriend
- talk to an angry friend, family member, or neighbor for you
- be your travel partner on a trip
- help you study
- listen to your problems and give you advice

B Work with a partner and create your own *benriya* service.

- What services do you offer (doing housework, running errands, fixing things, etc.)?
- How much do you charge for each service?
- What is your company's name and when do you work?

Company name: ______________________
Hours of operation: ______________________

Service	Price
1.	
2.	
3.	
4.	
5.	

C What things would you pay a *benriya* to do for you? List 2 or 3 ideas below.

____

D Get together with a new partner. Imagine you are calling his or her *benriya* service. Tell your partner what you need. Find out what he or she charges. Then switch roles.

A: Hello, Handy Helpers Service. How can I help you?

B: Yes, hello. I'm calling because I want to break up with my boyfriend. I need some help.

A: No problem! We can do that for you.

B: Great. Could you tell me how much you charge, please?

E Repeat **D** with three other partners. When you finish, ask your partners: Which *benriya* are you going to hire? Why?

7 Communication **My *benriya* service**

Warm Up

5 min

With books closed, ask, *What difficult things have you done in your personal life? Did you ever have to apologize to a friend? Did you break up with your boyfriend or girlfriend? Did you think, "I don't want to do this! Why can't somebody else do this for me?"*

A Read the information below. Then tell a partner: What does a *benriya* do? Do you think it is a good service?

20–25 min

Read the title aloud. (Note that in casual speech and writing, native speakers sometimes omit the subject of a sentence if it's clear from the context.) Explain vocabulary after reading, but first have students try to guess it. Possible difficult words are *household, annoying, break up with, travel partner.*

Teaching Tip: Explaining vocabulary

Try putting more responsibility on the class as a whole to understand vocabulary. Tell students you will explain only one word (or two, or three, depending on your class). Let individuals tell you which words they want to know and write them on the board. Read down the list word by word asking if anyone knows the word. If not, and if possible, help them figure it out from the context, from other words they know, or from parts of the word itself. Once a word is explained, cross it off the list. If there is more than one word left at the end (there may be none), make them vote for the one you'll explain. Tell students that they don't need exact definitions—a general idea is good enough when reading.

B Work with a partner and create your own *benriya* service.

10–20 min

Review the chores and errands in the ad on page 46. Students can choose some of them for their *benriya* service. Tell them to start each service with a verb. Copy the chart on the board. Ask for one or two examples, and write them in the left-hand column. *Price* can be in dollars or the local currency. The price should be for the whole service (not by the hour). Leave the chart on the board for **D**.

C What things would you pay a *benriya* to do for you? List 2 or 3 ideas below.

5 min

Students should write down services they would really pay for (if they had the money). They can do this alone or discuss their ideas with the same partner.

D Get together with a new partner. Imagine you are calling his or her *benriya* service. Tell your partner what you need. Find out what he or she charges. Then switch roles.

10–15 min

You might have students make their phone calls with books closed. Since this is a phone call, they should not make eye contact while they speak. Tell them to sit side by side and look straight ahead. The service that a caller wants may not be offered by the company they call. Write this on the board for students to practice:

A: Hello, Handy Helpers Service. How can I help you?

B: Yes, hello. I'm calling because . . .

A: I'm sorry. We don't offer that service here.

B: Oh. Thanks anyway.

E Repeat D with three other partners. When you finish, ask your partners: Which *benriya* are you going to hire? Why?

10–15 min

In **D** and **E**, each student has a total of eight conversations with four different partners. You can let students find their own partners, or tell them whom to talk to next. As a pair finishes, they raise their hands. When another pair finishes, assign the new partners.

Large Class Option

In a large class, it may be too disrupting for students to move across the room to a new partner. Before **D**, put students in groups of eight. Have them work in pairs, but switch partners within the group.

Instructor's Notes

This is my neighborhood.

Unit 5, Lesson B

1 Vocabulary Link

How's your commute?

Warm Up

5 min

With books closed, ask, *How do students get to your school? Do most people drive? Do you know anyone who walks? Rides a bike? What other ways are there?*

A Read the question and three responses. Then complete the chart below. Check answers with a partner.

15–20 min

Tell students to look at the web page, the title, and the photographs. What kind of information do they think it has? *Commute* can be a noun or a verb. Tell students to scan the website and find one example of each. How do they know which is which? (The noun has a possessive pronoun: *your commute*; the verb has a subject: *I commute*.) If students ask about vocabulary, tell them they can ask about blue words after doing activity **B**.

Questions about other words can be answered now. If there's a question about *it takes about 10 minutes* (Tara), use the information in the i-box to explain.

Students can complete the chart individually and check answers with a partner. To follow up, ask students for sentences about themselves using the information in the chart. Prompt a sentence with *bike* and call on a volunteer who says, for example, *I go to soccer practice by bike.* Then point to the other side of the chart and ask for the other form. (*I ride my bike to soccer practice*.)

Language Tip: *Catch* vs. *take a cab*

A *cab* is a *taxi*. When you are in a hurry, you try to catch a train, bus, or taxi. When you are relaxed, you are more likely to take the train, bus, or taxi.

B Answer the questions with a partner

20–25 min

Use the information box to explain *it takes* + time. Pair students to ask and answer the questions. Now answer questions about vocabulary in **A**, but help the class figure it out together as much as possible.

EXTRA! Colorful language

10–15 min

There are several colorful expressions in **A**. Write these neutral sentences on the board with blank lines as shown. Have students find more colorful expressions in **A** with the same meaning. Write them on the board.

I'm late. I'm running late.

The traffic around me isn't moving. I'm stuck in traffic.

It took an hour, so I read. It took an hour, so I passed the time by reading.

I didn't like it. It was no fun.

I took a taxi. I was in a hurry, so I caught a taxi.

EXTRA! Dictation

15–20 min

With students' books closed, dictate Tara's answer in **A**. Choose one student to work at the board. Read the paragraph once at normal speed. Read it again, divided into natural "breath groups." Say *comma* and *period* as needed, but leave capital letters up to the students. Read each breath group twice. Finally, read the paragraph once more at normal speed. Thank the student at the board and let him or her sit down. Then, still with books closed, the whole class corrects the work on the board. When it's correct, students should correct their own papers from the board or from the text in their books. While they work, you might speak with the student who wrote on the board, to give some personal feedback.

Teaching Tip: Dictation

Dictation is a fully individualized learning technique that works well, even in very large classes. In addition to listening, it gives practice in spelling, vocabulary, and grammar. Typically, the teacher chooses and reads a text aloud, phrase by phrase, and students try to write the whole text accurately. But there are many other possibilities. The text can be read aloud by a partner, a group member, a volunteer from the class, or a recorded voice. Students can write the entire text, a particular type of word, or just the sentences they agree with. Texts can come from the textbook, other books, or student writing. The text can be read in phrases, sentences, or as a whole text. Students can work alone, in pairs, or in groups to reconstruct the text. And finally, correction can be done individually on students' papers, or on the board as a class (giving further opportunities to work with difficult areas).

Lesson B This is my neighborhood.

1 Vocabulary Link **How's your commute?**

A Read the question and three responses. Then complete the chart below. Check answers with a partner.

The Question Lady

The Question Lady wants to know ... How's your commute?

I often ride my bike to school. It takes about 25 minutes, but I like the exercise. If I'm running late, then I take the bus so I can get to class on time. By bus, it only takes about ten minutes.

I live outside of Sao Paulo and I commute into the city every day by car. I'm often stuck in traffic for an hour or more, and that's no fun. For a short time, I took the subway to work, but that was worse. Sure, I could pass the time by sleeping or reading, but the crowded trains were terrible. Driving takes longer, but I prefer it.

About a year ago, my company moved from Seoul to Pusan so now I've got a really long commute—about 227 km (142 miles). My wife and kids stay in Seoul, and every Monday morning I catch the bullet train to Pusan and spend the week there. On Friday nights, I go back to Seoul and spend time with my family on the weekend.

You can go or travel somewhere . . .	To go or travel somewhere, you can . . .
by bike, ___bus___, ___car___, plane, subway, taxi, train. **on** foot. (= walking)	___ride___ your bike. **drive** your car. **catch** / ___take___ a bus, cab, plane, subway, train.

B Answer the questions with a partner.

1. How does each person in **A** commute (travel) to and from school or work?
   Tara rides her bike; Felipe drives; Yoon takes/catches the train.
2. Whose commute is the shortest? Whose is the longest?
   Tara's commute is the shortest; Yoon's is the longest.
3. Does it take Tara a long time to take the bus to school?
   No, it takes her a short time. OR It only takes about ten minutes.
4. When Felipe took the train, how did he pass the time? *He slept or read.*
5. Does Yoon spend a lot of time with his family? Why or why not? *No, Yoon doesn't spend a lot of time with his family because he only sees them on the weekend. On the other days, he's in another city.*
6. Your class starts at 10:00 and it's now 9:55. You're still at home. Are you running late or are you on time? *You're running (very) late.*

***It takes* + time**

It takes 30 minutes to bike to class.

It took 2 hours to do my homework.

It takes a long time to learn a language.

ASK ANSWER

How do you commute to and from school or work? How long does it take?

2 Listening Commuters around the globe

CD 1 Track 32

A You are going to hear the first part of a news report. Read the questions below. Then listen and choose the best answer for each one.

1. The average person's commute is __________ one way.

   a. 40 minutes b. one hour c. nearly 2 hours

2. What question is this news show going to answer?

   a. Why are people's commutes getting longer?

   b. Who has the longest commute time in the world?

   c. How do people pass the time while commuting?

CD 1 Track 33

B You will hear four people giving an answer to question 2 in **A**. Read the statements below. Then listen and match a statement with a speaker. One statement is extra.

Speaker 1	I make plans for the day.
Speaker 2	I study or phone people.
Speaker 3	I read while I drive.
Speaker 4	I sleep or listen to music.
	I listen to stories.

CD 1 Track 33

C How does each person commute to work or school? Listen again and write the type(s) of transportation (bus, subway, bike, car, etc.) each person uses.

Speaker 1: by / on car

Speaker 2: by / on subway

Speaker 3: by / on foot

Speaker 4: by / on subway and bus

ASK ANSWER

How would you answer the question from the news report?
Is your answer similar to any of the ones in **B**?

3 Reading Surprising neighborhoods

A Look at the photos and the names of the cities and neighborhoods on page 53. Then read the statements below. Which neighborhood do you think each sentence describes? In some cases, both answers are possible.

1. To enter this neighborhood, you go through a gate.	Inwood	Fes-al-Bali
2. You can go to this neighborhood by subway.	Inwood	Fes-al-Bali
3. It has an old forest.	Inwood	Fes-al-Bali
4. You can see animals in this neighborhood.	Inwood	Fes-al-Bali
5. You can't drive cars here.	Inwood	Fes-al-Bali
6. It has a university.	Inwood	Fes-al-Bali
7. You can get lost here.	Inwood	Fes-al-Bali
8. Its streets are very narrow.	Inwood	Fes-al-Bali
9. Its streets are usually very crowded.	Inwood	Fes-al-Bali

2 Listening Commuters around the globe

Skills: Identify the main idea; Listen for details; Make and check predictions; Infer information; Restate what you've heard

Warm Up

5 min

Ask, *What do you think is the average commute time in this city/town—the average time one way for people to get to work? Do you think this is about average in the world? Or longer or shorter?*

CD 1 Track 32 — 10 min

A You are going to hear the first part of a news report. Read the questions below. Then listen and choose the best answer for each one.

Read the two questions. Play the audio, check the answers, and play it again to confirm them.

CD 1 Track 33 — 10 min

B You will hear four people giving an answer to question 2 in A. Read the statements below. Then listen and match a statement with a speaker. One statement is extra.

Copy the exercise on the board, read the statements, and show students how to match the statements and speakers. When you play the recording, say *Speaker 1*, etc., so students don't lose their place. You may play the audio a second time to confirm answers.

CD 1 Track 33 — 10 min

C How does each person commute to work or school? Listen again and write the type(s) of transportation (bus, subway, bike, car, etc.) each person uses.

Students also need to choose *by* or *on*. Review *by* and *on* in the chart on page 51. Play the audio again and check answers. (*On the subway* is also correct, but *on the* is not covered in this lesson.)

ASK ANSWER

Students discuss the questions in groups of three to five. *Yes* or *no* is not a sufficient answer to the second question. Students should volunteer more information, and other students should ask one or two follow-up questions.

3 Reading Surprising neighborhoods

Skills: Use photos and background knowledge to make predictions; Categorize information

Warm Up

5 min

With books closed, tell students they're going to read about two neighborhoods, one in New York City and one in Fes, Morocco. Find out what they know or think Morocco and New York are like, and make two lists on the board.

10–15 min

A Look at the photos and the names of the cities and neighborhoods on page 53. Then read the statements below. Which neighborhood do you think each sentence describes? In some cases, both answers are possible.

In this activity, remember students are predicting or guessing. Do not check the answers. You may ask volunteers to give some answers with their reasons, but do not confirm or deny if their guess is correct.

Teaching Tip: Prediction

The purpose of prediction as a pre-reading strategy is to create a context in the reader's mind and help them make sense of information as they read. This works just as well if they guess wrong. For example, students might guess that Fes-al-Bali has an old forest because of the word *old*, or that Inwood has a university because there are a lot of universities in New York City. As much as possible, students should give reasons for their guesses.

Instructor's Notes

20-25 min **B** **Kyle and Farid made web pages about their neighborhoods for a class project. Read about their neighborhoods. Were your answers in A correct? Make any necessary changes.**

After reading, check answers with the class. (Answers in **A** on page 52 are the correct answers.) Answer questions about vocabulary, but help students share information with each other and figure out as much as they can for themselves.

5-10 min **C** **Quickly scan the reading to find what each number describes. Write your answers. The first one is done as an example.**

Remind students that scanning is reading to find specific information. It is often found on standardized tests, with a time limit. Students should make notes in incomplete sentences like the example—or shorter, as long as they understand them. Time the task and give students two to three minutes at the most.

ASK ANSWER

Discuss the first question with the whole class, and make notes of their answers on the board. Is anyone's neighborhood similar to Inwood or Fes-al-Bali? In what ways? Students can discuss the second, more personal, question in pairs or groups.

10-30 min

EXTRA! Post-reading

Choose a city in another country to visit. Using the Internet, search for the following information.

1. Find out how much it will cost for transportation both ways by plane.
2. Find out how much a tour of the city costs.

Write down the websites where you find your information.

10-30 min

EXTRA! Discussion questions

1. Kyle wrote that the farmhouse in Inwood was over 200 years old. This is pretty old in the United States. Farid's neighborhood is over 1,200 years old. What is considered "old" in your country? Is your neighborhood old or new? Would you rather live in an old neighborhood or a new one? Why?
2. How many neighborhoods can you name in your city or another city that you know? Which is the oldest? The most interesting? The most comfortable to live in?
3. Do tourists visit your neighborhood? If they do, what do they want to see and do there? If they don't, do you think they should? Why or why not?

20-30 min

EXTRA! Writing prompt

If you could change one thing in your neighborhood, what would you change? Why?

20-30 min

EXTRA! Additional reading

For more practice predicting, see Heinle's Footprint Reading Library *Wild Animal Town*.

For more practice reading at this level, see Heinle's Page Turners Reading Library *Dead Before Midnight*.

Culture Tip: Souk

Souk in Arabic means *market*, but it is usually the oldest part of a city. Some of them are thousands of years old. Souks usually have small narrow streets with lots of people buying, selling, and talking. The large ones, like in Damascus, Syria, and Tunis, Tunisia, are easy to get lost in!

Instructor's Notes

B Kyle and Farid made web pages about their neighborhoods for a class project. Read about their neighborhoods. Were your answers in **A** correct? Make any necessary changes.

City: **New York City, USA** Neighborhood: **Inwood**

When you hear the word "Manhattan," what do you think of? Tall buildings, the Statue of Liberty, theaters, crowded streets? Well, all of those things are in Manhattan. My neighborhood—Inwood—is in Manhattan, too, but it's very different from the rest of the city. Why? Well, for one thing, there's a lot of greenery in this neighborhood. In fact, we have a forest in Inwood. Many of its trees are hundreds of years old and there are lots of small animals and wild birds. You can go hiking in some parts of it and get lost!

Many buildings in this neighborhood are old, too. For example, there's a farmhouse near my home. It's over 200 years old. Today it's a museum.

Inwood is an interesting neighborhood. It's a quiet place where you can hike in the parks. But then you can take a subway and, in 20 minutes, you can be in busy midtown Manhattan.

If you're ever in New York City, come and visit Inwood and see a part of Manhattan you didn't know existed. You'll be glad you did!

City: **Fes, Morocco** Neighborhood: **Fes-al-Bali**

My name is Farid and I live in Fes-al-Bali—a neighborhood in Fes that's over 1,200 years old. You can find everything in my neighborhood—restaurants, shops, cafes, tearooms, and theaters. There are something like 10,000 businesses. We've also got one of the oldest universities in the world—the University of Al-Karaouine. It opened in the year 859.

The whole neighborhood of Fes-al-Bali is surrounded by a high wall with gates. You can drive inside the main gate, but once in, you can only travel through the streets on foot, by bicycle . . . or donkey! In fact, Fes-al-Bali is one of the largest car-free areas in the world. Still, the streets get pretty crowded—mostly because they're very narrow. Oh, and speaking of the streets, there are over 9,000 of them. It takes about 40 minutes to walk from one end of my neighborhood to the other, but be careful—the streets aren't straight. They're very long and winding and it's easy to get lost. Just last week I had to help some tourists from Australia.

If you're ever in Morocco, be sure to spend some time in Fes—and in my neighborhood, Fes-al-Bali. It's a place you'll never forget!

C Quickly scan the reading to find what each number describes. Write your answers. The first one is done as an example.

20: the number of minutes it takes to go from Inwood to midtown Manhattan

40: the number of minutes it takes to walk from one end of Fes-al-Bali to the other

200: the age of (in years) a farmhouse in Inwood

859: the year that the University of Al-Karaouine opened in Fes-al-Bali

1,200: the age (in years) of Fes-al-Bali

9,000: the number of streets in Fes-al-Bali

10,000: the number of businesses in Fes-al-Bali

ASK ANSWER

How are these neighborhoods different from yours?

Which neighborhood would you like to visit? Why?

4 Language Link **Intensifiers: *really, very, pretty***

A Study the information in the chart. Then complete the sentences below with *really, very,* and/or *pretty.* Which sentences have more than one answer? Tell a partner.

		adverb	adverb	
I (don't) talk		really / very	loudly	in class.
I talk		pretty		
		adverb	adjective	noun
I (don't) have	a	really / very	long	commute.
I have		pretty		
		adverb	verb	
I (don't)		really	like	my new bike.

Really, very, and *pretty* make adjectives and adverbs stronger.

Really and *very* are stronger than *pretty.*

Really can come before a verb. *Very* cannot.

1. I don't know Joan ___very OR really___ well. Do you?
2. I usually take the subway to work. I don't ___really___ like to drive.
3. A: Who's that man over there?
   B: I'm ___pretty___ sure it's Leo, but I'm not certain.
4. That was a ___very OR really___ good movie. I loved it.

You can use "at all" with negatives to mean "zero" or "never":

I **didn't** like that movie **at all**.

B Unscramble the words and make sentences. Then tell a partner: Are the sentences true for you? If they aren't, change them so they are true.

1. busy / I / a / have / pretty / schedule ___I have a pretty busy schedule.___
2. live / I / noisy / really / in / neighborhood / a ___I live in a really noisy neighborhood.___
3. don't / movies / really / scary / like / I ___I don't really like scary movies. OR I really don't like scary movies. Also possible: I don't like really scary movies.___
4. close / family / isn't / my / very ___My family isn't very close.___
5. commute / it's / on / very / crowded / my ___It's very crowded on my commute. OR On my commute, it's very crowded.___

Some possible ways that Ss can rewrite sentences 1–5 if they aren't true for them: **1.** I have a really/very busy schedule. OR I don't have a really/very busy schedule. OR I don't really have a busy schedule. OR I don't have a busy schedule at all. **2.** I don't live in a really/very noisy neighborhood. OR My neighborhood isn't really/very noisy. OR My neighborhood isn't noisy at all. **3.** I (really) like scary movies. **4.** My family is (very/really) close. **5.** It isn't very/really crowded on my commute. OR It isn't crowded at all on my commute.

5 Writing **Come to my neighborhood**

A Read the paragraphs on the right. Then tell a partner: Where does the writer live? What are the good things about his neighborhood? What are the bad things?

B Think about your neighborhood's good and bad points. Make a list of each. Then write two or three paragraphs about your neighborhood.

C Exchange your writing with a partner. Would you like to live in your partner's neighborhood? Why or why not?

I live in a busy neighborhood in Seoul called Jamsil. There are good and bad things about living here.

The best thing about my neighborhood is it's convenient. It's pretty easy for me to get to school by subway, bus, or cab. There are also a lot of stores and restaurants in my neighborhood, and there's a big park too. It's a great place to ride your bike or relax and it only takes five minutes to walk there from my house.

The worst thing about my neighborhood is it's really noisy. There are a lot of big apartment buildings and I live on a pretty busy street. It's not the quietest neighborhood in Seoul, but I like living here!

4 Language Link

Intensifiers: *really, very, pretty*

Warm Up

5 min

With books closed, ask students, *What do you really like about your neighborhood? What do you not like at all?* Don't require answers with *really* or *at all;* prompt them with *I like . . .* and *I don't like . . . .*

A 10–15 min **Study the information in the chart. Then complete the sentences below with *really, very,* and/or *pretty*. Which sentences have more than one answer? Tell a partner.**

Ask students to read each sentence in the chart or read them yourself. Review the rules in the grammar box. Ask which word is not used in negative sentences (*pretty*). You may want students to practice the sentences in the chart in pairs. Students should complete the sentences alone and check answers with a partner.

B 5–10 min **Unscramble the words and make sentences. Then tell a partner: Are the sentences true for you? If they aren't, change them so they are true.**

Use the information box to introduce *at all*. Write the sentences on the left on the board and have students say or write a negative sentence with *at all*.

I really liked their house. → I didn't like their house at all.

She speaks very good English. → She doesn't speak (very) good English at all.

My commute is pretty long. → My commute isn't (very) long at all.

Then students should unscramble the sentences and write the true sentence for themselves.

5 Writing Come to my neighborhood

Warm Up

5 min

With books closed, ask, *What's the nicest neighborhood you know? Why do people like it?* Help with vocabulary, and make a list on the board.

A 10–20 min **Read the paragraphs on the right. Then tell a partner: Where does the writer live? What are the good things about his neighborhood? What are the bad things?**

Students should read the paragraphs on their own, make notes, and compare their answers. Follow up by discussing the organization of the model with the class. Paragraph two is about good things. What different kinds of things does the writer mention (convenience, shopping, and recreation)? What specific examples does he give? Paragraph three is about the bad things. What examples does the writer give (just one: noise)?

B 20–30 min **Think about your neighborhood's good and bad points. Make a list of each. Then write two or three paragraphs about your neighborhood.**

Tell students to list more good and bad points than they need for their paragraphs. Then they can choose the ones that are most important or most interesting. Tell them to try to use *really, very, pretty,* and *at all* in their writing.

C 10–15 min **Exchange your writing with a partner. Would you like to live in your partner's neighborhood? Why or why not?**

If the paragraphs are typed, students can exchange papers. If they are written in class, students can read their papers aloud while the partner sits next to them and reads silently.

Some students may not be comfortable telling their partner that they wouldn't like to live in his or her neighborhood. In this case, have them ask questions instead. For example, they might ask the writer of the model paragraphs the name of the park, if he goes there often, if he rides his bike other places in the city too, etc.

C Teaching Option **Process writing**

Instead of a personal response, peer feedback can focus on clarity. Partners can say what parts aren't easy to understand. What would make them clearer? Are the ideas mixed up? Would an example help? Students can consider their partner's suggestions when they revise their work.

Teaching Tip: Peer feedback

It isn't easy for students to give useful feedback—it takes practice. If possible, use anonymous student papers for practice on a regular basis. Distribute copies or show an image onscreen for discussion. Start with papers that have only one or two problems. Be ready with your own suggestions until students are able to give useful feedback themselves.

6 Communication

Improving your community

Warm Up

5 min

With books closed, ask, *What makes a city good to live in?* (Examples may include clean air, parks, good transportation, etc.) *What makes it bad to live in?* (Examples may include noise, dirty streets, heavy traffic, etc.) Make two lists on the board.

A Cities around the world have different problems. Read about one city below. Then discuss the questions with a partner.

10–15 min

Tell students to look at the photograph. Does it show a problem or a solution? After pairs have finished, discuss the second question again with the whole class. Do they think that their city has the same problems as Bogota? If so, could their city do the same as Bogota? Would it be enough?

B With a partner, think of a problem in your city or neighborhood or choose one from the box below. Then think of at least one solution for the problem and explain why it's a good idea.

25–35 min

Do the exercise on the board with the information about Bogota. Have students tell you the problem, the solution, and why it's a good idea. Assign pairs and give them 10 minutes for each part of the exercise. Walk around, helping with ideas and vocabulary if needed. Monitor their progress and adjust the time limits. Tell them when to move on to the next part.

Large Class Option

This activity is called Jigsaw Conversations. Divide the class in half (A and B), and each half into equal groups of three or four. (Depending on your classroom, it may be possible to do this activity without moving students around. Make a B group next to every A group so the two groups can work together for exercises C and D.) Assign two problems—one problem to the A groups and the other to the B groups. When groups are ready with their problems and solutions, and have practiced their explanations, put every A group with a B group for exercises C and D. Finally, check with the groups and list their solutions to the two problems on the board. Which solutions does the whole group really like? Get a show of hands. Which ones won't work at all? Give groups a chance to defend their solutions if the class rejects them.

C Get together with another pair.

15–25 min

Review the three responses with *really, kind of,* and *at all*. Explain *kind of* as an intensifier. (It's positive—like *really, very, pretty*, even weaker than *pretty*. Like *pretty*, it doesn't go in a negative sentence.) Tell students to use these responses to talk about the other pair's solution.

If students don't think a solution can work, they should explain why and discuss it with the other pair. Is there any way to change the solution so it will work? Together, can they think of a better solution?

D Switch roles and repeat C.

20–25 min

Pair B presents their idea, Pair A comments. Follow up with the whole group. Write their problems on the board (in note form). How many different ones are there? Ask volunteers to explain their solutions. Which solutions does the class really like? Get a show of hands. Which ones won't work at all? Give students a chance to defend their solutions if the class rejects them.

World Link

Students should guess the answer, and you confirm it. Do students know, or can they guess, why Beijing and San Francisco are not very bike-friendly? (Beijing has pollution and heavy traffic. San Francisco has lots of hills.) Write these additional discussion questions on the board:

Is your city bike-friendly? Do many people ride bikes there? Why or why not?

World Link Video and World Link website

Remind students of the value of further practice outside the classroom. Ask students who have watched the video or done online practice to share their experiences.

Instructor's Notes

Check out the World Link Video. Practice your English online at http://elt.heinle.com/worldlink

6 Communication Improving your community

A Cities around the world have different problems. Read about one city below. Then discuss the questions with a partner.

1. What is the city of Bogota doing? Why?
2. What do you think of the idea? Could it work in your city? Why or why not?

Problem: People in cities need open areas to exercise, but often there are too many cars and not enough parks.

One city's solution: Every Sunday from 7:00 A.M. to 2:00 P.M., Bogota, Colombia, closes its main city streets to cars and other motor vehicles. People can ride their bikes, walk, skate, play music, and spend time with friends and family on car-free city streets. The event helps people be healthier. Today, other cities around the world, including Melbourne, Australia and Quito, Ecuador, have similar events.

B With a partner, think of a problem in your city or neighborhood or choose one from the box below. Then think of at least one solution for the problem and explain why it's a good idea.

- Too many people commute to work or school every day by car.
- Children have no place to get exercise because there are no parks in my neighborhood.
- Your idea: ______________________________

Problem: ______________________________

Our solution: ______________________________

____

Why it's a good idea: ______________________________

C Get together with another pair.

Pair A: Present your problem and explain your solution(s).

Pair B: Listen to Pair A's ideas. When they finish, answer the question below about their presentation. Explain your opinion to them.

What do you think of Pair A's idea?

- ☐ I really like the idea because . . .
- ☐ I kind of like the idea, but . . .
- ☐ Sorry, but I don't think the idea can work at all because . . .

What is the most bike-friendly city in the world?
a. Amsterdam, Holland
b. Beijing, China
c. San Francisco, USA

D Switch roles and repeat **C**.

Check out the World Link video.

Practice your English online at http://elt.heinle.com/worldlink

6 Student Life

Lesson A Starting out

1 Vocabulary Link Applying to college

A Read the posting on the website. Then answer the questions with a partner.

1. What is Kento's problem?
2. Do you think Sergei's advice is good? Why or why not?

Student Forums **Topic: Choosing a college**

I'm trying to choose a college. My family wants me to go to Tokyo University or Waseda University. They're two of the best colleges in Japan, but there's a lot of competition. Thousands of people apply to these schools every year, but they only admit a couple of hundred. It's a lot of work to get into these schools. And I'm not even sure I want to go to college right now! It's a really hard decision and I need some help!

~Kento (Tokyo, Japan)

Hi, Kento: Some students get accepted to a school, but they're not really ready for university. Here's my recommendation: After graduation from high school, study abroad and improve your language skills, or apply for an internship* for a year. Later, when you're ready for college, you can show how your "year off" prepared you for university. Good luck!

~Sergei (Moscow, Russia)

*internship: a job, usually done for a short time, in which you learn about a certain type of work

B Complete the chart with a word in blue from **A**. Then use the correct form of a word in the chart to complete the sentences below.

Verb	Noun
admit	admission
apply (to/for)	application
compete	competition
decide	decision
graduate	graduation
recommend	recommendation

The suffixes ***-ion, -ation, -ition***, and ***-sion*** change verbs into nouns.

graduate + ion = graduation

recommend + ation = recommendation

compete + ition = competition

decide + sion = decision

1. My brother ___graduated___ from Oxford University last year.
2. If you want to go to IES Language School, you can ___apply___ online, or they will mail a(n) ___application___ to you.
3. These days, there's a lot of ___competition___ for jobs. For one job, we interviewed over 100 people!
4. Leo got into Harvard and Yale, but he can't ___decide___ which university is better.
5. Wesley College ___admits___ students twice a year—you can enter in August or January.
6. I'm new to this neighborhood. Can you ___recommend___ a good place to eat?

ASK ANSWER

How many universities are you going to (or did you) apply to? Did you get into them?

Can you recommend a good place to study English?

Starting out
Unit 6, Lesson A

1 Vocabulary Link

Applying to college

Warm Up

5 min

Ask students, *In your country, who goes to college? Is it hard to get into college? How much does it cost?*

A **Read the posting on the website. Then answer the questions with a partner.**

15–20 min

Tell students to look at the website and guess what it is for. (Online, a *forum* is a place where people share information and advice.) Students should read the posting on their own, and then check their answers to the questions with a partner. Explain vocabulary or tell students to use dictionaries to look up unknown words.

Teaching Tip: Monolingual dictionaries

At this level, students can make good use of a monolingual intermediate-level dictionary, such as the *Collins COBUILD Intermediate Dictionary of American English*. Point out to students the advantages of a monolingual dictionary, which lets them work entirely in English. When looking up a word, remind students to look up the unknown words in the exact forms needed—for example, *apply to*, not just *apply*. If the dictionary does not have *apply to*, help students choose the correct definition of *apply* (there will be at least two) and then figure out what *apply to* means in the context. Learning to use a dictionary will help your students become independent learners and explore vocabulary that is relevant to their own interests.

Language Tip: *College, university,* and *school*

In the United States, people say *going to college*, not *going to university*. In the United States, college follows high school, and *college* can refer to a community college (two years, earning an associate's degree), a college that stands on its own (four years, earning a bachelor's degree), or a university. It is also acceptable to ask, *Where do you go to school?* when someone is asking what university you attend. In British English, *college* and *university* are distinctly different and *school* is only for younger people.

B **Complete the chart with a word in blue from A. Then use the correct form of a word in the chart to complete the sentences below.**

20–25 min

Copy the i-box on the board and use it to explain the suffixes. After students complete the chart, practice pronunciation of the words with them. Then, have students fill in the blanks individually and compare answers with a classmate before checking the answers as a class.

B Teaching Option **Support/challenge**

Challenge students to do more with the vocabulary and play with the parts of speech. In groups of three or four, assign students to write a sentence with each verb in the chart. They should also write a sentence each for *get into* and *get accepted*. The subject of each sentence should be *colleges* or *students*. For some verbs, either subject is possible. Then students can write sentences for the nouns.

ASK ANSWER

Students can answer the questions in pairs. For a longer and more natural conversation, they can add information to their answers and ask their partners follow-up questions. Have two volunteers demonstrate such a conversation for the class. Prompt them with ideas and words as needed.

Instructor's Notes

2 Listening Not your typical school

Skills: Make and check predictions; Listen for details; Draw conclusions; Guess the meaning of words from context

Warm Up

5 min

With books closed, ask students, Did (Does) your high school have sports? Which ones? Are sports important in the school, or not very important? What percentage of students play sports, approximately?

A **You're going to hear an interview about a special school. Look at the profile below. Why do you think Stratton Mountain School is special? Tell a partner.**

5–10 min

Tell students to look at the profile and the photo of the snowboarder. What seems to be different about this school? Students should compare their answers and say why they think so. Still in pairs, students should guess the words to complete the profile.

B **A student is going to talk about the school below. Listen and complete the profile. Use only one word per blank.**

CD 1 Track 34

10–15 min

For interest, tell students that Stratton Mountain School is a real school, and it has a website. Play the audio first with books closed so that students listen to the whole interview. Play it again once or twice while students complete the profile. Check answers with the class and write them on the board to confirm.

C **Review your notes in B. Then tell a partner: Why is Stratton an unusual high school?**

10 min

Students can discuss this in pairs with books closed.

C Teaching Option **Expand the conversation**

You can bring in the Ask & Answer questions at this point if you wish. Tell students to include not only the information in the profile, but anything else they think is interesting about the school, including questions they may have that are not answered in the interview.

D **Read sentences 1–3 below. Then listen again. Choose the correct answer for each one.**

CD 1 Track 35

10–15 min

Play the first segment of the recording and pause while students answer. Check the answer immediately. Students should listen again and remember the sentence that gave them the answer. (*Yeah, it admits both boys and girls.*) Write what they remember on the board. Finally, play the segment again to confirm or correct the sentence on the board.

Do the same with segments 2 and 3. (2. *So students are living in dorms?* 3. *After graduation, many Stratton alumni compete in the Winter Olympics.*) In question 2, the key word is *living.* Students must infer the meaning of *housing* to answer the question. In question 3, *graduates*, as a noun, is a new word. Again, students need to infer its meaning.

Language Tip: *Graduate,* verb and noun

Graduate and *graduates* can be verbs or nouns. They are pronounced slightly differently. Verb: *GRA jew ate*. Noun: *GRA jew it.*

ASK ANSWER

Add more questions on the board.

Do you know anyone who would like a school like Stratton?

Stratton is for winter sports. What other special high schools could there be?

3 Pronunciation

Reduced pronunciation of *going to*

A **Listen to the sentences. Notice the reduced pronunciation of *going to* in each sentence.**

CD 1 Track 36

5–10 min

Play the audio, pausing after each sentence to repeat it yourself. (It helps students to hear new pronunciation features from more than one speaker.) Then play the sentences without pausing.

B **Listen to the sentences and write the missing words you hear.**

CD 1 Track 37

10 min

Choose one or two volunteers to work at the board. Pause after each sentence for students to write the answers (you may want to do this twice). Thank your volunteers and let them sit down. Check answers on the board with the class.

C **Take turns saying the sentences in A and B with a partner.**

10–15 min

Students do not alternate sentences; both say each sentence before moving on to the next one. They say the sentences at least three times, alternating who starts. You can play the audio again so they can listen once more before they switch partners and continue practicing.

2 Listening **Not your typical school**

A You're going to hear an interview about a special school. Look at the profile below. Why do you think Stratton Mountain School is special? Tell a partner.

CD 1 Track 34

B A student is going to talk about the school below. Listen and complete the profile. Use only one word per blank.

School Profile

Name: Stratton Mountain School (for students ages __14__ to __18__)

Where: Vermont, USA

Students: Most are __skiers__ and snowboarders.

After graduation, many compete in the Winter __Olympics__.

A typical day at Stratton:

7:00 A.M.: __breakfast__

8:00 A.M. to __noon__: Students are in __training__.

12:30 to 5:00 P.M.: Students have __classes__.

C Review your notes in **B**. Then tell a partner: Why is Stratton an unusual high school?
The students are skiers or snowboarders and their schedule is very different.

CD 1 Track 35

D Read sentences 1–3 below. Then listen again. Choose the correct answer for each one.

1. A *coed* school admits . . .
   A: boys only.
   B: girls only.
   (C:) both boys and girls.

2. A *dorm* is a type of student . . .
   A: activity.
   (B:) housing.
   C: training.

3. A school's *alumni* are . . .
   (A:) graduates from the school.
   B: students now at the school.
   C: teachers at the school.

ASK ANSWER

Do you think Stratton is an interesting school? Why or why not?

3 Pronunciation **Reduced pronunciation of *going to***

CD 1 Track 36

A Listen to the sentences. Notice the reduced pronunciation of *going to* in each sentence.

1. I'm going to apply to three colleges.
2. He's going to clean the house next week.
3. We're going to study together for the big exam.
4. They're not going to finish in time.

CD 1 Track 37

B Listen to the sentences and write the missing words you hear.

1. __I'm not going to__ meet them before 3:00.
2. __We're not going to__ take a vacation this summer.
3. __She's going to__ call us tomorrow.
4. __He's not going to__ attend Harvard University.

C Take turns saying the sentences in **A** and **B** with a partner.

4 Speaking Look on the bright side.

CD 1 Track 38

A Listen to the conversation. Then answer the questions with a partner.

1. Tom is unhappy about something. What?
   Tom's unhappy because he didn't get into McGill University.
2. How does Hans make Tom feel better? Underline Hans's advice.
3. What do you think "look on the bright side" means?

Hans: Hey, Tom. How's it going with the college applications?

Tom: So-so. I didn't get into McGill University.

Hans: Really? Sorry to hear that. Did you apply to any other schools?

Tom: Yeah, three others.

Hans: And?

Tom: I got into all of them.

Hans: Well, that's great!

Tom: Yeah, but I really wanted to go to McGill.

Hans: Well, look on the bright side—three other schools accepted you.

Tom: Yeah, I guess you're right.

Hans: So, which school are you going to attend?

Tom: I'm not sure. Maybe I'll go to Queen's University.

B Practice the conversation with a partner.

5 Speaking Strategy

Useful Expressions: Offering another point of view	
I didn't get accepted to McGill University.	
Look on the bright side . . . Well, the good news is . . . Look at it this way . . . Yes, but on the other hand . . . (Yes, but) then again . . .	three other schools accepted you.

A Read the problems. For each, add one more "positive" point of view to the chart.

The problem	A positive point of view
You applied to two English schools: one in the UK and one in Australia. You really wanted to study in the UK, but only the school in Australia accepted you.	1. You got accepted to a good school. 2. ______
You're invited to a party at the beach. You're not sure if you want to go. You're worried you won't know many people.	1. You can meet new people. 2. ______

B Choose one situation from **A**. With a partner, create a short conversation like the one in Speaking. Use the Useful Expressions in your dialog.

C Change roles. Use the other situation and repeat **B**.

4 Speaking Look on the bright side.

Warm Up

5–10 min

With books closed, say, *A disappointment is when something that you want to happen doesn't happen.* Write the word *disappointment* on the board. Tell about a disappointment of your own. Ask, *Have you ever had a disappointment? What was it?* Let students volunteer to answer.

A Listen to the conversation. Then answer the questions with a partner.

CD 1 Track 38

10–15 min

With books closed, write the questions on the board, except leave out *Underline Hans's advice.* Play the audio once, and students can check answers with a partner. With books open, show students the rest of question 2. Play the audio again while students read along, verify the answers they've already checked, and underline the missing answer to question 2. Ask them what *bright* means. (In this context, *good.*) They should be able to infer it from the context.

B Practice the conversation with a partner.

15–20 min

Play the audio, pausing after each line for students to repeat it. Students can practice the conversation in pairs, changing roles. Play the audio again, then students should change partners to practice again. You can add two lines on the board to practice the pronunciation of *going to*:

Hans: When are you going to decide?

Tom: I don't know. I'm going to think about it for awhile.

5 Speaking Strategy

A Read the problems. For each, add one more "positive" point of view to the chart.

10–15 min

Introduce the Useful Expressions. Read the statement aloud. Then read the five responses (other points of view) and explain vocabulary. Read the first problem in the chart and the positive point of view (number 1). The class can brainstorm other possible positive points of view. Write these on the board. (For example, *You can go to the UK later. Australia is interesting and Australians are really nice. The Australian school is cheaper.*) Students can work in pairs to read the second problem and add another positive point of view. Until everyone finishes, assign the faster students to keep listing other positive points of view. To check answers, list all the ideas on the board.

B Choose one situation from A. With a partner, create a short conversation like the one in Speaking. Use the Useful Expressions in your dialog.

10–20 min

Develop two or three first lines for each conversation with the class and write them on the board. (*What's happening with your school applications? Did you hear from your schools yet? Did you decide to go to that beach party? What are you doing on Saturday?*) Students can use them to get started, or they can write their own first lines. Remind them to use one of the Useful Expressions in their conversation. If time allows, students can switch roles in the same conversation before doing **C**.

C Change roles. Use the other situation and repeat B.

10 min

Write the Useful Expressions on the board so that students can do this with books closed, not referring to the conversation in **A**.

C Teaching Option Support/challenge

On the board, list the Useful Expressions from 5, Speaking Strategy. Ask students to recall the disappointments they talked about in the Warm Up for 4, Speaking. List them on the board, too. With books closed, pairs choose a disappointment from the list, create a conversation (using one of the Useful Expressions), and practice it. Call on volunteers to perform their conversations for the class.

Language Tip: *Gonna*

Students may sometimes see *going to* written as *gonna.* Make sure they understand that the written contraction of *be going to* is *I'm, he's/she's/it's, we're, you're, they're going to. Gonna* is for pronunciation only, in rapid speech only; not for writing.

Instructor's Notes

6 Language Link

Plans and decisions with *be going to* and *will*

Warm Up

5 min

Ask students, *What do students have to consider when they choose a college?* Make a list on the board. (Ideas: Can I get financial aid? Can I live at home? Do they teach what I need? Do I want a big school or a small one?)

Grammar Tip: *Be going to* and *will*

Sometimes *be going to* and *will* are taught as interchangeable to discuss the future. *Be going to* is used to state an already-made plan: *We're going to the beach this weekend* (We agreed that is the plan for this weekend.). Use *will* to make an offer: *I'll take you to the beach on Saturday* (If you would like to go to the beach, I am offering to drive you there.).

There is only a slight difference between *I'm going to get the ice before the party* (It's been agreed upon that I will bring ice. That is the plan.) and *I'll get the ice before the party* (I'm offering to help you by getting the ice so you don't have to do it.). The meaning is slightly different but the ultimate action is the same so they are often taught as interchangeable here.

Here, *be going to* is used for things that are planned. *Will* is used for more sudden decisions.

A **Read these conversations. Then complete sentences 1 and 2 below.**

10–15 min

First read the two sentences in the box. Explain *sudden* if necessary. (In this context, it means that the person didn't think it over.) Students can read the conversations silently, or you can read them aloud, or ask four students to read them. Explain *register* if necessary. Remind students that contracted forms are typical in speaking (*I'm going to* and *I'll*) and that *going to* sounds like *gonna*. Students should repeat the conversations and practice in pairs. Then students can check the boxes to complete the sentences. After checking answers, write this on the board for **B**:

will = a sudden decision

be going to = a plan already made

Teaching Tip: Inductive learning

As teachers, it is easy to provide answers and explanations to students. It is more challenging to sit back and wait for students to figure out a grammar rule. In fact, having students figure out the rule themselves will help students remember it better and will give them confidence in their own abilities to understand English.

B **Complete these sentences with *be going to* or *will*. Then check your answers with a partner.**

10–15 min

Refer students to the information on the board while they work. Alternatively, students can complete the sentences in pairs, discussing whether each sentence expresses a sudden decision or a plan already made. Note that number 1 uses the simple present *I'm going* as a future tense.

C **Read what these new students are planning to do. Make sentences using *be (not) going to* with a partner.**

10–20 min

In pairs, students can take turns making affirmative or negative statements. They should do the exercise twice so that both students say all the sentences.

Word Bank: Places on campus

administration building
auditorium, theater
bookstore
computer center, computer lab
dining hall, cafeteria
gymnasium
classroom, lecture hall, laboratory
library
student union, student center
dormitory

ASK ANSWER

Students can discuss the questions in pairs or groups. Tell them to extend the conversation with follow-up questions and more information.

6 Language Link Plans and decisions with *be going to* and *will*

A Read these conversations. Then complete sentences 1 and 2 below.

Ana: I got accepted to college.
Pablo: Congratulations!
Ana: Thanks. I'm going to attend McGill University in the fall.

Yuri: I want to register for the grammar class.
Advisor: I'm sorry. That class is full.
Yuri: OK. I'll register for the writing class, then.

1. Ana uses be going to to talk about . . .
   - [ ] a. a sudden decision.
   - [x] b. a plan she already made.

2. Yuri uses will ('ll) to talk about . . .
   - [x] a. a sudden decision.
   - [ ] b. a plan he already made.

B Complete the sentences with *be going to* or *will*. Then check your answers with a partner.

1. I graduate from high school in June. Then I 'm going to ______ attend college in the fall.
2. I'm bored and don't know what to do. Wait, I know . . . I 'll ______ read and watch TV.
3. Waiter: What would you like today?
   Customer: Let's see . . . I 'll ______ have the chicken and rice, please.
4. I bought my ticket last month. I 'm going to ______ visit Paris from July 1 to July 14.
5. A: This box is too heavy!
   B: Wait! I 'll ______ help you.

C Read what these new students are planning to do. Make sentences using *be (not) going to* with a partner.

Carlos

Ariana

Max and Sara

Carlos:
- [x] live at home
- [ ] apply for scholarships
- [x] study business

Ariana:
- [x] major in law
- [x] live in the dorms
- [ ] go to a large university

Max and Sara:
- [ ] live in student housing
- [x] study together
- [x] work part-time

Carlos is going to live at home. He's not going to apply for scholarships.

ASK ANSWER

What about you? What are your future plans for school or work?

1. Carlos is going to live at home and study business. He's not going to (OR He isn't going to) apply for scholarships.
2. Ariana's going to major in law and live in the dorms. She's not going to (OR She isn't going to) go to a large university.
3. Max and Sara are going to study together and work part-time. They aren't going to (OR They're not going to) live in student housing.

7 Communication **Find someone who . . .**

A The two questions in the chart ask about someone's future plans. Read the answers. Then complete each question with *be going to*. Check answers with a partner.

***yes / no* questions**	Are you going to **study** English this summer?	Yes, I am. / Maybe. / No, I'm not.
***wh-* questions**	What are you going to **do** after graduation?	I'm going to take a trip.

B Read the questions on the left side of the chart. In the "Me" column, check (✔) the activities you're planning to do in the future. Then add your own question.

Are you going to . . .	Me	Classmate's name	Question	Answer
graduate from high school or college soon?			When . . . ?	
take a trip somewhere this summer?			Where . . . ?	
go out this weekend?			Who . . . ?	
study after class today?			What . . . ?	
take a test in English (like the TOEFL) soon?			Which . . . ?	
keep studying English after this session?			Where . . . ?	
______________ ?				

C Interview your classmates. For each question, find a different person who answers *yes*. Write the classmate's name. Ask another question to get more details.

D Look at the answers you got in **C**. Which one was the most interesting? Tell the class.

7 Communication

Find someone who ...

Warm Up

5 min

With books closed, ask students, *Do you have any big plans for the future?* Students answer, for example, *My plan is to graduate from college, go to graduate school, get married in June, become a fashion designer,* etc. Or, *No, I don't.* List their plans on the board in note form.

A 10 min

The two questions in the chart ask about someone's future plans. Read the answers. Then complete each question with *be going to*. Check answers with a partner.

To check answers, choose two students to write the complete questions on the board. Ask the questions of several students, until all four answers have been given.

B 10 min

Read the questions on the left side of the chart. In the "Me" column, check (✓) the activities you're planning to do in the future. Then add your own question.

Hold up your book and point to columns 1 and 2 as you explain what to do. (In a large class, copy the first line of the chart on the board.)

C 20-25 min

Interview your classmates. For each question, find a different person who answers *yes*. Write the classmate's name. Ask another question to get more details.

Again, point to the columns as you explain the activity. Students should write down their classmates' names and answers.

C Teaching Option **Support/challenge**

Some students may find it difficult to ask follow-up questions (column 4) without preparation. Students can work out the questions in advance and write them in their books before they begin talking. You might write the questions on the board.

Large Class Option

Walk-and-talk activities can be difficult to manage with very large groups. Instead of walking around, students can interview only the person next to them. Each student can ask all six questions of one other student, and write the answers on a piece of paper. To follow up, students can write 12 complete sentences about their partner and hand it in.

D 15-20 min

Look at the answers you got in C. Which one was the most interesting? Tell the class.

Students can chare in smaller groups of four to six. The groups can then choose their one or two most interesting answers to share with the class.

EXTRA! What are you going to do?

20 min

Prepare small slips of paper, one for each student, with a different amount of money written on each one, from very small—for example $1—to very large—for example, $1 million. Assign students to groups of five or six. Appoint a reporter for each group. Tell students they have all won money in a contest, now they have to decide what to do with it. Let each student pick a slip of paper from a bag or box. Give them a little time to think before telling their group what they are going to do. Let the group vote on which two answers they want to share with the whole class. The reporter tells the class.

Instructor's Notes

After graduation

Unit 6, Lesson B

1 Vocabulary Link

One of these days . . .

Warm Up

5 min

Copy this chart on the board and ask questions about future plans. (*Whose plans for the future are more definite—yours or your best friend's?*, etc.) Ask for a show of hands on each question, and write the totals under *You* and *Your best friend.*

	You	*Your best friend*
plans are more definite		
plans are harder		
will succeed first		

A Read about these two people. Then answer the questions with a partner.

10–15 min

Before students read, tell students that Carmen and Gabe are going to graduate soon. Tell students to look at the photos (Carmen has books and Gabe has a surfboard.) and guess who might have more serious plans for the future. What makes them think so? Read the two questions in the book. Check answers with the class. Ask two to four students to support their answers to question 2 by referring to the text. Read the Language Tip below and help explain these expressions to students.

> **Language Tip: Sooner or later**
>
> *Sooner or later*, *one of these days*, and *someday* all express a desire to do something without a definite plan to make it happen. In the case of Carmen's statement, "… someday I plan to be a doctor," she probably will become a doctor because she knows she is going to medical school, but the details after that are not as defined.

B Complete the chart with the blue time expressions in A.

10–15 min

Copy the first two lines of the chart on the board. Write *tomorrow* under *definite time*. Write *soon* and *in a few days* under *indefinite time*. Tell students to find one more definite time and one more indefinite time in the texts, and write them in the correct places on the board. To check answers, fill in the rest of the chart.

> **Language Tip: *This* and *next***
>
> Native English speakers do not always agree about using *this* and *next* in time expressions. For example, from Monday the 1st through Friday the 5th, *this weekend* means Saturday and Sunday, the 6th and 7th. *Next weekend* might mean the 6th and 7th, or the 13th and 14th. Usually, information known by both the speaker and the listener (the context) prevents confusion. Otherwise, the speaker has to explain.

C Complete the sentences. Then check your answers with a partner.

10–15 min

Tell students to write words in 1 and 2, and circle words in 3–6. Students can do this in pairs, or work alone and check answers in pairs. If they disagree, they should discuss the answer until they agree.

> **Culture Tip: Definite and indefinite plans**
>
> Native English speakers sometimes make social invitations with a very indefinite future time reference, such as *Let's have coffee soon!* This is meant as a friendly gesture rather than an actual invitation. A real invitation is always for a specific time—for example, *Let's have coffee soon. Are you free tomorrow?* Then the two people agree on a time and place. *You should come over for dinner some time* does not mean that the person is welcome at dinnertime any day. *Would you like to come over for dinner on Friday?* is a real invitation.

D Are you going to do any of these things in the future? When? Tell a partner.

5–10 min

To follow up, call on a student (A) at random to ask another student (B) one of the questions. When B answers, have a third student (C) ask a follow-up question. Or do this in groups of six to eight. After B answers, C asks the next question, and so on.

Instructor's Notes

Student Life

Lesson B After graduation

1. Carmen is going to volunteer at a hospital and study for the medical school exam this summer. Next year, she wants to enter medical school. Someday (in the future), she wants to be a doctor. Gabe doesn't really have any clear plans for the future. He wants to take a trip and sooner or later (at some time in the future) he needs to get a job.

1 Vocabulary Link **One of these days . . .**

A Read about these two people. Then answer the questions with a partner.

1. What is each person planning to do in the future? When is he or she planning to do it?
2. Which person has more of a definite plan about his or her future?
   Carmen's plans for the future are more definite than Gabe's.

Carmen

I'm going to graduate **the day after tomorrow**. I'm finishing school, but I've already got lots of plans for the future. **This summer**, for example, I'm going to study for the medical school exam. **Next year**, I hope to enter medical school, and **someday**, I plan to be a doctor.

Gabe

I'm going to graduate **in two weeks**. I'm a little nervous because **after graduation**, I don't have any clear plans. I'd like to take a short vacation **in the near future**—maybe **next month**. **Sooner or later**, I also need to get a job, but I don't know what I want to do exactly. I'm sure I'll make a decision—**one of these days**.

B Complete the chart with the blue time expressions in **A**.

Future Time Expressions	
Talk about a definite (specific) time	**Talk about an indefinite (uncertain) time**
tomorrow	soon
the ___day after tomorrow___	**in** a few days
in two hours / days / ___weeks___ / months / years	**in** the ___near future___
next week / ___month___ / ___year___	___sooner or later___
this ___summer___ / spring / fall / winter	someday / one ___of these days___
___after___ graduation / school / work	

C Complete the sentences. Then check your answers with a partner.

1. If today is Thursday, *the day after tomorrow* is ___Saturday___.
2. It's 2:00. You say, "I'll be home *in two hours*." You'll be home at ___4___:00.
3. It's May. You say, "I'm going to graduate *next June*." This means you're going to graduate next month / (in 13 months).
4. It's May. You say, "I'm going to graduate *this June*." This means you're going to graduate (next month) / in 13 months.
5. Your friend says, "We should have coffee *one of these days*." He or She is / (isn't) making an appointment with you.
6. If you tell a friend, "I'm going to Jamaica *in a few days*," you (are) / aren't going to Jamaica very soon.

D Are you going to do any of these things in the future? When? Tell a partner.

complete this English class | have children | take a trip somewhere | see my friends

2 Listening **Career Day**

A Look at the photos. What are the people doing? How do you prepare for these activities?

a written exam

a physical exam

CD 1 Track 39

B You're going to hear an ad for Career Day. Read the questions. Then listen and check the correct answers.

1. Who is Career Day for? ☑ students ☐ teachers ☐ parents
2. What is another word for *career*? ☐ school ☐ child ☑ job

CD 1 Track 40

C Listen to Jeff, a speaker at Career Day, describe a process. Put the steps in order from 1 to 5. Then complete the sentence.

__2__ take a written exam   __5__ take final exams   __4__ go to school for four months

__1__ take training courses   __3__ take a physical exam

Jeff is going to be a __firefighter__.

ASK ANSWER

Jeff completed all the steps in **C**. Which step would be the hardest for you? Why?

3 Reading **An opportunity of a lifetime**

A The people below are talking about Stephanie. Read what they say. What do you think Stephanie is going to do this summer? Share with a partner.

She's going to travel alone for six months. It's a great opportunity!

Mrs. Lee, mother

This is a perfect job for her. She loves to take photos and meet new people.

Mr. Lee, father

After she finishes her work assignment, I'm going to meet her in Europe.

Tommy Farr, boyfriend

B Now read the web page. Was your guess about Stephanie's summer plans correct?

2 Listening Career Day

Skills: Make and check predictions; Listen for gist; Listen for details; Infer information; Identify a sequence of events

Warm Up

5 min

With books closed, ask students, *What is your "dream job"? How does someone get a job like that? What do you have to learn or do first?* Make notes on the board of some jobs and their requirements. Which one is the hardest to get?

10 min

A Look at the photos. What are the people doing? How do you prepare for these activities?

Ask students to name some things that require written exams (such as school courses and degrees, a driver's license, citizenship in a new country, some jobs). How do they prepare for written exams? From the photo, what do they think a physical exam is like? What things might require a physical exam? (Examples could include military service, police work, firefighting, or construction work.) Based on the photos, what do students think they may hear in the listening?

> **Language Tip: Physical exam**
>
> Another kind of physical exam is given by a doctor. This exam checks your general health or looks for specific medical problems. This is different and distinct from the physical exam explained here.

CD 1 Track 39
15–20 min

B You're going to hear an ad for Career Day. Read the questions. Then listen and check the correct answers.

Read the two questions. If students think they already know the answers, they should listen to verify them. Play the audio as many times as necessary for students to understand it.

CD 1 Track 40
10–15 min

C Listen to Jeff, a speaker at Career Day, describe a process. Put the steps in order from 1 to 5. Then complete the sentence.

Play the audio once while students listen. Then play the audio again for them to listen and answer the questions. In pairs, students should compare answers and discuss any differences. Play the audio once more so students can verify the answers they disagreed about.

> **Culture Tip: Firefighters**
>
> Becoming a firefighter has different requirements around the world. In some places, fire departments are made up of volunteers. They are usually required to do a certain number of hours of physical and mental training. Ask your students if they know what requirements are needed to be a firefighter in their community.

> **ASK ANSWER**
>
> Students can discuss this question in groups of four or five. Instruct them to ask follow-up questions. Walk around to all the groups (if possible) as they talk. Listen to their follow-up questions and answers. Comment or ask a question of your own. Finally, with the whole class, ask each group which step got the most votes as the hardest. Tally these on the board.

3 Reading An opportunity of a lifetime

Skills: Use background knowledge to make and check predictions; Read for details; Guess the meaning of words from context

Warm Up

5 min

With books closed, ask students, *Have you ever traveled alone? Where did you go? How long were you gone? Was it a good experience?* If no one has traveled alone, ask what they think it would be like.

10–15 min

A The people below are talking about Stephanie. Read what they say. What do you think Stephanie is going to do this summer? Share with a partner.

Ask three students to read the people's names and comments aloud. Working with a partner, students can find facts about Stephanie's plans for the summer. As a class, pairs can share their answers. Write them on the board in note form. (Examples: travel alone – six months – have a job – take photos – meet new people – be near Europe, or in it.) Tell students to guess Stephanie's plans from the clues. Write their guesses on the board.

20–25 min

B Now read the web page. Was your guess about Stephanie's summer plans correct?

With books closed, ask students exactly what Stephanie is going to do this summer. Write the first student's response on the board and revise it as other students suggest improvements. Compare the statement to the students' guesses in **A**. If no guess was completely correct, which were the closest?

10–15 min **C** **Find a word or phrase in the text that has the same meaning as the words below.**

While checking answers, ask students how they figured out the four words. After checking answers, explain any other vocabulary if necessary, but first ask students to try to figure them out from the context. (*Highlight* is clear enough from the context—they don't need an exact definition; so are *turned back, made it all the way, miss, pass,* and *punctual.*)

10–15 min **D** **Complete the sentences about Stephanie's new job with words from the box. (You will not use all the words.)**

Give students two to three minutes to scan the text to remind themselves how the words are used. Then, with books closed, students should answer without looking back at the text. They can look at the text to check answers.

D Teaching Option **Support/challenge**

Recall details from the reading: To follow up, write some other words from the text on the board (*family business, Mount Kilimanjaro, give up*). After scanning for the words, students should write sentences about Stephanie using each of the words. They can work alone or in pairs. Have one or two volunteers work at the board and check answers there.

ASK ANSWER

Students can discuss their answers in groups or as a class. Give this follow-up for question 1: *In applications and interviews in Canada and the United States, people expect you to say good things about yourself—for example, that you are self-sufficient and a hard worker, that you never give up, and so on. Is this true in other cultures that you know about? Would it be (Is it) hard for you to do?*

Culture Tip: Self-presentation in applications

In Canada and the United States, self-confidence is one of the most important qualities that people look for in applicants. For this reason, applicants are expected to talk about their best talents, skills, and successes. They can even praise their own character and personality. On the other hand, they should not sound self-satisfied or arrogant. This is not easy, and many applicants have trouble finding the right tone.

10–20 min **EXTRA! Post-reading**

In groups of three to five, students can invent another contest like the one Stephanie won. What is the prize? Describe it. Write four or five questions for the contestants to answer.

15–20 min **EXTRA! Discussion questions**

1. Was Stephanie's prize a good one? Why or why not?
2. Which places in Europe should Stephanie and Tommy visit after her work assignment?
3. What advice would you give her before her trip?

20–40 min **EXTRA! Writing prompts**

1. Think of a job you would like to have. Why would you be good at it? What would be the hardest part of the job for you?
2. Agree or disagree with this statement: Some people take time off after college to travel. This is not a good decision. They should begin their career or start graduate school immediately.

20–30 min **EXTRA! Additional reading**

For more practice making predictions and checking facts, see Heinle's Footprint Reading Library *Chuckwagon Racing.*

For more practice reading at this level, please see Heinle's Classic Graphic Novel Collection *Henry V.*

Instructor's Notes

Travel

NEWS | UPDATE | PHOTOS | CONTACT US

We now have a winner! Stephanie Lee from Vancouver, Canada, answered our questions and won the top prize: she's going to be our youth travel reporter in Europe! A week after college graduation, Stephanie starts her six-month travel adventure. She'll write about her experiences for our World Link website. Here were some of Stephanie's answers to our questions:

Do you have any international travel experience and what does this tell us about you?
Yes, I do. Two years ago, I spent the summer in Hong Kong. I stayed with my grandmother and worked in the family business. I also visited Africa last year. I think this shows that I'm self-sufficient—I can do things on my own—and that I'm not afraid of new experiences.

In Africa, I went to Tanzania. The highlight was climbing Mount Kilimanjaro. It's the highest mountain in Africa. The climb was very hard. Two people turned back before they reached the top. I made it all the way! Once I start something, I never give up.

What do you think will be the hardest part of this job?
I'm going to be visiting over 25 countries where people speak lots of different languages so communicating with others might be difficult sometimes. I speak some French and German, and English, of course. I'll also be traveling with a translator in many places so I'm sure that will help. I'm also sure that sooner or later, I'm going to miss my family and friends. It's normal. But I also know from experience that this feeling will pass—especially when you meet new people.

Why should we choose you?
Because I love to travel and meet new people. I'm also a hard worker and will have no trouble filing reports on time. I'm always very punctual!

Stephanie

C Find a word or phrase in the text that has the same meaning as the words below.

1. independent ___self-sufficient___
2. quit ___give up___
3. speaking ___communicating___
4. lively, with a lot of energy ___energetic___

D Complete the sentences about Stephanie's new job with words from the box. (You will not use all the words.)

Africa	punctual	school	reporter	translator
photographing	Europe	popular	talking to	website

1. Stephanie Lee is going to spend her summer in ___Europe___.
2. She's going to work as a ___reporter___ for a ___website___.
3. The hardest part of the job will probably be ___talking to___ new people.
4. Stephanie is perfect for the job because she's very ___punctual___.

ASK ANSWER

1. Look at answer 4 in **D**. What other reasons is Stephanie perfect for the job?

2. Would you like to do Stephanie's job? Why or why not?

4 Language Link **Predictions with *be going to* and *will***

A People use *be going to* and *will* to make predictions (guesses about the future). Look at the pictures and read the captions. Then complete sentences 1 and 2 with *be going to* or *will*.

I'm sure you're going to be very successful.
or
I'm sure you'll be very successful.

"Look! That truck is going to go through that red light!"

1. In picture A, the man is making a general prediction about the student's future, so he can use ___be going to___ or ___will___.
2. In picture B, we can see that the action is happening now or very soon, so we use ___be going to___ but not ___will___.

B The sentences below all make predictions. Complete each with *be going to*, *will*, or both. Then explain your answer choices to a partner.

1. Liam did really well in college. I'm sure he ___'s/is going to OR 'll/will___ get a good job.
2. I think you ___'re/are going to OR 'll/will___ like this movie. It's a comedy and you like funny movies.
3. The score is 5 to 1 and there's only one minute left in the game. Our team ___'s/is going to___ lose for sure.
4. Scientists now believe there ___'re/are going to OR 'll/will___ be nine billion people on Earth by the year 2040.
5. Look at those dark clouds. It ___'s/is going to___ rain soon.

C Study the information in the chart. Then read the predictions below. Do you think each one will happen? Why or why not? Tell a partner.

Making predictions about the future		
Leo studied hard.	**I'm sure / I bet**	he's going to / he'll pass the test.
Mona didn't study.		she isn't going to / she won't pass the test.

- It's common to use *I'm sure* and *I bet* to make a prediction you are certain about.
- Use *probably* or *maybe* when you aren't 100% sure about your prediction:
  He'll probably pass the test.
  She probably won't pass the test.
  Maybe we'll find a cure for cancer someday.

1. We'll find life on other planets.
2. Scientists will cure diseases like AIDS and cancer.
3. Newspapers and magazines will disappear. All information will be online.

In the near future, we'll probably find life on other planets . . .

Really? Maybe it'll happen, but not in the near future . . .

4 Language Link

Predictions with *be going to* and *will*

Warm Up

5 min

Every year, in American high schools, a graduating student is named "Most Likely to Succeed" by his or her classmates. Ask students to think of their friends or classmates. Who do they think is most likely to succeed in the future? Why will he or she be successful?

10–15 min

A People use *be going to* and *will* to make predictions (guesses about the future). Look at the pictures and read the captions. Then complete sentences 1 and 2 with *be going to* or *will*.

Before students complete the sentences, discuss the pictures. In picture A, what is the situation? Who are the three people? Who is speaking? What is he predicting? When is the student going to succeed? In picture B, what is the situation? What are the women looking at? What is the speaker predicting? When is it going to happen?

Language Tip: *Be going to* and *will*

Sometimes *be going to* and *will* are taught as interchangeable to discuss the future. *Will* is used to make a prediction of what we think is likely to happen in the long term: *You will get married someday.* (There is no plan for you to get married but the speaker thinks it is likely to happen someday.) Use *be going to* to talk about something that is about to happen: *Careful! You're going to spill your coffee.* (The speaker thinks this is about to happen now, unless something changes now.)

There is only a slight difference between *You're going to do great at your new job!* (The speaker knows you are starting a new job soon and predicts you will be good at it when you start.) and *You'll do well in your new job.* (The speaker predicts that when you work you'll do a good job because you're so smart.) The meaning is slightly different, but the ultimate prediction is the same, so they are often taught as interchangeable here.

Here, *be going to* is used for things that are likely to happen soon. *Will* is used for more general predictions.

10–15 min

B The sentences below all make predictions. Complete each with *be going to, will,* or both. Then explain your answer choices to a partner.

Tell students to be sure to write two answers if both are correct. Follow up by asking several students to explain their answers to the class, referring to the rules in the box. Then explain to students that the order of the two sentences (or phrases as in number 4) can be switched to connect them. Point out that when switching the order in number 1, native English speakers would use the subject's name in the first sentence rather than the second.

B Teaching Option Support/challenge

Before completing the sentences, read them one by one with the class. What is the time of the action—an unspecified time in the future? Or now or very soon? How do you know? Ask students to explain. (Note that in 2, the movie may be starting now, but it will be over later.)

25–35 min

C Study the information in the chart. Then read the predictions below. Do you think each one will happen? Why or why not? Tell a partner.

Remind students that in Unit 3 they used *I bet, probably,* and *maybe* to talk about possibility in the present. Now they can use the same expressions for predictions. Point out the expressions for 100% certain predictions versus less certain ones. Review the future time expressions on page 61 and write them on the board for reference. Let the whole class create the first conversation together and write it on the board. Walk around while they practice to help with grammar and vocabulary.

C Teaching Option Support/challenge

Some students may find it challenging to think of reasons for or against the predictions. You might brainstorm ideas with the whole class and make notes on the board for reference during practice. Alternatively, let students work in groups and write their conversations to share with the class.

Instructor's Notes

5 Writing My life now and in the future

Warm Up

5 min

With books closed, ask students if they think their life will get better, stay about the same, or get worse in the future. What parts of their life do they think will change the most?

20–25 min

A Use the topics below or ones of your own. First, write about what you are doing now. Then write about your future. Use *be going to* and *will* to make predictions.

Read the model composition with the class. What is the first paragraph about? What verb tenses does it use? What about the second paragraph? Read the instructions aloud and show students how the model follows them. Assign students to write a first draft. Remind them to use future time expressions (page 61).

A Teaching Option Speaking

Students should make notes and prepare to tell a partner their ideas about their future, making predictions and using some of the time expressions on page 61. Remind them that examples make their ideas more interesting. Partners comment on the predictions.

20–40 min

B Exchange papers with a partner. Do you think your partner's predictions will come true?

Write some of the Useful Expressions from Lesson A on the board (page 58): *Look on the bright side, … ; But the good news is … ; Look at it this way … .* Suggest that students use them if they don't think their partner's prediction will come true. (Examples could include: *I'm not sure you'll get accepted to Harvard. But the good news is you're definitely going to go to graduate school.* or *Maybe you won't get married this year, but look on the bright side. Next year you'll both be more mature.*)

Teaching Tip: Errors in communication

It's generally not very effective to correct students' English during spoken communication. Their attention is focused on conveying meaning, and any corrections you make will probably not be internalized. Instead, it's best to make notes of common mistakes you hear (including the whole sentence) and work with them as a class after the activity is finished. It is not necessary to name the student who produced a particular sentence, as learners can often identify their own sentences. Instead, talk about several examples at a time, and help the class work out what the correct form should be.

6 Communication

Predicting the future

Warm Up

5 min

With books closed, ask students what they know about the British royal family, especially Princes William and Harry.

10 min

A Read this profile of Prince William. With a partner, make some predictions about his future.

Read the profile with the whole class, or students can read it on their own. While students practice, walk around and help them remember to use what they've learned in the unit—to pronounce *going to* as *gonna,* and use future time expressions (page 61) and expressions of probability (page 64). Follow up with students sharing some of their predictions. Were there some things that almost everyone predicted?

10–15 min

B Now complete your own personal profile.

The profile can be written in the third person, like Prince William's. If students are working now, they can include their jobs under *Schooling*. Tell students to write about their personality objectively—some good points and some less good ones. This will be more interesting for their partner.

25–30 min

C Exchange profiles with a partner. Make predictions about your partner's job, travel, school, family, and love life.

Give students time to read the profiles, ask the writer about anything that's not clear, and make notes about their predictions. This is a conversation, so both partners should ask questions, make comments, and explain what they mean. Walk around as they talk to comment, help, and participate.

30 min

EXTRA! Writing prompt

Would you like to trade places with Prince William—to live his life instead of yours? Why or why not?

Instructor's Notes

5 Writing **My life now and in the future**

A Use the topics below or ones of your own. First, write about what you are doing now. Then write about your future. Use *be going to* and *will* to make predictions.

family   job   travel   school   love life

My Life Now and in the Future

Right now, I'm taking an English class. I'm working part-time at a cafe. I live at home with my parents and two brothers. I have a boyfriend.

Someday, I'm going to get married and live in a house by the ocean. Sooner or later, I'll . . .

B Exchange papers with a partner. Do you think your partner's predictions will come true?

6 Communication **Predicting the future**

A Read this profile of Prince William.
With a partner, make some predictions about his future.

Birthday:	June 21, 1982
Schooling:	He attended university at St. Andrews in Scotland. He studied art history. After graduation, he also lived and worked for a short time in Chile, Belize, and parts of Africa. He is now a pilot with the Royal Air Force.
Hobbies:	He loves sports, including rugby, hockey, swimming, skiing, and running. He likes to listen to music.
Personality:	He is shy in public. In private, he is strong-willed and independent.

Someday, he's probably going to be the King of England.

I bet he'll marry someone famous, too, like a movie star.

B Now complete your own personal profile.

Schooling:

Hobbies:

Personality:

C Exchange profiles with a partner. Make predictions about your partner's job, travel, school, family, and love life.

I think you're going to get a good job someday. And you'll probably also . . .

Check out the World Link video.

Practice your English online at http://elt.heinle.com/worldlink

Review: Units 4-6

1 Storyboard

A Ruben is talking to his teacher, Gina Walker. Complete the conversations. Then tell a partner: Why does Ruben want to talk to Professor Walker?

Later in Ms. Walker's office . . .

B Practice the conversation with a partner. Then change roles and practice again.

Review: Units 4–6

1 Storyboard

Warm Up

10-15 min

Look at the phone conversation between Minh and Martina (on page 48) again. With books closed, ask *Who was Minh? Who was Martina? What did Minh want? Did he get it?* Write two list heads on the board: *Making appointments* and *Polite requests.* Tell students to brainstorm expressions for the lists. Write correct expressions and sentences on the board (even if they weren't in the original conversation or the charts on pages 48 and 49).

A **Ruben is talking to his teacher, Gina Walker. Complete the conversations. Then tell a partner: Why does Ruben want to talk to Professor Walker?**

20 min

Read the instructions and write the question on the board. Students should read through the conversation quickly to get the gist and answer the question. They should not fill in the missing words yet. Tell them they have two minutes. Stop them and check the answer to the question. (He wants to ask for a recommendation.) Tell students to look at the last frame. Do they think she's going to write the recommendation? There may be disagreement because of the *no.* Don't confirm the answer yet. Students can work independently or with a partner to complete the conversation. Before checking answers, repeat the question about the last frame. By now everyone should agree that the answer is *yes.* To check answers it would be helpful, if possible, to enlarge the storyboard enough for everyone to see.

B **Practice the conversation with a partner. Then change roles and practice again.**

5-10 min

Read the Storyboard conversation with students repeating. Pay special attention to reductions like *I'd like to make* (tuhmake) and *would you mind* (wouldja).

Teaching Tip: Choral repetition

When a speech includes long sentences, you have to break them up for repetition. Look for natural breath groups marked by commas or tied together by meaning. Then try the "backward buildup" technique. Say the whole sentence while students listen. Say the last breath group of the sentence, then have students repeat. Say the next-to-last breath group, then have students repeat. Say the last two breath groups together, then have students repeat. Continue this way until students are able to repeat the whole sentence. Then move on to the next one. Finally, put the whole speech together, one full sentence at a time. You can tell the whole group to repeat, then smaller groups or rows, then individuals. Work on pronunciation with smaller groups, so you can hear students better and avoid embarrassing anyone.

B **Teaching Option** **Support/challenge**

Make a grid of six squares on the board, three over three (like the frames in the storyboard). Draw two speech bubbles in each one with these words in the bubbles:

Hello? appointment	office hours time	tomorrow Sure
help applying	OK recommendation	So No

Students should practice until they think they can say the whole conversation from memory, with only these cues. Let volunteers try in front of the class. As soon as one person says the wrong thing (and doesn't correct it immediately), he or she sits down, and another student takes his or her place for the rest of the conversation. (The next student should be standing by so time isn't lost.) The first student(s) to get all the way through, win the round. For more students to have a chance, this can be done in groups. The students are very capable of catching others' errors, and they'll be paying attention while others are speaking. Keep yourself free to referee if any disagreements arise.

2 See It and Say It

Warm Up

10–15 min

Review vocabulary from units 4–6. This is a good time for students to pull out their vocabulary notebooks and share some of their new words with the class. If a student doesn't have a notebook, they can use the Language Summaries in the back of the book. Write the words on the board.

A Look at the neighborhood and discuss the questions with a partner.

20–25 min

With books closed, students can brainstorm a list of chores, errands, and things people do on the street. Write them on the board. With books open, working in pairs, students should study the picture and say what the people are doing. Tell students to look in the windows. Check answers with the class, writing students' sentences on the board until all the possibilities are covered. If students miss something you think they can say, point to it and have them create a sentence together.

A Teaching Option True or false?

With books closed, students can brainstorm a list of chores and errands and things people do on the street. Write them on the board. With books still closed, assign students to groups, and assign part of the list to each group. Groups should write sentences using the word someone in addition to their assigned words. (*Someone is driving to work. Someone is taking a dog for a walk.*) Now students can open their books to the picture and read their sentences aloud one by one as true/false statements about the picture. Everyone should study the picture to decide if each sentence is true or false. Students should explain and justify their answers. In the same groups, ask students to discuss the third question and find a consensus. One student from each group should report to the class.

EXTRA! Writing prompt

20–30 min

Use the last question in **A** as a topic for writing. Tell students to begin by saying whether the neighborhoods are similar or different. Then ask them to describe the buildings, the businesses, the people on the street, and what they are doing. Finally, they should say whether they prefer their neighborhood or the one in the picture, and briefly explain why. They can share their writing with a partner and make notes of their partner's comments.

B Do the following:

20–25 min

(See student book page 67 for complete instructions.)

With books closed, talk about what kinds of places are good for people to meet or relax in their town (cafés, malls, parks, plazas, etc.). What makes them good meeting places? With books open, read the instructions and review means of transportation. Suggest that students recommend a place that's easy to get to from the school—in their neighborhood, near the school, or somewhere else. It isn't necessary to give block-by-block directions. Write a complete conversation on the board:

Student A: Where's a good place to meet my friend after class tomorrow?

Student B: Bix's Café in my neighborhood is nice.

Student A: How can I get there from here?

Student B: Take Bus 11 to North Avenue. It takes about 10 minutes.

If you wish, Student B can go on to give exact directions from the bus stop to the café.

C Switch roles and do B again.

10–25 min

Students can also switch partners, practicing a total of four times in **B** and **C**.

Instructor's Notes

2 See It and Say It

A Look at the neighborhood and discuss the questions with a partner. Answers will vary.

- What household chores and errands can you see people doing?
- What are other people in the picture doing?
- Do you think this neighborhood is a good place to live? Why or why not?
- Is this neighborhood similar to or different from yours? Explain your answer.

B Do the following:

Student A: Where is a good place for people to meet or relax in your neighborhood? Tell your partner.

Student B: Imagine you want to go to this place. Ask your partner to . . .

- give you directions from school.
- tell you how long it takes to get there.

C Switch roles and do **B** again.

How can I get to Bix's Cafe from here?

Take Bus 211 to . . .

3 I Need Your Advice!

A Read sentences 1-6. What advice would you give to someone who made these statements? Think about your answers.

1. I'm always running late.
2. I forgot to bring today's English homework and it's 25% of the class grade.
3. My parents don't like my friends.
4. I have a terrible commute. It takes over two hours every day.
5. I get really nervous when I have to talk to others in English.
6. I bought a new cell phone and it's not working.

B Get into a group of three people. Write the numbers 1 to 6 on six small pieces of paper. Put the numbers in a bag or hat.

- When it's your turn, choose a number. Read aloud the problem in **A** that goes with your number. Explain the problem in more detail.
- Your partners will listen and give you advice.
- Think about their suggestions. Which person gave you the best advice? Why?

4 *Be going to* or *Will*?

A The chart shows the different uses of *be going to* and *will*. Complete the sentences below with *be going to*, *will*, or both.

	to talk about plans you already made	to talk about a sudden decision	to talk about an action that is about to happen	to make a general prediction about the future
be going to	✓		✓	✓
will		✓		✓

1. I decided to take the TOEFL exam. I __am going to__ take it next spring.
2. It's a beautiful evening. I think I __will__ take a walk.
3. The score is 10 to 1 and there's a minute left in the game. Our team __is going to__ lose for sure.
4. I bet there __will OR are going to__ be thousands of people at the free concert in the park tomorrow.
5. What __are you going to__ do this weekend? Do you have any plans?
6. A: The two o'clock movie is sold out, but we still have seats for the four o'clock show.
   B: OK, I __will__ take two tickets for the 4:00 show.
7. Hurry! Class starts in two minutes. We __are going to__ be late!
8. She's really smart. I bet she __is going to/will__ get accepted to a good school.

B Compare your answers with a partner's. Explain why you chose *be going to*, *will*, or both in **A**.

3 I Need Your Advice!

Warm Up

5–10 min

What words and expressions do students recall for giving advice? (Suggested modals: *could, should, ought to, had better.*) What are their negative forms? Write all the forms on the board. How strong is each one? Have students create one or two sentences with each form.

A 10–15 min **Read sentences 1–6. What advice would you give to someone who made these statements? Think about your answers.**

Read the statements with the class. Tell students to prepare advice to give these people. Answer any questions about vocabulary. Write this alternate for number 3 on the board: *I don't like my son's/daughter's friends,* and tell students to prepare different advice for children and parents. Give students enough time to think of advice for each situation. Tell them to make notes of their ideas. Walk around as they work to check their notes, and help with vocabulary and ideas as needed.

B 25–30 min **Get into a group of three people. Write the numbers 1 to 6 on six small pieces of paper. Put the numbers in a bag or hat.**

Write the expressions below on the board while students are working on **A**. These expressions can be used by anyone in the conversation, depending on what has already been said:

Look at it this way.
I know what you're saying, but . . .
OK, but look on the bright side.
Are you serious?
Oh, come on! Really?
I hear you, but . . .
Yes, but on the other hand . . .

These expressions are for Student A:
That's a really good idea, but . . .
That's a pretty good idea. Maybe . . .
Thank you.
Thanks for your help.

Review the expressions on the board and the instructions. Explain that in each conversation, one person is asking for advice (Student A), and two people are giving advice (Students B and C). Say that Students B and C can also ask Student A questions to understand the situation better. Student A comments on their advice and thanks them both. Walk around as they talk, helping as needed, and noting which groups are speaking more easily and comfortably. At the end, ask some of the more comfortable groups to perform their conversations for the class.

4 *Be going to* or *Will?*

Warm Up

10 min

With books closed, give a brief "quiz" on *be going to* and *will.* Write these questions on the board. Remind students that the answer can be both *be going to* and *will.*

Which do you use to talk about plans you already made?

Which do you use to talk about a sudden decision?

Which do you use to talk about an action that is about to happen?

Which do you use to make general predictions about the future?

Have them answer orally. Write all of their answers on the board—right or wrong. You will check answers in **A**.

A 10 min **The chart shows the different uses of *be going to* and *will.* Complete the sentences below with *be going to, will,* or both.**

Students can complete the chart by themselves. Check the answers and compare them with the notes on the board from the Warm Up. Ask students to tell you which answers on the board are wrong. Cross them out. Were there right answers for all of the questions? Go on to the next sentences. Students should be able to understand all of them without explanation, except possibly number 6. Explain or have them tell you that A is selling tickets and B wants to see the movie. Show them the instructions for exercise B, below, and tell them to think about the rules in the chart as they complete each sentence.

B 10–15 min **Compare your answers with a partner's. Explain why you chose *be going to, will,* or both in A.**

Students should explain their answers by referring to a rule in the chart and explaining why the sentence fits that rule: What plans? What decision? What action? What prediction?

Instructor's Notes

5 Listening

Warm Up

5 min

Review percents and fractions in English. Write on the board randomly: $\frac{1}{4}$, 50%, 66%, $\frac{1}{10}$, $\frac{2}{3}$, 25%, 10%, $\frac{1}{5}$, $\frac{1}{2}$, 20%. Ask students to pronounce them. (*One fourth or a quarter, fifty percent,* etc.) Then tell students to match every fraction with a percentage. (*One fourth is twenty-five percent,* etc.)

A **Read the poll below and choose your answer. Then take a class vote. What was the most common answer in your class?**

10–20 min

Students can ask each other the question in pairs, reading the question and all of the answers (including the letters a-c, as in a telephone poll). Partners should answer with just the letter. For the class results, students report their partners' answers. Ask for a show of hands for each answer, and write the totals on the board.

Some of your students may be married already. In this case, substitute a different poll question and answers. You can supply one yourself or have the class create one together. Rule out topics that might embarrass anyone.

B **A magazine asked a group of university students for their opinions on different topics. Listen and put the charts in the order (1–4) you hear them talked about.**

CD 1 Track 41
10–20 min

Show students where to write the numbers—over each chart. Tell them that to identify a chart, they need to listen for the quantities it shows. Ask what words they might hear about the chart on the left. Write their possible ideas on the board (such as *50%, half, the same number,* etc.). Play the audio one to three times, until most of the students have numbered the charts. Walk around as they work so you know when they are ready. Check answers with the class.

If students ask about the meaning of *plastic surgery*, use the information box in **D** to explain it. Ask quickly if they know of anyone (personally or a celebrity) who has had plastic surgery. What did they change? Do they look better now? Are they happy with the result?

C **Listen again and label the parts of each chart in B with the correct numbers / percentages. Some numbers will not be given. You have to guess them.**

CD 1 Track 41
10–20 min

Students should listen for the same quantities again, but this time they write them. Point out that two quantities have already been written on the charts. Explain to students that they aren't just guessing the numbers that are not in the audio, they have to figure them out logically by doing the math. Again, play the audio until most of the students have finished. Sketch the four charts on the board, and write the numbers on them when you check answers. Leave them on the board.

D **Look at your answers (1–4) in B. What do the students interviewed think? Read the sentences below and then choose the correct answer.**

15–20 min

Review quantity expressions. With students' books closed, turn to page 39 in your book, and sketch the information box (top right) on the board. Include the percentages and the vertical arrow. Also include *all (of)* and *none (of)*. Do not include the other four quantity expressions. Ask students to brainstorm all the quantity expressions they think might go on the scale. Write correct expressions on the board randomly. (Some possible additions to the original list: *half (of), a quarter (of),* etc.) Tell students to discuss and decide in what order the words should go. When the order is correct, write them in the scale from 100% to 0%. (If you have not explained plastic surgery yet, do it now as described in **B**.)

Tell students to open their books. Explain the instructions, tell students to scan the sentences for unfamiliar words, and answer their questions about vocabulary. At the end, check answers with the class. Point to the charts on the board to explain answers.

E **What do you think about the four opinions in D? Compare your ideas with a partner's. Explain your reasons.**

10–20 min

Review useful expressions for disagreeing (page 38). Pairs will work well if both students are confident speakers and have strong opinions. Otherwise, for a greater range of opinions and a livelier discussion, put students in groups of three or four.

Instructor's Notes

5 Listening

A Read the poll below and choose your answer. Then take a class vote. What was the most common answer in your class?

POLL:

Do you think you'll get married?

a. Yes, definitely. I want to get married.
b. Yes, maybe someday, but I'm not sure when.
c. No, never. Marriage isn't for me.

CD 1 Track 41

B A magazine asked a group of university students for their opinions on different topics. Listen and put the charts in the order (1-4) you hear them talked about.

____

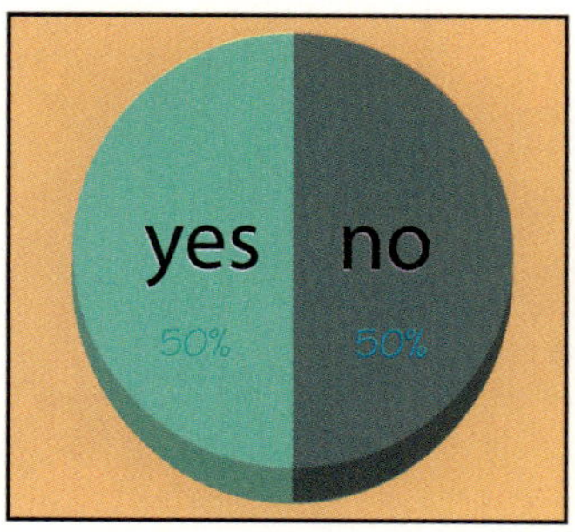

____

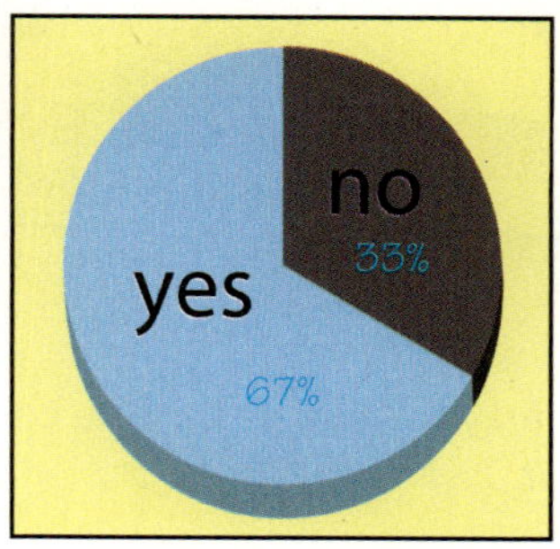

____

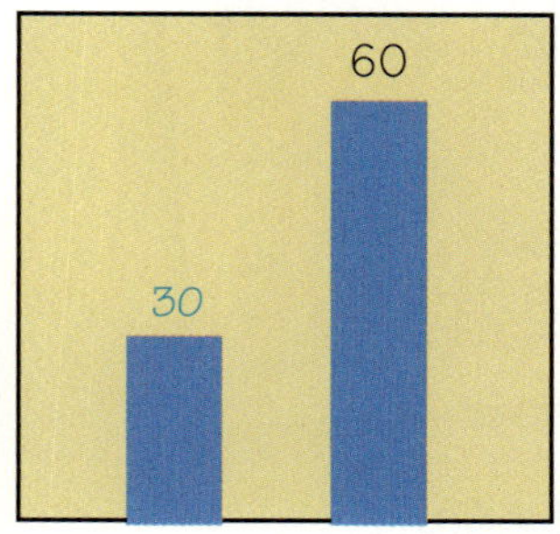

____

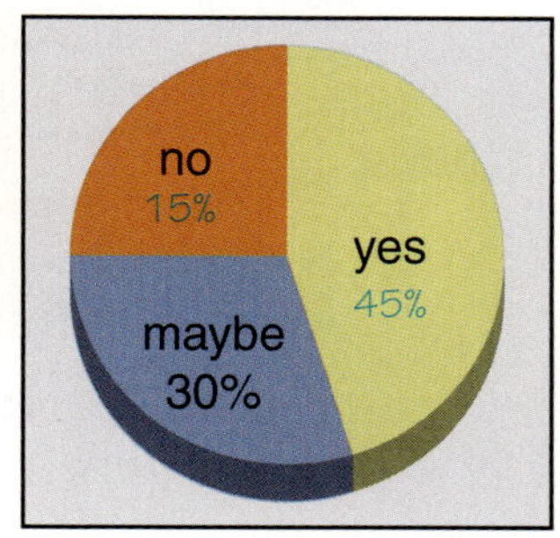

CD 1 Track 41

C Listen again and label the parts of each chart in **B** with the correct numbers / percentages. Some numbers will not be given. You have to guess them.

D Look at your answers (1-4) in **B**. What do the students interviewed think? Read the sentences below and then choose the correct answer.

Chart 1: Most / Some of the students think it's OK for couples with children to get divorced.

Chart 2: This year, a couple / more of them think studying abroad is good.

Chart 3: Most / Half of them think the university entrance exam is too difficult.

Chart 4: A lot / Almost none of them think plastic surgery is OK.

plastic surgery: a medical operation that changes or improves your looks

E What do you think about the four opinions in **D**? Compare your ideas with a partner's. Explain your reasons.

I think it's OK for couples with kids to get divorced.

Sorry, but I don't agree . . .

7 Let's Celebrate

Lesson A Party time!

1 Vocabulary Link **Different kinds of parties**

A Look at the photos of the different parties. Then take the quiz below. Circle the correct words.

American Party Quiz

1. When you turn 21, your friends may have a party for you. Everyone celebrates you *getting your first job* / *becoming an adult.*
2. A rave is an all-night party. Lots of people get together to dance and have a good time. It's usually outdoors or in a large building. It's often pretty *quiet* / *wild.*
3. When people get a new house or apartment, sometimes they throw a housewarming party. If you're invited to this type of party, bring the host *a gift* / *some money* for his or her new house.
4. Before the wedding, a *man's* / *woman's* friends may plan a bachelor party for *him* / *her.* It's often a rowdy celebration of the person's last "free" days before marriage.
5. Every February, two American football teams compete in a big sporting event called the Super Bowl. Many people get together at friends' houses to eat, drink, and root for their favorite *team* / *player.*
6. You have a baby shower for a pregnant woman *before* / *after* her baby is born. A close female friend or relative hosts the party and the woman gets presents for the child.

B With a partner, check your answers on page 154. Then discuss these questions.

1. In your country, are there parties like the ones in the United States? How are they similar to or different from the American ones?
2. When was the last time you went to a party?
   - What kind of party was it?
   - Who threw it?
   - How many people were invited?
   - Did you have a good time?

What two phrases in **A** mean the same thing as *have a party*?

Phrases that mean have a party: throw a party, host a party

Party time!
Unit 7, Lesson A

1 Vocabulary Link

Different kinds of parties

Warm Up

5–10 min

Ask students, *What was the best party you ever went to? Why was it special?*

A 15–20 min **Look at the photos of the different parties. Then take the quiz below. Circle the correct words.**

Ask students to describe what they see in the photos. Who are the people? Where are they? What are they doing? They may not be able to answer all of the questions for all of the photos. Students should read the quiz once, but not circle the answers yet. Write the words in blue on the board. Students should try to figure out as many as possible together, before you explain any words. Then students should read again and circle the answers.

Word Bank: Things at parties

birthday girl *or* boy, birthday cake, candles

spotlights, light show

host, hostess, gift, guest

buddies, bachelor, groom

football, sandwich, pitcher of beer, salads, chips and salsa

pregnant, mother-to-be, expectant mother, bib

Language Tip: Collocations with *party*

Verbs: **go to a** party, **crash a** party, **have a** party, **give a** party, **throw a** party

Adjectives: **a big** party, **small** party, **boring** party, **fun** party, **good** party, **noisy** party, **rowdy** party, **wild** party

B 20–25 min **With a partner, check your answers on page 154. Then discuss these questions.**

With the class, brainstorm other types of parties, and list them on the board (possibilities: anniversary party, going-away party, beach party, costume party, dinner party, graduation party, office party, pool party, retirement party, surprise party). If students are from the same country, use question 1 for pair work. To follow up, two pairs should get together and compare their ideas. Do they agree completely or only partly? They can tell the class. If your students are from different countries, form mixed groups of three to five students. Ask each group to report to the class about one type of party that is similar in each country, or is different. Students should discuss question 2 in pairs or groups of four.

Language Tip: Wild *and* rowdy

Wild and *rowdy* can have different meanings for different age groups and cultures. *Wild* typically means excited or energetic behavior, such as a lot of dancing or talking loudly. But it can also mean out of control with too much drinking. *Rowdy* is usually meant to describe loud parties (perhaps from music). But it can also mean rough or causing problems, such as fights. As the teacher, you can determine your students' ability to comprehend that these words can have negative as well as positive meanings.

Culture Tip: Baby showers

In the Americas and most European countries, baby showers are parties given to a mother-to-be before her child is born. The gifts are usually for the baby or for preparing the house for the baby's arrival.

In some cultures, it is bad luck to bring gifts for the baby before it is born. In Asia, it is typical to have a party for the baby after it is 100 days old. In Arabic countries, people often bring presents of gold for a baby after it is born.

Culture Tip: Gift giving

In the Americas and most European countries, when someone gives you a wrapped gift, you react with pleasant surprise and then accept it and open it in front of the giver. It is important to say how lovely it is.

In Asia, people usually do not open gifts in front of the giver. They thank the person and place it aside. They open the gift later, after everyone has left.

2 Listening An important day

Skills: Listen for main idea; Categorize information; Synthesize information in order to summarize

Warm Up

5 min

With books closed, say, *Some parties are for everyone, like a New Year's Eve party or an office party. Others are for just one person, like a birthday party. What other kinds of parties are given for just one person?* Make a list on the board.

A CD 2 Track 2 10–15 min

Two speakers are going to talk about an important celebration in their countries. Read sentences 1 and 2. Then listen and complete them.

Write these questions on the board: *Where is the first speaker from? How about the second speaker?* Play the audio once while students complete the answers. Read the questions and play the audio again. If students think they already know the answers, they should listen to confirm them the second time they hear the audio.

B CD 2 Track 3 10–15 min

Read sentences a–l below. Then listen and match a celebration with the correct answers. Some answers are true for both celebrations.

As a way to help students understand the sentences and keep them in mind, show them that some of the sentences are pairs: *a* and *b* are about age, *e* and *g* are about who it's for, etc. Tell students to look for other pairs before listening (*a/b, c/d, e/g, h/i, k/l*). Play the audio two or three times, or until most of the students have filled in the lines.

C 20–25 min

Choose one celebration from above. Use your answers in A and B and describe it to a partner.

Students can do this as a short, prepared talk rather than a conversation. Put students with the same topic in pairs to prepare what they're going to say. They should not write out their talk and read it; they should write their ideas in note form. When pairs have finished, each student should find a new partner who prepared a different topic. Walk around as they work and remind them to read, look up, and speak.

C Teaching Option **Support/challenge**

Some students are eager to work more independently and try more challenging activities. You can let them describe another celebration that they are familiar with, one that is not described in the book. They should provide the same kind of information as is given for the Rose Party and Coming of Age Day. Check while they are working to help and make sure they are on task. When it's time to speak, pair them with another student like themselves.

ASK ANSWER

Students from the same country can discuss how their ceremony is similar and how it's different. If they don't have a similar one, would they like to? Why or why not? Walk around and listen while they talk. If there's something that everyone would be interested in, ask those students to tell the class.

Culture Tip: Coming of age celebrations

Many cultures have coming of age celebrations. In Judaism, children have a *bar mitzvah* (for boys) or *bat mitzvah* (for girls). They recite parts of their holy book (*Torah*) and have a large party.

In many Latin American countries, the *Quinceañera* is a big celebration held for a girl when she turns 15. Often there is a symbolic candle lighting ceremony.

3 Pronunciation Reduced *want to*

A CD 2 Track 4 10–15 min

Listen and notice the pronunciation of *want to* in the sentences and questions.

Students should read the sentences and notice that they are invitations. Remind students that they worked with *gonna* (reduced pronunciation of *going to*) in Unit 6. Read the i-box aloud, emphasizing that *wanna* is for speaking only, not writing. Students should read the sentences aloud, then you can answer any questions about meaning. Play the audio once. The second time, pause after each sentence for students to repeat. If necessary, model the verbs yourself for separate repetition.

B CD 2 Track 5 10–15 min

Listen and complete the dialog. Then practice it with a partner.

Tell students to skim the dialog and say what the situation is. Play the audio once while students read it. Play it again line by line, pausing to give students time to complete the sentences. Check the answers on the board. Before pairs practice, play each sentence for students to repeat. Pairs should switch roles to practice both parts. For pairs that finish quickly, tell them to practice again, extending the conversation until they agree on something to do this weekend.

2 Listening An important day

CD 2 Track 2

A Two speakers are going to talk about an important celebration in their countries. Read sentences 1 and 2. Then listen and complete them.

1. Both speakers are talking about a type of __________ celebration.
   a. birthday b. graduation c. pre-wedding
2. In both countries, this celebration is important because it's when a person becomes an adult / is officially an adult.

CD 2 Track 3

B Read sentences a–l below. Then listen and match a celebration with the correct answers. Some answers are true for both celebrations.

The Rose Party: b, d, e, f, i, j, k

Coming of Age Day: a, c, f, g, h, j, l

a. You are 20.
b. You are 15.
c. It happens in Japan.
d. It happens in El Salvador.
e. It's only for young women.
f. You wear special clothes.
g. Everyone celebrates together on a day in January.
h. There's a ceremony at City Hall first.
i. There's a religious ceremony first.
j. You get gifts.
k. Many people come to your home to eat and dance.
l. You go with friends to different clubs and parties.

C Choose one celebration from above. Use your answers in **A** and **B** and describe it to a partner.

ASK ANSWER

Is there a similar celebration in your country? When is it and what happens?

3 Pronunciation Reduced *want to*

CD 2 Track 4

In spoken English, *want to* is often pronounced *wanna*.

A Listen and notice the pronunciation of *want to* in the sentences and questions.

1. Do you want to have coffee after class?
2. We want to have a party on Saturday.
3. Do you want to get together this weekend?
4. My parents want to invite you to dinner.

CD 2 Track 5

B Listen and complete the dialog. Then practice it with a partner.

A: What do you want to do this weekend?

B: I'm not sure. Oh, wait . . . I know. I want to see that new sci-fi movie. Do you want to come with me?

A: I don't really want to see that movie.

B: OK. What do you want to do?

4 Speaking Do you want to go with me?

CD 2
Track 6

A Listen to the conversation. Then answer the questions with a partner.

1. Omar is going to a party. What kind of party is it? How does Omar invite Lane? *Omar is going to a costume party. Omar invites Lane by saying, "Do you want to go with me?"*
2. Does Lane accept? What does she say? *Lane accepts by saying, "I'd love to go."*

Omar: Hey, Lane. My classmate Sayuri is having a party this weekend.

Lane: Really?

Omar: Yeah, it's a costume party.

Lane: Sounds like fun.

Omar: Do you want to go with me?

Lane: Are you sure? I don't really know Sayuri.

Omar: No problem. She said I could invite a friend.

Lane: OK, then. I'd love to go. When exactly is it?

Omar: On Saturday night.

Lane: Wow, that's the day after tomorrow! I need to get a costume.

Omar: Me, too. There's a good place near here that rents them. Let's go there after school.

Lane: Sounds good!

B Practice the conversation with a partner.

5 Speaking Strategy

A Use the Useful Expressions and the words in the box below to form invitations.

How'd = How would

Useful Expressions

Inviting someone to do something		Accepting or refusing an invitation
Do you want **Would you like** **How'd you like**	to go with me?	Sure, I'd love to. That sounds great. I'm sorry, but I can't. I have plans. Unfortunately, I can't. I have to work. I'd love to, but I'm busy.

study for our English test	see a movie	after class	tomorrow
come to my birthday party	your idea:__________	this weekend	tonight

1. *How'd you like to study for our English test after class?*
2. ____________________
3. ____________________
4. ____________________

B Take turns inviting your partner to the events in **A**. Refuse two of your partner's invitations. Give an excuse (a reason for saying "no").

We have an English test this Friday. How'd you like to study for it after class?

I'd love to but . . .

4 Speaking Do you want to go with me?

5 min

Warm Up

With books closed, ask students what kinds of things they invite people to do. List their suggestions on the board.

CD 2 Track 6

15–20 min

A Listen to the conversation. Then answer the questions with a partner.

Tell students to read the title, look at the pictures, and guess the situation. With books closed, write two of the questions on the board: *What kind of party is Omar going to? Is Lane going to go with him?* Play the audio and check answers. With books open, read the other questions. Tell students to write down Omar's and Lane's exact words, one sentence for each.

10 min

B Practice the conversation with a partner.

Play the conversation sentence by sentence, with students repeating. Model the longer sentences in parts until students can repeat them completely.

> **Teaching Tip: Stand and deliver**
>
> If your students' energy level falls during the class, energize the class by telling them to stand and face each other for a practice conversation. Holding their books, they should use the "read-look up-speak" technique, making eye contact with their partner. If they are able to try the conversation without the book, this is even more energizing.

> **Culture Tip: Fancy dress**
>
> "Fancy dress" in British English means the same as "costume" in American English. In American English, "fancy dress" could mean formal clothes. Check before you go!

5 Speaking Strategy

20–25 min

A Use the Useful Expressions and the words in the box below to form invitations.

Read the Useful Expressions. Choose one student to read the invitations aloud and five students to read the answers. Remind students to use the reduced pronunciation of *want to* and *would you.* Point out the information box and model the pronunciation of *How'd*. You could also preview *have to*, pronounced *haftuh*, which is practiced in Unit 12. Students can work alone or in pairs to write sentences of invitation. Walk around while they work, and ask individuals to say one of their invitations for you. Help with pronunciation as needed.

10–15 min

B Take turns inviting your partner to the events in A. Refuse two of your partner's invitations. Give an excuse (a reason for saying "no").

Students should review the refusals in Useful Expressions. With the class, brainstorm a list of other excuses for refusing an invitation. Write these on the board. Ask one or two pairs to demonstrate the conversation for the class. Students can switch partners for more practice.

> **Culture Tip: Saying "no" or "maybe" to an invitation**
>
> When refusing an invitation in the UK, the U.S., Canada, Australia, and New Zealand, a specific excuse (*I have a test the next day.*) sounds more sincere than a general one (*I have plans*). In fact, a very weak or general excuse is sometimes a kind way to say that you are not interested in the person. (In jokes, people say, "I have to organize my sock drawer," or "I have to wash my hair.") On the other hand, sometimes you would like to go but are not sure that you can. In that case, you can say, *Can I get back to you?*, or *I'm not sure I can. I need to check my schedule.*

Instructor's Notes

6 Language Link

Similarity and agreement with *so, too, either, neither*

Warm Up

5 min

Ask a series of questions that will allow you to respond to a student's answer with *So do I, Neither do I, So am I,* or *Neither am I.* Make sure you know what the student's answer will be! For example, *Do you speak Hawaiian? No, I don't. Neither do I.*

A 10–15 min **Study the information in the chart. Then match each of student A's statements below with the correct response. Check your answers with a partner.**

Hold up the chart while you explain it, or copy it on the board. Point out that the answers have affirmative or negative verbs, but all of them say that you are the same, or you agree. You can't say, "I'm different from you" with these expressions. Draw students' attention to the information box and read it aloud. They should understand that *casual* doesn't mean *incorrect.* Ask four pairs of students to read the four statements in the chart and give a response for each one. Tell students to look at the verbs in the matching exercise and make their responses agree with the statements. In number 5, the verb is *wasn't.* They need to find a negative response with *be* in the past tense—the second one, *Neither did I.*

B 10–15 min **Agree with each statement in at least two ways.**

To prepare, students should read each statement aloud. Respond to them with some right answers and some wrong ones. Tell students to raise their hands for right answers and sit still for wrong ones. Explain that there are three possible answers for each statement; students write two.

C 5–10 min **Complete the statements below with information about yourself.**

Explain that this is not grammar practice—it's preparation for the conversations in **D**. Conversations are more interesting with true information, so students can change the statements to make them true. For example, if someone hates to clean the house on weekends, they can change statement 1 to *I hate to . . .* or *I don't like to . . . .* This means that partners will need to pay careful attention in **D** in order to answer correctly.

D 10–15 min **Compare your opinions in C with a partner. Then switch roles and do the exercise again.**

These are true conversations, so students can disagree. Point out the new response: *Not me.* Ask two pairs of students to demonstrate the example conversations, one with *So do I . . .* (and continuing with student A's answer), and the other with *Not me . . . .* Tell students to extend the conversations with at least one question and answer.

EXTRA! Find someone the same as you.

20–30 min

Students write five statements about things they like, enjoy doing, and/or are good at. This is more fun if the things are unusual or if most people don't like them. Give a few examples to get them started: *I love opera! I really enjoy doing laundry. I'm pretty good at fixing cars.* Walk around while they work to help with vocabulary. When they're ready, they should stand up with their papers, walk around, and say their statements to different classmates. They should say, not read, the statements. When they find someone who likes the same thing, they write the person's name next to the statement. To follow up, ask students to report something interesting they heard: *Kimiko designs her own clothes, but I don't. Yuri sings with a band, and so do I.*

Teaching Tip: Vocabulary one-on-one

Personal interactions with their teacher can be a powerful motivator for students. For this reason, accustom students to asking you for vocabulary help during conversations with partners. They can raise a hand to call you. Just as important, tell them to keep talking with their partners until you can get to them—they will understand if you can't get to each one before the end of the exercise. In a large class, to distribute your attention more evenly, go to a different part of the classroom each time. Tell students to put the words you give them in their vocabulary notebooks.

6 Language Link **Similarity and agreement with *so, too, either, neither***

A Study the information in the chart. Then match each of student A's statements below with the correct response. Check your answers with a partner.

	Affirmative Answers	Negative Answers
with *be*	I am going to Sayuri's party. So am I. / I am, too. / Me, too.	I'm not going to Sayuri's party. Neither am I. / I'm not, either. / Me, neither.
other verbs	I need a costume for the party. So do I. / I do, too. / Me, too.	I don't have a costume for the party. Neither do I. / I don't, either. / Me, neither.

Student A says . . .	**Student B responds . . .**
1. I'm having a party this weekend.	Neither was I.
2. Tim and Monica speak Spanish.	Neither did I.
3. I missed the bus this morning.	So do I.
4. I was late for my first class.	So did I.
5. The teacher wasn't here yesterday.	I was, too.
6. I didn't have a good time at that party.	So am I.

Me, too and *me, neither* are common in casual conversation.

B Agree with each statement in at least two ways.

1. I like to go to parties.
   So do I. / I do, too. / Me, too.
2. I'm never late to class.
   Neither am I. / I'm not, either. / Me, neither.
3. I don't speak Italian.
   Neither do I. / I don't, either. / Me, neither.
4. I'm planning to study abroad next year.
   So am I. / I am, too. / Me, too.
5. I think I did well on the exam.
   So do I. / I do, too. / Me, too.

C Complete the statements below with information about yourself.

1. I like to ______________________ on the weekend.
2. I don't like to ______________________ during class.
3. I need to ______________________ before I graduate.
4. I think ______________________ parties are fun.

D Compare your opinions in **C** with a partner. Then switch roles and do the exercise again.

I like to go out with my friends on the weekend.

So do I. Where do you usually go?

Not me. I like to hang out and relax at home.

7 Communication **Party planning**

A Plan a party with a partner. Choose an item from each category or think of an item of your own.

Type of party

a. a costume party

b. a pool party

c. a birthday party

Place

a. a friend's house

b. a nightclub

c. a park

Type of food

a. finger foods

b. barbecue

c. pasta and salad

B Invite four other pairs to your party. Ask and answer questions about their parties. Complete the invitations below.

Would you like to come to our party next week?

What kind of party is it?

It's a surprise birthday party for Antonio. He turns 22 next Friday.

Type of party: ______________________
Place: ______________________
Food: ______________________

Type of party: ______________________
Place: ______________________
Food: ______________________

Type of party: ______________________
Place: ______________________
Food: ______________________

Type of party: ______________________
Place: ______________________
Food: ______________________

C Discuss the parties in **B** with your partner. What do you think of each one? Choose your favorite together and then share your choice with the class.

I really like the surprise birthday party.

So do I. But the costume party sounds fun too.

7 Communication Party planning

Warm Up

5 min

With books closed, ask students about their favorite things to do at a party. List their suggestions on the board.

A Plan a party with a partner. Choose an item from each category or think of an item of your own.

15–20 min

Brainstorm additional ideas for the three categories and write them on the board. Tell students to look at **B**. They need to prepare all the information to complete the invitations. They should also prepare additional information for every answer. Point out that in the example in **B**, the answer is not just, "It's a surprise party."

Culture Tip: Fingers or forks

In many countries around the world, including India, Ghana, the Philippines, and Afghanistan, it's customary to eat most things with your fingers, but only with the right hand. In Italy, utensils (knife, fork, spoon) are used for almost everything, and in Japan, chopsticks. In the United States, many things are eaten with the fingers that would not be acceptable in Europe or Japan. In casual eating—especially on the street, which is very common—almost anything can be eaten with the fingers unless it makes a mess. Good manners require utensils for most things at the table. At cocktail parties where people do not sit down, finger foods are served for convenience.

Word Bank: Finger foods for a party

sandwiches
savory pastries
mini pizzas
small skewers of meat
cheese and crackers
nuts and dried fruit
olives
pretzels
chips and dip, chips and salsa
sliced raw vegetables
sliced fruit

B Invite four other pairs to your party. Ask and answer questions about their parties. Complete the invitations below.

20–30 min

Students can walk around the classroom in pairs inviting their classmates to their party. The invited pair asks at least three questions to complete one of their invitations. The hosts of the party give additional information with every answer.

Large Class Option

Students can make more elaborate invitations. These should include more information than what is printed in **B**. Include time, activities, food, and if there is any special dress required. Students may decorate the invitation if they'd like. Then have the students turn to the people closest to them and invite them to the party. They should find at least two people who will attend their party. They should use the language in **B** and **C** with their partners.

C Discuss the parties in B with your partner. What do you think of each one? Choose your favorite together and then share your choice with the class.

10–20 min

With their original partners, students should look at the information they wrote on the four invitations. They can discuss the parties and decide which one will probably be the most fun. Each pair then reports their choice to the class and explains their reasons.

Large Class Option

As the teacher, choose five invitations randomly from the class and read them aloud. Students should vote on a favorite party by raising their hands.

EXTRA! Writing prompts

30 min

1. Describe a party planned by you or someone you know. Answer some of these questions. What kind of party was it? Where did it take place? How many people attended? What food and drink was served? What did the guests do during the party? Was it a successful party? Did you have a good time?
2. What was the best party you ever attended? Describe it. What made it so good?
3. What was the worst party you ever attended? Describe it. What made it so bad?

Instructor's Notes

Festivals and holidays

Unit 7, Lesson B

1 Vocabulary Link

International festivals

Warm Up

5–10 min

To introduce the idea of international festivals, give a mock quiz. Students can work together to match the festivals, countries, and the years they were first held. The answers are matched below. Write the festivals on the board, then write the countries and years in a different order.

Cannes Film Festival	France	1946
Festival of San Fermín	Spain	1591
Montreal International Jazz Festival	Canada	1980
Oktoberfest	Germany	1810
South by Southwest	United States	1987

Culture Tip: Festival facts

The Cannes Film Festival is the world's oldest and most influential film festival.

The Festival of San Fermín is a traditional festival honoring the patron saint of Pamplona, but it is most famous for the "running of the bulls." Bulls run from their pen to the bullring, and hundreds of (mostly) young men run with the bulls, trying to stay ahead of them.

The Montreal International Jazz Festival is the largest jazz festival in the world.

Oktoberfest is all about drinking beer and eating. It attracts as many as 6.5 million people a year.

South by Southwest has music, film, and an interactive conference for emerging technology.

A 15–25 min **Read about the three festivals. Then match a word or phrase in blue with the correct definition below.**

Choose three students to read aloud about the festivals. Then students can read the definitions below. Students should place the definitions below in the sentences above to see which ones work. Say that 4. defines an adjective. Which define nouns? (2., 3., 8.) Which define verbs? (1., 5., 6., 7., 9.) Students should then read all three texts in **A** and complete the definitions. Tell them to write the number of the text (1–3) next to each answer. This will be helpful when checking answers.

Point out the box labeled *Complete the chart.* The three verb forms are in **A**. *Performance* is not in **A**. Students can work alone or in pairs to complete the chart. Check answers by drawing the chart on the board and students telling you how to complete it. Tell students that if a word can have *the* before it, it's a noun; if a word can have *to* before it, it's a verb. Write *the* and *to* in the chart and have students repeat the noun and verb phrases.

Culture Tip: Carnival

Carnival is a festival that takes place before the start of the Christian period of Lent, a 40-day period of fasting and prayer. Lent begins on a Wednesday (in February or March). In the days before Lent begins, people celebrate Carnival by eating, drinking, dancing, and having fun. Probably the most famous Carnival celebration is the one in Rio de Janeiro, Brazil, but many other cities around the world celebrate it too.

B 15–20 min **Get into a group of three people. Each person chooses one festival from A. Use your own words to tell your group about it by answering these questions:**

(See student book page 75 for complete instructions.)

In groups, assign each student a festival (tell students to count off from 1 to 3). Tell them that when they talk about it, their books will be closed. They should re-read about their festival with the three questions in mind and to remember the answers. Then tell them to close their books and talk about their festival to their partners.

ASK ANSWER

In pairs or small groups, students should ask each other the questions and discuss their answers. To follow up, ask whose partners chose Carnival. Write the total number on the board and quickly find out the reasons why. Do the same with the other two festivals.

Lesson B Festivals and holidays

1 Vocabulary Link International festivals

A Read about the three festivals. Then match a word or phrase in blue with the correct definition below.

World Link Adventure

World Link Adventure | Home | Destinations | Video | Blogs | Maps | Search

International Festivals: Where do you want to go?

Carnival *(Trinidad)*

One of the largest Carnival celebrations in the world takes place in Trinidad in mid-February or early March every year. The streets of Port of Spain (the capital) are full of thousands of people watching colorful parades and dancing to music. People also compete in contests to win first prize for best costume or musical performance.

The International Festival of the Sahara *(Tunisia)*

For four days at the end of December, thousands of people gather together in Douz, a village near the Sahara Desert, to celebrate the traditions of the desert people. There are horse and camel races, and dancing and musical performances.

The Rainforest World Music Festival *(Malaysia)*

In early July, musicians from many different countries participate in this three-day "world music" event. Many afternoon performances are held in small village houses. In the evening, artists usually perform on large outdoor stages.

1. happens ___is held___, ___takes place___
2. a competition ___contest___
3. a competition in which one tries to be the fastest ___race___
4. filled, having a lot of something ___full___
5. to sing, dance, act, or play music in front of people ___perform___
6. to do the best in a competition ___win (first prize)___
7. to come together in a group ___gather___
8. something given to the winner ___prize___
9. to join in an activity ___participate___

Complete the chart.

Noun	Verb	Person (noun)
participation	participate	participant
performance	perform	performer
win	win	winner

ASK ANSWER

Which festival in **A** would you like to go to? Why?

B Get into a group of three people. Each person chooses one festival from **A**. Use your own words to tell your group about it by answering these questions:

- What's the festival called?
- Where and when does it happen?
- What happens at the festival?

2 Listening The Race of Hope

CD 2 Track 7

A Read the sentences below. Then listen to a news report. Choose the best answer for each item.

1. The main topic of the news report is ___.

   a. Cameroon b. a prize
   c. a race d. a performance

2. This year, the woman, Nichelle, is a ___.

   a. reporter b. winner
   c. watcher d. participant

3. She's from ___.

   a. Cameroon b. Kenya
   c. Ethiopia d. the U.S.

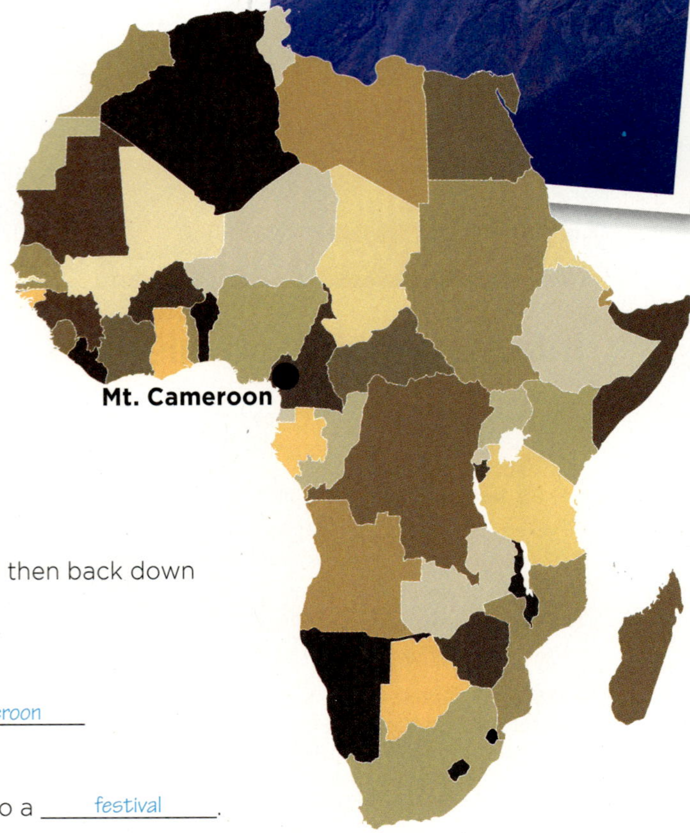

CD 2 Track 7

B Listen again and complete the notes.

1. Where the event is held: Cameroon
2. When it takes place: In February
3. What people do: run up a mountain OR volcano and then back down
4. Distance: 42 km
5. Number of participants: about 600
6. To date, country all winners are from: Cameroon
7. Prize: $10,000
8. Other events: During the weekend, there's also a festival.

CD 2 Track 8

C Why do you think this event is called "The Race of Hope"? Listen to part of the interview again. Then tell a partner your ideas. Two reasons why it might be called "The Race of Hope": 1. It's a tough race—42 km up and back down an active volcano. People hope to finish the race, but many start and can't finish. 2. The race winner gets $10,000 and that's a lot of money in Cameroon.

3 Reading Get ready to get dirty

A You are going to read about two festivals. Look at the title of the reading and the photos on the next page. Answer the questions. Then read the article and check your answers.

1. What's happening in the photos?
2. What kind of festivals do you think they are?

B What does each festival item symbolize? Match an item with its meaning. Two answers are extra.

Festival item	symbolize(s) . . .
the oranges	the end of all bad things
the red hat	a beautiful woman
the large fire	the rocks people originally used
the colored powder	an evil man
	you don't want to fight
	a new beginning

2 Listening The Race of Hope

Skills: Listen for main idea and key details; Infer information; Draw conclusions

Warm Up

5 min

With books closed, ask students if they (or anyone they know) have ever participated as a runner in a big race. Where was it? How long was the race? Why did they run?

A CD 2 Track 7 10–15 min

Read the sentences below. Then listen to a news report. Choose the best answer for each item.

Point out the title, "The Race of Hope." Tell students to locate Mt. Cameroon on the map of Africa. What do they think the photograph shows? Review the questions and tell students to guess any answers they can. Give them time to do this, and then play the audio so they can check and complete their answers.

> **Language Tip: *Mt.***
>
> *Mt.* is the abbreviation of *Mount*. It's the first word in the names of many mountains: Mt. Fuji, Mt. Kilimanjaro, Mt. Everest. In writing it is abbreviated. *Mt.* never comes at the end of the name. In that case, *Mountain* is used: Bear Mountain, the Rocky Mountains.

B CD 2 Track 7

Listen again and complete the notes.

Before listening again, students should complete any notes they can.

B 10 min **Teaching Option** Support/challenge

Explain that notes are normally written for the note-taker's own use, when speed is important and grammar isn't. Ask one student to read a note and one volunteer to say the note as a *wh-* question. If necessary, prompt their questions with these words: 1. *Where is*, 2. *When does*, 3. *What do*, 4. *How long*, 5. *How many*, 6. *Where are*, 7. *How much,* 8. *What other*. Or, students can work in pairs to write the questions.

C CD 2 Track 8 10–15 min

Why do you think this event is called "The Race of Hope"? Listen to part of the interview again. Then tell a partner your ideas.

Tell students that the question is not directly answered in the interview. They are to make an informed guess based on the interview and their own knowledge of the world.

3 Reading Get ready to get dirty

Skills: Use photos and background knowledge to make predictions about what you will read; Scan for specific information; Guess the meaning of words from context; Categorize information; Summarize

Warm Up

5 min

With books closed, ask students if their country (or countries) has any festivals that take place in just one town. What happens at the festival? Do tourists go, or just local people?

A 10–15 min

You are going to read about two festivals. Look at the title of the reading and the photos on the next page. Answer the questions. Then read the article and check your answers.

Before students read, point out the footnotes. If appropriate, explain their purpose and show students where the numbers are in the text. You can stop and ask comprehension questions between readings if you want to make sure everyone is moving at the same pace.

B 10–15 min

What does each festival item symbolize? Match an item with its meaning. Two answers are extra.

Explain vocabulary as needed. Help students figure out the meaning of *symbol* from its context (line 8 of Holi text). *Symbol* is something that means or substitutes for something else. Tell them that *-ize* is a verb ending, and *symbolize* is a verb. Students should scan the text to find the festival items, then read more closely to find what they symbolize.

Instructor's Notes

10-15 min

C **Circle the festival each sentence describes. In some cases, both answers are possible.**

Students may be able to answer all or most of these questions without reading again. Tell them to answer what they can and then search the text for the missing answers. Check answers with the class.

D **Choose a festival from the reading and explain it to a partner in your own words.**

10-20 min

You can let students choose their festival, in which case both may choose the same one. Or you can assign the festivals so that both are explained. Tell students they'll do this with books closed and as if it were an informal lecture, not a conversation. Give them enough time to prepare. You can also let the partner comment at the end. Write a few ideas for comments on the board. For example, *Did the speaker include all the important points? Did the speaker seem interested in what he or she was saying?*

Teaching Tip: Performance targets for speakers in class

It's helpful for students to understand exactly what is expected of them as speakers. For example, what is most important for them to focus on? Some possible performance targets: speaking clearly, including all the important points, presenting points in a logical order, speaking without many hesitations, maintaining eye contact, seeming interested in what they're saying. For any speaking assignment, tell speakers to concentrate on one or two targeted areas. At the end, listeners comment on how well the speaker met his or her performance targets. This can be helpful to the speaker and also keeps the listeners actively involved during the talk. You can choose the targets yourself, or sometimes let the class choose them. With a list of possible performance targets on the board, students vote to choose one or two of them for speakers to concentrate on. You can also let the speakers choose for themselves, telling their listener(s) before they begin.

10-25 min

EXTRA! Discussion questions

1. Are there any old, traditional festivals in this country? What are they? Are they important to the culture? Why or why not?
2. Are there any recently started festivals here? What are they? What, if anything, do they add to life here?
3. Do you have a favorite festival? Why do you like it so much? If you don't have a favorite, why don't you?

20-30 min

EXTRA! Writing prompt

Agree or disagree with this statement: Traditional festivals are important in modern life.

20-30 min

EXTRA! Additional reading

For more practice summarizing, see Heinle's Footprint Reading Library *One Boy's Journey.*

For more practice making predictions, see Heinle's Footprint Reading Library *Gliding Across the Gobi.*

Teaching Tip: Guessing before reading (or listening)

Students may appreciate an explanation of why they are asked to do this. Explain that it is perfectly fine if their guesses are incorrect. The point is not to get the answers right, but to help them when they start reading. Guessing ensures that they already have some ideas about the text, so the information makes more sense, and it's easier to figure out unfamiliar vocabulary.

Instructor's Notes

C Circle the festival each sentence describes. In some cases, both answers are possible.

1. It's celebrated in different countries. — Orange Festival / Holi
2. It's based on an old story. — Orange Festival / Holi
3. It's a celebration of good over bad. — Orange Festival / Holi
4. You throw things at other people. — Orange Festival / Holi
5. You need to join a team to participate. — Orange Festival / Holi
6. People wear costumes. — Orange Festival / Holi

GET READY TO GET DIRTY

It's a cool February afternoon in the small town of Ivrea in Northern Italy. The streets are usually quiet, but today they're full of people as the four-day Orange Festival begins. The "Carnevale di Ivrea" is over 900 years old. It celebrates the story of a young girl named Violetta. She killed the town's evil[1] leader and set the people of Ivrea free. Today's festival remembers the fight that took place between the people of Ivrea and the evil leader's guards.[2] In the original fight, people threw beans or rocks at the soldiers. Today, participants wear colorful costumes and throw oranges instead.

The Orange Festival begins with a parade from City Hall to the center of town. A young woman dressed as Violetta speaks to the crowd and throws candy to the people. After that, the orange fights begin. Men, women, and children will run throughout the town and throw oranges at each other.

To participate in the orange-throwing contests, you need to join a team—you can be on a team that fights for freedom or you can be one of the evil leader's soldiers. If you don't want to join the fighting, you must wear a red hat (red hats are sold everywhere during the festival). Then no one will throw oranges at you. Put it on, watch out, and have fun!

[1] **evil**: very bad [2] **guard**: a protector (e.g., a soldier or police officer)

The Festival of Color, also known as Holi, is a popular spring celebration. It takes place every year in late February or early March in India and many other countries, including Nepal and Sri Lanka.

In Indian mythology,[3] an evil woman tried to kill a young man named Prahlad by burning him in a fire. Because Prahlad was a good person, he escaped from the fire unhurt. Today, people remember this event by lighting large fires in the streets on the night before Holi. The fire is a symbol of burning all things evil. The next day, Holi, is a new beginning. To celebrate, people gather in the streets. They throw colored powder into the air and shout "Holi Hai!" Others throw brightly colored water or powder on each other. By the end of the festival, the streets are filled with color and smiles!

[3] **mythology**: a collection of very old, traditional stories

D Choose a festival from the reading and explain it to a partner in your own words.

4 Language Link Time clauses with *before*, *after*, and *when*

A Study the sentences in the chart. Notice the two ways of writing each sentence.

1a. Before the festival starts, you rent a costume. b. You rent a costume before the festival starts.	Both sentences tell us that first you rent a costume, and then the festival starts.
2a. After Violetta speaks to the crowd, the fights begin. b. The fights begin after Violetta speaks to the crowd.	Both sentences tell us that first the woman speaks, and then the fights begin.
3a. When people throw the powder into the air, they shout "Holi Hai!" b. People shout "Holi Hai!" when they throw powder into the air.	Both sentences tell us that people shout "Holi Hai!" at about the same time they throw powder into the air.

B Match a clause on the left with one on the right to make sentences about a typical day. Use each answer only once.

__b__ 1. After I eat breakfast, a. I take off my shoes and relax.

__c__ 2. Before I leave the house, b. I brush my teeth.

__e__ 3. I check my e-mail c. I say "goodbye" to my cat.

__d__ 4. I have lunch d. after I work all morning.

__f__ 5. I make my last phone calls e. after I turn on my computer.

__a__ 6. When I get home from school, f. before I leave the office.

C Read about Paloma's Three Kings Day activities. Then with a partner, combine the different sentences using *before*, *after*, and *when*. Answers will vary.

January 5

9:00 p.m. Paloma and her family go to the Three Kings Parade.

January 6

7:00 a.m. Paloma's younger brothers get up.
7:00 a.m. They wake Paloma up.
7:15 a.m. The family gathers in the living room.
7:20 a.m. They open presents.
8:00 a.m. Everyone relaxes and enjoys the morning.
11:00 a.m. Paloma and her mom prepare lunch.
2:00 p.m. Paloma's grandparents arrive at her house. Everyone has lunch.
3:00 p.m. The family eats a special cake called a *Roscón*.
3:30 p.m. The adults talk and the children play games.
10:55 p.m. Paloma kisses her parents good night.
11:00 p.m. Paloma goes to bed.

Paloma's brothers wake her up after they get up.

4 Language Link

Time clauses with *before, after,* and *when*

Warm Up

5 min

With books closed, ask what holidays students know. List them on the board. How is a holiday different from a festival? (Usually one day vs. several, usually celebrated at home vs. in public.)

A Study the sentences in the chart. Notice the two ways of writing each sentence.

10–15 min

With books closed, write sentence 1a on the board. Read the sentence aloud, and ask which clause happens first. (Pointing) *Does the festival start first or do you rent a costume first?* Do the same with 2a and 3a (in 3a, students must see that they happen at the same time). Write 1b next to 1a and ask the same question again. With books open, review the chart. A student reads the two examples aloud; you read the rule at the right.

Language Tip: Commas with time clauses

When the time clause is first, there is a comma after it and before the main clause. When the main clause is first, no comma is used.

B Match a clause on the left with one on the right to make sentences about a typical day. Use each answer only once.

10–15 min

Students should scan the clauses to find the one with *when* (6). Remind them to pair it with something that happens at the same time. To check answers, call on one student to read a numbered clause and another to read the matching lettered clause. Write the number and letter on the board.

C Read about Paloma's Three Kings Day activities. Then with a partner, combine the different sentences using *before, after,* and *when*.

10–15 min

The exercise can be done orally as suggested by the example at the bottom of the page. This is a good option if your students are comfortable with time clauses and if the energy in the classroom needs a boost.

C Teaching Option Written work

If your students need more controlled practice with time clauses, tell them to write out the sentences. (1) You can let students decide which sentences to combine. In that case, answers may vary considerably and it will be difficult to correct them in class. However, you can collect the papers to correct individually. (2) Alternatively, you can tell students which sentences to combine. Answers will be predictable and in-class correction will be possible. Write these combinations on the board. Possible time words are in parentheses. If your students need support, you can write them on the board; otherwise, choosing them should be part of the task.

7:00 and 7:00 (when)
7:15 and 7:20 (after)
8:00 and 11:00 (after, before)
2:00 (when)
3:00 and 3:30 (after)
10:55 and 11:00 (after, before)

Culture Tip: Three Kings Day

Three Kings Day is celebrated in Spanish-speaking countries, such as Spain and Mexico. It is called *Día de los Reyes Magos*, and is the traditional day for giving presents. However, today, many children get presents from both the Three Kings on January 6, and Santa Claus on December 25. Three Kings Day is also celebrated in many other countries, including Brazil, Greece, Ireland, Italy, the Netherlands, and the Philippines.

Culture Tip: More holidays

Eid ul Fitr – Muslim holiday celebrating the end of Ramadan, the month of fasting

Christmas – Christian holiday celebrating the birth of Jesus

Passover – Jewish holiday remembering the story of the Exodus, when the ancient Israelites were freed from slavery

Halloween – American holiday, originally religious, for children and adults to dress up at night in costumes, ask neighbors for treats, and be mischievous

Valentine's Day – American holiday to recognize love, especially romantic love. There are similar holidays in other countries; in many it is principally about family love or friendship.

5 Writing In my country

Warm Up

5 min

Tell students to look at the photo on page 79 for 7–8 seconds, then to close their books. What did they see in the photo? Where do they think the location is? What kind of holiday could it illustrate?

Language Tip: *Holiday*

A *holiday* in the United States is a *bank holiday* in the UK. A *holiday* in the UK is a *vacation* in the United States.

A **Read the paragraphs on the right. Then tell a partner:**

10–15 min

(See student book page 79 for complete instructions.)

In pairs, students collaborate in answering the questions. Tell them to have a conversation and to try to agree on their answers. Check the answers with the whole class.

B **What is a famous festival in your city or country? Use the questions in A to write a paragraph or two about it.**

20–30 min

If your students are from the same country, make sure there are enough different festivals written about so that there can be mixed pairs in **C**. Students all from one country should imagine that they are writing for a foreign reader.

C **Exchange papers with a partner. Ask your partner one question about his or her festival.**

15–20 min

If partners are from the same country, tell the one asking a question to pretend to be a foreigner.

C Teaching Option **Speaking**

Students should extend the conversation with more questions and answers about the holiday. Follow up with students reporting one or two interesting facts about their partner's holiday to the class or a smaller group.

6 Communication An unusual holiday

Warm up

5 min

With books closed, ask students to give the reasons for some holidays. For example, *Chusok* is for giving thanks and honoring ancestors; Three Kings Day is for giving gifts and being together as a family.

A **Look at these unusual holidays. Then ask and answer the questions below with a partner.**

10–15 min

In pairs, students should study the pictures and the names of the holidays. They can guess what happens on the holiday or what the holiday is for.

Culture Tip: Unusual holidays

World Hello Day was begun in 1973 and has been observed by people in 180 countries. People greet each other to show world leaders that they want communication, not force, to settle conflicts.

The United Nations World Tourism Organization celebrates World Tourism Day in a different host country every year. Its purpose is to raise awareness of the importance of tourism in the international community.

B **Use the questions to invent an unusual holiday.**

10–15 min

Tell students the holiday can be serious or silly.

C **Present your holiday to the class. Which is the most interesting?**

20–30 min

Give students time to practice their presentations. You can choose to let them use their notes when speaking, or not. If they use notes, they should read, then look at the listeners, and speak. The listeners will take notes. Allow time after each presentation for students to complete their notes.

World Link Video and World Link Website

Remind students of the value of further practice outside the classroom. Ask students who have watched the video or done online practice to share their experiences.

Check out the World Link Video. Practice your English online at http://elt.heinle.com/worldlink

5 Writing **In my country**

A Read the paragraphs on the right. Then tell a partner:

1. Is the person writing about a festival or holiday?
2. What is it called?
3. Where and when does it happen?
4. What do people do?

B What is a famous festival in your city or country? Use the questions in **A** to write a paragraph or two about it.

In Korea, we have a holiday called *Chusok*. It usually takes place in September. It is a holiday for giving thanks and honoring ancestors.

Many people travel home to spend Chusok with their families. After they arrive home, people eat special rice cakes called *songphyun*. Then everyone goes to the cemetery. When they visit the cemetery, they offer rice and fruit to their ancestors.

C Exchange papers with a partner. Ask your partner one question about his or her festival.

6 Communication **An unusual holiday**

A Look at these unusual holidays. Then ask and answer the questions below with a partner.

World Tourism Day
September 27

National Ice Cream Day
July 20

National Men Make Dinner Day
November 7

1. What do you think happens on each day?
2. Which one(s) would you like to celebrate? Why?

B Use the questions to invent an unusual holiday.

- What is the name of the holiday?
- What is the date of the holiday?
- What is the reason for the holiday?
- Who celebrates it?
- What do people do on the holiday?
- Do people celebrate it at home or outside the home?
- What do people wear?
- Are there any special foods or decorations?

C Present your holiday to the class. Which is the most interesting?

Check out the World Link video.

Practice your English online at http://elt.heinle.com/worldlink

8 Storytelling

Lesson A What's the story?

Person 1 is talking about a soap opera called *The Good Girls*. He/She thinks the show is corny (silly) and too predictable. Person 2 is talking about a TV drama series called *The Tudors*. He/She really likes the show because the characters are great and the stories are interesting.

1 Vocabulary Link **I love that show!**

A The people below are talking about TV shows. Read their opinions. Then discuss the questions with a partner.

1. What kind of show is each person talking about? 2. Does the person like the show? Why or why not?

My friend watches this nighttime soap opera called *The Good Girls*. The show **tells the story** of a group of teenagers in Hong Kong. They go to an elite high school. Anyway, the show is so **predictable**—always **the same old story**. A boy and girl fall in love. Then they fight. And, finally, there's **a happy ending**: they get back together. I think the show is boring, but my friend loves it.

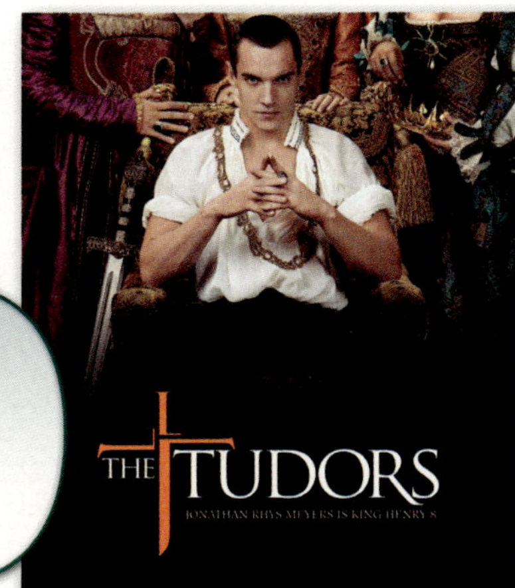

I'm totally **hooked on** a TV **series** called *The Tudors*—I never miss it! It's **based on** a **true story** about King Henry VIII of England and his family. Some stuff in the show is **made up**, but usually, the story is very **realistic**—it's based on actual events. The **characters** are great (especially King Henry) and the stories are really interesting. But you have to watch every episode or the story is hard to **follow**.

B Complete the sentences with a blue word or phrase from **A**.

1. I'm _hooked on_ the *Harry Potter* books. I can't stop reading them.
2. Everything about this movie is so _predictable_. You can guess what happens next.
3. This painting of you is very _realistic_. It's like a photograph!
4. A lot of the stories about her childhood are _made up_. Most of them aren't true.
5. Sorry, but I don't _follow_ you. Can you explain what you mean?
6. The story has a _happy ending_. The poor boy gets rich and marries his girlfriend.

C Think of a popular TV drama. Tell a partner about it.

- Who are the main characters?
- What's the show about?
- Are the show and characters realistic?
- Do you have to watch every episode to follow the story?
- Do you like the show? Why or why not?

What's the story?
Unit 8, Lesson A

1 Vocabulary Link I love that show!

Warm Up

5-10 min

Write heads for two lists on the board: *TV shows I like* and *TV shows I don't like*. Ask a student to name a show he or she likes; write it on the board. The next student names a show he or she doesn't like, and so on. When you have several shows in each list, discuss the lists briefly with the class. Is one show or one kind of show very popular? Are any shows on both lists?

A **The people below are talking about TV shows. Read their opinions. Then discuss the questions with a partner.**

15-20 min

Tell students that these are posters for two TV shows. Ask what they can guess about the two shows, based on the posters. Assign students to pairs, and read the two questions before they read the speech bubbles. When they finish reading, they should discuss their answers together. Students should work with the same partner to figure out the meaning of any words in blue that they don't know. These words can be guessed from the context. They can also consult with other pairs sitting near them. Notice that in the texts on this page, nothing tells us the gender of the two speakers.

Language Tip: *He, she,* and *they*

Historically, English used *he* as the pronoun for subjects that might be either male or female. Today, people want to use a gender-neutral pronoun, but there isn't one in general use. In informal speech, many native speakers just say *they*, even when the subject is clearly singular. In more careful speech, many say *he or she*, but this is long. Some people now choose to say *she* when gender is unspecified. Many other people still say *he*.

B **Complete the sentences with a blue word or phrase from A.**

10-15 min

Point out that each pair of sentences includes context clues about the meaning of the missing word. When you check answers, tell students to say the word and then read the clue that gave them the answer.

C **Think of a popular TV drama. Tell a partner about it.**

15-20 min

The questions fit dramas best. Brainstorm a list of current TV dramas with the whole class and write them on the board as examples. Students can describe a show on the list or any other TV drama. This is a conversation—one partner talks about a show and the other asks questions. Point out the first sentence in the two descriptions in **A** as ways to begin the conversation. Ask students for two or three more possible first sentences and write them on the board.

Instructor's Notes

2 Listening One sentence at a time

Skills: Listen for details; Identify a sequence of events

5 min

Warm Up

Ask students about their reading outside of school. Do they read books or magazines, read online, download e-books? Is there a technology for reading that they would like to try?

CD 2 Track 9 · 15–20 min

A Read the sentences below. Then listen to an interview with writer Roberto Gonzalez. Circle *True* or *False*. Then explain your answers to a partner.

Ask a student to read the sentences aloud or you can read them yourself. Play the audio once, then again, while students check and complete their answers. To explain their answers, students should correct the false statements if they can. Finally, review the answers and explanations with the class.

CD 2 Track 10 · 10–15 min

B Roberto is working on a new story. Read the sentences below. Then listen to the rest of the interview and circle the correct answers.

The chart shows Roberto's process for writing his new story. Give students time to read the sentences before playing the audio.

CD 2 Track 10 · 10–15 min

C Listen again and check your answers in B. Then answer the questions with a partner.

Play the audio again. Before checking answers, read the follow-up questions. Then students can compare their answers and discuss any differences. Using the information in **B**, they can collaborate to answer the questions.

Culture Tip: Cell phone novels and crowd-sourced fiction

Novels written on cell phones are very popular in Japan and China. Some have been bestsellers as published books, but most are available free online. *Crowdsourcing* refers to projects, including fiction writing, on which people collaborate anonymously over the Internet.

ASK ANSWER

Students can discuss what they like about Roberto's way of writing and what they don't like. If they would like to try it themselves, there are websites where writers post their cell phone stories, or they can post their story to their own social networking page.

20–30 min

EXTRA! Your writing process

Have students make charts like Roberto's to show the process they use when they write. This might help them see their process more objectively and perhaps see ways to improve it. They can show their charts to each other for discussion and comment. What parts work OK? What parts give them trouble? Can they think of ways to make those parts easier? Do their classmates do anything that they might want to try?

3 Pronunciation

Was* vs. *wasn't*; *were* vs. *weren't

CD 2 Track 11 · 10–15 min

A Listen and check (✓) the sentence you hear.

Make sure students notice that only one word is different in each pair of sentences. Check answers with the class and play the audio again to confirm the answers. Students may find it hard to hear the differences even after hearing the recording twice.

Language Tip: *Was* vs. *wasn't*; *were* vs. *weren't*

In American English, the final *t* of *wasn't* and *weren't* is often "lost" in the next word. As a result, learners may have difficulty distinguishing *was* from *wasn't* and *were* from *weren't* in connected speech. Explain to students that *was* has one syllable, while *wasn't* has two. Same for *were* and *weren't*. Even though students may not hear the *t*, they should listen for the second syllable. Do they hear *was'n* or *were'n*? Then it's the negative!

15–20 min

B Read the sentences in A aloud. Practice with a partner.

Before students practice together, read the sentences aloud yourself. Read one pair of sentences at a time, but vary the order of the two sentences. Tell students to raise their hands when they hear *was* or *were*, and sit still for *wasn't* and *weren't*. Then read the sentences in the order they are in the books so that students can read as they repeat, paying special attention to the verbs. Finally, they should practice together several times in pairs, taking turns.

2 Listening One sentence at a time

CD 2 Track 9

A Read the sentences below. Then listen to an interview with writer Roberto Gonzalez. Circle *True* or *False*. Then explain your answers to a partner.

1. Roberto writes love stories. True **False**
2. Many of his stories are based on real people and events. **True** False
3. His newest story has a happy ending. True **False**
4. One of his stories will be made into a movie. True **False**
5. These days, Roberto is writing a story about a Japanese cell phone. True **False**

CD 2 Track 10

B Roberto is working on a new story. Read the sentences below. Then listen to the rest of the interview and circle the correct answers.

Roberto types a **sentence** / chapter from his story on his **phone** / computer.

↓

He sells / **posts** it online.

↓

People read it. Then they can buy / **suggest ideas for** this part of the story.

↓

Roberto then writes his next story / **sentence** for people to read.

CD 2 Track 10

C Listen again and check your answers in **B**. Then answer the questions with a partner.

1. How is Roberto writing his new story?
2. How do his readers help him?

ASK ANSWER

Do you think this is a good way to write a story?

3 Pronunciation *Was* vs. *wasn't*; *were* vs. *weren't*

CD 2 Track 11

A Listen and check (✔) the sentence you hear.

1. [x] He was reading a story. [ ] He wasn't reading a story.
2. [ ] She was walking to work. [x] She wasn't walking to work.
3. [ ] They were working hard. [x] They weren't working hard.
4. [x] They were having fun. [ ] They weren't having fun.

B Read the sentences in **A** aloud. Practice with a partner.

4 Speaking So then what happened?

CD 2 Track 12

A Mia is telling Nico a story. Listen and then answer the questions with a partner. See answers below.

1. Who is the story about? 2. Where is he from? 3. What happened to him?

Mia: Hey, Nico, listen to this story. It's like something from a fairy tale.

Nico: Yeah? What's it about?

Mia: It's about this guy from Uganda. He came to the U.S. as a student.

Nico: Yeah?

Mia: Yeah, but then things got really difficult in his country and he couldn't go back. So, he stayed in the U.S. He got two jobs, but he was still poor.

Nico: Sounds like a hard life.

Mia: Yeah, but then a month ago, he finally returned to his country. It turns out he was really a prince!

Nico: Wait . . . he was living in the U.S. and he was really poor, but he was a *prince*?

Mia: Yeah!

Nico: So, then what happened?

Mia: Well, in the end, he stayed in Uganda and became king of his tribe[1].

Nico: Wow, what a great story!

[1] **tribe**: group of related families who live in the same area

1. & 2. The story is about a man from Uganda.
3. He went to the U.S. as a student, but then things got difficult in his country, so he had to stay in the U.S. He had to get two jobs and he was poor. But then, a month ago, he went back to his country. It turns out he was a prince. He stayed in his country and became king of his tribe.

B Practice the conversation with a partner.

5 Speaking Strategy

A On a separate piece of paper, write a word or single sentence for the following:

1. a person's name
2. another person's name
3. a place
4. how the two people met
5. what happened to the two people

Useful Expressions: Telling a story

Introducing the story	Continuing the story	Ending the story
It's (a story) about . . .	So (then), . . .	In the end, . . .
The story begins / starts in . . .	Later . . .	Finally, . . .
One day . . .	After that, . . .	
	It turns out that . . .	

Asking about a story

What's it about?
So then what happened?
Really? / Yeah?

B Exchange papers with a partner. Use your partner's notes and the Useful Expressions to make up a story.

C Get together with a new partner and do the following:

Student A: Tell your story.

Student B: Listen. Then tell your partner: What did you like about the story?

D Switch roles and do **C** again.

What's your story about?

It's about a high school student named Jonah. One day on the subway, he found a wallet full of money . . .

4 Speaking So then what happened?

Warm Up

5–10 min

Ask students if they remember stories from when they were very young. Who told or read the stories to them? Did they hear them at bedtime or other times? Did they have a favorite story?

CD 2 Track 12

A Mia is telling Nico a story. Listen and then answer the questions with a partner.

10–20 min

With books closed, write the questions on the board. Play the recording once. Still with books closed, students should compare their answers in pairs. Play it again if necessary to confirm the answers.

B Practice the conversation with a partner.

20–25 min

Before students practice in pairs, play the recording in short segments so that they can repeat it. For longer speeches, play them once, then read them aloud using the backward build-up technique.

Teaching Tip: Repetition by backward build-up

This technique works well for choral repetition. When something is too long for students to repeat all at once, start from the end of the sentence and work toward the beginning until they can put it all together without hesitating. For example, build Mia's first speech of the conversation like this:

- *from a fairy tale.*
- *something from a fairy tale.*
- *It's like something from a fairy tale.*
- *to this story.*
- *listen to this story.*
- *Hey, Nico, listen to this story.*
- *Hey, Nico, listen to this story. It's like something from a fairy tale.*

It is easier for students to repeat this direction than adding words from the beginning of the sentence.

5 Speaking Strategy

15–20 min

A On a separate piece of paper, write a word or single sentence for the following:

(See student book page 82 for complete instructions.)

Introduce the Useful Expressions quickly and tell students to close their books. Write the i-box questions on the board. Read them aloud, with students repeating. Write some example story notes and this question on the board: *What's your story about?*

To model this activity, tell a story using some of the Useful Expressions and the story notes on the board. Point to questions from the i-box to prompt the students to express interest. Finally, give students time to write their own story notes.

Teaching Tip: Photographs

Some students have difficulty with exercises that require imagination or creativity. Bring in magazine illustrations that suggest a story with two characters. Offer them to anyone who wants one—some may not.

B Exchange papers with a partner. Use your partner's notes and the Useful Expressions to make up a story.

15–25 min

After exchanging papers, students should work alone to make up a story. This will probably not be the same story their partner imagined. Point out the speech bubbles at the bottom of the page. The storyteller is adding information that was not in the notes; they need to do the same.

C Get together with a new partner and do the following:

15–20 min

(See student book page 82 for complete instructions.)

Write the Useful Expressions on the board with the i-box questions so students can look up while they speak. Tell students to read the speech bubbles. Explain the instructions. Both partners should talk; in fact, the listener begins the conversation. Write this on the board as a reminder: *Tell a story; Express interest.*

D Switch roles and do C again.

10–15 min

Student B can comment right after hearing the story or wait and share what they liked with the whole class.

Large Class Option

Make groups of six with three pairs from **D**. Students share what they liked with the group rather than the whole class.

6 Language Link

Past continuous vs. simple past

Warm Up

5–10 min

Ask students what they did yesterday. On the board, list the students' names and the verbs in their answers. For each verb, write the approximate time they did it. For actions that took some time to complete, write the approximate time they ended. Write *n/a* (not applicable) for actions that were very short. Leave the list on the board. It won't be in chronological order:

Alicia	*got dressed*	*6:25*	*6:45*
Jiro	*got up*	*6:00*	*n/a*
Irina	*drank a cup of coffee*	*6:50*	*n/a*
Jin	*took a shower*	*6:10*	*6:20*

A **Look at the pictures and read the sentences. Then answer the questions below with a partner.**

10 min

After students have done the exercise in pairs, follow up with the whole class. Use the pictures to explain *an action in progress* and *an action completed or finished*. You can also act out the sentences for pictures 1 and 2 as you say them aloud. Check answers by writing the verbs on the board circled or underlined.

Language Tip: Duration of actions

In the example, *stop* and *turn around* must be in the simple past because they express "sudden" actions. They can be used in continuous tenses when the action expressed is not sudden, but has duration. (*I shouted, "Stop!" but he was already stopping. We shouted, "Look out!" but she was already turning around.*)

B **Maya and Sami are talking about a TV show. Complete the dialog with the simple past or the past continuous of the verbs in parentheses.**

25–30 min

Introduce the past continuous using the chart. A student can read one sentence with each verb, or you can read them yourself. Tell students about the need to avoid progressive tenses with stative verbs. Point out the i-box. Ask volunteers for sentences with *be, have, need,* and *know* in the simple past; write them on the board.

B **Teaching Option** Support/challenge

Before students complete the conversation, go back to the verbs you listed on the board during the Warm Up. Point to one of the verbs that took some time to complete. Say, *Alicia got dressed from 6:25 to 6:45.* Then say and write, *At 6:30, Alicia was getting dressed.* Circle *was getting.* Point to one of the actions that was very short. Say and write, *Jiro got up at 6:00.* Underline *6:00.* Have students tell you what to write, circle, and underline for the other verbs.

B **Teaching Option** Support/challenge

Say pairs of sentences with stative verbs in the simple past and the past progressive. Students raise their hands for the correct sentences and sit still for the wrong ones. (*I was knowing him in primary school. I knew him in primary school.*)

Word Bank: Some stative verbs

be	have	need	know	feel like
look like	own	love	think	sound
look	belong to	like	believe	smell
appear		hate	remember	taste
seem		want	understand	

C **Check your answers in B with a partner. Then practice the conversation together.**

10–20 min

After students have checked their answers, confirm them with the whole class. Write the answers on the board and examine the past tense verbs. Tell students to look at the dialog and say which are stative and which are completed actions. (Only *be* and *have* are used in the dialog.) It would be good for students to repeat the conversation before practicing in pairs. However, if students are tired and energy is low, you can move right on to practice. Walk around while they practice to listen and help as appropriate.

D **Take turns asking and answering the questions with a partner.**

10–15 min

Students should do this twice so that both partners answer all the questions.

D **Teaching Option** Support/challenge

As pairs finish, tell them to continue with their own questions and answers.

Instructor's Notes

6 Language Link **Past continuous vs. simple past**

A Look at the pictures and read the sentences. Then answer the questions below with a partner.

Tom was walking down the street.

Suddenly, he stopped and turned around.

Someone was following him.

Which verbs describe . . .

- an action in progress at a certain time in the past? Circle them.
- a completed or finished action in the past? Underline them.

B Maya and Sami are talking about a TV show. Complete the dialog with the simple past or the past continuous of the verbs in parentheses.

The past continuous		
I / He / She	was walking	down the street.
You / We / They	were walking	

Sami: Hey, Maya. I (1. try) _tried_ to call you last night. Where (2. be) _were_ you?

Maya: I (3. watch) _was watching_ that show *Lonely Hearts*. I guess I (4. not hear) _didn't hear_ my phone.

Sami: Oh, I love that show! I (5. miss) _missed_ last night's episode. What (6. happen) _happened_ ?

Maya: Well, in the opening scene, Stefano (7. talk) _was talking_ on the phone to Nicole.

Sami: Wait . . . Nicole is Stefano's girlfriend, right?

Maya: Yeah, remember? Nicole and Stefano (8. be) _were_ together in Sydney.

Sami: In Sydney? What (9. do) _was_ Stefano _doing_ in Sydney?

Maya: He (10. go) _went OR was going_ to college there three years ago. He (11. meet) _met_ Nicole there. They (12. fall) _fell_ in love while they (13. work) _were working_ on a project together.

Sami: Oh, yeah . . . now I remember. But then Stefano (14. have) _had_ to return to Italy because his father (15. die) _died_ suddenly.

Maya: Right. Then later, Stefano (16. get) _got_ a job in Rome. But he never (17. forget) _forgot_ about Nicole.

Don't use stative verbs (*be, have, need, know*, etc.) with the past continuous. Use the simple past.

C Check your answers in **B** with a partner. Then practice the conversation together.

D Take turns asking and answering the questions with a partner.

1. What were you doing last night at 8:00?
2. What were you wearing two days ago?
3. What were you studying in last Monday's class?
4. Who were you sitting next to in class yesterday?

7 Communication **Who's telling the truth?**

CD 2 Track 13

A Both Jenna and Ryan say they were in a car accident. One person is lying. Listen to each person's story and take some notes below.

	Jenna	Ryan
When did it happen?	yesterday, after school	yesterday
Where did it happen?	near school	near school
What happened?	Someone hit her car.	Someone hit his car.
What color was the car?	blue	blue or black
Who was driving?	a woman in her 30s	He doesn't say; he isn't sure.

B In **A**, who do you think is making up a story? How do you know? Discuss your ideas with a partner.

Ryan is probably making up the story. He isn't sure of some of the answers. He hesitates a lot. Jenna always answers quickly.

C Think about something funny or unusual that happened to you. Then do the following steps with a partner:

1. **Student A:** Tell your story.
   Student B: Listen and take some notes on *who, what, where, when,* and *why.*
2. Change roles and repeat step 1.
3. Now choose one of your stories. You are both going to tell this same story to another pair.

D Get together with another pair.

- **Pair 1:** Each person should say one sentence to start your story.
- **Pair 2:** Ask each person in Pair 1 questions about their story. You have one minute. Then guess: who is telling the truth and who is making up the story? How do you know?

E Switch roles and do **D** again.

I was on TV once.

I was on TV once.

OK, Person 1: What were you doing on TV?

7 Communication

Who's telling the truth?

Warm Up

5 min

With books closed, ask students if they sometimes think people are lying. What if they don't know someone well? What might make them think that person is lying? Write their ideas on the board.

A CD 2 Track 13 10–15 min

Both Jenna and Ryan say they were in a car accident. One person is lying. Listen to each person's story and take some notes below.

Review the instructions and the chart. Set the context. These people are on a TV show, trying to win a prize. The students are the judges. Who is telling the truth? The person they pick is the winner, even if they pick the liar. (This activity is loosely based on the old TV show called *To Tell the Truth*.) Students listen and take notes in the chart. Check answers on the board.

B 5–10 min

In A, who do you think is making up a story? How do you know? Discuss your ideas with a partner.

After discussion in pairs, follow up with the whole class. Ask for a show of hands that Jenna is telling the truth, and the same for Ryan. Students should tell you the reasons for their votes. Finally, reveal that Jenna told the truth; Ryan did not. Were the judges right?

C 15–25 min

Think about something funny or unusual that happened to you. Then do the following steps with a partner:

(See Student Book page 84 for complete instructions.)

This is a conversation. Student A tells a story. Student B asks questions and takes notes. Student B can ask any questions he or she wants. In steps 1 and 2, both partners must tell the truth. Do steps 1 and 2 before introducing step 3.

In step 3, partners choose the story they will both tell in **D**. One will be lying and the other telling the truth. Both will try to convince the judges (the new pair) that they're the one who's telling the truth. Since students will be competing with each other, don't have them practice together now. Move on to **D** as soon as students have chosen their stories.

D 15–20 min

Get together with another pair.

The goal of every contestant is to make the judges believe him or her. Remind students that one contestant must tell the truth, but the other can invent information. The two stories do not have to match except at the beginning. Have three students demonstrate the beginning of the conversation at the bottom of the page. Questions are for *Person 1* and *Person 2*, as on a TV show. Enforce the one-minute time limit. Allow time at the end for the judges to give and explain their decision and for the contestants to reveal who told the truth.

E 15–20 min

Switch roles and do D again.

Pair 2 are contestants; pair 1 are judges. If one minute was too long or too short in **D**, adjust the time limit.

Large Class Option

It's important that judges not know who's telling the truth before they begin the activity. So, the two pairs should not sit near each other for **C**. In a large group, it may be too difficult to move so many pairs several seats away or across the room. As alternatives, you could (1) Do only **D** with several pairs of volunteer contestants going to the front of the class, and all the other students as judges, or (2) Make groups of six (judges) and move just one pair (of contestants) to another group. Move one pair at a time clockwise around the room to minimize confusion.

Instructor's Notes

Happily ever after
Unit 8, Lesson B

1 Vocabulary Link Modern fairy tales

Warm Up
5-10 min

With books closed, tell students they're going to read about two "feel-good" movies; write the expression on the board. What do they think a feel-good movie is? Do they enjoy that kind of movie? Can they name some feel-good movies?

10-15 min

A Read about the two movies below. Use the definitions in the box to help you.

Study the glossary as a class. Ask students to use the words in a sentence to show they understand the meaning. Tell students to look at the titles and photos in the two movie blurbs. Ask if anyone has seen either movie. Then students should read the passages. Remind them to use the glossary if they have trouble understanding the passage.

A Teaching Option Support/challenge

As you study the glossary and look at the words in context, ask students to identify what part of speech the words are. Check their answers with the class.

15-20 min

B Work with a partner. Choose one of the movies from A and answer the questions about it.

First, introduce the chart of prefixes. Tell students to find the three *un-* and *in-* words in **A**, and write them on the board. The prefixes mean *not*. Ask students to define four words in complete sentences: *Unpredictable means you can't predict it,* etc. Working alone, students should scan the blurbs in **A** to find the blue words with *in-* and *un-*. Students can read the word aloud and give the definition.

Then pair students to answer the questions. Each student should re-read only one blurb from **A** and answer questions about that one movie.

10-15 min

EXTRA! Dictionary work

Tell students with dictionaries to turn to the pages with *un-* and *in-*. Tell them to find words they think their classmates can figure out. Write their words on the board for other students to guess the meanings. Students with dictionaries can check the answers.

5-10 min

EXTRA! Movie interview

Ask for a volunteer who has actually seen one of the movies. The student should give some details that are not in the blurb. The other students can ask questions.

ASK ANSWER

Students share their stories in groups. Each group chooses their best story to tell the class and chooses the student to tell it.

10-20 min

EXTRA! Internet research

This is fun if no one knows anything about the movies. Students can search online to find out details of the story of one of the movies (two or three interesting details are enough). Then they report back another day, speaking to groups or to the whole class. If more than one student has researched the same movie, they can all contribute.

Instructor's Notes

Storytelling

Lesson B Happily ever after

1 Vocabulary Link **Modern fairy tales**

A Read about the two movies below. Use the definitions in the box to help you.

brave: not afraid, without fear	**overcome:** to successfully deal with a problem
clever: smart, quick thinking	**struggle:** to try hard to do something difficult
eventually: finally	**survive:** to stay alive
incredible: hard to believe, amazing	**uneducated:** having little or no schooling

Homeless to Harvard tells the story of 16-year-old Liz Murray. After her father leaves home and her mother dies, Liz has to live on the streets of New York City. Alone and afraid, she struggles a lot. She survives by sleeping in subways or at friends' houses. In time, this brave teen overcomes many difficulties and eventually she graduates from Harvard University.

Slumdog Millionaire tells the story of 18-year-old Jamal, a poor boy from one of Mumbai's worst neighborhoods. When Jamal starts winning money on a TV quiz show, people ask: How can an uneducated boy be so successful? Is he cheating or is he really clever? *Slumdog Millionaire* is an incredible story you'll never forget!

B Work with a partner. Choose one of the movies from **A** and answer the questions about it.

1. What's the movie about? Describe it in your own words.
2. Have you ever seen the movie? If yes, did you like it? If not, would you like to see it?

The prefixes *un-* and *in-*

Find the words in **A** that begin with *un-* or *in-*. What do these prefixes mean?

What do you think the words below mean?

unpredictable	incorrect
unbelievable	inexperienced

ASK ANSWER

Do you know a story about a person who overcame some difficulty? What did the person do?

2 Listening **The moral of the story is . . .**

A Which words in the box do you know? Which words do you think describe the animals in the picture? Tell a partner.

arrogant	patient	quick	slow

B Marnie and her dad are talking. Read sentences 1–3. Then listen and circle the correct answer(s).

CD 2 Track 14

1. There's a contest / game / test at school and Marnie thinks she's going to fail / lose / win.
2. Laura Sanders is Marnie's best friend / competitor / teacher.
3. Laura is very talented / funny / kind.

C Marnie's dad tells her the story "The Tortoise and the Hare." Listen and write *H* for hare and *T* for tortoise.

CD 2 Track 15

1. The _T_ challenges the _H_.
2. The _H_ thinks he will win the race.
3. The _H_ takes a rest during the race.
4. The _T_ finishes the race first.
5. The _H_ was arrogant.
6. The _T_ was clever.

D Listen again. Marnie's dad gives her some advice by telling the story of the tortoise and the hare. What is his advice? List your ideas in two or three sentences.

CD 2 Track 15

Marnie's dad gives her this advice: ____________________

Be like the tortoise. Be patient, work hard, and you'll do fine.

Laura is like the hare. She's fast, but it doesn't mean she will win.

ASK ANSWER

Do you agree with the father's advice? Why or why not?

3 Reading **The Cinderella story**

A Look at the title and the photos on page 87. What do you know about the fairy-tale character Cinderella? Tell a partner.

B Read the passage on page 87. Then write the headers below in the correct places in the reading. Two headers are extra.

One story, many cultures
Cinderella in the movies
Why we love her
A present-day Cinderella
The African Cinderella
A famous fairy tale

2 Listening

The moral of the story is . . .

Skills: Identify key details in a story; Draw conclusions based on information you heard

Warm Up

5–10 min

Tell students that traditional stories (fables) were told both to entertain and to make a point—usually about good vs. evil, smart vs. dumb, etc. Do they know any such stories? Briefly, who are the characters and what is the moral or point of the story?

A **Which words in the box do you know? Which words do you think describe the animals in the picture? Tell a partner.**

5 min

Talk about the words in the box and the picture as a class. Allow students to explain what the words mean or use a dictionary to define them. (Note: Although they look similar, hares and rabbits are different species, as are tortoises and turtles.) Check vocabulary comprehension by asking students to use the words in a sentence. Then in pairs, students can decide which words in the box describe each animal.

B **Marnie and her dad are talking. Read sentences 1–3. Then listen and circle the correct answer(s).**

CD 2 Track 14 — 10–15 min

Give students time to read the sentences. Very generally, ask what they think they will hear. Play the audio twice. Check answers and write them on the board.

C **Marnie's dad tells her the story "The Tortoise and the Hare." Listen and write *H* for hare and *T* for tortoise.**

CD 2 Track 15 — 15–20 min

Students should read the sentences, and complete any they can guess from the picture in **A**. Do students still need to understand any of the boxed words in **A**? Tell them to listen for them now. Let them hear the recording more than once. Check the words first, then check answers on the board, having students read the sentences aloud.

D **Listen again. Marnie's dad gives her some advice by telling the story of the tortoise and the hare. What is his advice? List your ideas in two or three sentences.**

CD 2 Track 15 — 15–20 min

After students listen, they can write down the advice working alone, or in pairs, or as group writing. Walk around as they work and send students with good answers to write them on the board. Correct answers will vary, so it's good to have more than one answer per question to discuss.

ASK ANSWER

Students discuss the questions in groups, explaining their reasons as fully as they can. Walk around as they work. Do many students disagree with the father's advice? Are their reasons the same or different? A group reporter should share different reasons with the class.

3 Reading **The Cinderella story**

Skills: Identify main ideas in paragraphs; Scan for details

Warm Up

5 min

Many fairy tales have been adapted for animated films. How many can students name? Which ones have they seen? Possibilities: *Sleeping Beauty, Snow White and the Seven Dwarfs, Cinderella, The Little Mermaid, Beauty and the Beast, The Princess and the Frog.*

A **Look at the title and the photos on page 87. What do you know about the fairy-tale character Cinderella? Tell a partner.**

5 min

Continue the conversation begun in the Warm Up, noting students' ideas on the board. There may be disagreement about details, and this is OK. The goal is to get students thinking about the story before reading. (And the reading is about different versions of the story.)

B **Read the passage on page 87. Then write the headers below in the correct places in the reading. Two headers are extra.**

20–30 min

Read the headers, and point out the write-on lines where they go in the text on page 87. Explain the purpose of headers—to tell the reader the main idea of a section of text before reading. Tell students that they are not looking for details; they need to understand the main idea of each paragraph. (They will read for details in **C**.) Some students will finish before others. Tell students to raise their hands when they finish so you can pair them to compare their answers. When most students have finished, check the answers with the whole class. Tell your students to tolerate unfamiliar vocabulary for now.

10–15 min

C **Match the names on the left with the information on the right to make true sentences. One answer is extra.**

Students don't need to understand everything in order to do this exercise either, so wait to explain vocabulary. Tell students to scan quickly to find the names on the left, then read enough to make complete sentences with the phrases on the right. If you have a sense of how long this should take your students, set a time limit. Finally, after checking the answers, answer questions about unfamiliar vocabulary.

Teaching Tip: Unfamiliar vocabulary in reading texts

After reading, allow students a very limited number of "free" vocabulary explanations. But first, guide them through guessing as many unfamiliar words as possible. At that point, write their remaining vocabulary requests on the board. Let students vote on which ones you'll explain. In the end, they may not need any "freebies." Tell them to add their individual choices of interesting or useful words to their vocabulary notebooks.

ASK ANSWER

Add this question: *People sometimes say that someone's life is "a real Cinderella story." What do they mean?* Students can discuss their opinions in groups. The class can choose one question for all the groups to report on.

5–10 min

EXTRA! Discussion questions

1. What was your favorite story as a child? Why did you like it?
2. Have you ever read a fairy tale from another country? Did the lesson seem clear to you?
3. Why are some fairy tales popular worldwide, while others stay in their country of origin?

20–30 min

EXTRA! Post-reading

There are many versions of the Cinderella story available on film. For this film review project, volunteers watch one of them, take notes about a few details that are different from the version they read in paragraph 1, and report to the class. The rules: (1) The title of the film must be "Cinderella," (2) It must be in English, not dubbed (at this level, subtitles would be a plus), and (3) It can't be about the heavy metal group, Cinderella.

20–25 min

EXTRA! Writing prompt

In the Cinderella story, Cinderella's life began to change when she was helped by a fairy. Do you think lives often change because of one amazing event? Give at least one example to support your opinion, yes or no.

20–30 min

EXTRA! Additional reading

For more practice reading at this level, see Heinle's Page Turners Reading Library *Light*.

For more practice identifying main ideas, see Heinle's Footprint Reading Library *Killer Bees!*

Teaching Tip: Accommodating late finishers

1. End when most students are ready. Don't wait for all students to finish.
2. Keep faster students busy with an additional challenge. Make it fun, not a punishment for finishing early.
3. Work with slower students as often as you can to help them finish.
4. Let them ask you questions after or before class instead of during the activity.
5. Be sure it's not a physical problem—can't see the board or hear the audio clearly.

Instructor's Notes

The Cinderella Story

1. A famous fairy tale

The Cinderella story is a famous one. Cinderella was living happily with her family when her mother died. Her father remarried. Cinderella's new stepmother and two stepsisters treated her poorly. She had to wear old clothes and work hard while the sisters wore fancy clothes and had fun.

You know the rest of the story. A good fairy helped Cinderella. She turned Cinderella's old clothes into a beautiful dress. Cinderella went to a party and a prince fell in love with her. Cinderella left the party in a hurry and didn't tell the prince her name. But she did leave a glass slipper and the prince used that to find her. Eventually, Cinderella and the Prince married and lived happily ever after.

2. One story, many cultures

That's one telling of the story, but the Cinderella fairy tale is found in many different countries with minor differences. In an African version, for example, there is one stepsister, not two. In a version from the Philippines, a forest spirit helps the Cinderella character. Settareh, a Middle Eastern Cinderella, goes to a New Year's party. And Cinderella is not always a woman. In an Irish story, a young boy, Becan, marries a princess and lives happily ever after.

3. A present-day Cinderella

There are also modern retellings of the Cinderella story. In one, a girl named Cindy Ella is a student at a Los Angeles high school. Her fashionable stepmother and older stepsisters care a lot about shopping and money. Cindy doesn't. When she writes a letter to her school newspaper against a school dance, she becomes very unpopular with both students and teachers. Only her two best friends—and later the school's most handsome boy—support her.

4. Why we love her

Why is the Cinderella story so popular and found in so many cultures? There are several reasons. First of all, it's a romantic story, which is a popular style. Also, Cinderella is a kind girl with a hard life. That makes people want to root for her. But maybe most important is that in the Cinderella story, a person faces many challenges but overcomes them in the end. That's a story that everyone—boy or girl, young or old— wants to believe can come true.

C Match the names on the left with the information on the right to make true sentences. One answer is extra.

1. The African Cinderella
2. Becan
3. Cindy Ella
4. The Philippine Cinderella
5. Settareh

a. attends a New Year's party.
b. has a forest spirit help her.
c. has only one stepsister.
d. is a "boy" Cinderella.
e. is an unpopular high school student.
f. was a movie version of the Cinderella story.

ASK ANSWER

Why is the Cinderella story so popular? The reading lists three reasons. Do you agree with these reasons?

Is there a Cinderella story in your country? If so, what is the story?

4 Language Link **Adverbs of manner**

A Read the sentences in the box. Notice the adverbs in blue. Then complete sentences 1–3 below.

Cinderella danced happily with the prince. She ran quickly down the stairs and lost a shoe.	The tortoise walked slowly across the finish line. The hare ran fast, but he still lost the race.

1. Adverbs of manner tell you how / why something is done.
2. Adverbs of manner usually come before / after a verb.
3. Adverbs of manner often / always end in *-ly*.

> **i** Stative verbs (*be, seem, look,* etc.) are followed by an adjective.

B Circle the adjective or adverb to complete Daniel Tammet's profile.

Daniel Tammet was born with a brain disorder (a type of illness). Because of it, Daniel was different / differently from other children. As a boy, he liked to play alone and acted strange / strangely around others. In school, he struggled to do good / well. To many of his classmates, Daniel seemed unusual / unusually and they laughed at him. This hurt Daniel deep / deeply, and he became very shy / shyly.

As a teenager, things changed. Daniel discovered he had an incredible ability. He could solve difficult math problems almost instant / instantly. He also discovered another talent: he could learn to speak a language very quick / quickly. Today, he is fluent / fluently in twelve languages.

As an adult, Daniel has overcome his shyness. He wrote two books and now he travels constant / constantly to talk to people about his life and his experience.

Daniel Tammet
Nickname: Brain Man
From: the UK

C Discuss the questions with a partner.

1. As a child, how did Daniel act? Why?
   As a child, Daniel was different from other children. He liked to play alone and acted strangely around others.
2. How did people treat Daniel? How did this influence him?
   His classmates laughed at him and Daniel became very shy.
3. What two special abilities does Daniel have?
   He can solve difficult math problems almost instantly. He can also learn to speak a language very quickly.
4. Does Daniel's story end happily? Why or why not?
   His story ends happily because he overcame his shyness and wrote two books about his life and his experience.

D Get into a group of 3–4 people. Add two more verbs and adverbs to the chart below.

Verbs		Adverbs	
climb	sing	calmly	nervously
dance	________	carefully	quickly
laugh	________	gracefully	quietly
run		happily	________
		terribly	________

E Choose a verb and an adverb. Then act out the combination. Can your group guess what you're doing? Take turns with the people in your group.

> You're singing terribly!

4 Language Link Adverbs of manner

Warm Up

5 min

Ask students if they have ever known someone who was exceptionally smart. What was the person like?

10-15 min

A Read the sentences in the box. Notice the adverbs in blue. Then complete sentences 1–3 below.

Tell students to underline the verbs in the box. Stress that the words in blue are called *adverbs of manner*. After the activity, turn to the i-box. Remind students that they learned stative verbs in Unit 3, and in this unit on page 83 [*be, have, need,* and *know* (with the simple past tense)]. Write a few adjective/adverb pairs on the board as examples: *clear/clearly, unhappy/unhappily, good/well, fast/fast.*

Grammar Tip: Stative verbs

Stative verbs refer to the condition of something or describe something that is not likely to change. The four categories of stative verbs are *thinking verbs, having verbs, feeling verbs,* and *sensing verbs*. Stative verbs usually cannot be used with the past continuous. They take the simple past.

10-15 min

B Circle the adjective or adverb to complete Daniel Tammet's profile.

Tell students to look at the photo and caption. Have they heard of Daniel Tammet? If not, what can they guess about him? Tell students to read the profile and circle the answers. Students should underline the verb for each adverb or adjective as they work. When they're ready, check answers with the class. For more explicit grammar practice, when students give an answer, they should say the verb and the answer they circled, then *action verb plus adverb* or *stative verb plus adjective*.

10-20 min

C Discuss the questions with a partner.

Students should look for the answers and discuss if they are correct and complete. Then they should write their answers using a verb + an adverb of manner or an adjective. Walk around to check their work. When you see a correct answer, send the student to write it on the board. It's OK if there's more than one correct answer for each question. Check the answers on the board with the class. Respond to other answers that students aren't sure about.

10 min

D Get into a group of 3–4 people. Add two more verbs and adverbs to the chart below.

Tell students to add <u>at least</u> two action verbs and adverbs of manner. Tell them that in **E**, they'll be acting out the verbs and adverbs in the chart, so they should choose ones that are easy to act out. For example, *succeed* might be impossible. Help with vocabulary that they want to use but don't know in English. Or they can use bilingual dictionaries.

Large Class Option

To minimize noise and confusion, allow only verbs that can be acted out sitting down. Eliminate *climb, dance,* and *run*. Possibilities: *eat, wash, knit, write, wait, type, sleep, read,* etc.

20-25 min

E Choose a verb and an adverb. Then act out the combination. Can your group guess what you're doing? Take turns with the people in your group.

Students shouldn't announce their choices; the others have to guess. Allow students to act out the same two words as someone else if they wish. This may help shy students feel more confident.

E Teaching Option **Competition**

Make groups of four or five, and have each group appoint a scorekeeper who doesn't play. The first actor begins acting out his or her words. The others guess. They must guess both words correctly. The scorekeeper counts how many guesses it takes the group to guess the actor's words. The number of guesses is the score. Each person guessing (not the actor) gets that score. Add up individual scores at the end. The <u>lowest</u> score wins. To be fair, everyone must have the same number of turns—one, two, whatever. If the group runs out of words and wants to keep playing, have actors come up with their own words. Before starting, have them write them down and give them to the scorekeeper.

Grammar Tip: Disappearing adverbs

English speakers frequently use adjectives when an adverb is called for.

Common examples:
**I did good on the test.* I did well on the test.
**We played bad.* We played badly.

Students should learn the grammatically correct use of adverbs, but should also be aware that they will often hear adjectives used in place of adverbs.

5 Writing A fairy-tale diary

Warm Up

5 min Ask if students have ever kept a diary. When was it? What kinds of things did they write in it?

A Look at the picture from the Cinderella story. Answer the questions with a partner.

10-15 min

Students can answer the questions with a partner in groups of three or four. If they're not sure of all the characters, any reasonable guess will do.

Add questions to the discussion: *What time is it? What's going to happen at midnight? What is each person thinking or feeling?*

B Look again at the picture and follow the instructions.

30-35 min

(See Student Book page 89 for complete instructions.)

Introduce the diary entry and tell students to find the three *-ly* adverbs. In their diaries, students can use action verb + *-ly* adverb, as on page 88, or they can use some different structures, as in the model.

Poll the class to find out which character each one wants to write for.

Form groups of students who chose the same character. They should discuss what the person is like and how he or she is feeling the next day. Tell students to think about the character's feelings while writing the diary.

B Teaching Option Process writing

The model diary page is a narrative in chronological order. Students may find this the most natural way to organize their own diary writing. The Teacher's Resources CD-ROM found in the back of this Lesson Planner includes a reproducible chart, *Chronological Order*, which may be useful for generating and organizing ideas.

B Teaching Option Support/challenge

If a student is having trouble getting started, or has trouble with writing in general, you might offer the option of completing the model diary, adding six sentences to the two that are there, with three more *-ly* adverbs.

6 Communication Guess who I am

Warm Up

5-10 min List some classroom activities on the board. Ask for a show of hands—which do students prefer to do?

read to yourself silently / read to a group out loud

role play with a partner / role play in front of the class

tell a story to a partner / tell a story to the whole class

It's likely that most students prefer the left-hand choices. Ask what bothers them about the right-hand choices. What could make them easier?

A Get into a group of three to four people and do the following:

10 min

(See Student Book page 89 for complete instructions.)

Before students begin reading, remind them that their characters had some strong feelings while they were writing their diaries. Ask students to say what different feelings the characters had. Write them on the board. Tell students to decide on the right feeling for their character and read the diary that way.

B Switch roles and repeat A again.

20-30 min

Students can do the activity two or three more times, until everyone has read his or her diary and gotten feedback. Walk around while students work to comment and offer help. Praise expressive reading when you hear it.

World Link

Tell students to guess the country. Before giving the answer, ask students why they chose as they did.

World Link Video and World Link Website

Remind students of the value of further practice outside the classroom. Ask students who have watched the video or done online practice to share their experiences.

Check out the World Link Video. Practice your English online at http://elt.heinle.com/worldlink

5 Writing A fairy-tale diary

A Look at the picture from the Cinderella story. Answer the questions with a partner.

- Who is in the picture?
- Where are they?
- What's happening?

B Look again at the picture and follow the instructions.

- It's the next day (the day after the party).
- Choose a character from the picure in **A**. Write a diary entry in that character's words. You can make up information.
- Write at least eight sentences in your entry. Use at least three *-ly* adverbs.

6 Communication Guess who I am

A Get into a group of three to four people and do the following:

Student A: Read your diary entry from Writing to your group. Try to act it out with feeling.

Students B, C, and D: Listen to Student A's entry. Then answer these questions:

1. Who is Student A?
2. What did you like most about his or her diary entry?

B Switch roles and repeat **A** again.

WORLD LINK

The world's oldest Cinderella story was written in 850 A.D. and comes from ______.

a. Germany
b. China (circled)
c. Iran

Check out the World Link video.

Practice your English online at http://elt.heinle.com/worldlink

9 The World of Work

Lesson A Work history

1 Vocabulary Link Job qualities

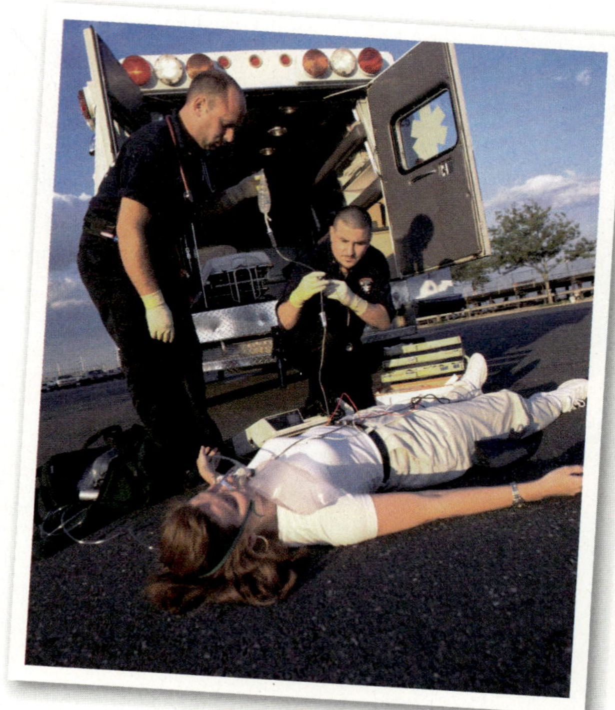

A Read about the job of a paramedic. Then tell a partner: could you be a paramedic? Why or why not?

- In an emergency, paramedics are often the first to arrive. They have to be knowledgeable about different ways to help sick and injured people. They also have to be courageous in dangerous situations.
- Paramedics need to be efficient in their actions and work quickly. At the same time, they have to be cautious—especially when moving an injured person.
- Sometimes, the injured person can be rude. Whatever happens, a paramedic must stay calm and be pleasant.
- Paramedics need to be independent and able to make good decisions on their own. They also need to be punctual when coming to work. An emergency call can come at any time.
- Finally, a paramedic's job is unpredictable. Every day and every situation is different. Paramedics have to be flexible and able to deal with changes as they happen.

B Match a blue word in **A** with its definition.

1. friendly, nice to people pleasant
2. knowing a lot knowledgeable
3. on time punctual
4. careful cautious
5. able to change easily flexible
6. able to work alone independent
7. brave courageous
8. always changing unpredictable
9. organized and fast efficient

List other words from B that end in *-able / -ible*, *-ent / -ant*, or *-ous*. Which part of speech (noun, verb, adjective) are these words? Do you know other words that end in these suffixes?

-able / -ible	knowledgeable,
-ent / -ant	independent,
-ous	courageous,

C Discuss the questions with a partner.

1. What is the hardest thing about being a paramedic?
2. What other jobs have unpredictable schedules? Which ones require you to be courageous? pleasant? flexible?
3. Which words in **B** describe you? Explain.

Work history
Unit 9, Lesson A

1 Vocabulary Link Job qualities

Warm Up

5 min

With books closed, ask students to name jobs in the health care industry. If they don't know the names of all the jobs, they can describe them. Write the names they know on the board. If you wish, tell them the missing names or have them find out for the next class.

A Read about the job of a paramedic. Then tell a partner: could you be a paramedic? Why or why not?

10-15 min

Tell students to look at the photo and the caption. Ask if they know anyone who works as a paramedic. Does the person like the job?

Read the discussion question. (If there's time, add this one: *Have you ever helped someone who was injured? What happened?*) Tell students to begin discussing their answers as soon as they finish reading. Follow up the pair work with the whole class. Ask for a show of hands for who said *Yes* and who said *No*. Ask a few students their reasons. If necessary, explain the bold words in the text; all the blue words are defined in **B**.

B Match a blue word in A with its definition

10 min

Students can work alone to match the words and definitions. Check answers with the class and write them on the board. Challenge students to do this activity without a dictionary. Students can compare answers with a partner for support before you check answers as a class.

Point out suffix box in **B** and read it aloud. Write *knowledgeable* as a list head on the board; students should find three words in the matching exercise to complete the list. Students should complete the other two lists on their own and check with a partner. (*Punctual* has a different suffix and doesn't belong in any of the lists.) Write *independent* and *courageous* on the board, and tell students to think of other words for the three lists. Some possibilities:

-able/-ible: reliable, capable, responsible, terrible
-ent/-ant: confident, excellent, competent, different
-ous: ambitious, generous, adventurous, courteous

Culture Tip: Ambition

In some cultures, ambition is always seen as a negative quality. In others, including the United States, ambition can be good or bad, depending on a person's behavior. If ambition makes a person energetic and motivated, it's a good thing. If it makes a person harm other people, it's a bad thing.

Word Bank: More job qualities

helpful	organized
outgoing	creative
cooperative	efficient
positive	motivated
caring	thorough

C Discuss the questions with a partner.

10-20 min

Read the questions. Questions 1 and 3 ask for a personal response. Tell students to discuss them in pairs. Each pair should join another pair to discuss question 2. Follow up question 2 with the whole class.

20-30 min

EXTRA! Writing prompt

What are your one or two strongest job qualities? Are they important in your present job, or a job you hope to have someday?

Instructor's Notes

2 Listening It's hard work.

Skills: Use background knowledge to build context; Infer information; Make and check predictions; Take notes; Listen to determine the speaker's attitude or feeling

Warm Up

5 min

Ask students about the hardest jobs they've ever had (or someone they know has ever had). Why was the job hard? Was it the work? The people? The place?

A Look at the jobs below. What are the advantages (good things) and disadvantages (bad things) of each job? Tell your partner.

10–25 min

After discussion in pairs, students can share some of the advantages and disadvantages they identified. List them on the board. Help with vocabulary as needed.

B You will hear a man talking about his job. Which job in A does he do? Circle it. What information helped you choose your answer?

CD 2 Track 16

5–10 min

Tell students to listen for keywords related to one of the jobs, and to write down as many as they can in note form while listening. Tell the whole class to call out the answer. Students should then use their notes to paraphrase what the speaker said. (For example, *You travel a lot. Your work schedule changes. You have to help with their luggage.*)

C What are the disadvantages and advantages of this job?

CD 2 Track 16

10–15 min

While students listen and complete the chart, have one or two volunteers work at the board like this:

1. away	*2. health*	*3.*
home	*etc.*	
twenty		
social		

Play the audio twice if students need it. Check answers on the board.

D The man suggests certain qualities are important for his job. What are they? Circle the correct answers. Two words are extra. Explain your choices to a partner.

5–10 min

Tell students to explain by giving specific examples of what the man said. Again, they should paraphrase—they don't have to remember the exact words. (An example for *pleasant*: You always have to be friendly and helpful, even when people get angry.) Ask a few students to explain one of their choices to the class.

ASK ANSWER

Students can discuss the questions in groups. Tell them there may be disagreement on question 1. They should defend their opinions with their general knowledge of the world and specific things the man said.

Teaching Tip: Review

It is always helpful to recycle and reuse items taught earlier in the course. When a moment allows, remind students of words, grammar, or skills they've studied before. For example, remind students that they practiced disagreeing in Unit 4. Brainstorm expressions for disagreeing or turn to page 38 for a quick review.

3 Pronunciation

Reduced *for* in time expressions

A Listen to the sentences. Notice the reduced pronunciation of *for*.

CD 2 Track 17

5 min

After listening, ask students what *for* sounded like (more like *fur*). If you wish, have students repeat the sentences. Play the audio, pausing after each one. Or model it yourself. (It helps students to hear two different voices.)

B Listen to these sentences and write the time expression you hear.

CD 2 Track 18

5–10 min

Choose a student to work at the board. Then check those answers with the class.

C Complete the sentences with information about yourself. Then say the sentences to a partner. Use reduced *for*.

5 min

Introduce *for a long time*. Like *for years*, it's useful if students don't remember the exact length of time.

Instructor's Notes

2 Listening **It's hard work.**

A Look at the jobs below. What are the advantages (good things) and disadvantages (bad things) of each job? Tell your partner.

taxi driver | flight attendant | tour guide

CD 2 Track 16

B You will hear a man talking about his job. Which job in **A** does he do? Circle it. What information helped you choose your answer?

Disadvantages	Advantages
1. You're __away__ from __home__ a lot—about __twenty__ days a month. • It's hard to have a __social__ life. 2. The job is hard on your __health__. • You __stand__ a lot. • It's difficult to get enough __sleep__ and to __eat__ right. 3. Sometimes, there's a __rude__ person. You have to be __friendly__ and __helpful__.	1. You meet __interesting people__. 2. You get to __visit__ lots of __places__.

CD 2 Track 16

C What are the disadvantages and advantages of this job?

1. Read the statements in the chart. Try to guess the answers.
2. Listen again and complete the statements. Use one word in each blank.

ASK ANSWER

Do you think the speaker likes his job? Why or why not?

Would you like to do this job? Why or why not?

D The man suggests certain qualities are important for his job. What are they? Circle the correct answers. Two words are extra. Explain your choices to a partner.

It's important to be . . .

punctual | (pleasant) | cautious | (flexible) | (patient)

3 Pronunciation **Reduced *for* in time expressions**

CD 2 Track 17

A Listen to the sentences. Notice the reduced pronunciation of *for*.

1. My father has worked there for decades.
2. I've lived in the same city for years.
3. He hasn't been in class for a week.

CD 2 Track 18

B Listen to these sentences and write the time expressions you hear.

1. He's been sick __for 2 days__.
2. I haven't eaten __for 6 hours__.
3. She's taught school __for years__.
4. I haven't seen him __for years__.

C Complete the sentences with information about yourself. Then say the sentences to a partner. Use reduced *for*.

1. I haven't been sick for ______________.
2. I've lived in ______________ for ______________.
3. I've studied English for ______________.

I've lived in the same house for ten years. I've studied English for three years.

4 Speaking Tell me a little about yourself.

CD 2
Track 19

A Read the job ad. Then listen to an interview.
Is Ines the right person for the job? Why or why not? Answers will vary.

ZOOMA MAGAZINE NEEDS STUDENT BLOGGERS!

You ...

- are 18–22.
- know a lot about pop culture.
- have good writing skills.
- are punctual and can work independently.

Simon: So, Ines, tell me a little about yourself.

Ines: Well, I'm a first-year student at City University, and I'm majoring in journalism.

Simon: And you're working for your school's online newspaper, right?

Ines: Yeah. I write a blog. It focuses on pop culture, fashion, music . . . stuff like that.

Simon: How long have you worked there?

Ines: For about six months. I post an entry once a week.

Simon: Excellent. But if you work here, you'll need to post every Tuesday and Friday—by noon.

Ines: No problem. I'm very punctual.

Simon: Great. Now, we need someone right away. When can you start?

Ines: On Monday.

Simon: Perfect. Let me talk to my boss and I'll be in touch with you later this week.

blog: an online diary

blogger: someone who writes a blog

B Practice the conversation in **A** with a partner.

5 Speaking Strategy

Useful Expressions: Interviewing for a job		
	The interviewer	**The applicant**
Starting the interview	Thanks for coming in today.	It's great to be here. / My pleasure.
Discussing abilities and experience	Tell me a little about yourself.	I'm a first-year university student. I'm majoring in journalism.
	Can you (work independently)? Are you (punctual)?	Yes, I can. For example, . . . Yes, I am. For example, . . .
	Have you ever (done this kind of work)?	Yes, I work for my school newspaper now.
Ending the interview	Do you have any questions?	Yes, I do. / No, I don't think so.
	When can you start?	Right away. / On Monday. / Next week.
	I'll be in touch.	I look forward to hearing from you.

A Imagine that you're applying for the student blogger job. Create a new dialog with a partner. Use the interview in Speaking and two or three Useful Expressions.

B Perform your conversation for another pair.

4 Speaking

Tell me a little about yourself.

Warm Up

5 min

With books closed, ask students about the term *pop culture*. What do they think it means? Which of these definitely do not belong to pop culture? Opinions can differ.

opera	sailing	soap operas	sushi
wrestling	baseball	action movies	hip hop
jazz	pizza	car racing	hiking

Point out the i-box and read it aloud. Ask if students read blogs—often, sometimes, or never? Ask for a show of hands. Ask what blogs they read and what they're about.

CD 2 Track 19

5-10 min

A Read the job ad. Then listen to an interview. Is Ines the right person for the job? Why or why not?

Tell students to read the job ad. Does the job sound interesting? Introduce the interview and write the discussion question on the board. Play the interview while students read it in their books. In pairs, students should compare the ad's requirements and what Ines says in the interview. Follow up with the whole class.

15-20 min

B Practice the conversation in A with a partner.

Play the audio again without pausing. Tell students to mark in their books where the voices are louder and circle *for* in two places. Play it again, pausing after every breath group so students can repeat. Or read it yourself. While students practice, walk around to listen and remind them to reduce *for*. Students should switch roles and practice again.

Teaching Tip: Reading speed

Reading aloud, or with lips forming words, slows students down. Recommend that students read silently. Conversely, having students follow with their fingers with a recorded reading will force students to move more quickly than if they are reading it aloud themselves. For the Speaking conversations, sometimes have students follow the conversation with their fingers. Stop the audio program randomly in the middle and have students show you where their finger is. Did they stop on the correct word? Are they able to follow the audio?

5 Speaking Strategy

15-25 min

A Imagine that you're applying for the student blogger job. Create a new dialog with a partner. Use the interview in Speaking and two or three Useful Expressions.

Read the Useful Expressions. Ask two students to read them as an interviewer and an applicant. Point out that applicants are expected to provide examples of their qualifications. What shows that they're punctual, for example? (They're never late for work, they never miss a deadline.) Also point out that Ines made points about herself, even if Simon didn't ask. (*Simon: How long have you worked there? Ines: For about six months. I post an entry once a week.*) This is a great interview technique that students should practice. Students can refer to the conversation in Speaking, but should not follow it.

Culture Tip: Informal language in "formal" situations

Although this is a job interview, both people speak quite informally. Some workplaces are much less formal than others, even for a job interview. Simon seems to prefer informality, and Ines takes her cue from him. In fact, in many business situations, Canadians and Americans prefer to maintain a casual tone. They feel it helps everyone relax and do better work.

15-20 min

B Perform your conversation for another pair.

After pair A performs, pair B should comment on one thing that was especially good. Then the pairs switch roles.

Teaching Tip: Partner work

It's easy for students to work with the same partner throughout the course. It's important sometimes to mix students up so they can work with new people. Some ideas of how to break students up:

1. Students with the same first initials work together.
2. Students wearing the same colors work together.
3. Students line up by age, and the youngest works with the oldest (if appropriate).

6 Language Link

The present perfect; *for* and *since*

Warm Up

5 min

Ask students if they have ever changed jobs. How many times? In the United States, workers between the ages of 18 and 38 change jobs an average of 10 times. If your students don't work, ask them if they have ever changed houses or schools.

A 5–10 min **Look at the time line. Then read sentences 1 and 2 below. Notice the verb forms in blue.**

On the time line (or a copy on the board), show the period of time that Sonia has been a flight attendant, and that she has not been a receptionist. Point to the green box and read it aloud. Again pointing to the time line, show how being a flight attendant began in the past and continues in the present. Do the same with not being a receptionist.

Present the rules for *for* and *since*, and relate them to the information in the time line. Ask for a time line sentence with *for three years*. (Sonia hasn't been a receptionist for three years.) Say, *Sonia finished her flight attendant training two years ago*, and ask for a sentence with *since*.

B 10–15 min ***For* and *since* are often used with the present perfect. Fill in the blanks with *for* or *since*.**

Relate the activity instructions to the i-box. Read the first few items with students saying if they are a period of time or a point in time, and which word is correct. Put those answers on the board for reference and let them do the rest on their own. When students are ready, check the remaining answers on the board.

C 10–15 min **Complete these profiles. Use the present perfect with the verbs in parentheses and *for* or *since*.**

Tell students about past participles. *Live*, *study*, and *talk* use the same form as the past tense. *Sleep*, *drink, be,* and *come* are irregular. Check answers for the first profile before students do the second.

C Teaching Option **Pair work**

Break students into pairs. In each pair, one student completes the first box only and the second student completes the second box only. Then in pairs, one student dictates the whole box with his or her answers to the partner. The student writing the answers can challenge any answer he or she thinks is incorrect.

D 10–15 min **Use the verbs in parentheses to form questions. Then ask and answer them with a partner.**

Study is a regular verb; the other verbs are irregular. Students can complete the questions alone, then practice them with their partner. They should switch roles to answer all of the questions.

EXTRA! A personal time line

15–25 min

Students can make time lines of their answers in **D**, including the beginning dates. In groups, students should ask *How long . . . ?* plus other questions about each classmate's time line. (*How long have you studied English? Where did you first study it? Do you like it?*) Each student should answers a question from each member of the group.

Teaching Tip: Learner's dictionary

Students can find the participial form of verbs in a learner's dictionary. For example, in the *Collins COBUILD Intermediate Dictionary of American English*, when a student looks up the word *eat*, the different verb tenses, including "*eaten*" as the past participle form, are given with the definition.

Instructor's Notes

6 Language Link **The present perfect; *for* and *since***

A Look at the time line. Then read sentences 1 and 2 below. Notice the verb forms in blue.

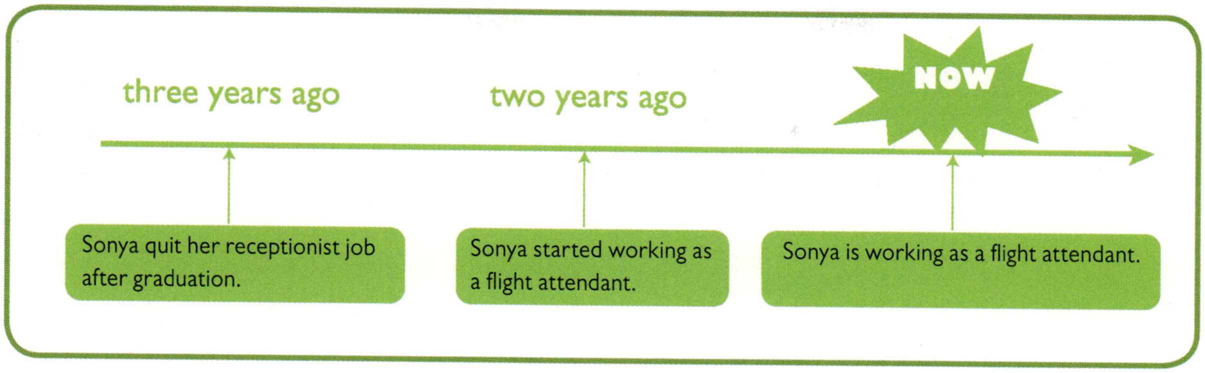

1. Sonya has worked as a flight attendant **for** two years.
2. She hasn't worked as a receptionist **since** graduation.

Use the present perfect (*have / has* + past participle) for an action that started in the past and continues up to now.

B *For* and *since* are often used with the present perfect. Fill in the blanks with *for* or *since*.

1. ___for___ half an hour
2. ___since___ last year
3. ___since___ noon
4. ___for___ one month
5. ___since___ yesterday
6. ___for___ three hours
7. ___since___ I started the job
8. ___for___ decades

for + a period of time: *for two years*
since + a point in time: *since 2010*
since + a past time clause: *since she graduated*

C Complete these profiles. Use the present perfect with the verbs in parentheses and *for* or *since*.

"I ___have/'ve lived___ (live) in the United States ___since___ August. I ___have/'ve studied___ (study) English ___since___ I was in high school. I'm studying for an exam right now. I ___have not/ haven't slept___ (not / sleep) well ___for___ two days. I ___have/'ve drunk___ (drink) three cups of coffee ___since___ 9:00."

"He ___has/'s been___ (be) in college ___for___ three years. He ___has not/ hasn't come___ (not / come) home ___for___ a year. I miss him. He ___has/'s lived___ (live) overseas ___since___ 2003. We ___have not/ haven't talked___ (not / talk) on the phone ___for___ a month."

D Use the verbs in parentheses to form questions. Then ask and answer them with a partner.

How long have you . . .

1. ___studied___ (study) English?
2. ___been___ (be) at this school?
3. ___known___ (know) your best friend?
4. ___had___ (have) the same hairstyle?

7 Communication **I really want this job!**

A Complete the job ads below with the qualities and abilities / experience needed. You can use the answers in the box more than once. Add your own ideas, too.

Qualities	Abilities / Experience	
	be able to . . .	**have experience . . .**
a fun, energetic person who loves the outdoors	swim well	caring for animals
good with computers	work flexible hours	working with children
patient and kind to animals	walk long distances	playing video games
a cautious, responsible person	work independently	
	speak English well	

Metro Classifieds Your Guide to Great Jobs

Work from home!
Part-time VIDEO-GAME TESTER needed!

Qualities needed: ______________________________
____
____

Abilities needed: ______________________________
____
____

Qualities needed: ______________________________
____

Abilities needed: ______________________________
____

Weekend LIFEGUARDS needed now!

Qualities needed: ______________________________
____

Abilities needed: ______________________________
____

Afternoon DOG WALKERS needed Mon.—Fri.

Qualities needed: ______________________________
____
____

Abilities needed: ______________________________
____
____

B Choose a job in **A** to apply for. Tell your partner your choice. Then do the following:

- Complete the questions. Then use them to interview your partner. Take turns.
- After the interview, decide if your partner is good for the job. Why or why not?

> Thanks for coming in today. So, tell me ... what do you do now?

Interview questions

Name: ______________________

Job he/she is applying for: ____________

1. What do you do now? How long have you done it?

2. Are you ______________ *? Give me an example.*
(quality)

3. Have you ever ______________ *?*
(experience)

4. Can you ______________ *? Please explain.*
(ability)

5. Your question: ______________ *?*

7 Communication

I really want this job!

5 min

Warm Up

Ask students where they (or people they know) look for jobs when they need one. Do they go to the newspaper? Online job search sites? Where else?

5–10 min

A Complete the job ads below with the qualities, abilities, and experience needed. You can use the answers in the box more than once. Add your own ideas, too.

Tell students to use a piece of their own paper so that more requirements will fit, and to work alone to complete the ads. If convenient, they can check their ad with a partner, but not the same partner they'll interview in **B**.

15–20 min

B Choose a job in A to apply for. Tell your partner your choice. Then do the following:

Review the Useful Expressions on page 92. The interview notes are to guide students while they're interviewing their partner. Students should get the applicant's name and the name of the job from their partner, and complete the questions by themselves. They are free to make up other questions, too. Tell students to look at their partner's job ads so they know what the partner's requirements are, because they may vary somewhat from the student's own ad.

Large Class Option

As is sometimes done in real interviews, have three people interview each applicant. After the interview, they confer to decide whether to hire him or her or not.

20–30 min

EXTRA! Writing prompt

In this activity, students write a letter of interest to a company. Students imagine that they would like to do a certain kind of job for a certain company, but there hasn't been an ad for it. For example, they might want to be a video-game developer for Activision. They write to the company to introduce themselves, name the job they want, and describe their one or two strongest qualifications with examples. They know the name of the person to write to. They begin the letter *Dear Mr.* ______ or *Dear Ms.* ______.

10–15 min

EXTRA! Role play: Information interview

As job seekers, students are interested in a specific kind of job—they want to be a paramedic, for example. They need information about the job's qualifications and advice about how to get the job. They ask an expert (played by a student) in the field for an informational interview. As "experts," students choose any job they can talk about. Match experts with job seekers to role play an interview. If the group is large, or if some students don't know any job well enough to be experts, one expert can talk to two or three job seekers at once.

Culture Tip: Job interviews

In many countries, interviews are an important part of the job search process. Usually a company receives many letters and résumés and invites only a few for interviews. At the interview, the representative of the company asks for more details about the applicant's background and tries to get a feeling for what kind of person the applicant is, and whether he or she would be a good "fit" with the company. The fit is often as important as the applicant's résumé.

There are many books that prepare applicants for job interviews, and they all give similar advice: dress neatly, arrive on time, answer all questions completely, and show interest in the position and knowledge of the company. Be ready to explain what you can contribute to the company.

Instructor's Notes

Dream jobs
Unit 9, Lesson B

1 Vocabulary Link

Not your typical job

Warm Up

5–10 min

With books closed, tell students they are going to read about some jobs that are not typical. Ask how they would describe a "typical" job. Where do people do it? How many hours a week do they work? What do they do during a typical work day? How long do people stay in a typical job? Do they like their job?

A Read about these people's jobs. Then tell a partner: What does each person do?

10–15 min

Before reading, tell students to look at the photographs and guess the people's jobs. After reading, discuss the advantages and disadvantages of each job, according to the people. Note them on the board.

Look at the word partnerships (collocations). Students should work with a partner to put the verbs in time order from first to last (*be out of a job / look for / apply for / get / quit*—and then be out of a job again). Then they should list the adjectives from best to worst, in their opinion. With a show of hands, compare the choices for best and worst with the whole class.

B Match a word or phrase in blue from A with its definition below.

10–15 min

Students can complete the sentences individually. Since all the blue words can be guessed from the context, check the answers with the whole class, and ask students to explain how they figured out each word.

B Teaching Option **Definition matching**

Give a group of three to four students 20 index cards. On 10 cards, write the definitions supplied in **B**. On 10 other cards, write the blue words in **A**. The challenge for the groups is to be the first to match all of the definitions and words. Walk around the room and determine if a group's matches are right or not.

EXTRA! Speaking

10–15 min

Tell students to work in pairs. Each student chooses one of the people in **A**. They should close their books and say what the person said, but in their own words. Then partners switch.

C Write the name of a job for each adjective in the chart. Compare your ideas with a partner.

5–10 min

Point out the questions in Ask and Answer so students know how their answers will be used. Help with vocabulary if needed; students may also use dictionaries or ask their partner.

ASK ANSWER

In pairs, students should discuss at least one job that each of them would like to do and one they wouldn't. They should explain their reasons, asking each other questions and commenting. Do they have similar ideas, or very different ones?

Instructor's Notes

The World of Work

Lesson B Dream jobs

1 Vocabulary Link Not your typical job

A Read about these people's jobs. Tell a partner: What does each person do?

I'm a crab fisherman in Alaska for part of the year. It's a physically demanding job—you work 12 to 14 hours a day, often in terrible weather. It's also one of the most hazardous jobs in the world—a lot of people die doing it every year. I do it because I can make a lot of money fast —about $50,000 for eight weeks of work. But it isn't steady work. After two or three months, I'm out of a job.

After graduation, I was in a dead-end job with no future. It was terrible. But now I've found a dream job. I work as a youth director on a cruise ship, organizing activities for kids. The job is really rewarding. When you teach kids to swim, for example, it feels really good. The job can be exhausting, though, because you're always busy. But the travel, plus working with a diverse staff from many different countries, means the job is never dull.

Word partnership *job*
(v.) apply for / be out of / get / look for / quit *a* **job**
(adj.) a dead-end / desk / dream / full-time / part-time / steady **job**

B Match a word or phrase in blue from **A** with its definition below.

1. dangerous ___hazardous___
2. boring ___dull___
3. satisfying, pleasing ___rewarding___
4. unemployed ___out of a job___
5. a perfect job ___a dream job___
6. continuing, not changing ___steady___
7. varied, different ___diverse___
8. hard, challenging ___demanding___
9. a job with no hope for growth ___a dead-end job___
10. very tiring ___exhausting___

C Write the name of a job for each adjective in the chart. Compare your ideas with a partner.

type of job	name of job	type of job	name of job
physically demanding		dead-end	
hazardous		dull	
rewarding		dream	

ASK ANSWER

Look at the jobs in **A** and the ones you wrote in **C**. Which would you like to do? Which would you never do? Why?

2 Listening **It's worth it.**

A Gino is a storyboard artist. What do you think he does? Choose the best picture.

CD 2 Track 20

B Listen and check your answer in **A**. Then circle the true sentence about Gino's job below.

a. He illustrates comic books.
b. He draws pictures for children's books.
c. He draws pictures of events in a movie.
d. He takes photos of famous actors.

CD 2 Track 21

C Read sentences 1–4. Then listen again and circle *True* or *False*.

Gino thinks . . .

1. the best part of his job is meeting famous people.	True	False
2. his job is dull sometimes.	True	False
3. working with a director is usually pretty easy.	True	False
4. it's common to work long hours in his job.	True	False

1. Gino says the most rewarding part of the job is helping to make a movie.
2. Gino says he's worked on many different types of movies. He also says he is always learning something new.
3. Gino says the job can be demanding. The director often changes his mind.
4. Gino says the job can be exhausting. He's worked all night many times.

CD 2 Track 21

D Gino gives people advice about becoming a storyboard artist. Which advice does he NOT give? Circle it. Listen again to check your answer.

a. Be knowledgeable about making films.
b. Be able to work independently.
c. Be a good artist.
d. Be a hard worker.

ASK ANSWER

Does Gino's job sound interesting to you? Why or why not?

3 Reading **I love my job.**

A Look at the photos. What do you think these people's jobs are?

B Look quickly at the two interviews on the next page. Match a photo in **A** (1, 2, 3, or 4) with a person.

Jonas ___3___ Tye ___4___

2 Listening It's worth it.

Skills: Make predictions; Listen for the gist; Listen for details; Infer information

Warm Up

5 min

With books closed, tell students they are going to hear an artist talking about his job. What kinds of jobs do artists do? (Possible answers include website designer, greeting card artist, courtroom artist, T-shirt designer, fashion illustrator, etc.)

5 min

A Gino is a storyboard artist. What do you think he does? Choose the best picture.

Students should look at the pictures and quickly circle their best guess. (They may recognize the word *storyboard* from the Review Units in this book.)

CD 2 Track 20

5–10 min

B Listen and check your answer in A. Then circle the true sentence about Gino's job below.

Students listen once to check A and answer B. You could follow up with a question: *When does Gino create a storyboard—before or after the movie finished?* (Before.) Students need to figure out the answer (infer it) using their own knowledge and what Gino says. There is more practice with inference in **C**.

CD 2 Track 21

5–10 min

C Read sentences 1–4. Then listen again and circle *True* or *False*.

Tell students that Gino doesn't say these things directly—they need to figure out the answers indirectly (infer them). Tell students to circle all the answers they think they know before listening, and compare their answers with a partner's. Play the recording once more while they complete and confirm their answers. When checking answers, students should change the false answers to make them true according to what Gino said.

CD 2 Track 21

5 min

D Gino gives people advice about becoming a storyboard artist. Which advice does he NOT give? Circle it. Listen again to check your answer.

Before listening, students should try to guess the sentence that Gino doesn't say. You may want them to briefly discuss their choice with a partner. Why did they guess it? Then play the audio and check the answer with the whole class.

Teaching Tip: Standardized tests

Questions that require students to identify what a speaker does NOT say is common on standardized tests, such as the TOEFL. To answer these types of questions, students must be able to identify what the speaker does say, and eliminate that as a possible answer. For this reason, it is harder than positive fact questions.

10–15 min

EXTRA! Discussion: *It's worth it.*

Students can discuss the idea of what makes a hard job "worth it" (the title of this Listening section). Gino says the best part of his job, the part that makes the job worth it, is that he's helping to make a movie. The man on page 95 says the money makes his dangerous job worth it. Tell students to think of people they know with difficult jobs. Are the jobs worth it to them or not? If they are, what makes them worth it?

3 Reading I love my job.

Skills: Make predictions; Skim for gist; Summarize a text

Warm Up

5 min

Take a few minutes to play *Job Alphabet*. Students try to think of a job for every letter of the alphabet. Write A–Z on the board as a list, and add the jobs, starting with A. Give the class one point for every job they name, and subtract a point for every letter standing alone at the end.

5 min

A Look at the photos. What do you think these people's jobs are?

You may have students guess together as a class, or discuss the photos in pairs. Either way, their guesses may be very different. They will find out what two of the jobs are in **B**.

5–10 min

B Look quickly at the two interviews on the next page. Match a photo in A (1, 2, 3, or 4) with a person.

Students should skim the interviews to match photos to the interviews. Remind students that skimming is reading fast to get a general idea of what's in a text (the gist of the text). (Another kind of fast reading is scanning—looking for certain specific information and ignoring the rest of the text.) Explain that choosing the right photos is only part of their task. It's just as important to do it as quickly as possible. At this point, they don't need to read every word.

10-15 min

C **Read these job profiles. Then complete the summaries of Jonas's and Tye's jobs below. Use the words in the box. Two are extra.**

Explain that a summary is a very short version of a text with just the most important points. Tell students to look at the summaries and the words in the box. Then they should read through the interviews, looking for the information they need for the summaries.

C **Teaching Option** **Support/challenge**

After checking answers, you could ask students to look at the summaries again. They are selective—that is, they don't try to include all of Jonas' and Tye's answers. Tell students to find the answers that were left out of each summary. Then they can try to state them very briefly, so they could be added to the summaries.

25-30 min

D **Work with a partner. One person will be Jonas and the other Tye. Read through your profile once more. Then follow the directions.**

Explain the task to students before they re-read the interviews. Point out that they will be answering the same questions as if they were Jonas or Tye (role playing), but without looking at their books. As they read, they should think about the task. What are the most important things to remember? Before students role play, you might want to have each of them copy the questions only on a separate piece of paper, or write them yourself on the board. Then students can simply close their books while they interview each other.

20-30 min

EXTRA! Post-reading

1. Students can interview someone outside of class about his or her job and report to the class (or a smaller group) in English. Prior to conducting the interviews, the whole class should brainstorm a list of possible interview questions—things they are interested to know about any job. The interviewers choose two or three questions from the list for their reports.
2. Students can write an ad for their dream job. Distribute copies to the class, pass the ads around for groups to read and comment on, or post the ads in the classroom or hallway.

5-10 min

EXTRA! Discussion questions

1. Interns work for a company for a short time, often without pay. They do this in order to get work experience. Are unpaid internships a good idea or a bad idea?
2. Many young people want to work and need to work, but they can't get jobs. One reason is that they don't know how. All schools should teach their students the skills they need to get a job.

30 min

EXTRA! Additional reading

For more practice skimming, see Heinle's Footprint Reading Library *Living with a Volcano.*

For more practice summarizing, see Heinle's Footprint Reading Library *The Lost Temples of the Maya.*

Instructor's Notes

C Read these job profiles. Then complete the summaries of Jonas's and Tye's jobs below. Use the words in the box. Three are extra.

Interview 1 - Name: Jonas

What do you do? I'm a V.J. or "video jockey."

How would you describe your job? I'm on TV. I introduce music videos and talk about them. I also interview singers who appear in videos.

What is the best part of your job? I get to meet a lot of famous people. That's very exciting. Also, I love music. This is definitely my dream job.

What is the worst part of your job? Well, it's fun meeting famous people, but some of them aren't very nice. They think they are better than me.

What was your most memorable moment? Last year, I presented an award on TV at a music awards show. I couldn't believe it. They flew me to Los Angeles and I stayed in Beverly Hills. I was on the TV show for a whole 45 seconds! I got to meet a lot of stars.

I want to be a V.J. How do I get the job? Well, first you have to make a video of yourself. You need to talk about certain things on the video. In my case, there was a list of questions, like "What did you do last weekend?" and "What's on your iPod right now?" After you talk about yourself, you send the video in to the TV station. They call you if they like it.

Interview 2 - Name: Tye

What do you do? I'm a car courier.

How would you describe your job? Sometimes a person or a company needs a car moved from one place to another. They may not have time to do it themselves. They hire me to drive the car.

What is the best part of your job? The freedom—I'm glad it's not a desk job. Also, I like to drive, so it's fun for me. Last summer, I drove all the way from New York to California. The weather was great. I had the music on and enjoyed my trip very much.

What is the worst part of your job? The schedule—it's demanding. If I say I'll arrive on Monday at 6:00, I have to be there by Monday at 6:00. Sometimes that means driving long distances in a short time. There are days when I work 12 to 14 hours straight. It can be exhausting and stressful.

What was your most memorable moment? I once drove a famous actor's car from Miami to New York City and he gave me a really big tip.[1] It was incredible!

I want to be a car courier. How do I get the job? That's a good question. My mother started this business, so she hired me. You'd have to call my mom to find out!

[1] **tip:** extra money you give someone for a service they've done

tiring	mom	interviews	loves	unusual	hates
famous	punctual	introduces	moves	friend	video

Jonas (1) ___interviews___ singers and (2) ___introduces___ music videos. He meets a lot of (3) ___famous___ people. That's the good and the bad part of the job. He (4) ___loves___ his job. He made a (5) ___video___ to get his job.

Tye (6) ___moves___ cars from one place to another. You have to be (7) ___punctual___ to do his job and it can be (8) ___tiring___. Tye's (9) ___mom___ gave him the job.

D Work with a partner. One person will be Jonas and the other Tye. Read through your profile once more. Then follow the directions.

1. **Student A:** Ask your partner the six questions in the reading.
2. **Student B:** Cover the reading and answer your partner's questions in your own words.
3. Change roles and repeat steps 1 and 2.

4 Language Link **Verb + infinitive**

A Study the chart.

These verbs can be followed by another verb in the infinitive form (*to* + verb):					
agree	choose	forget	learn	need	start
arrange	decide	hate	like	plan	try
attempt	expect	hope	love	prepare	want

B Read each sentence. Then do the following:

- Underline the main verb.
- Which verbs are followed by an infinitive? Circle the infinitive forms. Not all the sentences have one.

1. They plan to move to Mexico.
2. I chose to go to a large university.
3. I need a snack before I go to bed.
4. I like to buy presents for my friends.
5. I forgot the key to this door.
6. He hopes to meet her parents.
7. I expect him at ten minutes to three.
8. Do you want to work in an office?

C Complete the sentences below with the infinitive form of the verbs in the box. Check your answers with a partner.

go	help	open	~~speak~~	work	attend
become	graduate	perform	sing	work	

Sanjay: I've always liked (1) to speak foreign languages. I decided (2) to work as an interpreter. I work at the United Nations.

Teresa: I chose (3) to go to medical school because I wanted (4) to help people. I'm planning (5) to work in a clinic in my hometown.

Dan: My sister is learning (6) to sing. She wants (7) to perform in an opera someday.

Camille: I want (8) to become a flight attendant. I need (9) to attend a six-week training course. I expect (10) to graduate in August and start (11) to work in September.

5 Writing **Writing about jobs**

A Choose one of the topics below and write about it.

- a part-time or summer job you had
- your dream job

B Exchange your writing with a partner. Ask your partner one question about his or her job.

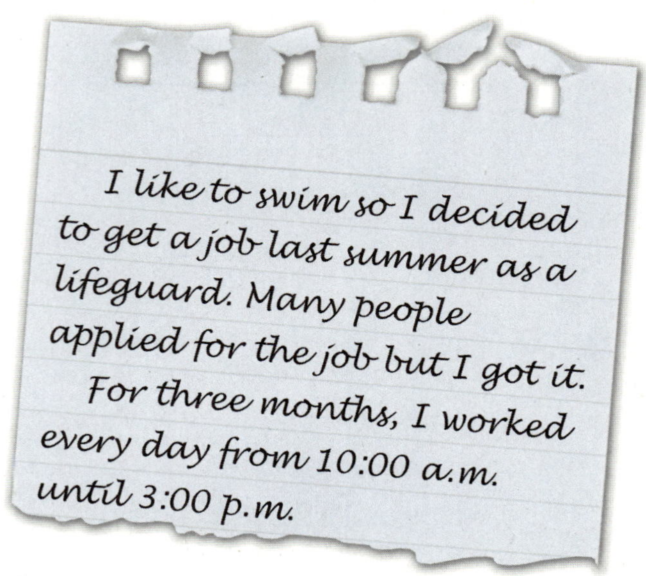

4 Language Link Verb + infinitive

Warm Up

5 min

With books closed, tell students something you like to do on weekends. Ask several students what they like to do on weekends and if they plan to do it this weekend.

5 min

A Study the chart.

Explain that these verbs and others—but not all verbs—can be followed by a verb in the infinitive. (*I like to play soccer. I'm planning to go shopping. I forgot to invite them.*) Unfortunately, there is no way to identify these verbs. Students just have to learn them.

5–10 min

B Read each sentence. Then do the following:

(See Student Book page 98 for complete instructions.)

Make sure students understand the two parts of the task. You might talk them through it by writing sentence 1 on the board and explaining what you're doing as you underline and circle. Students can compare their answers and change them if they think they should. Then check all answers on the board.

5–10 min

C Complete the sentences below with the infinitive form of the verbs in the box. Check answers with a partner.

Students can work alone to complete the sentences. To keep both partners engaged while checking answers, student A reads the sentence up to the number, and student B reads the rest.

15–20 min

EXTRA! Further practice

If possible, type up and copy a practice exercise. At the top, type the list of 18 verbs in the box in **A**. Below, type the exercise in **C**, leaving out the main verb and putting in the infinitive. (*I've always (1) ______ to speak foreign languages.*) Distribute copies for students to complete the sentences with any verbs that make sense. (You be the judge of what makes sense.) Check answers on the board, including alternate answers: *(1) liked, loved, wanted*, etc.

5 Writing Writing about jobs

Warm Up

5 min

With books closed, poll the class about what part-time or summer jobs they have had. Have most people had one? If not, have they had a regular (full-time, steady) job? How many people have not had a job yet?

Culture Tip: Jobs

Most people from English-speaking countries see working as an honorable thing. The first question many people ask each other when they meet is *What do you do?* Jobs are identifiers. However, many other cultures see work as something that is necessary for money only, and if you have money, it is undesirable to work. In these countries, students don't work part-time jobs. People may study to earn PhDs in order to show that they are intelligent, and don't need to work. Sometimes it can be a clash of cultures when those who see work as a class disadvantage meet those who take pride in their work.

15–20 min

A Choose one of the topics below and write about it.

If few of your students have had jobs, most of them will write about their dream job.

A Teaching Option Process writing

Introduce a spider diagram as a way of brainstorming and organizing ideas. There's a photocopiable master on the Teacher's Resources CD-ROM found in the back of this Lesson Planner. Try using the example in the book to demonstrate the spider diagram.

Introduce the diagram on the board. The topic in the center is *a summer job*. Main ideas might be (1) *lifeguard*, (2) *my work day*, (3) *advantages and disadvantages*, (4) *it was worth it*. For the first main idea, related details might be (a) *I like to swim*, (b) *a lot of applicants*. Complete the diagram with ideas from the class. Emphasize that things change when they start writing. They may drop some ideas, add others, and move them around. The spider diagram is just to help them get started.

Also point out that different writers have different ways of writing. Some writers say a diagram helps them see their ideas more clearly. But students shouldn't feel they have to use it. There are other ways to get started, including just starting to write.

10–15 min

B Exchange your writing with a partner. Ask your partner one question about his or her job.

Partners read each other's writing, or read it aloud to each other. Then each one asks at least one question based on the writing. (Will you work as a lifeguard again? Why not?) Tell them to take their time and read carefully before they start talking.

6 Communication Guess my job!

Warm Up

5 min

With books closed, ask students if they watch game shows on TV. What makes them fun? If they had a chance, would they be a contestant?

A **Get into groups of four: Students A, B, C, and D. Get ready to play "Guess my job!" Read the instructions below.**

5-10 min

It's important that students understand the rules before they begin to play. Demonstrate by taking the part of Student A. Ask three students to take the roles of Students B, C, and D, and coach them through one round of questions, according to the rules. Secretly tell the other students the job you choose.

A Teaching Option **Keep score**

Since it's a game, students may enjoy keeping score. Give one point to Student A for every question answered before his or her job is guessed. Give one point to Student B, C, or D for a question with verb + infinitive. Other questions are OK, but do not give points.* Students keep score together, writing down points after every question, answer, and guess. At the end, the student with the highest score wins.

*You may prefer to allow only questions with verb + infinitive. The advantage is that students will get much more concentrated grammar practice. A possible disadvantage is that students may find it difficult to come up with useful questions and may lose interest in the game.

Teaching Tip: Competitive games

Some students may temporarily forget they are learning a language if you add a competitive element. Students are motivated to win and will do their best to perform the task at hand. Assign points to completing tasks, and give candy when students are the first to complete something correctly. But be alert to students who find competitiveness aggressive and stop performing due to fear of losing for the team or being put on the spot.

B **Take turns being Student A and play "Guess my job!" again.**

25-30 min

Walk around while students play. Help with vocabulary and pronunciation (sparingly), comment on their questions, and referee disputes. When the energy in the room starts to drop, stop the game.

EXTRA! Writing prompt

20 min

Imagine that you have begun a new job. Monday was your first day. Write about it on your social networking page. Tell everyone your new job title (receptionist, customer service representative, etc.) and the name of the company. Then choose some of these to write about: your responsibilities, your boss, your co-workers, a typical day, lunchtime, your desk—or use your own ideas.

World Link Video and World Link Website

Remind students of the value of further practice outside the classroom. Ask students who have watched the video or done online practice to share their experiences.

Instructor's Notes

Check out the World Link Video. Practice your English online at http://elt.heinle.com/worldlink

6 Communication **Guess my job!**

A Get into groups of four: Students A, B, C, and D.
Get ready to play "Guess my job!" Read the instructions below.

taxi driver

flight attendant

rafting tour guide

ski instructor

film director

police officer

astronaut

forest ranger

fashion designer

1. Student A secretly chooses one of the jobs above. Don't say the job you choose!
2. Students B, C, and D take turns asking one question each to discover Student A's job. Use a verb from the box below or one of your own.

try	choose	want	learn	need	plan
attempt	expect	hate	like	hope	love

How do you learn to do your job?

3. Student A answers the three questions. Then together, Students B, C, and D take one guess to discover the job.
4. If the guess is incorrect, the game continues. Repeat steps 2 and 3 until someone guesses correctly.

B Take turns being Student A and play "Guess my job!" again.

Check out the World Link video.

Practice your English online at http://elt.heinle.com/worldlink

Review: Units 7-9

1 Storyboard

A Harry is telling Linda about his dream. Complete the story. For some blanks, more than one answer is possible.

B Cover the story. Take turns telling it to your partner.

ASK ANSWER

Have you ever dreamed you were lost, flying, or falling? What do you think causes these kinds of dreams?

Review: Units 7–9

1 Storyboard

Warm Up

5 min

With books closed, ask students if they remember their dreams after they wake up. Do they enjoy dreaming? Why or why not?

A 10–20 min

Harry is telling Linda about his dream. Complete the story. For some blanks, more than one answer is possible.

Remind students that they practiced the past continuous and the simple past in Unit 8. Write examples of both tenses on the board, and see if students remember how each is used. If necessary, write descriptions on the board, or have students turn back to page 83. (Examples: *An action finished sometime in the past,* and *an action that was in progress at a certain time in the past.*)

Introduce the activity. Tell students that some of the blanks need verbs and some don't. When you check answers, put them on the board and number them for the frames of the story. (*1. happened; 2. was flying,* etc.)

B 10–20 min

Cover the story. Take turns telling it to your partner.

Tell students they are just telling Harry's story and only one partner speaks—they don't role play Linda or the farmer. Tell the story the way they should tell it, so they can see what to include and what to leave out. Give them some time to study the story before speaking. One partner closes the book and speaks. The other partner follows in the book and helps if the speaker gets stuck. If there's time, have each of them practice twice.

EXTRA! Telling a dream

15–20 min

Tell students to think of a dream they had that was like a story (first this happened, then something else happened, etc.). Alternatively, they can invent a dream-like story. They should use the simple past and the past continuous. Students can tell their story to a partner, or in a small class, they can tell the whole class. In a large class, students can tell their stories in groups. Let the speakers use notes, but not write out the dream and read it. Listeners should ask questions and say at least one thing they liked about the story.

Teaching Tip: Correcting grammar in speaking activities

When your students speak at some length without memorizing or reading a script, it's a good opportunity to observe their control of grammar. While they're speaking, correct individuals very little or not at all (grammar corrections at this time tend not to stick). Instead, walk around and note grammar problems for later attention. Focus your notes on one or two points, and don't collect too many examples—five or six are enough. Talk about them when the activity is over, and don't mention names!

EXTRA! Chain writing

20–30 min

Divide the class into large groups of six to eight people. Tell them they are going to create stories together. The stories should be dreams like Harry's, where one thing happened, then another thing happened, and so on. The storyteller is *I* (first person singular), and the verbs are in the simple past and the past continuous.

Each student takes a piece of paper, writes the first sentence at the top, and passes the paper to the next student. That student has two minutes to read the sentence, write a new sentence that follows it, and fold the paper so that only the new sentence shows. After two minutes, give a signal, and everyone passes their papers to the next student. Continue until the papers have gone all the way around the group. Students should unfold the papers and read the stories to the group. If you wish, have each group choose their best story to read to the class.

ASK ANSWER

Students can discuss their answers in groups of three or four. Also, many people find meaning in their dreams. What do students think dreams "mean," if anything? Have they known anyone whose dream seemed to predict the future?

Instructor's Notes

2 See It and Say It

Warm Up

5 min

With books closed, ask students what they know about movie premieres. What is a premiere? Who goes to them?

A Yesterday there was a movie premiere at the Galaxy Theater. Look at the picture. What were the people doing when the movie star arrived? Tell your partner.

5-10 min

Still with books closed, tell students they're going to look at a picture of a movie premiere held last night. Tell them to guess who was there and what they were doing when the star arrived. List their ideas in note form (*photographers—taking pictures; fans—waving, cheering; actors—walking on the red carpet*, etc.). Leave the notes on the board.

Now tell students to look at the picture and say who was at the premiere (*police officer, photographer, reporter, fans, driver*). If they're not sure, they can say *a man* or *a woman,* or they can guess an identity. Ask, *What were the fans doing when the star arrived?* Students should work in pairs to say everything they can about the picture. To check answers, compile a list of sentences on the board.

To follow up, look at the guesses that students made earlier. Which ones are not in the picture? See if they can make sentences about what was not happening. (*Actors weren't walking on the red carpet.*)

B Think of a movie you know. Write the name of the movie on the sign in the picture. Invite your partner to the premiere. Your partner should ask one or two questions.

15-20 min

Ask students to recall expressions for inviting, accepting, and refusing an invitation, or review them on page 72. Then introduce the pair activity and the situation: Student A has an extra ticket to a movie premiere right after class tonight. Have two volunteers demonstrate a possible conversation, prompting them as needed. After pair work, find out how many students said yes to the invitation and how many said no. What questions did they ask? Then move on to **C** for more practice.

Culture Tip: Accepting and refusing invitations

Students should remember not to seem impolite when responding to an invitation. This can happen if they ask a lot of questions and then say no. It can sound as if they are deciding whether they want to go, not whether they can go. Tell them to accept or refuse as soon as they know when the event is happening. They should ask about other details after that.

C Invite other friends to see the movie. Practice inviting and accepting or refusing invitations.

10-15 min

Students should choose a new movie for which they actually have three extra tickets. They keep inviting classmates until all the tickets are taken. This can be done as a mixer, with students moving around the room and finding their own partners. With a large group, divide the classroom in half or even smaller areas.

Instructor's Notes

2 See It and Say It

A Yesterday there was a movie premiere at the Galaxy Theater. Look at the picture. What were the people doing when the movie star arrived? Tell your partner.

B Think of a movie you know. Write the name of the movie on the sign in the picture. Invite your partner to the premiere. Your partner should ask one or two questions.

How'd you like to see the new *Twilight* movie with me?

Sure. When?

After class.

I'd love to, but ...

C Invite other friends to see the movie. Practice inviting and accepting or refusing invitations.

3 Listening

CD 2 Track 22

A Read the information in the box. Then listen and complete each person's profile below. Use one word in each blank.

Every year, the Dream Big Foundation gives $10,000 to a person between the ages of 17 and 22 so that he or she can do something important—go to college, study abroad, start a business, etc. This year, the foundation received thousands of applications from all over the world. There are now two finalists—Teresa Silva and Daniel Okoye. Who should get the prize?

Name: Teresa Silva **Age:** 21

What she does:
- She created a _website_ to help poor artists sell their products to the _world_.
- When a product sells, she takes _10_ % and gives _90_ % to the artists.
- Since _January_, she has already sold _1500_ items.

Why she needs the money:
- There's a lot of _work_ to do.

What she plans to do with the money:
- She plans to _hire_ one more person.
- She hopes to sell _twice_ as many items.

Name: Daniel Okoye **Age:** 18

What he does:
- He's a _student_.

Why he needs the money:
- His parents _died_ when he was _15_.
- He has no money for _college / university_

What he plans to do with the money:
- He wants to study _medicine_.
- He hopes to become a _doctor_ and help others.

B You work for the Dream Big Foundation. Review your notes in **A**. Follow the directions.

- Which words in the box below would you use to describe Teresa and Daniel? Why?
- In your opinion, which person should win the money? Why? Give at least two reasons.

brave / courageous	cautious	clever	efficient	flexible
motivated / ambitious	careless	independent	pleasant	punctual

C Get into a group of 3 or 4 people. Compare your answers in **B**. Together choose the winner of this year's prize. Then share your answer with the class.

I think Teresa should get the money because she's very clever . . .

So do I.

Yeah, but Daniel lost his parents as a teenager and . . .

3 Listening

Warm Up

5 min

Have students brainstorm words for describing people (Unit 9, page 90). When they can't think of any more, write these suffixes on the board and see if they suggest more words: *-able/-ible, -ent/-ant, -ous*.

CD 2 Track 22

10–15 min

A Read the information in the box. Then listen and complete each person's profile below. Use one word in each blank.

Write a pre-reading question on the board: *What does the Dream Big Foundation do?* After reading, tell students to look at the two profiles and notice the information that is missing. Play the audio once, check answers, and play it again.

A Teaching Option Further practice

In **B** and **C**, students will talk about the finalists in detail. For extra preparation, students can close their books and tell a partner about Teresa. The partner can do the same for Daniel. They can switch partners so that everyone talks about both finalists.

5–10 min

B You work for the Dream Big Foundation. Review your notes in A. Follow the directions.

Preview the activity in **C** so students know how they're going to use this information. Students can use the adjectives in the box, the ones on the board from Warm Up, or others. Walk around as students work to answer questions and to see how much more time they need.

B Teaching Option Support/challenge

In **C**, students will be talking with supporters of the other finalist. Students should work in groups so they can help each other—different groups for Daniel and Teresa. Tell them to prepare (1) reasons why their choice should win, and (2) reasons why the other finalist should not win. They can also try to predict what people will say against their choice, and think about how they can respond.

15–20 min

C Get into a group of 3 or 4 people. Compare your answers in B. Together choose the winner of this year's prize. Then share your answer with the class.

Explain the activity, but before forming groups, play the recording once more. Students can update their notes if necessary. Make sure the groups include supporters of both finalists. Suggest that Daniel's supporters speak first, then Teresa's (or the other way around). Then everyone discusses the two and votes on the winner—the majority wins. To follow up, find out who won in each group. Was the vote close? Did anyone change his or her mind?

10–15 min

EXTRA! Dictation

Use the paragraph in the blue box for a dictation. Read it through once, then again, breaking the sentences into meaningful phrases. (There are only three sentences in the paragraph.) Dictate punctuation: comma, dash (—), period. Let students be responsible for capitalization. Finally, read it through again for students to check anything they missed. Then one or two students write at the board.

Teaching Tip: Class-controlled dictation

Dictation is a very useful activity for teaching and review. In addition to listening, it gives students practice in spelling, vocabulary, and grammar. An alternative to traditional dictation is to have the students use you like an audio device. This teaches students to speak up in class and ask questions. Tell students you are going to read the passage. They should tell you when to stop, when to slow down, and when to start up again. They can ask any questions about spelling or punctuation, but you can only do what they tell you to do. (Usually you will get quite far into the dictation before a brave student dares to tell you to stop and start again!)

Instructor's Notes

4 Spot the Error

Warm Up

5 min

Ask students what's good about making mistakes. How can mistakes be useful in learning English, especially in writing?

10 min

A **Find and correct the mistake(s) in the sentences below. You have five minutes.**

Explain the activity. Tell students to pay special attention to verbs. Not all the mistakes are with verbs, but a lot are. Is the tense right? Is the subject singular or plural? Is the form correct? Show students how to make clear corrections, like the answers in this book. This is also the clearest way for students to correct something they have written by hand. Walk around while students are working to see how they're doing.

5-10 min

B **Compare your answers in A with a partner. If you have different answers, explain your corrections.**

After pair work, give students a chance to check answers that they didn't agree on with you. Or, if you know that the group missed a lot, check all the answers on the board. Explain (or students can explain) why each correction was necessary.

5 Speak for a Minute!

Warm Up

5-10 min

With books closed, ask students how long they think they can talk without stopping in their first language. 10 minutes? 5 minutes? 2 minutes? Would it be hard to do, or pretty easy? Ask a volunteer to talk for one minute on any topic. Then ask how long they could speak in English. Go on to **A**.

(Note that in **B**, it would be good to have a box or small bag available for each group to pick numbers from. But if necessary, pick them from someone's book bag, sweater—whatever. You'll need a watch or cell phone to time one minute.)

5-10 min

A **Read the questions below and think about your answers. Do not talk about your answers with anyone.**

Explain the whole game. **A** is preparation for **B**; in **B** they will talk about the topics in **A**. **B** is a competition, so they should prepare alone and not share their ideas. Point out that they have already talked about topics 1–4 in Units 7–9. They may need to think more about topics 5 and 6. They can make notes now to help them with their ideas, but they can't use notes in **B**. Do not let them write notes in their books.

10-20 min

B **Work with 3 other people.**

Have a watch for timing one minute—the time should be the same for everyone, so counting seconds in your head isn't ideal. Help students get ready to play. When you say, *Pick a number,* the first student picks a number, shows it to the group, and checks the topic in **A**. When you say, *Go!*, the students begin talking. When you say, *Stop!*, they stop. If someone stops speaking for more than three seconds, they don't win a point. To be fair, everyone should have the same number of turns. They can play two rounds by returning the numbers to the bag and picking again. Students shouldn't talk on the same topic twice.

B **Teaching Option** **Don't keep score!**

If you want to minimize the competitive aspect of this game, change the rules. The goal is for everyone in the group to succeed in speaking for a minute. If a student stops speaking, the others can suggest something to say, or even speak for the student until he or she is able to begin speaking again. Tell students to encourage speakers before they start, and congratulate them (even cheer) when they finish. You might practice congratulating in English before they begin. To follow up, ask which groups succeeded in having everyone talk for a minute, and congratulate them.

Teaching Tip: Competition in the classroom

Competition can energize a class and spark learning, or it can make students uncomfortable and stressed. Some of this relates to culture, some to the individual students, and some to conditions in the classroom. You are the best judge of whether your students will respond well to competitive activities. You may decide it's best to reduce the intensity of competitive activities by keeping them short or not keeping score.

5-10 min

EXTRA! **Speak for a minute**

Students can select a topic that they are comfortable talking about for a minute. Then each student can talk for a minute in front of a large group or the class. (Someone should be the timekeeper.) The group should provide feedback to the speaker on what else they could have said.

4 Spot the Error

A Find and correct the mistake(s) in the sentences below. You have five minutes.

1. **A:** I really liked that movie.
   B: So ~~am~~ did I.
2. After graduation, I hope ^to visit my cousin in New York City.
3. Sorry I missed your call. I ~~watched~~ was watching TV and I didn't hear the phone.
4. You seem ~~quietly~~ quiet today. Are you OK?
5. Maya's worked for the same company ~~since~~ for two years. Now she wants ^to quit and get a new job.
6. **A:** How long ~~you know~~ have you known John?
   B: Since high school. We ~~are~~ have been friends for many years.

B Compare your answers in **A** with a partner. If you have different answers, explain your corrections.

5 Speak for a Minute!

A Read the questions below and think about your answers.
Do not talk about your answers with anyone.

1. Talk about the last movie you saw. What was the story about?
2. Talk about a festival or holiday that you know. Where and when does it take place? What happens?
3. Which would you prefer to do—work for a company or work for yourself?
4. Talk about the last party you went to. What was it for? Who hosted it? Did you have a good time? Why or why not?
5. To speak English well, what do you need to do? What should you try not to do?
6. Name something you've wanted to do for a long time. Why haven't you done it yet?

B Work with 3 other people.

1. On six small pieces of paper, write a number 1 to 6. Put the six numbers in a hat or bag.
2. Take turns. Pick a question out of the hat or bag.
3. Answer the question. Talk for one minute without stopping and you get one point.
4. Continue until there are no more questions. The winner is the person with the most points.

10 Telecommunications

Lesson A Telephoning

1 Vocabulary Link **Give me a call.**

A Tell your partner: What kind of cell phone do you have? What do you like most about your phone?

B Look at the phrases in the chart. Then ask your partner: Which phrases do you know? What do they mean?

Phrases with *phone*	Phrases with *call*	Phrases with *message*
answer the phone	call (someone)	check your (text / phone) messages
be on the phone	call (someone) back	get a (text / phone) message
hang up the phone	get a call (from someone)	leave a message
turn on your phone	make a call	send (someone) a text message
turn off your phone	screen (your) calls	take a message

C Complete the sentences below. Use the <u>correct form of a verb</u> in the chart. Use each verb only once.

1. Before the movie starts, please _turn off_ your cell phones.
2. **A:** Carlos?
   B: Yeah, wait a minute . . . I _'m OR am_ on the phone. I'm talking to Marta.
3. **A:** I heard the phone ring. Who called?
   B: It was probably a wrong number. When I _answered_ the phone and said, "Hello," the person _hung up_.
4. **A:** Good morning, Barr and Associates.
   B: Mr. Choi, please.
   A: He's busy at the moment. Can I _take_ a message?
   B: No, thanks. I'll _call_ back later.
5. **A:** Ann, you _got_ a call from Bill earlier.
   B: Did he _leave_ a message?
   A: Yeah. He said to meet him at the library at 3:00.
6. **A:** Your phone is ringing. Aren't you going to answer it?
   B: No, I'm _screening_ my calls. I don't want to talk to Sam.
7. **A:** _Check_ your messages. I think Mom called you.
   B: No, I haven't _gotten_ a message from her. Oh, wait—she _sent_ me a text message. It says, "Dinner at 7:00."
8. Can I use your phone for a minute? I need to _make_ a call.

D Discuss the questions with a partner.

1. Do you talk on the phone a lot?
2. In one day, how many calls do you make? How many texts do you get? How many texts do you send?
3. Do you always answer your phone or do you sometimes screen your calls?

Telephoning

Unit 10, Lesson A

1 Vocabulary Link Give me a call.

Warm Up

5 min

With books closed, ask students about their first cell phone. What features did it have? Write them on the board.

A Tell your partner: What kind of cell phone do you have? What do you like most about your phone?

5 min

The most natural thing for students to do is to take out their cell phones and show each other their features. They'll want to know the names of the features in English, so they can ask you or each other. Or they can note the words to look up later, probably on the Internet, as print dictionaries aren't likely to have all of the terms. Follow this up in the next class.

Word Bank: Cell phones

camera
GPS (global positioning system) navigation
headset
keypad
music player
OGM (outgoing message)
PDA (personal digital assistant)
QWERTY keyboard
ringtone
speakerphone
touch screen
video
voice command
WiFi

(not) have a signal
be out of range
charge (a cell phone)

B Look at the phrases in the chart. Then ask your partner: Which phrases do you know? What do they mean?

10–15 min

Students should repeat the phrases in the chart with their partner. They should explain as many phrases as they can. You could also let them ask other students sitting near them—but don't tell them yourself. When all pairs have explained as many as they can, explain only those phrases with the whole class. (Some of them can be demonstrated using a cell phone.) It's better not to explain all of the phrases before doing **C**.

C Complete the sentences below. Use the <u>correct form of a verb</u> in the chart. Use each verb only once.

10–15 min

Working alone, students should fill in the phrases they know and guess the rest. Now is the time for them to learn any phrases that were not explained in **B**, so check answers with the whole class. You can ask two students to write answers on the board as you confirm them, writing alternate answers to keep up with you.

C Teaching Option Speaking

Check the answers as a class and then students can repeat and practice the mini-conversations (items 2–7). They can practice in pairs, or you can say one part and the class say the other, or you can divide the class into two groups to say them.

D Discuss the questions with a partner.

5 min

Read the questions. Say that after they talk, you're going to ask about some of their partners' answers. Suggest that they take notes. When they're ready, ask, *How many calls does your partner make in one day? More than 20? More than 50?* Find out the highest number of calls, then repeat for text messages received and sent.

Instructor's Notes

2 Listening On the phone

Skills: Choose an appropriate response; Listen for details; Make predictions

Warm Up

5–10 min

1. (In a non-English-speaking country) With books closed, ask if students have had phone conversations in English. Ask them, *Who made the call, you or the other person? How long did the call last? Was the call successful?* (That is, did both people give/get the necessary information?)
2. (In an English-speaking country) With books closed, ask how often students talk to strangers—people who work at doctors' offices, government offices, stores, etc.—on the phone in English. Is that easier or harder than reading the newspaper in English?

A CD 2 Track 23 — 10–15 min

Read the sentences below. Then listen to six conversations. In each conversation, what would the man say next? Choose the best response.

Give students time to read the sentences silently, or ask students to read them aloud. Play the audio once, giving enough time after each conversation for students to read and circle their answers. Play it again straight through while students circle any answers they missed.

Teaching Tip: Listening

Some students find it difficult to understand native speakers on a recording. If this is true of your students, you can read the script aloud. Listen to the script in advance and make notes about the feelings expressed by the actors. Also mark the places that are stressed. When you read, say *A* and *B* or write the letters on the board and point to them. After this, when you play the audio, students will understand it much better. If you wish, distribute copies of the script so that students can follow along as they listen to the recording. The audio scripts are found on pages T156–T170 and on the Teacher's Resources CD-ROM found in the back of this Lesson Planner.

B CD 2 Track 23 — 5 min

Listen to the conversations again and check your answers.

To check answers, play each conversation while a student reads the man's next line. Write the letters of the answers on the board.

ASK ANSWER

Students can answer the questions in groups of any convenient size. Tell them to choose the funniest or most interesting outgoing message (OGM) to tell the class.

World Link

Ask for a show of hands on the three answers, and tell students the correct answer. You can have them discuss these questions in pairs, small groups, or as a whole class.

1. How can you explain this? (Some possible explanations: second or multiple phones for business, people living "double" lives, pre-paid phones bought one after the other.)
2. Do you think other places may have more cell phones than people? Where? (In fact, more than 30 countries have more phones than people.)

3 Pronunciation

Repeating to clarify information

A CD 2 Track 24 — 5 min

Listen to this conversation. Notice the intonation of B's sentence. Why does B stress the underlined number?

Tell students that to stress something means to say it louder. B stresses 7 to ask if it's correct. B's voice rises at the end to make the statement into a question.

B CD 2 Track 25 — 10 min

Listen and complete the conversations. Then practice saying them aloud.

As students complete the conversations, they should also underline the stressed parts. Play the conversations or read them aloud for students to repeat. Make sure they are using stress and rising intonation correctly.

C 10–15 min

Practice the conversations in B with a partner. Then use your own phone number and practice again.

Since these are phone conversations, students should not look at each other. They can sit back to back (or side by side if the room is noisy).

They should practice at least twice, switching roles. For freer practice with their own numbers, write some first lines on the board for reference, and they can improvise conversations with books closed.

Language Tip: Phone numbers

The numbers 1 and 4, 3 and 8, 5 and 9 are often confused because the vowel sounds are similar. For the digit *O* in phone numbers, Americans often say the letter *O*, but may also say *zero*. In the United States, all phone numbers have seven digits. Americans customarily pause after the first three digits and say phone numbers as a series of single-digit numbers (5-5-5, 1-2-1-2—not *five fifty-five, twelve twelve*). The area code 800 is said *eight hundred*.

2 Listening On the phone

CD 2 Track 23

A Read the sentences below. Then listen to six conversations. In each conversation, what would the man say next? Choose the best response.

1. a. OK, I'll check my messages.
   b. No, thanks. I'll call back later.
   c. Yes, I left a message.
2. a. Please leave me a message and I'll call you back.
   b. Would you like to leave a message?
   c. May I ask who's calling?
3. a. When is a good time to call?
   b. No, nobody called.
   c. Thanks, I will.
4. a. No, he sent me a text message.
   b. He can't come to class today.
   c. I don't know. He hung up.
5. a. Why? Are you screening your calls?
   b. No, can I take a message?
   c. Sorry, I think you have the wrong number.
6. a. Hang up and try the number again.
   b. Oh, I think my cell phone was turned off.
   c. No, sorry. I don't know the answer.

CD 2 Track 23

B Listen to the conversations again and check your answers.

ASK ANSWER

Which item (1–6) in **A** is a voicemail recording? What does the outgoing message on your cell phone say?

WORLD LINK

Which capital city has more cell phones than people?
a. Washington, D.C. (U.S.)
b. Beijing (China)
c. Mexico City (Mexico)

3 Pronunciation Repeating to clarify information

CD 2 Track 24

A Listen to this conversation. Notice the intonation of B's sentence. Why does B stress the underlined number? *B is asking if they heard the number 7 correctly.*

A: My number is 555-6749.

B: 555-6<u>7</u>49?

A: Yes. 6-7-4-9.

CD 2 Track 25

B Listen and complete the conversations. Then practice saying them aloud.

1. **A:** My number is 555-2526.
   B: Did you say 555-*2926*?
   A: No, it's 2-5-2-6.
2. **A:** My work number is 800-221-5348.
   B: *5348*?
   A: That's correct.
3. **A:** You can call me at 555-1661.
   B: Was that 555-*6061*?
   A: No, it's 1-6-6-1.

C Practice the conversations in **B** with a partner. Then use your own phone number and practice again.

4 Speaking May I speak to Lisa, please?

CD 2
Track 26

A Celia and Lisa are chatting when their phone call is interrupted. Listen to the conversations. Which one is more formal?
The conversation with Prof. Larson is more formal.

Lisa: Hello?

Celia: Lisa? Hi. It's Celia.

Lisa: Oh, hey, Celia. How're you doing?

Celia: Pretty good. So, are you ready for the big test tomorrow?

Lisa: Almost, but I have one question. . . . (phone beeps) Oh, Celia, . . . can you hang on? I've got another call coming in.

Celia: Yeah, no problem.

Lisa: Hello?

Prof. Larson: Yes, hello. May I speak to Lisa Sanchez, please?

Lisa: Speaking.

Prof. Larson: Lisa, this is Professor Larson. You left me a message earlier today. You had a question about tomorrow's exam.

Lisa: Oh, right. Professor Larson, could you hold for a moment?

Prof. Larson: Of course.

Lisa: Hello, Celia? Can I call you back? I have to take the other call.

Celia: Sure. Talk to you later.

B Practice the conversation in **A** with two classmates. Use your own names in the dialog.

5 Speaking Strategy

A Make the conversation below more polite by changing the underlined words. Then practice it with a partner.

A: Hello?

B: Hi. Is Kurt there? *Hello. May/Could/Can I speak to Kurt, please?*

A: Who's calling? *May I ask who's calling?*

B: This is Martin.

A: OK, hang on. *Would/Could you hold (for a minute)?*

B: Sure.

A: Sorry, he's not in. Can I take a message? *May I take a message? / Would you like to leave a message?*

B: No, thanks. I'll call back later.

B Create two phone conversations with your partner. One should be informal. The other should be more formal.

C Perform your conversations for another pair. Can they guess which one is more formal?

Useful Expressions: Using the telephone	
Asking for someone & responding	Hi, Lisa? / Hi. Is Lisa there? Hello. May / Could / Can I speak to Lisa, please? [formal] This is Lisa. / Speaking.
Asking for identification of caller	Who's calling? May I ask who's calling? [formal]
Asking someone to wait	Hang on. / Can you hang on (for a moment / second)? Would / Could you hold (for a moment / second)? [formal]
Taking a message	Can I take a message? May I take a message? [formal] Would you like to leave a message? [formal]

4 Speaking **May I speak to Lisa, Please?**

Warm Up

5 min

With books closed, ask students if they speak the same way to their friends as to a professor, a boss, or a doctor. What's different?

CD 2 Track 26

10–15 min

A Celia and Lisa are chatting when their phone call is interrupted. Listen to the conversations. Which one is more formal?

Play the recording once with books open. Tell students to notice where the second conversation begins and which conversation is more formal. Follow up and ask what expressions make the second conversation more formal. In the first conversation, what are some much-less-formal expressions? (*Oh, hey, Celia. How're you doing?* and *Pretty good. So, are you ready . . .* and *Yeah, no problem.*) Notice that Celia's *Pretty good* is not strictly grammatical—that would be *Pretty well*—but it's correct because it's what everyone says.

10–15 min

B Practice the conversation in A with two classmates. Use your own names in the dialog.

Play the audio again if you wish, then read it line by line, with students repeating. Before practicing with their own names, students need to decide who answers the phone (Lisa), who is the caller (Celia), and who is the professor. If possible, students should practice three times so that everyone plays all three roles.

5 Speaking Strategy

15–20 min

A Make the conversation below more polite by changing the underlined words. Then practice it with a partner.

Read the Useful Expressions, pointing out which are formal and which are not. Introduce the activity, and tell students to write their changes on the blank lines or a separate piece of paper. They should work alone at first, then with a partner, to combine their ideas into a conversation that both of them like. Check answers with the whole class, approving all appropriate sentences. Finally, pairs can practice the conversation, back to back.

Grammar Tip: Formal vs. polite

In most world languages, formality is designated through grammar. For example, in Spanish, Portuguese, and French there are different verb forms for a formal *you* and an informal *you*. In Korean there are different verb endings depending on the relationship of the speakers. In Japanese there are different forms to be used depending on age, gender, and relationship to the speaker.

English doesn't use grammar to designate formality, but it does require the learner to consider which phrases a person chooses to use in different situations.

10–15 min

B Create two phone conversations with your partner. One should be informal. The other should be more formal.

If practical, students should work with new partners. Tell students that they are to create entirely new conversations, not to follow the ones in **A** and Speaking. They should start by deciding the situation for each conversation. They can treat one situation both formally and informally, or have two different situations. Give them time to practice their conversations.

10–15 min

C Perform your conversations for another pair. Can they guess which one is more formal?

Students should perform their conversations without reading—and if possible without notes—and sit back to back. If students can't guess which is more formal, the four students should work together to revise the conversations as needed. Probably only one or two changes will be necessary.

Large Class Option

Rather than students working in groups of four, they can work in larger groups. In this case, put the pairs in **B** into groups of six or eight to perform their conversations in **C**.

6 Language Link

Permission with *may, can, could, would / do you mind if . . .*

Warm Up

5 min

Ask students, *What do you ask permission to do? Who do you ask? Who asks you?*

A 10–15 min

Study the chart. Then complete the sentences below with the correct word or phrase from the chart. Sometimes more than one answer is possible.

In the chart, point out the formality scale at the left. Also point out the different verb forms in the questions, even though the meaning in all three is *now*. The conditional question, *Would you mind if . . . ?* takes the past tense form of the verb. The other two questions take the simple present tense. Emphasize that *Would you/Do you mind if . . . ?* require negative verbs to say *yes* or to give permission. After students complete the sentences, review all the acceptable answers before they go on to **B**.

B 10–15 min

Work with a partner and do the following:

(See Student Book page 107 for complete instructions.)

Suggest that students mark the formal questions (2, 5, and 7) with an *F*. Remind them that formal questions should be answered formally. Model the questions and have students repeat them before practicing. If you feel your students need more preparation, two to four pairs can demonstrate the first question and answer. Walk around while they practice to notice any problems and facilitate the activity. Follow up by reviewing one or two problems you noticed.

C 10–15 min

Read each situation below. Use the verbs in parentheses to ask permission.

Students should refer to the chart—the questions and the formality scale—to compose their questions. Do the first one on the board with the whole class to show them what to do (or make up a new one to use as an example). Review all the possible answers with the whole class to be sure their questions are correct before going on to **D**.

D 5–10 min

With a partner, take turns asking and answering the questions in C. Refuse (say *no* to) one request and give a reason why.

Review the responses in the chart again before students practice responding to requests for permission. To follow up, ask four pairs to perform a question and a refusal for the class.

Instructor's Notes

6 Language Link **Permission with *may, can, could, would / do you mind if . . .***

A Study the chart. Then complete the sentences below with the correct word or phrase from the chart. Sometimes more than one answer is possible.

Asking for permission			Responding
most formal	**Would you mind if**	I used your phone?	No, not at all. / No, go ahead. Sorry, but . . .
↕	**Do you mind if**	I use your phone?	
least formal	**May / Could** **Can**		Certainly. / Of course. Sure, no problem. / OK. Sorry, but . . .

1. Do you mind if/May/Could/Can I use your dictionary? I need to look up a word.
2. Would you mind if I borrowed your notes from yesterday's class? I was sick.
3. Do you mind if / May / Could / Can I call you back in ten minutes? Someone is at the door.
4. Excuse me, Professor Walker. Do you mind if / May / Could / Can I talk to you for a minute?
5. It's cold in here. Would you mind if I closed the window?
6. Do you mind if / May / Could / Can I sit here or is this seat taken?
7. Would you mind if I made a phone call in here?

B Work with a partner and do the following:

- Review your questions in **A**. Which ones were formal? Which questions were more informal?
- Take turns asking and answering the questions. Use the responses in the chart to help you.

C Read each situation below. Use the verbs in parentheses to ask permission.

1. Your friend is doing his / her homework. You have finished your homework, and you want to watch TV. Ask permission very informally. (turn on)
   Can I turn on the TV?
2. You're invited to a party on Saturday night. You want your friend to go, too. Ask the host's permission a little formally. (bring)
   May / Could / Do you mind if I bring a friend to the party on Saturday night?
3. You were sick yesterday and missed an important test in class. You want to take it this Friday. Ask your teacher's permission formally. (take)
   I missed the test yesterday because I was sick. Would you mind if I took the test this Friday?
4. Your teacher doesn't allow cell phones turned on in class. You just got an important text and need to read it. Ask your teacher's permission formally. (check)
   Would you mind if I checked my messages? This message is very important.

D With a partner, take turns asking and answering the questions in **C**. Refuse (say *no* to) one request and give a reason why.

7 Communication **Good news!**

A Get into groups of three: Student A, Student B, and Student C. Read the instructions.

Student A: Choose one piece of good news from the list below.

☐ I bought a cool new scooter!	☐ I got an "A" on my exam!	☐ I've got two tickets to a concert!
☐ I found your lost wallet!	☐ I got a new job!	☐ your idea: ____________

Student B: Have a piece of paper and a pen ready to write down a message.

Student C: Choose a reason you are busy from the list below.

☐ You're taking a nap.	☐ You're out with friends.
☐ You're at the library.	☐ your idea: ____________

B Role play these three conversations.

Step 1: Student A wants to give some good news to Student C, but Student B answers the phone. Student B explains why Student C is busy and takes Student A's message.

A: Hello. May I speak to Bianca, please?

B: I'm sorry, she's taking a nap. Can I take a message?

A: Yes. This is Ernesto. Would you tell her I found her wallet?

B: Sure, no problem. What's your number?

A: It's . . .

> **Remember! How to make a request**
>
> **Can/Could/Will/Would** you answer the phone?
> OK. / Sure, no problem. / I'd be glad to.
>
> **Would you mind** answering the phone?
> No, not at all. / No, I'd be glad to.

Step 2: Student B writes down the message and gives the information to Student C.

:: WHILE YOU WERE OUT ::
Ernesto **called.**
Time: 12:30
Message: He found your wallet.
Phone number: 555-9733

Step 3: Student C calls Student A back to find out about the good news. Ask at least two questions.

C: Hi, Ernesto. It's Bianca.

A: Hi, Bianca. I have some good news. I found your wallet.

C: That's great! Where did you find it?

A: In the school cafeteria.

C: Thanks a lot, Ernesto. Could you bring it to school tomorrow?

C Switch roles so everyone gets a chance to play each role.

7 Communication Good news!

Warm Up

5 min

With books closed, tell students to think of something really good that happened to them lately—some good news that they wanted to tell their friends about. Ask some volunteers to say what happened.

A **Get into groups of three: Student A, Student B, and Student C. Read the instructions.**

5–10 min

This activity is preparation for the role plays in **B** and **C**. Preview the activity in **B** so that students understand what they're doing in **A**. In **B** and **C**, all students will play all three roles; they should prepare for them now. Every student chooses a piece of good news to tell (as Student A), takes out a piece of paper to write a message on (as Student B), and chooses a reason why they can't take a phone call (as Student C). Encourage them to use their own ideas as Students A and C.

Teach this before going on to **B**. Students practiced requests in Unit 5. Review the verb forms: the base form with *Can/Could/Will/Would*, and the *-ing* form (present participle) with *Would you mind . . . ?* Tell students to underline a request in **B**, Step 1. (*Would you tell her I found her wallet?*) How can they say this formally? (*Would you mind telling her . . . ?*) How can they answer it formally? (*I'd be glad to. or Sorry, but . . . .*) Ask the same about the request in Step 3.

(Note that *Can I take a message?* in Step 1 is not a request—it's an offer to help.)

B **Role play these three conversations.**

10–15 min

Students are still in their groups from **A**. Review the instructions. Before they start, Student C must tell Student B why he or she can't take Student A's call. Tell them that in Step 2, Student B "leaves" the message where Student C will find it—there is no conversation. (Student C should "find" it immediately!) Tell students to follow the model conversations in the book, using their own names and the information they prepared in **A**. Walk around while they talk to see if there are any problems that need immediate attention. Help groups separately unless the problem is general. In that case, stop the class and review or explain it so that they can continue practicing effectively. In any case, pause after this first round to give feedback and answer questions. Then go on to **C**.

Teaching Tip: Students who were absent for A

If you have not been able to do **A** and **B** on the same day, some students may be present now who were absent when you did **A**. Ask those students to wait a few minutes while you organize groups for the students who are up to speed with the activity. These students should still have the information they prepared from the last class. Review the activity quickly, put them in new groups of three, and get them started. Then bring the absentees together, prepare them, and put them in groups together.

B–C Teaching Option Support/challenge

If students handle the first round of conversations easily, they may become bored practicing the same ones three times. For the second or third round, they should close their books and improvise similar conversations but use their own words. Now Student B could hand the message to Student C, and they could improvise a short conversation. You might also recommend this challenge to selected groups while the others continue with the original conversations.

C **Switch roles so everyone gets a chance to play each role.**

20–25 min

For rounds two and three, again walk around to notice problems. To follow up, congratulate the class! Review one or two points you noticed during practice.

Instructor's Notes

Cell-phone society
Unit 10, Lesson B

1 Vocabulary Link

How polite are you?

Warm Up

5 min

With books closed, introduce the topic of cell-phone use in public. Ask if students have ever seen two strangers having an argument about cell-phone use. Where did it happen? What was the problem? How did the argument end?

A 15-20 min

Read the quiz. Pay attention to the words and phrases in blue. Use your dictionary to help you.

Tell students to read the title of the quiz. What do they think *etiquette* means? (Answers may include correct behavior or good manners.) They should be able to guess pretty closely. Tell them not to answer the quiz yet—they'll do that in **C**. If there are blue words that they can't figure out, explain how to use a dictionary while reading.

Teaching Tip: Using a dictionary while reading

Always impress upon your students that the best way to deal with unknown words while reading—even in their first language—is to get the general meaning from the context. They shouldn't lose their concentration to work on vocabulary. However, if students wish to learn the exact meaning, suggest that they mark the word and go back to it later to use a dictionary.

1. Find the word in the dictionary and read the definition.
2. Look back at the word in context to see if the definition makes sense. If it doesn't, try a bigger dictionary that gives more definitions.
3. If there is more than one definition, try each one in the context until they find the one that fits.
4. Add the word to their vocabulary notebook.

B 15-20 min

Complete the chart of opposites with a word or phrase in blue from A. Then explain the meaning of the words with a partner.

Students should work alone to complete the chart, or as much of it as they can. Then in pairs, they can explain the meaning of each word and its opposite, and fill in any words that they missed. There are many possible ways to express the meaning of each word. For this reason, check answers with the whole class and get more than one explanation for each one.

C 10-15 min

Now take the quiz in A. Then explain your answers to a partner.

Students should fill in their own answers before discussing them with their partners. Follow up by asking about students' *My idea* answers. Find out who wrote their own ideas and what they said.

Instructor's Notes

Lesson B Cell-phone society

1 Vocabulary Link How polite are you?

A Read the quiz. Pay attention to the words and phrases in blue. Use your dictionary to help you.

High-Tech Etiquette: How polite are you?

1. You're on a date and you get a text from a friend. It says, "How's it going?" What do you do?

- ☐ Check it and respond right away.
- ☐ Ignore the message. Answering it now would be rude.
- ☐ My idea: ____________

2. You're on the bus. The person next to you is listening to really loud music on his MP3. What do you do?

- ☐ Ask him to turn down the music. You don't want to hear it!
- ☐ Put on your headphones and turn up your music loud, too.
- ☐ My idea: ____________

3. I think cell phones should be . . .

- ☐ banned in crowded places like subways and airplanes. No one should be able to use them.
- ☐ allowed everywhere. I should be able to make a call wherever I want to.
- ☐ My idea: ____________

4. When talking on my cell phone in public (on the bus, in a restaurant), I usually . . .

- ☐ raise my voice so the caller can hear me clearly.
- ☐ lower my voice. I don't want others to hear my conversation.
- ☐ My idea: ____________

5. You want to put some funny pictures of your friend on your social networking site, but the photos might make your friend uncomfortable. What do you do?

- ☐ Show your friend the photos first. It's the thoughtful thing to do.
- ☐ Just post the photos. If he doesn't like them, you can delete them.
- ☐ My idea: ____________

B Complete the chart of opposites with a word or phrase in blue from **A**. Then explain the meaning of the words with a partner.

What does *respond* mean?

Well, if you *respond* to a question, you answer it. The opposite is *ignore*.

Word	Opposite
respond	ignore
polite	rude
turn down	turn up
banned	allowed
raise your voice	lower your voice
thoughtless	thoughtful
add, post	delete

C Now take the quiz in **A**. Then explain your answers to a partner.

2 Listening Do you mind?

CD 2 Track 27

A Read the items below. Then listen to the conversations and choose the best answers for each one.

Conversation 1

1. The speakers are in a ___________.

   a. classroom
   b. restaurant
   c. movie theater

2. The man is asking the girl to ___________.

   a. turn off her phone
   b. lower her voice
   c. turn down her music

Conversation 2

1. The speakers are ___________.

   a. on a plane
   b. at a concert
   c. in a movie theater

2. After the woman talks to him, the man probably ___________.

   a. listens to an announcement
   b. ends his phone call
   c. stops using his MP3

Conversation 3

1. The girl is worried because ___________ on the website Linkbook.

   a. she doesn't have any friends
   b. a friend wrote an angry message to her
   c. she doesn't want to be friends with someone

2. What will the girl probably do next?

   a. become friends with Manny
   b. ignore Manny's request
   c. call Manny at home

CD 2 Track 27

B Listen to the conversations again. Then ask a partner:
What information in each conversation helped you choose your answers?

ASK ANSWER

Think about the situations in the three conversations. Have these things ever happened to you?

3 Reading Phone free in the car?

A Read the title and first paragraph on page 111. Then tell a partner:
What new law passed recently? Is the law working?
The new law bans all cell-phone use while you are driving—including talking on the phone, texting, and e-mailing.

B Read the readers' comments. Then match each person with his or her opinion. (Two readers have the same opinion.)

Person	Opinion
Simon	Some cell-phone use in the car should be allowed.
Alexis	
Yalun	All cell-phone use in the car should be banned.

C Look at your answers in **B**. Why does each person have this opinion? Give a reason for each person from the reading.

1. Simon:
   Using your cell phone and driving at the same time causes accidents . . . or worse.
2. Alexis:
   Sometimes we have to use our cell phones to help others while we are driving (for example, if we see an accident).
3. Yalun:
   Talking on the phone while driving (using a hands-free device) is the same as listening to music or talking to a passenger while you are driving. The last two are OK, so using the hands-free device to talk while driving should be, too.

2 Listening Do you mind?

Skills: Listen for the gist; Draw conclusions; Infer information

5 min

Warm Up

With books closed, ask students if they and their friends all have the same ideas about using cell phones in public. Do they agree about when it's OK and when it isn't? If not, what different ideas do they have?

CD 2 Track 27

10–15 min

A Read the items below. Then listen to the conversations and choose the best answers for each one.

Students should read the questions for Conversation 1. Ask if the speakers are male or female. Who is probably younger? (The female, because of the word *girl*.) Play the conversation (twice if necessary) and allow time for students to answer the questions. Check the answers immediately. Before playing Conversations 2 and 3, ask students what they can guess about the speakers.

CD 2 Track 27

10–15 min

B Listen to the conversations again. Then ask a partner: What information in each conversation helped you choose your answers?

Tell students to make notes of the words and expressions that helped them in **A**. For example, in 1, how did they know it was a restaurant? What told them that the man wanted the girl to lower her voice? Play each conversation again, giving students time to make notes. Students can compare their ideas in pairs. If there are different ideas, you may want to follow up at the end by playing the conversations again so that students can verify what they heard. You might also copy the script so students can follow as you play the conversations again.

15–20 min

EXTRA! Role play

Make groups of six—three pairs per group. Each pair takes one conversation and role plays it for the group using their own words.

ASK ANSWER

Students can discuss the question in pairs or groups. Students who say *yes* should tell the story of their experience. What was the situation, and how did it end?

3 Reading Phone free in the car?

Skills: Understand the main ideas and supporting details; Identify opinions; Read for details; Understand referents

5 min

Warm Up

Ask students if they talk on their cell phones or text message while driving. Get a show of hands. Ask if there are any driving situations when they don't use their phones. (If students don't drive, ask about the habits of friends or family members.)

10–15 min

A Read the title and first paragraph on page 111. Then tell a partner: What new law passed recently? Is the law working?

Before students read, review the questions. What does the second question mean? How do you decide if a law is working? On the next page, point out the footnotes for the first paragraph. Tell students to underline the information that tells them the answers. When students have finished and are ready to talk, put them in pairs. At the end, if you think some students may not have gotten the answers, review them with the whole class.

10–15 min

B Read the readers' comments. Then match each person with his or her opinion. (Two readers have the same opinion.)

Introduce the matching activity and point out that there are three readers and two opinions. On the next page, be sure that students understand this is a news website; readers write comments about articles that interest them. Tell students to use the context to figure out unfamiliar words while they read. If they can't do the matching activity without a certain word, tell them to underline it and keep reading. At the end, answer vocabulary questions if students say they couldn't complete the activity without the word.

10–20 min

C Look at your answers in B. Why does each person have this opinion? Give a reason for each person from the reading.

Students read again if necessary to find the reasons each person gives for his or her opinion. They should write the reasons as complete sentences. Walk around looking for correct answers, and send those students to the board to write them. Try to get two answers about each reader, expressed in different words. Discuss the answers with the class. Finally, ask students to tell you about any mistakes in grammar or spelling that they see, and make appropriate corrections.

5-10 min

D **Look at the highlighted words in the passage and complete the sentences with the correct answer.**

In this activity, the highlighted words are reference words. Read the instructions and the sentences. If you wish, use *things like this* to demonstrate the task. After checking answers, if you think more examples would be helpful, use *this* in line 3 and *they* in the next-to-last line.

Teaching Tip: Referents in readings

Understanding referents is a valuable reading skill. Readers who are aware of referents are not confused when words like *this, they, it,* and *that* refer to words mentioned earlier in a passage. When doing any reading, take the time to stop and ask students what a pronoun refers to. See if students have the same answer. Tell students to place the proper noun/noun in place of the pronoun and see if the sentence makes sense.

ASK ANSWER

Students can discuss their answers in groups. Do they agree with the reasons the reader gives, or just the opinion? If they have the same opinion but different reasons, they should explain and discuss their reasons.

20-40 min

EXTRA! Poster project

A public service sign or poster tries to encourage people to think about certain issues and maybe change their behavior. In pairs or groups, students can design public service posters about behavior in public places. They should say where their poster should be displayed (on buses, in doctor's waiting rooms, in libraries, in schools, etc.). After students present their posters to the class, hang them where students can see them and discuss them. The class can then vote for the best ones. Some possible topics are:

1. Using cell phones in public places
2. Using MP3 players in public places
3. Walking dogs without a leash
4. Riding bicycles on the sidewalk
5. Littering
6. Using rough language in public places
7. Having loud conversations in public places
8. Smoking in public places

10 min

EXTRA! Discussion questions

Have students discuss these questions in groups.

1. In your country, is there a law like the one in the reading? If there is, do most people obey it or break it? If there isn't such a law, do you think there should be one? Explain your reasons.
2. In your country, do young people and older people usually have different feelings about cell phones? If they do, how are they different? Who do you agree with, mostly? Do you understand the other point of view?
3. In your country, do most people like their cell phone service? If not, how could it be better?

20-30 min

EXTRA! Additional reading

For more practice with opinions, see Heinle's Footprint Reading Library *Making a Deal*.

For more practice reading at this level, see Heinle's Page Turners Reading Library *Bad Blood*.

Instructor's Notes

NewOnline

NEWSONLINE

World | National | Regional | Business | Technology | Science

Phone free in the car?

Back to article »

A new law passed recently. It bans all cell-phone use while you are driving—including talking on the phone, texting, and e-mailing. The fine[1] for breaking the law[2] is high, but many drivers are ignoring the ban. What do you think about this problem?

Add your comment

Readers' Comments

Look—I've got a cell phone, and I'm glad to have it. But come on! Talking on the phone or texting while you're driving is crazy. And yet, I see people doing **things like this** every day. Using your cell phone and driving at the same time causes accidents . . . or worse. There have been many studies to prove this. My question is: Where are the police? **They** don't seem to care, so it's easy for drivers to ignore the law. When people are afraid of getting a large fine, cell-phone use in the car will stop. Everyone needs to learn that when you drive, you should turn off your phone. It's very simple! ~Simon

OK, I agree—texting or having a long phone conversation while driving is hazardous. But can we really ban all cell-phone use in cars? For example, yesterday I was driving home and I saw an accident on the road. I made a call and reported **it**. Did I stop driving to make the call? No. But did I help someone? Yes. We need to talk more about this new law. I just don't think the answer to the problem is so simple. ~Alexis

I don't think we can ban all cell-phone use in cars—especially if you use a hands-free device while driving, like I do. Look, I listen to the radio in my car. Isn't the music distracting[3]? Sometimes my friend is in the car with me. I talk to her while I'm driving. Isn't **that** dangerous? I mean, isn't talking on the phone (hands-free) the same as listening to music or talking to a passenger? In my opinion, they ARE all the same, and so I think we should be able to chat on the phone while we're driving. ~Yalun

[1] A **fine** is money you pay when you break a law.
[2] If you **break a law**, you do something illegal.
[3] If something is **distracting**, it makes it hard to pay attention.

D Look at the highlighted words in the passage and complete the sentences with the correct answer.

In the reading, . . .

1. *Things like this* means ___________.
   a. talking on the phone while driving b. texting while driving c. both a and b
2. *They* means ___________.
   a. the drivers b. the police c. both a and b
3. *It* means the ___________.
   a. accident b. driver c. call
4. *That* means ___________.
   a. talking while driving b. using a hands-free device c. listening to music

ASK ANSWER

Whose opinion(s) do you agree with? Why?

4 Language Link **Verb + gerund vs. verb + infinitive**

A Read the note on the right and study the chart.

Verbs followed by infinitive only		Verbs followed by gerund only		Verbs followed by gerund or infinitive	
agree	plan	appreciate	feel like	can't stand	prefer
choose	prepare	avoid	finish	continue	start
decide	seem	can't help	imagine	like	try
hope	want	dislike	keep	love	
learn	would like	enjoy	suggest		
need		(not) mind			

an infinitive (*to* + verb):
I like **to talk** on the phone.

a gerund (verb + *-ing*):
I like **talking** on the phone.

B Notice the use of the gerund or the infinitive in each sentence. Check (✔) the sentences that are correct. Change the incorrect sentences.

1. ☑ I learned to speak Spanish when I was four.
   Correct
2. ☐ I avoid to use cell phones in public places.
   Incorrect: I avoid using cell phones in public places.
3. ☑ I like playing sports.
   Correct
4. ☐ I appreciated to receive such a beautiful gift.
   Incorrect: I appreciated receiving such a beautiful gift.
5. ☐ I agreed turning down the music on my MP3.
   Incorrect: I agreed to turn down the music on my MP3.
6. ☑ I prefer to respond to messages quickly.
   Correct

C How do you feel about the activities below? Use the verbs in the box with the phrases in parentheses to write sentences. Answers will vary.

avoid hate need can't stand enjoy like (not) mind want

1. (study on weekends) I hate to study on weekends.
2. (talk on the phone) ______________
3. (get wrong numbers) ______________
4. (eat junk food) ______________
5. (cook at home) ______________
6. (go to the beach) ______________

D Compare your ideas in **C** with a partner.

I hate to study on weekends.

Me, too. I can't stand studying on weekends.

5 Writing **Opinions about cell phones**

A Look back at question 3 on page 109. Then, on a separate piece of paper, complete the information in the box.

I think cell-phone use should be ______________
Reason: ______________
Reason: ______________
Concluding sentence: For these reasons, I think . . .

I think cell phones should be banned in places like subways and airplanes for two important reasons. First, these places are very small and crowded. People often raise their voices when they talk on the phone. Imagine everyone talking on their phones at once. How noisy! Second . . .

B Use your outline in **A** to write a short paragraph like the example on the right.

C Exchange papers with a partner. Are your opinions similar or different?

4 Language Link

Verb + gerund vs. verb + infinitive

Warm Up

5 min

With books closed, have a short discussion. Students have been talking about people's use of cell phones and MP3 players in public. What other public behavior causes discussion? Smoking? Littering? List their ideas on the board. How do they feel about these things personally?

A Read the note on the right and study the chart.

5–10 min

Write the two sentences in the i-box on the board. Point out the two different structures after the verb *like*. *To talk* is an infinitive; *talking* is a gerund. Have students find *like* in the chart. It's in column 3 because it can have either an infinitive or a gerund after it. Column 1 verbs can only be followed by an infinitive; column 2 verbs, only by a gerund. Explain that there is no rule to predict which group a verb belongs to—students have to learn them one by one. (Note that many of the verbs in columns 1 and 3 were introduced with infinitives in Unit 9.)

Language Tip: *Gerund*

An *-ing* verb form (present participle) is called a gerund when it's used as a noun.

I enjoy *conversation*.	(noun)
I enjoy *it*.	(pronoun)
I enjoy *talking*.	(gerund)

B Notice the use of the gerund or the infinitive in each sentence. Check (✓) the sentences that are correct. Change the incorrect sentences.

10–15 min

Make sure students understand that they need to look for the first verb in the chart (*learned, avoid,* etc.). Then they should check to see if the next verb (*to speak, to use,* etc.) is in the correct form. Check answers with the whole class. Write the changed sentences on the board or call on students to write them.

C How do you feel about the activities below? Use the verbs in the box with the phrases in parentheses to write sentences.

10–20 min

Walk around checking students' papers while they work. Give a checkmark if the verb form is correct or an X if it's wrong. Try to get to as many students as possible, even if you check only one sentence on each paper, but try to find a mistake that they can correct.

D Compare your ideas in C with a partner.

5–10 min

Point out the example conversation and have two students read it aloud. Ask one or two pairs of students to demonstrate with their own sentences for 3 and 4. Then students can compare their sentences with similar conversations.

5 Writing **Opinions about cell phones**

Warm Up

5 min

Discuss student writing. Refer to the fact that students often read each other's writing in class. What kinds of things make their classmates' writing more interesting? Ask for examples.

A Look back at question 3 on page 109. Then, on a separate piece of paper, complete the information in the box.

5–10 min

Explain that this is preparation for **B**, in which they will write a paragraph with these ideas.

B Use your outline in A to write a short paragraph like the example on the right.

15–25 min

Ask a student to read the example paragraph aloud. Show how it follows the outline in **A**. Point out that the writer has four sentences for the first reason, not just one. Students should support and explain their reasons in the same way.

C Exchange papers with a partner. Are your opinions similar or different?

10–15 min

As students finish writing, pair them to read each other's papers. Remind them that hard-to-read papers can be read aloud by the writer. Students should compare their opinions and discuss the differences. You can also have students comment on one thing they like in their partner's paper, even if they disagree.

C Teaching Option Process Writing

Students can revise their writing after discussing it with their partner. They can revise in class or at home. Follow up in the next class by asking students to exchange papers with a new partner. Students should tell the partner what they changed and why.

6 Communication

How young is too young?

Warm Up

5–10 min

With books closed, ask how old students were when they got their first cell phone. Have they ever had an argument with their parents (or children) about cell phones? What was the reason for the argument?

A 15–20 min

Take this quiz about children and cell phones. Compare your answers with a partner. Then check your answers on page 154. Are any of these statistics similar in your country?

Ask if students were surprised by the answers on page 154. Pairs should join together to make groups of four to compare their country to the countries in items 1, 3, and 4. They don't have statistics, so they can discuss and guess as a group. Appoint a reporter for each group. At the end of the discussion, have the reporters give their group's best guesses. Were the groups' ideas different, or similar?

B 10 min

Evan is twelve years old. He wants a cell phone. Read what each person thinks about the situation.

Tell students this is preparation for **C**, and briefly explain the role play. Give students time to read and remember what each person thinks.

C 20–30 min

Get into groups of four. Each student role plays a person in B. Discuss whether Evan should get a cell phone. What is your group's final decision? Explain it to the class.

Students can chose their roles, or you can assign them. The role play has two parts. In part 1, everyone says what he or she thinks. In part 2, they have to make a decision. They must find a compromise—an agreement so that Evan gets a cell phone (now or soon), and his mother, father, and doctor are all happy. The group should work out the details together, and Mr. or Mrs. Logan reports them to the class.

Large Class Option

Students can write out a conversation between two of the people in **B**.

EXTRA! Writing prompt

20–25 min

1. Agree or disagree with this statement. Today, mothers are always in touch with their children by cell phone. As a result, children are growing up without learning how to be independent and make their own decisions.
2. Agree or disagree with this statement. Children today spend much more time with TV, cell phones, and video games than they do playing physically active games. As a result, they are obese (too fat) and have other serious health problems.

World Link Video and World Link website

Remind students of the value of further practice outside the classroom. Ask students who have watched the video or done online practice to share their experiences.

Instructor's Notes

Check out the World Link Video. Practice your English online at http://elt.heinle.com/worldlink

6 Communication How young is too young?

Do you think young children should have cell phones? Why or why not?

A Take this quiz about children and cell phones. Compare your answers with a partner. Then check your answers on page 154. Are any of these statistics similar in your country?

Cell Phone Quiz

1. A survey in the U.S says ___ of 8- to 12-year-olds have a cell phone.
   a. 4%
   b. 21%
   c. 45%

2. A study in Britain says that cell phones may be dangerous for children's ___.
   a. brains
   b. ears
   c. voices

3. A recent law in Bangladesh says that children under 16 cannot ___ cell phones.
   a. buy
   b. sell
   c. use

4. In Japan, more than 80% of teenagers and ___ of junior high school students have cell phones.
   a. 5%
   b. 25%
   c. 60%

B Evan is twelve years old. He wants a cell phone. Read what each person thinks about the situation.

Evan Logan

"I want to get a cell phone. All my friends have one. I need one to make phone calls and play games."

Mrs. Logan

"I can't relax unless Evan has a phone. I want to be able to reach Evan immediately if I have to."

Mr. Logan

"Why does a 12-year-old need a cell phone? He's a kid! He should be playing, not making phone calls."

Evan's doctor

"Cell phones are convenient, but it may not be safe for children to use them a lot."

C Get into groups of four. Each student role plays a person in **B**. Discuss whether Evan should get a cell phone. What is your group's final decision? Explain it to the class.

Dad, I want to get a cell phone. All my friends have one!

Evan, you don't need to have a cell phone. I think you should wait until you're sixteen to get one.

Check out the World Link video.

Practice your English online at http://elt.heinle.com/worldlink

11 Technology Today

Lesson A Then and now

1 Vocabulary Link They make life easier.

A Read the ads. Pay attention to the words in blue. Then match the sentence parts below to form correct definitions. One answer is extra.

*recycling bin = container in which glass, paper, and plastic are collected for reuse.

> **i** The suffix ***-able / -ible*** = *can.*
>
> If something is *affordable*, you can afford it.
>
> What do you think the words below mean? What are their opposites?
>
> breakable separable
> predictable visible

1. If something is affordable, . . .	it costs a lot of money.
2. If something is convenient, . . .	you can probably buy it.
3. If something is practical, . . .	it makes life easy or more comfortable.
4. If something is disposable, . . .	you can carry it from one place to another easily.
5. If something is durable, . . .	you can trust it.
6. If something is portable, . . .	you throw it away after you've used it.
7. If something is reliable, . . .	it is a useful and logical thing to do.
	it is strong and lasts a long time without breaking.

B Discuss the questions with a partner.

1. Choose one of the ads in **A** and answer the questions. Use your own words.
   a. What is the ad selling? b. Why should you buy it?
2. Would you ever have LASIK eye surgery or use a disposable camera? Explain your answer. Do you think these things make our lives better? Why or why not?
3. Which words in blue in **A** would you use to describe your MP3 player? Phone? Car?

Then and now

Unit 11, Lesson A

1 Vocabulary Link

They make life easier.

5 min

Warm Up

With books closed, tell students that Unit 11 is called *Technology Today*. Ask, *What is the coolest or most important thing technology has done for you recently?*

This i-box teaches the suffixes *-able/-ible*. With books closed, write the example on the board and add a second one: *If something is affordable, you can afford it; If something is visible, you can see it.* Ask students what *-able* and *-ible* mean. When they say they mean "can," have them open their books. Check their understanding by asking what *breakable, predictable,* and *separable* mean.

15–20 min

A Read the ads. Pay attention to the words in blue. Then match the sentence parts below to form correct definitions. One answer is extra.

After students look at the ads, ask them what product or service each one is selling. (Note that *LASIK* is laser-assisted vision surgery. It's a general term, not a brand name.) After students read and do the matching exercise, ask them to read the definitions, and repeat them yourself so that everyone hears them. You may want to do **B**, item 1, with the whole class as a comprehension check for the reading.

A Teaching Option Support/challenge

Challenge students to find the opposite of *affordable, convenient, practical,* and *reliable* (unaffordable, inconvenient, impractical, unreliable). They may use their dictionaries again to check their answers.

10–15 min

EXTRA! Definitions

Students can work in pairs to write definitions of the adjectives in the i-box (breakable, predictable, separable, visible). The definitions should be like the ones in **A**, so they can't use any form of the word in its definition. For example, in the exercise, the definition of *affordable* isn't *you can afford it.* Students should share their definitions in new groups of four (the partners now in different groups). Have each group choose their best definition to share with the class.

10–15 min

B Discuss the questions with a partner.

Students should discuss the questions as instructed. To follow up, students can share their ideas in groups formed of two pairs, new groups of four, or as a whole class.

20–30 min

EXTRA! Writing prompt

Use a question in **B**, item 2, as a topic for writing: *Would you ever have LASIK eye surgery? Explain your answer.*

Instructor's Notes

2 Listening Predicting the future

Skills: Listen for the main idea and details; Answer factual detail questions; Identify a sequence of events

Warm Up

5 min

With books closed, ask how students watch movies. (In theaters, on TV, with DVD players, or on computers?) How many watch them each way?

A How do these two items make our lives more convenient? Tell a partner.

5–15 min

For some classes, you may want to personalize and structure the conversation more. Write some or all of these questions on the board: *Do you have a laptop/portable DVD player? Where do you use it? How many hours a day/week do you use it? How long have you had it? Has it changed the way you live? How?*

B Read the questions and answers below. Then listen to the lecture and choose the best answer for each.

CD 2 Track 28

20–25 min

(Question 1 is answered in the first part of the script, questions 2 and 3 are answered in the second part, and questions 4 and 5 in the third part.) You may prefer to treat the three parts of the audio separately to make the task less challenging. For each part, have students read the questions and guess the answers, then listen to the audio at least twice to confirm or correct their guesses. Tell students they are going to hear a lecture by a university professor. This activity is followed up in Ask and Answer.

Culture Tip: IBM

IBM (International Business Machines) is the world's biggest technology company. The company has scientists, engineers, consultants, and sales professionals in more than 200 countries, and has more than 407,000 employees worldwide.

ASK ANSWER

Discuss questions 1 and 3 with the whole class. Ask a Student A to state the prediction in 1. Ask a Student B if it was correct or not. Then ask Student B what has actually happened. Do the same with question 3. (Do students think the prediction in 3 might still happen?) Put students in groups to discuss the other questions. Each group should choose a reporter to report their ideas to the class (or to another group). The group should help the reporter prepare, and the report should take less than a minute.

3 Pronunciation

Pronunciation of *s* in *used to* and *use* / *used*

A Listen to the sentences. Notice the different pronunciation of the *s* in *used to* and the *s* in the verb forms *use* or *used*.

CD 2 Track 29

5 min

Write *used to, didn't use to, use,* and *used* on the board, and circle the *s* in each word. Tell students this is the pronunciation point—the sound of *s* in these words and expressions. Review the chart, write the phonemic symbols /s/ and /z/ on the board, and say them in isolation. Play the recording, pointing to the symbols as students hear the sounds.

B Listen to how the words *use* and *used* are pronounced. Check (✓) /s/ or /z/. Then take turns reading the sentences aloud with a partner.

CD 2 Track 30

10–15 min

Let students hear the audio twice while they check /s/ or /z/. Check answers and play the sentences once more to confirm. Play the sentences again with students repeating before they practice with a partner. Or if you're comfortable doing it, model them yourself. This lets students hear the sentences in a different voice, and they can watch you pronounce them.

Instructor's Notes

2 Listening Predicting the future

A How do these two items make our lives more convenient? Tell a partner.

CD 2 Track 28

B Read the questions and answers below. Then listen to the lecture and choose the best answer for each.

1. In the 1940s, the president of IBM made a prediction about computers. What was it?
   a. They will never be popular with most people.
   b. Someday, they will be small and portable.
   c. In the future, people will use them in their homes.
2. In the 1980s, seeing movies changed. What happened?
   a. Movie tickets became more affordable.
   b. People began watching movies online.
   c. Renting movies became popular.
3. In the 1980s, people were making a prediction about movies. What was it?
   a. All movie theaters will close.
   b. Someday, all movies will be free.
   c. No one will watch movies anymore.
4. What prediction are people making today?
   a. In the future, people won't make movies.
   b. In the future, people won't watch traditional TV.
   c. Someday, everyone will use computers.
5. Look at your answer in 4. Why are people making this prediction?
   a. More people are getting news and entertainment online.
   b. Movies are becoming too expensive.
   c. Computers are becoming cheaper.

ASK ANSWER

Look at your answers to questions 1 and 3. Were these predictions correct? Why or why not?

Look at your answers to questions 4 and 5. Do you agree with this prediction? Why or why not?

3 Pronunciation Pronunciation of *s* in *used to* and *use / used*

CD 2 Track 29

A Listen to the sentences. Notice the different pronunciation of the *s* in *used to* and the *s* in the verb forms *use* or *used*.

used to / didn't use to: s = /s/	use / used: s = /z/
1. People used to go to movie theaters a lot more.	3. What kind of computer do you use?
2. I didn't use to wear glasses.	4. I used my brother's cell phone.

CD 2 Track 30

B Listen to how the words *use* and *used* are pronounced. Check (✔) /s/ or /z/. Then take turns reading the sentences aloud with a partner.

	/s/	/z/
1. She used the phone in her office.	☐	✔
2. He used to paint his own house.	✔	☐
3. Do you use a laptop?	☐	✔
4. I didn't use to eat meat.	✔	☐

4 Speaking **The fact is . . .**

A Listen to Alan and Kim's conversation. Then answer the questions with a partner.

CD 2 Track 31

1. How would most people describe Kim's sister?
   Most people would say Kim's sister is a quiet, shy person.
2. What is Kim's sister really like?
   Kim's sister is actually very talkative and friendly.

Alan: Hey, Kim. I saw your sister on Facebook the other day. She's really changed a lot.

Kim: Yeah? Why do you say that? She still looks the same.

Alan: Yeah, but now she's got all these friends and she's really funny. She used to be so different—you know, kind of shy.

Kim: A lot of people say that about my sister. They think that she's this quiet person, but, actually, she's very outgoing.

Alan: Really?

Kim: Yep. Once she feels comfortable with you, she's really friendly and she talks a lot.

Alan: Wow, I had no idea.

B Practice the conversation with a partner. Do you know anyone like Kim's sister?

5 Speaking Strategy

Useful Expressions: Stating facts		
Stating what other people think	A lot of people say (that) . . . Some people think (that) . . .	she's really shy.
Explaining what you think	(But,) actually, . . . (But,) in fact, / in reality, . . . (But,) the truth / fact / reality is . . .	she's very outgoing.

A Read the statements below and check (✔) the ones you agree with.

____ Learning English is easy.

____ Playing video games is bad for you.

____ You should get married some day.

____ The more expensive something is the better quality it is.

____ Computers make our lives better and easier.

____ Men are more aggressive than women.

B With a partner, compare your opinions about the statements in **A**. Talk about the statements you don't agree with. Use the Useful Expressions to help you.

> Some people say learning English is easy, but, actually, it's hard—especially the grammar.

C Tell a partner something surprising about you or your country.

> A lot of people think it's warm in Spain all year, but, in reality, it's very cold in the winter.

> Wow, I had no idea.

4 Speaking The fact is . . .

Warm Up

5 min

With books closed, say to students, *Some people are easy to know, but with others it takes time.* Ask students to think of someone they know who is slow to open up. What do most people think that person is like? What are they *really* like? Students can answer each question with just one or two adjectives.

A **Listen to Alan and Kim's conversation. Then answer the questions with a partner.**

CD 2 Track 31

10–15 min

Read the instructions and the two questions. Students should listen first with books closed and try to answer the questions. Then they can listen again, following along in the book, and working in pairs to answer the questions in complete sentences. Answers can be expressed in more than one way, and students should be able to figure out vocabulary from the context.

> **Language Tip: *This* and *these***
>
> These demonstrative pronouns are sometimes used in casual speech for emphasis rather than identification. ***All these*** *friends* = a lot of friends; ***this*** *quiet person* = a quiet person.

B **Practice the conversation with a partner. Do you know anyone like Kim's sister?**

5–10 min

Read the conversation with students repeating. Break up long sentences and use backward buildup when needed. Students can practice in pairs, and of course they should look at their partner when either of them is speaking. They should switch roles and practice at least twice. If desired, they can change partners for additional practice.

B Teaching Option **Role play**

If you wish, students can go on to role play the conversation—standing, with books closed, and in their own words. Or they can revise it before role playing to talk about someone else (not Kim's sister) and speak as themselves. In this case, have them perform it.

5 Speaking Strategy

A **Read the statements below and check (✓) the ones you agree with.**

5–10 min

Present the Useful Expressions. Read the expressions in the chart as sentences so that students can see how they go together: *A lot of people say she's really shy, but the truth is, she's very outgoing.* In the statements, explain the unusual structure, *The more . . . the better . . . .* Say, *If something is expensive, it's good quality. If it's more expensive, it's better quality.* After students check the statements they agree with, ask for a show of hands on the ones they don't agree with. Make sure they know these are the ones they'll be talking about in **B**.

B **With a partner, compare your opinions about the statements in A. Talk about the statements you don't agree with. Use the Useful Expressions to help you.**

10–20 min

Ask a student to read the example aloud, and point out that Student A adds some extra information. Give an example yourself about a different statement, with different Useful Expressions and extra information. Give students time to make notes about what they're going to say. Then, in pairs, they take turns disagreeing.

B Teaching Option **Support/challenge**

Students should continue the conversation. Student B says, *What do you mean?*, and Student A explains.

C **Tell a partner something surprising about you or your country.**

10 min

Students should repeat the example, and again, give another example yourself. If students are from the same country, Student B can pretend to be a foreigner. Or they can speak only about themselves or their hometown if it is different from other students. Students should change partners several times and make a new statement to each partner. Give them time to think of several things to say.

> **Large Class Option**
>
> Rather than practice with several random partners, students can practice in groups of 8 or 10. Students may work with people sitting near them, so they stay within the group's limited space.

6 Language Link *Used to*

Warm Up

5 min

With books closed, ask students to name something that they don't do now, but they did a lot in the past. Note their ideas on the board.

A Study the chart. Notice the different forms of *used to*. Then complete sentences 1–3 below.

10–15 min

With books closed, write the mini-dialogs on the board, and underline the words in blue. Add this sentence to **B** in the second dialog: *He didn't used to have a job.* Ask these questions and call on able students to answer:

1. *What tense are the underlined verbs in?* (the simple past)
2. *What form is the verb after* used to? (base form)
3. *How do you start a yes/no question with used to?* (did)
4. *Which kinds of sentences use* used to *with a d? Affirmative?* (yes) *Negative?* (no) *Yes/no question?* (no)

Finally, ask what *used to* means, what it expresses. Let everyone try out answers and say *yes* or *partly right* if they are. Now, with books open, read the explanation of *used to* at the top of the chart, and students can complete the sentences.

> **Teaching Tip: Teaching inductively**
>
> Inductive teaching means giving students examples and allowing the students to generalize patterns from them. Here are some things to keep in mind:
>
> - Choose examples thoughtfully to show the pattern in the simplest form possible.
> - Use as few examples as possible.
> - Give students time to study the examples and look for the pattern.
> - Ask basic, general questions, and allow enough time for students to think.
> - Call on individual students—and choose ones you're sure will know the answer!

B Each sentence below contains one mistake. Correct the mistakes. Then compare answers with a partner.

10–15 min

Students should correct the sentences working alone. Remind them to check the chart and statements in **A** if they're not sure. Both partners should agree on every answer. Tell them to discuss it until they do. They can also ask nearby students.

C With a partner, use the verbs in the box to describe each situation in Mary's life ten years ago and now. Use *used to* and the simple present.

10–15 min

Students can work these out together orally, referring to the pictures. Both of them should say their final sentences, then write them on a separate piece of paper. Walk around checking the papers, and send a student to the board to write each one. Check them with the whole class.

D Look again at the pictures and ask your partner: How else has Mary's life changed?

10–15 min

Students should take turns saying sentences with *used to* based on the pictures. When they can't think of any more, they can get together with another pair and compare their observations.

D Teaching Option Who's got the most sentences?

After students complete the exercise in groups of six to eight, they should appoint a recorder (or two) to write down their sentences about Mary. Give them a convenient time limit, perhaps five to eight minutes. When they can't think of any more statements based on the pictures, the recorders then draw a line across the page and begin to invent Mary's life. (*She used to have a boyfriend, but he married her best friend.*) When time is up, each group should pass their paper to another group to check the sentences. Only correct sentences count. The group writes the total number of correct sentences at the top and returns the papers. The original group makes sure the score is correct, and they all report their scores to the class.

> **Large Class Option**
>
> Do **D**'s Teaching Option with a large class.

EXTRA! Interview: Life back in the day

30–45 min

Students prepare 15–20 questions and interview an older person (in the native language) about his or her memories, taking notes. Later, they write 10 sentences with *used to* about the world back then. To follow up in class, put students in groups of four. Have them read their sentences aloud and discuss what they found out. Each group appoints a recorder and directs him or her in preparing a short summary of the most interesting things they learned. It should include sentences like *Kids used to . . . , Parents used to . . . , Nobody used to . . . , Students didn't use to . . . ,* etc. Finally, they appoint a reader who reads their summary to the class.

6 Language Link *Used to*

A Study the chart. Notice the different forms of *used to*. Then complete sentences 1-3 below.

We use *used to* to talk about situations that were true or happened regularly in the past. These situations are not true now or do not happen anymore.

A: This computer used to be really expensive.
B: I know, but now most people can afford it.

A: Did your brother use to spend a lot of time on Linkbook?
B: Yeah, he used to, but he doesn't anymore.

1. Use *used to* to talk about the ________.	a. present	(b.) past
2. *Used to* is followed by ________.	(a.) the base form of a verb	b. a gerund (*-ing* form)
3. Use *use to* in negative statements and ________.	a. responses	(b.) questions

B Each sentence below contains one mistake. Correct the mistakes. Then compare answers with a partner.

1. I use to talk on the phone a lot.
   I used to talk on the phone a lot.
2. Did you used to have long hair?
   Did you use to have long hair?
3. My computer never use to crash so often.
   My computer never used to crash so often.
4. Didn't you used to wear glasses?
   Didn't you use to wear glasses?
5. We used live in the city, but we moved last year.
   We used to live in the city, but we moved last year.
6. He never used to watching TV.
   He never used to watch TV.

C With a partner, use the verbs in the box to describe each situation in Mary's life ten years ago and now. Use *used to* and the simple present.

listen to	go to	wear
watch	work on	

1 Before: hip-hop music / Now: jazz
   She used to listen to hip-hop music. Now she listens to jazz.
2. Before: glasses / Now: contacts
   She used to wear glasses. Now she wears contacts.
3. Before: movie theater / Now: DVDs at home
   She used to see movies at the movie theater. Now she watches DVDs at home.
4. Before: large PC / Now: small laptop
   She used to work on a large PC. Now she works on a small laptop.

Mary used to listen to hip-hop music. Now she ...

D Look again at the pictures and ask your partner: How else has Mary's life changed?

Answers may vary.
She used to have long, blond hair. Now she's got short, dark hair.
She used to wear casual clothes. Now she wears more stylish clothes.
She used to wear braces, but she doesn't anymore.

7 Communication Things have changed.

A Two years ago, Tetsuya and his family moved from Tokyo to Los Angeles. Look at his old Tokyo web page and his new Los Angeles web page. How has his life changed? Make sentences with *used to* and *didn't use to*.

People used to call him Tetsuya. Now everyone calls him . . .

Tokyo Homepage

- My name is Tetsuya.
- I live in Tokyo with my parents.
- I wear a uniform to school.
- I ride my bicycle to school.
- I belong to the soccer club.
- I study all the time, but my English isn't very good.

last updated: three years ago

LA Homepage

- Everyone here calls me "Ted." I like L.A. a lot.
- Guess what? I have a new niece! Her name is Risa.
- I don't wear a uniform.
- I have a car! I drive to college.
- I'm a member of my college's swim team.
- I have a lot of friends and we speak English together!

last updated: yesterday

B Make notes about your life five years ago and now. Try to write down things that are different if possible.

Five years ago	**Now**
Home: ____________	Home: ____________
Family: ____________	Family: ____________
Friends: ____________	Friends: ____________
Work / School: ____________	Work / School: ____________
Favorites (movies, magazines, TV programs): ____________	Favorites (movies, magazines, TV programs): ____________
Other: ____________	Other: ____________

C Tell your partner how your life has changed in the past five years. Whose life – yours or your partner's – has changed the most?

My family and I used to live in a small apartment. Now we live in a bigger place.

7 Communication

Things have changed.

Warm Up

5–10 min

With books closed, ask students if they have ever moved from one city to another. What changed when they moved? (If no one has moved, ask about starting at a new school or when a younger sibling was born.)

A 10–20 min **Two years ago, Tetsuya and his family moved from Tokyo to Los Angeles. Look at his old Tokyo web page and his new Los Angeles web page. How has his life changed? Make sentences with *used to* and *didn't use to*.**

Explain the situation—put the web pages in context. Students should look at the photos and guess: In the Tokyo photo, which one is Tetsuya? How old was he then? For pair practice, students can answer in simple sentences, like the answers in blue on the opposite page. Or you can ask for two sentences, like the example. Or sentences with *but*: *People used to call him Tetsuya, but now they call him Ted.* Give examples with the pattern you want (or write examples of all of them on the board). You could also let students work in groups of three to five. To support weaker students, put two to four of them in a group with a stronger student. Walk around to check on how they're doing; stop and help as needed. If there are general problems, work with the whole class for a few minutes.

B 5–10 min **Make notes about your life five years ago and now. Try to write down things that are different if possible.**

These don't have to be big changes, but students need changes to talk about in **C**. Tell them that if most things haven't changed to use the line for *Other*. (*bit my nails/don't bite them, braces/perfect teeth!, loved purple/only wear black*, etc.)

C 10–20 min **Tell your partner how your life has changed in the past five years. Whose life—yours or your partner's—has changed the most?**

This activity is open-ended; students speak in their own words. If you would like to remind them of language available from this lesson, write the vocabulary words on the board (page 114) and quickly review the Useful Expressions (page 116). Or you could distribute photocopies of the Language Summary from the back of the book (page 143). Instruct students not to take turns making statements, but have a natural conversation. Student A describes the changes in his or her life; Student B reacts (*Wow!*), comments, and asks questions. When Student A has finished, Student B speaks.

C Teaching Option **Support/challenge**

To follow up, tell the students to "play back" each other's information. Student B tells Student A's story and vice versa. (*You and your family used to live in a small apartment.*) For large classes, do the Playback Challenge option in a group of four to six students.

Teaching Tip: Setting up groups

If your classroom has movable seating, you're probably already using groups. There are many ways to assign students to groups. Some of them work better with different classes, and sometimes you'll want to vary your groupings just for a change of pace.

- In a very large class, routines are important for smooth classroom management. You can assign permanent groups for the entire course, or change them periodically.
- You can let students choose who they want to work with. This takes a lot of class time and results in some students always working together. Use it occasionally, as a treat.
- Assign students randomly. Have them count off with the number of groups you want. (For six groups, each student counts off up to six.) Then direct groups to different areas of the classroom: *Ones go over there, twos here. . . ,* etc.
- Group students to achieve a certain mix—all weaker students in one group so you can work with them while other groups work more independently, or all stronger students in one group with a more challenging task, or a stronger student with weaker ones (not two strong students because they may prefer to work together and ignore the others).

Instructor's Notes

Making life better
Unit 11, Lesson B

1 Vocabulary Link Too much plastic

Warm Up
5 min

With books closed, ask students what plastic items they throw away every day. List them on the board. If there is plastic recycling locally, ask how much plastic students recycle.

Culture Tip: Recycling household trash

- Recycled items are not used again in the same form. They are used as material for making new items.
- The most common items recycled around the world are aluminum cans, steel cans, paper, plastic bottles, and glass.
- In most places, plastic bags and fast-food containers are not recycled.
- Each ton (2,000 pounds) of paper recycled means a 64% energy savings, a 58% water savings, and 27 kilograms less of air pollution.
- Recycling a glass bottle causes 20% less air pollution and 50% less water pollution than making a bottle from raw materials.
- In the United States, people use 2,500,000 plastic bottles every hour. Most of them are thrown away.
- In the United States, people use over 80,000,000,000 aluminum soda cans every year. But, because of recycling, this is less than 1% of the country's total trash.

A Read the information. Then match a word or phrase in blue with its definition below.

10–15 min

Students should look at the three questions in the text before reading and point out the definitions below. Remind them to check each definition by reading the context of the blue word. Does it make sense? Tell students to check their answers with a partner when they finish, but check them on the board with the whole class so that late finishers can check their answers, too.

Tell students to close their books. Write the example sentences on the board and underline *effect* and *affects*. Ask which one is a noun (effect). How do they know? (It's preceded by *the*.) What part of speech is *affects*? (It is a verb.) Suggest they think of a word or letter association to help them remember which is which—it can be silly as long as it works for them. For example, *effect* and *elephant* sound similar and both start with *e*—and an elephant is a really big noun! If you wish, ask students for one or two sentences with each word and put them on the board. Finally, open the books again and quickly go over the i-box so students can refer to it later.

Language Tip: Pronunciation of *effect* and *affect*

In both *effect* and *affect*, the first syllable is unstressed, and the words usually sound identical in natural rapid speech. Only the context tells you what the word is, and most people won't notice if students mix them up. Of course, the difference is obvious in reading and writing.

B Read the information in A again. Then with a partner, take turns asking the three questions in the reading. Use your own words to answer.

10–15 min

Write the questions on the board and tell students to close their books while they do this.

ASK ANSWER

Students can discuss the question in groups, choosing a reporter to take notes on their ideas. Which ones would they actually do? Which ones are they already doing? At the end, ask the reporters to talk about their group's ideas. But tell them to report only ideas that have not been mentioned yet by another group.

Instructor's Notes

Lesson B Making life better

1 Vocabulary Link Too much plastic

A Read the information. Then match a word or phrase in blue with its definition below.

What is the Great Pacific Garbage Patch?

It's an area of water located in the Pacific Ocean. It is hundreds of kilometers wide and is filled with trash—most of which is plastic.

Why is this area a problem?

- It is killing animal and plant life.
- Eventually, it may have a negative effect on humans. For example, fish that consume plastic because they think it is food, won't be safe for people to eat.

What are scientists doing about the problem?

They're trying to …

- prevent the growth of this area. We can stop it, they say, if we use less plastic and recycle plastic goods we already have.
- rescue injured or sick animals in the area.
- use advanced technology to transform the plastic so that it breaks down faster. In time, this will reduce the amount of plastic in the area to almost nothing. Eventually, scientists hope to restore the area to its original, cleaner state.

plastic bottles and other trash

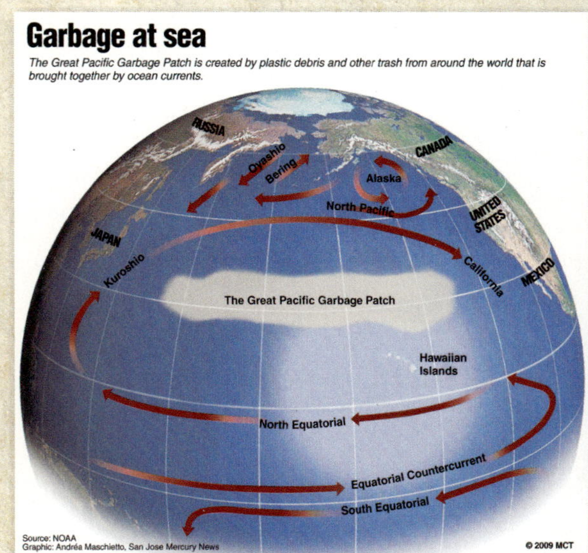

1. a specific place ___area___
2. stop something from happening ___prevent___
3. decrease ___reduce___
4. save ___rescue___
5. reuse ___recycle___
6. change something completely ___transform___
7. eat or drink ___consume___
8. have a bad influence ___have a negative effect___
9. found in a certain place ___located___
10. make something like it was in the past ___restore___

Notice!

effect = *a noun* | *affect* = *a verb*

Scientists are studying the effect of TV on children.

This problem affects everyone.

B Read the information in **A** again. Then with a partner, take turns asking the three questions in the reading. Use your own words to answer.

ASK ANSWER

In addition to recycling, how else can we reduce the amount of plastic we use?

2 Listening Now you see it.

a computer chip

A Complete the sentences below with the words *blind, sight,* and *vision*. Use your dictionary to help you.

1. __Sight__ or __vision__ is the ability to see things.
2. If you are __blind__, you can't see.

CD 2 Track 32

B Look at the photos and read the sentences below. Then listen and choose the best answer to complete each one.

1. The man is talking about a tool he and others are working on. This tool will __________.
   a. prevent blindness from happening
   (b.) restore blind people's vision
   c. give blind people perfect vision
2. The glasses have a __________ inside.
   a. computer chip b. pen (c.) video camera

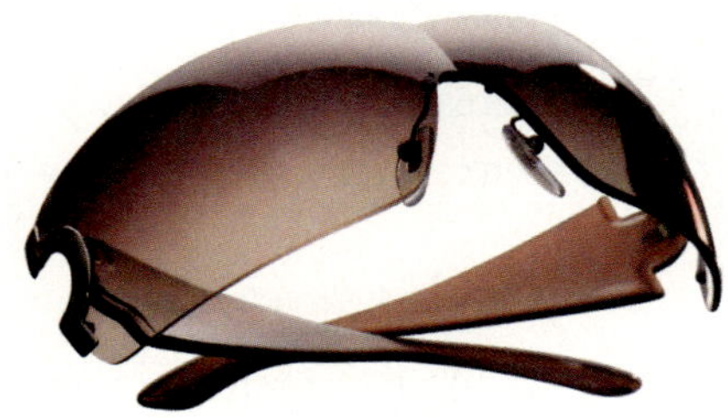

a pair of glasses

CD 2 Track 32

C How does the tool work? Read the sentences below. Then listen again and put the steps in the order (1–5) they happen.

__5__ The person can see the pen.
__2__ The blind person puts on special glasses and looks at an object, such as a pen.
__4__ The picture is sent to the chip in the person's eye.
__1__ Doctors put a computer chip in a blind person's eye.
__3__ The glasses take a picture of the pen.

ASK ANSWER
Use your answers in **B** and **C** to explain how this new technology works. What do you think of this tool?

3 Reading Rescue robots

A Read the title of the news article on page 121. Look also at the photos and read the captions. What do you think this article is about? Tell a partner. Then read the article to check your ideas.

B Find the four bold words in the passage and read the sentences they are in. Then match each word with its definition. One definition is extra.

Word	Definition
collapsed	discovered
trapped	put something down
position	fell down
identified	unable to escape or move
	location, place

C Morgan is telling people what happened to her. Number the events (1-9) in the order they happened.

__8__ They took me to the hospital.
__4__ Then the roof of the gym fell down, and I passed out.
__2__ I went into the gym for my class.
__9__ I have to stay for a couple of days, but I'm feeling much better!
__6__ Then suddenly, this little robot appeared.
__1__ It was snowing really hard on Tuesday morning.
__7__ A few minutes later, a couple of men found me.
__5__ When I woke up, I tried to move, but I couldn't. I was scared.
__3__ I heard this really loud sound.

2 Listening Now you see it.

Skills: Listen for the main idea and details; Listen for specific information; Identify a sequence of events

Warm Up

5–10 min

With books closed, write the word *tool* and this definition on the board: *a small device that you use to do a specific kind of job*. A knife is a tool. So is a ruler. Ask what other tools students can name in English or in their native language. (Some possibilities include a hammer, spoon, bottle opener, and flashlight.) Is a pencil a tool? A computer mouse? A hearing aid? (Opinions may vary. There is no need to give a "right" answer, and native speakers might not agree on all the answers.)

5 min

A **Complete the sentences below with the words *blind, sight,* and *vision*. Use your dictionary to help you.**

Remind students that their dictionary may have more than one definition. They should choose the one that makes sense in the sentence.

CD 2 Track 32

10–15 min

B **Look at the photos and read the sentences below. Then listen and choose the best answer to complete each one.**

Students should look at the photos and captions. Tell them they are going to hear about a new tool being developed to help blind people. The tool uses the items in the photos. Ask students how they think the two are connected. Read the instructions and the sentences. Play the audio, give students time to answer, and then check answers with the whole class. Ask what they heard that gave them the answer to question 1. Play the beginning of the track again so students can hear that part.

CD 2 Track 32

10–15 min

C **How does the tool work? Read the sentences below. Then listen again and put the steps in the order (1–5) they happen.**

Give students time to read the sentences. They should guess or remember and write the numbers, then listen and check their answers. Play the audio more than once so that students can sequence the process correctly.

ASK ANSWER

Choose how you want to use this question with your students.

- Students work alone to prepare a short talk about the tool. They give their talk for a partner, and listen to the partner's talk.
- In pairs, students study the information in **B** and **C**, then close their books. They explain the tool together, taking turns saying the next sentence.
- Students write short articles on the topic and share them with a partner.

3 Reading Rescue robots

Skills: Use photos, captions, and titles to make predictions about what you will read; Guess the meaning of words from context; Understand a sequence of events; Infer information

Warm Up

5 min

With books closed, write the word *robot* on the board and ask for word associations. That is, when you say *robot*, what words do students think of? (Possibilities include R2D2, *Star Wars*, man-made, cute, Sony AIBO puppy, dangerous, Roomba, etc.) Accept words in the native language, write them on the board, and have students look them up in their dictionaries.

5–10 min

A **Read the title of the news article on page 121. Look also at the photos and read the captions. What do you think this article is about? Tell a partner. Then read the article to check your ideas.**

Put students in pairs before they look at page 121. Tell students to look at the title, photos, and captions quickly and not to read the article. Then they should discuss their prediction with their partner.

5–10 min

B **Find the four bold words in the passage and read the sentences they are in. Then match each word with its definition. One definition is extra.**

When students are ready, read the instructions and point out the matching box. The boldface words from the article are on the left. Students should read again and do the matching. Check answers with the class or in pairs before going on to **C**.

5–10 min

C **Morgan is telling people what happened to her. Number the events (1–9) in the order they happened.**

Tell students to number the events before reading again, then read to check the order.

ASK ANSWER

Do this before **D**, which is longer and more challenging. Students should discuss their ideas in pairs or groups of three to five. Tell them that a simple list of situations is not enough. They should explain why or how a rescue robot could help in the situations. Walk around as they talk to ask questions and comment, encouraging them to say more. Follow up with the whole class. Ask several students to share an idea.

D **Imagine you are Morgan and you're talking to reporters. With a partner, use your answers in C and take turns retelling her story. Use your own words.**

25–30 min

Read the direction line together as a class. Students should tell you what they are going to do. Help students prepare for it. Select some expressions for continuing a story and ending a story from Unit 8, page 82. Write them on the board under the head *Morgan*. Also on page 82, select expressions for asking about a story, and write them under *reporter*. Read the expressions with students repeating them. To help students learn Morgan's story, they can copy the sentences in **C** in the correct order on a separate piece of paper. Have them read the sentences several times to themselves—you might suggest that they read aloud in a soft voice. When students are ready, put them in pairs and tell them to close their books. Student A tells Morgan's story while Student B listens and asks about it. Then they switch roles so that everyone plays both parts.

Teaching Tip: Paraphrasing instructions

If you want to be sure students understand what they are being asked to do, read the instructions together and then ask more than one student to tell you what they are going to do.

Large Class Option

Three or four reporters can interview Morgan together. A caution: if everyone plays Morgan once, this may begin to get boring for the students. It might raise the energy level to impose a time limit for each story—perhaps a minute. Be the timekeeper yourself, so that all Student As start and stop together. Limit Student B to comments (*Really? Wow!*), not questions, so Student A doesn't have to say anything extra that would take more time. Adjust the time limit as needed.

15–25 min

EXTRA! Post-reading

Play a game: Test your classmates. This game requires close reading and accurate writing. Put students in groups of three to five and appoint a secretary. Each group (as Group A) writes a certain number of comprehension questions about the article *Local Girl Rescued*. Choose the number of questions based on the time available. On your signal, students should close their books and exchange their questions with Group B. Group B answers the questions. Again, on your signal, Group B returns the questions and answers to Group A. Group A checks the answers and marks the paper with the number of correct answers over the total number of questions. (Three correct answers to four questions = 3/4.) Then the two groups get together to discuss any disagreements.

20–30 min

EXTRA! Additional reading

For more practice making predictions, see Heinle's Footprint Reading Library *One Village Makes a Difference.*

For more practice with sequence, see Heinle's Footprint Reading Library *Cupid the Dolphin.*

Teaching Tip: Extensive reading

Extensive reading is reading longer passages on topics of interest for general understanding. Carried out during class time or as homework, it is an effective way to develop and practice reading skills. At this level, students can practice extensive reading with graded readers, such as levels 1300-1600 in Heinle's Footprint Reading Library or Heinle's Page Turners Reading Library. If possible, students should be allowed to choose their own reading material from the selection available, and instead of being assigned a set number of pages, they should be encouraged to read as much as they can.

Instructor's Notes

B1

The Fairview Herald

Local Girl Rescued

She may have a broken leg, but she couldn't be happier. Morgan Bailey, 15, is happy to be alive.

Tuesday was like any other day for Morgan. She was at school. It was fourth period, and she was the first student to arrive in the gymnasium for her physical education class.

Suddenly there was a loud noise.

"There was a sharp cracking noise and then a loud boom. After that, I don't remember anything," said Morgan. "I guess I passed out[1]."

The roof of the gymnasium had **collapsed** under the heavy snow. Morgan was **trapped** underneath. She couldn't escape.

"I woke up and there was a big piece of wood on my leg. I couldn't move it. I was starting to get cold."

Fortunately, help was nearby. A new program using "rescue robots" was tried for the first time.

"We were nervous about using the robot," said Derrick Sneed, the man in charge of the program. "But in the end, the robot gave us reliable information. It went extremely well."

The rescue robot was able to go into the gym and locate Morgan's exact **position**.

"We send in robots first because it may not be safe for humans," said Mr. Sneed. "People are not as useful as robots in some situations. A gas leak, for example, could kill you or me but wouldn't hurt a robot."

Although it didn't happen in Morgan's case, some rescue robots can bring fresh air or water to people who are trapped.

Rescue robots go into rough, dangerous places. They work in life-or-death situations. They have to be durable.

"Once we **identified** Morgan's location and knew it was safe, a couple of our men went in to rescue her," says Sneed. "Her leg was broken and she was scared, but thankfully, she was alive."

Doctors say that Morgan is doing well. She should be going home in two or three days. What is the first thing she wants to do after she gets out of the hospital?

"I want to meet my hero," laughs Morgan, "That little robot saved my life!"

[1] If you **pass out**, you become unconscious.

Rescue robot

A dangerous mess

D Imagine you are Morgan and you're talking to reporters. With a partner, use your answers in **C** and take turns retelling her story. Use your own words.

ASK ANSWER

In what other kinds of situations could rescue robots be used?

4 Language Link *As . . . as*

A The photos below show a regular vacuum cleaner and two robotic ones. Read the sentences in the box. Then answer questions 1-3 with a partner.

- The Roomba weighs as much as the Vacuum Cleaner Pro.
- The regular vacuum cleaner is not as light as the Roomba or the Vacuum Cleaner Pro.
- The regular vacuum cleaner doesn't cost as much as the Roomba or the Vacuum Cleaner Pro.

9 kilos / $80

4 kilos / $130

4 kilos / $130

1. Which vacuum cleaners weigh the same? What phrase in the box is used to show this?
   The Roomba and the Vacuum Cleaner Pro weigh the same. The phrase "as much as" shows they are equal.
2. Which vacuum cleaner is the cheapest? What phrase is used to show this?
   The regular vacuum cleaner is the cheapest. The phrase "doesn't cost as much as" shows it costs less than the Roomba or the Vacuum Cleaner Pro.
3. Which vacuum cleaners cost the same? How can you say this using *as . . . as*?
   The Roomba is as expensive as the Vacuum Cleaner Pro.

B Look at the comparisons below. Use the words in parentheses to write sentences using *as . . . as*. Then check your answers with a partner.

	regular vacuum cleaner	the Roomba	
1. expensive	☐	☑	1. (vacuum cleaner) A regular vacuum cleaner isn't as expensive as the Roomba.
2. work well	☑	☐	2. (the Roomba) The Roomba doesn't work as well as the regular vacuum cleaner.
3. durable	☑	☑	3. (the Roomba) The Roomba is as durable as the regular vacuum cleaner.
4. easy to use	☐	☑	4. (vacuum cleaner) The regular vacuum cleaner isn't as easy to use as the Roomba.
5. popular	☑	☐	5. (the Roomba) The Roomba is not as popular as the regular vacuum cleaner.

5 Writing **Comparing two products**

A Read the paragraphs. What two things is the writer comparing? Which one does she like more? Why?
She is comparing MP3 players. She likes the iTouch better because she can do more things with the iTouch than the iListen.

B Think of two similar products. Choose from the list below or use your own idea. Then write a short paragraph. Explain which product you think is better.

two MP3s	two cell phones
two video games	two similar websites

I used to own an iListen, but two months ago, I got an iTouch. Of the two MP3s, I like the iTouch better.

With the iTouch, I can listen to music, watch and make videos, play games, surf the Web, and many other things. The iListen doesn't have as many features. Also, the iListen's battery doesn't last as long as the iTouch's. And finally, . . .

C Exchange papers with a partner. Answer the questions in **A** about your partner's writing.

4 Language Link *As . . . as*

Warm Up

5 min

With books closed, ask students how they decide what product to buy when making a major purchase like a cell phone, car, bicycle, TV, or computer. Do they think about it? For example, do they look at ads? Ask their friends? Read about products?

A The photos below show a regular vacuum cleaner and two robotic ones. Read the sentences in the box. Then answer questions 1–3 with a partner.

10–15 min

Students should look at the photos and captions. (Explain robotic vacuum cleaners if necessary.) Call on volunteers to read the examples in the box. Put students in pairs to look at the captions and examples and answer questions 1–3. Check the answers with the class and write them on the board in note form.

> **Culture Tip: What a robotic vacuum cleaner does**
>
> You can program a robotic vacuum cleaner to clean whenever you want. When it begins to clean, its sensors tell it how big the room is. The robot "knows" when it gets to a wall, or when it could fall downstairs, and adjusts. If it hits something, it backs up and finds a way around. When it finishes cleaning, it goes back and connects to its charger. There are videos on YouTube that demonstrate how it works.

B Look at the comparisons below. Use the words in parentheses to write sentences using *as . . . as*. Then check your answers with a partner.

10–20 min

Tell students to use the information in the comparison chart and the examples in **A** to write sentences. As students finish, they can check answers with a partner. Finally, check answers on the board. You could also ask students to reverse the comparison, with the other vacuum cleaner as the subject. (*1. The Roomba is more expensive than a regular vacuum cleaner.*)

5 Writing Comparing two products

Warm Up

5–10 min

With books closed, ask students, *Who do you know with a different MP3 player from yours, or a different cell phone? Which do you like more, theirs or yours? Why?*

A Read the paragraphs. What two things is the writer comparing? Which one does she like more? Why?

5–10 min

Tell students that in **B**, they're going to write a product review for a shopping website, like the one in the example. Read the directions. After students read the review, check their answers to the questions. The reviewer compares features and battery life, and is going to compare one other thing. ("And finally, . . . ") What else could she compare? (Some possibilities include design, weight, speed, and storage capacity.)

> **Culture Tip: Online product reviews**
>
> Online shopping sites like Amazon.com invite their customers to write reviews about the products they sell. Customers comment on what they like and don't like about a product they own, and new customers can read the comments before they decide what to buy. Reviewers also rate the product by giving it from one to five stars. Shoppers rate the reviews as helpful or not helpful.

B Think of two similar products. Choose from the list below or use your own idea. Then write a short paragraph. Explain which product you think is better.

20–30 min

Tell students to think of products that they know well. They should compare three or four different things about the products, as in the example. Students can compare electronics, like the products in the box, but they might also compare sneakers (U.K. *trainers*), fast food, cars, guitars, bicycles, etc.

B Teaching Option **Support/challenge**

If students have trouble getting started on their own, they can work with a partner to brainstorm products and features they can compare. Tell them to use their bilingual dictionaries for needed vocabulary, or let them ask you.

C Exchange papers with a partner. Answer the questions in A about your partner's writing.

5–10 min

Students should tell their partner their answers. This lets the reviewer know if the review wasn't clear or complete, and it provides an answer check for the person who read the review.

C Teaching Option **Process writing**

Publishing work is the final step in process writing. If you and your students are comfortable, students can write a review for a product they really know and use. Post an actual review on a website.

6 Communication

Design your own robot.

5 min

Warm Up

With books closed, ask students if they have ever seen a real, useful robot (including on TV). They should not include fictional robots from movies. What did it look like? What did it do?

A 10–20 min

With a partner, design a robot that will do something useful for people. Discuss the questions below.

Tell students they're going to design their own robots. Then, in **B** and **C**, they'll present and evaluate each other's robots. Tell students to look at the photo and read the caption. Read the instructions and tell them to answer the questions talking about Paro. For question 4, they need to imagine possible answers. In pairs, have students plan and design their robots.

B 10–15 min

Get together with another pair and take turns doing the following.

The chart is in a different order from the questions in **A**. Students should present the information in the same order as the chart. Partners can share each presentation, or they can take turns. When students are ready, presenters show their drawing to the listeners and begin their presentation. Listeners should fill in the chart for *Pair 1*. Make sure listeners understand that they are to fill in the first three squares while listening, then in **C**, they fill in square 4. Remind listeners that in **C**, they have to choose their favorite robot, so they should ask questions to help them do that.

Large Class Option

Pair students and seat four pairs together. They can switch around within their groups to work with three different pairs in **B** and **C**.

C 10–20 min

Repeat B with two other pairs. When you have finished, compare notes with your partner and choose your favorite robot. Explain your choice to the class.

As students finish their presentations in **B**, make new groups for **C**, and do the same for the third round. As students finish the third round, have pairs discuss the robots they've heard presented and choose their favorites.

15–20 min

EXTRA! Writing

Students can write an email to a friend and tell them about the robot they're going to buy. They begin with the header, start with *Hi!*, and explain why they want a robot and what they like about it.

From:

Date:

To:

Subject:

World Link Video and World Link website

Remind students of the value of further practice outside the classroom. Ask students who have watched the video or done online practice to share their experiences.

Instructor's Notes

Check out the World Link Video. Practice your English online at http://elt.heinle.com/worldlink

6 Communication **Design your own robot.**

Paro is a Japanese robotic toy used in hospitals. It looks like a seal and helps to reduce stress in patients.

A With a partner, design a robot that will do something useful for people. Discuss the questions below.

1. What is the purpose of the robot? Choose from the list below or write your own idea.

to be a friend to children or adults	to do household chores
to work in schools	to work in hospitals
to do factory work / to build things	other: ___________

2. What will the robot do?
3. What will the robot look like? Draw a simple picture on a separate piece of paper.
4. Why is the robot as good as (or better than) a human?
5. What will you call the robot?

B Get together with another pair and take turns doing the following:

Presenters: Present your robot.

Listeners: As you listen to the other pair's presentation, complete "Pair 1" in the chart below. At the end of the presentation, you may ask questions.

	Pair 1	Pair 2	Pair 3
Robot's name			
What it does			
Why the robot is as good as (or better than) a human			
Would you use this pair's robot? Why or why not?			

C Repeat **B** with two other pairs. When you have finished, compare notes with your partner and choose your favorite robot. Explain your choice to the class.

Check out the World Link video.

Practice your English online at http://elt.heinle.com/worldlink

12 Let's Go Somewhere!

Lesson A Before you go

1 Vocabulary Link **Tasks before a trip**

A Andrew and Becky are going on a trip. What will they do before they leave home? Match 1-5 with a-e. Then match 6-10 with f-j.

1. unplug	a. the trash
2. empty	b. money
3. exchange	c. the bills
4. give away	d. any electrical items
5. pay	e. any fresh foods

6. give	f. the house keys to a friend
7. stop	g. the plants
8. turn off	h. the lights
9. confirm	i. the mail delivery
10. water	j. the flight plans

B Look at the pictures. With a partner, take turns telling what Andrew and Becky did. Use the vocabulary in **A**.

Andrew called to confirm the flight plans.

Becky called to . . .

C Discuss the questions with a partner.

1. Think of a trip you've taken. Which tasks did you do before you left home?
2. What might happen if you forget to do some of the tasks in **A**?

Before you go
Unit 12, Lesson A

1 Vocabulary Link Tasks before a trip

Warm Up

5 min

With books closed, ask students, When you and your family go on a trip, who takes care of your house and your pets?

A 5–10 min **Andrew and Becky are going on a trip. What will they do before they leave home? Match 1–5 with a–e. Then match 6–10 with f–j.**

Students should look at the pictures in **B**. Explain that they show people getting ready for a trip, and that most of the words in the matching exercise are illustrated. Point out that the matching exercise is not words and definitions this time, but words that can be used together (verb + noun/noun phrase; here, specifically, verb + object). Use the example to show students how the numbered (blue) and lettered (black) words go together. Check answers before going on to **B**.

B 5–15 min **Look at the pictures. With a partner, take turns telling what Andrew and Becky did. Use the vocabulary in A.**

Students should number the pictures 1–5, and cross out verbs as they use them. Sentences can vary. (For example, *Betty stopped the mail delivery.* vs. *Betty called to tell the post office to stop the mail delivery.* Or *Betty gave away any fresh foods.* vs. *Betty took some fruit to give to their neighbor.*) For this reason, check answers with the whole class, and get more than one sentence for each verb. To follow up, ask for sentences with any verbs that students haven't used yet, and ask where in the storyboard those things probably happened.

> **Language Tip: *Call to do something***
>
> *Called to confirm* looks like verb + infinitive, but it isn't. The meaning is *called in order to confirm*, or *called so he could confirm*. Other verbs often used this way are *stop (to let her pass me), wait (to hear the schedule change), listen (to know if it's him),* and *go (to see them).*

C 5–10 min **Discuss the questions with a partner.**

Question 1 is answered in the simple past tense. Students may want to name tasks that aren't included in **A**. Direct them to use their dictionaries, but if they aren't able to find the words they need, pause the activity to deal with vocabulary. Put a list of their tasks on the board in the native language, and give them the English words they need. (Make sure students add the words to their vocabulary notebooks.) Then restart **C**.

Question 2 is phrased to be answered in the present conditional and simple present. Make sure students don't try to answer about a past trip, where they'd need the past conditional. (Tell them to think of their next trip.) You might want students to talk about the tasks they mentioned in Question 1—their own tasks.

Instructor's Notes

2 Listening

While we're away, could you . . . ?

Skills: Listen for details; Identify speakers

Warm Up

5 min

With books closed, ask if students have ever done a favor for a neighbor. What did they do?

A **Paula is asking Leticia for help. What does she ask Leticia to do? Check (✓) the task.**

CD 2 Track 33 · 5 min

Read the instructions and choices with the students; have them say what Paula is going to do. Play the audio once and check the answer.

> Explain the meaning of *kennel*. If kennels are not common locally, tell students that a kennel is a place that boards dogs while their owners are away. Dog owners may not want to ask friends or neighbors to feed and walk their dog, and they may feel the dog will get more attention in a kennel.

B **Listen again. Write *P* for Paula or *L* for Leticia**

CD 2 Track 33 · 20 min

Give students time to read the statements. Play the audio once and tell them to complete as many as they can before listening again. Play the audio again while students complete any incomplete answers. Then check the answers.

B **Teaching Option** **Support/challenge**

Ask students how they knew the answers—what did Paula and Leticia say, exactly? Tell them they're going to find out. Put them into six groups. Students should number off by sixes and form six groups—all the ones together, all the twos, etc. (In a large class, make 12 groups—two Ones, two Twos, etc.) Tell students they'll hear the audio twice more. Their job is to write down exactly what Paula and Leticia say about one task (Ones about task 1, Twos about task 2, etc.). Explain that it's OK if they don't catch all the words, but they should write as many as they can. After listening, ask groups to put together what they wrote. A group reporter should read the final version aloud or write it on the board. Play the audio one more time or hand out copies of the script.

ASK ANSWER

Students can discuss their answers in groups. They can make notes of their "why not" answers. To follow up, write them on the board for discussion. Are the reasons personal (for example, they're shy)? Or social (for example, they live in a big city and don't know their neighbors very well)? Or cultural (for example, in their country it's bad manners to ask for help)?

World Link

(This means busiest by number of passengers.) Get a show of hands for each answer. Did most students guess right or wrong? What were the reasons for their guesses?

3 Pronunciation

Reduced *have to* and *has to*

A **Listen to these sentences. Notice the reduced pronunciation of *have to* and *has to*.**

CD 2 Track 34 · 5 min

Read the sentences and ask who says each one (a passenger and a flight attendant). Students will hear /hæft / and /h st / (and in 1, they'll also hear /g n / for *going to*). Students should repeat the sentences several times: with the audio, or modeling them yourself, and by speaking all together, by halves of the class, by rows, or individually.

B **Imagine that you and a friend are going on a trip to another country. How will you prepare? Make a list of tasks you and your friend have to do.**

5 min

First students need to choose a foreign country or city to visit and decide who they're going with. Tell them to extend their lists of tasks as much as they can. Let them confer with nearby classmates if they don't have many ideas.

C **Now tell a partner about the tasks. Use the reduced form of *have to* and *has to*.**

10–15 min

Students can begin by saying where they're going and who's going with them, then they should talk about everything they have to do. Partners can listen and ask a few questions. (*Are you sure you have to have a visa?*) After they switch roles, they could also switch partners. Follow up by asking if any tasks they heard were surprising or funny. Ask students to report what their partner said. (*He has to tell his parents about his plans. Her friend has to say goodbye to her cat.*)

Instructor's Notes

2 Listening **While we're away, could you . . . ?**

CD 2 Track 33

A Paula is asking Leticia for help. What does she ask Leticia to do? Check (✔) the task.

- ☐ feed the dog
- ☐ pick up the mail
- ☑ water the plants

kennel = a place where pets stay when their owners leave town

CD 2 Track 33

B Listen again. Write *P* for Paula or *L* for Leticia.

1. __P__ is taking a trip for two weeks.
2. __L__ is going to water the plants.
3. __P__ is going to put the dog in the kennel.
4. __L__ asked about the mail.
5. __P__ stopped the mail delivery.
6. __P__ will give the keys to __L__.

ASK ANSWER

Do you ever ask your friends or neighbors for help? Why or why not?

WORLD LINK

Which is the busiest air route in the world?
a. Paris to New York City
b. Hong Kong to Taipei
c. Rio de Janeiro to Lisbon

3 Pronunciation **Reduced *have to* and *has to***

CD 2 Track 34

A Listen to these sentences. Notice the reduced pronunciation of *have to* and *has to*.

1. I'm going to miss my flight. I have to hurry.
2. Everyone has to sit down before this plane can take off.

B Imagine that you and a friend are going on a trip to another country. How will you prepare? Make a list of tasks you and your friend have to do.

I have to . . .	My friend has to . . .
______________	______________
______________	______________
______________	______________
______________	______________

C Now tell a partner about the tasks. Use the reduced form of *have to* and *has to*.

I have to pack my suitcase.

My friend has to get some traveler's checks.

4 Speaking **I can't remember where it is.**

CD 2
Track 35

A Mina and Esther are preparing to leave on a trip. Listen to their conversation. What is the problem?

Esther: We have to leave in thirty minutes. Have you finished packing?

Mina: Yes, I have . . .

Esther: You look worried. What's wrong?

Mina: I can't remember where I put my passport.

Esther: Oh, no!

Mina: It's here somewhere.

Esther: When did you last have it?

Mina: About ten minutes ago. Let me think . . . Oh, there it is. I put it on the dresser.

Esther: What a relief!

ASK ANSWER

Talk about a time when you lost something. What did you do?

B Practice the conversation with a partner.

5 Speaking Strategy

A Study the Useful Expressions in the chart. Practice saying the sentences.

Useful Expressions	
Saying you've forgotten something	
I forgot + noun	I forgot my bus pass.
I forgot + infinitive	I forgot to empty the trash.
I don't remember + gerund	I don't remember turning off the lights.
I can't remember where + clause	I can't remember where I put my car keys.

B You are going to perform a short conversation about forgetting something. Follow the steps below.

Step 1: Choose a location.

- ☐ the airport
- ☐ school
- ☐ the office

Step 2: Choose something you forgot to take or do.

- ☐ ticket
- ☐ report
- ☐ textbook
- ☐ get traveler's checks
- ☐ feed the dog
- ☐ other: ________________

Step 3: Write and practice a short conversation with your partner. Then perform it for the class.

OK, it's time to get on the plane.

Oh, no! I forgot my ticket.

4 Speaking

I can't remember where it is.

Warm Up

5 min

With books closed, ask students if they are nervous travelers or relaxed travelers. That is, do they worry while getting ready for a trip, or stay calm? If they worry, do they ever get stressed out enough to start losing and forgetting things?

CD 2 Track 35

5 min

A Mina and Esther are preparing to leave on a trip. Listen to their conversation. What is the problem?

With books closed, describe the situation and write the question on the board. Play the audio and check the answer.

10-15 min

B Practice the conversation with a partner.

Play the audio again while students listen and read, then listen and repeat. If needed, students can repeat it after you. In pairs, students should practice the conversation as a role play with books open, always looking at their partner when they speak, and switching roles. If you wish, you can go on to less-supported role play with books closed. Students should stay as close to the script as they can without reading it.

ASK ANSWER

Students can tell this as a story in pairs or groups. When did this happen? What was the situation? What did they do? How did it end?

5 Speaking Strategy

Saying you've forgotten something

5-10 min

A Study the Useful Expressions in the chart. Practice saying the sentences.

After practicing the sentences, ask students for additional examples with each structure on the left. Write them on the board and tell students to repeat them.

15-20 min

B You are going to perform a short conversation about forgetting something. Follow the steps below.

(See Student Book page 126 for complete instructions.)

In pairs, students choose a location, decide what they forgot, and write short conversations, four to six lines long. Write these sentences from **A** on the board for reference: *Oh, no!, It's here somewhere, When did you last have it?, What a relief!* Also suggest *Are you sure?* and *Why don't you . . . ?*, which could be useful for continuing a conversation like the one in the example. Partners practice their conversation until they can say it without reading. While they practice, walk around and remind them to use reduced forms of *could you, would you, going to, want to,* and *have to*. Also urge them to speak with appropriate feeling—model what they should do. Finally, have all the groups perform for the class.

Teaching Tip: Role plays

At this level, students should be role playing and not reading. Don't let students write out full scripts. Encourage students to just take notes as they create their role plays. They can practice multiple times with their partner until the language feels natural. Then, when they present their role play to the class, they shouldn't have notes with them. They should act it out with the phrases they've been practicing and feel comfortable with.

Large Class Option

Pairs can perform in groups of four or five pairs.

Instructor's Notes

6 Language Link

Modal verbs of necessity

Warm Up

5 min

With books closed, ask students, *When you take a trip, where do you stay? With relatives? With friends? In a hotel? Do you camp? Where are some other places you can stay?*

A **Study the chart. Then complete sentences 1–4 below with a partner. For one sentence, more than one answer is possible.**

10–15 min

You can teach this as presented in the book, or teach it inductively, following up with the chart and sentence completion, as follows. With books closed, write only the six sentences from the chart on the board. Tell students they will work with modal verbs like *may, might,* and *should.* Ask, *What are the modals in these sentences?* Underline them. Ask which sentences are affirmative, negative, past, and present. Write +, –, *past* and *present* next to them. Continue asking questions:

Which modals can we use in the present? (all three)
Which in the affirmative? (all three)
Can we use must *in the negative? In the past?* (no, no)
Can we use have to *in the negative? In the past?* (yes, yes)
Can we use have got to *in the negative? In the past?* (no, no)

Now have students in pairs refer to the chart and complete the sentences.

> **Teaching Tip: Inductive vs. deductive learning**
>
> Some students prefer to have the rule laid out for them before they start practicing the language. Others learn better if they work out the rule for themselves. In class, challenge students to figure out the rules for themselves. Remember that there are charts in the back of the book (pages 144–154), which students can use later when trying to study a rule.

B **These people are preparing for a trip. Look at their lists. They have finished the tasks that are checked (✓). On a separate piece of paper, write eight sentences with *has / have to* or *doesn't / don't have to*. Compare your answers with a partner.**

10–15 min

Tell students to look at the photos and lists. Explain vocabulary as needed. Ask them to guess about the three people. Who probably owns a house? How will Jake's trip probably be different from Doris and Jim's? After students have written their sentences and checked them with a partner, call on volunteers to say their sentences for the class or write them on the board.

> **Language Tip: *First-aid kit, shot, youth hostel***
>
> *First-aid kit:* You can buy a first-aid kit or prepare your own, including what you think is important. Possibilities are adhesive bandages (U.K.: sticking plasters), your favorite pain relief medicine, such as aspirin or acetaminophen, antiseptic wipes, sterile gauze pads and tape, etc.
>
> *Shot:* The common U.S. term for *injection*. Jake needs some immunizations that are for travelers where he's going.
>
> *Youth hostel:* A place where travelers can stay, generally cheaper and less comfortable than a hotel. A typical hostel has dormitory sleeping (several people in one room) and shared bathrooms. Jake wants a card showing that he's a member of an international youth hostel organization.

C **Correct the error in each sentence.**

5–10 min

Students should make the corrections in their books and check answers with a partner. Alternatively, six students can write the sentences on the board and correct them there. Review their corrections with the whole class.

Instructor's Notes

6 Language Link Modal verbs of necessity

A Study the chart. Then complete sentences 1-4 below with a partner. For one sentence, more than one answer is possble.

Use *must*, *have to*, and *have got to* to say that something is necessary.		
	Present forms	**Past forms**
affirmative	You must show your ID to get on the plane. I have to buy a backpack for my trip. We have got to get some cash.	I had to wait at the airport for an hour.
negative	I don't have to check any luggage.	I didn't have to wait long.

1. You can use ____________ in the present to express necessity.
   a. must b. have to c. have got to *All 3 answers are possible.*
2. Only ____________ can be used to talk about things that were necessary in the past.
   a. must (b.) have to c. have got to
3. ____________ is often used to talk about rules or laws. It is stronger than *have (got) to*.
   (a.) Must b. Have to c. Have got to
4. You can only use ____________ in the negative.
   a. must (b.) have to c. have got to

B These people are preparing for a trip. Look at their lists. They have finished the tasks that are checked (✔). On a separate piece of paper, write eight sentences with *has / have to* or *doesn't / don't have to*. Compare your answers with a partner.

Jake

✓ *buy a backpack*
prepare a first-aid kit
get shots
✓ *apply for a youth hostel card*

Jim and Doris

✓ exchange money
✓ pay the bills
change the voicemail message
stop the mail delivery

C Correct the error in each sentence.

1. She ~~doesn't~~ has to pack her suitcase.
2. They ~~must~~ *had to* leave yesterday.
3. I ~~haven't~~ *don't have* to reserve a hotel.
4. All passengers must ~~to~~ board the flight now.
5. We didn't ~~had~~ *have* to pay in cash.
6. You don't have ~~got~~ to buy traveler's checks.

7 Communication **What should we take?**

A Imagine you and your partner are going on a camping trip for three days. You will be in the forest, far away from any towns or cities. With your partner:

- Circle the items that are necessary for your trip.
- Check (✔) the items that you would like to bring, but that are not necessary.
- Cross out the items that are not necessary.

B Join another pair. Together you must decide what to take on your trip. You can only take six items. Choose four items pictured above. Think of two more items. Consider these things:

- food
- water
- shelter
- first aid
- safety

> We have to take the tent for shelter.

C Tell the class the items your group has decided to take and explain your reasons.

7 Communication

What should we take?

Warm Up

5–10 min

With books closed, ask if students have ever been camping. If they haven't, ask if they would like to. Why or why not? If they have, where did they go and how did they like it?

A **Imagine you are going on a camping trip for three days. You will be in the forest, far away from any towns or cities. With your partner:**

5–10 min

(See Student Book page 128 for complete instructions.)

Explain the tasks in **A**–**C**. Students make their first choices in **A**. In **B**, they make their final decisions in a group of four—everyone has to agree. Finally, in **C**, they have to explain their choices as a group. Tell students that their campsite will have only what you normally find in a forest. They have to take everything else with them.

Students should circle, check, and cross out items by themselves before discussing them with a partner. They do not have to agree on six items in **A** unless you want them to. To tell their partners their choices, they can say, *We have to take . . . , I'd like to take . . . , We don't have to take . . . .* Write these sentences on the board and remind students to use reduced forms in speaking.

B **Join another pair. Together you must decide what to take on your trip. You can only take six items. Choose four items pictured above. Think of two more items. Consider these things:**

10–15 min

(See Student Book page 128 for complete instructions.)

Students can choose two new items not pictured in **A**, but you could let them choose all six from **A** if they can explain their reasons. Students can use their dictionaries and/or ask classmates or you for needed vocabulary. To discuss the items and agree on six, they can say: *We have to/should take . . . for . . . , We don't have to/shouldn't take . . . because . . . .*

C **Tell the class the items your group has decided to take and explain your reasons.**

15–20 min

Groups should choose reporters to present their ideas to the class. In a small class, every group can explain every item on their list. In a class of up to 40 students (10 groups from **B**), reporters could read the list, then the other students could ask them to explain one of the items. In a very large class, divide the class into groups of 12 or 16 (three or four groups from B). Follow up with a show of hands—which groups chose each item for their final list? Or tally the numbers on the board as the lists are read. Were any items chosen by all groups? Were any items rejected by all?

EXTRA! Writing prompt

15–20 min

In some places, campers are not allowed to leave anything in the forest when they leave. Everything must be taken away—empty cans and bottles, food, even human waste and toilet paper. Are such rules necessary or unreasonable?

Instructor's Notes

Adventures in traveling

Unit 12, Lesson B

1 Vocabulary Link Airline travel

Warm Up

5 min

With books closed, have students brainstorm different ways to travel (by car, train, etc.). Ask which is their favorite way and why.

10–15 min

A Match a word on the left with one on the right to form compound nouns about air travel. Write each compound noun below the picture it describes. Then check your answers with a partner.

Students may already know some of these compounds, or they may know one half and be able to guess the other. Instruct them to use dictionaries for those they can't guess. You might also let them ask nearby students. Check answers on the board.

A Teaching Option Support/challenge

Students can do this in groups. Make sure each group has at least one dictionary. First, students fill in as many compound nouns as they can and cross them off in the boxes. Then a student with a dictionary looks up one unknown word and tells the group. Together, the group tries to figure out the other half of the compound. In the meantime, the student looks up another word, and so on.

Language Tip: Compound nouns

A compound noun is two nouns used together that have a new meaning different from either noun alone. *Tray* and *table* each refer to a specific thing. A *tray table*, however, is neither a kind of tray nor a kind of table.

5–10 min

B Use the compound words in A to complete the sentences below.

Students should complete the sentences alone and check answers with a partner or the whole class. Answer questions about vocabulary that students weren't able to figure out. Check answers in pairs or with the whole class.

B Teaching Option Speaking

Imagine that the sentences are the script for a video telling travelers what to expect at the airport and on the plane. Model the sentences. Have students repeat and then practice in pairs. Each student reads half the script, then they switch and read the other half.

15–20 min

EXTRA! Record your voiceover

Again, **B** is the script for a video voiceover. If playback equipment is available, ask one or two volunteers to practice the script, record it outside of class, and burn a CD. In the next class, play it back. If the quality is good, you might use part of the students' audios for a short dictation.

ASK ANSWER

If few students have been on a plane, those who haven't flown can interview those who have. In any case, add these questions: *Do you enjoy flying? What is your favorite thing about flying? What do you dislike about it?*

Instructor's Notes

Let's Go Somewhere!

Lesson B Adventures in traveling

1 Vocabulary Link Airline travel

A Match a word on the left with one on the right to form compound nouns about air travel. Write each compound noun below the picture it describes. Then check your answers with a partner.

baggage	carry-on	flight	oxygen
boarding	check-in	overhead	tray

attendant	compartment	luggage	pass
claim	counter	mask	table

1. tray table

2. boarding pass

3. check-in counter

4. overhead compartment

5. flight attendant

6. oxygen mask

7. carry-on luggage

8. baggage claim

B Use the compound words in **A** to complete the sentences below.

1. When you arrive at the airport for your flight, you go to the check-in counter first.
2. When your departing flight is announced, pick up your carry-on luggage and go to the gate.
3. Before you get on the plane, you must show your boarding pass.
4. When you enter the plane, you put your luggage in the overhead compartment. You may need to ask a flight attendant for help.
5. Before takeoff, you learn about safety. They show you how to use an oxygen mask in an emergency.
6. During the flight, you are served drinks on your tray table.
7. After the flight is over, you go to the baggage claim area to get your luggage.

ASK ANSWER

Have you ever been on a plane?

2 Listening A long weekend

Many students and workers look forward to a holiday that happens on a Monday or Friday because they can enjoy a "long weekend." What do you like to do on a long weekend?

CD 2 Track 36

A Listen. What did Jun do? Circle the correct answers.

Jun flew / drove to three / four countries in three / four days.

CD 2 Track 36

B Listen again. Check (✔) the statements that are true for Jun.

- [x] 1. Jun loves flying.
- [ ] 2. Jun didn't go shopping.
- [x] 3. Jun was in a hurry.
- [ ] 4. Jun had two pieces of luggage.
- [x] 5. Jun didn't make a reservation.
- [ ] 6. Jun's flights were expensive.
- [x] 7. Jun works for an airline.
- [x] 8. Jun works in sales.

ASK ANSWER

Would you like to take a trip like Jun's? Why or why not?
Where would you like to go on a long weekend?

WORLD LINK

The shortest scheduled flight in the world is between the Isle of Westray and Isle of Papa Westray in Scotland. How long is this flight?

a. 2 minutes
b. 15 minutes
c. 20 minutes

3 Reading Traveling alone

Would you like to take a vacation by yourself? Why or why not?

A Read the title of the article on page 131. What do you think the author is writing about? Check (✔) your answer. Then read the article and see if you were right.

- [x] 1. the advantages of traveling alone
- [ ] 2. some memories of traveling alone
- [ ] 3. the expense of traveling alone

B Read the article again. What topics does the author mention about solo travel? Check (✔) your answers.

- [ ] 1. the cost of solo travel
- [ ] 2. the dangers of traveling alone
- [x] 3. study vacations
- [x] 4. using your vacation to learn a sport
- [ ] 5. packing for a trip alone
- [x] 6. options for solo travelers

2 Listening A long weekend

Skills: Listen for facts; Listen for details; Identify speakers

Warm Up

5 min

With books closed, tell students the information in the box in your own words. Discuss the question with them: *What do you like to do on long weekends?*

CD 2 Track 36

5–10 min

A Listen. What did Jun do? Circle the correct answers.

Tell students they're going to hear someone who just had an unusual weekend. Review the sentence and the choices. Then play the audio. Give students a little time and check the answer.

CD 2 Track 36

10–15 min

B Listen again. Check (✓) the statements that are true for Jun.

Read the statements, and students can check the ones they know. Play the audio again so students can confirm and complete their answers. Students can compare answers with a partner or check them with the whole class. Call on students to correct the three false statements so that they are true. You might want to ask some follow-up questions too, as an extra challenge: *Where did Jun go shopping?* (Seoul); *What kind of luggage did he have?* (carry-on); *How much did his flights cost?* (They were almost free.)

B Teaching Option What do the words mean?

Jun uses these expressions in his conversation with Ashley, and their meaning is explained by the context. Play the audio again. Have students raise their hands when they hear the meaning of one of the expressions.

airplane freak
connecting flights
standby passenger

B Teaching Option Catch the mistake!

Read the script, changing some information. Students raise a hand when they hear a mistake and then they correct it. If the student can't remember the correct information, let anyone try.

You might say I'm a travel freak.
I visited Taiwan, Hong Kong, and Vietnam.
No, I didn't have any luggage.
Basically, yes. I fly first class.
I'm a flight attendant for Twin Star Airlines.
I know most of the flight attendants, so I don't have to pay.

ASK ANSWER

Have students discuss the questions in groups.

10 min

EXTRA! Interview Jun

This activity depends on having at least one imaginative and eager communicator in your class. Jun's weekend trip was unusual, and there may be questions students would like to ask him if that were possible. One student can role play Jun and answer questions about his trip. (Possible questions: *When did you sleep? When did you take a shower? What was in your carry-on? What did you buy?*) If there's more than one volunteer, divide the class into groups.

World Link

Tell students to guess and then give them the answer. Ask them to imagine that flight. What questions does it make them think of? Write a list on the board and have them guess possible answers. (Possible questions: *Why do people fly between two islands—why not take a boat? Who lives on those islands, and what do they do there?*, etc.)

3 Reading Traveling alone

Skills: Use photos and title to make predictions; Find examples to support answers; Identify topics

Warm Up

5 min

Ask students the questions in the green box. Students can answer as a class discussion or in pairs. Ask if anyone in the class has travelled alone. Where did he or she go?

10–15 min

A Read the title of the article on page 131. What do you think the author is writing about? Check (✓) your answer. Then read the article and see if you were right.

In addition to the title, students could also look at the photos. What do they illustrate? (Responses should include scuba diving and archeological excavation.) Students can guess what the article might say about them. After reading, check their guesses.

5–10 min

B Read the article again. What topics does the author mention about solo travel? Check (✓) your answers.

Review the topics and have students check the ones they already know. Then they can read again and complete their answers.

5-10 min **C** **Look at the items you checked in B. For each item, give examples from the reading.**

Checked items in **B** were 3 (study vacations), 4 (using your vacation to learn a sport), and 6 (options for solo travelers). Students should make notes of their answers and check them with the class.

ASK ANSWER

Students can discuss the questions in groups. Follow up by asking each group to share their most interesting idea about what to do on a solo vacation.

20-25 min

EXTRA! Writing

After students have discussed the questions in Ask and Answer, assign one as a writing activity. (Limit the destinations question to just one city.)

25-45 min

EXTRA! Post-reading

If students' out-of-class time is limited, let them volunteer for one of these projects. Students can find an appropriate website in English and answer the questions. Afterwards, students can discuss their experience with others who answered the same questions. How did they find the information? Is their information very different?

1. A youth hostel
   - What country is it in?
   - How much does it cost for one night?
2. A city tour
   - What city is it in?
   - How much does a tour cost?
3. A restaurant menu
   - Where is the restaurant?
   - What do they have for dessert (name one)?

Teaching Tip: Authentic reading material

At this level, students can work with authentic reading material if the items are short and the tasks well chosen. The chance to read "real English" can be very motivating. Some possible texts include photos of signs, short advertisements, train or bus schedules, sections of menus, simple comic strips, very short articles from the local English newspaper, product packages, etc. Many useful and authentic texts are available online where you can print them or make screenshots. Hand out photocopies or use a classroom computer monitor or overhead projector so that everyone can see the text. Write a few simple comprehension questions that can be answered by locating specific information in the text (for example, a menu: *Can you get ice cream?*; a movie ad: *Where can you see this movie?*; hotel rules: *What time do we have to check out?*), and have students work individually or in pairs to find the answers.

15-30 min

EXTRA! Discussion questions

1. Do you think solo travel would be more expensive than traveling with another person, less expensive, or about the same? Why do you think so?
2. In general, do you think travel is dangerous? How can travelers avoid danger and still have fun?

20-30 min

EXTRA! Writing prompt

1. What is your favorite thing to do on a vacation? Explain.
2. Would you ever travel as part of a tour group? Why or why not?

20-30 min

EXTRA! Additional reading

For more practice making predictions, see Heinle's Footprint Reading Library *Solar Cooking.*

For more practice reading at this level, see Heinle's Page Turners Reading Library *The Road to Lucca.*

Travel Today

GOING SOLO IS THE WAY TO GO!

by D. Toor

How do you usually travel? Do you go with a close friend or a group of friends? Do you join a tour group? Do you travel with your family?

Have you ever imagined "going solo"? In the mid 1990s, it was estimated that 9 million Americans were planning a summer vacation alone. Since then, the number of solo travelers has increased.

You may think that traveling alone would be scary or boring. Well, according to people who do it, that's not exactly true. Solo travelers often have positive experiences: they make new friends, get to know themselves better, and can make their own schedules.

There are many different things you can do on a vacation alone. Some solo travelers use the time to learn or practice a sport such as golf, mountain climbing, or scuba diving. Others go and stay on a ranch and learn how to ride a horse. You can pretend to be a cowboy or a cowgirl for a day!

You may not believe this, but some travelers like to study on their vacation. They even go to "vacation college" at a university or join a research team as a volunteer worker. It's hard but satisfying work. You can "play scientist" for a week or two while you help someone with their project.

For solo travelers of different ages and genders, there are many travel options. There are tours for women only and for people over the age of 60. And, of course, there are trips for singles who are looking for romance. One company offers trips that focus on fine dining—there is time for sightseeing during the day and for sharing a delicious meal with new friends at night.

The next time you take a trip somewhere, why don't you consider going solo?

Bon voyage!

C Look at the items you checked in **B**. For each item, give examples from the reading.

1. ______________________________
2. ______________________________
3. ______________________________

ASK ANSWER

What would you do on a vacation by yourself?

What cities do you think are good destinations if you're traveling solo? Why do you think so?

4 Language Link The present perfect for indefinite time

A Study the chart. Notice how the present perfect is used in the conversations.

The present perfect is used to talk about past actions, when the time they happened is unknown or unimportant.

Questions	Answers	
Have you ever been to Brazil?	Yes, I have. I was there two years ago. No, I haven't. Have you?	*ever* = at any time in the past up to now **Notice!** When you mention a specific time (yesterday, two years ago), use the simple past.
Have you packed yet?	Yes, I've already packed. No, I haven't packed yet. / No, not yet.	Use *already* in affirmative statements. Use *yet* in questions and negative statements.

B Read each conversation and the statement below.
Write *T* for true, *F* for false, or *N* for not enough information.

1. **Man:** Do you want a sandwich?
   Woman: I've already eaten, thanks.
   • The woman is hungry. __F__

2. **Woman:** Have you ever visited Rio?
   Man: Yes, I have.
   • The man went to Rio last year. __N__

3. **Man:** Should I call a cab for you?
   Woman: No, Fred has already called one.
   • A cab was called. __T__

4. **Woman:** What does Maria want?
   Man: I don't know, but she's called three times.
   • Maria called an hour ago. __N__

5. **Man:** Have you been to London?
   Woman: I haven't. But I've been to the UK twice.
   • The woman visits London often. __F__

6. **Woman:** Have you put the suitcases in the car?
   Man: Not yet.
   • The suitcases are in the car. __F__

5 Writing Travel experiences

A Write about a place you've visited.

- Describe the things you did.
- Explain why you liked or didn't like the place.

I've been to Barcelona, a city in Spain. It's a great city. I was there last summer for a month. I was studying Spanish at a school and I lived with a host family.
In Barcelona, I visited many famous sites, such as La Rambla and …

B Exchange papers with a partner.

- Have you ever visited the place in your partner's writing?
- Ask your partner one question about the place he or she visited.

4 Language Link

The present perfect for indefinite time

Warm Up

5 min

With books closed, ask a series of questions with *Have you ever . . . ?* Students answer just *yes* or *no*. *Have you ever been to Brazil/taken a tour/ridden a horse/seen the Statue of Liberty?*, etc. If a student answers *Yes*, ask, *When?*

10–15 min

A Study the chart. Notice how the present perfect is used in the conversations.

With books closed, write on the board:
A: Have you ever been to Brazil?
B: Yes, I have.
Say, *Do you know when I went to Brazil?* (No) *That's why we use the present perfect, because we don't know when it happened.* Add to B: I was there two years ago. *Now do you know when I went?* (Yes) *That's why we use the simple past here.*

Write these choices on the board and ask which is close to the meaning of *ever*: *often, in the past, recently* (Correct answer: in the past).

Write:
A: Have you packed yet?
B: Yes, I've already packed./No, I haven't packed yet.
Ask which is close to the meaning of *yet* and *already*: *before now, soon, quickly* (Correct answer: before now).

Now have students open their books and look at the chart. Go over it, taking time to relate rules to examples. Ask a few follow-up questions with *ever* and *yet*.
Have you ever seen Avatar*/eaten a hot dog/stayed in a youth hostel?*
Have you had breakfast/lunch/dinner yet?

Remind students that the present perfect is used differently with *for* and *since* (Unit 9, page 93). In *Sonya has worked as a flight attendant for two years*, the action is continuing now, and we know when it started. In *I've been to Brazil*, the action is not continuing now—it finished in the past—and we don't know when it happened.

10–15 min

B Read each conversation and the statement below. Write *T* for true, *F* for false, or *N* for not enough information.

You might want students to work in pairs, reading the conversations aloud, and choosing their answers together. But also check answers with the whole class and make sure the reason for each one is explained.

5 Writing Travel experiences

Warm Up

5 min

Tell students they're going to write about a place they've visited. Point out that these might be quiet places nearby or big cities in other countries—anyplace can be interesting to read about. With books closed, help students make a collective list of places they've been.

10–15 min

A Write about a place you've visited.

Read the example with the class. Which would be more interesting to read next, a list of places in Barcelona or more information about La Rambla? What questions could they ask the writer to help him or her think of more to say about it? Write their questions on the board. Before students write, tell them that they should try to imagine their readers' questions and answer them in their writing.

A Teaching Option Process writing

This activity focuses on generating ideas. In pairs, one student tells where he or she went and the things he or she did there. His or Her partner says one or two things he or she would like to know more about. The first student gives some details, his or her partner comments, etc. When the first student has some good ideas, they should switch and the first student helps his or her partner.

5–10 min

B Exchange papers with a partner.

Read the response questions with the class. In pairs, students can read and respond to each other's writing.

B Teaching Option Process writing

This activity focuses on peer feedback. When students read their partner's writing, they first comment personally—saying if they've been to the same place or not, if their experience was similar or different, etc. But then they should say what part of the writing is most interesting and why. If none of the writing is very interesting, they can suggest something else to say. After this feedback, give students an opportunity to improve and rewrite their paper.

6 Communication

Find someone who has . . .

Warm Up

5 min

With books closed, say, How much do you know about your classmates? Do they like to try new things? Give an example of something a classmate has done that you haven't done.

A Follow these instructions.

10–15 min

(See Student Book page 133 for complete instructions.)

This is a "mixer" activity. Students should stand up and walk around speaking to classmates at random. Make sure students understand that only people who say *Yes, I have* are added to the list. If the person says, *No, I haven't,* students can try another question or say *OK. Thanks,* and move on. Review the list of activities. Some are common, so everyone should be able to say *Yes* more than once. Students may find it more comfortable to write on a separate piece of paper.

Large Class Option

Divide the classroom into smaller areas and tell students in each area to speak only with each other.

B Get to know your classmates. Listen to your teacher read each item in A. If you've ever done the activity, raise your hand.

5–10 min

Read the items as complete questions. Then, one by one, call on each student with a hand raised. The student gives additional information. For example, you say to the class: *Have you ever visited a big city?* Beto's hand is up, so you call on him. Beto says, *I visited Buenos Aires last year.*

B Teaching Option **Students call on classmates**

You need a list of students' names for this activity. As a whole class or in smaller groups, students call on each other and ask questions. They should refer to their list in **A** and call on students that they know will answer *Yes*.

Demonstrate the activity. Show students that Beto is on your list for question 1. Ask, *Beto, have you ever visited a big city?* Beto answers and you ask a related question (or two or three—tell them how many), such as, *What city? When did you go there? How long did you stay?* Beto answers your questions, then calls on another student and asks questions. That student calls on a third student, and so on. Any related questions are OK, and it's not necessary to follow the order of the list in **A**.

Give a list of students' names to a checker and have the checker check them off as they speak. At the end, if some students haven't been called on, ask who has them on their list and have that student call on them.

EXTRA! Memory race

10–25 min

For this game, you need a watch or cell phone to keep time. In groups, students put their book and papers away and choose a secretary who writes fast. Only the secretary has a piece of paper. Set a short time limit (so there won't be too many sentences to check). When you say, *Go!*, students start dictating sentences to the secretary, one sentence about each classmate, with information they remember from **A** and **B**. Secretaries write complete sentences, like *Beto has visited Buenos Aires.* If the secretary gets tired, he or she can pass the paper to another student. When you say, *Stop!*, secretaries stop writing and put their pencils down. Each group counts their sentences, writes the total at the top, and passes the paper to the next group. That group crosses out extra sentences about the same person and writes the new total at the top. Now find out the highest number of sentences. Have the sentences read aloud, and ask the class to say if any are wrong. Wrong sentences are crossed out. If they still have the highest score, that group wins. If not, check the next highest score until there's a winner.

World Link Video and World Link Website

Remind students of the value of further practice outside the classroom. Ask students who have watched the video or done online practice to share their experiences.

Check out the World Link Video. Practice your English online at http://elt.heinle.com/worldlink

6 Communication **Find someone who has . . .**

A Follow these instructions.

1. Ask your classmates questions with the present perfect. Complete as much of the chart as you can.
2. When someone answers "Yes" to a question, ask another question to get more information. Then write the person's name and the piece of information in the chart.

Jin Sung, have you ever visited a big city?

Yes, I have.

Which city?

Seoul.

Find someone who has . . .	Name	Information
1 visited a big city		
2 joined a group tour		
3 talked to a flight attendant		
4 ridden on a train		
5 gone on a trip and forgotten something		
6 spent time on a beach		
7 participated in a festival		
8 seen a TV show about a foreign place		
9 eaten food from another country		
10 overpacked for a trip		
11 gone on a day trip		
12 taken a lot of photos of something		

B Get to know your classmates. Listen to your teacher read each item in **A**. If you've ever done the activity, raise your hand.

Check out the World Link video.

Practice your English online at http://elt.heinle.com/worldlink

Review: Units 10–12

1 Storyboard

A Pia is calling Bob, her boss, at work. Complete the conversation. For some blanks, more than one answer is possible.

B In groups of three, practice the conversation. Then change roles and practice again.

C Think of an interesting place to make a telephone call from. Then make your own conversation like the one above. Practice with your group.

Review: Units 10–12

1 Storyboard

Warm Up

5 min

With books closed, ask students to remember what they learned about making phone calls and leaving messages. As they say all the words, expressions, and sentences they can think of, list them on the board. If you wish, tell students to look back at Unit 10 (pages 104 and 106) to find more examples.

A 10–15 min **Pia is calling Bob, her boss, at work. Complete the conversation. For some blanks, more than one answer is possible.**

Explain the situation: Pia isn't at work, and she's calling her boss. Tell students to look at the pictures. Ask where Pia is and what she's doing. Who do they think she's talking to in pictures 5 and 6? What do they think she's saying? Students can work in groups of three to complete the conversation. To check answers, a different group should read the speech bubbles for each picture. Ask if other groups have different answers. Confirm all correct answers, and write them on the board.

B 10–15 min **In groups of three, practice the conversation. Then change roles and practice again.**

In new groups of three, students should practice the conversation three times so everyone reads all the roles. Tell them to make it sound like a real phone call, and remind them to look up at the person they're speaking to. Walk around while they practice to help with pronunciation and expression. To follow up, have a group of expressive readers perform it for the class.

C 10–20 min **Think of an interesting place to make a telephone call from. Then make your own conversation like the one above. Practice with your group.**

Assign students to new groups of three. First they should decide where they're calling from, whom they're calling, and what they want. Then they should create a conversation that includes two phone conversations and leaving a message. Set a time limit for preparation, and after that, all groups should be practicing. If they have not finished, they must improvise the rest of their conversation. They should switch roles so everyone plays every part. Walk around as they work and note the most amusing or interesting conversations. At the end, ask those groups to perform for the class.

EXTRA! Speaking: Telephone stories

10–15 min

Have students choose one of these topics to tell a story to a group.

1. Have you ever called your boss when you were out of the office? What was the situation? What did you say?
2. Have you ever expected a call that you didn't want to answer? What did you do? What was the result?

EXTRA! Vocabulary contest

20–30 min

This is a vocabulary review game for two or more teams. Each team makes a list of words for the other team to define. (Allow definitions, examples of when to say something, opposites—any good explanation.) They may choose from the blue words on pages 109, 119, and 129 (there are 29 words in all). The team should be able to define every word they choose. (Decide how many words are allowed per list, and set a time limit for making the lists.) Teams also should choose a speaker.

Next, the two teams exchange lists. Team 1 chooses a word from their list, agrees on the definition, and tells their speaker. (You may want to limit the time the speaker has to answer before they lose their turn.) If the definition is correct, the team gets a point. (You decide what's correct.) If it's wrong, Team 2 gets a chance to define the same word. If they're right, they get a point. Right or wrong, Team 2 has the next turn, and so on. The winning team is the one with the highest score when all the words have been used.

Instructor's Notes

2 See It and Say It

Warm Up

5 min

Ask volunteers, *What was the worst thing you ever forgot to do? What was the best (or luckiest) thing you ever remembered to do?*

Language Tip: *Remember to do* vs. *remember doing*

Remember can be followed by either a gerund or an infinitive, but the meaning is different. *I remembered to call* means that I didn't forget. *I remembered calling* means first I called, and then later I remembered that I called. Gerunds are used when you are talking about a memory. (*I remember as a child going to my grandmother's house.*)

5–10 min

A Look at the picture of Leo's house. He went on a trip, but he forgot to do many things before he left. On a separate piece of paper, make a list of what he forgot to do.

Students should work in groups to list all the things Leo forgot to do. If you wish, set a time limit. To check answers, in turn, groups can say one thing they saw, and make a master list on the board. Continue until students feel the list is complete.

10–15 min

B Pretend you are Leo and call a friend. Choose three things you forgot and ask for help. Then switch roles.

In pairs, students can role play the whole telephone call, beginning with the friend's *Hello?* and ending with *Goodbye*. To prepare, have them talk about what Leo is going to ask. Is the task important? (Will he ask his friend to empty the trash?) What exactly does Leo want the friend to do? (Bring his passport to the airport?) When students are ready, have them role play, switching roles until they have asked for all the important things on their list.

B Teaching Option **Write to Leo**

Give this assignment: Leo is still away on his trip, but he is checking his e-mail. You are the friend he called for help. Write Leo an e-mail telling him what you have done. Also tell him if you didn't do something and why. Share your e-mail with a partner.

10–15 min

EXTRA! Discussion

In pairs or groups, have students discuss what they think of Leo. Would they like to have him as a friend?

Instructor's Notes

2 See It and Say It

A Look at the picture of Leo's house. He went on a trip, but he forgot to do many things before he left. On a separate piece of paper, make a list of what he forgot to do.

Leo forgot to ...
- stop the mail.
- water the plants.
- unplug and turn off the computer.
- turn off the lights.
- pay the bills.
- put out the trash.
- take his passport.
- take/bring his keys (or give his keys to a friend).
- feed the dog (or put the dog in the kennel).
- take his cell phone.

B Pretend you are Leo and call a friend. Choose three things you forgot and ask for help. Then switch roles. Answers will vary.

I don't remember turning out the light in the living room. Can you do it for me?

Sure. No problem.

3 A TV Ad

A Read the ad. Circle the correct verb forms in the sentences. Then unscramble the adjectives. Check your answers with a partner.

This Week's Best Buy!

★ **Are you planning (buying / to buy) a new TV?**

★ **Can't stand (viewing / to view) movies on a small screen?**

★ **When you watch sports, do you want (feeling / to feel) like you're actually at the game?**

★ **Would you like (saving / to save) energy when you watch TV?**

Try our new flat screen HDTV!

And you'll appreciate (watching / to watch) TV in a whole new way!

★ ___excellent___ (cellxente) *picture quality!*

★ ___affordable___ (roffadable) *Now only $900!*

★ ___convenient___ (venconient) *Easy to use and perfect for any room in your home!*

B With a partner, compare your TV to the one in the ad using *(not) as . . . as.*

> My TV is not as expensive as the TV in the ad.

4 Old Favorites

A Complete the chart with your favorites.

	When you were younger	Now
Snack food		
Music group or singer		
Piece of clothing you own(ed)		
Hobby		
Weekend activities		

B With a partner, ask and answer questions about your present and past favorites. Use *used to* for the past favorites. Have you changed a lot?

> What snack food did you use to eat?

> I used to eat a lot of sweets, but these days, I eat healthier snacks.

3 A TV ad

Warm Up

5–10 min

Review verbs that take infinitives only, gerunds only, or either gerunds or infinitives. If students don't remember many of them, turn to page 111 and briefly review. If you wish, leave the lists on the board for students to refer to in **A**.

A **Read the ad. Circle the correct verb forms in the sentences. Then unscramble the adjectives. Check answers with a partner.**

5–10 min

This is a two-part activity. In the first part, students choose a gerund or an infinitive. They should identify the main verbs in the sentences first. In the second part, they unscramble adjectives. Check all answers on the board.

B **With a partner, compare your TV to the one in the ad using *(not) as . . . as.***

5–10 min

Since students' TVs may be bigger, more expensive, etc., than the one in the ad, you may wish to include comparatives (Unit 2) in the activity.

This exercise gives information about size, price, picture quality, and convenience. You can have students add other categories for comparison (see pages 114 and 122). If additional practice is desired, students can list information about an imaginary cell phone, car, skateboard, etc., and compare theirs to it.

5–15 min

EXTRA! Pop quiz

A *pop quiz* is a short, unannounced test. This one follows up on the Warm Up activity for this section, but can be done at any later point in the unit. Tell students to take out a piece of paper and a pen and put everything else away. Write three column heads on the board: *Infinitive only, Gerund only,* and *Infinitive or gerund*. From the list on page 112, dictate verbs in random order, noting the ones you choose. Check answers on the board or with the help of "Assistant Teachers."

Teaching Tip: "Assistant Teachers" for in-class correction

When class work results in a set of papers that (1) are not too long, (2) have only one possible answer per item, (3) you want to score for the students, and (4) are not going to count for a grade, you can correct them immediately with the help of "Assistant Teachers." This works even in large classes.

Tell students to raise their hands when they have finished. Start with the ones who finish first, giving a checkmark next to correct answers and an X next to wrong ones. Students correct their wrong answers, bring them to you (where you are correcting other papers), and you check them again. As soon as a student has all correct answers, he or she becomes an Assistant Teacher and begins correcting other students' papers in the same way. When an Assistant Teacher says all corrections have been made, that student shows you his or her paper and is promoted to Assistant Teacher.

Since the number of Assistant Teachers increases exponentially, the process goes very fast. Students are motivated to learn from their mistakes, and it's a lot of fun.

4 Old Favorites

Warm Up

5 min

With books closed, ask students if their favorite things are different now from when they were younger. Ask about movie stars, sports, video games, places to hang out, role models, friends, and relatives.

A **Complete the chart with your favorites.**

5 min

Students can work in pairs and extend their list of categories before they complete the chart. They will each have the same list and complete the chart about themselves.

B **With a partner, ask and answer questions about your present and past favorites. Use *used to* for the past favorites. Have you changed a lot?**

5–10 min

Students work in the same pairs as in **A**. They should tell each other if they think their partner has changed a lot, a little, or not at all.

5 First Trip

Warm Up

5 min With books closed, ask students if they know any very old people (90 or older). What are they like?

10–15 min **A Emma Goldstein is ninety years old. She took her first trip on an airplane last month. Read what she said. Then correct the mistake(s) in each sentence. It can be a mistake in grammar or vocabulary.**

Remind students how to correct mistakes clearly. In this exercise, they only need to cross out wrong words and write the correct words above them. To check answers, have several students at once write the sentences on the board (or write them yourself), then have others tell you how to correct them.

> **Teaching Tip: Alphabet/spelling review**
>
> When students tell you words to write on the board, ask them to spell the words instead of just saying them. Write exactly what they spell, including mistakes. When a mistake is noticed, students must tell you how to correct it. (*No, not a! Write e.*) Pretend you are a robot and that you don't know what they mean unless they are very specific. For example, if they just say, *No, e!,* you write *e* anywhere on the board.

10–15 min **B Ask your partner about a trip he or she has taken.**

Make sure students haven't already done this with the same partner in Unit 12—or you might like to try this variation. Students can work in groups of three. One acts as the timekeeper; the other two alternate telling the story of a fictitious trip. They stop and start speaking when the timekeeper says *Change!* You can have the timekeeper count 20 or 30 seconds, or say *change* at good points in the story. Each student telling the story should speak at least twice, or until the story is over. Students should switch roles so that everyone tells two stories and is timekeeper once.

6 Listening

Warm Up

5 min With books closed, say, *These days, most telephone messages are left on voice mail or answering machines, not written down. Can you think of situations where written messages are still needed or used?* Make a list of the responses on the board.

CD 2 Track 37, 5–10 min **Read the phone messages below. Then listen and circle the correct answer for each question.**

Read the messages with the class. How are they different? Point out that Ted's message is for Penny's brother. Play Sheila's call, then pause the audio while students circle their answers. Continue with Ted's call and give students time to answer. Then play the recording again without pausing. Check answers with the whole class.

Ask what they heard in Sheila's call that gave them the answer (two sentences). What about Ted's call? (This is more complicated. Ask them to give the gist of what they heard.) Play the conversations again if needed, then students can tell a partner their answers. Play them once more to confirm.

20–30 min **EXTRA! Writing or discussion**

Tell about one of these phone messages.

1. A missed message—an important message that you didn't get.
2. A wonderful or terrible message.

World Link Video and World Link website

Remind students of the value of further practice outside the classroom. Ask students who have watched the video or done online practice to share their experiences.

Check out the World Link Video. Practice your English online at http://elt.heinle.com/worldlink

5 First Trip

A Emma Goldstein is ninety years old. She took her first trip on an airplane last month. Read what she said. Then correct the mistake(s) in each sentence. It can be a mistake in grammar or vocabulary.

1. I used to ~~was~~ [be] afraid of flying.
2. Last month, I ~~made~~ [got] a call from my daughter.
3. She said, "You ~~must to~~ [have to] pack your bags. We're taking a trip."
4. I didn't want to ~~going~~ [go] at first because I disliked ~~to fly~~ [flying].
5. I took two pieces of ~~boarding passes~~ [carry-on luggage] on the plane.
6. The flight attendant was nice. She helped me put everything in the ~~oxygen mask~~ [overhead compartment].
7. Airplane travel is not as ~~scarier~~ [scary] as I thought.
8. I can now proudly say, "I have ~~flying~~ [flown] on an airplane!"

B Ask your partner about a trip he or she has taken.

6 Listening

CD 2
Track 37

Read the phone messages below. Then listen and circle the correct answer for each question.

1. What message did Sheila leave for Tom?

WHILE YOU WERE OUT
Sheila called. She wants to meet soon. She will call again at 5:00.

WHILE YOU WERE OUT (circled)
Sheila called. She can't meet tomorrow. Please call her.

WHILE YOU WERE OUT
Sheila called. She can't meet today. She wants to meet tomorrow at 2:00.

2. What message did Ted leave for Penny's brother?

WHILE YOU WERE OUT
Ted called. His computer crashed and won't start. He wants you to fix it. Can you call him? His number is 555-9083.

WHILE YOU WERE OUT
Ted called. He has a question about his new laptop. Please call him back.

WHILE YOU WERE OUT (circled)
Ted called. He wants you to help him buy a new computer. He'll call you later.

Language Summaries

Unit 1 All About Me

Lesson A

Vocabulary Link

acquaintance
attend/go to (a school)
close friends
co-worker
date (someone)/go out (*with* someone)
just friends
work together

Speaking Strategy

Introducing a person to someone else

I'd like to introduce you to Andres.
I'd like you to meet Andres.

Junko, this is Ricardo.
Junko, meet Ricardo.
Junko, Ricardo.

Responding to introductions

It's (very) nice to meet you.
(It's) nice/good to meet you, too.

Nice/Good to meet you.
You, too.

Lesson B

Vocabulary Link

get a good - bad grade
have (name of sport) practice
meet (*for* a time/*on* a day)
pass - fail (an exam/a class)
prepare (*for* something)
take a class
take a lesson
tutor

Unit 2 Let's Eat!

Lesson A

Vocabulary Link

delicious/tasty
fried
juicy
salty
spicy
sweet
tastes like

Speaking Strategy

Making suggestions

Let's have Thai food.
Why don't we have Thai food?
How/What about having Thai food?

Responding to suggestions

Great idea!
(That) sounds good (to me).
Fine with me.
I don't really want to.
I don't really feel like it.

Lesson B

Vocabulary Link

a (balanced/healthy) diet
a (bad/unhealthy) habit
benefit
cut back (*on* something)
eat out
eliminate
increase
lifestyle
plenty (*of* something)
protect (*against* something)

Unit 3 Unsolved Mysteries

Lesson A

Vocabulary Link

by accident - on purpose
good luck - bad luck
lucky/fortunately - unlucky
luckily - unfortunately
miss a chance - take a chance
reunite - separate
work out (for the best)

Speaking Strategy

Talking about possibility

Saying something is likely

I bet (that) Marco plays drums.
Marco probably plays drums.
Maybe/Perhaps Marco plays drums.

Saying something isn't likely

I doubt (that) Marco plays drums.

Lesson B

Vocabulary Link

explain/explanation
figure out
investigate/investigation
make sense
mystery/mysterious
prove/proof
solve/solution
theory

Unit 4 Today's Trends

Lesson A

Vocabulary Link

a quarter/one-fourth/twenty-five percent
almost/nearly
average
drop/decrease
half/fifty percent
over
percent
rise/increase
thousands
trend
twice/two times as high as (something else)

Speaking Strategy

Disagreeing

Politely
I know what you're saying, but …
Sorry, but I disagree. / I don't agree.
I hear you, but …

Strongly
That's not true.
I totally/completely disagree.
Oh, come on! / Are you serious?

Lesson B

Vocabulary Link

a look/style
in (style)/**out** (of style)

(body) piercings
baggy/oversized
casual
conservative
dramatic (hairstyle, makeup)
retro
ripped (clothes, jeans)
pointy (shoes, boots)
skinny/fitted (jeans)
sloppy
sporty

Unit 5 Out and About

Lesson A

Vocabulary Link

do the chores
do the dishes
do the laundry
go grocery shopping
mail (something)
make a reservation
make an appointment
make dinner
pick up – drop off (something)
run an errand
sweep (the floor)
take (someone) to (a place)
take a break
take the dog for a walk
vacuum (a rug)

Speaking Strategy

Making appointments

Explaining why you're calling

I'm calling to make a dental appointment.
I'd like to make a dental appointment.

Scheduling the time

Can you come in tomorrow at 2:00?
Can you make it tomorrow at 2:00?
How/What about tomorrow at 4:00?

That's perfect. / That works great.
No, that day/time isn't good for me.

Lesson B

Vocabulary Link

ways to travel

by bike, bus, car, plane, subway, taxi, train
on foot
catch/take a bus, cab, plane, subway, train
ride a bike

talking about time

It takes . . . (+ time period)
a short time - a long time
(be) on time - (be) running late
pass (the) time (doing something)
spend time (*with* someone)

commute
stuck in traffic

Unit 6 Student Life

Lesson A

Vocabulary Link

admit/admission
apply to (a school)/ application
apply for (something)/ application
compete/competition
decide/decision
get into/get accepted to (a school)
graduate/graduation
recommend/ recommendation

Speaking Strategy

Offering another point of view

I didn't get into Yale.

Look on the bright side . . .
Well, the good news is . . .
Look at it this way . . .
Yes, but on the other hand . . .
(Yes, but) then again . . .

three other schools accepted you.

Lesson B

Vocabulary Link

Definite time expressions

after graduation/school/work
in two hours/days/months
next week/month/year
this summer/spring/fall/winter
the day after tomorrow

Indefinite time expressions

in a few days
in the near future
someday/one of these days
soon
sooner or later

Unit 7 Let's Celebrate

Lesson A

Vocabulary Link

a host
celebrate/celebration
get presents
get together (*with* others)
have/throw/host a party
have a good time
invite (someone to something)
plan a party
root for (something or someone)
wild/rowdy

Speaking Strategy

Inviting someone to do something

Do you want to go with me?
Would you like to go with me?
How'd you like to go with me?

Accepting or refusing an invitation

Sure, I'd love to.
That sounds great.

I'm sorry, but I can't. I have plans.
Unfortunately, I can't. I have class.
I'd love to, but I'm busy.

Lesson B

Vocabulary Link

be held/take place
full (*of* something)
gather
participate/participation/participant
perform/performance/performer
race
win/winner
(win) a contest
(win) first prize

Unit 8 Storytelling

Lesson A

Vocabulary Link

a (TV/drama) series
a soap opera

a true story
be based on (a true story)
make up (a story)
tell a story
the same old story

a happy ending
be hooked on (something)
character
follow (something or someone)
predictable
realistic

Speaking Strategy

Telling a story

Introducing the story
It's (a story) about . . .
The story begins/starts in . . .
One day, . . .

Continuing the story
So (then), . . .
Later, . . .
After that, . . .
It turns out that . . .

Ending the story
In the end, . . .
Finally, . . .

Lesson B

Vocabulary Link

brave
clever
eventually
incredible/unbelievable
overcome
struggle
survive
uneducated

Unit 9 The World of Work

Lesson A

Vocabulary Link

cautious
courageous
efficient
flexible
independent
knowledgeable
pleasant
punctual
unpredictable

Speaking Strategy

Interviewing for a job

Thanks for coming in today.
It's great to be here. / My pleasure.

Tell me a little about yourself.
I'm majoring in journalism . . .

Have you ever (done this kind of work)?
Yes, when I was in college.

When can you start?
Right away. / On Monday.

I'll be in touch.
I look forward to hearing from you.

Lesson B

Vocabulary Link

a dead-end job
a dream job
be out of a job
demanding
diverse
dull
exhausting
hazardous
rewarding
steady

Unit 10 Telecommunications

Lesson A

Vocabulary Link

phone
answer the phone - hang up
be on the phone
turn on - turn off your phone

call
call (someone) back
get a call (*from* someone)
make a call
screen your calls

message
check your messages
get a message
leave a message
send a text (message)
take a message

Speaking Strategy

Using the telephone

Hi. Is Lisa there?
Hello. May/Could/Can I speak to Lisa?
This is Lisa. / Speaking.

Who's calling?
May I ask who's calling?

Hang on.
Can you hang on (for a moment)?
Would/Could you hold (for a moment)?

Can I take a message?
May I take a message?
Would you like to leave a message?

Lesson B

Vocabulary Link

allowed - banned
delete - add
ignore - respond
lower your voice - raise your voice
polite - rude
thoughtful - selfish/thoughtless
turn up - turn down

Unit 11 Technology Today

Lesson A

Vocabulary Link

affordable
convenient
disposable
durable
portable
practical
reliable

Speaking Strategy

Stating what other people think

A lot of people say (that) …
Some people think (that) …

Explaining what you think

(But,) actually, …
(But,) in fact,/in reality, …
(But), the truth/fact/reality is …

Lesson B

Vocabulary Link

affect/effect
area
consume
locate/location
prevent
recycle
reduce
rescue
restore
transform

Unit 12 Let's Go Somewhere!

Lesson A

Vocabulary Link

confirm the flight plans
empty the trash
exchange money
give away fresh foods
give the house keys to a friend
pay the bills
stop the mail delivery
turn off the lights
unplug electrical items
water the plants

Speaking Strategy

Saying you've forgotten something

I forgot + noun:
I forgot my bus pass.
I forgot + infinitive:
I forgot to empty the trash.

I don't remember + gerund:
I don't remember turning off the lights.

I can't remember where + clause:
I can't remember where I put my car keys.

Lesson B

Vocabulary Link

baggage claim
boarding pass
carry-on luggage
check-in counter
flight attendant
overhead compartment
oxygen mask
tray table

Grammar Notes

Unit 1 All About Me

Lesson A Language Link: The simple present vs. the present continuous

I always **take** a shower in the morning. The express train **arrives** at 9:03 a.m. They **don't speak** Italian. They **speak** French.	Use the simple present to talk about habits, schedules, and facts.
Clara **isn't studying** right now. She**'s talking** on the phone at the moment.	Use the present continuous to talk about actions that are happening at the time of speaking. Notice the time expressions.
How many classes **are** you **taking** this term? Hiro **is living** in Singapore these days.	Also use the present continuous to talk about actions happening in the extended present (nowadays). Notice the time expressions.

Lesson B Language Link: Review of the simple past

Subject	Verb		Time expressions	
I You	**missed** **didn't miss**	a tennis lesson	yesterday. two days/weeks ago. last week/month.	The past tense ending of regular verbs is *-ed*. For irregular verbs, see the list on the next page.
He/She We They	**had** **didn't have**			

	***Yes / No* questions**	**Answers**
With *be*	Were you in class today?	Yes, I was./No, I wasn't.
With other verbs	Did you pass the test?	Yes, I did./No, I didn't.
	***Wh-* Questions**	**Answers**
With *be*	Where were you last night?	(I was) at my friend's house.
With other verbs	When did you meet your girlfriend?	(We met) last year.

Regular past tense verbs				Irregular past tense verbs			
Base form	**Past tense**	**Base form**	**Past tense**	**Base form**	**Past tense**	**Base form**	**Past tense**
change	changed	pass	passed	be	was/were	know	knew
die	died	play	played	come	came	make	made
enter	entered	prepare	prepared	do	did	meet	met
finish	finished	practice	practiced	eat	ate	read	read
graduate	graduated	study	studied	give	gave	run	ran
help	helped	talk	talked	get	got	take	took
live	lived	travel	traveled	go	went	think	thought
marry	married	use	used	have	had	win	won
move	moved	work	worked	keep	kept	write	wrote

Unit 2 Let's Eat!

Lesson A Language Link: The comparative form of adjectives

This restaurant is **bigger than** that one.	Use the comparative form of an adjective to compare two things.
Your cooking is **better than** my mom's. My cold is **worse** today **than** it was yesterday.	The comparative of *good* is *better*. The comparative of *bad* is *worse*.
I'm tall, but Milo is **taller**.	Sometimes, you can use the comparative form without *than*.

One syllable	sweet/sweet**er**	Add *-er* to many one-syllable adjectives.
	large/large**r**	Add *-r* if the adjective ends in *-e*.
	big/big**ger**	Double the final consonant and add *-er* if the adjective ends in a vowel + consonant.
Two syllables	simple/simple**r** quiet/quiet**er**	Add *-r* or *-er* to two-syllable adjectives that end in an unstressed syllable.
	spicy/spic**ier**	Change the final *-y* to *-ier* if the adjective ends in *-y*.
	crowded/**more** crowded famous/**more** famous	Add *more* to other adjectives, especially those ending in *-ing*, *-ed*, *-ious*, or *-ful*.
Three syllables	relaxing/**more** relaxing delicious/**more** delicious	Add *more* to all adjectives with three or more syllables.

Lesson B Language Link: The superlative form of adjectives

It's **the oldest** restaurant in Paris. (= The other restaurants are not as old.)	Use the superlative form of an adjective to compare something to an entire group.
It's **one of the oldest** restaurants in Paris. (= It's one of many old restaurants in Paris.)	Use *one of* ... to show that something or someone is part of a group.
Mario's has **the best** pizza in the city. It was **the worst** movie of the year.	The superlative of *good* is *the best*. The superlative of *bad* is *the worst*.

One syllable	sweet/**the** sweet**est** large/**the** large**st**	Add *the* and *-est* or *-st* to many one-syllable adjectives.
Two syllables	quiet/**the** quiet**est** simple/**the** simple**st**	Add *the* and *-est* or *-st* to two-syllable adjectives that end in an unstressed syllable.
	spicy/**the** spic**iest**	Add *the* and change the final *-y* to *-iest* if the adjective ends in *-y*.
	crowded/**the most** crowded famous/**the most** famous	Add *the most* to other adjectives, especially those ending in *-ing* ,*-ed*, *-ious*, or *-ful*.
Three syllables	relaxing/**the most** relaxing delicious/**the most** delicious	Add *the most* to all adjectives with three or more syllables.

Unit 3 Unsolved Mysteries

Lesson A Language Link: Stative verbs

He **seems** like a nice person. Not: ~~He is seeming like a nice person.~~	Stative verbs describe states and feelings (not actions). Usually, they are not used in the present continuous.
I think he is dangerous. [think = believe] I am thinking about the problem. [think = consider] She has a lot of money. [have = own, possess] She's having coffee with a friend. [have = drink]	Some stative verbs (for example, *have, feel, look, see, think*) can be used in the continuous. When used this way, their meaning changes.

Lesson B Language Link: Modals of present possibility

Subject	Modal	Main verb		
Luis	**may** **might** **could**	be	sick. He's not in class today.	Use *may, might*, and *could* to say something is possible.
	can't **couldn't**	be	sick. I just saw him in the cafeteria.	Use *can't* or *couldn't* to say something is not possible.

	Questions	Short answers
With *be*	Is Ian from the UK?	He might/could be. He can't/couldn't be.
With other verbs	Does Marta have a brother?	She might/could. She can't/couldn't.

Unit 4 Today's Trends

Lesson A Language Link: Quantity expressions

	With count nouns		With noncount nouns	
100%	**All of**	my friends live with their parents.	**All of**	my homework is finished.
	Most of		**Most of**	
	A lot of		**A lot of**	
	A couple of		______	
0%	**None of**		**None of**	

Quantity expressions are used to talk about amounts.

a couple = two
Don't use *a couple* (*of*) with noncount nouns.

General	**Most students** work hard.	[students everywhere]
Specific	**Most (of the) students** in my class work hard.	
General	**Some families** have children.	[families everywhere]
Specific	**Some (of the) families** in my neighborhood have children.	
General	**All teachers** are strict.	[teachers everywhere]
Specific	**All (of the) teachers** at my school are strict.	

Most, *some*, and *all* can be used to make general statements about people or things everywhere. Notice the difference between the sentences in each pair.

Lesson B Language Link: Giving advice with *could*, *should*, *ought to*, and *had better*

You **should/ought to** wear a suit to your job interview. You **shouldn't** wear jeans. They're too casual.	Use *should* or *ought to* to give advice. Use *shouldn't* in the negative.
You **could** wear a suit to the interview. You **could** wear your blue suit or the black one.	Use *could* to make a suggestion. It isn't as strong as *should* or *ought to*. *Could* is often used when there is more than one choice.
You**'d better** leave now or you'll miss your flight. We**'d better not** drive to the concert. It will be hard to park.	Use *had better (not)* to give strong advice. It sounds like a warning.

Unit 5 Out and About

Lesson A Language Link: Polite requests with modal verbs and *mind*

Making requests				Responding to requests
informal	**Can/Will** you **Could/Would** you	help	me, please?	OK./Sure, no problem. / I'd be glad to./Certainly. / Of course. Sorry, but . . .
formal	**Would you mind**	helping		No, not at all./No, I'd be glad to. Sorry, but . . .

- Use *Can you*, *Will you*, *Could you*, or *Would you* + verb to make requests.
- To make a formal request, use *Would you mind* + verb+ *-ing*.
  Note: To agree to a *Would you mind* . . . request, answer with *No. (No, I don't mind.)*
- To make a request more polite, add *please*.

Lesson B Language Link: Intensifiers: *really*, *very*, *pretty*

	Adverb	Adjective		
I (don't) live	really/very	close	to school.	*Really*, *very*, and *pretty* make adjectives and adverbs stronger. *Really* and *very* are stronger than *pretty*. Only *really* or *very* can be used in the negative.
I live	pretty			
	Adverb	**Adjective**	**Noun**	
I (don't) have a	really/very	long	commute.	
I have a	pretty			
	Adverb	**Verb**		
I (don't)	really	like	my new bike.	*Really* can come before a verb. *Very* cannot.

I don't know John **at all**. (I've never met him.) I didn't like that movie **at all**.	You can use *at all* with negatives to mean *zero* or *never*.

Unit 6 Student Life

Lesson A Language Link: Plans and decisions with *be going to* and *will*

Subject + *be*	*(not)*	*going to*	Verb		Time expressions
I'm You're He's/She's We're They're	not	going to	attend	Harvard	next month/year. this fall. in the summer. after graduation.

Use *be going to* to talk about definite future plans (plans you have already made).

A: What are your plans for today? **B:** I don't know. Maybe I'**ll** see a movie. **A:** Are you feeling OK? **B:** No, not really. Maybe I **won't** go to class today.	Use *will* to talk about a sudden decision (one you make as you're speaking). *Will* is followed by the base form of a verb. *Won't = will not*

Contractions

I'll = I will
you'll = you will
he'll = he will
she'll = she will
we'll = we will
they'll = they will

Lesson B Language Link: Predictions with *be going to* and *will*

Leo gets all As. I'm sure he**'s going to**/he**'ll** get a scholarship to college. She didn't study. I bet she **isn't going to**/she **won't** pass the test.	You can use *be going to* and *will* to make predictions about the future. It's common to use *I'm sure* and *I bet* when you make a prediction you are certain about.
He'll probably get a scholarship to college. She probably won't pass the test. Maybe we'll find a cure for cancer someday.	You can use *probably* or *maybe* when you aren't 100% sure about your prediction. *Probably* is stronger than *maybe*.
Look! That rock **is going to** fall.	Use *be going to* (not *will*) to make a prediction about an action that is about to happen very soon.

Unit 7 Let's Celebrate

Lesson A Language Link: Similarity and agreement with *so, too, either, neither*

	Affirmative answers	Negative answers
With *be*	I am going to Sayuri's party. **So am I./I am, too./Me, too.**	I'm not going to Sayuri's party. **Neither am I./I'm not, either./Me, neither.**
Other verbs	I need a costume for the party. **So do I./I do, too./Me, too.**	I don't have a costume for the party. **Neither do I./I don't, either./Me, neither.**

- Use the expressions above to show similarity or to agree with something said.
- *Me, too* and *Me, neither* are common in casual conversation.

Lesson B Language Link: Time clauses with ***before***, ***after***, and ***when***

Time clause	Main clause	
Before the party,	you put on a costume.	A time clause explains when something happens. It is always connected to a main clause. A time clause can come before or after the main clause.
Main clause	**Time clause**	
You put on a costume	before the party.	

After she had dinner, Paloma went to bed.	Use *after* in a time clause to show that the event happened first. (Paloma had dinner, and then she went to bed.)
Before I left, I turned off the lights.	Use *before* in a time clause to show that the event happened second. (I turned off the lights, and then I left.)
When you see a friend, you say, "Hello."	Use *when* to show that the two events happen at the same time or one happens immediately after the other.

Unit 8 Storytelling

Lesson A Language Link: Past continuous vs. simple past

Subject	be	Verb + *-ing*		
I He/She	**was(n't)**	**watching** TV	at 8 o'clock last night.	Use the **past continuous** to talk about an action in progress in the past.
You We They	**were(n't)**			

A: I called you last night. **B:** I didn't hear the phone. I **was watching** TV.	Use the simple past (not the **past continuous**) to talk about a completed action. Use only the simple past (not the past continuous) with stative verbs (*be, hear, need, know, etc.*).
I **was taking** a shower *when* the phone rang. *While* I **was taking** a shower, the phone rang.	You can use the past continuous with the simple past to show that one action was in progress when another happened. Notice the words *when* and *while*.

Lesson B **Language Link:** Adverbs of manner

Cinderella danced **happily** with the prince. He speaks twelve languages **fluently**. He was different from other children. Mary seems unhappy.	**Adverbs of manner** tell how something is done. They often come after a verb and end in *-ly*. Remember: Adjectives, not adverbs, come after stative verbs (*be, have, hear, need, know, seem,* etc.).
She drives too **fast**. He often works **late**. They didn't do **well** in school.	Some common adverbs of manner don't end in *-ly*. Some examples are *fast, hard, late,* and *well*.

Unit 9 The World of Work

Lesson A **Language Link:** The present perfect; ***for*** and ***since***

Subject	*have/has*	Past participle		*for/since* phrase
I/You/We/They	**have(n't)**	**lived**	here	for five years. since graduation.
He/She	**has(n't)**			

- Use the **present perfect** for an action that started in the past and continues up to now.
- For many verbs, the past participle is the same as the simple past form. Some irregular past participles are in parentheses: *be (been), go (gone), did (done), begin (begun).*

Contractions
I've = I have you've = you have he's = he has she's = she has we've = we have they've = they have

Questions	Answers	
How long **have** you **lived** here? How long **has** she **lived** here?	(I've lived here) **for** two years. (She's lived here) **since** June 20. **since** she graduated.	**for** + a period of time **since** + a point in time **since** + a past time clause

Lesson B **Language Link:** Verb + infinitive

I **like** to sing. I **wanted** to become a singer. I **was planning** to move to New York. Then I got a job in London so I **needed** to move there.	Certain verbs can be followed by an infinitive (*to* + verb). Some examples are *agree, arrange, choose, decide, expect, forget, hate, hope, learn, like, love, need, plan, prepare, start, try,* and *want*. Note: The **main verb** can be in different tenses.

Unit 10 Telecommunications

Lesson A Language Link: Permission with *may, can, could, would / do you mind if* . . . ?

Asking for permission			Responding
most formal ↑	**Would you mind if**	I used your phone?	No, not at all. / No, go ahead. Sorry, but . . .
	Do you mind if	I use your phone?	
↓ least formal	**May/Could** **Can**		Certainly. / Of course. Sure, no problem. / OK. Sorry, but . . .

- Use *May I, Could I,* or *Can I* to ask permission to do something.
- To ask for permission formally, use . . .

  Do you mind if I + verb.

  Would you mind if I + the past tense of the verb.

Note: To agree to a *Would / Do you mind if* . . . request, you answer with *No.* (= No, I don't mind.)

Lesson B Language Link: Verb + gerund vs. verb + infinitive

I **need** to buy a new cell phone.	Certain verbs can be followed by an infinitive (*to* + verb).
I **avoid** talking on the phone when I'm driving.	Other verbs can be followed by a gerund (verb+ *-ing*).
I **like** to talk/talking on the phone.	Some verbs can be followed by an infinitive or a gerund. See p.112 for a list.

Unit 11 Technology Today

Lesson A Language Link: *Used to*

Subject	*used to*	Verb		
I	**used to**	wear	glasses in high school, but I don't anymore.	*Used to* is a special past tense form. Use it to talk about things that were true or happened regularly in the past, but are not true or do not happen now.
	didn't use to		glasses, but I do now.	

Questions	Answers
Did you **use to** have long hair? **Did** they **use to** live in Tokyo?	Yes, I did. / No, I didn't. Yes, they did. / No, they didn't.

Lesson B Language Link: *As … as*

Phone A costs $100. Phone B costs $100. Phone A costs **as** much **as** phone B.	Use *as* + adjective/adverb + *as* to show that two things are equal.
Jon **isn't as** tall **as** his brother. (= His brother is taller.) Russia **doesn't** have **as** many people **as** China. (=China has more people.)	You can use *not as … as* to show that things are not equal.
My phone works as well as your phone. = My phone works as well as yours.	Sometimes after *as … as*, you can end a sentence with a pronoun.
She studies as hard as he studies. (not common) She studies as hard as he does. (common) She studies as hard as him. (very informal) You're as tall as I am. You're as tall as me. (very informal)	In spoken English, it's common not to repeat the verb after *as … as*, but to say things as shown.

Unit 12 Let's Go Somewhere!

Lesson A Language Link: Modal verbs of necessity

	Present forms	Past forms
Affirmative	You **must** show your ID to get on the plane. I **have to** buy a backpack for my trip. We**'ve got to** get some cash.	I **had to** wait at the airport for an hour.
Negative	I **don't have to** check any luggage.	I **didn't have to** wait long.

- Use *must, have to,* and *have got to* + the base form of a verb to say that something is necessary.
- In spoken and written English, *have to* is used most commonly.
- *Must* is often used to talk about rules or laws. *Must* is stronger than *have (got) to.*
- Only *have to* can be used in the negative or to talk about things that were necessary in the past.

Lesson B **Language Link:** The present perfect for indefinite time

Present perfect	Simple past
I'**ve been** to Korea. He'**s taken** the driving test three times.	I went to Korea last year. He took the test in March, May, and July.

- Use the **present perfect** to talk about past actions when the time they happened is unknown or unimportant.
- When you mention a specific time (*last year, March*), use the simple past.

Questions	Answers	
Have you **(ever)** been to Brazil?	Yes, I have. No, I haven't. No, I've **never** been there.	*Ever* = at any time in the past up to now *Never* = at no time in the past
Have you packed **yet**?	Yes, I've **already** packed. (I'm done). Yes, I've packed **already**. No, I haven't packed **yet**.	Use *yet* or *already* to talk about whether an action has been completed. Use *yet* in questions and negative statements. Use *already* in affirmative statements.

Answer Keys

Answers to page 70, Vocabulary, Activity A

1. becoming an adult **2.** wild **3.** a gift **4.** man's, him **5.** team **6.** before

Answers to page 113, Communication, Activity A

1. b **2.** a **3.** c **4.** b

Listening

Answer factual detail questions, p. 115a

Categorize information, pp. 23a, 71a

Choose an appropriate response, pp. 47a, 105a

Draw conclusions, pp. 3a, 8a, 57a, 76a, 86a, 110a

Guess the meaning of words from context, p. 57a

Identify key details in a story, p. 86a

Identify the main idea, pp. 23a, 37a, 52a

Identify a sequence of events, pp. 62a, 81a, 115a, 120a

Identify situations, p. 47a

Identify speakers, pp. 125a, 130a

Infer information, pp. 18a, 52a, 62a, 76a, 91a, 96a, 110a

Listen for details, pp. 3a, 8a, 18a, 37a, 42a, 47a, 52a, 57a, 62a, 76a, 81a, 96a, 105a, 115a, 120a, 125a, 130a

Listen to determine the speaker's attitude or feeling, pp. 37a, 91a

Listen for facts (including negative factual information), pp. 13a, 130a

Listen for gist, pp. 3a, 8a, 18a, 23a, 42a, 47a, 62a, 96a, 110a

Listen for main idea(s), pp. 71a, 76a, 115a, 120a

Listen for specific information, p. 120a

Make and check predictions, pp. 3a, 13a, 18a, 42a, 52a, 57a, 62a, 91a, 96a, 105a

Organize information, p. 28a

Predict the topic, p. 28a

Restate what you've heard, p. 52a

Synthesize information in order to summarize information, p. 71a

Take notes, pp. 42a, 91a

Understand cause and effect, p. 28a

Use background knowledge to build context, p. 91a

Use visual aids to aid in listening, p. 28a

Reading

Categorize information, pp. 52a, 76a

Draw conclusions, p. 42a

Find examples to support answers, p. 130a

Guess the meaning of words from context, pp. 62a, 76a, 120a

Identify main ideas in a text, pp. 28a, 86a

Identify opinions, p. 110a

Identify topics, p. 130a

Infer information, pp. 42a, 120a

Make and check predictions, pp. 8a, 18a, 42a, 96a

Read for details, pp. 18a, 28a, 42a, 62a, 110a

Scan for specific information, pp. 18a, 76a, 86a

Skim for gist or main idea, pp. 8a, 96a

Summarize a text, pp. 8a, 76a, 96a

Understand the main ideas and supporting details, p. 110a

Understand referents, p. 110a

Understand a sequence of events, p. 120a

Understand text organization, p. 42a

Use background knowledge to make predictions, pp. 52a, 62a, 76a

Use captions to make predictions, p. 120a

Use photographs to predict content, pp. 18a, 28a, 52a, 76a, 120a, 130a

Use titles to make predictions, pp. 18a, 120a, 130a

Unit 1, Lesson A

Page 3, Listening (CD 1, Track 2)

Woman: So, Linda, how do you know Michael?
Linda: Michael? Oh, we went out for a while.
Woman: He's your boyfriend?
Linda: Not anymore, but we're still friends.
Woman: Really?
Linda: Yeah. In fact, I saw him last weekend. A group of us went out together.

Andres: Excuse me? Are you Miriam?
Miriam: Yeah. And you must be Andres.
Andres: Right.
Miriam: Hi. It's nice to meet you.
Andres: Nice to meet you, too.
Miriam: So, Andres, is this your first day working here?
Andres: No, I started yesterday.

Rakesh: Clara? Clara Goldman?
Clara: Uhm . . . yeah? Do I . . . do I know you?
Rakesh: I'm Rakesh . . . Rakesh Patel. . . . We were in the same English class last year . . .
Clara: Oh, yeah! Rakesh. Now I remember you. How are you doing?
Rakesh: Fine. How about you?

Page 3, Pronunciation (CD 1, Track 3)

1. Clara: Now I remember you. How are you doin'?
   Rakesh: Fine. How about you?
2. Lisa: Hey, Josh. Are you busy?
   Josh: Yeah. I'm writin' a paper for my English class.

(CD 1, Track 4)

1. I'm tryin' to finish my homework.
2. I'm fixin' my car.
3. She's workin' in her garden.
4. We're goin' to the movies.

Page 4, Speaking (CD 1, Track 5)

Conversation 1
Maria: Hi, Junko.
Junko: Hi, Maria. It's good to see you again! How are you?
Maria: Fine. How about you?
Junko: Pretty good.
Maria: Oh, and this is my friend Ricardo. We both go to City University.
Junko: Hey, Ricardo. Nice to meet you.
Ricardo: Yeah, you too.

Conversation 2
Mr. Otani: Morning, Miriam.
Miriam: Good morning, Mr. Otani. . . . Oh, Mr. Otani, I'd like you meet Andres Garcia. He started working here yesterday. Andres, Mr. Otani is our V.P. of Sales.
Mr. Otani: Nice to meet you, Andres.
Andres: It's very nice to meet you, too, Mr. Otani.

Unit 1, Lesson B

Page 8, Listening (CD 1, Track 6)

Are you planning to go to college or graduate school? Do you want to study in an English-speaking country? Do you need to pass an exam to get a job or to move up in your current job? GBL Learning Center can help you to prepare for these and other important exams.

(CD 1, Track 7)

Are you planning to go to college or graduate school? Do you want to study in an English-speaking country? Do you need to pass an exam to get a job or to move up in your current job? GBL Learning Center can help you to prepare for these and other important exams. Listen to what some of our recent graduates have to say . . .

Student: I'm a student. To go to college in the U.S., I had to take the TOEFL test. The first time I took it, my score was really low. Then I took one of GBL's classes and my score went up fifty points!
Engineer: I'm an engineer and needed to pass an exam to move up in my job and make more money. The first time I took the test, I failed. Then I met with one of GBL's tutors twice a week. Last month, I retook the test and passed!
Medical student: I knew I needed help to get into medical school. So, I went to GBL Learning Center. They were great, and guess what? I took the test for medical school once and I passed it! Now I'm studying to be a doctor!

So, what are you waiting for? To learn more about GBL Learning Center, visit us online at www. . . .

Unit 2, Lesson A

Page 13, Listening (CD 1, Track 8)

Bill: Hi, Marta. What did you do last night?
Marta: Oh, I had dinner at a friend's house. Her mom cooked.
Bill: Really? What was on the menu?
Marta: It was a big meal. Let's see . . . we had fried chicken, grits, fried green tomatoes, and . . . oh yeah, Mississippi mud pie for dessert.

Bill: Grits? Fried green tomatoes? Never heard of them.

Marta: Yeah, I'm not surprised. They're common in the southern United States. That's where my friend's mom is from.

(CD 1, Track 9)

Bill: Hi, Marta. What did you do last night?
Marta: Oh, I had dinner at a friend's house. Her mom cooked.
Bill: Really? What was on the menu?
Marta: It was a big meal. Let's see . . . we had fried chicken, grits, fried green tomatoes, and . . . oh yeah, Mississippi mud pie for dessert.
Bill: Grits? Fried green tomatoes? Never heard of them.
Marta: Yeah, I'm not surprised. They're common in the southern United States. That's where my friend's mom is from.
Bill: Interesting! So, did you like the food?
Marta: Yeah . . . the chicken was delicious.
Bill: How about the grits? What *are* grits anyway?
Marta: They're made from crushed corn, and they kind of taste like . . . um, oatmeal . . .
Bill: Oatmeal? Like a hot breakfast cereal? Hmmmm. Were they any good?
Marta: Yeah, They were. . . . They had a strong buttery flavor. I liked them.
Bill: And the tomatoes?
Marta: They were a little oily, but I have to say they went well with the chicken and the grits.
Bill: Sounds like a lot of food.
Marta: Yeah, it was! So you can imagine how I felt when dessert came out . . .
Bill: What did you have again?
Marta: Mississippi mud pie.
Bill: What is it exactly?
Marta: It's a really thick chocolate pie.
Bill: Wow! So how was it?
Marta: It was really sweet—too sweet for me. I only ate a little.

Page 13, Pronunciation (CD 1, Track 10)

ORanges are SWEETer than GRAPEfruit.
PoTAto chips are SALTier than CRACKers.

(CD 1, Track 11)

1. MATH is HARDer than ENGlish.
2. APPles are JUIcier than CARRots.
3. The CURry is SPIcier than the CHILi.
4. JANuary is COLDer than FEBruary.

Page 14, Speaking (CD 1, Track 12)

Jose: So, Jill, where do you want to go to dinner tonight?
Jill: I don't know. Why don't we go to the pizza place on the corner?
Jose: Pizza again? I don't really feel like it.
Jill: OK, how about Thai food instead?
Jose: Fine with me. Where do you want to go?
Jill: Well, Thai House is near here. And there's another place — The Thai Cafe — but it's downtown.
Jose: Thai House is closer. Let's go there.
Jill: Sounds good!

Unit 2, Lesson B

Page 18, Listening (CD 1, Track 13)

Alison: On today's show, we're talking with Alessandro Moretti about his book *The Future of Slow Food*. Thanks for joining us today, Mr. Moretti.
Alessandro: My pleasure, Alison.
Alison: So, Mr. Moretti, why don't you tell us a little about the Slow Food Movement. It started in the late nineteen eighties, right?
Alessandro: Yes, in 1989—in Italy, actually, but today, there are more than a hundred thousand members worldwide.
Alison: Uh-huh. And when you say "slow food," what exactly do you mean?
Alessandro: Well, in many ways, it's the opposite of fast food.
Alison: You mean food like you buy in fast-food restaurants?
Alessandro: Yes, but also instant, prepared foods you buy in the supermarket. One of the things slow food supporters want to do is to eliminate this food from their diets.
Alison: Can people really do this—especially busy people?
Alessandro: Yes, definitely! You *can* change your eating habits. And, of course, by cutting back on processed foods, you'll be healthier.
Alison: Yeah, I guess that's true. So, slow food supporters don't eat fast food . . .
Alessandro: Right, but we also believe it's important to *protect* traditional foods.
Alison: What do you mean by that?
Alessandro: Well, for example, think about the dishes your grandmother cooked—things you really liked. Can you prepare any of these dishes?
Alison: Uhm, well, no, not really, well, maybe one . . .
Alessandro: Exactly. The fact is many people don't learn to cook anymore . . .
Alison: Yeah, sometimes it's just easier to buy something in the supermarket or to eat out.
Alessandro: Right. So, it's important to learn how to prepare these dishes and to keep food traditions alive.

Unit 3, Lesson A

Page 23, Listening (CD 1, Track 14)

Everyone wants to be lucky—to do well in school, get a good job, make a lot of money, fall in love. And when these things happen—when we pass a test or meet the perfect boyfriend or girlfriend—maybe we think, "Wow, I sure am lucky." But maybe you have a friend . . . he lost his job, failed the university entrance exam, or he can't get a date. Maybe people look at this guy and say, "He's so unlucky!" So the question is why are some people lucky but others aren't? Dr. Richard Wiseman, a professor at a university in the UK, asked this same question. He and his team did a study and they found something interesting—there are important key differences between lucky people and those who aren't.

(CD 1, Track 15)

Everyone wants to be lucky—to do well in school, get a good job, make a lot of money, fall in love. And when these things happen—when we pass a test or meet the perfect boyfriend or girlfriend—maybe we think, "Wow, I sure am lucky." But maybe you have a friend . . . he lost his job, failed the university entrance exam, or he can't get a date. Maybe people look at this guy and say, "He's so unlucky!" So the question is why are some people lucky but others aren't? Dr. Richard Wiseman, a professor at a university in the UK, asked this same question. He and his team did a study and they found something interesting—there are important key differences between lucky people and those who aren't.

Okay, so what are those things? First, Dr. Wiseman says that lucky people aren't afraid to meet new people or try new things. Because they are open, they increase their chances of having good luck. Unlucky people, on the other hand, are often too careful and so they miss many chances. How else are they different? Unlucky people focus too much on the facts. Lucky people, on the other hand, use their intuition and often follow their feelings. For example, you meet someone and he asks you on a date. You don't know him . . . should you go? You have to make a quick choice. You try to "feel" what's right. That's your intuition. What is the feeling telling you? "Yes, go on the date!" Or "No, don't go!" Pay attention to that feeling. It's usually right. A third way that lucky and unlucky people are different is this: Unlucky people often worry about the future . . . they expect things to be difficult. But lucky people believe good things will happen, and even when bad things happen, a lucky person says, "Next time, things will be better."

Page 23, Pronunciation (CD 1, Track 16)

1. I heard an interesting story on the radio last night.
2. Steve and Carmen met in England.
3. Later, she took a job in Paris and they separated.
4. Steve knew he still loved Carmen, so he wrote a letter to her.
5. Carmen's mother got the letter, but then she lost it.
6. Later, workmen found the letter and Carmen read it. What luck!
7. I thought this was a good story.

Page 24, Speaking (CD 1, Track 17)

Sandra: Anything interesting in today's news?
Nico: Yeah, I'm reading about a woman in New York City. She just won $25,000.
Sandra: That's a lot of money. Did she win the lottery?
Nico: No, she guessed the correct number of candies in a jar.
Sandra: Really? How many were there?
Nico: 7,954.
Sandra: Wow. That was a lucky guess!
Nico: Oh, I doubt she guessed. I bet she's good at math. The article says she won a similar contest in the past.
Sandra: So, what's she going to do with the money?
Nico: I don't know. She'll probably go on vacation or use it for school.

Unit 3, Lesson B

Page 28, Listening (CD 1, Track 18)

Stuart: And now for our last report of the evening, we go to London, where city officials are planning to put more police on the street on nights when the moon is full. For that story, we turn now to Mia Curtis. Mia?
Mia: Yes, Stuart, it's true. Soon, there might be more police out when the moon is full. . . . The city is saying that there are more car accidents and more people hurt in fights on these nights. . . . It's all very mysterious.

(CD 1, Track 19)

Stuart: And now for our last report of the evening, we go to London, where city officials are planning to put more police on the street on nights when the moon is full. For that story, we turn now to Mia Curtis. Mia?
Mia: Yes, Stuart, it's true. Soon, there might be more police out when the moon is full. . . . The city is saying that there are more car accidents and more people hurt in fights on these nights. . . . It's all very mysterious.
Dr. Wong: Well, I'm a doctor here at City Hospital in London and I'll tell you, yesterday was a full moon and there were *a lot* of people in here. Not because the moon makes people more dangerous—there's no proof that's true.
Mia: So, why are full moon nights different? Dr. Wong says one explanation is this—full moon nights are brighter than other nights. There's more light, so more people go out.
Stuart: So, Mia, if more people are out, it makes sense to put more police on the street . . .
Mia: Right. Dr. Wong said the same thing. For KCTR news, this is Mia Curtis reporting live from London.

Review Units 1–3

Page 34, Listening (CD 1, Track 20)

Man 1: I'm about ten kilos overweight. To get in shape, I'm exercising more and I'm also on a diet right now. There are a lot of foods and drinks I've cut back on—sweets, sodas, stuff like that. But it's hard to eliminate the fried foods, especially when I eat out. I just like them too much!

Woman 1: I lived in Thailand for six months. It was really fun, but the best part was the food. Thai food is too spicy for some people, but not for me. The spicier, the better, I say! Now I'm back home, but the food here tastes so bland. It's very different than Thai food.

Man 2: I'm training for a swimming competition and I've completely changed my lifestyle. I've eliminated sweets and fried foods from my diet. . . . and I've increased the amount of fresh fruit and vegetables I eat every day. At first, it wasn't easy, but now I'm healthier . . . and a better swimmer!

Woman 2: My boyfriend is always telling me that I have a sweet tooth and actually, it's true. Dessert is my favorite part of any meal. My mother is always telling me I should eat less candy and more fresh fruit, but sometimes you just want some chocolate!

(CD 1, Track 21)

1. I'm about ten kilos overweight. To get in shape, I'm exercising more and I'm also on a diet right now.
2. Thai food is too spicy for some people, but not for me. The spicier, the better, I say! Now I'm back home, but the food here tastes so bland. It's very different than Thai food.
3. My boyfriend is always telling me that I have a sweet tooth and actually, it's true. Dessert is my favorite part of any meal.

Unit 4, Lesson A

Page 37, Listening (CD 1, Track 22)

Alessandro: My name is Alessandro, and I'm from Rome. I'm twenty-eight, and I still live at home. Actually, in Italy, the average age for moving out of your parents' house is thirty-six. In Italy these days, finding a good job is hard. Apartments are really expensive, so, I don't know, it's just easier to stay with your family and save money.

Aya: I'm Aya, and I'm from Hiroshima. In Japan, most people move out of their parents' home in their late twenties—you know, like twenty-eight or twenty-nine. These days, though, more people are living with their parents for a longer time—for lots of reasons. Like, for example, people are getting married later. I think the average age now is around thirty. And housing costs and other things are very high. It just makes sense to stay with your family.

Evan: My name's Evan, and I'm from London. In the UK, most people leave home between the ages of eighteen to twenty-four. Nowadays you see more people living with their parents longer. Why? Well . . . it costs a lot of money to go to university, so if you stay with your parents, it's easier to pay for school. But, you know, even after graduating, a lot of people still live with their parents because it's expensive to buy a house. Personally, I think kids should leave home early and work to make their own lives. Sure it's hard, but that's part of being an adult.

Page 37, Pronunciation (CD 1, Track 23)

1. Most of my friends still live with their parents.
2. A lot of people are getting married later.
3. Leaving your parents' house is part of becoming an adult.

(CD 1, Track 24)

1. None of the kids in my family still live at home.
2. A couple of my friends are studying in New York City.
3. Thousands of people get divorced every year.
4. Most of them have children.

Page 38, Speaking (CD 1, Track 25)

Carla: Dad, can I talk to you for a minute?
Dad: Sure, what's up?
Carla: Well, my friend Marta is going to see a concert tomorrow night and she invited me to go.
Dad: Tomorrow night? But tomorrow's Tuesday. Sorry, Carla, but no.
Carla: Dad! You *never* let me do anything.
Dad: That's not true, Carla. You do lots of things. But the concert ends late and you have school on Wednesday.
Carla: I know what you're saying, Dad, but it's just one night. And all of my friends are going.
Dad: Sorry, Carla, but the answer is still "no."
Carla: Oh, Dad, you're so unfair!

Unit 4, Lesson B

Page 42, Listening (CD 2, Track 26)

Marco: Welcome back to "You've Got the Look," your go-to source for the best in fashion makeovers. I'm Marco Reyes . . .

Lisa: And I'm Lisa Harris, and we want to help *you* to look your very best! OK, Marco, who are we working with today?

Marco: Well, Lisa, we've got three people. Our first makeover challenge is coming up on screen. . . .
Lisa: Wow. Overall, very sloppy . . . old jeans . . . a dirty shirt . . . the messy hair . . .
Marco: Yes, not a good look . . .
Lisa: Ok, this person definitely needs some work. Who else have we got today?
Marco: Next up is Tamara. Here comes the photo . . .
Lisa: OK. Overall, not *too* bad. It's kind of a cool look . . .
Marco: Right, but the clothes are a bit too baggy . . . there's no shape or style to them . . .
Lisa: Agreed.
Marco: Now, here comes our final makeover challenge . . .
Lisa: Hmmm, the whole look is *way* too dramatic . . . the bright colors . . . the different kinds of material . . .
Marco: And nothing matches.
Lisa: Well, it looks like we've got some work to do, Marco.
Marco: Then let's get started!

(CD 1, Track 27)

Lisa: OK, let's talk about our first makeover challenge, Brad.
Marco: Right. . . . At the moment, his whole look is much too sloppy, and that needs to change. Now, he's a casual guy and we can work with that style.
Lisa: Agreed. He could get rid of the old, dirty shirt and buy a nice new shirt . . .
Marco: Exactly! And fix the hair . . .
Lisa: Yeah—it would improve his whole look. . . . Now what about Tamara?
Marco: Well, as I mentioned, the clothes she wears are just too baggy. Oversized sweats are fine when she's relaxing or playing sports, but when she goes out, she should wear something a bit more fitted . . .
Lisa: Like a pair of skinny jeans.
Marco: Exactly! And a fun top.
Lisa: OK, Marco, we've only got a few minutes left, so let's talk about Mimi.
Marco: All right, let's bring her photo up again. . . . The trouble with Mimi is that her whole look is totally mismatched.
Lisa: Exactly. She needs to choose a single style . . .
Marco: Right, and one or two colors that match. Let's talk quickly about how we can help her do that . . .

Unit 5, Lesson A

Page 47, Listening (CD 1, Track 28)

Conversation 1
David: Good afternoon and thank you for calling Aziza. This is David speaking. How can I help you?
Elaine: Yes, hi. I have a dinner reservation for this evening at eight . . .
Man: Your last name, please?
Elaine: It's Mitchell. Elaine Mitchell.
Man: Yes, Ms. Mitchell, here you are. You have a reservation for six people tonight at eight o' clock.
Elaine: Right. I'm calling because we'd like to come in a little earlier. Is that possible?

Conversation 2
Woman: Hello. Blue Bird Cleaners.
Jose: Yeah, hi. I dropped off some pants on Monday to be dry cleaned, but I've lost my ticket. Could you tell me . . . when will they be ready?
Woman: Your name please?
Jose: Jose Martino.
Woman: Just a moment, Mr. Martino. . . . Hello? Yeah, they're ready today. Come by anytime.

Conversation 3
Sarah: Good morning. Dr. Chu's office. This is Sarah.
Leo: Uh, yeah, good morning. I'm calling to make an appointment to see the dentist.
Sarah: Okay, um, have you seen Dr. Chu before?
Leo: Yes, I have. My name's Leo Kwan. K-W-A-N.
Sarah: Thanks. Okay, Leo, let's see what Dr. Chu has open. . . . Can you come in tomorrow at ten?

Conversation 4
Bea: Hello?
Mona: Hi, Bea.
Bea: Oh, hi, Mona. What's up?
Mona: Are you driving to school this morning?
Bea: Yeah. Do you need a ride?
Mona: Yeah, but not to class. I have a doctor's appointment near school. Could you drop me off there? The office is near school.

Page 47, Pronunciation (CD 1, Track 29)

1. Could you open the window? It's hot in here.
2. Would you hold the door for me? Thanks.
3. Could you drop me off at school?
4. Would you help me lift this box?

(CD 1, Track 30)

1. That radio is really loud. Could you turn it down, please?
2. I think the computer is broken. Would you please look at it?
3. The phone's ringing. Could you answer it, please?
4. Let me see if he's in his office. Would you hold for a moment?

Page 48, Speaking (CD 1, Track 31)

Martina: Hello, ISS Language Center. This is Martina.
Minh: Yeah, hi. I'm in a TOEFL class that starts next week. I'd like to make an appointment to see the student counselor first.
Martina: Sure. I can help you with that. Let's see . . . Can you come in tomorrow at 10:30?
Minh: No, that time isn't good for me. Do you have anything later in the day?

Martina: Let me check. . . . Okay, how's 4:15?
Minh: That's perfect.
Martina: Great. Now, I just need to get your name.
Minh: It's Minh Nguyen.
Martina: Could you spell your last name for me, please?
Minh: Sure, it's N-G-U-Y-E-N.

Unit 5, Lesson B

Page 52, Listening (CD 1, Track 32)

Commute times for people are increasing all over the globe. According to a recent report, the average commute around the world is nearly 40 minutes one way. This means many people are spending over an hour every day just to go to and from work or school. In Thailand, the country with the longest commuting times of any nation, people spend almost two hours every day traveling by bus, subway, car, taxi, or on foot to get to school or their jobs. So the question is, what are people doing while they're stuck in traffic, or even when they're just going back and forth? We put the question out to our listeners and many phoned in with their responses. Let's see what they had to say . . .

(CD 1, Track 33)

So the question is, what are people doing while they're stuck in traffic, or even when they're just going back and forth? We put the question out to our listeners and many phoned in with their responses. Let's see what they had to say . . .

Man 1: There are so many books that I want to read, but I just never have the time, so I've started listening to audio books while I drive to work. They're pretty great. I just finished listening to a story about . . .
Woman 1: It's hard to do much on the subway because the cars are always really crowded, so I usually just take a nap or listen to songs on my Mp3 player.
Woman 2: It's only about a ten-minute walk to school for me, so not very long. On the way, I usually just think about the day and what I'm going to do after class.
Man 2: I have a really long commute to school. I have to take the subway across the city and then catch bus 44. All total, it takes about ninety minutes. Sometimes, I try to do homework, but usually I text or call my friends.

Unit 6, Lesson A

Page 57, Listening (CD 1, Track 34)

Host: Hello and welcome to our show, "Special Schools." Today we're talking to Bobby Ochoa, a student at Stratton Mountain School in the U.S. Thanks for joining us, Bobby.
Bobby : My pleasure.
Host: So, Bobby, tell us a little bit about Stratton. What kind of school is it exactly?
Bobby: Well, it's a four-year high school . . .
Host: For our international listeners, that means that students attend Stratton between the ages of 14 to 18. So, what makes Stratton different from your typical high school?
Bobby: Well, for one thing, almost all of the students are skiers or snowboarders. I'm an alpine skier myself.
Host: So, it's a school for athletes . . .
Bobby: Right.
Host: And Stratton's coed, right?
Bobby: Yeah, it admits both boys and girls.
Host: So, what's a typical school day like for a student at Stratton?
Bobby: Well, it depends on the season. In the winter, for example, the day starts at 7:00 a.m. with breakfast.
Host: So, students are living in dorms?
Bobby: Right, you live on campus So, like I was saying . . . you have breakfast at 7:00 and then from eight to noon, you're in training . . .
Host: Which means . . . .?
Bobby: Students are out on the snow skiing or snowboarding. . . . They're practicing . . .
Host: So, no class . . .
Bobby: Right. Regular classes are in the afternoons from 12:30 to 5:00.
Host: Wow, that's very different from an average high school student's day. Is Stratton a hard school to get into?
Bobby: Yeah, there's a lot of competition because the school is basically preparing students to be professional athletes. In fact, after graduation, many Stratton alumni compete in the Winter Olympics.
Host: What about you . . . are you going to compete in any games in the future?
Bobby: I hope so!
Host: And I hope so, too. Best of luck to you, Bobby!
Bobby: Thanks a lot!

(CD 1, Track 35)

1. Host: And Stratton's coed, right?
   Bobby: Yeah, it admits both boys and girls.
2. Host: So, what's a typical school day like for a student at Stratton?
   Bobby: Well, it depends on the season. In the winter, for example, the day starts at 7:00 a.m. with breakfast.
   Host: So, students are living in dorms?
   Bobby: Right, you live on campus . . .
3. Host: Is Stratton a hard school to get into?
   Bobby: Yeah, there's a lot of competition because the school is basically preparing students to be professional athletes. In fact, after graduation, many Stratton alumni compete in the Winter Olympics.

Page 57, Pronunciation (CD 1, Track 36)

1. I'm gonna apply to three colleges.
2. He's gonna clean the house all week.
3. We're gonna study together for the big exam.
4. They're not gonna finish in time.

(CD 1, Track 37)

1. I'm not gonna meet them before 3:00.
2. We're not gonna take a vacation this summer.
3. She's gonna call us tomorrow.
4. He's not gonna attend Harvard University.

Page 58, Speaking (CD 1, Track 38)

Hans: Hey, Tom. How's it going with the college applications?
Tom: So-so. I didn't get into McGill University.
Hans: Really? Sorry to hear that. Did you apply to any other schools?
Tom: Yeah, three others.
Hans: And?
Tom: I got into all of them.
Hans: Well, that's great!
Tom: Yeah, but I really wanted to go to McGill.
Hans: Well, look on the bright side—three other schools accepted you.
Tom: Yeah, I guess you're right.
Hans: So, which school are you going to attend?
Tom: I'm not sure. Maybe I'll go to Queen's University.

Unit 6, Lesson B

Page 62, Listening (CD 1, Track 39)

Every year, City University hosts a Career Day for college seniors. Are you wondering what to do after graduation? *Or* are you trying to decide which job is right for you? If so, be sure to attend Career Day next Saturday, September 7, from noon to five. Speakers will talk about their jobs and how they got them. Until then, here's a clip from one of last year's speakers talking about his job and how he got it . . .

(CD 1, Track 40)

Here's a clip from one of last year's speakers, talking about his job and how he got it . . .

Jeff: Actually, I always wanted to be a firefighter . . . you know, it looked like a pretty cool job—of all the things you see on TV and in the movies. And I thought, "Oh, this will be an easy job to get." Boy . . . was I WRONG! In reality, there are *a lot of* things you have to do to get this job. Here are some of them . . .

First, you have to take health-training courses—and that's just to start. Then you can actually apply to become a firefighter. After that, there's a written exam. If you pass the written test, you then have to take a physical exam. It's really hard and a lot of people fail, so make sure you're in good shape. Finally, you go to the fire academy—a school. You study all day, every day for four months. At this school, you learn to become a firefighter. Finally, you have to pass your final exams. It's totally stressful, but worth it.

Luckily, I passed all my courses, and in a couple of weeks, I'm going to graduate from the fire academy. I'm really excited. So, that's a little bit about how you become a firefighter. Any questions?

Review Units 4–6

Page 69, Listening (CD 1, Track 41)

Students had some pretty clear feelings about divorce—as you can see in the first chart. When we asked them this question: "Should a couple with children get divorced if they are unhappy?," a third of the students said "no." The other two-thirds say a couple should.

Turning to the second chart, this year, sixty of the students interviewed say they are going to study in another country. That's twice as high as it was last year.

When we asked them this question: "Is the university entrance exam too difficult?," students' answers were divided evenly—as shown in the third chart.

And finally, when we asked the students, "Would you have plastic surgery to change your looks?," almost forty-five percent of them said "yes." Another thirty percent said "maybe," and the rest said "no."

Unit 7, Lesson A

Page 71, Listening (CD 2, Track 2)

In El Salvador, a girl's fifteenth birthday is very important. It's the day she celebrates becoming a woman. When I turned fifteen, my family had a big party for me . . .

The second Monday in January is an important day in Japan. We call it "Coming of Age Day." When you turn twenty, you're officially an adult in Japan. Anyone who turned twenty in the last year celebrates on Coming of Age Day . . .

Page 71, Listening (CD 2, Track 3)

In El Salvador, a girl's fifteenth birthday is very important. It's the day she celebrates becoming a woman. When I turned fifteen, my family had a big party for me. . . . We call this party "La Fiesta Rosa" or "The Rose Party" because everything you wear to the party is pink—a pink dress, pink shoes, pink flowers. Anyway, the celebration lasts all day. In the morning, you go to church. Then later there's a big party either at your family's house, or some people rent a place. Lots of friends and family members are invited so you need a big space. Anyway, at the party, there's lots of food and dancing. And people give you presents—like jewelry and clothes. I'll never forget my party . . . . it lasted until four in the morning. It was pretty wild . . .

The second Monday in January is an important day in Japan. We call it "Coming of Age Day." When you turn twenty, you're officially an adult in Japan. Anyone who turned twenty in the last year celebrates on Coming of Age Day. . . . So, what happens? Well, most people get dressed up. Girls wear traditional kimonos and guys wear dark suits, though some also wear traditional clothes. Then in the morning, you and your parents go to City Hall. There's a big ceremony—for you and all the other twenty-year-olds in your city. Important leaders give speeches. After the ceremony, you get a small present and take a lot of pictures. Then later, you get together with your friends. Most people go to parties or nightclubs. I remember when I celebrated Coming of Age Day. I had a lot of fun . . .

Page 71, Pronunciation (CD 2, Track 4)

1. Do you wanna have coffee after class?
2. We wanna have a party on Saturday.
3. Do you wanna get together this weekend?
4. My parents wanna invite you to dinner.

(CD 2, Track 5)

A: What do you wanna do this weekend?
B: I'm not sure. Oh, wait. I know. I wanna see that new sci-fi movie. Do you wanna come with me?
A: I don't really wanna see that movie.
B: OK. What do you wanna do?

Page 72, Speaking (CD 2, Track 6)

Omar: Hey, Lane. My classmate Sayuri is having a party this weekend.
Lane: Really?
Omar: Yeah, it's a costume party.
Lane: Sounds like fun.
Omar: Do you want to go with me?
Lane: Are you sure? I don't really know Sayuri.
Omar: No problem. She said I could invite a friend.
Lane: OK, then. I'd love to go. When exactly is it?
Omar: On Saturday night.
Lane: Wow, that's the day after tomorrow! I need to get a costume.
Omar: Me, too. There's a good place near here that rents them. Let's go there after school.
Lane: Sounds good!

Unit 7, Lesson B

Page 76, Listening (CD 2, Track 7)

Sandra: And now for our final story of the evening, we turn to Stuart Kaplan, reporting live from the West African country of Cameroon—where every year, usually in February, the Race of Hope takes place. For more on this, we turn now to Stuart. . . .
Stuart: Yes, hello Sandra. I'm standing here in the town of Buea, Cameroon, where the Race of Hope is about to begin. Behind me you can see some of the participants . . . about six hundred people will be running 42 kilometers up and then back down Mount Cameroon, the highest mountain in western Africa and . . . an active volcano. Thousands of people from different countries also come to watch. I spoke to one woman earlier today about her reason for coming to the race . . .
Stuart: Hello, Nichelle. Thank you for talking to me.
Nichelle: My pleasure.
Stuart: So, is this your first time here?
Nichelle: Oh, no. I've watched the race many times before. This year, though, I'm *in* it — for the first time!
Stuart: That's great! Do you think you'll win? It's a tough race . . . a lot of people start but can't finish . . .
Nichelle: I know, but I'm hopeful. I also know I have some strong competition. The other runners, especially from Kenya and Ethiopia, are very fast. But, you know, all the winners to date are from Cameroon. I hope to be the next winner from my country.
Stuart: Well, you know the prize, right? If you win first place, you get 10,000 U.S. dollars.
Nichelle: Yes . . . that's a lot of money for people here. I could certainly use it to help my family. We don't have much . . .
Stuart: I'll be rooting for you, Nichelle. Good luck!
Nichelle: Thank you!
Stuart: Now, during the weekend of the race . . . there's also a festival in the town of Buea with music, dancing, sports, and local foods. For those who cannot travel to Cameroon, there's also a documentary film about the race called *Volcanic Spirit* . . .

(CD 2, Track 8)

Stuart: I spoke to one woman earlier today about her reason for coming to the race . . .
Stuart: Hello, Nichelle. Thank you for talking to me.
Nichelle: My pleasure.
Stuart: So, is this your first time here?
Nichelle: Oh, no. I've watched the race many times before. This year, though, I'm *in* it — for the first time!
Stuart: That's great! Do you think you'll win? It's a tough race . . . a lot of people start but can't finish . . .
Nichelle: I know, but I'm hopeful. I also know I have some strong competition. The other runners, especially from Kenya and Ethiopia, are very fast. But, you know, all the winners to date are from Cameroon. I hope to be the next winner from my country.
Stuart: Well, you know the prize, right? If you win first place, you get 10,000 U.S. dollars.
Nichelle: Yes . . . that's a lot of money for people here. I could certainly use it to help my family. We don't have much . . .
Stuart: I'll be rooting for you, Nichelle. Good luck!
Nichelle: Thank you!

Unit 8, Lesson A

Page 81, Listening (CD 2, Track 9)

Interviewer: You write a lot of crime stories . . . and many of your characters and situations are very realistic. Are your stories based on real people and events?
Roberto: Yeah, they are, but I do change people's names in the stories. You have to . . .
Interviewer: Now . . . I hear that your bestseller—*Endless Night*—might be made into a movie . . .
Roberto: Yeah, I doubt that will happen.
Interviewer: Really?
Roberto: Yeah. The movie studio wants to change the story's ending. They don't like it.
Interviewer: Well . . . the ending is kind of sad . . .
Roberto: Yeah, but that's how things are in life. There isn't always a happy ending. . . . That's how I feel and I won't change what I wrote. So . . . no movie, I guess.
Interviewer: OK, well, let's talk a bit about your new project. I hear that you're doing something interesting with a story you're working on these days . . .
Roberto: Yeah, I'm basically writing a short story—mostly on my cell phone. It's about a detective in Tokyo . . .

(CD 2, Track 10)

Interviewer: OK, well, let's talk a bit about your new project. I hear that you're doing something interesting with a story you're working on these days . . .
Roberto: Yeah . . . I'm basically writing a short story—mostly on my cell phone. It's about a detective in Tokyo . . .
Interviewer: How exactly are you writing it?
Roberto: I type a sentence from the story—usually on my phone. Then I post it online.
Interviewer: So, you're building your story one sentence at a time . . .
Roberto: Right, and readers are following the story this way—usually on their phones . . .
Interviewer: Where did you get the idea to do this?
Roberto: I got it when I was visiting Japan last year.
Interviewer: So, do you already have the entire story planned from start to finish?
Roberto: Yes and no. I *do* have a plan for the story. But the cool thing is that people can suggest ideas to continue the story.
Interviewer: What do you mean?
Roberto: Well, let's say I write a sentence in the story and then you read it. Maybe you have an idea for what could happen next, right? You can post your idea. If I like it, I'll use it.
Interviewer: That's cool. It's like I'm not only reading your story . . . I'm helping you write it, too.
Roberto: Exactly! That's the best part!

Page 81, Pronunciation (CD 2, Track 11)

1. He was reading a story.
2. She wasn't walking to work.
3. They weren't working hard.
4. They were having fun.

Page 82, Speaking (CD 2, Track 12)

Mia: Hey, Nico, listen to this story. It's like something from a fairy tale.
Nico: Yeah? What's it about?
Mia: It's about this guy from Uganda. He came to the U.S. as a student.
Nico: Yeah?
Mia: Yeah, but then things got really difficult in his country and he couldn't go back. So, he stayed in the U.S. He got two jobs, but he was still poor.
Nico: Sounds like a hard life.
Mia: Yeah, but then a month ago, he finally returned to his country. It turns out he was really a prince!
Nico: Wait . . . he was living in the U.S. and he was really poor, but he was a prince?
Mia: Yeah!
Nico: So, then what happened?
Mia: Well, in the end, he stayed in Uganda and became king of his tribe.
Nico: Wow, what a great story!

Page 84, Communication (CD 2, Track 13)

Jenna: My name's Jenna, and I was in a car accident.
Man: Really? When?
Jenna: Yesterday—after school.
Man: Where?
Jenna: Near school.
Man: What happened exactly?
Jenna: Well, I was driving and someone hit my car.
Man: What color was the car?
Jenna: Blue.
Man: Are you sure?
Jenna: Yeah, definitely.
Man: Who was driving the other car?
Jenna: A woman in her thirties . . .
Ryan: My name's Ryan, and I was in a car accident.
Man: Really? When?
Ryan: Uhm, let's see . . . yesterday.
Man: Where?
Ryan: It was near here . . . near school.

Man: What happened exactly?
Ryan: Well, this person hit my car.
Man: What color was the car?
Ryan: What color? Uhm . . . let's see. . . . It was blue . . . no, wait . . . black . . .
Man: Who was driving?
Ryan: Who was driving?
Man: Yeah, the car that hit you . . .
Ryan: Uhm . . . . Uhm . . . it was a man.
Man: How old was he?
Ryan: How old? Uhm . . .

Unit 8, Lesson B

Page 86, Listening (CD 2, Track 14)

Dad: Hey, Marnie, are you OK? You look kind of down.
Marnie: Oh, hey, Dad.
Dad: What's up?
Marnie: Well, there's a speech contest at school next week and I'm in it. But I know I won't win.
Dad: Why do you say that?
Marnie: Because I'm competing against Laura Sanders. You know her . . . she's the best at everything.
Dad: Marnie, that's not true. And I've read your speeches before. They're really good.
Marnie: Yeah, but I struggle to write well. And I'm shy in front of large groups. But not Laura . . . she does *everything* perfectly. When she heard we were competing, she even laughed!

(CD 2, Track 15)

Dad: Look, just because Laura's good doesn't mean she'll win. It's like that story *The Tortoise and the Hare* . . .
Marnie: I don't know it.
Dad: Yeah, you do! It's an old story. In it, the hare is always laughing at the tortoise because he is slow . . .
Marnie: Dad, what does this story have to do with me?
Dad: Just listen. So one day, the tortoise challenges the hare to a race . . .
Marnie: A race? There's no way a tortoise can beat a hare.
Dad: That's what the hare thinks, too. And sure enough, at the start of the race, the hare goes really fast.
Marnie: And he wins.
Dad: Nope. During the race, the hare decides to rest. He's so arrogant, he thinks, "I can't lose this race." And then he falls asleep. When the hare wakes up, he sees the tortoise walking slowly across the finish line.
Marnie: So, the tortoise wins?
Dad: Yeah . . . and you need to be like that clever tortoise.
Marnie: What do you mean?
Dad: Laura thinks she's the best right now—just like the hare. But you can still win the contest.
Marnie: But *how*?
Dad: I'll tell you again, Marnie . . . you can write a good speech. And you can overcome your shyness, too. You just need to practice a lot. Be patient, work hard, and you'll do fine. I bet you'll even win.
Marnie: Yeah . . . maybe you're right. Thanks, Dad!

Unit 9, Lesson A

Page 91, Listening (CD 2, Track 16)

A lot of people think I've got a fun and easy job, but I've been in this position for about five years and I'm telling you, it's harder than it looks. For one thing, you're away from home *a lot*—about twenty days a month. It's really hard to have a social life because you're traveling so much and your work schedule is always changing. You have to be able to deal with this.

This job is also hard on your health. You know, you stand a lot and are serving people, helping them with their luggage. For example, I was on a sixteen-hour trip last week and that's not good for your back. Also, with the time changes, it's difficult to get enough sleep and to eat right.

Oh, and then there are the passengers. Usually, they're fine. Sometimes, though, there's a rude person, but, you know, you have to be friendly and helpful—no matter what. Believe me . . . it's not easy to stay calm at times. The worst is when a flight is late and people start getting angry.

Still, there are advantages. You meet some interesting people in this job. And, of course, you get to visit lots of places. I've been to eight different countries in the last five years. But I'll say it again, this job is NOT an easy way to travel. Most of the time, it's hard work.

Page 91, Pronunciation (CD 2, Track 17)

1. My father has worked there for decades.
2. I've lived in the same city for years.
3. He hasn't been in class for a week.

(CD 2, Track 18)

1. He's been sick for two days.
2. I haven't eaten for six hours.
3. She's taught school for years.
4. I haven't seen him for years.

Page 92, Speaking (CD 2, Track 19)

Simon: So, Ines, tell me a little about yourself.
Ines: Well, I'm a first year student at City University and I'm majoring in journalism.
Simon: And you're working for your school's online newspaper, right?
Ines: Yeah. I write a blog. It focuses on pop culture, fashion, music . . . stuff like that.
Simon: How long have you worked there?
Ines: For about six months. I post an entry once a week.
Simon: Excellent. But if you work here, you'll need to post every Tuesday and Friday—by noon.
Ines: No problem. I'm very punctual.
Simon: Great. Now, we need someone right away. When can you start?
Ines: On Monday.
Simon: Perfect. Let me talk to my boss and I'll be in touch with you later this week.

Unit 9, Lesson B

Page 96, Listening (CD 2, Track 20)

Interviewer: So, before we take questions from the audience, tell us a little about your job, Gino.
Gino: I'm a storyboard artist.
Interviewer: And what exactly do you do?
Gino: Well, storyboard artists can do lots of different things. In my case, I work with film directors to make movies.
Interviewer: How exactly?
Gino: Well . . . I create a picture story of the movie on the computer. These pictures show the events in the film. The director and actors use these pictures to understand and make the movie.

(CD 2, Track 21)

Interviewer: Interesting . . . so . . . what do you like most about your job?
Gino: Well, I guess the most rewarding part is that I'm helping to make a movie.
Interviewer: How many films have you worked on?
Gino: Eight, including the one I'm working on now. I work on all different kinds—action movies, romantic comedies, science fiction . . .
Interviewer: Wow! That's cool.
Gino: Yeah, I really enjoy it. I'm always learning something new.
Interviewer: So, what's the hardest part?
Gino: Well . . . the work can be very demanding. Sometimes, for example, a film director will say he wants one thing. Then he changes his mind, then he changes his mind again. It's hard. You really have to be flexible . . . *and* patient.
Interviewer: It sounds like it.
Gino: Yeah, and the job can be exhausting, too. I've worked all night many times . . . but in the end, I helped to make the movie and like I said, then it's all worth it.
Interviewer: So, if a person wants to be a storyboard artist, what advice would you give?
Gino: I'd say first—be good at your art, of course. Second—learn everything you can about movies and movie making. And finally, and maybe most important—work hard and have a good attitude. If you do these things, you'll never be out of a job.

Review Units 7–9

Page 102, Listening (CD 2, Track 22)

Teresa: My name's Teresa Silva, and I'm twenty-one years old. Even though I'm young, I already have my own business. I work with artists here in my country. Many of these people are poor and until recently, they could only sell their art in their own towns and villages. I created a website to help them and now they can sell their products . . . clothing, jewelry, paintings . . . to the world. When something sells online, I take ten percent. The other ninety percent of the money goes to the artist. Since January, we've already sold over fifteen hundred items. I've made money *and* have helped many people in my community. But now I need your help. There's a lot of work to do and I can't do it alone. With the money from the Dream Big Foundation, I plan to hire one more person and with the extra help, I hope to sell twice as many items as this year. Please, your support will not only help me. It will also help the people of my country. Together we can make this dream a reality.
Daniel: My name is Daniel. I'm eighteen years old and I'm a student. I'm originally from Nigeria, but at age eleven, I moved to London with my parents and older brother. When I was fifteen, both my parents died in a car accident, and since then, life hasn't been easy. My older brother had to leave school and get a job. I've stayed in school and want to go to university, but there's very little money for it. And now I'm asking the Dream Big Foundation to help me pay for college. I want to study medicine and eventually, I hope to become a doctor. Since my parents died, life hasn't been easy. My brother and I have struggled many times, but I still have hope for the future. With your support, we can give this story a happy ending.

Unit 10, Lesson A

Page 105, Listening (CD 2, Track 23)

1. Man: Hello, can I speak to Dr. Allen?
   Woman: Sorry, he's not in. Can I take a message?
2. Man: Hi, this is Ethan. Sorry I missed your call.
3. Man: Thanks for showing me around London. I had a great time.
   Woman: My pleasure. The next time you're visiting, give me a call.
4. Man: I got a text from Leo a minute ago.
   Woman: Really? What did he say?
5. Man: Hello?
   Woman: Uhm . . . hello? Is this five-five-five, two-seven-four-two?
6. Man: Lena, I've been waiting for your call for an hour.
   Woman: I called and texted you several times. Why didn't you answer?

Page 105, Pronunciation (CD 2, Track 24)

A: My number is five-five-five, six-seven-four-nine.
B: Five-five-five, six-*seven*-four-nine?
A: Yes. Six-seven-four-nine.

(CD 2, Track 25)

1. A: My number is five-five-five, two-five-two-six.
   B: Did you say five-five-five, two-*nine*-two-six?
   A: No, it's two-*five*-two-six.
2. A: My work number is eight hundred, two-two-one, five-three-four-eight.
   B: Five-three-*four*-eight?
   A: That's correct.
3. A: You can call me at five-five-five, sixteen-sixty-one.
   B: Was that five-five-five, *sixty*-sixty-one?
   A: No, it's one-six-six-one.

Page 106, Speaking (CD 2, Track 26)

Lisa: Hello?
Celia: Lisa? Hi. It's Celia.
Lisa: Oh, hey, Celia. How're you doing?
Celia: Pretty good. So, are you ready for the big test tomorrow?
Lisa: Almost, but I have one question. . . . *(beep)* Oh, Celia . . . can you hang on? I've got another call coming in.
Celia: Yeah, no problem.
Lisa: Hello?
Prof. Larson: Yes, hello. May I speak to Lisa Sanchez, please?
Lisa: Speaking.
Prof. Larson: Lisa, this is Professor Larson. You left me a message earlier today. You had a question about tomorrow's exam.
Lisa: Oh, right. Professor Larson, could you hold for a moment?
Prof. Larson: Of course.
Lisa: Hello, Celia? Can I call you back? I have to take the other call.
Celia: Sure. Talk to you later.

Unit 10, Lesson B

Page 110, Listening (CD 2, Track 27)

Conversation 1
Girl: Hello? Oh, hi, Tony. How're you? Oh, no! Well, are you OK? Yeah, I know . . . that class is really hard and I . . .
Man: Excuse me, miss?
Girl: Umm . . . yeah?
Man: I'm trying to have a meal and talk to my friend, but it's really hard to hear over your conversation.
Girl: Oh, I'm sorry. I didn't realize I was being so loud. I'll be quieter.
Man: Thanks a lot.

Conversation 2
Woman: Excuse me, sir? Sir?
Man: Oh, uh . . . yes?
Woman: I'm sorry, sir, but I need to ask you to turn that off.
Man: Is the music too loud?
Woman: No, sir. We're getting ready to land and electronics must be turned off. You can turn it on again when we're on the ground in London.
Man: Oh, right. I guess I didn't hear the announcement.
Woman: Thank you very much.

Conversation 3
Guy: Hey Veronica. What's wrong?
Girl: Well, you know Manny? That guy in our math class?
Guy: Yeah, I know him. . . . Why?
Girl: Well, we're both on LinkBook—you know that website, right?

Guy: Yeah, of course.
Girl: Well, Manny sent me an email three days ago. He asked to be my friend online.
Guy: Okay . . . and?
Girl: Well, I don't know. . . . He's OK, but I'm not sure I want to be his friend on the site.
Guy: So, don't respond.
Girl: You mean I should ignore him? That's kind of rude . . .
Guy: Have you ever talked to him at school?
Girl: No, not really.
Guy: Then he's not your friend.
Girl: Yeah, I guess you're right.

Unit 11, Lesson A

Page 115, Listening B (CD 2, Track 28)

So, in our last class, we were talking about different types of technology and we were making predictions about the future. We ended with this example: In the nineteen forties, the president of IBM—the computer company—made this prediction, "Most people will never use computers at work or in their homes." Imagine—the president of IBM saying that. We laugh because we know he was wrong. But he wasn't the only one to make incorrect predictions about technology. People have done it for years. And they're still doing it.

Let's take another example: movies. In the early nineteen eighties, videos, and later DVDs, started to appear. This gave people a choice. They could either go to a theater to see a film *or* they could rent the movie and watch it at home. For many people, it was more convenient and affordable to stay home and rent a movie. As renting became popular, people started making predictions. They said things like, "Renting DVDs will cause movie theaters to close everywhere." But, of course, theaters haven't closed. In fact, a lot of people today *still* go the theater to see a movie.

Nowadays, people are predicting the death of traditional television. As we all know, more people today get their news and entertainment online. You can watch movies and TV shows—often for free. You can also make and post your own videos. And you can do all of these things on your laptop or phone. These tools are portable—and interactive. Your television isn't.

So, will traditional TV disappear? What do you think?

Page 115, Pronunciation (CD 2, Track 29)

1. People used to go to movie theaters a lot more.
2. I didn't use to wear glasses.
3. What kind of computer do you use?
4. I used my brother's cell phone.

(CD 2, Track 30)

1. She used the phone in her office.
2. He used to paint his own house.
3. Do you use a laptop?
4. I didn't use to eat meat.

Page 116, Speaking (CD 2, Track 31)

Alan: Hey, Kim. I saw your sister on Facebook the other day. She's really changed a lot.
Kim: Yeah? Why do you say that? She still looks the same.
Alan: Yeah, but now she's got all these friends and she's really funny. She used to be so different—you know, kind of shy.
Kim: A lot of people say that about my sister. They think that she's this quiet person, but actually, she's very outgoing.
Alan: Really?
Kim: Yep. Once she feels comfortable with you, she's really friendly and she talks a lot.
Alan: Wow, I had no idea.

Unit 11, Lesson B

Page 120, Listening (CD 2, Track 32)

Interviewer: Dr. Spenser, thanks for joining us today.
Dr. Spenser: My pleasure.
Interviewer: So, what exactly are scientists at your company doing?
Dr. Spenser: We're developing a tool to help blind people see again. I'm talking about people who could see at one time, but then lost their vision . . .
Interviewer: You mean people who lost their sight because of, uh, you know, an accident.
Dr. Spenser: Exactly.
Interviewer: So, tell us about the tool you're working on now.
Dr. Spenser: Well, it uses a computer chip and special glasses. We start by putting the chip in the blind person's eye. The chip is very, very small, of course.
Interviewer: Okay . . .
Dr. Spenser: And the glasses . . . they have a very small video camera inside.
Interviewer: So, how do the computer chip and glasses work together?
Dr. Spenser: Well, a blind person puts on the glasses and "looks at" something—for example, this pen.

Interviewer: Okay . . .
Dr. Spenser: Then the video camera—in the glasses—takes a picture of the pen. Then the camera sends the picture to the computer chip in the person's eye.
Interviewer: And then the person can see the pen!
Dr. Spenser: Exactly! This whole process happens very quickly, of course.
Interviewer: Wow! Now, using this tool, will a blind person be able to see as well as a normal person?
Dr. Spenser: No, they won't have perfect vision, but they will be able to see many things. This tool is still new, but for many of the people in our study, it's transformed their lives . . .

Unit 12, Lesson A

Page 125, Listening (CD 2, Track 33)

Leticia: Hello?
Paula: Hi, Leticia. It's Paula.
Leticia: Hi, Paula. How are you? Have you finished packing yet?
Paula: Almost.
Leticia: You must be excited. When's your flight?
Paula: Tomorrow. At 9 a.m. Listen, Leticia, I need your help.
Leticia: OK. What's up?
Paula: Well, as you know, I'm going on vacation—for two weeks. Do you think you could water my plants while I'm away?
Leticia: Sure. No problem.
Paula: Great. They need water twice a week. There's one plant in the bedroom and one in the kitchen.
Leticia: OK, say, how about your dog? Should I feed her, too?
Paula: No, that's OK. I'm putting her in a kennel.
Leticia: All right, then, I'll water your plants, and . . . oh, how about the mail? Should I pick it up for you?
Paula: Actually, I've already asked the mailman to stop mail delivery. Thanks for asking, though.
Leticia: Well, have a great trip!
Paula: Thanks, Leticia. I really appreciate your help.
Leticia: My pleasure. Wait a second. I don't have any keys to your place.
Paula: Oh, that's right. Will you be home around 8 tonight?
Leticia: Yeah, I think so.
Paula: OK, I'll drop by . . . I'll give you the keys then.
Leticia: OK! See you tonight. Bye!
Paula: Bye! Thanks again!

Page 125, Pronunciation (CD 2, Track 34)

1. I'm going to miss my flight. I hafta hurry.
2. Everyone hasta sit down before this plane can take off.

Page 126, Speaking (CD 2, Track 35)

Esther: We have to leave in 30 minutes. Have you finished packing?
Mina: Yes, I have . . .
Esther: You look worried. What's wrong?
Mina: I can't remember where I put my passport.
Esther: Oh, no!
Mina: It's here somewhere.
Esther: When did you last have it?
Mina: About ten minutes ago. Let me think . . . Oh, there it is. I put it on the dresser.
Esther: What a relief!

Unit 12, Lesson B

Page 130, Listening (CD 2, Track 36)

Ashley: Wow, Jun, you look relaxed. Did you enjoy the long weekend?
Jun: I sure did, Ashley. Actually, I took a big trip.
Ashley: Over the weekend? We only had three days off!
Jun: Yep, but I visited four countries in three days.
Ashley: What?
Jun: I love to fly. You might say I'm an "airplane freak."
Ashley: That's interesting. . . . Where did you go?
Jun: I visited Korea, Thailand, Singapore, and the Philippines.
Ashley: Sounds like you were busy!
Jun: I was. I had only four hours in Seoul, so I had to finish my shopping *very* quickly. Sometimes I had to run between connecting flights.
Ashley: Wait a minute! What about your baggage? Didn't you have to wait for it?
Jun: No, I didn't have much—only one carry-on bag. It just fits in the overhead compartment.
Ashley: So, let me get this straight . . . you spent your weekend in an airplane? Flying around?
Jun: Basically, yes. I fly standby.
Ashley: Standby?
Jun: Yes. As a standby passenger, I don't have a reservation. At the last minute, they let me know if there is a seat available. They give me a boarding pass and I get on.
Ashley: All this flying must be expensive!
Jun: Well, I'm an airline employee. I'm a sales representative for Twin Star Airlines. So I know most of the flight attendants and I can almost fly for free.
Ashley: Lucky you!

Review Units 10–12

Page 137, Listening (CD 2, Track 37)

Conversation 1

Sheila:	Hello, could I speak to Tom Herman, please?
Receptionist:	May I ask who's calling, please?
Sheila:	This is Sheila Banks.
Receptionist:	Thank you, Sheila. I'll ring him now. I'm sorry. His line is busy. Would you like to leave a message?
Sheila:	Yes, I would. Would you tell him Sheila called? I can't make our meeting tomorrow at 2:00 . . . I have to cancel it.
Receptionist:	Does Mr. Herman have your phone number?
Sheila:	Yes, he can call me back. I'll be here until 5 p.m.

Conversation 2

Penny:	Hello?
Ted:	Penny? Hey, it's Ted.
Penny:	Hi, Ted. What's up?
Ted:	Well, my computer has crashed again and I can't get it to start.
Penny:	Sorry to hear that. Do you want me to come over and try to help you fix it?
Ted:	No, I've decided to get a new one. I'm going to try a place downtown tomorrow. Can you come with me?
Penny:	Sorry, but I can't. I've got class. But listen, I think my brother can go with you. He knows everything about computers and can help you make a good choice.
Ted:	That'd be great.
Penny:	What are you looking for?
Ted:	Something small . . . portable . . . . oh, and affordable, of course.
Penny:	Okay. I'll leave a message with my brother.
Ted:	Thanks a lot, Penny. Tell him I'll call him around eight tonight. What's his number again?

Unit 1, Lesson A:

1. Vocabulary Workout

A. 1. a close friend 2. a coworker 3. an acquaintance 4. a date 5. a coworker 6. a date
B. Answers may vary.

2. Conversation Workout

A. The more formal introduction is number 1. The phrases *I'd like you to meet* and *It's nice to meet you* make it more formal.
B. Answers will vary.

3. Language Workout

A. Answers will vary. Usually: Richard teaches English. He writes on the board. He doesn't like his job. He works hard. Today: He is relaxing at the beach. He is wearing sunglasses. He is listening to music. He is smiling.
B. 1. am 2. doesn't like 3. am watching 4. plays 5. am studying, study 6. is winning 7. cooks, is cooking 8. doesn't drink / likes
C. 1. ~~he is speak~~ = he is speaking 2. ~~Do you~~ = Are you 3. ~~are having~~ = have 4. ~~writes~~ = is writing

Unit 1, Lesson B:

1. Vocabulary and Language Workout

A. 1. c 2. g 3. a 4. f 5. e 6. b 7. h 8. d
B. 1. lived 2. moved 3. got 4. wanted 5. finished 6. went 7. was 8. found

2. Reading and Writing

A. Answers will vary.
B. No response required.
C. Answers may vary. 1. making beautiful books to hold special memories 2. newspaper clippings, postcards, tickets, report cards, letters 3. Who, What, Where, When, and Why 4. School days, Family travel, Memories of my grandparents, Baby's first year 5. design the pages, decorate the pages
D. 1. took 2. went 3. felt 4. said 5. got 6. talked 7. sat 8. met 9. took 10. stayed 11. had 12. was 13. saw 14. didn't want
E. Answers will vary.

Unit 2, Lesson A:

1. Vocabulary Workout

A. 2. spicy 3. healthy 4. sweet 5. fried 6. crunchy 7. juicy 8. crispy 9. sour 10. salty
B. 1. juicy 2. spicy 3. salty 4. sweet 5. buttery

2. Conversation Workout

A. 1. How about going to a movie tonight? 2. Why don't we have some ice cream after class? 3. How about the new Italian restaurant? 4. Why don't we meet at 8:00? 5. How about playing tennis tomorrow?
B. 4, 2, 5, 6, 1, 3
C. Answers will vary.

3. Language Workout

A. Answers may vary. 1. Dogs are friendlier than cats. 2. Computer games are more difficult than chess. 3. Mexico City is more interesting than Tokyo. 4. Fried chicken is greasier than French fries. 5. Lying on the beach is more relaxing than swimming. 6. Donuts are sweeter than cookies. 7. Cleaning the house is harder than cooking. 8. Sharks are more dangerous than snakes. 9. and 10. Answers will vary.
B. Answers will vary.

Unit 2, Lesson B:

1. Vocabulary and Language Workout

A. 1. strict diet 2. habits 3. eliminate / cut back on 4. diet 5. cut back on / eliminate 6. increase 7. lifestyle 8. plenty of
B. 1. c 2. a 3. e 4. b 5. d
C. Answers will vary.

2. Reading and Writing

A. Answers will vary.
B. No response required.
C. 1. c 2. b 3. a 4. e 5. f 6. d
D. 1. F, 5 2. T, 3 3. F, 8 4. F, 2 5. T, 5 6. F, 4
E. 1. most famous 2. spicy 3. most popular 4. milder 5. spiciest 6. healthier 7. most delicious
F. Answers will vary.

Unit 3, Lesson A:

1. Vocabulary Workout

Down: 1. by accident 2. reunite 4. separate 5. good luck 8. lucky
Across: 3. miss a chance 6. on 7. out 9. take a chance

2. Conversation Workout

A. Answers may vary. 1. I doubt the dog ate the fish. 2. I bet the dog ate the ham. 3. It's unlikely the dog ate the fish. 4. It doesn't seem possible the monkey ate the fish. 5. There's a good chance that the monkey was hanging from the light.
B. Answers will vary. 1. I doubt she will hurt the cat. 2. I bet she will buy a new fish. 3. There's a good chance she will get angry.
C. Answers will vary.

3. Language Workout

A. Answers include the following: love, like, tastes, see, smell, hear, feel, believe
B. 1. smells 2. am doing 3. know 4. don't believe 5. hate, feel 6. is learning, is teaching 7. own, am taking 8. belong 9. looks 10. seems, understand
C. 1. I, ~~I'm not understand~~ = I don't understand 2. I, ~~we look at~~ = we're looking at 3. C 4. C 5. I, ~~is tasting~~ = tastes 6. C 7. I, ~~is having~~ = has 8. C

Unit 3, Lesson B:

1. Vocabulary and Language Workout

A. 1. mysteries 2. prove 3. theories / explanations 4. make sense 5. figured out 6. theory / explanation 7. investigation 8. solution
B. Answers will vary. 1. It may be a weather balloon. 2. It might be a new type of airplane. 3. It could be a toy plane. 4. It can't be a spaceship. 5. It couldn't be a flying saucer.

2. Reading and Writing

A. 1. A terrible explosion rocked the forest. 2. It happened in eastern Russia. 3. It happened in 1908.
B. No response required.
C. 4, 1, 3, 5, 2
D. 1. explain 2. investigations 3. explanation 4. proof 5. sense 6. theories 7. mystery 8. solved
E. Answers will vary.

Unit 4, Lesson A:

1. Vocabulary Workout

A.

- On the first graph, the bar above the year 2000 should reach up to the level of the number 20 at the left.
- On the second graph, half of the circle should be marked off and labeled to represent "50% Every day." A quarter of the circle should be marked off and labeled "25% 2 or 3 times a week."
- On the third chart, the "Now" column should read $2.00, $125, $13,000, $120,000.
- On the fourth graph, the line for high school students should meet the 4 million horizontal mark on the vertical "Now" line. The line for university students should reach the 3 million horizontal mark on the vertical "Now" line.

B. Answers will vary.

2. Conversation Workout

A. 1. e 2. a 3. d 4. b 5. c
B. Answers will vary.

3. Language Workout

A. Answers will vary.
B. 1. Most 2. all of 3. a couple of 4. Some 5. A lot of 6. Many 7. some of 8. None of
C. 1. Most of the houses have trees. 2. None of the houses are white. 3. Some of the houses have flowers. 4. Some of the houses have three windows. 5. None of the houses are very large.

Unit 4, Lesson B:

1. Vocabulary and Language Workout

A. 1. pointy 2. sporty 3. unique 4. oversized / ripped 5. fitted 6. retro 7. ripped / oversized 8. colorful
B. Answers will vary.

2. Reading and Writing

A. Lana = 2, 3; Dave = 1, 4
B. Answers will vary. 1. a list of things that employees can and cannot wear to work 2. change the color something 3. says negative things about something or someone 4. think well of someone or something 5. agree with
C. 2. ~~clothings~~ = clothing 3. ~~trennds~~ = trends 4. ~~freinds~~ = friends 5. ~~slopy~~ = sloppy 6. ~~uniqe~~ = unique 7. ~~develope~~ = develop 8. ~~styleish~~ = stylish
D. Answers will vary.

Unit 5, Lesson A:

1. Vocabulary Workout

A. 1. Go 2. Pick up 3. Mail 4. Sweep 5. Vacuum 6. Do 7. Make 8. Run 9. Take
B. Answers will vary.

2. Conversation Workout

A. 1. 4, 1, 6, 2, 3, 5 2. 2, 1, 3, 5, 4, 6 3. 3, 1, 4, 6, 2, 5 or 5, 1, 4, 6, 2, 3

3. Language Workout

A. Possible answers: 1. Could you repeat the question, please? 2. Could I borrow five dollars? 3. Would you mind turning the TV down? 4. Can you speak a little louder, please? 5. Would you help me move this sofa? 6. Can you check this paper for mistakes in English? 7. Would you get me some coffee? 8. Would you stop talking for a minute so you can help me?
B. 1. No, not at all. 2. I'd be glad to. 3. Sure. 4. OK.
C. 1. Would you mind turning off the radio? 2. Will you lend me your cell phone for a minute? 3. Could you close the window, please? 4. Can you explain that to me again? 5. Would you mind helping me with this computer?

Unit 5, Lesson B:

1. Vocabulary and Language Workout

A. 1. ride 2. travel 3. stuck 4. commute 5. short 6. train 7. spend 8. late
B. 1. commute 2. train 3. travel 4. ride 5. short 6. late 7. stuck 8. spend
C. 1. really 2. a pretty 3. a very 4. very 5. really 6. really

2. Reading and Writing

A. 5 (cars, buses, subway, bicycling, walking)
B. 1. Neither 2. Both 3. Bogota 4. Both 5. Both 6. Curitiba 7. Neither 8. Boota
C. a. is b. becomes c. solve d. Build e. Decrease f. Buy g. Increase h. Don't let i. make
D. Answers will vary.

Unit 6, Lesson A:

1. Vocabulary Workout

Down: 1. decision 2. application 3. graduation 4. competition 7. recommend
Across: 5. admission 6. apply 8. into 9. compete

2. Conversation Workout

A. 1. d 2. a 3. e / c 4. b 5. c / e
B. 1. 4, 1, 2, 3 2. 3, 1, 4, 2 3. 2, 3, 1, 4
C. Answers will vary.

3. Language Workout

A. 1. B 2. B 3. A 4. A 5. A 6. B
B. 1. am going to 2. will 3. will 4. is going to 5. are going to 6. will
C. Answers will vary.

Unit 6, Lesson B:

1. Vocabulary and Language Workout

A. 5, 2, 6, 4, 1, 3

B. 1. I 2. D 3. I 4. I 5. D 6. I 7. D 8. I

C. Possible answers: 1. I'm going to have dinner with Angela tomorrow. 2. I'm going to a concert the week after next. 3. I have an English test the day after tomorrow. 4. I have a computer class on Saturday. 5. I have a dentist appointment a week from Friday.

2. Reading and Writing

A. No response required.

B. Jameela: major: biology and chemistry; day care center job; be a doctor; travel and volunteer in West Africa
Jennie: studied business; cooking; start own business; move to New York and work for Giant Corporation
Shane: major: computer science; playing music; play music; get a job

C. Answers may vary. 1. will have 2. will work 3. will become 4. is going to get 5. will start

D. Answers will vary.

Unit 7, Lesson A:

1. Vocabulary Workout

A. 1. invite 2. celebrate 3. host 4. plan 5. rowdy 6. presents 7. wild 8. root for 9. throw 10. get together

B. 1. got together with 2. hosted 3. had a bad time 4. invited 5. presents 6. rooted for 7. celebration 8. rowdy

C. Answers will vary.

2. Conversation Workout

A. 1. 2, 5, 4, 1, 3, 6; 4, 5, 6, 2, 3, 1

B. Answers will vary.

3. Language Workout

A. 1. d, b, c, a 2. d, a, b, c 3. d, c, b, a

B. 1. Neither 2. So 3. too 4. neither 5. So 6. too

C. Answers will vary.

Unit 7, Lesson B:

1. Vocabulary and Language Workout

A. 1. c 2. f 3. a 4. h 5. b 6. e 7. d 8. g

B. 1. a. participant, b. participation, c. participate 2. a. performer, b. perform, c. performance 3. a. win, b. win / winner, c. winner

C. 1. before 2. When / After 3. After, before 4. Before / When 5. after

2. Reading and Writing

A. No response required.

B. 1. F, You might need glasses, a jacket, an umbrella, or all three. 2. T, For the popular Sunday night parade, find a space in the morning. 3. F, Many hotels start taking reservations for Mardi Gras in August. 4. T, Jump up to catch beads, plastic coins, cups, and toy animals. 5. F, There are over 70 parades of dazzling floats. 6. T, Many streets are closed to cars, and bus and streetcar schedules are often changed.

C. 1. jacket, sunglasses and umbrella 2. beads, coins, cups, and toy animals

D. 1. Before 2. after 3. before 4. After 5. before 6. after

E. Answers will vary.

Unit 8, Lesson A:

1. Vocabulary Workout

A. 1. happy ending 2. predictable 3. true story 4. follow 5. character 6. hooked on 7. make up 8. soap opera

B. 1. d 2. a 3. c 4. e 5. f 6. b

C. Answers will vary.

2. Conversation Workout

A. 1. It's a story about money. 2. The story begins in a big bank. 3. One day a robber enters the bank. 4. Then he walks up to a teller. 5. After that, he can't ask for money. 6. It turns out that he is too afraid. 7. Finally, the teller asks him what he wants. 8. In the end, he just leaves the bank.

B. Answers will vary.

3. Language Workout

A. Answers will vary.

B. Possible answers: 1. Tiffany was studying. 2. Kevin was playing the guitar. 3. Marcus was cooking. 4. Kaitlyn was helping Marcus. 5. Mrs. Lee was reading the newspaper. 6. Mr. Lee was exercising. 7. Chester was sleeping.

Unit 8, Lesson B:

1. Vocabulary and Language Workout

A. 1. bravely 2. unbelievably 3. inadequately 4. eventually 5. courageously 6. cleverly 7. slowly 8. easily

B. 1. slowly 2. inadequately 3. bravely / courageously 4. easily 5. Unbelievably 6. eventually 7. courageously 8. cleverly

C. 1. saw, was wearing 2. tried, ran 3. was running, dropped 4. picked 5. was standing, returned 6. smiled

2. Reading and Writing

A. 4, 5, 7, 1, 2, 6, 3

B. Answers will vary.

C. 1. was sleeping 2. opened 3. saw 4. was flying 5. said 6. heard 7. agreed 8. picked up 9. went 10. were flying 11. said 12. opened 13. fell

D. Answers will vary.

Unit 9, Lesson A:

1. Vocabulary Workout

Down: 1. punctual 3. efficient 4. courageous

Across: 1. pleasant 2. knowledgeable 4. cautious 5. flexible 6. independent 7. unpredictable

2. Conversation Workout

A. 1. Have you ever done this kind of work? 2. Can you work independently? 3. Are you punctual? 4. Do you have any questions for me? 5. When can you start? (Students' answers to these five questions will vary.)

B. Answers will vary.

3. Language Workout

A. 1. gone 2. been 3. had 4. studied 5. drunk 6. slept 7. come 8. read 9. taken 10. met 11. known 12. done

B. Julie's list: 2. She has gone to the bank. 3. She hasn't written letters yet. 4. She hasn't read the company report yet. 5. She has met with Mr. Sung.

Mr. and Mrs. Silva's list: 1. They have taken the kids to the dentist. 2. They haven't gone shopping yet. 3. They have cleaned the apartment. 4. They haven't made lunch yet. 5. They haven't washed the dishes yet.

Takeshi's list: 1. He has done his English homework. 2. He has bought a dictionary. 3. He hasn't studied for computer class yet. 4. He hasn't sent e-mails yet. 5. He hasn't had dinner with Carol yet.

C. Answers will vary.

Unit 9, Lesson B:

1. Vocabulary and Language Workout

A. 1. f 2. c 3. a 4. h 5. b 6. d 7. e 8. g

B. 1. dead-end job 2. out of a job 3. dream job 4. dream job 5. dead-end job 6. out of a job

C. Answers will vary.

2. Reading and Writing

A. No response required.

B. Name: Melissa Hayes; Job: recording messages; Company: National Telephone; Schedule: three days a week; Good points: three days a week, she's helping people; Bad points: Has to be careful about her voice, can't go to horror movies.

C. 1. Melissa 2. the job 3. a cassette she recorded 4. the recorded voice

D. 1. to become 2. to study 3. to work 4. to graduate 5. to find 6. to start

E. Answers will vary.

Unit 10, Lesson A:

1. Vocabulary Workout

A. 1. hang up 2. turn on 3. screen calls 4. wrong number 5. message 6. answer 7. text 8. turn off

B. 1. screen calls 2. text 3. answer 4. wrong number 5. turn off 6. hang up 7. message 8. turn on

C. Answers will vary.

2. Conversation Workout

A. Conversation 1: 6, 3, 1, 5, 7, 2, 4, 8, 9 Conversation 2: 4, 1, 7, 2, 5, 3, 6

B. Answers will vary.

3. Language Workout

A. 1. Can I call you back tomorrow? 2. May I ask who's calling? 3. Could you hold for a minute, please? 4. May I take a message? 5. Could you spell that please? / Could you please spell that? 6. Does Marty have your telephone number? 7. May I please speak to Rosa? / May I speak to Rosa, please? 8. Would you like to leave a message?

B. **Less polite:** Call back later. Who are you? Is Carl there? **More polite:** May I speak to Dolores, please? May I take a message? Can you call back later, please? Could you hold for a minute, please? Would you like to leave a message?

C. The more polite ones

Unit 10, Lesson B:

1. Vocabulary and Language Workout

A. 1. ban 2. ignore 3. raise 4. lower 5. responds 6. allow 7. Thoughtful 8. turn 9. rude 10. delete

B. Answers will vary.

2. Reading and Writing

A. 1. Everyone loves cell phones. 2. Choose the right plan. 3. What phone is right for you? 4. Don't talk and drive. 5. Use your cell phone politely.

B. 1. emergency 2. illegal 3. private 4. risky 5. disturb 6. budget 7. co-workers

C. 1. to get 2. talking 3. working 4. getting 5. to buy 6. to answer 7. to call

D. Answers will vary.

Unit 11, Lesson A:

1. Vocabulary Workout

Down: 1. affordable 2. reliable 6. practical

Across: 3. disposable 4. convenient 5. durable 6. portable

2. Conversation Workout

A. 1. Some people say that cell phones are dangerous. But in reality, they save lives. 2. Some people think that video games are too expensive. But the truth is they aren't. 3. Some people say that I'm crazy. But actually, I'm not. 4. Some people think that everyone should have a cell phone. But the truth is it's not necessary.

B. Answers will vary.

C. Answers will vary.

3. Language Workout

A. Answers will vary.

B. 1. Did you use to be 2. Did you use to make 3. Did you use to travel 4. Did you use to have 5. Did you use to live in 6. Answer will vary.

C. 1. I, ~~used~~ = use 2. C 3. I, ~~playing~~ = play 4. C 5. C 6. C 7. I, ~~uses to visit~~ = visits 8. I, ~~used to~~ = use to

Unit 11, Lesson B:

1. Vocabulary and Language Workout

A. 1. c 2. f 3. a 4. h 5. d 6. b 7. e 8. g

B. Answers will vary.

C. 1. isn't as tall as 2. doesn't play / as well as 3. doesn't play / as well as 4. is as old as 5. doesn't have as many problems as 6. isn't as happy as

2. Reading and Writing

A. toaster, microwave, coffee maker, clock, washing machine, refrigerator (Lights, heaters, and telephones aren't usually considered appliances.)

B. 1. T 2. T 3. F 4. T 5. F 6. F

C. 1. d 2. e 3. b 4. a 5. c

D. 1. communicate 2. pervasive 3. technology 4. design 5. appliances

E. Answers will vary.

Unit 12, Lesson A:

1. Vocabulary Workout

A. 1. unplug 2. toaster 3. stop 4. newspaper delivery 5. exchange 6. money 7. pay 8. bills 9. confirm 10. flight plans 11. water 12. plants 13. give 14. house keys

B. Answers will vary.

2. Conversation Workout

A. 1. d 2. c 3. b 4. a

B. Answers will vary.

C. Answers will vary.

3. Language Workout

A. Answers will vary.

B. Answers will vary.

C. Answers will vary.

Unit 12, Lesson B:

1. Vocabulary and Language Workout

A. 1. g 2. f 3. e 4. h 5. b 6. a 7. c 8. d

B. 1. I've unplugged, already 2. I haven't exchanged, yet 3. I've given away, already 4. I haven't left, yet 5. I've paid, already 6. Bill hasn't emptied, yet 7. I haven't turned off, yet 8. Bill has watered, already

2. Reading and Writing

A. 1. Pre-trip planning 2. Tagging luggage 3. Saving space 4. Your carry-on bag 5. Other ideas

B. 1. Bad Idea 2. Good Idea 3. Bad Idea 4. Good Idea 5. Good Idea 6. Bad Idea 7. Good Idea 8. Good Idea 9. Bad Idea 10. Good

C. 1. have visited 2. I've been 3. have seen 4. went 5. don't have to 6. took 7. ate 8. are planning

D. Answers will vary.

A Quick Start Guide to Using the *World Link* Videos

The *World Link* Videos

The *World Link* video program provides stimulating and exciting video material, offering both audio and visual input as well as opportunities for follow-up conversation practice. Each *World Link* video unit features three video segments: "Good Morning World," "City Living," and "Global Viewpoints."

- The **"Good Morning World"** segments are a morning show program featuring interviews, discussions, and demonstrations in the style of talk shows. The hosts, Jay Jones and Kim Kimal, welcome many guests and discuss various topics associated with the themes and language presented in the *World Link* student books.
- The **"City Living"** segments are original dramatic episodes, filmed in an engaging sitcom-like style. They focus on the lives of six young people from a variety of international backgrounds living in New York City. Each episode reinforces and expands upon the language presented in the corresponding unit of the student books.
- The **"Global Viewpoints"** segments consist of real-life interviews in which a wide range of students and professional people from around the world present their personal views on issues related to unit topics.

The *World Link* Video Worksheets

Each *World Link* Lesson Planner contains 36 photocopiable video worksheets that correspond to the video units. The worksheets are designed to facilitate effective use of the *World Link* videos in the classroom. There are three worksheets per unit, one for each video segment. The first worksheet focuses on the "Good Morning World" video segment, the second on the "City Living" video segment, and the last on the "Global Viewpoints" segment. The worksheet activities integrate previewing, viewing, and postviewing activities into complete video-based lessons.

Using the "Good Morning World" Segments

The "Good Morning World" worksheet includes two viewing activities and one communicative activity.

- Viewing activities (1A/1B) focus on video comprehension by asking students to watch and listen for specific information. Activity formats vary from unit to unit but typically take the form of true/false, multiple choice, circling, checking, or sentence-completion exercises.
- Communicative activities (1C) encourage students to apply in the classroom what they learned in the video. These activities are intended to motivate students to think about the practical applications of the topics and the language presented in the video.

Using the "City Living" Segments

The "City Living" worksheet contains three activity types: previewing, viewing, and postviewing.

- Previewing activities (2A) usually take the form of a schema-generating discussion question ("Are you nervous at job interviews? Why or why not? Tell a partner."), or a brainstorming activity ("Why do people use cell phones so often? List all the reasons you can think of."). Previewing activities are most effective when presented in class as discussion-generating exercises and sufficient time is allowed for all students to present and discuss their views.

- Viewing activities (2B) focus on video comprehension. As with "Good Morning World," students are asked to watch and listen for specific information. Discussion is invited by having students compare answers with a partner. More involved classroom discussion may be stimulated by asking students to give reasons for their answers.
- Postviewing activities (2C) encourage students to express their personal opinions and reactions to the characters and events in the "City Living" episode. As with the viewing activities, more elaborate discussion can be encouraged by asking students to provide reasons for their answers. In some cases, postviewing activities can be used as the basis for optional writing assignments. For example, students can be asked to write a paragraph explaining one or all of their answers.

Using the "Global Viewpoints" Segments

The "Global Viewpoints" worksheet contains two activity types: two viewing activities followed by a communicative activity.

- Viewing activities (3A/3B) are similar to those found on the "Good Morning World" and "City Living" worksheets. On the "Global Viewpoints" worksheet, these activities typically take the form of true/false, multiple choice, circling, checking or sentence completion activities.
- Communicative activities (3C) are always fun or game-like communicative activities designed to stimulate conversation in pairs, groups, or the whole class. Activities often take the form of opinion surveys and discussions that involve students in sharing personal experiences, ideas, and feelings related to the themes explored in the unit.

General Suggestions for Using the *World Link* Videos

- Familiarize yourself with the videos. Before showing a segment to the class, view it yourself and try doing the activities. In this way, you will be able to anticipate questions students may have about the segment.
- Allow students to view the videos more than once. The video icon indicates activities during which the video should be shown. In order to carry out these viewing activities, students may need to view an individual segment several times. Play the segment as often as the students feel is necessary to complete the activity.
- Clarify directions for viewing activities. Focus students' attention more effectively on the task at hand by making sure they understand the directions before you play the video segment.
- Know your video equipment. Practice with the DVD player you will be using in class, so that you can easily locate and play the appropriate segment.

Using Video in the Classroom

Video is one of the most useful aids available for language teaching. It is motivating. It shows how people speak to each other. It is excellent for teaching both behavior and body language. It shows the culture of the people using the language. It is one of the best ways of communicating meaning and stimulating students to talk. But how can you exploit these advantages most effectively in the classroom? There are several useful techniques you can use to add variety to your classroom lessons and to make more effective use of video in the classroom.

The following is a description of five basic techniques for using video in the classroom: silent viewing, pause/freeze frame, sound only, split viewing, and normal viewing. With these descriptions are suggestions for specific teaching activities based on each technique.

1. *Silent Viewing*

This technique, which involves playing the video with the sound off and showing only the pictures, can be used to stimulate student interest and language use about what is being shown on the screen (rather than what can be heard on the soundtrack), or to get students to focus on what is being said, through the use of a variety of guessing and prediction tasks. Playing a short video sequence with the sound turned off not only helps students concentrate on the situation, but it also stimulates their imagination. Some classroom activities based on the Silent Viewing technique are:

- **What are they saying?**
  Show a dramatic scene with short exchanges of dialog, where the action, emotions, setting, and situation give clues to what is being said by the characters. Students watch the scene with the sound off and guess or predict what the characters are saying. Then they watch the scene with the sound on and compare their guesses and predictions with what the characters actually say.
- **What's happening?**
  Write the following three questions on the board, or dictate them to students:
  Where are the people?
  Who are they?
  What's happening?
  Students watch a dramatic scene and use the questions as a guide to help them guess the gist of the situation rather than the exact words used by the characters.
- **What's the conversation?**
  Students watch a dramatic scene, preferably one involving a conversation between two people. Then they work in pairs and try to write an appropriate dialog to accompany the pictures. Students practice their dialog in pairs and then take turns performing the dialog in front of the class. Finally, students watch the scene again, this time with the sound on, and compare their dialog with the dialog that is actually used in the video.
- **What did you see?**
  Students watch a video sequence and then write a descriptive commentary on what they see.

2. *Pause / Freeze Frame*

This technique, which involves using the pause button to stop the video while keeping a still picture frozen on the screen, can be used with either the sound on or off. The Pause / Freeze Frame technique is useful for concentrating on a single image or sentence in a video sequence. It is ideal for studying language in detail. For additional language reinforcement, it can be used in conjunction with displaying the subtitles that accompany each *World Link* video sequence. Some classroom activities based on the Pause / Freeze Frame technique are:

- **Listen and say**
  Students watch a video sequence twice with the sound on. During the first viewing they simply follow the story. During the second viewing, use the pause function to stop the video from time to time so that students can repeat the line just spoken. Encourage students to use the same intonation and stress patterns as the speakers. Offer opportunities for individual students to repeat the lines, as well as for the whole class to repeat the lines in chorus.
- **Tell me what you see**
  Play a video sequence with the sound off and pause at a convenient point to show a still picture. Students work in pairs and take turns describing what they see in the picture. As a variation, instead of using a single picture, you can pause at several different points where specific items come into prominence.
- **Guess the next line**
  Students watch a dramatic sequence, preferably one involving a dialog between two characters, with the sound on. During the viewing, pause the video at several different points, always just after one character has asked a question or said a sentence to which the second character is expected to respond. Students guess what the second character will say in response to what the first character has said. After eliciting suggested responses from the students, play the video and allow students to hear the actual response used in the video. After going through a sequence in this manner, play the entire sequence again, straight through without pausing, so that students have a chance to follow the dialog spoken at its natural pace.

3. *Sound Only*

This technique involves playing the video with the sound on and no picture. (Cover the screen with a cloth, a coat, or a large piece of paper.) With Sound Only, students listen and concentrate on what they hear, rather than on what they see. As with Silent Viewing, the creation of an information gap stimulates the imagination and student language use. Some classroom activities based on the Sound Only technique are:

- **Describe the person**
  Choose a video sequence in which one character speaks continuously for at least 10 or 15 seconds. On the board, write a list of words that students are likely to need to describe the character, for example, *old, young, tall, short, dark, fair, nice, nasty.* Play the video sequence with sound only. Students listen and write down the words they feel describe the character. Students then work in pairs or small groups, comparing and giving reasons for their answers. Elicit some answers (and reasons for them) from the class. Then replay the sequence with sound and picture so that students can modify or confirm their original answers.
- **Describe the scene**
  Select a video sequence with a soundtrack in which some clues are given as to the location, number of characters, and general situation of the scene. Write the following questions on the board, or dictate them to the students:
  Where does the scene take place?
  How many characters are in it?
  How are they dressed?
  What are their ages?
  What is their relationship?
  What are they doing?
  Play the sequence with sound only. Students listen and then work in pairs or small groups asking and answering the questions and giving reasons for their answers. Finally, play the scene again, this time with sound and picture. Students discuss the questions again, taking into consideration the new information they now have from the pictures.

4. *Split Viewing*

The technique of Split Viewing involves having some students see a video sequence and hear the soundtrack, while other students only hear the soundtrack. Some activities based on the Split Viewing technique are:

- **Tell me what happened**
  This activity is a lot like a game. Divide the class into pairs. One student in each pair is a listener who faces away from the screen. The other student is a watcher who faces the screen. Play the video episode. Listeners listen only. When the sequence ends, the watchers have three minutes to tell the listeners what they saw. At the end, encourage one or two listeners to sum up the story. Then replay the episode for all students to watch. At the end, the listeners and the watchers compare their earlier versions with what actually happens in the video.
- **Find out what happened**
  This activity follows a procedure similar to that described above, but instead of watchers telling listeners what happened, the listeners have to ask the watchers questions to find out what happened. After listeners have interviewed watchers, call on listeners to report the information they found out. This is all useful practice in asking questions and reporting information.

5. *Normal Viewing*

As you would expect, the technique of Normal Viewing involves watching the video with sound and picture, the way most people normally watch TV or a video. There are numerous activities based on this technique, and only a few of them are listed here. The most common and popular techniques that involve Normal Viewing are:

- **Role play**
  Select a video sequence with a dialog involving two or three characters. Divide the class into groups composed of the same number of students as there are characters in the video sequence. Play the sequence twice. The students' task is to study the situation in the video and then role-play the same situation using whatever words or other means they wish. After students have viewed the sequence twice, allow the groups five minutes or so to practice role-playing the situation in the video. Finally, groups take turns performing their role plays for the class, using their own words, actions, and gestures. Role play is an excellent way of having students use the language they have learned. With role play, students concentrate not just on the language people use, but also on how they behave.
- **Change!**
  This is a variation of role play (above). In large classes, each group prepares the role of one character. It then nominates one of its members to play that character. During the role play, members can be substituted by the teacher calling "Change!" or by another group member tapping the role player on the shoulder and replacing him or her.
- **Behavior study**
  In this activity, students watch a dramatic sequence, imagine a similar situation in their own country, and examine the differences in behavior. Select a video sequence that illustrates two or three incidents of behavior that are culturally different from the students' own culture. Ask the students to observe the video carefully. Play the video sequence and pause after each incident. Elicit information about what the people in the video said and did and how this differs from the students' culture. For example: Watch how the people greet each other. Play the relevant part of the sequence and elicit from the class:
    a. where the people are
    b. what they say
    c. what they do
    d. what their relationship is
    e. how they would act differently in the students' own language and culture

- **Comparing situations**
  Two or three incidents or sequences can be contrasted to allow the students to compare behavior in two different situations (e.g., people greeting each other at a party, and people greeting each other at a business meeting).
- **Prediction**
  Before having students watch a scene, tell the class where the scene takes place and ask them to predict eight to ten things they might see in the video. For example, for a scene that takes places in a kitchen, students might predict the following: *an apple, a cake, a cook, a stove, a table, a spoon, a sink, a chair, a refrigerator.* Play the video. Students watch and call out the names of the predicted items as they see them on the video.
- **Thinking and feeling**
  As much as the words we use, our body language—such as posture, gestures, and facial expressions—conveys what we really think and feel. An interesting and valuable activity involves describing what characters in a video are thinking and feeling, using clues from the dialog and the body language they use. To carry out this activity, start by preteaching a number of words students can use to describe feelings exhibited by a character or characters in the video, for example, *angry, irritated, furious, curious, surprised, disappointed, unhappy, worried.* The students' task is to watch the video and name the feelings being expressed. Play the video, stopping at crucial points to focus on a character. Ask students which word describes the character's emotions or feelings at that point, and have them give reasons for their answers.
- **Telling the story**
  Students can watch a video episode and then produce an oral or written summary of the story. Alternatively, they can watch a video episode and make up a story about the events leading up to the episode they saw on the video or about what may happen next. Using video to get students to make up a story is an excellent way of getting students to recycle language they have learned and use it in original ways for their own purposes.

The *World Link* Video Characters

"Good Morning World" is an exciting and entertaining morning show hosted by Jay Jones and Kim Kimal. On "Good Morning World," Jay and Kim reveal much about their unique personalities as they discuss numerous topics every morning. The co-hosts welcome a variety of guests to the show, including a chef, a doctor, a fashion expert, a movie star, a politician, and many others. They are joined by Rashid, the show's quiet but hard-working assistant. Start every morning off right with "Good Morning World!"

Jay Jones

Kim Kimal

"City Living" follows the lives of six friends living, studying, and working in New York City. Takeshi Mifune is a film student from Osaka, Japan. He lives with his best friend Mike Johnson, an actor from Minneapolis, Minnesota. Tara Greene is a student and waitress from Nottingham, England. Her roommates are Sun-hee Park, a computer instructor from Seoul, Korea, and Claudia Oliveira, a software sales manager from Rio de Janeiro, Brazil. Claudia's boyfriend, Roberto Chavez, is a financial analyst from Mexico City, Mexico. Interesting, exciting, and always fun—that's "City Living"!

Takeshi Mifune

Sun-hee Park

Mike Johnson

Claudia Oliveira

Tara Greene

Roberto Chavez

1 World Link 2 Video Worksheet

1 Good Morning World | You, Adrian

Name: ____________________

Date: ____________________

A Who is speaking? Watch the video and circle the answers. Then check your answers with a partner.

1. "Do we have a new co-worker?" Jay / Kim / Adrian
2. "You always forget who she is." Jay / Kim / Adrian
3. "It's nice to meet you." Jay / Kim / Adrian
4. "It's like I'm taking a class." Jay / Kim / Adrian
5. "Are you learning a lot from me?" Jay / Kim / Adrian
6. "I think she's learning a lot about you." Jay / Kim / Adrian
7. "You are going to pass." Jay / Kim / Adrian
8. "I want to get good grades." Jay / Kim / Adrian
9. "Before Good Morning World, we were just acquaintances." Jay / Kim / Adrian
10. "Ah, I know what that means." Jay / Kim / Adrian

B Now watch the video again. Circle the answers. Then compare your answers with a partner's.

1. Adrian is a new co-worker / an intern at Good Morning World.
2. Adrian works during the day and attends classes / takes tennis lessons at night.
3. Adrian wants to be a news reporter / teacher.
4. Adrian doesn't work / get a grade as an intern.
5. Kim says that Adrian is going to pass / fail.
6. Adrian has soccer / basketball practice twice a week.
7. Jay says that you don't have to study a lot / get good grades to be on television.
8. Adrian and Rashid play sports / go to school together.
9. Adrian and Rashid are just friends / dating.
10. Kim says that Jay passed / failed the "get to know Adrian" exam.

C Group activity. Work in a group of three. Role-play a conversation. Two of the people have never met. One person introduces them to each other. Then each person says something about work or school.

I'd like to introduce you to . . .	It's good to meet you.	take a class
I'd like you to meet . . .	It's nice to meet you.	work together
This is . . .	Nice to meet you.	co-worker
Meet . . .	You too.	attend
		get good / bad grades

1 World Link 2 Video Worksheet

2 City Living | A favorite keepsake

Name: ______________________

Date: ______________________

A **What's your favorite keepsake? Take notes in the chart. Describe it to the class and explain why it's so important.**

My favorite keepsake is:
Description:
It is important because:

B **What happens? Watch the video and match the correct information to make true sentences. Then compare your answers with a partner's.**

1. Tara has a blind date with ______________
2. The bracelet was a present from ______________
3. Tara got the bracelet when ______________
4. The ring is a souvenir from ______________
5. Tara's first trip to the U.S. was when ______________
6. The pendant is ______________
7. Tara's grandmother gave Tara the pendant when ______________
8. Tara's grandmother told Tara a story about ______________
9. Tara's grandmother got the pendant from ______________
10. Tara is going to wear the pendant on ______________

a. Tara's favorite keepsake.
b. Claudia's co-worker.
c. a blind date tonight.
d. she was seventeen.
e. she was five.
f. Tara's first trip to the U.S.
g. Joe, her first boyfriend.
h. her difficult childhood.
i. she was eighteen.
j. her mother.

C **Summarize the story and tell it to a partner. Write notes in the space below. Include as many details as you can remember.**

____

____

____

____

____

____

1 World Link 2 Video Worksheet

3 Global Viewpoints | Special people / Memories

Name: ____________________

Date: ____________________

A **Watch the interviews about "Special people" and circle *True* or *False*. Then correct the false sentences. Check your answers with a partner.**

1. The most important people in Alex's life are his family members. True / False
2. Alex has two brothers and one sister. True / False
3. Alejandra's grandmother is very important to her. True / False
4. Alejandra's grandmother's name is Ester and she's 70 years old. True / False
5. Kumiko says her father is always kind and supportive. True / False
6. Calum can talk to his friends about most things. True / False
7. Calum's three brothers are the most important people in his life. True / False

B **Now watch the interviews about "Memories." Match the names with the things these people mention. Make short notes with details as you watch. Then compare your answers with a partner's. Discuss any details you can remember.**

a. a trip to an amusement park in France

b. his/her first day at school

c. a shoe box full of letters, pictures, and other keepsakes

d. a visit to his/her grandfather

1. Catherine ____________
   Details: ____
2. Agnes ____________
   Details: ____
3. Calum ____________
   Details: ____
4. Julianna ____________
   Details: ____

C **Group work. Think about a favorite memory. Make notes in the boxes. Then describe your memory to the group and answer any questions they have.**

When did it happen?	Where were you?	Who was with you?	What happened?

2 World Link 2 Video Worksheet

1 Good Morning World | Fit to be fit

Name: ____________________

Date: ____________________

A Watch the video. Check (✓) the sentences that are true. Then work with a partner to correct the false sentences.

1. ☐ All week on Good Morning World they are going to talk about how to have a healthier lifestyle.
2. ☐ Kim thinks that running is the best idea ever.
3. ☐ Jay says that it is going to be easier tomorrow.
4. ☐ Jay says, "Why don't we stand up?"
5. ☐ Jay says that dinner is the most important meal of the day.
6. ☐ Kim says that the grapes are juicy, sweet, and delicious.
7. ☐ Jay says, "Let's try some eggs."
8. ☐ Kim says the cereal tastes like a cookie.
9. ☐ Jay says that Kim is running faster now.

B Now watch the video again and circle *a* or *b*. Then compare your answers with a partner's.

1. What does Jay say that you need to do for a balanced diet?
   a. He says you need to eliminate spicy foods and cut back on crunchy foods.
   b. He says you need to eliminate sweet foods and cut back on fried foods.
2. How does Kim compare grapes and cookies?
   a. She thinks that cookies are sweeter and more delicious than grapes.
   b. She thinks that grapes are sweeter and more delicious than cookies.
3. How does Jay compare grapes and cookies?
   a. He says that cookies have greater health benefits than grapes.
   b. He says that grapes have greater health benefits than cookies.
4. What has plenty of vitamins for a balanced diet?
   a. Toast with butter has plenty of vitamins for a balanced diet.
   b. Cereal with milk has plenty of vitamins for a balanced diet.
5. Does Jay tell Kim to eat faster or slower?
   a. He tells her to eat slower.
   b. He tells her to eat faster.

C Pair activity. Role-play a conversation between two friends. They are going to go out to dinner and have to choose a restaurant. Use the words from the boxes to talk about the restaurants and their food.

Let's have __ for dinner.	bigger than	it's the best . . .
Great idea!	better than	the worst . . .
Fine with me.	crowded / more crowded	the most delicious
I don't really feel like it.	relaxing / more relaxing	the biggest

2 World Link 2 Video Worksheet

2 City Living | The spicier the better

Name: ____________________

Date: ____________________

A **Do you like spicy food? What's the spiciest dish you've ever eaten? Describe it to the class and say when and where you ate it. Write notes in the chart.**

The spiciest dish I've ever eaten:	When and where I ate it:

B **What happens? Watch the video and number the events in order from 1 to 8. Then retell the story to a partner. Include any details you can remember.**

_______ Chef Jackson Dupree comes out of the kitchen.

___1___ Roberto tastes Mike and Takeshi's chicken.

_______ Roberto says, "I told you, the spicier, the better!"

_______ The chef tastes the Mike and Takeshi's chicken.

_______ Mike adds more hot sauce.

_______ The chef tastes the other contestants' food.

_______ The chef gives Mike and Takeshi first prize for their chicken.

_______ Roberto suggests adding more hot sauce to the chicken.

C **What do you think Mike, Takeshi, and Roberto will do now? Complete the chart. Then compare and explain your answer(s) with a partner.**

	I . . .	**My partner . . .**
1. They will eat the chicken.	agree / disagree	agrees / disagrees
2. They will celebrate.	agree / disagree	agrees / disagrees
3. They will go out to eat.	agree / disagree	agrees / disagrees
4. They will ________.	agree / disagree	agrees / disagrees

2 World Link 2 Video Worksheet

3 Global Viewpoints | Favorite foods / International foods

Name: ____________________
Date: ____________________

A **Watch the interviews about "Favorite foods" and circle *True* or *False*. Then correct the false sentences. Check your answers with a partner.**

1. Brad says jambalaya is a Cajun dish from New Orleans. True / False
2. Jambalaya contains chicken, beans, and pasta. True / False
3. Dennis likes spicy food. True / False
4. Dennis loves overcooked vegetables. True / False
5. Dayanne likes rice and beans that are salty and buttery. True / False
6. Thales likes grilled chicken because it's healthy. True / False
7. Dan says there's nothing better than juicy chicken. True / False
8. Julianna likes to eat bacon. True / False
9. Alejandra doesn't like oily foods. True / False
10. Alejandra doesn't enjoy sweet foods like chocolate. True / False

B **Now watch the interviews about "International foods." Circle the answers. Then compare your answers with a partner's.**

1. Catherine says the Trident Café serves typical / delicious / expensive American food.
2. Catherine's favorite food at the Trident Café is the pizza / hamburgers / french fries.
3. Dave says that *chilaquiles* are fried pieces of chicken / steak / tortilla with salsa.
4. Dave likes *chilaquiles* because they are very spicy / crunchy / salty.
5. Lourdes says Colombians make a dessert out of rice, sugar, and honey / milk / chocolate.
6. Lourdes says Colombians eat rice at least once / twice / three times a day.
7. Woo Sung's favorite food is a Korean / Mexican / Colombian dish.
8. *Yukkae-jang* is a soup made with fish / beef / chicken and vegetables.

C **Class survey. Ask six classmates the questions below. Write their names and answers on the chart. Then report the information to the class.**

1. What's your favorite food?
2. Why do you like it?
3. How often do you eat it?

Name	Favorite food	Why	How often
1.			
2.			
3.			
4.			
5.			
6.			

3 World Link 2 Video Worksheet

1 Good Morning World | Sister, meet sister

Name: ____________________

Date: ____________________

A Watch the video and circle *True* or *False*. Then correct the false sentences. Check your answers with a partner.

1. Today's show is about two sisters separated as children. True / False
2. Jay thinks that the last time he cried was the day he was born. True / False
3. Marla never remembered she had a sister. True / False
4. Maria did not know about Marla. True / False
5. Jay does not like a good mystery. True / False
6. Marla was trying to prove that she had a younger sister. True / False
7. Marla and Maria went to the library on the same day. True / False
8. At the library, Marla did not remember her sister. True / False
9. Now the Lopez sisters are reunited after many years. True / False
10. Jay does not cry after hearing the story. True / False

B What do they say? Watch the video again and circle the words you hear. Then compare your answers with a partner's.

1. Jay: "Fortunately / Unfortunately, I came prepared."
2. Kim: "I know / doubt that. Everyone, please welcome . . ."
3. Maria: "It happened by accident / on purpose."
4. Kim: "And I bet / doubt that no one figured out the truth."
5. Marla: "Fortunately / Unfortunately, no. I tried to explain . . . "
6. Kim: "And Maria, did you think / know about Marla?"
7. Jay: "Ooh, how interesting / mysterious!"
8. Maria: "I could / couldn't have a sister."
9. Marla: " . . . I was trying to prove that / figure out if I had a younger sister named Maria Lopez."
10. Kim: "Wow, what good / bad luck!"

C Summarize the story and tell it to a partner. Write notes in the space below. Include as many details as you can remember.

reunite	mystery	It seems . . .
separate	figure out	I think . . .
unfortunately / fortunately	prove / proof	can / can't
by accident	remember	could / couldn't

____

____

____

____

____

____

3 World Link 2 Video Worksheet

2 City Living | Elementary, my dear Tara!

Name: ______________________

Date: ______________________

A **Do you think borrowing or using something without asking is a crime? Why or why not? Write your thoughts below. Explain your viewpoint to a partner.**

____

____

____

B **Who is speaking? Watch the video and circle the answers. Then check your answers with a partner.**

1. "She said something about solving a crime..." Takeshi / Roberto / Sun-hee
2. "Arresting a criminal?" Sun-hee / Tara / Claudia
3. "Someone in this room has committed a crime." Roberto / Tara / Takeshi
4. "Well, my yogurt is missing." Claudia / Sun-hee / Tara
5. "Who knows where it will end?" Takeshi / Claudia / Tara
6. "I only use my key for emergencies." Takeshi / Sun-hee / Claudia
7. "I have an alibi. I was out of town last week" Mike / Roberto / Takeshi
8. "Confess! You're always too busy to go shopping!" Tara / Sun-hee / Mike
9. "No! No! It's not true!" Mike / Claudia / Roberto
10. "Nice hat! What's up?" Claudia / Roberto / Mike

C **What's your opinion? Check (✓) *I agree* or *I disagree.* Then work with a partner. Compare and explain your answers.**

	I agree	I disagree
1. It's OK to take food from a friend's refrigerator without asking.	❑	❑
2. People should ask for food before taking it from other people.	❑	❑
3. Drinks and snacks are OK to take, but not expensive items.	❑	❑
4. Roommates should always share food with each other.	❑	❑
5. Tara's investigation was a good idea.	❑	❑
6. Tara did a good job solving the crime.	❑	❑
7. What Mike did is a crime.	❑	❑
8. Sun-hee should be mad at Mike.	❑	❑

3 World Link 2 Video Worksheet

3 Global Viewpoints | Mysteries and strange events

Name: ____________________

Date: ____________________

A What mystery or event does each person mention? Watch the video "Mysteries and strange events" and match the names with the information. Then compare your answers with a partner's.

1. Agnes ______________
2. Dave ______________
3. Catherine ______________
4. Lourdes ______________
5. Alejandra ______________
6. Calum ______________

a. a scary event that happened in his or her dorm
b. the Jersey Devil
c. UFOs
d. a Mexican tale about a woman who wanders the streets
e. a strange event that happened in her grandfather's village
f. the Pyramids

B Now watch the video again and circle the answers. Compare your answers with a partner's. Then decide which is the most interesting story.

1. Agnes says the women went to a special place to make the rain stop / fall.
2. Dave says *La Llorona* is a woman weeping for her dead sons / husband.
3. Dave says people say you can hear *La Llorona* when there is a strong / no wind.
4. Catherine says the Jersey Devil is big, hairy, and very sneaky / slow.
5. Catherine says that the Jersey Devil moves from house to house / tree to tree.
6. Lourdes's favorite mysteries / stories are about UFOs.
7. Lourdes would like to think that UFOs are real / a hoax.
8. Alejandra would like to know when / how the Pyramids were made.
9. Alejandra wonders how they brought in the heavy pieces of stone / wood.
10. Calum says the lights in his dorm turned on / off suddenly.

C Pair work. Interview a partner about a strange or interesting event he or she has witnessed, or have them make one up. Ask questions like the ones below. Then tell the class about your partner's experience.

Q: Where did you witness the event?

A: ____________________

A: What happened?

A: ____________________

Q: When did you witness it?

A: ____________________

Q: How did you feel?

A: ____________________

Q: Who was with you?

A: ____________________

Q: Would you like to see it again?

A: ____________________

4 World Link 2 Video Worksheet

1 Good Morning World | Passion for fashion

Name: ____________________

Date: ____________________

A Who is speaking? Watch the video and circle the answers. Then check your answers with a partner.

1. " . . . do you agree that it's expensive to be in style?" Jay / Kim / Isadora
2. "There ought to be a better way." Jay / Kim / Isadora
3. "These are the clothes you should buy." Jay / Kim / Isadora
4. "Oh, come on!" Jay / Kim / Isadora
5. "Ooh, that's a hard one." Jay / Kim / Isadora
6. "Some of them are expensive designer brands, and . . . " Jay / Kim / Isadora
7. "Which pair is designer?" Jay / Kim / Isadora
8. "What? Those jeans are ripped!" Jay / Kim / Isadora
9. "Ripped and sloppy are in style . . . " Jay / Kim / Isadora
10. "All of the kids love retro." Jay / Kim / Isadora

B Watch the video again and circle *a* or *b*. Then compare your answers with a partner's.

1. Kim says that Jay is ______________.
   a. very stylish b. out of style
2. Isadora is going to talk about how to get the look you want ______________.
   a. without spending a lot of money b. by paying thousands on designer clothes
3. Isadora says that the clothes you should buy ______________.
   a. are expensive designer brands b. look designer but are nearly half the cost
4. The designer jeans are ______________.
   a. the darker fitted ones b. the ripped ones
5. The designer shirt is ______________.
   a. the one that has a retro look b. the sporty one

C What's your opinion? Check (✓) *I agree* or *I disagree.* Then work with a partner. Compare and explain your answers.

	I agree.	I disagree.
1. Jay shouldn't wear designer clothes. They are too expensive.	☐	☐
2. Kim should have a more dramatic hairstyle.	☐	☐
3. Most people can't spend a lot of money on designer clothes.	☐	☐
4. A lot of people buy clothes that look designer, but at half the cost.	☐	☐
5. None of my friends are out of style.	☐	☐
6. A couple of my friends wear retro clothes.	☐	☐

4 World Link 2 Video Worksheet

2 City Living | You ought to get more exercise!

Name: ______________________

Date: ______________________

A **Should people exercise to be healthy? What are the best ways to exercise? What are the best ways to be healthy? Make two lists. Then compare your lists with a partner's and tell the class.**

Ways to exercise	Ways to be healthy

B **What do Roberto and Mike think? Watch the video and circle *thinks* or *doesn't think*. Then compare your answers with a partner's.**

1. Roberto thinks / doesn't think Mike should get more exercise.
2. Mike thinks / doesn't think most people exercise.
3. Roberto thinks / doesn't think more people are exercising nowadays.
4. Roberto thinks / doesn't think more than one-third of his co-workers exercise.
5. Mike thinks / doesn't think going to the gym is a trend.
6. Mike thinks / doesn't think most people enjoy exercising.
7. Mike thinks / doesn't think that they should eat ice cream after jogging.
8. Roberto thinks / doesn't think it's a good idea to eat ice cream after exercising.

C **What's your opinion? Talk about exercise with a partner. Ask and answer questions like the ones below. Then share your information with the class.**

How often do you exercise?

____

Is exercising fun? Why or why not?

____

What kind of exercise do you do?

____

Do you prefer to exercise indoors or outdoors? Why?

____

Do you think people exercise more now than before? Why or why not?

____

4 World Link 2 Video Worksheet

3 Global Viewpoints | Family trends / Personal style

Name: ____________________

Date: ____________________

A Watch the interviews about "Family trends." Match the countries with the family trends. Then compare your answers with a partner's.

1. Ukraine ________ a. In traditional families, males usually work.
2. Colombia ________ b. People get married when they're about 25.
3. Brazil ________ c. People get married very early.
4. Korea ________ d. Children live with their parents until they get married.
5. Japan ________ e. People usually get married in their late 20s.
6. Argentina ________ f. People usually get married when they're around 30.

B Now watch the interviews about "Personal style" and circle *True* or *False*. Then correct the false sentences. Check your answers with a partner's.

1. Dave thinks his sister's style is very independent. True / False
2. Calum's says his friend Alex wears very nice clothes. True / False
3. Dayanne talks about a friend who wears a baseball cap to work. True / False
4. Dayanne thinks her friend should wear something more stylish. True / False
5. Dennis likes the way Robert Redford sings. True / False
6. Dennis doesn't like Robert Redford's hair. True / False
7. Woo Sung thinks it's time to change his hairstyle. True / False
8. Dayanne thinks gaining weight will improve her appearance. True / False
9. Dayanne thinks she should get a haircut. True / False
10. Calum thinks new glasses could improve his appearance. True / False

C Pair work. Talk to a partner about his or her style. Ask and answer the questions below. Then tell the class about your partner's style.

Whose style do you admire most? Why?

____

How would you describe your personal style?

____

Do you like to shop? Why or why not?

____

What's your favorite store? Why?

____

Are clothes important to you? Why or why not?

____

What could you do to improve your style?

____

5 World Link 2 Video Worksheet

1 Good Morning World | Where are you going?

Name: ____________________

Date: ____________________

A Watch the video. Check (✓) if the errand or chore is mentioned. Then compare your answers with a partner's.

1. run errands ☐
2. take the dog for a walk ☐
3. mail letters ☐
4. go grocery shopping ☐
5. make dinner ☐
6. make a reservation ☐
7. make an appointment ☐
8. do the dishes ☐
9. do laundry ☐
10. sweep ☐
11. vacuum ☐

B What happens? Watch the video and number the events in order from 1 to 8. Then retell the story to a partner. Include any details you can remember.

_______ Kim says she doesn't mind grocery shopping.

_______ Ana says she is running errands this morning.

_______ Paul runs in and says he is looking for the restaurant La Belle Petite.

___1___ Kim and Jay are outside the Good Morning World studios.

_______ Ana leaves because she is running late.

_______ Jay asks a woman, "Would you mind talking to us for a minute?"

_______ Jay calls La Belle Petite to make a reservation for Ana and her husband Paul.

_______ Ana says that when she goes home she still has to do the dishes, do the laundry, and vacuum.

C Class activity. Go around the class. Ask questions and complete the chart. Then report your information to the class.

Find someone who . . .	Name
doesn't like to run errands	
is usually on time	
is usually running late	
has a pretty long commute	
lives really close to school or work	
rides a bike	
takes a bus	
takes a dog for a walk	

5 World Link 2 Video Worksheet

2 City Living | Claudia's errand service

Name: ______________________

Date: ______________________

A **What kinds of errands do you usually do every week? When do you do them? Make a list and share it with a partner. Compare your lists. Do you and your partner do the same errands?**

My errands	My partner's errands

B **Watch the video and circle *True* or *False*. Then correct the false sentences. Check your answers with a partner's.**

1. Roberto doesn't feel well. True / False
2. Claudia volunteers to do Roberto's errands. True / False
3. Roberto asks Claudia to get some groceries for him. True / False
4. Claudia forgets the grocery list. True / False
5. Most of the places Claudia has to go are near each other. True / False
6. Claudia picks up Roberto's dry cleaning first. True / False
7. Claudia gets the movie last. True / False
8. Claudia doesn't like Roberto's neighbors. True / False
9. Roberto wants to watch the movie alone. True / False
10. Claudia agrees to go and get some ice cream for Roberto. True / False

C **In the video Claudia says, "Don't push your luck." What does she mean? Circle *Yes* or *No*. Then work with a partner to write a definition.**

1. Is Claudia talking about doing errands for Roberto? Yes / No
2. In Claudia's opinion, has she done enough to help Roberto? Yes / No
3. Does Claudia think that Roberto is lucky? Yes / No
4. The expression "Don't push your luck" means: ______________________________

____

____

5 World Link 2 Video Worksheet

3 Global Viewpoints | Running errands / My neighborhood

Name: ____________________

Date: ____________________

A **Watch the interviews about "Running errands." Check (✓) the errands each person mentions. Then compare your answers with a partner's.**

1. Brad goes to . . .

☐ the Laundromat ☐ the dry cleaners ☐ the pharmacy ☐ the supermarket

2. Alejandra goes to . . .

☐ the bank ☐ the post office ☐ the dry cleaners ☐ the pharmacy

3. Calum goes to . . .

☐ the Laundromat ☐ the grocery store ☐ the bank ☐ the post office

B **Watch the video about "My neighborhood." What do these people say? Circle the words you hear. Then compare your answers with a partner's.**

1. Julianna: "In Brazil, my neighborhood is very safe / busy."
2. Julianna: "I live close to movie theaters / restaurants, parks . . . "
3. Alejandra: "My neighborhood in Buenos Aires is a residential / commercial neighborhood."
4. Alejandra: "It is close to shops, and I can bike / walk to the shops."
5. Alejandra: "There are a lot of trees on the sidewalks / in the park . . . "
6. Lourdes: "There is a big school / grocery store near my house . . . "
7. Lourdes: "We have two buses / trains that pass by my house . . . "
8. Lourdes: "It's very easy to get around taking public transportation / using a car."

C **Pair work. Work with a partner and take turns asking each other about the neighborhoods you live in. Ask the questions below and take notes on your partner's answers. Then tell the class two things about your partner's neighborhood.**

Q: Do you like your neighborhood? Why or why not?

A: ____________________

Q: What do you like to do in your neighborhood?

A: ____________________

Q: What are your neighbors like?

A: ____________________

Q: What are the good points about your neighborhood?

A: ____________________

Q: What are the bad points, if any?

A: ____________________

Q: Would you like to move to a different neighborhood? Why or why not?

A: ____________________

6 World Link 2 Video Worksheet

1 Good Morning World | Apply yourself

Name: ____________________

Date: ____________________

A Who is speaking? Watch the video and circle the answers. Then compare your answers with a partner's.

1. "Well, this will be a big weekend, won't it . . . ?" Jay / Kim / Rashid
2. "I thought we decided not to do this." Jay / Kim / Rashid
3. "It's mine from when I graduated." Jay / Kim / Rashid
4. "Maybe I'll go to dinner with my family." Jay / Kim / Rashid
5. "I'm talking about in a few months or next year." Jay / Kim / Rashid
6. "I'll probably learn a lot more about the television business if I take more classes." Jay / Kim / Rashid
7. "Someday I want to produce my own television show." Jay / Kim / Rashid
8. "You won't leave!" Jay / Kim / Rashid
9. "Who will remember that I like water and not coffee?" Jay / Kim / Rashid
10. "You are going to learn more about television, too." Jay / Kim / Rashid

B Now watch the video again and circle *a* or *b*. Then check your answers with a partner.

1. When is Rashid's college graduation?
   a. His graduation is tomorrow.
   b. His graduation is next year.
2. What are Rashid's plans for the future?
   a. He's going to travel.
   b. He's going to apply to graduate school.
3. Why will Rashid leave Good Morning World someday?
   a. He wants to produce his own television show.
   b. He wants to be the host of a different morning show.
4. When is Rashid's application due?
   a. It is due in a few days.
   b. It is due in a few weeks.
5. Who will write a recommendation for Rashid?
   a. Jay will write a recommendation.
   b. Kim will write a recommendation.

C Pair work. Talk to a partner about his or her future plans. Ask and answer the questions below. Then tell the class about your partner.

What are you going to do tomorrow?

____

What are you going to do this summer?

____

What are your plans for next year?

____

What will you be doing in five years?

____

6 World Link 2 Video Worksheet

2 City Living | The letter

Name: ____________________

Date: ____________________

A **How do you share important news with people? How do people share important news with you? Put the methods for sharing and receiving news in order from 1 (most common) to 4 (least common). Write an example of the kind of news next to each one. Then compare your ideas with a partner's.**

How you share news	How you receive news
____ **Letter** Example: ____________	____ **Letter** Example: ____________
____ **Phone call** Example: ____________	____ **Phone call** Example: ____________
____ **Text message** Example: ____________	____ **Text message** Example: ____________
____ **E-mail** Example: ____________	____ **E-mail** Example: ____________

B **What happens? Watch the video and circle the answers. Then compare your answers with a partner's.**

1. Takeshi applied to Harvard University and was accepted / rejected.
2. He was accepted / rejected by the University of Southern California.
3. If he doesn't get into graduate school, he's going to travel / get a job.
4. Sun-hee will be happy / sad if Takeshi goes to Europe.
5. Mike thinks / doesn't think that Takeshi will be accepted to grad school.
6. Takeshi has received a letter from Columbia / New York University.
7. If he doesn't get into graduate school, Takeshi will / won't apply again.
8. If he gets into graduate school, he's going to become a film director / professor.
9. The letter for Takeshi says that he has been accepted / rejected.
10. Takeshi is going to travel around Europe / go to graduate school.

C **What's your opinion? Circle *I agree* or *I disagree*. Then work with a partner. Compare and explain your answers.**

1. Takeshi is probably a good student. — I agree / I disagree
2. Takeshi should go to graduate school. — I agree / I disagree
3. Takeshi should become a film director. — I agree / I disagree
4. Takeshi should travel before he goes to graduate school. — I agree / I disagree
5. Takeshi should not go to Columbia. — I agree / I disagree

6 World Link 2 Video Worksheet

3 Global Viewpoints | After graduation / Five years from now . . .

Name: ____________________

Date: ____________________

A **Watch the interviews about "After graduation." What are these people going to do? Match the names with the plans. Compare your answers with a partner's.**

1. Agnes ________ a. go to graduate school and study art
2. Brad ________ b. start a business in agriculture
3. Calum ________ c. move to Washington, D.C., and work for National Geographic
4. Dave ________ d. start an import-export business
5. Alex ________ e. find a good job, start a family, and buy a house
6. Julianna ________ f. get a job that pays a lot of money, travel, and see the world

B **Now watch the interviews about "Five years from now . . . " and circle *True* or *False*. Then correct the false sentences. Check your answers with a partner's.**

1. Dave will be studying five years from now. True / False
2. Dave knows where he's going to be living five years from now. True / False
3. Calvin plans to become a lawyer. True / False
4. Calvin thinks it will be ten years before cyber law is important. True / False
5. Woo Sung expects to be married in five years. True / False
6. Woo Sung wants four kids and a dog. True / False
7. Most of all, Woo Sung wants to enjoy his life. True / False

C **Group work. Think about your plans for the future. Make notes in the boxes. Then describe your plans to the group and answer any questions they have.**

Future Plans
Plans for school
Plans for a career
Plans for travel
Plans for family life

7 World Link 2 Video Worksheet

1 Good Morning World | Party time

Name: ____________________

Date: ____________________

A Watch the video and circle *True* or *False*. Then correct the false sentences. Check your answers with a partner's.

1. Jay is having a party this weekend. True / False
2. It will be held this Sunday at Penn Park. True / False
3. One week before the party, Jay invites Rashid and Kim to come. True / False
4. Before she goes to a party, Kim likes to know what she's celebrating. True / False
5. The party is for Jay's best friend. True / False
6. Jay wants Kim to bring presents and cake. True / False
7. Jay tells Kim to put on a costume before she comes to the party. True / False
8. Everyone at the party will participate in a costume contest. True / False
9. Jay will choose the winner of the contest. True / False
10. Jay's best friend is his sister Precious. True / False

B What do they say? Watch the video again and circle the words you hear. Then compare your answers with a partner's.

1. Jay: "She gave me some good ideas for my celebration / party this weekend."
2. Kim: "Celebration? Are you throwing / having a party?"
3. Jay: "Oh, maybe I forgot to invite / didn't invite you."
4. Kim: "Or are people celebrating / getting together just to have a good time?"
5. Jay: "I am the host / winner."
6. Kim: "I'm sorry / I'd love to, but I can't. I already have plans."
7. Kim: "It might be a surprise party, but I don't want to be surprised after / when I get there."
8. Jay: "OK, you win / are invited. The party is for my best friend."
9. Jay: "Before / After you come, put on a costume."
10. Kim: "I'd love to / I'm sorry, Jay, but I can't come."

C Pair activity. Role-play a conversation between two friends. They are talking about going to a party. Use the words and phrases from the boxes to help you.

celebrate get together have a party	Do you want to go with me? Would you like to go with me? How'd you like to go with me?	Sure, I'd love to. That sounds great. I'm sorry, but I can't. I'd love to, but I'm busy.
have a good (bad) time get presents participate	I am going to the party. I don't have a costume for the party. I need a costume for the party.	So am I. / Me too. Me neither. / Neither do I. So do I. / I do too.

7 World Link 2 Video Worksheet

2 City Living | Aloha everyone!

Name: ____________________

Date: ____________________

A **What's the most interesting party you've ever attended? Write some notes. Describe it to the class. Your classmates vote to decide whose party was the most interesting.**

____

____

____

____

____

B **What happens? Watch the video and number the events in order from 1 to 7. Then retell the story to a partner. Include any details you can remember.**

_______ Roberto tells Mike he can't go because he has to go to a "luau" with Claudia.

___1___ Claudia calls Tara and invites her to a luau.

_______ Mike calls Roberto and asks him if he'd like to go to "a party."

_______ Takeshi calls Mike and invites him to go to "a Hawaiian party."

_______ Roberto tells Claudia that Mike invited him to a party.

_______ Tara asks Sun-hee if she'd like to go to the luau.

_______ Sun-hee invites Takeshi to the luau.

C **What do you think happens next? Work with a partner to predict what will happen when Mike sees Roberto at the luau. Write down your prediction. Then share it with the class.**

____

____

____

____

____

____

7 World Link 2 Video Worksheet

3 Global Viewpoints | What a party! / Festivals and holidays

Name: ______________________

Date: ______________________

A Watch the interviews about "What a party!" and circle the answers. Then compare your answers with a partner's.

1. Alejandra went to a party where the dance floor was covered with soapsuds / sand.
2. The party was during the summer / fall.
3. People at Alejandra's party were dressed in formal / casual clothes.
4. There were 28 / 38 people at Dennis's birthday party.
5. Dennis's birthday party took place in his / a friend's apartment.
6. Dennis's friends / Dennis cooked the food for his birthday party.

B Now watch the interviews about "Festivals and holidays." Match the names with the holidays each person mentions. Make short notes with details as you watch. Compare your answers with a partner's. Discuss any details you remember.

a. The Day of Tradition
b. New Year's Day
c. Thanksgiving
d. Independence Day

1. Catherine ______________
   Details: ____
2. Lourdes ______________
   Details: ____
3. Kumiko ______________
   Details: ____
4. Alejandra ______________
   Details: ____

C Class activity. What's the most popular party activity in your class? What's the least popular? Interview six classmates. Check (✓) the things they like to do at parties. Then report your information to the class.

What do you like to do at parties?

Name	Listen to music	Eat special foods	Dance	Talk to friends	Play games
1. ______________	❑	❑	❑	❑	❑
2. ______________	❑	❑	❑	❑	❑
3. ______________	❑	❑	❑	❑	❑
4. ______________	❑	❑	❑	❑	❑
5. ______________	❑	❑	❑	❑	❑
6. ______________	❑	❑	❑	❑	❑

8 World Link 2 Video Worksheet

1 Good Morning World | A likely story

Name: ____________________

Date: ____________________

A Who is speaking? Watch the video and circle the answers. Then check your answers with a partner.

1. "But also, books are predictable." Jay / Kim / Anthony
2. "In the end, everyone lives happily ever after." Jay / Kim / Anthony
3. "It is written so well." Jay / Kim / Anthony
4. "Am I talking too fast?" Jay / Kim / Anthony
5. "It begins in Peru." Jay / Kim / Anthony
6. "It's unbelievable!" Jay / Kim / Anthony
7. "So the boy begins a journey to find his father." Jay / Kim / Anthony
8. "You can tell a story well." Jay / Kim / Anthony
9. "Does he eventually find his real father?" Jay / Kim / Anthony
10. "You said you wanted a realistic story!" Jay / Kim / Anthony

B Watch the video again and circle *a* or *b*. Then compare your answers with a partner's.

1. Anthony Guinness is a ______________.
   a. famous chef b. famous author
2. Jay thinks that books are ______________.
   a. predictable b. incredible
3. Kim thinks that the book is written ______________.
   a. badly b. well
4. The book *The Way It Was* is ______________.
   a. based on a true story b. a made-up story
5. In the book, the boy was looking for ______________.
   a. his father b. his grandfather
6. Anthony is ______________ in the story.
   a. the father b. the boy
7. Jay is now ______________ the story.
   a. unhappy about b. hooked on

C Summarize the story from the video and tell it to a partner. Write notes in the space below. Include as many details as you can remember.

It's a story about . . . It begins . . . a true story	So (then) . . . Later . . . After that . . . tell a story (well)	It turns out that . . . Finally . . . In the end . . . a (happy) ending

____

____

____

____

____

8 World Link 2 Video Worksheet

2 City Living | Takeshi presents "Cinderella"

Name: ____________________

Date: ____________________

A What do you know about the story of Cinderella? Make a list of details that you remember from the story. Then tell a partner.

Cinderella

____

____

____

____

____

B What do they say? Watch the video and circle the words you hear. Then compare your answers with a partner's.

1. Takeshi: "Once upon a time, there was a kind and humble / beautiful young woman named Cinderella . . . "
2. Claudia: "I was having fun until my two ugly / evil stepsisters moved in with me."
3. Tara: "Don't forget to wash my skirt / dress."
4. Mike: " . . . and I was enjoying / watching my Sunday afternoon football game until Takeshi asked me to be in his movie."
5. Claudia: "I want to go to the prince's ball tonight but I have too much to do / nothing to wear!"
6. Mike: "Fear not, Cinderella. You will see the brave and loyal prince tonight / soon."
7. Takeshi: "But when she was rushing / hurrying home just before midnight, she lost one of her slippers."
8. Roberto: "I'm looking / searching for the woman who wore this slipper last night."
9. Takeshi: "And so they ran away / got married and they . . . lived happily ever after."

C What's your opinion? Talk about Takeshi's film project with a partner. Ask and answer questions like the ones below. Then share your opinions with the class.

1. Did you like Takeshi's film? Why or why not?

   ____

2. Which parts did you think were funny?

   ____

3. Who was the best "actor"?

   ____

4. Who had the best costume?

   ____

5. What would you change about the film if you could?

   ____

8 World Link 2 Video Worksheet

3 Global Viewpoints | Favorite stories

Name: ____________________

Date: ____________________

A **Whose story is it? Watch the video "Favorite stories" and match the names with the stories. Make short notes with details as you watch. Compare your answers with a partner's. Discuss any details you can remember.**

a. a fable about a boy who sees a pretty girl in a library

b. Snow White and the Seven Dwarfs

c. a story about a princess who marries a sea prince

1. Julianna ______________

   Details: ______________________________

2. Reda ______________

   Details: ______________________________

3. Jackie ______________

   Details: ______________________________

B **Now watch the video again and circle *True* or *False*. Then correct the false sentences. Check your answers with a partner.**

Snow White and the Seven Dwarfs

1. Snow White was a beautiful witch. True / False
2. A bad princess gave Snow White a poisoned apple. True / False
3. A handsome prince kissed her and brought her back to life. True / False

Lithuanian Story

4. The princess's family wants her to go away with the prince. True / False
5. The princess turns herself and her children into frogs. True / False
6. The castle bursts into little pieces of amber. True / False

Korean Story

7. A pretty girl is standing in the library. True / False
8. The boy tells the girl to come forward. True / False
9. The girl has no legs or torso. True / False

C **Pair work. Think about a famous fairy tale or fable. Write details from the story in the boxes below. Then tell the story to your partner without saying the title or the name of the main character. Your partner guesses the fable or fairy tale.**

When?	Where?	Who?	What happens?

9 World Link 2 Video Worksheet

1 Good Morning World | Intern view

Name: ____________________

Date: ____________________

A Watch the video. Check (✓) the sentences that are true. Then work with a partner to correct the false sentences.

1. ☐ Kim wants to thank Adrian for her work on Good Morning World.
2. ☐ Adrian is almost finished with her internship at Good Morning World.
3. ☐ Kim doesn't think they should try to help Adrian with a practice interview.
4. ☐ Jay says to Adrian, "Tell us a little about your job."
5. ☐ Adrian will graduate from college next year.
6. ☐ Kim asks Adrian, "Have you ever worked in television before?"
7. ☐ Adrian has worked as an intern at Good Morning World since last fall.
8. ☐ Adrian has learned to be flexible.
9. ☐ Jay says that in television you have to work independently.
10. ☐ Adrian says that Jay is very knowledgeable.

B Now watch the video again. Circle the answers. Then check your answers with a partner.

1. Kim says that they need / want to take a moment to thank Adrian for all of her work.
2. Kim says that Adrian has been a very pleasant and efficient / punctual part of their team.
3. Adrian is going to finish school and then look for her dream / dead-end job.
4. Kim and Jay are going to do a stressful / practice job interview.
5. Adrian is a first-year / fourth-year university student and is majoring in journalism.
6. Adrian has worked / hasn't worked as an intern at Good Morning World since last fall.
7. Adrian says that her experience was very rewarding / dull.
8. Adrian has learned / hasn't learned to work independently sometimes.
9. Jay has watched / worked in television for a long time.
10. For Kim, the most stressful / demanding thing about her job is being pleasant to her co-workers.

C Pair work. Role-play an interviewer and an applicant at a job interview. Use the words and phrases in the box to help you. Then tell the class two things about the interview.

Interviewer	Applicant
Thanks for coming in.	My pleasure.
Tell me a little about yourself.	I'm a. . . . I'm . . .
Can you . . . ?	Yes, I can. For example . . .
Are you . . . ?	Yes, I . . .
Have you ever . . . ?	No, I . . .
Do you have any questions for me?	Right away.
When can you start?	I look forward to hearing from you soon.

9 World Link 2 Video Worksheet

2 City Living | The big job interview

Name: ______________________

Date: ______________________

A **What qualities and skills does a salesperson need? Work with a partner and make a list. Then share your list with the class.**

____

____

____

____

B **What do you learn about Claudia in this episode? Watch the video and circle *a, b,* or *c.* Then compare your answers with a partner's.**

1. What does Claudia say she's "really good at"?
   a. listening to customers
   b. designing software
   c. using software
2. How much experience has she had training people to use software?
   a. two years
   b. one year
   c. none
3. How long has she been with her present company?
   a. four years
   b. three years
   c. two years
4. How many times has she been salesperson of the month?
   a. four times
   b. three times
   c. twice
5. What subject is she taking graduate courses in?
   a. software design
   b. management
   c. marketing
6. Why is she taking graduate courses?
   a. to learn about software programs
   b. to understand the market
   c. to get a degree

C **In the video Ms. Li says, "We'll be in touch." What does she mean? Circle *Yes* or *No*. Then work with a partner to write a definition.**

1. Are Ms. Li and Claudia making plans together? Yes / No
2. Is Ms. Li planning to contact Claudia? Yes / No
3. Is Ms. Li waiting for Claudia to contact her? Yes / No
4. "We'll be in touch" means ____

____

9 World Link 2 Video Worksheet

3 Global Viewpoints | What do you do? / Dream jobs

Name: ____________________

Date: ____________________

A **Watch the interviews about "What do you do?" and check (✓) *True* or *False*. Then correct the false sentences. Check your answers with a partner's.**

	True	False
1. Natalie works for a television station that was launched seven years ago.	❑	❑
2. Natalie has worked for the television station for about a year.	❑	❑
3. Dan works for a computer company.	❑	❑
4. Dan has been working at his job for three years.	❑	❑
5. Gian is a managing editor.	❑	❑
6. Gian makes brochures, sends e-mails, and works on the Web.	❑	❑

B **Now watch the interviews about "Dream jobs." What is the dream job of each person? Match the names with the jobs. Compare your answers with a partner's. Discuss any details you can remember.**

1. Kumiko ______ a. helping people in developing countries
2. Dave ______ b. teaching Japanese and training dogs
3. Jackie ______ c. photographer
4. Vanessa ______ d. designing movie posters and CD covers
5. Dayanne ______ e. reporter
6. Jonathan ______ f. teaching children
7. Calum ______ g. computer animator

C **Pair work. Work with a partner and take turns asking each other about your dream jobs. Ask the questions below and take notes on your partner's answers. Then tell the class about your partner's dream job.**

Q: What's your dream job?

A: ____________________

Q: Why would you like to do the job?

A: ____________________

Q: What skills do you need for the job?

A: ____________________

Q: Have you had any experience related to the job?

A: ____________________

10 World Link 2 Video Worksheet

1 Good Morning World | Hello hangups

Name: ____________________

Date: ____________________

A What do they say? Watch the video and circle the words you hear. Then compare your answers with a partner's.

1. Erica: "She doesn't need / want to worry."
2. Erica: "Do you mind if I answer it / hang up?"
3. Erica: "No. I hate to eat / eating there."
4. Jay: "Do you mind answering / hanging up the phone?"
5. Erica: "I love / hate having cameras in my house to record every moment of my life."
6. Jay: "Kim means we wanted / decided to talk about your show."
7. Erica: "I just got a phone / text message from my boyfriend."
8. Jay: "You could turn on / off your phone."
9. Kim: "Or ignore / answer the call."
10. Jay: "Kim, raise / lower your voice."

B Now watch the video again and circle *a* or *b*. Then compare your answers with a partner's.

1. Who does Erica love talking to?
   a. her friend Renee b. Kim and Jay
2. How long does Erica say she'll be on the phone?
   a. a second b. a minute
3. Who does Erica say is rude sometimes?
   a. her boyfriend b. her agent
4. What does Erica think is always important to do?
   a. screen your calls b. take messages
5. What does Erica say when she answers the phone and doesn't know who it is?
   a. Hang on, Erica Allendez. May I ask who's calling?
   b. Hello, Erica Allendez. Who's calling?
6. Why is Erica so excited?
   a. She loves being on Good Morning World.
   b. She got a part.

C Class activity. Go around the class. Ask questions about phone habits and complete the chart. Then report your information to the class.

Find someone who . . .	Name
likes to talk on his or her cell phone	
hates sending text messages	
avoids talking on the phone while driving	
hates when people talk on the phone in public	
always screens his or her calls	

10 World Link 2 Video Worksheet

2 City Living | I can't stand cell phones!

Name: ______________________
Date: ______________________

A **Why do you think people use cell phones so often? Think of some reasons and make a list. Then share your list with the class.**

Reasons why people use cell phones:

____
____
____
____
____
____

B **What happens? Watch the video. Number the sentences in order from 1 to 8. Then retell the story to a partner. Include any details you can remember.**

_______ The woman who was on a cell phone earlier asks Mike to be quiet.
_______ Mike gets a call from his mother.
_______ Mike's dad gives him his new phone number.
_______ Roberto and Mike criticize people who use cell phones in public places.
___1___ Roberto and Mike see a woman chatting on a cell phone.
_______ Mike gets a call on his cell phone from his father.
_______ Mike's mom tells him her vacation plans.
_______ Mike uses his cell phone to connect his mother and father.

C **What do you think happens next? Work with a partner to predict what will happen after Mike hangs up. Write out the conversation between Roberto and Mike. Then act out your conversation for the class.**

ROBERTO: ______________________________________
MIKE: ______________________________________
ROBERTO: ______________________________________
MIKE: ______________________________________
ROBERTO: ______________________________________
MIKE: ______________________________________
ROBERTO: ______________________________________
MIKE: ______________________________________
ROBERTO: ______________________________________
MIKE: ______________________________________

10 World Link 2 Video Worksheet

3 Global Viewpoints | Cell phones

Name: ____________________
Date: ____________________

A **What are these people's opinions? Watch the video "Cell phones" and circle *True* or *False*. Then correct the false sentences. Check your answers with a partner.**

1. Catherine thinks cell phones are necessary nowadays. True / False
2. Brad always has his cell phone with him. True / False
3. Brad can't browse the Internet on his cell phone. True / False
4. Jackie doesn't like having a camera on her cell phone. True / False
5. Dayanne thinks that cell phones are always necessary. True / False
6. Alex likes being able to contact people whenever he wants. True / False
7. Calvin thinks he has more privacy with a cell phone. True / False
8. Lourdes likes cell phones more than she dislikes them. True / False
9. Dennis likes cell phones because they connect you with people. True / False
10. Dennis doesn't mind cell phones ringing at unexpected times. True / False
11. Alejandra likes to use her cell phone to tell people when she is running late. True / False
12. Alejandra hates cell phones when they ring in public places. True / False

B **Now watch the video again. Match the people with what each one says about cell phones. Then compare your answers with a partner's.**

1. Brad ________
2. Jackie ________
3. Dayanne ________
4. Calvin ________
5. Lourdes ________
6. Dennis ________
7. Alejandra ________

a. mentions the usefulness of cell phones in emergencies.
b. says that phones are very good for business.
c. says that they allow her to call people when she's late.
d. mentions browsing the Internet and downloading music.
e. mentions a camera phone.
f. talks about privacy.
g. says that cell phones help people reach each other anywhere.

C **Group work. Brainstorm the advantages and disadvantages of cell phones with your group. Complete the chart below. Then share your group's ideas with the class.**

Advantages of Cell Phones	Disadvantages of Cell Phones

11 World Link 2 Video Worksheet

1 Good Morning World | Okay computers

Name: ____________________

Date: ____________________

A Watch the video and check (✓) *Yes* or *No*. Then compare your answers with a partner's.

	Yes	No
1. Are computers as old as Jay is?	❑	❑
2. Does Kim have her laptop with her?	❑	❑
3. Is Kim's laptop portable and convenient?	❑	❑
4. Does Jay think that computers are disposable?	❑	❑
5. Does Kim say that old computers are as practical as new ones?	❑	❑
6. Does Jay say that old things are more reliable?	❑	❑
7. Is Jay's computer small and portable?	❑	❑
8. Did Kim's parents used to have a computer like Jay's?	❑	❑
9. Does Kim drop her laptop?	❑	❑

B Now watch the video again. Match the correct information to make true sentences. Then check your answers with a partner.

1. Jay says that some people think computers ________
2. Kim says that computers are as ________
3. Jay says that computers don't look as ________
4. Kim says she used to ________
5. Jay says a lot of people think computers ________
6. Kim says that old computers are not as ________
7. Kim says that Jay's computer is as ________
8. Kim is very happy with her new, attractive, ________

a. good as he does.
b. practical as new ones.
c. are disposable.
d. old as Jay is.
e. are a new technology.
f. big as a house.
g. and convenient laptop.
h. be more careful.

C Pair work. In pairs, make an advertisement about a computer. Include some of the words or expressions below. Then share it with the class, and everyone will vote on the most original advertisement.

It's . . . affordable / attractive / convenient / disposable / durable / portable / practical / reliable	Some people say / think A lot of people say / think	It costs as much as . . . It is as big as . . . It works as well as . . .
consume / prevent / recycle / reduce / transform	(But) actually / in fact (But) the truth / fact	Some people used to . . . Technology used to . . .

11 World Link 2 Video Worksheet

2 City Living | The first word processor

Name: ______________________
Date: ______________________

A **Have you ever had a problem with a computer, a cell phone, or another piece of technology? What happened? Discuss with a partner and take notes below. Which of you had the hardest problem to solve?**

My technology problem	My partner's technology problem

B **What do you learn in the video? Watch the video and circle *a*, *b*, or *c*. Then compare your answers with a partner's.**

1. What did the professor use to write her term papers when she was in high school?
   a. a computer
   b. a typewriter
   c. a word processor
2. What's the professor's opinion of the typewriters she used in high school?
   a. They were OK.
   b. They were really bad.
   c. They were amazing.
3. What does the professor say about the first computers?
   a. They were fast.
   b. They were unreliable.
   c. They were affordable.
4. What happened one spring when the professor was working on a term paper?
   a. The batteries in her laptop died.
   b. Her typewriter broke.
   c. The electricity went out.
5. What did the professor use to finish writing her paper?
   a. a laptop
   b. a typewriter
   c. a paper and pencil

C **What's your opinion? Circle *I agree* or *I disagree*. Then work with a partner. Compare and explain your answers.**

1. It's difficult to live without a personal computer. I agree / I disagree
2. The world could not function without computers. I agree / I disagree
3. Computers are not reliable. I agree / I disagree
4. People rely too much on computers. I agree / I disagree

11 World Link 2 Video Worksheet

3 Global Viewpoints | Technology today

Name: ______________________
Date: ______________________

A What do we learn about these people? Watch the video "Technology today" and circle *True* or *False*. Then correct the false sentences. Check your answers with a partner.

1. Reda knows a lot about electronics. True / False
2. Kevin likes his laptop because it's portable. True / False
3. Alejandra thinks instant messenger is affordable and fun. True / False
4. Denise uses her cell phone to stay in touch with her family. True / False
5. Jackie likes to search the Web and download music. True / False
6. Catherine usually phones her friends in New York. True / False
7. Dave sometimes uses his computer to write papers on the train. True / False
8. Julianna uses her computer to surf the Internet and do homework. True / False
9. Jonathan's computer is old and reliable. True / False

B Now watch the video again and circle the answers. Compare your answers with a partner's.

1. Reda thinks that cell phones with cameras / Internet access are very cool.
2. Kevin likes his laptop because it's very fast / thin.
3. Alejandra's favorite feature on her computer is the instant messenger / webcam.
4. Denise stays in touch with her friends / family in Brazil with instant messenger.
5. Jackie uses the computer for downloading pictures / music.
6. Catherine sends a lot of e-mails / text messages to her friends.
7. Dave thinks that his laptop / MP3 player is fun.
8. Julianna's computer was expensive / inexpensive.
9. Jonathan doesn't like his computer because it's slow / old and unreliable.

C Class activity. What kind of computer habits do your classmates have? Interview five classmates. Mark the correct column in the chart for each answer. Total the number of marks in each square and report the results to the class.

How often do you use a computer to . . .	once a day or more	once a week	once a month	hardly ever
check and send e-mail?				
surf the Web?				
write papers or do homework?				
play computer games?				
download music?				
watch videos?				
shop online?				
chat with friends?				

12 World Link 2 Video Worksheet

1 Good Morning World | Show on the road

Name: ____________________

Date: ____________________

A Watch the video and check (✓) *Yes* or *No*. Then compare your answers with a partner's.

	Yes	No
1. Did Kim turn off the lights this morning?	❑	❑
2. Did Jay empty the trash?	❑	❑
3. Did Kim unplug all of her electrical items?	❑	❑
4. Did Kim give away her fresh foods?	❑	❑
5. Did Kim give her apartment keys to her sister?	❑	❑
6. Did Jay put his dog in a kennel?	❑	❑
7. Is Jay's mother going to water his plants?	❑	❑
8. Has Jay ever been to Jamaica?	❑	❑
9. Has Jay ever been to India?	❑	❑
10. Did Jay forget to confirm that his passport is still good?	❑	❑

B What do they say? Watch the video and circle the words you hear. Then check your answers with a partner.

1. Jay: "I've / You've got to be excited about this trip!"
2. Jay: "Well, let's not think about carry-on luggage / boarding passes and overhead compartments . . . "
3. Kim: "Did you remember / forget to empty the trash?"
4. Kim: "Uh-oh. I remembered / forgot to do that."
5. Jay: "Precious? In a kennel / carry-on?"
6. Kim: "Have you ever been / travelled to Jamaica?"
7. Jay: "But I have travelled all over the world and I've visited / seen many beautiful places."
8. Kim: "I've / You've been to Egypt . . . Italy . . . Morocco . . . India . . . Argentina . . . "
9. Kim: "Jay Jones remembered / forgot to confirm that his passport is still good."
10. Jay: "I asked Mother / Precious to do this for me!"

C Class activity. Go around the class. Ask questions and complete the chart. Check off if each classmate *has* or *hasn't* done the items listed. Then report your information to the class.

Have you ever . . . ?	Name	Yes, he/she has.	No, he/she hasn't.
been to Jamaica	____________	❑	❑
written a poem	____________	❑	❑
forgotten your keys	____________	❑	❑
put a pet in a kennel	____________	❑	❑
flown on a plane	____________	❑	❑
been on television	____________	❑	❑
won a contest	____________	❑	❑
solved a mystery	____________	❑	❑

12 World Link 2 Video Worksheet

2 City Living | Mexico – here we come!

Name: ____________________

Date: ____________________

A **What are the three most important things to take on a vacation to a warm place? How about a cold place? Make lists for each and explain your choices to the class.**

Things to take on vacation to a warm place	Things to take on vacation to a cold place
1.	**1.**
2.	**2.**
3.	**3.**

B **What happens? Watch the video. Number the events in order from 1 to 8. Then retell the story to a partner. Include any details you can remember.**

________ Tara starts looking for her wallet.

____1____ Tara runs through the room looking for her bag.

________ Mike reminds Sun-hee to unplug the electrical appliances.

________ Sun-hee goes back into the apartment to get her ticket and traveler's checks.

________ Claudia runs through the room looking for her ticket.

________ Sun-hee ends her phone call with Mike.

________ Claudia, Tara, and Sun-hee leave the apartment.

________ Claudia starts looking for her cell phone.

C **What kind of traveler are you? Talk about travel with a partner. Ask and answer questions like the ones below. Then share your information with the class.**

How often do you travel?

____

What do you like to do when you travel?

____

Where do you usually go? Why?

____

How do you like to travel? By car? By train? By plane?

____

What things do you do before you go?

____

What do you usually take with you?

____

12 World Link 2 Video Worksheet

3 Global Viewpoints | Travel

Name: ____________________

Date: ____________________

A What do these people do before going on a trip? Watch the video "Travel" and check (✓) the things each person does. Then compare your answers with a partner's.

	Dave	Alejandra	Thales
confirm plans	❑	❑	❑
empty trash	❑	❑	❑
give out key(s)	❑	❑	❑
pay bills	❑	❑	❑
request meal(s)	❑	❑	❑
turn off items	❑	❑	❑
water plant(s)	❑	❑	❑

B Watch the video again. Check (✓) the sentences that are true. Then work with a partner to correct the false sentences. Discuss any details you can remember.

1. ____________ Before going on a trip, Dave gives a house key to a friend.
2. ____________ Before leaving on a trip. Alejandra requests a vegetarian meal.
3. ____________ Thales gives his keys to his brother when he goes on a long trip.
4. ____________ Julianna's story happened when she came to the U.S. by herself.
5. ____________ Julianna didn't speak English, so she used an interpreter to communicate.
6. ____________ Catherine's story happened on her first trip to Tanzania.
7. ____________ Catherine traveled in a helicopter.
8. ____________ Catherine had a detailed travel plan.
9. ____________ Dennis's story happened when he was a passenger on an airplane.
10. ____________ Dennis's co-worker lost her balance and accidentally moved a man's toupee.

C Group work. Think about an interesting travel experience. Write details from your experience in the boxes below. Then describe your experience to the group and answer any questions they have.

When did it happen?	Where were you?	Who was with you?	What happened?

Unit 1

Good Morning World – You, Adrian

Jay: Good Morning World! Thank you for joining us this morning! We are your hosts, Jay Jones . . .

Kim: . . . and Kim Kimal! How are you doing, Jay?

Jay: Well, I'm confused, Kim. Who were you talking to before the show? Do we have a new co-worker?

Kim: A new co-worker? No, we don't. Wait, are you talking about the woman with blonde hair? Jay! That's Adrian, our intern. You always forget who she is.

Jay: Adrian? Really? I thought the intern's name was Allison.

Kim: We have to do something about this. Adrian, can you come out here please? *(Adrian enters)* Ladies and gentlemen—and Jay—I'd like you to meet our intern at Good Morning World, Adrian!

Adrian: Hi, everyone. It's nice to meet you.

Kim: Adrian, Jay would like to get to know you. What can you tell him?

Adrian: Well, I am a student. I work here during the day and attend classes at night.

Jay: You work all day and then go to school? Why are you doing both?

Adrian: My job here is part of my education. It's like I'm taking a class.

Jay: That makes me your teacher. Are you learning a lot from me?

Kim: I think she's learning a lot *about* you.

Adrian: This is a great experience. I want to be a news reporter, so working here is going to help me after college.

Jay: *If* you get a good grade from me.

Kim: Oh, Jay. She doesn't get a grade. When you're an intern, you either pass or fail. And don't worry, Adrian. You are going to pass.

Jay: What else do you do?

Adrian: I have soccer practice twice a week. I tutor high school students on the weekends. And I study a lot.

Jay: Adrian, Adrian. You don't have to study a lot to be on television. I know.

Adrian: Well, I want to get good grades. It helps to study with people. In fact, Rashid is in my study group.

Jay: Really? So you and Rashid go to school together?

Adrian: Yes. Before Good Morning World, we were just acquaintances. But now that we work together, we're friends. I'm actually—

Jay: Friends? Ah-ha! I know what *that* means.

Kim: What are you talking about, Jay?

Jay: Come on, Kim. Friends? Adrian is dating Rashid!

Adrian: No! Rashid and I are just friends! I was going to say that I'm close friends with his girlfriend!

Kim: Jay, I think you failed the "get to know Adrian" exam.

City Living – A favorite keepsake

Sun-hee: Hey. What are you doing?

Tara: I'm getting ready for my blind date.

Sun-hee: A blind date? You don't know this man?

Tara: No, but he's a friend of Claudia's, so it should be OK.

Sun-hee: Oh. So where did she meet him?

Tara: They met at work. He's a colleague of hers. He's from Brazil too, but he's working in the U.S. office right now.

Sun-hee: Are you excited?

Tara: Excited and a little nervous! What jewelry should I wear?

Sun-hee: I don't know. Hey, what's that? That's nice.

Tara: This? Oh, this is a bracelet my first boyfriend, Joe, gave me. Isn't it beautiful?

Sun-hee: Yeah.

Tara: We were so in love. Too bad we were only 17. Too young.

Sun-hee: What's this?

Tara: That? Oh, that's a souvenir from my first trip to the U.S. I was five years old.

Sun-hee: Why are you still hanging on to it?

Tara: Oh, I'm keeping it for the memories.

Sun-hee: How about this?

Tara: Now that is my favorite keepsake. It's a pendant from my grandmother. She gave it to me when I was 18 years old.

Sun-hee: For your birthday?

Tara: No. I was in my first year of college and things were rough. I had no friends. I hated my classes. I didn't think I could make it. And one day, my grandmother told me a story.

Sun-hee: Yeah?

Tara: My grandmother's father died when she was only eight years old. Things were hard for her family after that. She went to school, she helped out at home, and she had a job.

Sun-hee: She was just a little girl!

Tara: I know. She worked really hard throughout her whole childhood. So when my grandmother turned 18, her mother gave her this pendant to say thank you.

Sun-hee: That was nice.

Tara: Yeah, so when life was difficult for me in college, my grandmother gave me the pendant as a reminder to be strong.

Sun-hee: That's beautiful. And it's perfect for tonight.

Tara: You know, you're right. Here goes.

Global Viewpoints – Special people

Alex: The most important people in my life are my mother, my father, my two sisters, and my brother.

Alejandra: My grandmother is a very important to me. Her name is Ester, and she is 80 years old.

Kumiko: The special person in my family is my grandfather, because he's always kind to me and supportive.

Calum: My friends are important to me because I like to go out with them and I can talk to them about most things. I think the three most important people in my life are my friends Tony, Dan, and David.

Memories

Catherine: Memories are very important to me. I have a shoe box where I put all the letters and pictures. And all the little things that I've collected for the past years. And, um. . . I have it in the shoe box.

Agnes: My favorite memory is my visit to my grandfather. He was a very old and wise man, and he told me a lot of interesting stories.

Calum: One of my happiest memories is when I was a child, and I went outside Scotland for the first time. I went to an amusement park in France, and I had a very good time there with my family.

Julianna: One of the happiest memories from my childhood was my first day of school. I was really excited, and the thing I wanted the most was to learn how to read.

Unit 2

Good Morning World – Fit to be fit

Jay: Good morning! It is Health Week on Good Morning World. All week we talk about how to have a healthier lifestyle. And to start it right, Kim and I went running before the show together! Kim, how do you feel? Kim?

Kim: Jay! How did you get here so fast? I can't believe you do this every morning. This was the worst idea ever.

Jay: You want healthier habits, right? It's going to be easier tomorrow.

Kim: You mean I have to do this again?

Jay: Why don't we sit down?

Kim: I'm glad we're doing Health Week, Jay. But really, I'm very healthy. I play a lot of sports.

Jay: Yes, I know you have an active lifestyle. But you also need a balanced diet. Breakfast is the most important meal of the day. Let's talk about how to eat a healthy breakfast.

Kim: Breakfast? Did you say breakfast? *(Rashid brings a tray of food)* No eggs? No toast with butter? No cookies?

Jay: You eat cookies for breakfast?

Kim: You don't?

Jay: For a balanced diet, you need to eliminate sweet foods like cookies and cut back on fried foods like eggs. How about eating some grapes?

Kim: Fine with me. I'm hungry! *(Kim eats a grape)* Mmm, they're juicy, they're sweet. . . Delicious! Cookies are sweeter and more delicious, though.

Jay: Grapes have greater health benefits than cookies.

Kim: These grapes are good. But I usually eat a lot more for breakfast.

Jay: Let's try some cereal.

Kim: Great idea! I never eat cereal for breakfast. *(takes a bite)* Mmm. It's crunchy. It tastes like a cookie!

Jay: Enough with cookies. We eliminated cookies from breakfast.

Kim: Sorry. Mmm. This is delicious too!

Jay: Cereal with milk is very nutritious. It has plenty of vitamins for a balanced diet. And also. . . Kim, you have to eat slower! You're going to get—

Kim: I don't feel very well.

Jay: —sick.

Kim: Umm. Excuse me a minute.

Jay: I notice that Kim is running much faster now.

City Living – The spicier the better

Mike: Let's add the grits! It'll make our plate look better.

Roberto: Hey, do you do takeout?

Mike: This isn't fast food! This is old-fashioned Southern home cooking!

Roberto: This looks delicious. Mmm. . . crispy!

Mike: Not too oily?

Roberto: No. And it's really juicy.

Takeshi: Not too spicy?

Roberto: Well, in my opinion, the spicier the better. Hey, how about some more hot sauce?

Mike: Yeah! My cousin is from down South. He lives in Louisiana, and man! The food down there is spicy. It's what you call Cajun cooking. Whoo! Is it hot!

Takeshi: I don't know.

Mike: Oh, come on Takeshi. Just a little.

Roberto: Look!

Takeshi: Oh my gosh! It's Chef Jackson Dupree!

Chef Dupree: All right, step away from your dishes. The taste testing is starting. No more cooking!

Roberto: Too late.

Chef Dupree: *(to first contestant)* Buttery. Not bad. Not bad at all. Quite tasty. *(to second contestant)* This is the oiliest chicken I have ever tasted! *(to Mike and Takeshi while tasting fried tomatoes)* Hmm. . . very good! A little sweet, but still crunchy. *(tastes grits)* Delicious! Try some chicken. Whoo! Now that's some good chicken! Hot and spicy, just like Mama's. You know, I'm an old Cajun boy myself.

Mike: You're from Louisiana?

Chef Dupree: Born and raised. And you two, you are the winners!

Roberto: I told you. The spicier, the better!

Global Viewpoints – Favorite foods

Brad: My favorite food is jambalaya, which is a Cajun food from New Orleans. Jambalaya contains chicken, beans, and rice.

Dennis: I like spicy food, and I like my vegetables really crispy. I don't want them overcooked or soggy.

Dayanne: My favorite food is rice and beans. And why do I like rice and beans? I'm Brazilian! Rice and beans are very healthy for you, but I don't like them if they are too salty or too buttery.

Thales: My favorite food is chicken. . . is grilled chicken, because it's healthy. It has less oil than other foods.

Dan: There's nothing better than a big, juicy steak.

Julianna: I do not like to eat greasy or buttery food, like bacon for example.

Alejandra: I do not like oily foods, but I do like sweet ones, like chocolate.

International foods

Catherine: I like this restaurant called Trident Café. They serve typical American food—pizza, hamburgers, French fries. My favorite dish from the restaurant is their hamburgers.

Dave: My favorite Mexican food is *chilaquiles*, which is fried pieces of tortilla with salsa. *Chilaquiles* are very spicy, and I love that.

Lourdes: I think the most popular food in Colombia is rice, and we make rice—or *arroz en espanol*—in all kinds of ways. We mix it with meat, we mix it with fish, we mix it with beans, vegetables. We make it as a dessert also with milk and sugar. You name it, we'll make rice any way possible. And we'll eat it at least twice a day.

Woo Sung: My favorite food is a Korean dish called *yukkae-jang*. It's a spicy soup with chunks of beef and vegetables. It's delicious. I love it, and I eat it once a week.

Unit 3

Good Morning World – Sister, meet sister

Kim: Welcome back! We have an amazing story for you today.

Jay: You said it, Kim. Two sisters separated as children and reunited as adults. You aren't going to believe how it happened. Fortunately, I came prepared. *(pulls out box of tissues)*

Kim: What are these for?

Jay: You might need them. I know how stories like this make you cry.

Kim: I'm not going to cry, Jay! This is a happy story.

Jay: You cry at weddings. Weddings are happy.

Kim: Everyone cries at weddings!

Jay: I don't. I think the last time I cried was the day I was born.

Kim: I doubt that. Everyone please welcome Maria and Marla Lopez! Thanks so much for joining us today! Now tell me, how do two sisters get separated for more than 30 years?

Maria: It happened by accident. Our parents died when we were very young, and I went to live with our aunt and uncle.

Marla: Before I went to live with a new family, someone wrote my name as "Maria." So everyone thought there was just one of us.

Kim: And I bet no one figured out the truth.

Marla: Unfortunately, no. I tried to explain that my name was Marla and that Maria was my sister. They didn't investigate. But I always remembered I had a sister.

Kim: And Maria, did you know about Marla?

Maria: No, I was too young. Then, earlier this year, before our aunt died, she said to me, "Go and find your sister Marla."

Jay: Ooh, how mysterious!

Maria: It didn't make sense to me. I couldn't have a sister. I doubted that it was true, but I like a good mystery.

Jay: So do I! What did you do?

Maria: I took a chance and started to look for proof that I had an older sister named Marla Lopez.

Marla: And at the same time, I was trying to prove that I had a younger sister named Maria Lopez.

Maria: One day I went to the library to investigate our family history.

Marla: I went to the library the same day to do the same thing.

Maria: I saw Marla . . .

Marla: . . . and I saw Maria . . .

Maria: . . . and I knew . . .

Marla: . . . and I remembered . . .

Maria & Marla: . . . and we hugged.

Kim: Wow, what good luck! And now you're reunited after all these years! Jay, wasn't that an amazing story? Jay?

Jay: Yes, amazing. And so . . . beautiful!

City Living – Elementary, my dear Tara!

Roberto: Does anybody know why Tara asked us to come here today?

Takeshi: She said something about solving a crime and arresting a criminal.

Claudia: Arresting a criminal?

Tara: Yes, a criminal.

Takeshi: Hey Tara. Nice hat!

Tara: Someone in this room has committed a crime.

All: What? Come on. What are you talking about?

Tara: A theft. Someone ate Sun-hee's yogurt!

Sun-hee: Well, my yogurt is missing, but it's OK. It's only yogurt.

Tara: It starts with yogurt. Next time it's your cookies, your ice cream. Who knows where it will end?

Sun-hee: OK . . . OK. Go on.

Tara: It's very likely one of you did it because you all have a key to this apartment.

Takeshi: I only use my key for emergencies. And besides, you live here, you have a key. Maybe you took it.

Tara: I'm the detective. I didn't do it. Now, the thief worked calmly, quietly, and very neatly. Note the weapon. *(holds up spoon)* Clean and dry.

Roberto: I didn't do it. I have an alibi. I was out of town last week. Just got home last night.

Tara: I know you didn't do it, Roberto. I asked you to come here today because you are a friend of the thief—Claudia!

Claudia: What?

Tara: Confess! You're always too busy to go shopping! You didn't have any yogurt. You were hungry. It was late. You waited until everyone went to bed, and then you slowly entered the kitchen. You made sure no one was there. Then you carefully took this spoon and—very quietly—opened the refrigerator door and ate Sun-hee's yogurt!

Claudia: *(jokingly)* No! No! It's not true!

Mike: *(enters apartment using key)* Hey, everyone! *(to Tara while taking spoon and walking towards fridge)* Thanks. *(to all while eating yogurt)* Nice hat! What's up?

Global Viewpoints – Mysteries and strange events

Agnes: When I was visiting my grandfather in his village, I witnessed a very strange event. It wasn't raining, and the women of the village went to a special place to make the rain fall. And that night it rained.

Dave: There's a strange tale in Mexico about *La Llorona*, who is a woman who wanders the streets weeping for her dead sons. When there is a strong wind, they say you can hear *La Llorona*.

Catherine: In New Jersey, there's a "thing" or a "monster" called the Jersey Devil. They say it's very big and hairy, but also very sneaky and that it moves from tree to tree.

Lourdes: My favorite mysteries are about UFOs, which means "Unidentified Flying Objects." I'm not sure if the UFOs are real or if they are a hoax, but I would like to think that they are real.

Alejandra: One of the mysteries that I find interesting and has not been solved yet is the one of the Pyramids. How they made them. How they brought in those very heavy pieces of stone to build the Pyramids.

Calum: My advisor and my teacher told us that the dorm that we lived in was haunted. And one time, late at night, all the lights turned off suddenly. And it was very strange and quite scary.

Unit 4

Good Morning World – Passion for fashion

Kim: It's time to talk fashion. Jay, do you agree that it's expensive to be in style?

Jay: Do you think it's cheap to look this good?

Kim: Yes, Jay, you are very stylish. But maybe you don't have to pay so much for that look. That's why Isadora Vestiti joins us again on Good Morning World. She is going to talk about how you can get the look you want without spending a lot of money. Welcome back, Isadora!

Isadora: Thank you, Kim. You look wonderful in that outfit.

Kim: Oh, why thank you, Isadora!

Jay: Ahem.

Kim: Isadora, someone could pay thousands on designer clothes. But most people don't have that kind of money. There ought to be a better way.

Isadora: There is a better way, Kim. Some people make clothes that look designer but at nearly half the cost. These are the clothes you should buy.

Kim: That's great! So you can be stylish and save money.

Isadora: Yes, and no one knows the difference.

Jay: Oh, come on!

Kim: Jay?

Jay: Sorry, but I disagree. Anyone who knows fashion—like me—knows if clothes are designer or not.

Isadora: Well Jay, let's see how good you are. I have some clothes here. Some of them are expensive designer brands, and some of them are more affordable clothes. I am going to show you two items, and you tell me which one is designer.

Jay: No problem, Isadora.

Isadora: Let's call these ripped jeans "A" and these darker fitted jeans "B." Which pair is designer?

Kim: Ooh, that's a hard one.

Jay: Are you kidding me? Pair "B" are the designer jeans. I think I have them at home.

Isadora: Ooh, I'm sorry Jay. The correct answer is "A." These jeans are twice as expensive as the others.

Jay: What?!? Those jeans are ripped! They look sloppy!

Kim: Ripped and sloppy are in style, Jay.

Isadora: Let's try shirts. This one is "A." And this one is "B." Which shirt is designer?

Jay: Shirt "A," the sporty shirt.

Isadora: Sorry, Jay. Wrong again. The shirt that has a retro look is the designer brand.

Kim: It's true, Jay. All of the kids love retro.

Jay: Well I bet "the kids" don't know a designer tie when they see one.

Isadora: Um, Jay? About that tie . . .

City Living – You ought to get more exercise!

Mike: I told you, I don't like to go running.

Roberto: You ought to get more exercise, Mike. It's good for you. You know, I think there's a definite trend. More and more people are starting to exercise.

Mike: You're just saying that because you think I should exercise more. The majority of the people I know don't exercise.

Roberto: Well, in my opinion, I really think more people are exercising nowadays.

Mike: What makes you say that?

Roberto: Well, when I came to New York five years ago, almost no one in my office exercised. Then, a few years ago, some people started going to the gym. And now, I just read in my office newsletter that 28 percent of the people in my office go to the gym three or more times a week. That's almost one-third of the employees.

Mike: Just because some of the people in your office go to the gym doesn't make it a trend. Maybe 28 percent go, but that means that 72 percent don't.

Roberto: Not necessarily. There's more ways to get exercise than going to the gym.

Mike: Such as?

Roberto: Some people walk to work. Some people play golf. Some people jog in the park.

Mike: Yeah, that's true.

Roberto: Look around you. Don't you see all the people exercising?

Mike: How many of them are enjoying it? None!

Roberto: Oh come on, Mike. All of them are enjoying it.

Mike: Not all of them.

Roberto: Well, most of them.

Mike: Maybe some of them, but not this one. I'm exhausted. I think we ought to go home.

Roberto: Yes, I think we'd better. And we'd better get you something to drink, too.

Mike: Hey, you know what?

Roberto: What?

Mike: I think we should get some ice cream too.

Roberto: What?

Mike: Yeah! You know, I read somewhere that 33 percent of all famous athletes recommend eating ice cream after a heavy workout.

Roberto: Yeah, right.

Mike: No, I'm serious. I read it in a magazine!

Global Viewpoints – Family trends

Yelena: In Ukraine, people get married very early.

Lourdes: In Colombia, people usually marry in their late 20s.

Paula: In Brazil, people get married around 25. Usually husbands and wives both work.

Calvin: I guess in a traditional family—traditional Korean family—you know, it is usually the males who work. There are a lot of parents who both have full-time jobs.

Kumiko: In Japan nowadays, people usually get married around 30. Husbands and wives both work until they have babies. And the wife stays at home with her children.

Alejandra: Children in Argentina live with their parents until they get married. Usually both the husband and the wife work. But if they have children, then the wife stays at home to take care of the children.

Personal style

Dave: I really admire my sister's style because she's very independent.

Calum: One person whose fashion I admire is my friend Alex. He wears really nice clothes.

Dayanne: I have a friend that always wears cowboy boots to go to work. I think that she should wear something more stylish.

Dennis: The person I most admire is Robert Redford. I like the way he moves, the way he stands, the way he carries his clothes, his hair.

Woo Sung: I've had this hair for a while, and I think it's definitely time for a change. I need a haircut.

Dayanne: To improve my appearance, I should have a haircut and lose weight.

Calum: I think I could improve my appearance by wearing contact lenses instead of glasses.

Unit 5

Good Morning World – Where are you going?

Jay: Welcome back! We are outside the Good Morning World studios this morning, and we're asking people on the street what they are doing and where they are going.

Kim: I think we're making people pretty nervous, Jay. Everyone is going on the other side of the street.

Jay: Here comes someone. Excuse me? Would you mind talking to us for just a minute? Hi. What's your name?

Ana: I'm Ana. Uh, is this Good Morning World?

Jay: How did you know?

Ana: Because you're Kim Kimal! I'm a really big fan.

Kim: Aww, thanks Ana. Could we ask you some questions about what you're doing this morning?

Ana: Sure. I can take a break from my errands.

Kim: Oh, so you're running errands this morning. What did you get done so far?

Ana: Well, I took my sister to our parents' house, I mailed some letters, and I just went grocery shopping. Ugh. I don't really like grocery shopping.

Kim: Oh, I don't mind going grocery shopping. But cooking? No thanks. I like to eat, but I don't like to cook at all.

Ana: Well fortunately, I don't have to make dinner tonight. My husband is going to take me to La Belle Petite.

Kim: Oh, I really like that restaurant.

Ana: He'd better not forget to make a reservation. When I go home, I still have to do the dishes, do the laundry, and vacuum.

Kim: Jay? We're kind of in the middle of something right now.

Jay: *(on phone)* Hello, La Belle Petite? This is Jay Jones. I'd like to make a reservation for two tonight at 7:00. Yes, Ana and. . . *(to Ana)* what's your husband's name?

Ana: Uh, Paul.

Jay: *(back to phone)* Ana and Paul. That's perfect. Thanks. *(hangs up)* What? It takes weeks to get a reservation there. I know the owner.

Ana: Wow! Thank you, Jay! Oh! I'm sorry, I have to go. I'm running late for an appointment. Bye Jay, bye Kim!

Kim: Jay, that was very nice! Are you feeling OK?

Jay: Look, I can tell you what's going to happen. Poor Paul calls La Belle Petite, he can't make a reservation, he comes into the city to talk to the owner, he gets stuck in traffic, so he tries to get there on foot, probably has to run—

Paul: Excuse me. Can you help me please? I'm looking for the restaurant La Belle Petite. If I don't make a reservation there for tonight, my wife—

Jay: You must be Paul.

Paul: What? Yes. How did you—

Jay: Don't worry about a thing. And welcome to Good Morning World!

City Living – Claudia's errand service

Claudia: Hi. How are you feeling?

Roberto: Awful. But I have some errands I have to do today.

Claudia: I think you'd better stay home. I can do your errands for you. I'm never in your neighborhood. It'll be fun.

Roberto: Thanks.

Claudia: Claudia's Errand Service.

Roberto: OK. Could you get some groceries for me at the Food Mart on Fourth Street? There's a grocery list right over there.

Claudia: OK.

Roberto: And would you mind picking up my dry cleaning? It's at the cleaners next to the supermarket. Across the street from the park.

Claudia: Park. Got it. Groceries, dry cleaning. Anything else?

Roberto: Yes, would you mind picking up a movie for me?

Claudia: OK. Where?

Roberto: Just go to the video store on the corner of Fourth Street and Bowery.

Claudia: OK. What kind of movie?

Roberto: You decide.

Claudia: OK. Anything else?

Roberto: Nope. That's it.

Claudia: OK.

Roberto: Don't forget the grocery list!

Claudia: Got it. Be back in an hour.

Claudia: *(to self outside grocery store)* OK. Got the groceries. Next, the dry cleaning.

Clerk: Thank you. Here you go.

Claudia: Thank you.

Clerk: Have a great day.

Claudia: *(to self outside dry cleaner)* Last stop, video store. Ah, there it is.

Claudia: Hi.

Roberto: Hi. How did it go?

Claudia: No problem! Your neighborhood's really convenient. Everything's in one place. Your neighbors are really friendly.

Roberto: Yeah, it's nice here. Safe. Not too crowded. Close to public transportation—both subways and buses.

Claudia: Oh, speaking of . . . I'd better get going. I have a bus to catch.

Roberto: Hey, there is one more thing.

Claudia: What?

Roberto: Would you mind staying and watching the movie with me? I hate being alone when I'm sick.

Claudia: Well, I suppose. Since you're sick.

Roberto: You know what would be really nice? Some ice cream. Could you go . . .

Claudia: Don't push your luck!

Global Viewpoints – Running errands

Brad: On weekends, I run errands. I go down the street to the Laundromat to do my laundry. And after that, I go to the supermarket to get my food.

Alejandra: In Argentina, I usually go shopping around the neighborhood or I go to the bank or I go out to buy food, groceries. Also, I generally go to the dry cleaners and the pharmacy.

Calum: When I'm not in class, I run a lot of errands. For example, I usually go to the shops to buy groceries and food. I also have to go to the bank to pay bills, and I usually have to go to the post office as well to check for parcels and packages.

My neighborhood

Julianna: In Brazil, my neighborhood is very safe. I live close to restaurants, parks, and close to the beach. My house is very well-located.

Alejandra: My neighborhood in Buenos Aires is a residential neighborhood. It is close to shops, and I can walk to the shops. There are a lot of trees on the sidewalks. And it is quite safe.

Lourdes: There is a big school near my house. There is also a very nice park nearby. There are many cars that pass through the neighborhood, so we have a lot of traffic. Also, we have public transportation. We have two trains that pass by my house, so you really don't need a car if you don't want to use a car. It's very easy to get around taking public transportation.

Unit 6

Good Morning World – Apply yourself

Jay: Good morning and welcome back! Well, this will be a big weekend, won't it Kim?

Kim: It will be for one of us! Rashid, come on out here!

Rashid: Hi Jay and Kim. I thought we decided not to do this.

Jay: Relax, Rashid! You only graduate from college once!

Kim: That's right! Rashid's college graduation is tomorrow! *(Jay puts cap on Rashid's head)* Where did you get that?

Jay: It's mine from when I graduated. I wear it around the house sometimes to make me feel smarter. Not that I need any help.

Kim: Rashid, we are very excited for you. What are your plans after graduation?

Rashid: I don't know. Maybe I'll go to dinner with my family.

Kim: No, I don't mean in the near future. I'm talking about in a few months or next year. What are your ambitions for the future?

Rashid: Oh. Well, I'm going to apply to graduate school. If I get accepted, I'll start taking classes next fall.

Jay: More school?!? Why do you want to do that, Rashid? You just finished school!

Rashid: Yes, but I'll probably learn a lot more about the television business if I take more classes.

Jay: Oh please. Jay Jones can teach you everything there is to know about television. And you won't have to sit through another boring class.

Kim: Jay, maybe Rashid wants to stay in school.

Rashid: I do! Someday I want to produce my own television show. That means sooner or later I'm going to leave Good Morning World.

Jay: Leave?!? Ha! You won't leave! You get to work with the greatest host. . . greatest *co*-hosts in the business! Good Morning World *is* your future!

Kim: Rashid can make decisions about his own future, Jay. But it won't be the same without you here!

Jay: Good Morning World without Rashid? Who will hold my mirror for me before the show? Who will remember I like water and not coffee?

Kim: When is your application due?

Rashid: In a few weeks. I need a recommendation with my application.

Kim: No problem! I will write it for you!

Rashid: Great! Thanks!

Jay: I think you are making a bad decision, Rashid. I'm sorry, but I will not write a recommendation for you.

Rashid: That's OK, Jay. I only need one.

Kim: Look on the bright side, Jay. You are going to learn more about television too.

Jay: How is that?

Kim: You'll learn how to hold your own mirror and get your own water. Those are very important skills in the business.

City Living – The letter

Mike: Do you think he was accepted?

Sun-hee: I don't know.

Mike: Any news from Harvard?

Sun-hee: He was rejected. He also applied to the University of Southern California, and they didn't accept him either. It's too bad. He studied so hard in film school. And he got really good grades.

Mike: I know. And he researched all those schools, and applied for all those scholarships. I hope he gets in. Hey, do you know what he's going to do if he doesn't get into grad school?

Sun-hee: No, what?

Mike: He's going to hit the road.

Sun-hee: I don't understand. What do you mean?

Mike: He's going to buy a nice camera and travel around Europe taking photos for his brother's website.

Sun-hee: Now that would be an experience. But it'll be sad if he goes.

Mike: He'll get in. I just know it!

Sun-hee: Takeshi!

Takeshi: *(enters front door)* Hi!

Mike: There's a letter for you from the Columbia Graduate School.

Sun-hee: *(takes letter from Mike)* Uh, uh, uh! Now let's think about this for a moment. What are you going to do if you aren't accepted?

Takeshi: Well, like I said, I'm going to travel around Europe for a while. And then I'll apply to graduate school in a few years, and I will get in!

Mike: *(takes letter from Sun-hee)* What will you do if you are accepted?

Takeshi: Oh, that's easy. I'm going to become a film director.

Mike: *(gives letter to Takeshi)* All right then. Here. *(waits for Takeshi to open letter)* Well what are you waiting for? Open it!

Takeshi: Here goes. *(opens letter)*

Sun-hee: Well?

Mike: Were you accepted?

Takeshi: I'm going to grad school!

Global Viewpoints – After graduation

Agnes: After I finish my Ph.D., I would like to go back to Senegal and start my own business in agriculture.

Brad: After I graduate, I will move to Washington, D.C., to work for National Geographic.

Calum: After I graduate, I'd like to have a good job that pays a lot of money. And to travel and see the world.

Dave: After I graduate from college, I will go to graduate school, and I'm going to study art.

Alex: After graduation, I plan to find a good job. I also plan to start a family and buy a house.

Julianna: I want to start my own business. An import-export business.

Alejandra: My students work very hard and get good grades to get into university. After finishing their degrees in the United States, they will go home and either work with their families or open a business.

Five years from now . . .

Dave: Five years from now, I will still be studying. And I don't know where I'm going to live.

Calvin: I'd like to become a lawyer, and I'd like to specialize in cyberlaw. I think cyberlaw will be pretty big within five, six years or so.

Woo Sung: I'll probably be married. I want about three kids, a dog, my own house, and a job that I enjoy. And you know, most of all I just want to be. . . just I guess. . . enjoy my life.

Unit 7

Good Morning World – Party time

Kim: We want to thank Violet Braun again for coming on the show to talk about how to host a great party.

Jay: I'm so glad she was here, Kim. She gave me some good ideas for my celebration this weekend.

Kim: Celebration? Are you having a party?

Jay: Yes, Kim. Did you forget already? Oh, maybe I didn't invite you. Well, I'm inviting you now. You and Rashid both. It will be held this Saturday at Penn Park.

Kim: OK. What's the occasion?

Jay: It's a surprise.

Kim: A surprise? Is the party for someone? Or are people getting together just to have a good time?

Jay: It is for someone. And yes, everyone is going to have a great time. After all, I am the host.

Kim: So you are planning a party for someone, but it's a surprise. And one day before the party, you invite Rashid and me to participate in it.

Jay: Exactly. Do you want to come?

Kim: I'm . . . sorry, but I can't. I already have plans.

Rashid: So do I.

Jay: What's wrong with you two? Don't you like to have a good time?

Kim: Well Jay, before I go to a party, I like to know what I'm celebrating. It might be a surprise party, but I don't want to be surprised when I get there.

Rashid: Neither do I.

Jay: OK, you win. The party is for my best friend.

Kim: Oh. Well, that is a surprise. I didn't know you had a best friend.

Jay: Of course I do. We met five years ago, and that is what we are celebrating.

Kim: Aww, that's very nice, Jay! Friendship is a good thing to celebrate. Should Rashid and I get presents for you and your friend?

Jay: No, you don't have to get presents.

Kim: Can I bring a cake?

Jay: Mmm, you'd better not. My friend can't eat cake.

Kim: No presents. No cake. Jay, I'm very confused. Is there anything more you can tell us about this party?

Jay: Oh, yes. Before you come, put on a costume. Everyone will participate in a costume contest, and the best costume wins first prize.

Kim: A costume? Are you and your friend going to wear costumes too?

Jay: I am. My friend will choose the winner of the contest by barking at the best costume.

Kim: Barking? Wait a minute. Your dog! This is a party for your dog?

Jay: Now it's not a surprise party. I hope Precious isn't watching.

Kim: Um . . . I'm sorry, Jay, but I can't come. I don't have a costume for the party.

Rashid: Neither do I.

Jay: Too bad. I always win the contest.

City Living – Aloha everyone!

Tara: *(phone rings)* Hello?

Claudia: Aloha! Tara, it's me, Claudia.

Tara: Hi Claudia. What's up?

Claudia: A friend of mine invited me to a luau tonight. She told me to bring friends. Would you like to join us?

Tara: Sure! What's a luau?

Claudia: It's like a Hawaiian barbecue. You wear Hawaiian shirts, drink pineapple juice, dance. It's fun, you know.

Tara: Sounds great! I'd love to go.

Claudia: Great! Is Sun-hee there? I'd like to invite her as well.

Tara: She's right here. Let me ask her. Sun-hee, would you like to go a luau tonight?

Sun-hee: The Hawaiian kind? Yeah, I would. Um . . . wait. I can't. I promised Takeshi I'd help him with his film project tonight.

Tara: Well, bring him along. Claudia said it's OK to bring friends.

Sun-hee: OK. *(into phone)* Takeshi?

Takeshi: Yeah?

Sun-hee: Hey listen, after we work on your film project tonight, would you be interested in going to a party? It's a Hawaiian luau.

Takeshi: That sounds interesting. I'd love to! Can Mike come?

Sun-hee: Sure! Tara said to bring friends.

Takeshi: Great. I'll call him right away. See you tonight.

Mike: *(phone rings)* Hello?

Takeshi: Hey Mike.

Mike: Hi Takeshi. What's up?

Takeshi: How would you like to go to a Hawaiian party tonight?

Mike: Sure! Hey, why don't we invite Roberto too? He loves parties.

Takeshi: Yeah. Sun-hee said we could bring friends.

Mike: OK, great. I'll give him a call.

Roberto: *(phone rings)* Hello?

Mike: Hi Roberto, it's Mike. Would you like to go to a party tonight? It's going to be really fun!

Roberto: Ah, that sounds great, but I can't. I have to go to some "luau" tonight with Claudia. Maybe next time. Have fun!

Mike: OK.

Claudia: Who was that?

Roberto: That was Mike. He invited me to some party tonight.

Roberto & Claudia: No . . .

Global Viewpoints – What a party!

Alejandra: I went to a party where the whole dance floor and party space was covered with soapsuds. So everything was very soapy and somewhat slippery. People at this party were dressed in summer clothes, because it was during the summer, and in casual clothes. Things that would not get ruined by the soap.

Dennis: I had a birthday party last month, and I had 38 people in my small apartment. There was a lot of food, which I cooked. And I had a lot of presents. And all my friends were there. It was fun.

Festivals and holidays

Catherine: My favorite celebration or holiday is Thanksgiving. In America, families get together in one place and have a big, big, huge dinner. And it's actually just a day where you eat a lot and where you think about or you reflect about the things you are thankful for.

Lourdes: The most important holiday in Colombia is Independence Day, which in Spanish is *Día de la Independencia***.**

Kumiko: I like New Year's Day, because when I was little, I got lots of *otoshidama*, which is money in little pretty envelopes.

Alejandra: In Argentina, one of the unique festivals is the Day of Tradition, or *El Día de la Tradición,* where we celebrate our *gaucho* heritage. A *gaucho* is an Argentinean cowboy. People usually perform traditional dances, dress as *gauchos*, and have huge barbecues.

Unit 8

Good Morning World – A likely story

Jay: Hello everyone! Our next guest is—

Kim: Anthony Guinness!!! I can't believe he is here! I am *so* excited. How do I look?

Jay: Kim, would you like to tell everyone who this famous guest is?

Kim: Anthony Guinness is only the best author in the world! He wrote my favorite book, *A Rose for Charly*. Did you read it?

Jay: No! I don't read much.

Kim: Really? Why not?

Jay: I'm a very busy man, Kim. But also, books are predictable. They tell the same old story every time: the hero struggles bravely and then cleverly overcomes incredible odds. In the end, everyone lives happily ever after. Give me something realistic!

Kim: Well, Anthony Guinness is very real. Please give him a warm welcome!

Anthony: Hello Jay and Kim!

Kim: He knows my name!

Jay: Your new book is called *The Way It Was*. Tell us about it.

Kim: It is wonderful! It is written so well. I think it's even better than *The Flower House*, but this book has a happy ending—

Jay: Kim!

Kim: I'm sorry. Am I talking too fast?

Jay: No. Let's hear it from the man who wrote it, hmm?

Kim: Right. *(to Anthony)* I'm a big fan.

Anthony: Thanks, Kim. Well, *The Way It Was* is based on a true story. It begins in Peru. A boy is separated from his father in a crowded market. The father looks for him everywhere, but he can't find him.

Kim: It's unbelievable!

Anthony: So the boy begins a journey to find his father. He is uneducated, he can't speak the language, and he struggles to survive far from home.

Jay: See, Kim? Predictable.

Anthony: Later, he meets a man who teaches him how to survive. The boy follows the man through Peru. It turns out that while the boy was looking for his old father, he found a new one.

Jay: So the boy has to decide if he wants to struggle hard to find his old home or live simply in his new home.

Anthony: Very good, Jay. You can tell a story well.

Jay: So what happens? Does he eventually find his real father?

Anthony: Well, I don't want to tell you the ending. But I can tell you this: *Yo soy el niño.*

Kim: Anthony is the boy in the story!

Jay: You? No way! Wait. You said that in Spanish. That means you stayed in Peru!

Anthony: Did I? You'll have to read the book.

Kim: Ha! Jay is hooked! You said you wanted a realistic story!

Jay: Yes, I did. I just didn't want to have to read it.

City Living – Takeshi presents "Cinderella"

Takeshi: *(to camera)* Once upon a time, there was a kind and humble young woman named Cinderella.

Claudia: *(to camera)* I'm Cinderella. I'm kind and I'm humble. I was having fun until my two evil stepsisters moved in with me. Now my life is terrible.

Tara & Sun-hee: *to camera)* We're the evil stepsisters, and I'm determined to marry the prince.

Tara: I'm going to marry him!

Sun-hee: I'm going to marry him!

Tara: Well, you're too skinny.

Sun-hee: Humph. Please.

Tara: Oh, please. You smell!

Takeshi: *(voice-over)* Cinderella always worked hard while her stepsisters relaxed. Her stepsisters never did a thing.

Sun-hee: It's the prince's ball tonight.

Tara: Don't forget to wash my dress.

Sun-hee: And fix my shoes!

Takeshi: *(voice-over)* Poor Cinderella. She didn't know what to do. There she was, crying all alone, when the good fairy appeared before her.

Mike: *(to camera)* I'm the good and compassionate fairy. And I was enjoying my Sunday afternoon football game until Takeshi asked me to be in his movie.

Takeshi: Come on Mike! You said you'd help me with my film project.

Mike: OK . . . OK.

Claudia: Oh, good and generous and compassionate fairy! I want to go to the prince's ball tonight, but I have nothing to wear!

Mike: Fear not, Cinderella. You will see the brave and loyal prince tonight. But remember—you must be home by midnight!

Claudia: I promise, good fairy. And thank you.

Takeshi: *(voice-over)* And so, Cinderella went to the prince's ball, met the prince, and fell in love. But when she was rushing home just before midnight, she lost one of her slippers. The next day, Cinderella had a visitor.

Roberto: *(to camera)* I'm the brave and loyal prince. I'm looking for the woman who wore this slipper last night. *(to Claudia)* Would you please try on this slipper?

Takeshi: And so the prince saw that it was indeed Cinderella's slipper. And he knew that she was the princess he loved. And so they got married, and they . . . *(Claudia and Roberto leave)* and . . . they lived happily ever after.

Global Viewpoints – Favorite stories

Julianna: My favorite story is *Snow White and the Seven Dwarfs*. Snow White was a beautiful princess. A bad witch gave her a poisoned apple putting her to sleep for many years, until a handsome prince kissed her and brought her back to life. And then they lived happily ever after.

Reda: There is a story in Lithuania about the princess who marries a sea prince. But the family doesn't want her to go away with the prince. So they trick the princess, and they kill her husband. She turns herself, her sons, and her daughter into trees. And the castle where they lived bursts into little pieces of amber. This necklace that I have is made of amber.

Jackie: My favorite stories to tell are *kaeshin* stories, and *kaeshins* are Korean fables. And they're based on women who have long black hair, and they usually wear white. They haunt people in their dreams and kill them in real life. My favorite *kaeshin* fable is when a boy is going to the library to study, and he stays there for long periods at a time. And he sees a pretty girl sitting at a table in the back. When she's sitting at the table, she's resting her chin on both of her palms—like this—on the table. And he tells her to come forward, and she does, by moving like this *(crawls on her elbows)* because she has no legs or torso.

Unit 9

Good Morning World – Intern view

Kim: Thank you for being with us again this morning! Before we go, we want to take a moment to thank Adrian for all her work on Good Morning World.

Jay: I'm sorry. Who?

Kim: Adrian. Seriously, Jay? Our intern!

Jay: Oh yes, of course. And why are we thanking her?

Kim: Adrian is almost finished with her internship at Good Morning World. She has been a very pleasant and efficient part of our team, and we're going to miss her.

Jay: She's leaving? What will she do next?

Kim: Well, she's going to finish school and then look for her dream job. So Jay, I think we should try to help Adrian with a practice job interview!

Jay: Hmm. What a great idea!

Kim: Adrian, will you come out please?

Adrian: Hi Jay and Kim! Thanks for doing this. I have enjoyed working—

Jay: Very good, Adrian. Let's begin the practice job interview!

Adrian: Oh . . . um . . . OK.

Jay: Good morning, Adrian. Thanks for coming in today.

Adrian: My pleasure.

Jay: My name is Jay, and this is Kim. Tell us a little about yourself.

Adrian: Well, I'm a fourth-year university student, and I'm majoring in journalism. I will graduate from college next month.

Kim: Have you ever worked in television before?

Adrian: Yes, I have worked as an intern at Good Morning World since last fall.

Jay: Who is your favorite person there? Is it Jay? Isn't he really smart?

Kim: Jay, an interviewer won't ask those questions! *(to Adrian)* Was the job demanding?

Adrian: Yes, but in a good way. My experience there was very rewarding. I have learned to be flexible because working in television can be unpredictable.

Kim: How so?

Adrian: I work with a diverse group of people. Some of them like to teach me things about the business, and some of them . . . Well, let's just say I have learned that sometimes you have to work independently.

Jay: Independently, hmm? No, no. In television, you have to work as a team!

Adrian: I agree, Mr. Jones. You are very knowledgeable.

Jay: Well, I have worked in television for a long time. Now, do you have any questions for me?

Adrian: For Kim, actually. What is the most stressful thing about your job?

Kim: Being pleasant to your co-workers.

City Living – The big job interview

Ms. Li: Hi, I'm Yvonne Li. Welcome.

Claudia: Hi. Claudia Oliveira.

Ms. Li: Please, have a seat. Thanks very much for coming in. Did you bring your résumé?

Claudia: Yes. Here you are.

Ms. Li: Great, thanks. First, let me tell you a little bit about the job. We're looking for someone to sell our new software product internationally. The job requires flexibility, independence, and, most importantly, a pleasant manner with customers.

Claudia: I agree. That's important. I've worked in sales for years and have always tried to really listen to my customers to find out what they need. I think I'm really good at that.

Ms. Li: That's great. So, tell me a little bit about your experience with software programs.

Claudia: Well, I've trained people how to use a similar software product for the past two years at my current job. So I really feel I know the product and customer needs.

Ms. Li: Hmm. . . interesting. And your sales experience?

Claudia: I've been with my present company for three years and in my present position since last year. In that time, I've been named salesperson of the month three times and have taken top sales awards several times as well.

Ms. Li: Impressive.

Claudia: I'm also taking graduate courses right now in marketing. I feel it really helps me understand the market better, especially the competition.

Ms. Li: You've been very busy, Ms. Oliveira. Well, thanks very much for coming in. We'll be in touch.

Claudia: Thank you.

Ms. Li: Hey Bill, I just interviewed a woman for that software sales position.

Mr. Howard: How did it go?

Ms. Li: Very well.

Mr. Howard: Do you think she's right for the job?

Ms. Li: I think so. She has a high energy level and a lot of experience.

Mr. Howard: OK. Let's offer her the job.

Ms. Li: Great.

Tara: Hello?

Ms. Li: Hello. Claudia Oliveira, please.

Tara: She can't come to the phone right now. May I take a message?

Ms. Li: Yes, please. Tell her Yvonne Li called.

Tara: OK.

Claudia: *(enters from bedroom)* Come on. We're going to be late for our aerobics class.

Tara: Oh, by the way there was a phone call from some woman called Yvonne. . . Yvonne something. *(door closes)*

Claudia: *(opens door and runs for phone)* Ah!

Global Viewpoints – What do you do?

Natalie: I work for a television station that was launched ten years ago, and I have been working there for about a year.

Dan: I work with computers at a hospital, and I have doing that for three years.

Gian: I'm a marketing manager. I make brochures, I send out e-mails, and I work on the Web.

Dream jobs

Kumiko: I have two ideal jobs, and teaching Japanese is one of them. The other one is training dogs. I like working with dogs, because they give me unconditional love all the time.

Dave: My ideal job would be designing movie posters and CD covers. To do this job, I need a strong foundation in art, and it helps to be able to speak two languages.

Jackie: Teaching is an ideal job for me, because I enjoy being around children, and I want to help them learn.

Vanessa: My dream job is to be a photographer, because I love taking pictures.

Dayanne: I would like to help people in developing countries. In order to do this job well, you need to be passionate, you need to be able to listen, and you need to communicate.

Jonathan: My future plans are to get into computer animation and hopefully become an animator in movies or video games. To be a computer animator, you have to be patient, work hard, and be creative.

Calum: My ideal job would be a reporter, or to work for a newspaper. And that way I could see the world and also keep up-to-date with events. For my job, you should be able to write well, and you should be well-informed, and you should be able to communicate well.

Unit 10

Good Morning World – Hello hangups

Kim: Good Morning World! Our next guest stars in a TV show about her life called "The Famous One." You have seen her picture in magazines everywhere. Please welcome Erica Allendez!

Erica: *(on phone)* Are you serious? That's so funny! You tell her I'll be there. She doesn't need to worry. . .

Kim: Um, hi. Erica?

Erica: Hey, I'll have to call you back. Yeah. I have a thing. OK. Buh-bye! *(hangs up)* Sorry, it was my friend Renee. I love talking to her. She is so funny!

Jay: Well, you must be very busy. We're glad you took the time to—

Erica: Ooh, I'm getting a call from my agent. Do you mind if I answer it? I'll be on the phone for just a second.

Kim: Sorry, but we—

Erica: *(answers phone)* Felicia, hi! No *you're* the best! Mmm-hmm. He didn't! He did? Right. We need to talk about this at lunch. Mmm-hmm. No, I hate eating there. No one takes my picture.

Jay: Erica, I'm sorry to interrupt, but we have viewers waiting. Do you mind hanging up the phone?

Erica: *(on phone)* Hey Felicia, I have to go. Remember Good Morning World? Yeah. Call my assistant and leave a message for me. Right. *(hangs up)* Sorry. My agent. She can be so rude sometimes. Now, what were we talking about?

Kim: We weren't, actually.

Jay: Kim means we wanted to talk about your show. What—

Erica: Aww. I just got a text message from my boyfriend. He is so sweet! I. . . *(Kim glares)* will respond to him later. Now, as I was saying about my show, I love having cameras in my house to record every moment of my life. The other day I—

Jay: You could turn off your phone.

Kim: Or ignore the call.

Erica: Hmm. I don't know this caller. Maybe it's a wrong number. It's always important to screen your calls. *(answers phone)* Hello, Erica Allendez. Who's calling? I did? I got the part? I got it?!? Hang on a minute. *(to Jay and Kim)* I got the part!!! *(on phone)* Yes! I'm so excited!!! Oh yes, I will. But I don't want to work with Nicole. She's impossible! Mmm-hmm. *(exits)*

Kim: Can you believe that?!?

Jay: Kim, lower your voice. It's not easy being famous. I know.

City Living – I can't stand cell phones!

Woman 1: *(talking loudly on cell phone)* No! No, no, no. . . Go. . . The taxi line. Find the taxi line. There's one just outside.

Woman 2: It's right outside.

Woman 1: It's right outside. . . No! It's right outside of the airport. Go inside and ask someone, OK? All right. We'll see you soon. Twenty minutes or so. OK. Bye.

Roberto: I can't stand cell phones. Why do people use them so often—especially in public places?

Mike: I know. I only use my cell phone when I need it. I find it to be a form of noise pollution. *(Mike's phone rings)*

Roberto: See what I mean?

Mike: *(into phone)* Hello?

Mr. Johnson: Hi Mike!

Mike: Hi Dad! How's it going?

Mr. Johnson: Oh, great. Listen, son, I just got a new cell phone, and I called to give you the number.

Mike: Oh, you just need to give me your new number.

Mr. Johnson: Yeah. You know, I really love these cell phones. They're so convenient. Your mother's addicted to hers. She's on it all the time.

Mike: Uh. . . Dad? The number?

Mr. Johnson: Oh, I'm sorry. I almost forgot. Here it is. The new area code is 651. . .

Mike: Did you say 691?

Mr. Johnson: No, no. 651. 5. 5. "F," like in "Frank."

Mike: Got it.

Mr. Johnson: And the telephone number is 555-2324.

Mike: *(phone beeps)* Dad? Can you hold on a minute? Mom's calling on the other line. *(into phone to mom)* Hello?

Mrs. Johnson: Hi sweetheart! It's your mom.

Mike: Hi Mom. I'm on the other line with Dad.

Mrs. Johnson: Oh that's nice, dear. I need to talk to him too. I'm planning our trip to New York. I'd prefer to come in September, but your father wants to come during the holidays. Now you tell him—

Mike: Wait a minute, I can't stand sending messages. Can you hold on a second? I'm going to try to connect you two. *(into phone to both mom and dad)* Hello? Is everybody here?

Mr. Johnson: Yeah, I'm here. Oh, this is what I call a family reunion.

Mike: Yeah!

Woman: Shh! Do you mind? I can't stand cell phones. Especially in public places.

Global Viewpoints – Cell phones

Catherine: I think these days you can't live without a cell phone.

Brad: I always have my cell phone with me so I can call my friends. I also can browse the Internet and download music.

Jackie: My cell phone has a camera on it. It's very useful when I don't have a camera with me. And if there's something funny happening, then I can take a picture.

Dayanne: I think that sometimes cell phones are unnecessary. However, they're very good for business.

Alex: What I like about cell phones is you can contact anybody you want any time you want.

Calvin: I feel like I lost some privacy because of cell phones.

Lourdes: I don't like cell phones that much. They're necessary, and they're very useful in emergencies. But in general, I think that they're not a good thing.

Dennis: I like cell phones because they connect you with people. Wherever you are people can reach you. What I don't like about cell phones is when they ring at the most unexpected times.

Alejandra: I like cell phones, because they allow me to call people when I'm running late and let them know that I'm running late. I don't like when cell phones ring in theaters, or movie theaters, or important talks, or even in the classroom. That's—I think—a lack of respect, so that's when I hate cell phones.

Unit 11

Good Morning World – Okay computers

Jay: It's Technology Week here on Good Morning World, and today we are talking about computers. Now some people think computers are a new technology, but in fact they have been used for a long time.

Kim: It's true, Jay. Computers are as old as you are!

Jay: Maybe. But they don't look as good as I do.

Kim: I don't know. Some computers these days are very attractive. Here, look at this. I brought my laptop with me today.

Jay: Hey, look at that. It fits on top of your lap.

Kim: Yes Jay, that's why they call it a laptop. So what do you think?

Jay: Well, it does look portable, and that makes it convenient to use. But is it durable?

Kim: Hmm. I think so. It looks strong. But I don't plan to drop it.

Jay: Kim, you drop everything. How many coffee mugs have you broken?

Kim: Only four! Fourteen. I used to be more careful. But look, even if this computer is not durable, that's OK—I can buy a new one! Laptops are very affordable.

Jay: Kim, Kim, Kim.

Kim: What?

Jay: A lot of people think computers are disposable, but actually they should be recycled.

Kim: But technology changes. Computers transform and become better, more convenient. Old computers are not as practical as new ones.

Jay: Kim always tells everyone that new things are better than old things, but in fact, old things are much more reliable. And now I will prove it. Rashid! My computer please! *(Rashid rolls computer on set)*

Kim: That's your computer? It's as big as a house! I think my parents used to have a computer like that 30 years ago.

Jay: But look, Kim. It's affordable. It's durable. It's portable.

Kim: Portable? It's on wheels! How did you get it here this morning. On your bike?

Jay: OK, that was a bit of a struggle. But I tell you, Kim. This is the best computer you can own.

Kim: No thank you, Jay. I am very happy with my new, attractive, convenient, dur—

Jay: Oh, Kim. Well, I guess that's a good way to see how durable it is. Do you want to prevent that from happening again? Use a computer that can*not* fit on top of your lap.

City Living – The first word processor

Mrs. Morgan: Good. So change the first part and make those corrections, and your paper will be great.

Tara: OK. Thanks for all your help, Professor Morgan. I'll e-mail my paper to you later today.

Mrs. Morgan: You know, technology is amazing. In high school, I used to write my term papers on a typewriter.

Tara: It must have taken a long time to write a paper on a typewriter.

Mrs. Morgan: Well, I was pretty fast, but I made some mistakes. Actually, the typewriters weren't that bad. Now, as for the first computers . . . Oh my gosh!

Tara: What do you mean?

Mrs. Morgan: The first computers were so unreliable. They used to crash all the time. And they were not as affordable or as fast as they are now.

Tara: Mine's pretty fast, but not as fast as some of the newer, more expensive ones.

Mrs. Morgan: I know! And nowadays, almost everyone has a computer. In those days, nobody had their own computer. We used to use the ones at the university.

Tara: In the computer lab?

Mrs. Morgan: Yeah, that's all we had. I'll never forget, one spring, during final exams. Everybody was working on their term papers, and the electricity went out!

Tara: So? No big deal. Laptops have batteries.

Mrs. Morgan: Yes, but remember, in those days we didn't have laptops. If your computer crashed, you lost everything.

Tara: Everything?

Mrs. Morgan: Everything. We used to lose information all the time. But that time it was terrible. Everybody lost their papers that afternoon. Including me.

Tara: What did you do?

Mrs. Morgan: I went back to the good old-fashioned way.

Tara: You mean typewriters?

Mrs. Morgan: Nope. I used something more affordable, portable, reliable, disposable—something that always worked.

Tara: What was that?

Mrs. Morgan: *(holds up pencil and paper)* The first word processor.

Global Viewpoints – Technology today

Reda: I really don't know a lot about electronics, but I think that new phones—new cell phones—with, ah, cameras, which have digital cameras, are very cool. And they're so easy to use. And you don't have to think all the time that you forgot the camera, you know? Because you always have it with you, and that's so smart.

Kevin: I like the laptop, because it's very, very thin. It's maybe less than one inch. It's about four pounds, and I can carry it anywhere I want.

Alejandra: My favorite feature of my computer is the instant messenger. The reason for this is that it's very affordable, fun, and convenient and allows me to chat with my friends from all over the world.

Denise: I stay in touch with my family in Brazil with, like, instant messenger.

Jackie: I use the computer for chatting online, searching the Web, and downloading music.

Catherine: I have a lot of friends in New York and Philadelphia and California. So instead of talking on the phone with them, I e-mail them constantly.

Dave: My laptop computer is fun, because I can do all sorts of things on it. I can write a paper while I'm on the train on the way home.

Julianna: I use my computer to surf on the Internet, to do my homework, and to work. My computer was expensive, but it is reliable.

Jonathan: I don't really like my computer, because it's old and not reliable.

Unit 12

Good Morning World – Show on the road

Jay: Good morning everyone! We have a little time left before we say goodbye. The next time you see us, Good Morning World will be coming to you from sunny Jamaica! Now Kim, I know you don't like to fly. But we are going to your old home! You've got to be excited about this trip!

Kim: Yes, Jay. I'm trying to be.

Jay: Well, let's not think about carry-on luggage and overhead compartments and oxygen masks and a heavy plane flying thousands of meters in the air over water. How about trip preparations! Let's make sure we remembered to do everything.

Kim: Good idea.

Jay: Before you left this morning, did you turn off the lights?

Kim: Yes I did. The lights are off. Did you remember to empty the trash?

Jay: No. But I've never had to empty the trash. That's Mother's job. Let's see, did you unplug all of your electrical items?

Kim: Yes I did. I even unplugged the refrigerator!

Jay: Good! But I hope you gave away your fresh foods.

Kim: Uh-oh. I forgot to do that. I gave my apartment keys to my sister. I'll have to call her. I hate to see good food go bad!

Jay: I bet you do.

Kim: Did you remember to put your dog in a kennel?

Jay: Precious? In a kennel? No, no, no. Mother will take care of Precious.

Kim: Is your mother going to do everything for you?

Jay: Of course not! She only has to watch the dog, water the plants, pay the bills, and open my fan mail. That's all! She's going to have a great time while I'm gone!

Kim: Well thank you, Jay. I don't feel so nervous now. I am getting excited! Jamaica is a beautiful place, and the people are very friendly. Have you ever been to Jamaica?

Jay: No, I've never been there. But I have travelled all over the world, and I've seen many beautiful places. I travel so often that the flight attendants know my name.

Kim: Probably because you always tell them.

Jay: Yes, this passport is like a book about the adventures of Jay Jones. *(hands passport to Kim)* Here Kim. Would you like to read it?

Kim: Not really. *(takes passport)* Wow. You've been to Egypt . . . Italy . . . Morocco . . . India . . . Argentina . . . I guess you really were telling the truth.

Jay: I don't make up stories. I live them.

Kim: Uh, Jay? Here's a story for you: "Jay Jones forgot to confirm that his passport is still good."

Jay: What?!?

Kim: The date has passed. You can't use this passport anymore.

Jay: No! It can't be! I asked Mother to do this for me!

Kim: Well, your mother will be very happy you're staying home. Don't worry; I'll tell the flight attendants that Jay Jones says "Hi." You know, suddenly I'm really looking forward to this trip!

City Living – Mexico—here we come!

Sun-hee: This is going to be a great trip! I've never been to Mexico. Have you?

Mike: No, I haven't. Have you finished everything?

Tara: Oh my gosh! Where's my bag?

Sun-hee: *(to Tara)* It's in the closet. *(into phone)* Of course! I'm the only one who's organized around here. I ran errands all day, and I'm ready. Exhausted, but ready.

Mike: What did you have to do?

Sun-hee: *(holds up ticket)* Well, first I had to confirm my flight.

Claudia: My ticket! Where's my ticket? Have you seen it?

Sun-hee: *(to Claudia)* I saw it in the bathroom.

Claudia: The bathroom? Are you sure? So strange. *(holds up her ticket)* Oh, you're right. Got it!

Sun-hee: *(holds up traveler's checks)* Then I had to get traveler's checks.

Tara: Oh! My money! I've lost my wallet! *(Sun-hee hands Tara her wallet)* Whew!

Sun-hee: *(into phone)* Then I had to pay the electricity and the phone bills, *(to Tara)* because someone forgot. *(into phone)* And then I had to change my voice-mail message.

Claudia: My cell phone! I don't remember where I put my cell phone!

Sun-hee: *(to Claudia)* It's in the kitchen.

Claudia: *(to self)* The kitchen. It's in the kitchen. *(holds up cell phone)* Ta-dah!

Sun-hee: *(into phone)* These two—they're never prepared! What would they do without me?

Mike: How true. Hey, don't forget to unplug your TV and electrical stuff before you go.

Sun-hee: *(holds up plug)* Done.

Tara: Sun-hee! We're late! It's time to go!

Sun-hee: OK! Hey Mike, I have to go. We're leaving for the airport.

Sun-hee, Tara, & Claudia: Bye Mike!

Mike: Cool! Have a great trip, girls. Bye.

Sun-hee: OK. Does everybody have everything?

Claudia: Yep.

Sun-hee: Tickets?

Claudia: Yes.

Sun-hee: Bags?

Claudia: Yep.

Sun-hee: Coats?

Claudia: Yep.

Sun-hee: Everything.

Claudia: Yep.

Tara: Let's go!

Sun-hee: OK. Mexico—here we come! *(all exit)*

Tara & Claudia: *(Sun-hee re-enters to get her ticket and traveler's checks)* Now . . . Mexico—here we come!

Global Viewpoints – Travel

Dave: Before going on a trip, I pay the bills, I empty the trash, and I give a house key to a friend.

Alejandra: Before I leave on a trip, I have to confirm travel plans and make sure that I have requested a vegetarian meal.

Thales: Before leaving for a long trip, I turn off the lights, I turn off my heater, I give my keys to my roommate, and I water my plant.

Julianna: The funniest story of my traveling experience was when I came to the U.S. for the first time by myself. They lost my luggage, and I didn't speak a word of English. I had to use my hands to explain myself. People understood what I meant, and they helped me out.

Catherine: My recent trip to Africa was one of the most amazing trips of my life. This was my second trip to Tanzania, Africa. We visited a lot of villages, some very remote that we had to travel by helicopter. In Tanzania, it's very different from America, so there are no maps. So, even traveling in a helicopter, we didn't really know where we were going to go. We didn't really know the village names, so we just kind of had no destination, and we got in the helicopter and just flew around. And if we saw some animals or some rooftops of hut houses, we said, "Let's go there," and we just kind of landed.

Dennis: I have a lot of funny experiences on the airline as a flight attendant. But one of the funniest I could recall was there was this passenger who had a toupee, and one of my flight attendants was serving . . . I think she was serving food. And she had this tray. And suddenly turbulence happened, and she lost her balance. And her hand landed on the guy's head, who had a toupee. When she caught her balance again, the toupee kind of shifted, so his sideburns were on his forehead. And I had to control my laughter, because you're not allowed to laugh.

Unit 1

1 Good Morning World – You, Adrian

1A

1. Jay; 2. Kim; 3. Adrian; 4. Adrian; 5. Jay; 6. Kim; 7. Kim; 8. Adrian; 9. Adrian; 10. Jay

1B

1. an intern; 2. attends classes; 3. news reporter; 4. get a grade; 5. pass; 6. soccer; 7. study a lot; 8. go to school; 9. just friends; 10. failed

1C Answers will vary.

2 City Living – A favorite keepsake

2A Answers will vary.

2B

1. b; 2. g; 3. d; 4. f; 5. e; 6. a; 7. i; 8. h; 9. j; 10. c

2C Answers will vary.

3 Global Viewpoints – Special people / Memories

3A

1. True; 2. False, Alex has two sisters and one brother.; 3. True; 4. False, Alejandra's grandmother is 80 years old.; 5. False, Kumiko says her grandfather is kind and supportive.; 6. True; 7. False, Calum's three friends are the most important people in his life.

3B

1. c; 2. d; 3. a; 4. b

3C Answers will vary.

Unit 2

1 Good Morning World – Fit to be fit

1A

True: 1, 3, 6, 8, 9.; False: 2. Kim thinks that running is the worst idea ever.; 4. Jay says, "Why don't we sit down?"; 5. Jay says that breakfast is the most important meal of the day.; 7. Jays says, "Let's try some cereal."

1B

1. b; 2. a; 3. b; 4. b; 5. a

1C Answers will vary.

2 City Living – The spicier the better

2A Answers will vary.

2B

Order: 4, 1, 8, 6, 3, 5, 7, 2

2C Answers will vary.

3 Global Viewpoints – Favorite foods / International foods

3A

1. True; 2. False, Jambalaya contains chicken, beans, and rice.; 3. True; 4. False, Dennis likes his vegetables really crispy.; 5. False, Dayanne doesn't like rice and beans that are salty and buttery.; 6. True; 7. False, Dan says there's nothing better than a big juicy steak.; 8. False, Julianna doesn't like to eat bacon.; 9. True; 10. False, Alejandra enjoys sweet foods like chocolate.

3B

1. typical; 2. hamburgers; 3. tortilla; 4. spicy; 5. milk; 6. twice; 7. Korean; 8. beef

3C Answers will vary.

Unit 3

1 Good Morning World – Sister, meet sister

1A

1. True; 2. True; 3. False, Marla always remembered she had a sister.; 4. True; 5. False, Jay likes a good mystery.; 6. True; 7. True; 8. False, at the library, Marla remembered her sister.; 9. True; 10. False, Jay cries after hearing the story.

1B

1. Fortunately; 2. doubt; 3. by accident; 4. bet; 5. Unfortunately; 6. know; 7. mysterious; 8. couldn't; 9. prove that; 10. good

1C Answers will vary.

2 City Living – Elementary, my dear Tara!

2A Answers will vary.

2B

1. Takeshi; 2. Claudia; 3. Tara; 4. Sun-hee; 5. Tara; 6. Takeshi; 7. Roberto; 8. Tara; 9. Claudia; 10. Mike

2C Answers will vary.

3 Global Viewpoints – Mysteries and strange events

3A

1. e; 2. d; 3. b; 4. c; 5. f; 6. a

3B

1. fall; 2. sons; 3. a strong; 4. sneaky; 5. tree to tree; 6. mysteries; 7. real; 8. how; 9. stone; 10. off

3C Answers will vary.

Unit 4

1 Good Morning World – Passion for fashion

1A

1. Kim; 2. Kim; 3. Isadora; 4. Jay; 5. Kim; 6. Isadora; 7. Isadora; 8. Jay; 9. Kim; 10. Kim

1B

1. a; 2. a; 3. b; 4. b; 5. a

1C Answers will vary.

2 City Living – You ought to get more exercise!

2A Answers will vary.

2B

1. thinks; 2. doesn't think; 3. thinks; 4. thinks; 5. doesn't think; 6. doesn't think; 7. thinks; 8. doesn't think

2C Answers will vary.

3 Global Viewpoints – Family trends / Personal style

3A

1. c; 2. e; 3. b; 4. a; 5. f; 6. d

3B

1. True; 2. True; 3. False, Dayanne talks about a friend who wears cowboy boots to work.; 4. True; 5. False, Dennis likes the way Robert Redford moves, stands, and carries his clothes.; 6. False, Dennis likes Robert Redford's hair.; 7. True; 8. False, Dayanne thinks losing weight will improve her appearance.; 9. True; 10. False, Calum thinks contact lenses could improve his appearance.

3C Answers will vary.

Unit 5

1 Good Morning World – Where are you going?

1A

Checked: 1, 3, 4, 5, 6, 8, 9, 11

1B

Order: 4, 3, 8, 1, 7, 2, 6, 5

1C Answers will vary.

2 City Living – Claudia's errand service

2A Answers will vary.

2B

1. True; 2. True; 3. True; 4. False, Claudia remembers the grocery list.; 5. True; 6. False, Claudia goes to the grocery store first.; 7. True; 8. False, Claudia likes Roberto's neighbors.; 9. False, Roberto wants Claudia to watch the movie with him.; 10. False, Claudia does not agree to go and get some ice cream for Roberto.

2C Answers will vary.

3 Global Viewpoints – Running errands / My neighborhood

3A

1. the Laundromat, the supermarket; 2. the bank, the dry cleaners, the pharmacy; 3. the grocery store, the bank, the post office

3B

1. safe; 2. restaurants; 3. residential; 4. walk; 5. on the sidewalks; 6. big school; 7. trains; 8. taking public transportation

3C Answers will vary.

Unit 6

1 Good Morning World – Apply yourself

1A

1. Jay; 2. Rashid; 3. Jay; 4. Rashid; 5. Kim; 6. Rashid; 7. Rashid; 8. Jay; 9. Jay; 10. Kim

1B

1. a; 2. b; 3. a; 4. b; 5. b

1C Answers will vary.

2 City Living – The letter

2A Answers will vary.

2B

1. rejected; 2. rejected; 3. travel; 4. sad; 5. thinks; 6. Columbia; 7. will; 8. film director; 9. accepted; 10. go to graduate school

2C Answers will vary.

3 Global Viewpoints – After graduation / Five years from now . . .

3A

1. b; 2. c; 3. f; 4. a; 5. e; 6. d

3B

1. True; 2. False, Dave doesn't know where he's going to be living five years from now.; 3. True; 4. False, Calvin thinks cyberlaw will be important in five or six years.; 5. True; 6. False, Woo Sung wants about three kids and a dog.; 7. True

3C Answers will vary.

Unit 7

1 Good Morning World – Party time

1A

1. True; 2. False, it will be held this Saturday at Penn Park.; 3. False, one day before the party, Jay invites Rashid and Kim to come.; 4. True; 5. True; 6. False, Jays doesn't want Kim to bring presents or cake.; 7. True; 8. True; 9. Jay's best friend will choose the winner of the contest.; 10. False, Jay's best friend is his dog Precious.

1B

1. celebration; 2. having; 3. didn't invite; 4. getting together; 5. host; 6. I'm sorry; 7. when; 8. win; 9. Before; 10. I'm sorry

1C Answers will vary.

2 City Living – Aloha everyone!

2A Answers will vary.

2B

Order: 6, 1, 5, 4, 7, 2, 3

2C Answers will vary.

3 Global Viewpoints – What a party! / Festivals and holidays

3A

1. soapsuds; 2. summer; 3. casual; 4. 38; 5. his; 6. Dennis

3B

1. c; 2. d; 3. b; 4. a

3C Answers will vary.

Unit 8

1 Good Morning World – A likely story

1A

1. Jay; 2. Jay; 3. Kim; 4. Kim; 5. Anthony; 6. Kim; 7. Anthony; 8. Anthony; 9. Jay; 10. Kim

1B

1. b; 2. a; 3. b; 4. a; 5. a; 6. b; 7. a

1C Answers will vary.

2 City Living – Takeshi presents "Cinderella"

2A Answers will vary.

2B

1. humble; 2. evil; 3. dress; 4. enjoying; 5. nothing to wear; 6. tonight; 7. rushing; 8. looking; 9. got married

2C Answers will vary.

3 Global Viewpoints – Favorite stories

3A

1. b; 2. c; 3. a

3B

1. False, Snow White was a beautiful princess.; 2. False, a bad witch gave Snow White a poisoned apple.; 3. True; 4. False, the princess's family doesn't want her to go away with the prince.; 5. False, the princess turns herself and her children into trees.; 6. True; 7. False, a pretty girl was sitting in the library.; 8. True; 9. True

3C Answers will vary.

Unit 9

1 Good Morning World – Intern view

1A

True: 1, 2, 6, 7, 8, 10.; False: 3. Kim thinks they should try to help Adrian with a practice interview.; 4. Jay says to Adrian, "Tell us a little about yourself."; 5. Adrian will graduate from college next month.; 9. Jay says that in television you have to work as a team.

1B

1. want; 2. efficient; 3. dream; 4. practice; 5. fourth-year; 6. has worked; 7. rewarding; 8. has learned; 9. worked in; 10. stressful

1C Answers will vary.

2 City Living – The big job interview

2A Answers will vary.

2B

1. a; 2. a; 3. b; 4. b; 5. c; 6. b

2C Answers will vary.

3 Global Viewpoints – What do you do? / Dream jobs

3A

1. False, Natalie works for a television station that was launched ten years ago.; 2. True; 3. False, Dan works with computers at a hospital.; 4. True; 5. False, Gian is a marketing manager.; 6. True

3B

1. b; 2. d; 3. f; 4. c; 5. a; 6. g; 7. e

3C Answers will vary.

Unit 10

1 Good Morning World – Hello hangups

1A

1. need; 2. answer it; 3. eating; 4. hanging up; 5. love; 6. wanted; 7. text; 8. off; 9. ignore; 10. lower

1B

1. a; 2. a; 3. b; 4. a; 5. b; 6. b

1C Answers will vary.

2 City Living – I can't stand cell phones!

2A Answers will vary.

2B

Order: 8, 5, 4, 2, 1, 3, 6, 7

2C Answers will vary.

3 Global Viewpoints – Cell phones

3A

1. True; 2. True; 3. False, Brad can browse the Internet on his cell phone.; 4. False, Jackie uses the camera on her cell phone.; 5. False, Dayanne doesn't think that cell phones are always necessary.; 6. True; 7. False, Calvin thinks he has less privacy with a cell phone.; 8. False, Lourdes dislikes cell phones more than she likes them.; 9. True; 10. False, Dennis doesn't like cell phones ringing at unexpected times.; 11. True; 12. True

3B

1. d; 2. e; 3. b; 4. f; 5. a; 6. g; 7. c

3C Answers will vary.

Unit 11

1 Good Morning World – Okay computers

1A

1. Yes; 2. Yes; 3. Yes; 4. No; 5. No; 6. Yes; 7. No; 8. Yes; 9. Yes

1B

1. e; 2. d; 3. a; 4. h; 5. c; 6. b; 7. f; 8. g

1C Answers will vary.

2 City Living – The first word processor

2A Answers will vary.

2B

1. b; 2. a; 3. b; 4. c; 5. c

2C Answers will vary.

3 Global Viewpoints – Technology today

3A

1. False, Reda doesn't know a lot about electronics.; 2. True; 3. True; 4. False, Denise uses instant messenger to stay in touch with her family.; 5. True; 6. False, Catherine usually e-mails her friends in New York.; 7. True; 8. True; 9. False, Jonathan's computer is old and unreliable.

3B

1. cameras; 2. thin; 3. instant messenger; 4. family; 5. music; 6. e-mails; 7. laptop; 8. expensive; 9. old

3C Answers will vary.

Unit 12

1 Good Morning World – Show on the road

1A

1. Yes; 2. No; 3. Yes; 4. No; 5. Yes; 6. No; 7. Yes; 8. No; 9. Yes; 10. Yes

1B

1. You've; 2. carry-on luggage; 3. remember; 4. forgot; 5. kennel; 6. been; 7. seen; 8. You've; 9. forgot; 10. Mother

1C Answers will vary.

2 City Living – Mexico—here we come!

2A Answers will vary.

2B

Order: 3, 1, 5, 8, 2, 6, 7, 4

2C Answers will vary.

3 Global Viewpoints – Travel

3A

Dave: empty trash, give out key, pay bills; Alejandra: confirm plans, request meal; Thales: give out keys, turn off items, water plants

3B

1. True; 2. True; 3. False, Thales gives his keys to his roommate.; 4. True; 5. False, Julianna used her hands to communicate.; 6. False, Catherine's story happened on her second trip to Tanzania.; 7. True; 8. False, Catherine didn't have a detailed travel plan.; 9. False, Dennis's story happened when he was working on a plane as a flight attendant.; 10. True

3C Answers will vary.